DATE DUE

MAR 1972

APR 13 1987   BIRD   APR 6 1987

THE DANFORTH STUDY OF CAMPUS MINISTRIES

THE COMMISSION ON
THE DANFORTH STUDY OF CAMPUS MINISTRIES

WILLIAM L. KOLB, *Chairman*
Dean, Beloit College

WILLIAM GRAHAM COLE
President, Lake Forest College

LUTHER HARSHBARGER
Professor of Religious Studies, Pennsylvania State University

EDITH M. LERRIGO
Executive Director, Young Women's Christian Association of the U.S.A.

CHARLES McCOY
Robert Gordon Sproul Professor of Religion in Higher Education,
Pacific School of Religion and Graduate Theological Union

ROBERT RANKIN
Vice President, The Danforth Foundation

PAUL REYNOLDS
Dean, The University of North Carolina, Wilmington

HAROLD VIEHMAN
Secretary, The Division of Higher Education, The United Presbyterian
Church, U.S.A.

ROBERT WATSON
Dean of Students, Harvard University

—

THE CHURCH, THE UNIVERSITY, AND SOCIAL POLICY

The Danforth Study of Campus Ministries

VOLUME I

REPORT OF THE DIRECTOR

THE CHURCH, THE UNIVERSITY,

AND SOCIAL POLICY

The Danforth Study of Campus Ministries

✍ VOLUME I ✍

REPORT OF THE DIRECTOR

BY

KENNETH UNDERWOOD

WESLEYAN UNIVERSITY PRESS

Middletown, Connecticut

Library of Congress Catalog Card Number: 69 – 17794
Manufactured in the United States of America
First edition

To my wife Marge, my daughter Valerie, and my son Keith, who gave me the affection and understanding which made work on this study possible.

CONTENTS

PUBLISHER'S NOTE

THIS book is the first of two volumes containing the basic reports and papers of the Danforth Study of Campus Ministries, appearing under the general title *The Church, the University, and Social Policy*. The present work is Volume I, the report of the director of the Danforth Study, on the process of inquiry, the data, and the resulting implications for policy. Volume II contains working and technical papers by scholars, ministers, university and church administrators, students, and others who participated in the study.

A number of collateral books and monographs have also arisen from this enterprise. These are published by a variety of presses and represent a variety of relationships to the Danforth Study. They include, for example, *The Campus Clergyman*, by Phillip E. Hammond (New York: Basic Books, 1966), begun before the Danforth inquiry was commissioned but completed during a leave supported by the Danforth Study; and *The Gathering Storm in the Churches*, by Jeffrey K. Hadden (New York: Doubleday, 1969), based on data from the ministers' survey prepared and conducted by the Danforth Study.

FOREWORD

O NE of the keenest pleasures a professional man has is that of calling attention to the work of a colleague when he regards that work as having considerable significance. The opportunity of introducing Kenneth Underwood's *The Church, The University, and Social Policy* provides such pleasure, tinged with sadness because of the illness and death of its author.

For the past five years William Cole, Luther Harshbarger, Edith Lerrigo, Charles McCoy, Robert Rankin, Paul Reynolds, Harold Viehman, Robert Watson, and I, as members of the Commission for The Danforth Foundation Study of Campus Ministries, have had the privilege of consulting, counseling, and advising with Kenneth Underwood as he designed and conducted the study of campus ministries of which *The Church, The University, and Social Policy* is his report. Such work went on almost until his death in the early fall of 1968. I know I speak for all members of the Commission when I say that the study and the report have great potential importance for the future of Christian ministry, higher education, and possibilities of humane existence in an urban technical society. This potential significance can be realized, however, only if the basic perspective of the study is understood and reflected upon, and only then if that perspective is utilized for continuing thought, reflection, research, and action by those in the Church and in higher education.

Knowledge, for Underwood, is not divorced from aesthetic and ethical valuation, nor from action within the structures of social life. Rather, together with valuation, it is the indispensable ingredient of social policy which can humanize the quality of modern life. The search for knowledge within this context of valuation, policy formulation, and social action is policy research, the kind of research which must increasingly come to characterize the higher learning. Since the primary locus of the higher learning is the university, it has become the central institution of the modern world, even though policy research within the context of the higher learning must become an integral part of all professions and institutions.

Campus ministries, of both the professional clergy and the laity, are ministries to students, faculty, and administrators as they struggle toward this conception of the centrality of the university. This does not mean an abandonment of the historical modes of ministry—priestly, pastoral, prophetic, and governing—but rather their reconception and reorganization in light of the central task of the higher learning. Thus worship and the preaching of the word of God must occur within the context of the worshiper's place within the complex modern order; counseling must recognize the problems of the person as he struggles to find direction and relevance in his occupation as it is a means of serving men in the urban world; prophecy must fuse technical knowledge and value; and governance and organization must be relevant to the task of transforming contemporary structures.

But for this to happen the Church must itself engage in policy research to reform itself. It must find structures of campus ministry that render possible the performance of the complex tasks, rather than expecting the impossible from the individual. It must utilize the knowledge that has been the result of the university's reflection upon itself, so that it knows the context of campus ministries. It must utilize the knowledge of personality that the higher learning provides concerning students, faculty, and administrators if counseling is to be meaningful. It must call upon all the disciplines of the modern world to understand that world if it is to minister to the university in such a way that its knowledge can be used for the sake of the life of man.

Underwood's own study of campus ministries exemplifies this kind of policy research enabling the campus ministry to reflect upon itself and its context of the university and the world. The disciplines of the social sciences are used without violating their integrity, and yet the knowledge they bring is inextricably intertwined with the judgments of value of the social ethicist. The campus ministers' own conceptions of their work and life are taken for what the ministers perceive them to be, yet causal analysis is constantly present as well as perceptions of failures and successes both of will and knowledge. Knowledge of the literature of student personality and social and political processes on campus is used to evaluate the data on the modes of ministry on specific campuses. Knowledge of the urban technical world is used to define the problems of relevance and governance. And all this knowledge and valuation is directed toward the understanding of the vocation of ministry on the contemporary campus.

It must be clear from the picture I have drawn of Underwood's perspective and of his study that *The Church, The University, and Social Policy* is not a work which falls within the ordinary categories of scholarly research. Perspective, knowledge, and valuation are fused throughout the work, and there is a constant working back and forth from concrete analysis to policy to theory. The book itself is a concrete instance of the complex stance that Underwood feels is necessary to do the work of God in the modern world. Yet those who will submit themselves to the discipline required will find clarity, comprehension, and commitment. And for those people, Churchmen, students, administrators, faculty and campus ministers, the clarity, comprehension, and commitment they find may be the starting point for a reformation of ministry, of higher education, and of the world.

To offer such a starting point has been Kenneth Underwood's intent —an intent to which he has devoted himself with that single-mindedness which all who know him recognize: a single-mindedness which carried him through the difficulties of the study, and in the last year to the near completion of the report at a time when his serious illness made it seem unlikely that he could come close to finishing his task. He did nearly complete this book, and with the work of his friends it is now finished. It is not only with pleasure but with the greatest respect and affection that I introduce both the man and his work, for they are inseparable.

WILLIAM L. KOLB

Beloit, Wisconsin
March 1969

PREFACE

No period in the history of American Christianity has been the occasion of so pervasive and anxious a reappraisal of structures and functions of ministry, of organizational saga, of personal meaning of faith and the processes forming beliefs in the world.

Three forces have converged on the churches to produce this occasion for critical reflection and decision. They are the actual and potential publics to whom this study seeks to speak. They have in varied stages of our inquiry spoken to us. The first consists of the clerical and lay ministries who regard the structures and acts of the institutional church as essential to the expression of the Christian faith and gospel and therefore worthy of preservation, reform, and radical renewal. The second is made up of the leaders of higher education who seek to enhance the capacities of people to act in the contemporary and emerging world. They are both the discoverers of systematic knowledge about what is happening to people and nature in the world and the evaluators of its use for human community. The third includes the public figures who seek to formulate policies of major organizations and professions in American society informed by the commitments and wisdom of the church and the university.

The internal motivation for reappraisal of the churches' ministry to contemporary society is the gospel itself. Those leaders who welcome attempts at an accurate and critical look at past and present actions of the churches believe that in the mysterious depths of their religion, ultimate powers forever seek to "make all things new." They ask, as do we in this study, what epistemologies and ways of learning keep alive the sense of wonder and awe, of power and goodness beyond man's capacity to manipulate? Are distinctions still to be made in the churches and universities between the scientific and technological accomplishments of this society and what God wills as worthy of man's being? What part do the religious leaders in our colleges and universities have in answering such questions? Is the chief task of the most educated and specialized ministry of the church—the campus clergy—that of providing a supportive religious ideology for a scientific, technological, urban society? Or are there more discriminating and constructive judgments about the design of cities and the management of open spaces to which faithful perceptions speak? These are the kinds of questions asked in this study.

The second force which we have seen at work pressing religious and educational leaders to open themselves to self-examination is created by the revolutionizing knowledge of the university. The vast intellectual, political, and social changes sweeping the world confront the leadership of the churches in the theories and data of the strategic centers of higher education. The crises of ministries over the contemporary meaning of ancient formulations of faith are poignant and recognizable to leaders of other professions and institutions—increasingly even to the originators of our new technical knowledge. They know of their own inadequacy to perceive, administer, and use the fund of knowledge accumulating in the major institutions of our society and ordered and transmitted by the colleges and universities.

This situation reminds us of the third force represented in this study leading to a critical reappraisal of the basis of actions in the churches: the search for leaders of our major bureaucracies and professions for social policies which are post-modern, which sense something of the shape of future alternatives. Such leaders concern themselves not only with the quantity of production but with its quality. They focus not only upon the specialization of role in religion, science, law, and medicine, but upon the relationships of special skills, theories, and norms in the acts of whole persons. They use creatively various ways of knowing in the university. They express a flexibility toward organizational life: reducing spontaneous responses to increase efficiency in some areas; eliciting in others creative and imaginative speculation about problems cutting across formal organization.

With only this much said about the approach of the study and the publics it seeks to serve, several potential problems for readers should be evident. We need to anticipate and describe these, for they introduce the three major concepts through which the study may best be viewed.

The problems and related concerns of the study are not confined to one of the publics but are of moment to all of them, though each public has traditionally been more concerned with certain ones than with others.

First, many readers are accustomed to dividing the world of experience and of research into relatively small pieces and parts so that they are more "manageable." Clergy pick one doctrinal or ethical theme, image, or role for a sermon, a demonstration, even a career. Faculty isolate particular areas or problems (such as church organization or ideology, university power structures, legislation on poverty) from their relationships on the margins. These they focus on with great intensity.

Our inquiry is of campus ministries, but in principle, we refuse to isolate the study of a part of a profession from its wider contexts. In this case, these are: the churches and their modes of ministry and ideologies; the universities and their structures of learning and teaching, the students and their aspirations and anxieties; the American culture and the basic trends, policies, and values of professional, technical, and popular subcultures. If the reader does not grasp a vision of these factors in relation to the Protestant ministries under intensive scrutiny, he is likely to be baffled by the scope and movement from one particular area or problem to the others.

For example, the study reports on the approach and findings of a survey which samples not only campus clergy but all types of ministries in six major denominations. The questions asked range from theological beliefs to views of educational and scientific developments, interpretations of their work and relation to political and social convictions, and even self-perceptions. These separate areas of the clergy's perspectives as seen in empirical, aggregate data are not introduced until the last part of this volume. Thus the reader can test other kinds of data (by interview, observation, historical reconstruction, for example) against the survey questions and data. The reader can see just how widespread the developments reported in the campus clergy of the Bay area of California, Madison, Wisconsin, Chapel Hill, Pittsburgh, Boston, New York, and Detroit are in the church, the university, and the larger society. If a trend away from an apologetic preaching-type ministry toward an inquiring and questing-type ministry is found to be present not only in the campus clergy but in the whole clergy, then perhaps some profound changes in religious education and missionary policies are called for.

The Danforth study calls the problems of adjudicating and justifying the relations between these various kinds of knowledge in order to engage in significant corporate and personal action: problems in the *morality of knowledge.* The churches, the universities, and public or community leaders are deeply involved in the task of evaluating what knowledge is relevant and meaningful to their work and of determining the best ways to acquire this knowledge. Hence all the talk about institutes, centers, leave-for-study-provisions in careers, student participation in governance of church and university, the limits of pulpit-centered worship, the opportunity of clergy for rich and broad reading (for example, a lifetime subscription to *The New York Times* as a gift of the denomination to a beginning minister) as well as intensive knowledge of a specialized area (for example, medical education).

If one asks what are to be the criteria for action in these matters, he deals with issues in the morality of knowledge. If one asks what is the good of such knowledge for personal and group care of others, then he asks the kind of question which permeates this book and the one to follow. If these are pressing questions for him, the reader will not mind that what he has been given when he completes his reading is a comprehensive vision rather than the detailed description of a particular speciality of ministry. He will hopefully have a sense of the need for establishing new ways of relating many factors and perspectives contained in the research in the task of restructuring and redefining corporate purpose.

If this is gained, then the reader will know that he has been engaged with others in an exercise in practical reason which is not the fabrication of a single discipline of knowledge, but the discovery of a reality seen by a number of observers and by testers of their observations. On such grounds, policy for organizations can be built.

Second, many readers are accustomed to dividing research reports from policy recommendations, or at least accustomed to having the research reports given with distinctive margins defining the sphere of inferences drawn from them for policy. Our study does not do this. The refusal to do this is not just a matter of personal style or habit, but of principle. We are in this study reaching for a way of knowing and understanding, indeed a method and theory of knowledge which prohibits such sharp differentiations. This approach is called *policy research.* It precludes a more normal way of writing a study director's report: that is, dividing the work into method of inquiry; description of findings; analysis of the findings in light of a theory developed out of them or brought to them; evaluation of the importance of data and theory for practical issues motivating the study; and recommendation of policy alternatives in the future. All these elements are present in varying degrees in parts of the study, but are interwoven with each other.

The particular academic discipline of the director of the study is social ethics. Historic aspects of this discipline give it special affinities to an emerging emphasis in the unversity and church upon the conscious and free movement back and forth between the descriptive and normative aspects of each problem in acquisition of knowledge and its use as these are confronted in the process of multifaceted inquiry. Social ethicists have never been content to know simply what are the realities of our past or present situation. They have speculated about its goodness, and about the possibility that the future might be influenced in a meaningful way. Thus, new developments would not be characterized as simply the incidents of constant change. Our common-sense experience of the world today anticipates and hopes for organizations with mission and legend inviting deep affection and support. These experiences are as real as the present structures under testing. The social ethicist, therefore, moves professionally in and out of academic clusters of theologians, social scientists, psychologists, and historians. He appropriates and supports their work in his own critical study of the forces which have shaped the moral actions of people in a particular society.

Policy research is not oriented toward the mastery of a particular strip of knowledge developed in a guild of scholars. The policy researcher, like the social ethicist, does not wish to be forced to choose between the claims of social science or theology in study of the sources of church commitment. He is seeking to provide knowledge of the alternatives of corporate action available to certain leaders, and these alternatives will be highly limited if the perspectives of only one discipline are brought to a problem. The policy researcher stops short of telling leaders of an institution what they are to do, what alternatives are to be chosen, and the time and place of the choice. He knows he cannot envision the concrete circumstances of decision. But he can as part of his responsibilities engage in illustrative speculation about the possible influence of certain choices.

For this reason, policy research is neither strictly science nor strictly art. The methods of inquiry and the criteria of success are in great flux and often disturbingly new, though they may draw upon humanistic concerns pronounced in earlier scholarship. Honesty in reporting, rigor in pursuit of truth, fairness toward the autonomy of other disciplines, are all basic to policy research. In our case these concerns explain our attempt to tell the reader in a forthright manner what really went on at each stage, why a certain type of inquiry was undertaken, what necessitated changes in approach, and what new explorations opened up over a five-year period of study.

The *third* potential problem in reading about this study is that the reader may be accustomed to a rather simple linear development in the presentation of materials and arguments. Each chapter is assumed to add some increment of information, theory, evaluation, and recommendation. Or each chapter is assumed to add one of these to the previous types of knowledge in an additive, tandem sort of way. The director's report and most of the technical papers are not arranged in this way.

If the concern of the writer is simply to establish a new fact, propose a new type or theory, illumine a variety of experiences with an image, then the traditional style is useful. But what is at stake in this study, as the title for both volumes indicates, is *social policy*, the ordering and reordering of the resources and personnel of whole institutions, organizations, and movements in the context of the needs and aspirations of nations, peoples, and societies. The first chapter of this book tries to make clear how the campus ministry is involved ultimately in profound social policy questions and why we cannot write of their history, their modes of ministry, their hopes for the church in the accustomed way. The picture of the whole intention of the study in the first chapter must be grasped and kept in mind as intensive forays are made into the elements of that intention in subsequent chapters.

The forays also move from intensive work (for example, in the Berkeley and Wisconsin studies of student religious commitment and dissidence) relatively swiftly to inference drawn from these to the wider, more general intention to illumine social policy choices. If the reader can empathize with the first three chapters, or be persuaded that these provide a rationale legitimizing the writing of a study report in the way we have described, his difficulties with the reading of the two basic volumes and collateral works will not be great. If he cannot, then he is likely to get the impression of more randomness than he is ac-

customed to or than is intended by the staff of the study. The difficulties
the reader may have are, in short, a function of the wholeness, complexity, and richness of the reality described and envisioned and the
variety of disciplines and perspectives brought by the participants to
the inquiry.

If the reader asks what he is likely to take with him after he completes his reading, it may be a comprehensive vision, or sense of the need
for establishing new ways of relating many factors and forces contained
in the research, the importance of social policies as a focus for restructuring and redefining the purpose and methods of their achievement.
Our hope is that the report will provide the direction for thinking carefully about what ought to be the course of events where religious,
academic, and ethical concerns impinge upon one another. While the
proposals are not radical in the sense of much contemporary use of this
term as a kind of iconoclasm, they are radical and long range in the
sense of showing what kind of reorientation is needed in the church and
university to meet the opportunities opening up to them in our time.

KENNETH UNDERWOOD

Round Hill Road
North Haven, Connecticut
August 26, 1968

PART I

The Valued People and the Evaluators

≫ 1 ≪

THE MAJOR PROTESTANT "EXPERIMENT"

IN SPECIALIZED MINISTRIES

At the most basic level the American people manifest a crisis of contemporary religious commitment and consciousness. We experience it in the daily multiform contradictions and discontinuities in our thought and action as we try to live with the vestiges of our traditional faith in a modern, technical, rapidly changing, mass society. We have reported to us daily the confusions and controversies of our theologians and clergy. We witness their agonizing on the TV panel shows and their cliché-ridden figures as caricature in the new comedy hours aimed for the "under-thirty" market. But we have not been able to focus on any one section of the ministry or church as a symbol for the religious problems and anxieties we sense most strongly.

This study singles out the most generally significant and illuminating sector of religious leadership for intensive investigation and analysis: the campus ministries. They symbolize and articulate best the spiritual problems and occasions that grip the nation. The Protestant campus ministry, of all religious leadership in this country, has been most involved with the intellectual, social, and moral movements of the best-educated youth in America. The problems and potentialities of faith and ethics which confront this particular ministry are likely to be those which most religious leaders will have to face as the questions, doubts, and hopes voiced by college and university leaders are brought out through the mass media, primary and secondary schools, and adult and continuing education into the main stream of the whole society.

This inquiry, though it begins with what is happening to the religious leadership of our colleges and universities, seeks to do this in a way that explores the major controversies over how we know what we know, how we judge what is right and wrong, and what ultimate loyalties and commitments stir the universities and churches deeply.

This is the first time in academic history that a substantial sum of money ($375,000 from the Danforth Foundation and about $50,000 from co-operating churches and universities) has been made available for intensive study of the religious commitments and actions of American church leaders and of their relations to the laity. The commitment of funds began with an interest in what was happening to campus ministers. But the sponsoring foundation leaders saw, as did the scholars, that they had as their object of study a manageable clue, in research terms, to what was happening to the clergy at large and to the major shifts occurring in the faith, intellectual formulations, and relations to organized religion of the laity.

It does not matter much that the study focuses on the Protestant churches, since in whatever major educational center we studied, the inquiry reveals the patterns of religious commitment and values of all students, relates the interactions of Catholic, Jewish, and Protestant leaders, and tries to envision ecumenical strategies. Moreover, by being a project in policy research, the study seeks to formulate proposals which broadly affect the whole field of religious activity. But more importantly, it seeks at the start to clarify those normative, primary tasks and missions which historically have justified the existence of a ministry and church, whatever the denomination, and then sets out to see what changes have taken place in their interpretation and if they now serve people in ways they really need and respect.

Our basic research will be reported in two volumes, of which this is the first. We see the relation of the stages of inquiry, the modes of ministry, the intensive analysis of educational centers, and the policy recommendations as inseparable parts of a report that we encourage the serious reader to treat in argument and reflection as an integral whole. The church has been the victim in recent years of the exploiter of the single theological theme, the quick-church-reform plan artist, the situational ethicist moving quickly from one problem to another with only love as the analytical guide. We must turn from these scholarly temptations to consideration of the more general, interrelated human movements and policy choices facing religion and education.

There are data in this study that were first collected in 1963 and are now made public, as well as data that barely made the press deadlines.

But we did not rush into print. We think we are dealing with factors of loyalties, world views, and institutional structures that do not change over a year or two, but will be present for decades of discussion and reflection, social change or reform. The study is oriented toward future policies the universities, churches, foundations, and public leaders can adopt to meet basic problems in achievement of significant goals— not toward the reporting of data from surveys of the past.

We begin with an inquiry into the meaning for the churches, for the universities, and for the larger society of the accelerating movement of clergy toward preference for work in "experimental" and "specialized" ministries, rather than the parish church. What does this mean as to the kind of adjustment the Protestant churches and young religious leaders are making to contemporary society? Once we can answer this in relation to the largest and longest-established of these "experimental" and "specialized" fields (the campus ministries), perhaps we can begin to say something about larger trends in the church. The majority of the students in the principal seminaries today say they hope to enter some field other than "leadership of a local parish." Only 17.6 per cent of the entering class of Yale Divinity School in 1967 wish a career in the parish ministry or as pastor of a local congregation. The Lilly study of pre-seminary education indicated that no more than a third of the 1961–1962 students in theological schools wished to go into parish churches.[1]

Meanwhile the absolute number of persons going into the ministry is declining, reversing population trends generally. With the leveling off, and in some denominations lessening financial support for organized religious activities, church leaders are being pressed for clarification of what ministries are essential for expressing Christian commitment in the modern world and of what are to be the future relations of clergy and laity in these primary ministries.

In periods of history when a society is in transition from one way of life, thought, and faith to another, its religious leadership is among the first and the most serious objects of criticism and rebellion, for religion symbolizes and articulates the society's most basic values and commitments. Confusions and loss of morale in the religious leadership of a society are usually an indication of serious problems of meaning and purpose to come in other leadership and institutions. What makes religious symbols different from other kinds of symbols, and therefore highly

---

1. Keith R. Bridston and Dwight W. Culver, *Pre-Seminary Education* (Minneapolis: Augsburg, 1965), p. 227.

sensitive to fundamental social change, Robert Bellah observes in his comparative study of *Religion and Progress in Modern Asia*, "is that they define in broadest terms the nature of reality" and therefore "of the self." The roles of priests and ministers project a set of "limit" and "possibility" images and bring social and personal actions within the framework of a "higher power" or "wider meaning."[2]

The church appears to most sensitive observers to be reflecting a time of crisis and transition not only in its own life but in the whole of American society, when the foundations of past courageous actions are shaking and an unknown future threatens old securities and statuses. An intensive study of the campus ministry may tell us a great deal, therefore, not only about a bellwether ministry in the churches but about the nature of more general changes and continuities in morals and faith in the larger society.

Although the campus ministry is the oldest and most generally supported of the so-called "experimental" and "specialized" ministries in the Protestant church, no comprehensive study has been made of its development, its future possibilities and options, and its relation to the other major forms of ministry. Such a study would seem to be long overdue. Aware of the need, the Danforth Foundation established in 1963 a commission and a staff to conduct a descriptive and evaluative inquiry into the Protestant ministries in higher education in the United States.

We have been both appalled by the cost of research—describing and evaluating the mission, methods, and results of institutional leadership —and challenged by the complexity of such inquiry. The Danforth grant may be only an important beginning in what the churches and universities will need to spend in policy research and advanced learning during the next two decades if the profound changes taking place in organized religion in this country are to be understood and the alternatives for corporate reform and renewal envisioned.

Some Basic Assumptions of the Study

Our study began with the conviction that the primary and inescapable responsibility it faced was the exploration and clarification of the

2. Robert N. Bellah (ed.) *Religion and Progress in Modern Asia* (New York: The Free Press, 1965), p. 174.

meaning of ministry not only for a particular place—the campus—but for the church as a whole. We began with the premise that ministry is Christian faith in action. We were investigating in this study the continuing and new modes by which Christians made known the truth about God's creation of the world and His love and compassion for it. The structures of ministry represent the convergence of belief, technical data about the world, personal talent and competence, and institutional resources in an act of loving service to others.

We see every Christian as a potential agent of ministry. By *Christian* we mean every member of a community who believes that Jesus Christ is his best insight into what God is like, is doing in the world, and wishes man to be and do. The subjects of our most intensive inquiry have been three thousand or so clergy on the major campuses of this country and their relations to the laity in higher education. Our study does not confine itself to the pastoral care, preaching, teaching and inquiry, or social reform carried on by the professional clergy; rather it seeks to open up the questions of what are religious and theological concerns on campus, what Christian commitments look like, and how they are experienced by all kinds of church members and leaders in the university.

In this study we are talking about the people from whom most of the educated leadership of future churches as well as the nation is likely to come. The major anxieties, problems, and structures of the future church are caught up in the controversies and power battles being waged now on the campuses in Berkeley, Madison, Ann Arbor, New York, Boston, Chapel Hill, Pittsburgh, and other centers of our study.

What consequences, if any, do Chritsian commitments and actions have for the life and work of these institutions of higher learning? The question is important, for these are the institutions from which our society expects the major inquiries into what is happening to human beings in the world, why it is happening, whether the deepest historic convictions of the citizenry can approve what is happening, and whether we have the wisdom to improve the conditions of human existence. Furthermore, the "knowledge industry," the "multiversity," the city and state systems of higher education, will provide the structure for global education on a mass scale for the rest of the century. Education is responsible for an increasingly large percentage of the gross national product in America alone; it is probably the most influential institution in our country.

The ministry working most closely with the structures of higher education and intellectual inquiry becomes, by nature of these developments, the proper focus for a study in depth of the contemporary ministry. The problems confronted by the campus ministry are those which in another decade will be consciously those of all the ministry. We are not speaking now simply of the fact that most leaders of church congregations will have been educated in these systems of research and learning. We are speaking of the impact of ideas and techniques that originate in the multiversity and change the whole culture. As Clark Kerr says, the "ideopolis" is now the center of the city. The university is increasingly the center of attempts by an entire people to know what is happening to them, to reflect critically on past actions, and to imagine policies that express enduring visions of the good life. The basic volumes of the Danforth study are called *The Church, The University, and Social Policy* to indicate that the campus ministries and their constituencies are being evaluated fundamentally in terms of their power to provide religious meaning, to draw upon, to integrate, and to refashion historic forms of service to others in a new social and technical age.

This is an age in which the leaders of expanding sciences and technologies are being asked to use their special knowledge and skills experimentally and flexibly in order to provide new corporate means of meeting pervasive human needs. Professionals and public leaders are trying to engage in continual, planned change, to discover the myths and hypotheses that give unity and direction to a society of increasingly diverse sciences and technologies. In such an age, experimental and specialized ministries like the ones we are studying are likely to be those which are in chief contact with the emerging leadership. But are they able to provide these leaders with a religious understanding of where they have been and where they are going, of the ground of humane organization and courageous action?

The crisis in contemporary religious commitment and consciousness is probably experienced most painfully by scholar and clergy alike as confusions over fundamental objectives of Christian ministry and legitimate criteria for evaluation of the work of the clergy and of laymen who support them. As a secretary for the National Lutheran Council's university work in the northeast region of the country noted to one of our researchers:

What is needed is a systematic attempt to define both the theological criterion for this kind of work and the actual expectations of those who legitimate it and then attempt to measure performance by the employment of a method designed distinctly to deal with these expectations. . . . How do you measure, just for instance, the degree to which students accept basic responsibilities in mutual pastoral care for each other? . . . I am not at all persuaded that the campus ministry, least of all in New York, would come off any better but until those who know about expectation and measurement . . . can supply us with methods, we are not likely to do anything but scare our legitimators into giving us more money.[3]

Much in the present situation of the church is not new to other times of crisis—profound anxiety beneath the surface of routine religious practice and the temptation to moral nihilism and wholesale anti-institutionalism among experimenters released from traditional responsibilities. But today these aspects of crisis are expressed in a new setting: a mobile, dynamic, secularized, scientifically informed, publicly educated, urban society. The plight of religious leadership is the subject of pop theology and panel polemic in the mass media often before it is empirically and systematically studied in major universities. Systematic study is called for, since the new setting does not permit the crisis to be understood or met simply by an analysis of a special ministry (the campus), one institution (the church), or one professional school complex (the seminaries).

The evidence and manifestations of the crisis will unfold with the study, but we need to note at the start what kinds of question the church leaders wished us to investigate and what we decided should have our greatest attention. Profound and serious divisions in the body politic of the church are clearly revealed in controversies now taking place over the status and function of the experimental and specialized ministries. Why do people want to enter them? Do such people no longer agree with many traditional or orthodox beliefs, or do they simply seek expression of deep religious convictions more relevant and significant than they believe the parish or local congregation provides? Do the people in these new ministries reflect more intensely than the parish ministries the crisis

---

3. Comment made to Robert Dentler during his study of the Protestant campus ministry in the New York metropolitan area. See report on this study in Chapter 17 of this volume.

of religious consciousness, or have they found ways of expressing new relationships between belief and action? (The question assumes that a major symptom of the crisis is the lack of cognitive and administrative power to integrate traditional religious beliefs, contemporary technical theory and data, and institutional resources of the church in one's ministry.) Are the traditional forms of church life—the local parish or congregation—more isolated from the technical, professional, and urban structures of contemporary society than the experimental and specialized ministries? Are the new ministers more isolated from financial and organizational realities of the church than the pastors of local congregations directly dependent on support by the constituencies they serve? Or are financial and political pressures becoming so pervasive in the church that in the future large numbers of clergy in every type of ministry will need to review whether they can expand their services by training more lay leadership and whether they should seek to earn their basic income through secular sources, such as teaching?

The Meaning of Experimentation in Ministry

Though many campus ministries are referred to in the churches as "experimental," the early investigations of the Danforth study produced few systematic efforts by the churches to make explicit what hypotheses the experiments were testing, what controls were introduced, or what provisions were made for gathering data on the consequences of various types of work. So honorific has the stance of innovation become in some church and university circles that in recent years the status of experimentation has been conferred retroactively, as it were, on church enterprises that are vague in conception and repetitive of past failures, but claim the magic of "relevance" and "newness" on the edge of a "major breakthrough." Only a few evaluative studies of these "experimental" ministries have been launched in the past few years under denominational and ecumenical auspices.[4]

The "experimental" ministries on campus are not really experiments

---

4. For example, Henry Clark's study of experimental ministries for the National Council of Churches, Samuel Gibson's study of Wesley Foundations for the Methodist Church, Paul Harrison's evaluation of the United Church Seminaries with special attention to the church as an instrument of social change.

in the sense in which most university scholars or administrators would use the term. Few new programs have been instituted by denominational or ecumenical leadership with the explicit purpose of finding out the potential and limit of a form of ministry and then of introducing it in a number of strategic places after careful evaluation. Few campus ministries are commended to the church at large as combining lay interests, historic convictions, and university knowledge so as to be exciting in the adult education of a parish as well as in week-end retreat at a college. Before the Danforth study, no plan of inquiry was developed by the churches to enlist the scientific and humanistic disciplines of the university in order to place the experience of campus ministries in the context of the whole church and to clarify normative models of future ministries. The churches have not devised policy controls to find out how people respond to new programs before activities go the limit of financial resources and personal endurance. When the aid of a university scholar has been sought by the church, little attempt has been made to encourage the academic community to explore how the varied activities of an experiment might support personal or corporate objectives; rather, church leaders have simply turned funds over to an expert whose chief interest has been in testing the claims of logic or the theories of his particular specialty.

Yet models of social and religious experimentation, of evaluative research, and of reflection on future policies are emerging in the university. They can inform the development of new ministries in the churches. Many scholars who are national leaders in their discipline, such as Elting E. Morison, historian, professor of history and American studies, and Master of Timothy Dwight College, Yale University, believe genuine experiments are going to become more widespread in all the professions and educational structures in mature, technical societies such as our own. Morison's hope is not for "some grand design to satisfy all the data in the disturbing new world" or for "settled doctrine from which all men can take their bearing," but for a style of action he calls "the experimental society":

> One of the purposes of the experimental society should obviously be to find out the potential and limit of the new machines and systems, but the larger context for the experiment is to find out, before things go too far, how men respond to new conditions. The successful organizing principle

for the new things is not likely to be found in . . . political man, forgotten man, or economic man, or statistical man, but the whole bundle appearing as single man.[5]

These convictions state in nontheological terms what many church leaders whom we shall be studying refer to as "being freed by Christ to minister to the whole man" and who view institutional forms as the "servant of the neighbor, not the object of ultimate Christian loyalty." The church they envision will be more of an experimental society, originating and conducting experiments in co-operation with the universities and with careful provision for continuing research on the results of their work and for the intensive, continuing education of leaders. Such plans are necessary if the churches are to begin new programs and ministries with the expectation that they are possibly going to inform the work of the whole church and to influence the actions of laity in a complex, technical society.

The campus clergy has been called the "greatest experimental, specialized ministry of the Protestant church—the largest and most firmly established of them all" by Parker Rossman, a devoted historian and interpreter of religion in higher education.[6] Certainly the campus ministries have attracted more people who are consciously trying to come to grips with the scientific and technical culture of the university world than have other ministries of the church. In no other ministry is so great a premium placed, at least verbally, on projects' and proposals' being "experimental," academically informed, directed to concrete professional and public problems, and willing to bring the church under "critical review." With such a range of factors being introduced into ministerial actions, it is not surprising that a recent study of Wesley Foundation leaders conducted by the Methodist church found that clarification of ministerial roles and search for adequate self-images were among their greatest concerns.[7] Even the traditional functions of

---

5. Elting E. Morison, *Men, Machines and Modern Times* (Cambridge: M.I.T. Press, 1966), p. 224.

6. Newton B. Fowler, Jr. (ed.), *Consultation on the Church's Ministry in Higher Education* (East Lansing: Kellogg Center for Continuing Education, Michigan State University, November 9, 1964, mimeographed).

7. Samuel N. Gibson, *A Study of the Wesley Foundations and the Campus Ministry of the Methodist Church* (Nashville: Board of Education, The Methodist Church, 1967, mimeographed); Woodrow A. Geier, *The Campus Ministry of the Methodist Church* (Nashville: The Methodist Church, 1967), a summary report of the Gibson study.

worship, pastoral care, and teaching are in the campus clergy usually carried out amidst considerable talk of change, crisis, and quest for the new. If the beginnings of institutionalization of "an experimental society" were to be found anywhere in the Protestant church, it would probably be in the campus ministry.

Yet it should be noted also that this ministry has been in existence long enough to have a considerable personnel and a physical establishment in hundreds of college chapels, denominational centers, foundations, and Christian associations. When many of these were founded, in the latter part of the last century, they represented not so much new forms of ministry as simply the extension to the campus of familiar church forms: the affectionate decision, as Clarence Shedd has noted, of each church "to follow its students" from private colleges into the public, urban universities. Today, however, most campus ministers interpret the support of this work as expressive of the church's determination to pay the price of understanding the work and significance of a major social institution and of the Christian commitments of those who shape its life. Most campus ministers regard higher education as the proper choice by the churches of a social structure for launching a major attempt to minister to a special parish or constituency. Their chief concerns now appear not to be with the wisdom of having a special ministry for this influential area of contemporary society, but with the churches' failure to sense the complexity and centrality of the work and with the weakness and marginality of the effort mounted.

Without evaluating these concerns at this time, we can at least note that this study has the responsibility of viewing church policies and strategies in relation to the whole system of education and intellectual inquiry in the great urban areas of the nation. Our focus is not primarily the private church-related colleges. The institutions of learning we have studied, for the most part, assume no official financial responsibility to support or to initiate the formation of Christian associations, congregations, communities, or church centers. The lay constituencies we are studying are faculty, students, and administrators in the professional, graduate, and technical schools, as well as in the liberal arts undergraduate colleges. The laity of our study are also as likely to include the leaders in research and development centers, in extension, continuing, and adult education, as the teachers and students in formal, degree-granting courses.

To look for campus ministries in such places and among such constituencies is to presume a major shift in the historic concerns of "religion and higher education." If a study is less interested in the question of how many schools require chapel attendance than in the use of university centers for continuing education, it is already saying that the legitimacy of the campus ministry is bound up with its ability to help the whole church appropriate creatively and critically the potentially revolutionizing knowledge of the university. Scholars who know the pace and complexity of the university research enterprise and of teaching those who must act on the research have a great deal of professional interest in how campus clergy select what new discoveries they bring to the study, prayers, and public worship of local churches and to the policy-making boards of denominational organizations. Whatever they discover about ways to bring church leadership into serious and effective confrontation with the knowledge revolution, and ways to guide university leaders into understanding of the problem of acting faithfully and ethically on the kind of information they develop, will be of great importance in the current education scene.

A decade ago many churchmen were more willing than now to say that campus ministries should be free from routine duties of local parish congregations so that "new ideas and ways of Christian service" could be discovered. But concern has grown in the church that the changing "experiments" and expanding "specializations" are simply the activities of people who do not know what they are doing. Early in this study a number of church and university leaders expressed to us concern that much campus ministry is highly idiosyncratic and private and the ideology ("anti-institutional," "antiestablishment") highly defensive and evasive of the question whether "innovations" can be given some objective measure of performance.

Phillip E. Hammond, in a sociological study undertaken before our own, seeks to apply a scientific theory of institutionalization or social structuring to the "occupation" of campus ministry. He has investigated the question of how widely understood were "the expectations relevant to the position, expectations held both by the occupants and by others who interact with the occupants." He has investigated the degree to which "the partners to the interaction are committed to the fulfillment of the expectation." And he found that this specialized ministry, after more than a half-century, "still looks like a new endeavor." Why, he asked, "after several generations of practitioners and many generations of clients, should it be unable to define its task clearly or hold on to its recruits firmly?"[8]

The campus ministry was not to this sociologist a successful experiment in institutionalization of either new or traditional ministries. It was not conceived and carried out with a clarity of purpose or with criteria for evaluation of possible achievement. The ambiguity of role and mobility of people in and out of this ministry were increasing, he concluded. Hope for its survival would be in further professionalization; that is, in the "development of specific standards, set and administered by the campus ministry itself." This would mean that "not only will individual persons and denominations have less freedom in appointments and promotion, but also there will be more limitation (self-imposed by the profession) in programming. What is a decrease in ambiguity is an increase in limitation. With the campus ministry a terminal occupation, denominations will lose some power to move persons in and out of positions."[9]

What this sociological view misses is the possibility of an experimental extension of historic forms of ministry. The church may have greater capacity for transmitting enduring but flexible modes of ministry than his theory of institutionalization and organization can perceive. Less attention to short-term proclamations, events, and attitudes and more attention to basic roles carried out over long periods of time, such as pastor and priest, teacher and prophet, governor and administrator, may be essential in understanding how the church changes while preserving its faith.

The campus ministries have generally represented to the parish churches a break from traditional roles of evangelist, preacher, and priest. But we have little data as to what these roles have meant to individual campus ministers and to different segments of the church. We do not know whether the campus ministers believe they are successfully carrying out these historic and primary functions in different ways and in different contexts, whether they believe that other roles are more important and possible in the places where they work, or whether their corporate ministries represent an even richer complex of historic roles than most parish churches.

---

8. Phillip E. Hammond, *The Campus Clergyman* (New York: Basic Books, 1966), p. xiii.
9. *Ibid.*, p. 149.

But the Hammond study highlights one characteristic of the campus ministry worthy of further inquiry: a commitment and manner which do not settle easily into an establishment. Clergy attracted to it often ask questions more than they affirm beliefs; they encourage unbelievers, as much as believers, to come to church meetings; many of the organizations they administer are so informal that they seem on the edge of dissolution; their ministerial roles blur, combine, and diffuse in response to varying situations. Many campus clergy will not try, as Hammond observes, to "hold on to recruits firmly" by putting them to work in the institutional church, but rather send them out on protest marches or into community decision-making structures or wherever they claim "the action is." And more recently, just when they seemed recognizable and controllable within the university environment, forming their own standards, conducting their own evaluations, and accepted by the church as a specialized ministry with little to say to the regular parish ministry, a number of their leaders have been insisting that they are not rebels who have seceded from tradition, but *precursors* laying new foundations of ministry within the old roles of pastoral care, preaching, teaching, and governance.

This distinction between the experimenter as precursor and as rebel may prove important in the future of the campus ministry. The precursor—at times while innovative and imaginative—believes he is shaping a new church, not that he is defining the edges of a disintegrating one.[10] He does not, like the rebel, despise the church and seek to live on the fringes of it, pursuing his own integrity and identity. He thinks rather that he has appeared on the scene of an institution that has become provincial or cut off from movements of history destined to pervade the culture. He seeks to shape his work in response to developments in higher learning and with an experimental stance toward the historic modes of ministry, using them as heuristic clues to continuing human needs and problems and to essential functions to be performed in all institutions of society.

Inquiry and experimentation as a disposition of mind and faith did not seem to us at the beginning of this study to be a specialty that the church should expect to be confined to the campus clergy. Certainly

---

10. George Kubler, *The Shape of Time* (New Haven: Yale University Press, 1962), pp. 90–93, has an analysis of the rebel and the precursor in art which has analogies to types of religious leadership.

campus ministries have the most ready access to the major research and educational resources in the nation. They therefore bear responsibility to stimulate and guide the church in the use of these resources. Whether an experimental stance toward the institutional church becomes more pervasive in future years depends greatly on the experience all kinds of ministries have in returning to the campus to look anew through varied perspectives and disciplines at their own patterns of action and thought. Do they sense in those who invite them to do this a compassionate understanding of their own situation? Do they sense an appreciation of church forms as finite but necessary instruments of religious commitment? By this study, the campus ministries are having their affections and attachments to old and new forms of the church explored in a way they may in time wish others to undergo.

The Meaning of Specialization in the Ministry

One of the continuing concerns pressed upon us from the start by the churches has been to clarify what specialization in the ministry now means and what significance it has for the future. Is the campus minister more specialized than the parish minister in the sense that he does not have the responsibility of conveying to one congregation, over a long period of preaching and teaching, the full range of the gospel as he understands it? Does he then become more expert at the quick, arresting presentation of a point of view? Is the campus minister more specialized by nature of concentration on a particular role and by reliance on a team of ministers to provide the other roles, in contrast to the parish minister who tries to do a little of everything? Or is he specialized by the limited constituency with which he tries to work intensively; for example, a few undergraduate students in a particular college, rather than a mixture of classes, vocations, ages, residences, and education possible as in a parish congregation?

The current classifications of specialized ministries are a mix of all these criteria. For example, a European study of specialized ministries, whose categories are reproduced in an American study sponsored by the American Association of Theological Schools, has four major divisions:

1) Chaplaincies to the armed forces, hospitals, prisons, migrants, and students with an orientation chiefly toward counselling and pastoral care;

2) Ministers engaged in Education, e.g. theological religious education of the young, university teaching, centers for lay teaching; 3) Ministries engaged in evangelism and communication in city and industrial missions, in press and films and TV, in music, drama and visual arts; and 4) Ministers engaged in Administration and Service Institutions such as central, regional and national church organizations, ecumenical bodies, coordinating positions in government, university, etc.[11]

In this scheme, students and institutions of higher education appear as constituency and locale for each separate, specialized role. Are all these roles essential for a full ministry to any one institution and its people, and are they to be carried out by leaders isolated in theory and function? What are the relationships, if any, for example, among a chaplain to prisons, a minister to a law school studying criminal law and rehabilitation, and a suburban parish minister with many successful lawyers in his church membership?

The churches reflect the problems of a society in which specialists find it difficult to understand the interactions of medical practice, education, and government on the health of a child. The secular, specialist mind is often said by the theologians to turn away from the problem of wholeness or holiness. Does the contemporary religious mind also do this in its own way? Can the minister now enter an era "beyond technology," to use Kenneth Keniston's phrase, in which questions as to the relation of specialized knowledge and the policies of institutions to the care of persons can come to the fore?

How is the parish minister related to the specialist? Local parish churches may have taken on their own selective forms of ministry, and those who support them have difficulty understanding the need to underwrite other kinds of ministry. Yet the constituencies of most experimental specializations, such as campus and inner-city ministries, are not financially self-supporting. Therefore, this study must seek answers to questions such as these: What basic beliefs, skills, and services do professional ministers provide to all Christians, no matter where they live and work? What are the primary ministries of the church that require the co-operation of laymen and clergy from varied places and responsibilities, and in what settings is this co-operation best achieved? The campus ministers work with a variety of students for short and in-

---

11. Charles R. Feilding, "Education for Ministry," in *Theological Education*, Vol. III, No. I (Autumn, 1966), 1–258.

tensive periods of time. Yet students are people trying to find the criteria by which to choose careers and mates, to decide on joining military or some other public service. The campus ministry may serve a specialized constituency, but its problems are human and universal. Has the substance of the historic faith and ministry been changed by specialization? Is the specialization such that its work and knowledge can inform other ministries? Have church experiments in the university led to a radical reconstruction of the Christian religion, in which fundamental and enduring modes of action in the church have been abandoned, reduced, or replaced, or are the campus ministries actually engaged in a restating and re-enacting of essential Christian commitment and modes of action?

The campus clergy have gone into the university, living and working there for almost a century. Do their ministries provide the laity with significant insight into their own mission and mode of faith in the modern world? The Protestant churches in America have claimed, perhaps more than any other religious movement, that each member had a chosen vocation: to express his love of God in those places that command his greatest energy and attention. The clergy, thus, are not offering laymen God's mystery in some cultic act, but leadership in a ministry which, by its care for persons, its symbolic presentation of the limits and possibilities of human existence, its prophetic teaching and inquiry, its governance in peace and justice, provides men with an important clue to the Kingdom of God.

⚜ 2 ⚜

DESIGN FOR SEARCH AND RESEARCH

I N the campus ministries, a whole new web of relationships and processes, which we term policy research and advanced learning, is being developed. The kinds of question posed by campus ministers to the scholars asked to undertake this study, the changing style of the leaders being evaluated, the research competencies drawn upon in this study, the attempts to help key leaders in the institutions studied to reflect on the implications of the data for corporate action, are all part of a new phenomenon. There is a kind of sociotechnical knowledge and learning being created by the university in its involvement with the problems of contemporary society. These factors reflect a new concern in all professions with understanding the relation of science, social ethics, and institutional policy.

The process of policy research and reflection is so new in the life of the church that none of the campus ministers asked to participate in the study had been instructed in this in their seminary education. Few thought of the process as one in which their own ministries might find important expression. Yet the beginning of such activity is so pervasive already in their work that a variety of research projects, colloquia, and seminars to which they were related could be linked with specific projects of the Danforth study. Many of the participants—such as Paul Schrading, now of the University Christian Movement; Jack Harrison, director of the Christian Faith and Higher Education Institute—have, for example, themselves begun to bring to their own organizations and institutions many of the characteristics of advanced learning. They are developing new modes of pastoral concerns by which machines serve scientific methods of inquiry and existential learning situations are adapted to community and church organizations. They wish to educate all age levels to have the courage and knowledge to act in the new society as humane persons with the power to change public policies. They see the process as crucial for the churches in their relation to the university and to public and professional leadership in our time. It signifies to them a new experience of religious reality, a new understanding of the relation of the church to scholarship, particularly that of science, and a new approach to Christian social ethics in response to the conditions of a technological, urban civilization.

American scholarship, more than that of any other nation, is now attempting to combine classical liberal arts with pragmatic-technological disciplines in education. Social surveys, psychological testing, economic analysis, cybernetics, management control systems, value engineering and programing, are all creating new kinds of knowledge that need no longer be looked on by the religionists and humanists as dealing with issues outside the reaches and interests of traditional theology and ethics. The Danforth study is policy research which has adapted such methods of gaining knowledge to social and religious experimentation and development. This has been done by a director who is not himself an expert or devotee of any one of these epistemological skills, but rather one who critically draws upon their understanding of people and institutions, as do other professional and institutional leaders.

This is not to argue at all that policy research and reflection have been fully accepted in higher education. We are exploring a way of thinking and acting in the university and church which has to win greater influence in hard struggles in the future. The kind of scholarship and learning we are trying to project in this study shares the risk of search for new and valid bases for corporate actions in response to real and pressing public problems. It seeks comprehensive models and images for service to others, not withdrawal from these responsibilities in the name of basic, pure, or even applied research.

This chapter describes the structures and processes of *search* in this study for models of ministry in the church and university and of *research* into the extent of their existence in the ministry at large in American society. We do this for two reasons: (1) so that those evaluated may test the legitimacy of the evaluation of themselves; (2) so as to increase knowledge about policy research and advanced, noncertification, noncredit education—an increasingly influential phenomenon in the modern university.

Actually the confusions in religion and education over the relation of the worlds of science, ethics, and theology to that of public action are so great that little has been written on the ways in which the evaluative character of knowledge may influence future developments in the churches.[1] Much contemporary scholarship assumes radical disjunctions between objectivity and engagement with the subject of study. Therefore the mutual effects of these realities on policies of institutions in the society such as the church and university are seldom studied.

Yet in the sociotechnical age emerging, the scholar will be increasingly asked to direct his studies to the clarification of alternatives of action confronting leaders in major institutions. In most of the inquiries which professional schools, foundations, and governmental boards are sponsoring today, the scholar is at work subtly changing the processes of decision-making. Scholars are asked not simply to report on what people think and do but to indicate possibilities for changing their ways of thinking and acting and to suggest what responsibilities may be assumed for influencing situations once thought to be the consequences of fate, providence, or someone else's initiative. The scholar is expected to be aware of the influence on policy which others see in his work and to recognize that his data-gathering does not take place through methods closed off from the people he studies. He is involved in a social and educational process which affects both the researcher and those who are the subjects of research.

Objective Involvement and Policy Research

The engagement of the director of this study with campus ministries began in 1963 in discussions with a commission established by the Dan-

---

1. There are some helpful leads: Daniel Lerner *et al.*, *The Policy Sciences: Reports on Developments in Scope and Method in the Behavioral and Social Sciences* (Stanford: Stanford University Press, 1951). François Houtart, *The Challenge to Change* (New York: Sheed & Ward, 1964), speculates some about the implications of social science for Roman Catholic church policies. Edward L. Long, Jr., *A Survey of Christian Ethics* (New York: Oxford University Press, 1967), is the best interpretation of his discipline in terms of policy concerns. One of the best statements made to the churches on evaluative policy research is Charles V. Willie's "Evaluation Resources and Their Use," *Information Service*, February 12, 1966. H. W. Richardson's *Toward an American Theology* (New York: Harper, 1967), particularly Chapter 1, is one of the most impressive theological statements of the significance of the sociotechniques of policy research for the churches.

forth Foundation to set the goals of a study of Protestant ministries in higher education and to select its director. The commission had sought a social ethicist who was as much a scholar able to understand a complex situation confronting the campus ministries and to use varied methods and perspectives in analyzing it as a methodologist interested in proving the validity of a particular type of inquiry. This was the commission's way of saying that they sought a director with an academic discipline whose subject of study was the practical reasoning of institutional or professional leaders about their moral, religious, and public responsibilities in contemporary society. As the chairman of the commission noted,

> The study will be conducted from the perspective of a particular discipline that draws freely upon both theology and social science; it will take careful account of the variety of ministries, and will arrive at the soundest conclusions possible as to future corporate actions on the basis of the facts and of value convictions shared by the people studied and the research director.

This point of view is not widely established in the university, but it was ours: the members of the study commission as well as the director accepted the objective reality of the subjects to be studied and the legitimacy of their calling.[2] The study accepted responsibility for reporting what was being done and thought by them as much as envisioning new possibilities of action. In somewhat the same way, the believer values the object of his faith. He trusts it, even if its actions are not what he expects. In this sense, at least, the objectivity of the scientist and the faithfulness of the believer are similar. Both may be present in the scholar who describes and evaluates the work of other persons. Thus, the objectivity with which this study began signified "the critical distance, the breathing-space necessary for inquiry and reflection."[3] To

---

2. A number of members of the commission either had been campus ministers or were now involved in their evaluation and direction as denominational or foundation executives or university administrators. Others were scholars, theologians, or sociologists who had made the church, education, and the Christian theology a subject of systematic study.

3. Julian Hartt, "The University: The Dilemmas of Academic Life in American Culture and Politics" (paper prepared for the Institute of Ethics and Politics, a Wesleyan University program which has influenced several campus ministries). The Institute is described by Kenneth Underwood in Volume II of the working papers.

discern the nature of what one values requires this kind of objective involvement.

The "critical distance" of the social ethicist is not to be confused with nonparticipation in the policy issues at stake in an inquiry. The scholar's critical powers are exercised both within and outside what is described and evaluated. He discerns what is happening to the people studied, but he is also a part of what is happening. His procedures of inquiry and judgment about new possibilities invite a response on the part of those he studies. The researcher is not mechanically or impulsively related to the church and the university; his deep investment of time and thought reflects hope that future ministries can be better informed of the realities of their situation, that they are as interested as he in what is good and truthful in it, and that policy research and reflection can contribute to this end. Richardson in his *Toward an American Theology* has sensed the importance of the stance of objective involvement in contemporary policy research when he notes that in it

> the "traditional" subject-object stance—characteristic of the disciplines of the modern intellectus—is overthrown. The investigator actually influences his subject matter by his questions (as in the effect of pollsters on elections), yet his questions are also affected by the answers he receives. On the basis of his participation, there is a continuing cycle of inquiry and feedback, which culminates not in "facts" but in "images." These images are the basis for a rational system of control.[4]

Thus, in the early months of the Danforth study, we attempted to discover what those who call themselves campus ministers meant by the phrase and what those who have studied them in the past had considered essential data. This was accomplished through analysis of literature, along with informal interviews and group consultations with clergy, faculty, and students in twenty centers of higher education in every region of the country.[5] We did not wish to develop a research de-

---

4. Richardson, *op cit.*, p. 18.

5. The preliminary survey of literature on campus ministries and of the types of institution in which they were developed was made by Charles S. McCoy and William L. Kolb, *The Campus Ministries in the Context of Higher Education* (mimeographed), on file in the archives on campus ministries, Yale University Divinity School. All unpublished monographs referred to in this study are to be found in this archive. Data having to do with individuals and of a confidential nature, such as copies of answered survey questionnaires, interview transcrip-

sign which reduced the campus ministers to less than they understood themselves to be or imposed visions of service on which they would never act. We sought to discover whether the campus ministries were moving toward a recognizable field of action that we could clarify and extend in all its particularity. Thus we would be evaluating these ministers in terms which were in part legitimized within their own faith and work.

Policy Research and the Actor

The kind of policy research and reflection the Danforth study represents has a view of the moral actor and the kind of problems he confronts, whether clergy or layman, which assumes that people may have some meaningful responsibility in specific situations, but that its discovery is difficult. The corporate policy issues our research deals with are not to be understood as the outgrowth of some immoral individuals. The problems are the cumulative effects of whole systems of action and actors. Systems, institutions, networks, or communication and interaction must be examined and ways found to change them at the initiative of committed, competent people. The relationship of the actors to other selves and organizations are seldom simply marked by "personal encounter" or "dialogue," but by a rich, varied mix of laws, customs, resource allocations and power alignments. The frontier literature of a number of academic disciplines is now recognizing these realities; and so policy studies such as our own can draw upon work in a variety of fields.[6] However, the situations the policy researcher confronts usually have been given no satisfactory order by the academic community; the order is his to discover and supply.

The new knowledge emerging from policy research may enable men to achieve some technique that will increase man's control over institu-

---

tions, and the like, are in the files of the director and are not available to the foundation. The purpose of this decision, agreed to fully by the foundation officials, is to assure participants in the study that none of the data will be used for evaluation of persons in connection with foundation grant programs.

6. For instance, moral philosophers such as Stuart Hampshire (*Thought and Action*) and Dorothy Emmett (*Rules, Roles and Relations*); theological ethicists such as James Gustafson and James T. Laney (*On Being Responsible*); the revisions of the meaning of canon law among the historiographers of Catholic ecclesiology and ethics, and so on.

tions. Thus man can initiate imaginative activity to change his world for the improvement of his life and that of others. Such technical knowledge does not develop in simple, voluntaristic, and individualistic moral views, but in complex and corporate ones. The latter sustain personal aspirations to discover political, educational, and religious policies which enable men to regulate and interact in a wide variety of systems.

Studies which talk about church policy are often regarded as attempts to reduce the gospel of "Christ crucified" to human engineering. To project rational goals for an institution also representing the mysteries of God is to presume a control of ultimate reality. Yet the policy researcher also sees the minister as living with the need to see what his institution can do best for others in its particular place and time and with an awareness that by its actions it may signify the presence of God in lives of men.

The occasions of deep religious commitment are not necessarily personal crises. They are also times when men act responsibly within their limited powers to avoid crises. More often than not choices are hardened and narrowed, and whole institutions and peoples destroyed, when whole movements of men and interactions of extreme commitments of social or human resources are not anticipated in policy. The imaginative judgment that fits one institution's plans into a pervasive cultural movement may be closer to religious commitment than a judgment that simply observes "what is happening in the world."

The pull of much of this new knowledge is away from the personalistic categories of "encounter" and "dialogue" and covenanted community" that have dominated much theology in the church during the past decade and gives attention to corporate, policy acts of institutional religion. The evaluators of the valued people under study in this project have lived in both personal and corporate worlds. This probably accounts for the fact that in our design of inquiry both career or case studies and social surveys were used. But they were used in very critical ways. We did not wish our research to emerge from a manipulative mentality. Many of the surveys of students and clergy we examined represented little attempt to understand the current options of belief and dissidence available in the church and university. And we discovered that many were being used by the churches with little understanding of their theological bias, or with a willing joining of the scientist in opinion manipulation. This is not to make of social survey an instrument of evil to be avoided, but to indicate that it must be used critically and developed co-operatively with university experts for clearly designated purposes.

Use of Personal "Cases" in Policy Research

Some church and academic leaders involved in this study tend first to see the nature of religiousness and of ministry in terms of individual orientations toward reality. Then they move conceptually to corporate actualities. They are aware that aspects of collective life shape religious belief, but they regard the individual's religious orientation itself as crucial. Therefore, interpretative reports and analytical use of some colloquia in this study (such as Chapel Hill) begin with persons. Their ministries and their perceptions of their situation are analyzed and placed in the context of developments in the church and university at large. But more often our "cases" are influential figures who catch the ethos of a ministry under review and move in and out of our analysis at various points.

The men whose personal views and actions receive attention are not cases in the sense that many behavioral and psychological studies use the term. These people are involved in a process of reflection and research, and they are presented as changing their way of thinking and acting in the course of the study. They are admittedly never seen by the reader except through the eyes of the director, for whom they take on significance in a whole field of action. This field and their relation to it emerge for him as he observes and reflects upon consultations and colloquia, working papers, and personal responses to survey questionnaires and data. Much of this raw material has been, and will be, available to others in scholarly work.

These people are cases in the sense of our claiming they are representative of the church's consciousness of major problems and dilemmas confronting the religious person in contemporary society. These leaders represent in ideal-typical terms the range and variety of campus ministries in the nation. But they are not cases from whom the marks of their own personal experiences have been removed in what they say and do. Such men are at once sentinel, representative, and unique figures. They say that their identity problems as Christians, whether in theology, sociology, or psychology, cannot be satisfactorily posed, let alone solved, in general terms, but they want the attempt made. The essential subject matter for them and for us—and hence their willingness to study and be studied—is human consciousness, the experience of men and women with the capacity for personal meaning and acting in the institutional structures of their age.

The Policy Researcher and His Sponsors

The policy researcher, as we have indicated, tries to maintain a critical distance between himself and the actors being studied. There exists an equally crucial relationship to the sources of support for his research. In our society it becomes increasingly important that these sponsors know why various ways of inquiry are being used. The researcher has to allow some times and places in the midst of the process of inquiry for the sponsor of an inquiry to formulate questions, be critical of emerging conclusions, adapt to new realities. The complex relation of the university to society through the funding agent is worthy of more analysis than it is getting. The relationship, if it is a responsible one, is not maintained without strains and conflict.[7]

The exploration of truth to be acted upon assumes that the researcher and the sponsor share a morality of knowledge which may not really exist. The professional researcher seeks respect for the soundness of his methods of inquiry and for the significance of the data he has obtained. When the data threaten established practices or bring to light the need

---

7. Jeffrey Hadden, the sociologist with whom we worked most closely in the conduct of the survey of ministers in the latter stage of the Danforth study, notes: "Traditionally the professionals' authority has been based on the fact that they professed 'to know better than others the nature of certain matters, and to know better than their clients what ails them in their affairs.' The client accepted the judgment of the professional as a matter of trust because he knew little if anything about the professional's field of competence. But today the client is often not ignorant of the professional's area of competence. To be sure, he is probably no more than a dilettante in the professional's subject matter, but he is at least aware of the fact that the profession does not stand as a monolithic structure on the truth of many subject matters. In the past, the frontiers of knowledge were debated in the shadows of Ivory Towers, but today they are exposed to the entire society through the mass media. The Kreboizen debate in medicine and the 'death of God' in theology are examples of the open public forum on issues that would have been largely confined to learned circles in an earlier era. And, unfortunately the mass media seem to inevitably portray intellectual issues in terms simpler than they actually are." Jeffrey Hadden, "The Crisis in Professional Identity: The Clergy as a Clue to its Nature," unpublished paper written in 1967 for staff of this study.

for innovative and new responsibilities, certain representatives of the sponsor organization with the greatest stake in programs under study may become defensive and refuse, or even be unable, to study the data and speculate about their implications for action. The same reaction may come from leaders of organizations who did not sponsor the study, but are subjects of investigation in it and of policy recommendations. Yet such people can hardly be expected to act upon data unless the methods of obtaining them are legitimate and justifiable to them. How then can professional research competence be combined with essential speculation by the sponsoring agents about the implications of the data for future action?

One answer we devised to the question was the establishment of a network of colloquia on policy research at the centers of education in which we wished to obtain data influencing future courses of action. Also the commission of the study included representation of the sponsoring foundation and consultation with its key staff members. The colloquia were set up for reflection on the nature of the campus ministries in relation to the church and university and on how information about their past thought and action and future possibilities could best be obtained and used. Through these colloquia the national staff initiated and tried out various interview schedules and survey instruments, reported preliminary impressions and data, and sought help in understanding their significance. The colloquia were able to engage the campus clergy as well as influential lay leaders among faculty, students, and public leaders in self-studies of their own situation. They used the intellectual resources available in a particular area, as well as materials developed by the national study staff.

The colloquia also, because they followed enthusiasms and concerns of local people, explored church-university-community relations in a depth that would not have been possible had the study staff imposed a rigid theoretical structure on their work. Basic questions growing out of concerns of the study commission were asked at the start by the staff, and methods of inquiry were suggested. But then the colloquia were helped to formulate their own particular inquiries. In this way interests both of the colloquia and of the emerging formal design of the national study were served. It was the early intention of the director of the study and the commission that the colloquia would be the nucleus in each area of leaders who would bring other key ministers, faculty, and administrators into intensive consultations to evaluate the study's conclusions. The way would then be prepared for the development of centers of advanced learning, institutes, private corporations for policy research, acting on recommendations of the study.

All this was a much too optimistic projection of what our financial and leadership resources represented and of the pace at which fundamental transformation of major educational and religious organizations takes place. At least by the time conclusions of this study were being formulated the methods of inquiry of the study could be seen as expressive of wide cultural and intellectual shifts in understanding forms of interaction between church, university, and social policy.

In the early stages of the commission's thoughts about the methods of the study and before a director was employed, self-studies were envisioned for "sixty to a hundred campuses." The varied histories, cultural and educational settings, and religious programs of American campuses were thought to demand this kind of broad sampling. A review of the developments in higher education, and a series of informal consultations with faculty, clergy, and students on a variety of campuses, led instead to a decision to seek a comprehensive and in-depth knowledge of the whole complex of educational and religious institutions in a few major centers.

The habitat in which we decided to study campus ministers was not to be simply that of a particular campus or that of a single city with all its higher educational and religious activities. Rather the backdrop of most of our inquiries has been the inchoate, infinitely diverse, fragmented, and confused product of our age and culture: the megapolis. Hence, our first research colloquium began with Berkeley, and our studies spanned out to survey campus ministries in the whole California system of higher education. Other areas we chose to study intensively represented places in America where rural and urban culture are meeting each other after both have gone through shattering transformations in the past century: Madison, Wisconsin, and the Twin Cities. The Chapel Hill–Durham area we studied is going through a similar development, but with the particular possibilities and problems of the South. Thus, we hope that in its design the study has taken regional variations seriously.

The metropolitan and rural-urban centers such as San Francisco, Boston–Cambridge, Madison, Raleigh–Chapel Hill, Pittsburgh, Ann

Arbor–Detroit offered us an opportunity to observe the extent to which significant interactions and interdependencies had developed between the major types of educational institution and the principle types of ministry. Most of the students, faculty, public leadership, and clergy were at least spatially locatable in such cosmopolises, and national developments were discernible. Also the extent of religious, social, and political pluralism in the United States could be noted.

With a smaller number of study units to administer, the director had a positive role in choosing leadership and assessing the significance of questions and research methods developed by these groups for the national study design. In the first year of the study, consultations were undertaken with campus clergy, faculty, and students known by our staff and commission to be influencing the relations of church and higher education in all the aforementioned centers and a number of others (for instance, Austin and Houston, Texas; Chicago and Urbana, Illinois; Cornell, New York) where no colloquia or special research projects were established. The director sought to encourage a disciplined and experimental use by campus ministries of the varied intellectual resources of their geographical area to aid in understanding their past actions and feed speculation about future social policies.

Where there was sufficient interest and leadership and the focus of concerns promised to advance our understanding of the national scene, the organization of a continuing colloquium was encouraged. Staff, membership, and consultative and financial resources were such as to ensure a look at the total situation from a number of perspectives: academic (theologians, sociologists, psychologists); administrative (college deans, presidents, denominational supervisors); participating laymen (students doing relevant studies, community and public leaders, doctors, lawyers and other professionals). These participants in a colloquium were not expected to be able to tell the church leaders what they were to do in the future, but to show them an aspect of their situation which they believed to have great human or religious significance.

Though we selected major centers with as fully developed ministries to education as any in the nation, we discovered that this was the first time in most of these that any group of clergy had gone to faculties of the universities and colleges asking them to use their professional skills to help them describe and evaluate the actions of the churches in their area. The colloquium coleaders, usually a faculty person and a clergyman, were asked to expand the core of participating personnel carefully, exploring what kinds of problems and future possibilities were most important to campus ministries and which scholars and lay leaders were most competent to study them. The varied focuses of the centers were periodically reviewed with the leaders, and financial requests for special study assistants were considered in relation to a total research strategy. Interpretative reports of the colloquium were accompanied by position papers, intellectual and career autobiographies of selected ministers, development of trial questionnaires, and so on produced in local studies.[8] Recordings and transcripts of special sessions of the colloquia were made.

It soon became evident to the national staff that most of the church leaders involved in this process were learning to appropriate critically and in a professional way data, methods, and perspectives which they had not known about before the colloquia began. The new resources represented the expenditure of millions of dollars and years of faculty and student time.[9] Thus, by the end of the first year of the study we were able to reach some consensus among the staff and the colloquia participants as to the major policy issues confronting the ministries in education, the major structures of ministry and faith in the church and the university which had to be reformed or abandoned, and the personal careers that had explored these possibilities most fully. We also had some idea of existing research we could utilize, of new data needed, and of competent personnel to obtain such data.

In the first year of our study the discernment of historic and persisting structures of primary ministry had taken on an importance not present in the early formulations of the project. It was clear after a year of discussion with church and academic leaders that institutional religion was under such severe attack, division, and disillusionment among the most educated leadership of the nation that it was difficult to get serious study of what present patterns and constituencies actually

---

8. In each center a director or codirector convened and moderated the research colloquium which met informally once or twice a month, usually for an afternoon and evening over a period of one or two years. Usually an interpretative reporter and a special researcher were also part of the local organization.

9. For example, the studies by the research staff of the Association of American Medical Colleges of intellectual, social, and religious factors involved in training for medical practice; studies by Joseph Katz, Nevitt Sanford, and others of the factors influencing on academic careers of students.

looked like and what had been their origins and significance. The faculty studying religion and clergy were seeking to speak to a generation of students reared on a popular mix of Spock permissiveness, Sartre existentialism, pietistic paternalism, and disillusionment with solemn assemblies. The difficult questions of which institutional forms of religious life are still viable and of what primary, essential services to human beings were represented in traditional ministries and the proliferating specialties, were for the most part being avoided in the university. We began with an analysis of the historic shape of the future church, therefore, not because we thought that the only normative sources of Christian service were in the past, but because we were trying to discern the occasions and movements in which men and women act corporately and institutionally. This has always been the prophetic-priestly stance in the main stream of Judaism and Christianity.

❧ 3 ❧

POLICY RESEARCH AND ADVANCED LEARNING

T HE initiative of decision as to what issues would be pursued in depth and the academic disciplines and methods to be used rested with the director and the scholars he chose to develop into a national team of inquiry. The Danforth study commission and director had to devise a flexible organization of inquiry that permitted scholars from a number of institutions to collaborate in work schedules adjusted to complex and varied professional commitments. The risk had to be taken that the national director, through the conscious and at times aggressive reflection with these scholars on the particular perception from which he and they saw the over-all task, could bring about an effective unity amid diversity. The scholars in this team varied in the ways in which they wished to use the research colloquia. But every man knew that the basic work of research and reflection does not get done in committee, but in the mind of each scholar.

Therefore, in the second year of the Danforth study the national staff members, with the co-operation of the research directors in each of our key centers, were doing considerable work on their own initiative. They conducted consultations on a national level with denominational executives, with leaders of professional and technical schools (particularly the seminaries and schools of medicine and urban studies), to determine the basis of past policies toward church-university relations and the plans for the future. An intensive study of Danforth interns and campus minister grant recipients was made in order to understand better the relations of formal seminary education to field experience of ministers in the universities. Arrangements were made for work on issues that invited further exploration by individual scholars who were not members of a particular colloquium or of the national staff.[1]

_____
1. Some of these papers are published in Volume II of this report; for example, Albert Rasmussen, "Religion and Education in a Secular Society"; Thomas Green,

Surveys of students and clergy were pretested in the second year of the study. They included items from colloquia and individual studies on religious world views and commitments, ministerial roles, social attitudes, church and academic experience, self-perceptions, and the like. The revised student survey instruments were administered in a wide enough sample of colleges and universities to show the kinds of constituency with which the campus ministers were working and the responses to their work. These plans were carried out by Professors N. J. Demerath, III and Kenneth Lutterman, sociologists at the University of Wisconsin, and by Parker Palmer, College Examiner at Beloit College, Wisconsin. A more extensive but similar survey questionnaire was sent to a broad range of American Protestant ministerial leadership—parish as well as campus. All the campus clergy and a 25 per cent probability sample of parish appointments in the American Baptist, American Lutheran, Episcopalian, Methodist, Missouri Synod Lutheran, and Presbyterian, U.S.A., denominations received the questionnaire. Approximately 70 per cent of the 12,000 sent out were completed and returned. Major responsibility for the development and administration of this survey was that of Jeffrey Hadden, of the department of sociology at Case Western Reserve University.

The research colloquia had indicated to us the importance of relating aggregate data to the institutional and personal context of survey respondents. The analysis of the national survey data was therefore accompanied by intensive studies of individual campus ministers (lay and cleric) and of the total program offering and resources allocations of churches in six centers. In these we attempted to bring together all our research resources: the extensive data of past studies, the reflections of the colloquia, interview and field observation following up student and ministerial surveys. The technical papers of Volume II and the separately published monographs, books, and articles and unpublished doctoral dissertations are all drawn upon for the director's report and conclusions in Volume I.

These academic resources had a wide range. They included the report of Robert Dentler and associates in the Columbia University Institute for Study of Urban Education on the effect of the New York metropolitan environment on campus ministries dominated by individualistic denominational assumptions out of the nineteenth century.

"Toward an Action Theory of Learning for the Churches"; David Duncombe, "An Experiment in Evaluation of Faith and Life Communities."

They also included doctoral dissertations by Yale students: Elden Jacobson's intensive study of the response of six campus clergy in Berkeley, California, to the student rebellion; Hoyt Oliver's imaginative examination of Talcott Parsons' theories of social action systems and professionalization as a tool for analyzing the ministry. The survey work of Demerath, Lutterman, and Hadden was considerably enhanced and extended by the use of students they had instructed in depth interviewing and field observation: "Mid City" interviews of clergy in the Great Lakes area by William Horvath, reproduced in Volume II. The secretaries of the director, Phebe Barth, Judy Long, and Lorna Borgstrom, and the editorial assistant for the series, Professor Burke Long, of Bowdoin College, have made important contributions to its substance and style.

Use of diverse sources of data and insight into policy alternatives has its obvious academic hazards (loss of analytical tidiness in the final reports, if not in the more specialized studies). But it invites the testing, clarifying, and integrating of technical fields that may turn out in this stage of higher education to be the most important source of new hypotheses about human and social motivation and institutional reform.[2] The director sought to make the early stages of the Danforth study primarily a free-wheeling, critical, interdisciplinary search for models of ministry which realistically reflected what was going on in the modern world and were expressive of what faithful action for others involved.

When the illness of the director in the crucial final year of the study made impossible his writing of the second volume alone, scholars associated with different phases of the inquiry, such as Jeffrey Hadden, Robert Dentler, Hoyt Oliver, Elden Jacobsen, and David Duncombe, helped him in writing particular chapters and in working out the impli-

---

2. For example, the relations between Jeffrey Hadden and the director reflected the fact that Hadden was seriously trying to come into an understanding of a world of theology and ethics absent from his graduate education and the director was trying to master the rudiments of the social-survey world in which Hadden was already a young star. The director was playing Hadden's views of what the Danforth study could get out of a questionnaire against those of his peers, in order to sense the technical possibilities in a discipline that seemed necessary to our work but whose practitioners had often displayed naïveté about the changes going on in the church and in religious commitment. For Jeffrey Hadden's interpretation of the purposes and approach of the clergy survey, see his "A Study of the Protestant Ministry of America," *Journal for the Scientific Study of Religion*, Vol. V, No. 1 (1965).

cations of his perspective and the data for policy recommendations. Obviously we had achieved an empathetic understanding of one another's approach. A community of scholarship and public concern had been attained that none of the participants quite knew was there.

The national staff continued its consultation with leaders in centers of higher education until a design emerged which made intensive inquiry into the changing meaning of each of the modes of ministry possible without destruction of the major concerns and experience of campus ministers, permitting us to see the relationship of all these modes, actual and potential. In the intensive study of denominational and ecumenical attempts to plan regional and national work and in the appraisal of seminary education in a few key institutions, we had our best opportunity to see what the churches understood to be the interrelations of these modes of ministry. The description of each center moves from an analysis of the particular mode of ministry which appears to dominate to a consideration of that mode in the context of the whole ministry and the possibilities for its expression in the future.

The San Francisco Bay area study was chosen by the national staff as the most fruitful center for beginning our inquiry into the nature of personal religious and moral commitments among students and into the kind of ministry the professional church leadership was providing in response. It was in this part of the nation that protest against the impersonality and bureaucratization of mass education and pleas for more existentially meaningful learning first became overt rebellion. Many of the campus ministers in the area had concluded that the first task of the church was pastoral: to know students as responsible selves and to provide the kinds of supportive community which permitted them to understand and assess the multiple claims being made upon them in a specialized society. They were particularly perplexed as to the connections between the personalistic religious concerns of contemporary students and their way of knowing and acting in the university, the church, and public life.

Our Wisconsin studies give chief attention to the kind of student parishioner that has been attracted by the present campus ministries, hoping to discern any significant correlations between religious commitment, social and academic values of students, and the patterns of preaching-priestly ministry to which they are attracted. The sources of intensive support for, and dissent from, traditional patterns of church life are particularly probed. Clerical expectations of their constituencies are compared with student interpretations of their own religious, social, and academic needs. The over-all intent of this aspect of the study is to see the actual tensions between laity and clergy and to see what constituencies of Christians are being given greatest support and attention by the professional leadership. Further, the study intends to discover what areas of university life offer new constituencies of people whose fundamental convictions are close to the historic and basic concerns of the Christian movement.

Chapel Hill, Raleigh, and Pittsburgh represent a series of attempts to explore the nature of effective teaching about the Christian faith in contemporary education and to begin to adumbrate the shape of a new posture of learning in the church. Attention is given to carefully planned institutes, workshops, and consultations that explore the consequences for action of various ways of inquiry and thinking about a scientific problem and produce the raw data of human compassion and concern that move others to act.

The Boston, New York, and Great Lakes area reports are the result of a Danforth inquiry asking groups of church and academic leaders— some professionally in the business of policy studies of urban education, or of Catholic and Protestant church reform—to think in terms of what responsible government of the church means. What does the church understand to be Christian exercise of power and influence in today's world? What kind of power—and whose—is being mobilized for reform? What are the natural and most faithful avenues to communication with decision makers?

In the Great Lakes region, we seek particularly to connect all our depth studies by answering questions such as these: Have denominational executives on a regional and national level governed in a way which produces social policy? If not, what have been the consequences on the commitments and work of dedicated laymen and clergy? Has a continuing ministry to people in all forms of educational life been developed? We look at the extent to which executives in a few major denominations discern relations between foreign and domestic religious education, church extension, and other traditional departments of the church ministering to higher education.

In the closing sections of Volume I, the relation of the campus ministers' situation to the seminaries and to other professional school systems is examined. Also the data from the clergy survey is reported and analyzed.

The common concern running through all of this is to define criteria, legitimate in terms of the historic faith and contemporary human need, for the church's work in the university and to measure the performance of the ministry in terms of these criteria. But more has been at stake. We are aware that we have been designating the fundamental responsibilities of all ministry, no matter whether in an academic community or not. The whole mission of the church and how it is to be fulfilled in an urban, university culture is under examination, not the rightness of specific doctrines or particular campus programs.

The effect of this general concern has not been to level the study of each place to some abstract theory of ministry. Each center grasps aspects of the Christian heritage and ministerial responsibility which have their unique gifts, while contributing considerably to an understanding of national problems. The church is revealed as the minister in the sense that not one man, but a community of men, makes possible Christian witness and service. The more concretely and profoundly special talents and callings are viewed, the more enduring and historic they seem—not exclusive or passing specializations of some one person or campus, but thoughtful and essential contributions to the full mission of the church in an urban area.

Self and Corporate Renewal through Policy Research and Reflection

Not the least important information gained in the Danforth study had to do with methods by which persons and organizations review their capacities to think and act in contemporary society. In the research colloquia, leaders of major institutions and professionals were asked to heighten consciousness of themselves and their particular responsibilities in the world. And they were asked to do what Christian men must do: to test and evaluate what they learn through the images of Christ and the vision of that more inclusive reality, the Kingdom of God.

This is an experience of self and corporate renewal that does not fit the stereotypical work of much academic social science or theology. For example, at some stage the dimensions of dramaturgy as well as the exposition of quantitative and qualitative data are involved in this learning process. The dialogic dimensions of education by which the participants affectionately sustain one another in the confrontation of complex and threatening data can be as important to the enterprise we are describing as statistical rigor and elegant factor analysis in social survey. Knowledge is not likely to be accumulated about the correlations of contemporary theological belief, role competencies, and social attitudes and then used in the forming of new ministries, if church leaders are not brought into an educational process in which future research is speculated about and the data of the research studied for their policy implications. The Danforth study sought to introduce church leaders to a process of continuing policy research and advanced learning that we expected to become a crucial part of a way of life for institutional leaders in our society and to encourage them to speculate about the contribution to that process the church could make out of its most basic historic religious convictions and actions.

Policy conclusions of a study staff or commission are not likely to be acted on if the way of thinking about the ministry, Christian faith, and education informing the study's design are not understood, debated, and adapted critically to the decision-making processes of various church bodies and agencies. One of the anticipated results of the study is a strategy of research, reflection, and continuing education for university religious centers, councils of churches, seminaries, and so on— a strategy abetted by the use of the materials and instruments of this study. What is at issue is whether this approach to church-university relations is valid for the educational life of local congregations and for whole urban or suburban areas as well as campus ministers. The method of the study, we now see, prepared us to recommend a considerable shift in the intellectual resources used by parish churches.

Policy Research and Historic Modes of Ministry

The policy research director must at some point in his work decide that the institutions, men, and regions to be studied intensively have considerable significance for the future; he has limited resources and time for study, and he must hazard that the people and places he chooses for his greatest attention will anticipate the most pressing future demands upon the institution he evaluates.

In the Danforth study, each center chosen for intensive inquiry had institutional problems and styles of ministry present in all other areas of the country. Each also represented an emphasis on a mode of ministry in the church which, when studied in depth, contributed to our understanding of the basic church-societal relationships which had to be incorporated in future work of organized Christianity expressing its faith in the modern world.

We began discussions with lay and clerical leaders in key educational centers and moved toward selection of ones for intensive study after a fairly simple recognition that what these leaders told us they were doing in ministry was the carrying out in new circumstances of certain basic, historic roles. They were engaged in pastoral care in the form of counseling, talking, and visiting with people they sensed were in deep personal trouble, sick and bereaved or facing decisions that deeply threatened and disturbed them. They were maintaining the institutional church and its proclaiming witness through preaching and administration of the sacraments and the securing of the financial support and polity for such minimal rituals. They were engaged in prophetic inquiry into the substance and meaning of faith and transmission of this knowledge in teaching. And finally they were trying to maintain some effective communication on concerns vital to the church between laity and clergy and other powers and influences embedded in a more general religious culture; this complex process of arriving at decisions as to what the church is going to say and do is one of politics and governance. It is a process essential to an institution seeking to serve corporate human needs and to transform the environment for the welfare of all. Activities of governance involve methods of education and of speaking the truth as much as they involve other interests, powers, and principalities; political roles must be fitted into whole systems of relationships in an institution or between institutions, or in and between any other agents or actors.

These four primary roles are freighted, therefore, with theological and moral beliefs and commitments, with skill competencies, technical data, institutional resources (such as allocations of personnel and funds). What the relationship of these modes and their priority are now and will be in the future in the whole structure of action of the church is a matter for serious empirical study, a subject of great controversy, and a policy question of first magnitude.

The Laity in the Polity and Economy of the Church

The first year of our preliminary interviews made clear that the basic maladjustment in the whole economy and polity of the church was in the powers and responsibilities given the laity in the church. They lacked general involvement in the issues and ideas sweeping through the clergy.[3] The campus clergy delighted in proposing educational reforms, for example, which only the more advanced graduate students, faculty, administration, trustees, professional and public leaders, could effect. But they knew little about the appraisal by these people of their own work. This study, therefore, set about early to give priority to those who put at the center of their concern the view and actions of laymen and the response of clergy to these.

This was a needed departure from the way in which large-scale studies appraising the church, the clergy, and seminary education have been conducted in this century. In the past three decades, for example, the major study of the Protestant ministry[4] began with the clergy and the seminary faculties and engaged in no systematic inquiry into lay reactions to the situation of theological education—even among non-seminary university leadership, let alone parish constituencies. The Danforth study begins with an attempt to understand what is happening theologically, religiously, and morally to the laity who are likely to constitute the future leadership of the church. We are interested in their commitments to the causes of education and work in the society around them. The study then moves to the response of the clergy and finally to the seminaries and their task. Furthermore, the Danforth study has used the social and behavioral sciences much more than the Carnegie study, but with a critical eye to the theological assumptions involved in surveys of lay and cleric beliefs, values, and roles. This is not meant as criticism of the Carnegie study data, which have influenced needed changes in seminary education. The Danforth study had financial and academic resources not available to the other inquiry.

---

3. Jeffrey K. Hadden analyzes these issues in detail in a collateral book of this study, *The Gathering Storm in the Churches* (Garden City: Doubleday, 1969).

4. The Carnegie Study by H. Richard Niebuhr, D. D. Williams, and James M. Gustafson, *The Advancement of Theological Education* (New York: Harper, 1957); H. Richard Niebuhr, *The Purpose of the Church and Its Ministry* (New York: Harper, 1956); H. Richard Niebuhr and D. D. Williams(ed.), *The Ministry in Historical Perspectives* (New York: Harper, 1956).

The only point we wish to make is that a major shift has taken place in the intellectual climate of the university and in the data considered essential for arrival at policy.

It may be that many of the disciplines used here will in another decade be more conscious than they are now of common concerns. Then the movement back and forth between specialties will not be as awkward and self-conscious as our own. In our time, many people will be disturbed by the director's running appropriation and criticism of various stages and actors in the inquiry. But perhaps those disturbed have settled in our time too easily for religious understanding in terms of a particular method or perspective in theology, ethics, or some other discipline dominating their professional or graduate education and are not capable, therefore, of participating freely in the process of policy research.

The religious issue is what God intends man to be and do for others as a thinking, social, moral person. Is man to act in the full context of life God has created for him or from within the isolated mechanisms of some one theory, role, or institution? The major religious and scientific deficiencies of design in research are not usually in the theoretical knowledge of the kerygma to be proclaimed or of the most influential factors in the institution and people to be dissected. Rather they lie in perceiving the field in which the interactions take place and the making of this field into something meaningful, manageable, and endurable for specific human beings who, for better or worse, have become the objects of one's service.

Style and Policy Research

A few words need to be said finally about the relation of the style of the director's report to its design of inquiry. The two basic volumes are intended to unfold a story of a *process* of inquiry. It is a process which reveals the methods and conclusions of the director using varied disciplines and scholars, some of whom work within an explicit religious framework, some of whom do not; it is a process which appropriates these disciplines in a way that illumines and expands the churches' Christian understanding of faith and the world, but does not distort or denigrate the integrity of these disciplines.

There have been increasing attempts to do this in the church and university,[5] but most still give little evidence (as we try to provide in Volume II) of what the parties to the encounter have really had to say to one another. The style of the report of policy research is finally what reveals the morality of minds at work in choosing among various possible expenditures of research funds, in resolving epistemological controversies between staff members, in using first one, then another, set of data to illumine the factors that influence the actions of men.

This can be done if the style takes the readers through the most significant twists and turns the writer has made in his journey to certain policy conclusions. The policy researcher does not know the strategic, over-all outcome of these until the end. He knows something of the power of the factors and modes of action emerging in the lives and work of those studied, but he does not know until the latter stages of his work their organic relation in social policy—in the impact on basic institutional financial allocations, on training and nurturing of types of leadership, on the attraction of certain kinds of constituency and neglect of others, on preoccupation with certain problems and issues, and on shifts in convictions, status, and power that *may* transform the whole mission of an institution or organization.

But to speak finally of the most fundamental aspect of the director's report—the hope is to convey a sense of the fun, excitement, and release that is beginning to show in the people studied. The basic hypotheses and anticipated finding of this study are that in the midst of profound crisis and division over the direction and purpose of the ministry, the basic lines for fundamental reform are emerging. And they have emerged first in that most troubled and self-conscious of all ministries: the campus religious leaders.

---

5. See, for example, from the church, the mimeographed report of the World Council of Churches special study commission on the *Church as Mission* (Geneva: 1967); Sallie McFague TeSelle, *Literature and the Christian Life* (New Haven: Yale University Press, 1967).

PART II

The Historic Shape of the Future Church

↣ 4 ↢

FROM VOLUNTARY RELIGIOUS ASSOCIATIONS

TO COLLEGE CHAPLAINCIES

Aт Cornell University, the clergy who minister to the people of that institution do not refer to themselves as campus ministers, but as "The Religious Ministry at Cornell University." The united ministries there (Congregational, Baptist, and Presbyterian) recently issued a common statement describing their work. The statement is not unlike that made in scores of other educational centers.

It affirms that the campus leaders of these three denominations are "ministers in motion" who hold "nothing sacred save the new commandment [new presumably with the New Testament] to love God with our total being and to love our neighbors as ourselves." The statement seeks to break from any view of clerical domination by stating that "the students, faculty and staff do the work of this ministry."

What are these works? Four, and their order is significant: the ministry is committed (1) "to reconciling the fragments of contemporary life"; (2) "to engaging in creative service within the world and the university"; (3) "to undertaking a thorough analysis of history and contemporary theology"; (4) "to participating in the authentic and relevant worship of God within the sanctuary and beyond its walls."

The statement then goes on to say, "Further, this is a ministry moving toward ecumenicity with the self conscious intent of becoming 'one people'." And "even more," the statement adds, "this is a ministry which encourages radical experimentation without fear of failure. The new world about us invites bold and courageous dialogue with the men and women who struggle amidst the implications of a Christian faith of our time."

The most significant indication of the future thrust of this ministry is found in a speech by one of its leaders, John Smith. He argues that there is emerging on his campus and many others a "prophetic militant community in the center of the university . . . of Jews, Catholics, Protestants, agnostics and humanists, as well as others," who are attempting "to recruit and mobilize professional experts within that community for the sake of providing greater clarity on and more direct involvement in policy issues of mutual concern." This community, he contends, shares at best "a margin of meaning" which theologically might be described as a "community of hope and expectation, whose unity is primarily constituted by a shared passion, shared action, and a shared vision of the future, rather than any common (organized) religious affection or theological affirmation." As far as Smith is concerned, these are the kinds of community and center which will be decisive as to whether significant theological inquiry and ethical research go on in the church and whether significant learning and reflection take place in the university.

We need to note the parallels of these works of ministry to the integrative-pastoral, the kingship and governance of Christ, prophetic inquiry and teaching, the priestly-sacramental themes central to the organization of this study. But they have taken on new expressions of service and new institutional or corporate form.

Where did these modes of service come from, and what is their current meaning? Are they simply the creations of a small clique of ministers, lay and cleric, who have covenanted as the Cornell group says to "be alive for the university, to be present in the world, to be responsible as one people, and to be conscious of our expanding possibilities?" Or are we dealing with forces that are moving whole institutions and peoples?

The term "campus minister" has been widely used for the past decade by professional leaders who wished to differentiate themselves from "religious workers with students" or leaders of a "home church away from home." Countless statements issued by denominational centers and the offices of chaplaincies and religious affairs have indicated that "campus ministry" implies that the Protestant churches are concerned with the problems and changes affecting all of higher education. But the name has seemed less and less adequate to leaders in the university Christian movement in helping perplexed church leaders understand that campus ministers are trying to alert the church to the fact that the university is becoming the institution around which the cultural life of modern society is being organized. This fact has profound implications for all ministries; the clergy on campuses, consequently, have new and crucial responsibilities to the whole church.

There is a growing awareness in church circles that we are in the midst of what Robert Lynn calls a great "turning point in American education."[1] The future will bring a quite different pattern with closer, co-operative relations among local churches, denominational offices, and university leaders; among elementary, secondary, and liberal arts educators; between Protestant and Catholic, public and private institutions of higher education. The campus ministry, therefore, will increasingly mean service to the total enterprise of education in an area with a variety of institutions: the experimental, mixed vocational and liberal arts centers in the ghettos of the city; the well-established two-year community colleges in complex state systems; the four-year state schools just making it out of normal, teacher college status; the large public, urban universities with their rich complex of graduate, technical, and professional, adult, and extension and TV mass educational enterprises.

Even a decade ago to talk of the "campus" denoted largely residential colleges and universities whose boundaries were fairly clearly marked; and "ministry" reflected an era when the presence of professional religious workers on each campus was still a hope and laymen were not yet seen as the principal agents of significant Christian witness in most American educational enterprises. The "ministers" were specialists in a particular area of Christian service. The vision of a corporate ministry expressing a whole range of structures and functions (as reflected in the Cornell statement) had not yet appeared. What is at issue in the new situation is whether the religious forces can produce social policies that in deed as well as word provide communities expressing the full field of action and thought of God's renewal of the world and man's discovery of a common humanity.

This occasion, which many influential campus ministers have perceived, arises from something quite special in their lives: the frustrating

---

1. Robert W. Lynn, *Education in the New America* (New York: Department of Higher Education, National Council of Churches, 1966), p. 1. See also his essay, "A Ministry on the Margin," in Volume II of this report.

experience of being crowded to the edge of the most vital and salient moral and religious concerns of the very people and institutions they seek to serve. The campus minister is often identified with the interests of an institutional church they regard as failing to put these human concerns at the center of its life. On many campuses, chapel attendance is declining. Courses on Christianity are taken over in the public universities by expanding departments of religious studies, while research and teaching by ministers is confined to extracurricular, noncertification status. Many of the students with whom campus ministers have worked closely in social action projects have become more realistic about the power of bureaucracies and professional structures to resist change and more concerned about influencing people of technical competency to institute reforms in the institution where they spend most of their time and energy—in education itself.

What do these developments mean for the ministry and for the church? Few religious leaders are sure. They look now with more seriousness than a few years ago to attempts at discerning the shifts in structures of power rather than to the latest cause needing a following. They are trying to discern the major processes and structures that have an objective and continuing reality to them, though they may be beyond the control of individuals or single organizations.

The occasions of God's actions in the past, so far as the director of the study can discern, are expressed in pervasive movements requiring fundamental decisions not only by religious institutions but by all major structures in society. Yet these forces can often be seen as part of one's personal calling. So the response made to an occasion is not some separate defense of a special ministry (for example, preserving it for the future), but a rereading of its history and potential in terms of the full field of God's action in the world. The scene of lay and clerical work now cuts across departments of higher education and religion in church and university, across traditional boards of supervision in higher education, and across academic interests of faculties in theological education and other departments and schools.[2]

What has happened in the past century to bring about this new

2. This is seen well in the "Report of the Committee to Study the Campus Ministry," Annual Conference, Methodist Church of California, February 1967. See also Charles McCoy and William Kolb, *The Campus Ministry in the Context of Higher Education* (St. Louis: Danforth Foundation, 1964, mimeographed). This paper reviews the literature of historians in religion and higher education.

occasion in the relation of the churches and the university can be seen in the changing meaning and relationship of the four traditional modes of ministry reflected in the Cornell statement. These modes are represented in four important phases in the history of campus ministries in this country and in the contemporary institutional establishment. These modes have been recast over a century in new vessels of service demanding close, selective, effective collaboration of laity and clergy.

The Voluntary Associations

The campus ministry as a special religious activity had its origins in voluntary associations established by students. They sought ways of expressing religious interests and convictions other than the regular services of worship and pastoral care provided by clergy and faculty controlling the daily life of the college. It is important to understand the environment within which these first associations were formed. It provides a clue to the lay-oriented, nonofficial, pastoral activity which has characterized much of the campus ministry ever since.

Virtually all colleges founded prior to the Civil War were under church auspices. Of 182 permanent colleges in the antebellum period, 175 were under religious control.[3] In these old liberal arts colleges, the faculty were primarily concerned "to transmit the learning of the past" in order to develop persons of strong character, "called" to "serve God and one's fellow man." The educated man in this tradition, even while carrying out the skills of a particular profession, was expected to be the bearer and critic of his culture.

The campus climate of opinion, the curriculum, the leadership of faculty and president, all were thought to minister to the student. Therefore a professional with specific responsibilities for the religion of the student was seldom designated. This ministry of the total college is indicated by Samuel Eliot Morison when he writes of Harvard:

> An important, and as many will think, an essential, ingredient of this early liberal education was the religious spirit of Harvard. Our founders brought over this medieval Christian tradition undiluted. The Harvard student's day began and ended with public prayer: daily he heard a chapter of Scripture expounded by the President; Saturday was given up to cate-

3. Donald G. Tewksbury, *The Founding of American Colleges and Universities before the Civil War* (New York: Columbia University Press, 1932), pp. 55, 90.

chizing and other preparations for the Sabbath, which was wholly devoted to worship, meditation—and surreptitious mischief. Harvard students were reminded in their college laws, and by their preceptors, that the object of their literary and scientific studies was the greater glory of God; and that the acquisition of knowledge for its own sake, without "laying Christ in the bottom, as the only foundation," was futile and sinful.[4]

Yet interest in orthodox doctrine and ritual did not exclude concern for advancement of learning.[5]

The establishment of religious societies by students—forerunners of the Young Men's and Women's Christian Association, the university Christian movements, and covenant communities—began in these eighteenth-century colleges.[6] Then, as now, these societies were organized primarily by laymen who wished to explore questions in greater personal depth than the regular curriculum permitted; they sought to discover what their religious convictions required of their careers and what changes in the church and the college might more adequately accomplish their proper purposes in the world. The Society of Brethren, begun in 1806, was, for example, dedicated to awakening the church and students to missionary responsibilities outside the nation.

The period of 1820 to 1860 was one of increasing rebellion by students against faculty and clergy. Both groups were many times seen as enforcers of rote learning in a fixed curriculum and snoopers into personal lives in order to detect infringements of moral codes. But this was not the dominant picture. The teaching and pastoral concerns of such influential administrators and teachers as Stephen Olin at Wesleyan University and other faculty and clergy who taught courses in Christian and public ethics during this period were of considerable influence among students. Their ideas were sometimes out of touch with a world beginning to emerge from the influence of the Industrial Revo-

4. Samuel Eliot Morison, *Three Centuries of Harvard* (Cambridge: Harvard University Press, 1937), pp. 24–25.
5. Manning M. Patillo, Jr., and Donald M. MacKenzie, *Church Sponsored Higher Education in the United States* (Washington, D.C.: American Council on Education, 1966), pp. 124–136. Perry Miller's explorations of the life of intellectuals among the Puritans, for example, reveal their breadth of learning, including an interest in the classics and the emerging physical sciences. See Perry Miller, *The New England Mind: The Seventeenth Century* (Cambridge: Harvard University Press, 1954), pp. 34–108.
6. Clarence P. Shedd, *Two Centuries of Student Christian Movements: Their Origin and Intercollegiate Life* (New York: Association Press, 1934), pp. 1–17.

lution and natural sciences, but they were trying to ask the basic questions about man's nature and destiny as posed in the new student societies and associations.[7]

There is not a great shift in tone from the charges the voluntary associations brought against the churches and colleges (such as "lack of missionary fervor," "indifference to the soul and spirit of the impoverished and destitute outside the college") to the protests of campus ministers such as Walt Herbert and the "student left" at Berkeley (for instance, against the "Silence" of the university on the big issues of "meaning" and against the doctrinaire reduction of educational experiences and the routine accreditation of people for bureaucratic position, without regard to their creative and innovative possibilities). From their beginnings these voluntary associations have been barometers of a younger generation's discernment of the indifference of established institutional leadership to the uniqueness, diversity, fervency, and authenticity of personal hopes and aspirations.

Growing out of the earlier voluntary student groups, the Christian Associations provided the most influential form of campus ministry between the Civil War and World War I. The first were formed in the 1850's. Six hundred twenty-eight chapters embracing 32,000 students were established in colleges, universities, preparatory school, and professional institutions by the turn of the century.[8] Both the YMCA and YWCA throughout their history, and more consistently than many other organizations in the campus ministry, have been sensitive to changing ethical religious interests of the laity. Academic and theological rigor has been less important than student initiative in the formation of programs. The movement began as an "interdenominational" effort expressive of the mission of a number of evangelical Protestant churches. The association was

> to unite the Christian college men of the world, to win to Christ the students who are not his followers; to guard college men against the many

---

7. Wilson Smith, *Professors and Public Ethics: Studies of Northern Moral Philosophers before the Civil War* (Ithaca, New York: Cornell University Press, 1956), is a worthy account of some teachers and chaplains who sought to explore with students the relations of personal Christian commitment to public issues.

8. For a history of the Christian Associations, see C. H. Hopkins, *History of the YMCA in North America* (New York: Association Press, 1951), and Shedd, *op. cit.*

temptations which assail them, not only in the body but also in the realm of the intellect; to deepen the spiritual life of the Christian men; to increase their efficiency in Christian work; and to lead them, as they go from college, to place their lives where they will count most in advancing the Kingdom of Christ.[9]

The growing religious and social mobility of Americans was reflected in the Y's expansion of its "associate" membership to include students who did not share the Protestant assumptions of its constituents. The social gospel movement, with its criticism of the indifference of American business and industry to human misery and poverty, and the new openness of biblical studies to historical and scientific insight, both found strong support in the student Y associations. Since the 1920's the stance of the Y's, and in particular that of the women's associations, has been that of providing a community of affectionate support for people of diverse creeds, races, skills, and talents in a world-wide network of voluntary communities.

In recent decades the student Christian "voluntary associations" have been increasingly criticized in campus ministry circles for offering pastoral concern cut off from academic learning, fellowship without significant public influence, and technical counseling weak on theological perspective. But they have represented an important bias toward reconstituting the pastoral functions of the laity and have provided an ecumenical base for activities in public educational institutions.

Evangelical conceptions of ministry dominating nineteenth-century Protestantism had a concern for individual "poore soules" not present in the priestly concepts of ministry dominating Anglican and other old-line establishment religion.[10] The chief emphasis was on authenticity of personal religious experience and on the "hard-sell" strategies of conversion rather than on critical, comparative reflection on the meaning of faith. It sought to meet serious social problems by saving souls one by one from an evil world.

The effect of this kind of religion in the twentieth century was to turn pastoral care from concern with responsible selfhood in an increasingly specialized society to vague, supportive counseling on private

9. Shedd, *op. cit.*, p. 625. Quotation is from a speech by John R. Mott.

10. Sydney Mead, "Evangelical Conception of the Ministry in America," in H. Richard Niebuhr and D. D. Williams (ed.) *The Ministry in Historical Perspectives*, (New York: Harper, 1956), p. 222.

moral and religious issues. Friendly pastoral care and the proliferation of discussion and other student-initiated groups became a noncontroversial service many ministers felt the church had competency to provide. The chief professional discipline required was the capacity to listen sympathetically and to spot the fad issues and popular phrases. Programmatic and organizational devices were available in the evangelical academies: "covenant communities," "dialogic education" and "ecumenical institutes." Little serious, critical study of the theological, social, and educational assumptions or consequences of these programs went on in the nineteen-forties, -fifties, and -sixties.

A number of forces have increased the demand in the past century upon the church for these informal groups which encourage affectionate support of individuals regardless of their function or status in society: the skill of organizations to manipulate personal guilt and anxiety; the harsh breaks in communication between generations; the indifference of academic leaders to the subtle policies of government and business which force career choices and retirement decisions. Many laymen hoped that at least the minister and lay association leader could be a nonofficial resource of personal counsel and absolution outside the record-keeping, efficiency-rating machinery of work and government. But could the church and its voluntary associations change anything in the very organizations that deepened these personal horrors? That was the question that came increasingly to the fore in the mid-twentieth century.

By the 1940's the private papers, sermons, and manifestoes of the precursors in the campus clergy begin to note that in the New Testament context, the pastoral functions and voluntary associations (such as Christ's disciples) of the church always have an *apostolic* aspect. The minister is *sent* out to serve others and to make known his hopes for the future. He is one who must go and find out what is happening to people, why they are forming associations outside the traditional organizations, and what possibilities they have for the larger society in the future.

But the shifts in emphasis in the pastoral mode have been vast in this century. Studies of the covenant communities, for example, a phenomenon of campus ministers but two decades old, indicate that the focus of activity has moved from internal concerns with authenticity of personal encounter and with the ordering of cultural change through major theological images, to exploration of basic career styles and responsible policy function in the technological and professional organizations of the society. The deep alienation of many students—not only those of the "hippy" subcultures—from the formal guidance and health services of the university have heightened the pastoral responsibilities of many in the faculty and clergy. The groping of students for personally meaningful education and for freedom to influence how that education proceeds is affecting church colleges and seminaries as well as the large public universities.

Origins of the College Chaplaincy

The second historic structure developed in the campus ministry was that of the chaplaincy. Until recently this mode regarded as basic the preaching and priestly offices of the church. Teaching, for the most part, was made an extension of its proclaiming, confessing, apologetic stance. In this tradition, a clergyman or faculty member was designated to direct the college chapel and to preside over occasions in the life of the institution when the whole community gathered in scholarly convocation or worship. He was to give symbolic expression to the normative religious convictions of the institution and presumably those of the wider culture. The polity of the office still reflects this assumption. Most of the current members of the Association of College and University Chaplains have administrative appointments in private schools, but because they usually hold teaching as well as preaching responsibilities, their appointments are subject to some sort of review by the faculty.

Some Protestant denominations, principally the Lutherans and Episcopalians, have in their official sponsorship of college work sought to maintain this image of chaplaincy for college congregations of their own tradition. In more recent years the ministers, if not the administrators, have seen the style of their chaplaincies as a charismatic proclamation that has its cognitive challenge to the central academic work of the university. They often view the office as an expression of religious convictions of a minority. To them this is more important than any attempt to speak the consensus of a majority. From Talcott Parsons to Charles Glock, the traditional chaplaincy has been the form of ministry most prominent in the sociological view of the church: guardian in sermon and rite of the organized and institutional power of religion in our society.

However, recent historical scholarship is complicating the picture of what these nineteenth-century chaplaincies were like. The images provided by Schmidt, Tewksbury, Rudolph, and Hofstadter are of colleges and religious leaders narrowly sectarian, ecclesiastically oriented, and dogmatically opposed to science and technology.[11] The new studies are usually of particular colleges and of their relations to surrounding communities and to general intellectual and social trends of their time. They show that the leaders of many of the influential denominational colleges, rather than being out of touch with the social and intellectual needs of their time or merely catering to them, appear to have enjoyed widespread support in the more progressive elements of business, professional, and academic sectors of their communities. Sermons delivered, for example, at Bethany College, the first college founded by the Disciples of Christ, sought to persuade the students when they became leaders to divest "literary institutions of a sectarian character . . . [and to give] reference solely to the public good as a measure of policy." Community leaders were urged to help furnish the colleges with "every species of apparatus for all the physical sciences and useful arts," and faculty were enjoined to "build up all the brethren, for the common cause which knows not state, territory, lineage, or blood on earth."[12]

---

11. Only two books, both written over thirty years ago, deal comprehensively and exclusively with the pre-Civil War colleges and both do not effectively relate the college and its leadership to its social context: George P. Schmidt's *Old Time College President* (New York: AMS Press, 1930) and Tewksbury *op cit.* Richard Hofstadter's *Academic Freedom in the Age of the College* (New York: Columbia University Press, 1955) mostly tells what the denominational college was not. Frederick Rudolph, in *The American College and University* (New York: Vintage, 1965), is also more concerned with the quality of scholarship in Jacksonian America than with the moral and social functions of the colleges. The problems in the historiography of higher education were reviewed by David Potts, Harvard University, Department of American History, for this study and in a Harvard dissertation, 1967. Case studies of the relationship between theology and education in the thought of college presidents, some of whom were also chaplains to their institutions, were done in a Yale University dissertation, 1967, by Larry T. McGhee, "Higher Education and Human Depravity on the Antebellum Frontier."

12. These quotations are from the sermons of Alexander Campbell in **The Millenial harbinger** . . . , 3rd Series, Vol. VII, 1850, p. 331; 4th Series, Vol. V, pp. 12–13; 5th Series, Vol. III, 1860, p. 370 (Bethany, Va: The editor, 1830–70).

The post-Civil War dissipation of religious energies in competitive denominational battles to found colleges and the shortsighted hostility of the churches to the expansion of the state universities are familiar in historical scholarship. So also is the incapacity of evangelical pietism to appreciate the religious and ethical dimensions of an urban, industrial environment and the natural and social sciences. Theological studies which continued to rely chiefly on a historical and classical humanities curriculum were increasingly identified with professional training for the ministry and not deemed suitable for informing action in a specialized, technical culture.

Institutions in higher education which remained closely related to the churches' preaching and priestly ministries continued to dominate the style of work into the twentieth century. These modes presumed a community of believers large and faithful enough to keep chapel services going, a congregation whose religious commitment was both particular and historical (to the God made known in Christ and the Scriptures) and in one important sense unreserved (the acknowledgment of the holy as the ultimate ground and condition of all learning and action). The chaplain and those he chose to preach were expected to keep alive this worshiping constituency.

With the increasing secularization of the society and the diversification of religious and academic backgrounds of students and faculty, this community of believers could no longer be assumed even in the church-related institutions. In some church-related colleges, in a century, attendance at chapel services was at first generally expected, then made "compulsory," then presented as one option in a lecture series, and finally either abandoned or apologetically presented as an alternative use of the general forum of the college. Faculty became more insistent that the study of religion be differentiated from liturgical practice. Administrators sought to employ only clergy whose scholarship met the academic standards of other faculty.

These developments were part of a larger struggle to free inquiry from the control of all orthodoxies. The struggle in the church was to gain some prophetic, independent perspective on education and culture, to learn to inquire as well as to proclaim, to manifest a corporate rather than purely personal conviction on issues that mattered to the academic world. Thus the chapel would be the full expression of an actual Christian community involved in the work of the university.

The dominant mode of Protestant chaplaincy has in this century been that of attempting to make a clear and careful confession to the world of the concrete meaning of its faith. As Richard Luecke, once a Lutheran chaplain at Princeton, has said, "Words are a first and basic kind of deed of the church, which cannot be replaced or subsumed by other kinds of deeds."[13] In his view, this presence of God is made known by signs in history; the human word is an indispensable element of such signs, because the proclaimed gospel alone joins together such realities as water, bread, information about suffering human beings, possible policies to help them, and the revealed signs of the hidden God. The word in this sense, then, is sacramental; it is God making Himself present in the history of man's free response to Christ's call to act for others. In such a tradition the presence of charisma, or a gift of grace, is dependent both on the objective fact of the proclaimed word and sacrament and on the subjective attitude of the worshiping community.

There are many college chapels which operate out of a more "liberal" or "modern" tradition. Their leaders say that they seek to reflect in the lecture stance of the "sermon" and in other aspects of the sabbath ritual a kind of "academic atmosphere of classroom objectivity." This does not necessitate the chaplain's assuming "each Sunday a proclaiming, confessing posture," but relies on presentation to the students of "a representative sample of the best of contemporary religious thought." The chapel is not seen as a place of confrontation with the theological and ethical reflection of a particular church or congregation, nor of participation in the usual covenants and sacraments of church life.

Other college chapels reflect a climate of subjective personalism. They rely on the appeal of a chaplain who is "with it" in the eyes of students, even if he may lack historical insight into the continuing dilemmas of human realities. In the course of this study we have observed chapels that have begun a school year filled with a rich mixture of students, faculty, and townspeople of varied religious commitments, genuinely seeking strong leadership in the exploration of the meaning of faith. And we have seen these constituencies reduced by spring to a score of students reporting experiences in experimental cults, reading plays to one another from *motive* magazine, imitating the esoteric music of communities other than their own, focusing on aesthetic innovation to the exclusion of moral and public hopes and frustrations of a

13. Richard H. Luecke, "A Lutheran Perspective" (unpublished, 1965).

city or region. Here the pastoral and teaching offices of ministry have become abstracted from proclamation and governance. The chapel becomes a platform for idiosyncristic expression of charismatic personalities and free-floating expression of oceanic joy in life, uninformed by the experience and study of any academic department, least of all religion. The short-run attraction of such chapels is that no theological commitment or study is presupposed, and the sacraments are confined to second features after the main service.

This kind of *sui generis* university chapel appears to be reaching the end of its day. So also is the end near for chaplaincies that equate the church with the college establishment. What is sought more often now is a setting for proclaiming the faith of a genuine congregation in the service of God—a congregation that knows what it is to be loyal both to their Lord, Jesus Christ, and to the best in education, a congregation whose particular confession of faith is informed by other ministries, not the least of which is that of serious social involvement and action.

In the broad view of a century of ministry the chaplaincy's chief contribution has been an insistence that proclamation and celebration of the ultimate commitment of the self must not be lost amid emphasis on adaptation to a changing environment. But the campus chaplaincy has historically been bound up for the most part with a particular kind of educational context—liberal arts, private colleges enabling students to organize fragments of information and experience into personally meaningful philosophies of life and fostering associations informed by their own sense of social purpose and religious commitment.

Now the leadership of campus ministries, in response to the trends described in the next chapter, has shifted to centers of mass, public education in order to keep some contact with major developments in education, religion, and social policy. But significant choices of what can be done with the voluntary associations and chaplaincies of the small, private church-related colleges remain; the choices are the kind that only administrators, faculty, community leaders, and hard-pressed chaplains can make in frank and open consort. The kinds of choice can best be indicated by a look at some of the church-related college chaplaincies we studied in depth.[14]

---

14. The colleges and personnel will not be named, and some changes have been made in their situation which do not change the essential issue so that dis-

College A is an academically strong institution in a classic way; it is what Barron's *Profile of American Colleges* rates as a "highly competitive" college, drawing students from the top fourth of their class with SAT scores ranging from 600 to 675. This college has had a long tradition of church relationship and of student liberal reform action. It is located in a small town, but within two hours of a major midwestern city. This is a college which has had in its structure a faltering denominational seminary with long historic ties to the school. The faculty of this seminary were not aware until too late how marginal or peripheral their work was considered in the academic enterprise of the college. The seminary was recently closed. Before it went under, concerned faculty in the college went to key administrators and scholars in the seminary offering to help it focus its concern on the campus clergy and the relations of the church to the changing intellectual life of America and to make the chapel an expression of this concern. The proposal was not acted on.

Now , as in the past, the administration of this college has thought of the chaplaincy as preaching-worship leadership and counseling of *a* minister and has placed a strong premium on personal qualities that seem to assure tender, loving care of each student. Indeed, a report prepared by outside consultants on what the college was to do with the chaplaincy did not dispel this image of the office in the minds of many administrative and faculty leaders deciding its future. The predicted "solution" was to be the employment of a "strong young preacher" who, by partial membership in a good eastern university department of religion, has shown his respect for orthodox academic circles.

Today the future of the chapel, including its relations to a strong department of religious studies and to new educational proposals in the college, is highly ambiguous. What our own study of the situation in College A revealed was strong and varied alumni support for the religious activities of the college, an awareness of heady changes under way in the church, and an estimate by a number of faculty that sizable funds could be easily found for a venturesome religious program outside the classroom that would also strengthen formal academic studies. But this would mean the development of a chapel staff, lay

guise is more effectual. Tensions over what to do in those institutions run fairly deep, and the people involved are so few as to make identification easy if the institutions are not treated as composite cases.

and clerical, that widened considerably the images of the primary modes of ministry. It would mean, for example, that the substance of faith proclaimed and the acts of worship would reflect the thought and experiences of an active, committed group concerned with basic academic and social policy issues. Thus when the chaplain preached, his voice would be more than the lonely cry of a dedicated man. The reform we envision would mean the soliciting of alumni funds to conduct carefully planned consultations into the moral and religious problems of a variety of leaders, so as to encourage faculty research on problems of religious commitment, personal development, and social policy and so that students might feel the chapel was a center of learning and inquiry not confined to the methods and rituals of the regular curriculum. Thus students might share with faculty in "task force" studies of some import to neighboring communities and cities, if no more than by depth interviewing and discussion of the data's significance.

College B is by Barron's standard's "very competitive." It is highly aggressive in its attempt to find a new role for the small, church-related college. It has a trimester system to give time for a change of academic pace and social involvement; it has a faculty trying to see how its courses can help students understand the problems of urban and suburban United States from which they come.

The administration of College B wants the chapel to be what was suggested for that of College A, but the chaplain shows signs of panic and genuine confusion as to how to act on the proposals. He has for years traded on the antichurch predilections of students and their love of discussion of the "hot" issues that stir dissent, but promise little lasting change in educational policy. His ties to the religion department have been strained by a running attack on its "outdated" theology which fails to grasp the Christian significance of the "death of God," the revolt against "Puritan sexuality," and the rise of a new feeling-based religion. The prediction of our study was that he would soon move on to development or personnel work in some college. There is no existing training center or denominational career evaluation that could help him learn to do what the college now wants from him.

College C, a denominational college born in the depression, recently met Barron's standards of being "competitive" academically. With an energetic and courageous president, this college has faced the fact that "it must either innovate radically to serve a regional and denominational constituency from which it draws what strength it has, or die as gracefully and as soon as possible." To the chaplaincy of this small-town college the president brought a Negro, fresh out of a national denominational staff, with ghetto experience freighted with possibilities for "revenge." But this was a man who cherished the values of small-town college life. In two years of chaplaincy he helped that college break out of a whole series of confining postures. He helped it discover new constituencies and issues for its summer religious conference programs, its drama school, and its social inquiries to serve. He helped put synod policies and local church adult education endeavors at the center of the opportunities for reflection which students and faculty offered the region. Over all, this is not the stuff of national policy action. But it is important to the life of particular communities and institutions which matter a great deal to the students, parents, and public leaders whom this college can educate at all levels of age and career. Its chapel offers in the midst of these inquiries, for those who wish them, the rituals of human forbearance and divine suffering and love.

In College C the chaplain's own personal encounter with an isolated WASP community was something like a northern *In The Heat of the Night*, except that the story line was more subtle. There was no obvious violence or murder committed on the new agent of social change. There is no single, ignorant, economically marginal culprit to be found by a smart, well-educated Negro pitying the ignorance, prejudice, and insularity of the whites trying to run the town. There is only the way of life of a fairly affluent, middle-class white community. And the non-heroic *provocateur* is simply a chaplain who likes a college and has persuasive ways of explaining what higher learning means to the life of a person and a town.

These colleges are not the places where most of the students and faculty and the scientific-technological research of this country are now located, but the decisions made in them as to their basic purposes are not without significance still to the lives of millions of persons.

⤜ 5 ⤛

FROM DIRECTORS OF DENOMINATIONAL CENTERS

TO CAMPUS RELIGIOUS PROFESSIONALS

By the end of the nineteenth century the leaders of the old-line denominations were beginning to be aware that most of their young people were no longer going to be educated in the private or church-related colleges, but in state and municipal universities. The third major structure of campus ministry then emerged as denominational student centers and foundations led by clergy who saw their work as a special, professional calling: chiefly to minister to the public and urban universities and technical schools.

Denominational Centers at the Technical-Research Universities

Some of the ministers who chose to serve them viewed these new institutions as an expression of values and social developments that challenged the meaning of the "faith of our fathers."[1] They represented an emphasis on developmental research and experimentation, extension of a specialized, elective curriculum, and unabashed application of learning to technology and social change; and they appealed fervently to egalitarian aspirations not present in many of the private schools.

The methods and the spirit of inquiry in the new public universities were to test basic convictions of the churches about the nature of God

---

1. Harry Smith, former director of the Westminster Fellowship at the University of North Carolina, notes in an unpublished paper of the Chapel Hill Colloquium, "Secularization and the American University," for example, that the state schools, the extension departments, and the technical institutes expressed fundamental shifts in world views, epistemologies, and learning processes which had dominated most private and church-related colleges.

and of how His actions are known in the world. Was God to be known only through historically oriented theological scholarship? Were religious knowledge and experience fixed and given or part of a dynamic process of emerging truth won in constant inquiry? Were religious and ethical principles capable of being tested in controlled experimentation for their operational meaning? Or were these matters strictly for private speculation? Did laymen have as much insight as clergy into the substance of faith and the processes by which beliefs are formed? These issues deal with ways in which Christian service or ministry is to be performed. The different responses made by Christian leaders to these issues continue to provide the major sources of conflict in American Christendom.

Today tremendous shifts are still taking place in values and in the power structures of higher education. They are not accurately described simply as shifts of influence from the private to the public sector. Rather the shifts in educational purpose, leadership, and resource go on in both these sectors. They go on in the church-school battles over how religious and educational convictions are to be tested and authenticated in the world. They go on in contests between the older land-grant colleges, the more prestigious (academically) state universities, and the emerging community colleges. They go on over the kind of academic research that will come to grips with pressing, corporate problems of an urban society and with world responsibilities of public leadership. They go on in controversies over the kind of extension and adult education that will serve long-range policy concerns. There are public and private institutions alike which have built great national reputations on traditional academic learning and on selection of only the most intellectually gifted students. Many of these institutions are now beginning to feel entrapped in situations where the conditions and values that made them great are disappearing or being transformed.

In such a revolutionary time, the chief problem for spiritual leaders who want to help the people who need it the most—the neglected, lonely, alienated persons of the educational system—is to discover where the crucial decision-making processes are and the issues being discussed. Yet the crucial decision-making processes are not easily located. The easy answer of the radicals is that these places are in the free universities, in store-front education a block from the factories and businesses where students work. The answer of the conservative is that the places are easily locatable on the formal organizational charts. The answers appear to us much harder to come by. The controversies fought in the history of higher education of the nineteenth century show us the difficulties.

The chief disputes over the nature of authentic pursuits of the mind and the relation of faith and science appear to have been waged in public universities. They were expanding and revising the classic humanities curriculum that dominated the private schools. They made vast public funds available for scientific experimentation and technological research. They increased faculty power, if not responsibility, in shaping the educational enterprise, in order to reduce control by denominations or other special interests outside the university. Even the fight for an elective course system for students represented a reaction against the fixed scholastic curriculum of institutions such as Cambridge and Oxford and their counterparts in this country. The reforms of Eliot of Harvard,[2] the establishment of Rensselaer Polytechnic Institute in 1826,[3] the passage of the Morrill Land Grant Act of 1862 providing federal money and land to states in support of colleges offering occupational training in agricultural and mechanical arts, were all manifestations of a growing conviction that truth was something to be discovered through the active engagement of men in reshaping the natural and social environment.[4]

The first experiments of the churches with student programs in these new public universities and technical institutes were largely attempts to repeat the voluntary associations and chaplaincies. In 1867 the Presbyterians began a program at the University of Michigan under the direction of the minister of an Ann Arbor parish church. In 1893, the Disciples of Christ established a Bible Chair at the University of Michigan to supplement a public education expected to remain devoid of formal religious studies.[5]

---

2. Frederick Rudolph, *The American College and University* (New York: Vintage, 1965).

3. Ray Palmer Baker, *After One Hundred Years* (Troy: Rensselaer Polytechnic Engineering and Science Series, No. 29, 1930).

4. This theme is particularly well developed by Solon T. Kimball and James E. McClellan, Jr., *Education and the New America* (New York: Random House, 1963), pp. 19–61.

5. Grey Austin, *A Century of Religion at the University of Michigan* (Ann Arbor: University of Michigan Press, 1957).

By 1913, however, a new and more influential form of campus ministry had emerged at the University of Illinois in the first Wesley Foundation. Its statement of purpose, by James C. Baker, reveals a mix of concerns: preservation of traditional church loyalties in face-to-face groups; an awareness that the opportunities for learning in the universities would necessitate an improvement in the quality of religious education in the churches; attention to the religious significance of the scientific atmosphere (hence a "laboratory for training lay leaders" was envisioned); reflection on the fact that in the university career decisions were made and that these were likely to be oriented toward "specialized tasks." The statement of objectives is not in this contemporary language, but beneath the pious vocabulary these hopes are clear. Baker sought for major campuses:

1. A shrine for worship. 2. A school for religious education. 3. A home away from home. 4. A laboratory for training lay leaders in church activities. 5. A recruiting station for the ministry, for missionary work at home and abroad, and for other specialized Kingdom tasks.[6]

By the time this pioneer of campus ministries had become a Methodist bishop he was convinced that such university-based centers were going to become more important to the work of the churches than their private colleges. These centers should be supplied with the kind of professional leadership, library, and study facilities to make possible the continuing re-education of clergy and laity and to foster critical analysis of the basic decisions made by the churches on publication of literature, investment in architecture, and community action. This pioneer church statesman believed that the mission of organized religion and the meaning of the gospel for a new urban, technical society must be formed in close co-operation with the intellectual resources of the university. For him, we now realize, much more was at stake than a ministry to students which satisfied the home-town churches. In 1966, the Michigan Association of Ecumenical Ministries, reviewing Baker's historic vision of what denominational work at universities might be, concluded that the

6. Board of Home Missions and Church Extension of the Methodist Episcopal Church, *Wesley Foundation Work* (pamphlet), cited by Clarence P. Shedd, *Two Centuries of Student Christian Movements: Their Origin and Intercollegiate Life* (New York: Association Press, 1934), p. 125. See also James C. Baker, *The First Wesley Foundation* (Nashville: Methodist Publishing House, 1960).

churches had often reduced the vision to superficial work spread thinly over the educational landscape and that most church administrators were just now beginning to understand what Baker meant by campus ministries.[7]

The sources of Protestant inability to act on such a vision are not hard to find. In the mid-twentieth century most Protestant churches were still trying to function within the institutional mechanisms and mind-set of nineteenth-century evangelical Christianity. This saw the secular, experimental, highly specialized research structures of the university as an alien, antireligious, dehumanizing development.[8] Even Baker's understanding of public education assumed that the task of the churches was to establish a center capable of appropriating the intellectual resources of the university for the evangelistic work of the church. The possibility that the university itself might become the major institution for the formation of belief and commitment among key leadership in the society was not foreseen.

Neither could the men who made church policy in this period anticipate that the historic modes of teaching and prophecy in the church might be recast in terms highly influenced by the scientific inquiry, historical consciousness, and technological imagination of the modern American university. The denominational student foundations were conceived as centers of religious education and training because the public universities were not expected themselves, by nature of their secular character, to be influential places for the formal study of Christian commitment. Therefore, Sunday schools and weekday, noncredit classes taught by the clergy were needed to supplement the curriculum of the state universities.

Yet the fact which now confronts the churches is that about 90 per cent of the nation's publicly supported, four-year-or-more colleges and universities offer some kind of studies in religion as part of their established curriculums, and the options are growing. A fourth of the nation's public universities have developed special departments of religion, and the percentage is fast increasing. The hindrances to such departmental developments are not legal now, but mainly political, cultural, and intellectual. Their chief support is the serious academic interest of students

7. Newton B. Fowler, Jr. (ed.), *Consultation on the Church's Ministry in Higher Education* (Kellogg Center for Continuing Education, Michigan State University, 1964, mimeographed).

8. Bernard Bailyn, *Education in the Forming of American Society* (New York: Vintage, 1960), p. 40.

and faculty. Many of these new departments display greater interest than most church-related colleges and seminaries in phenomenological and empirical studies of religious commitment; they are interested in ecumenical approaches to religious experience in a variety of cultures and traditions, rather than exclusive focus on Christianity; they seek to test the ways in which theological inquiry gives some personal order to academic specialization and how it heightens consciousness of the complementary uses to be made of varied epistemologies in discernment of responsibilities in complex social situations.[9]

In short, the churches and the universities have taken our society to a point where issues as to what forms of inquiry most enhance personal and corporate capacities to act creatively and responsibly in the world have become the crucial ones in the relations of men and institutions. This is a question of the morality of knowledge.[10] These issues cut across religious groups in complex ways.

The decisive questions to be answered about people with whom one may wish to work have to do more and more with how they inform themselves about the forces shaping a situation, whether their commitments and loyalties permit an openness to truth that may not fit previous interpretations of a problem, whether they are consciously able to use different languages and methods for perceiving the social realities they confront. These are not matters simply of formal indoctrination in beliefs or principle, the accumulation of religious fact or information, the acquisition of narrow technical ministerial skills. They have to do with intellectual resources to perceive the truth about the world and one's relation to it and the moral courage to act on such knowledge.[11]

9. Robert Michaelsen, *The study of Religion in American Universities: Ten Case Studies with Special Reference to State Universities* (New Haven: The Society for Religion in Higher Education, 1965); Milton D. McLean and Harry H. Kimler, *The Teaching of Religion in State Universities* (Ann Arbor: University of Michigan Press, 1960); M. Willard Lampe, *The Story of an Idea: History of the School of Religion at the State University of Iowa* (State University of Iowa, Bulletin No. 704, March 1955); Christian Gauss (ed.), *The Teaching of Religion in American Higher Education* (New York: Ronald, 1951); Erich A. Walter (ed.), *Religion and the State University* (Ann Arbor: University of Michigan Press, 1964).

10. Van Harvey, *The Historian and the Believer: The Morality of Historical Knowledge and Christian Belief* (New York: Macmillan, 1966).

11. Some of the best studies in the changing philosophies of education in America, tracing these themes: Thomas Molnar, *The Future of Education* (New York: Grosset and Dunlap, 1961); Theodore Brameld, *Education for the Emerging Age* (New York: Harper and Row, 1950); Laurence A. Cremin, *The Genius of*

Ministry on the Margins of Social Policy

The period of 1875 to 1920 seems to have been a formative one in American religion. This was the era in which the churches were being asked to come to grips with the human meaning of industrial, scientific, urban developments as epitomized, generated, and conceptualized in the public multiversity. By the second decade of the twentieth century all major denominations had established national church organizations, along with student movements and professional leadership on campus. By 1940, departments or commissions of university work had been formed with denominational and interdenominational boards of education. Professional leadership representing some main-line church bodies were present on most of the state or major private university campuses.

There was a period in the post-World War II religious boom when many Protestant church leaders entertained the illusion of placing a minister on every campus, or at least establishing a Christian Athletes organization in every locker room. Church organizations and personnel would visibly influence or transform every major institution and activity of society.

But the leveling off of financial support for ecclesiastical programs in the sixties, the loss of institutional morale, the increase in mobility of professional ministers in conversation with both church and university leaders, pressed Protestant leadership to some painful conclusions. The source of dedicated, informed talent in the Christian movement was very limited and increasingly critical of the policies which governed its placement and support. The choice of educational institutions to which men gave important years of their careers had to be made with care, a conscious philosophy, and a national strategy. The relations of religious leaders to other major institutions had to be related to the university programs, and the insight gained made the clue to the reconstituting of whole church programs. All of these conclusions reflected a movement of the church to the margins of formal power, status, and institutional resources in the society.

This marginal position in the society is viewed by some church leaders as an occasion for renewed interest in the theological and moral dimensions of education and urban life.[12] But it can also be an occasion

---

American Education (New York: Vintage, 1966); George F. Kneller, *Existentialism and Education* (New York: Wiley, 1958).

12. See Robert Lynn, "A Ministry on the Margin," in Volume II of this report.

for an increasing embrace of the eccentric gimmick. Both responses are symptomatic of anti-intellectual, antihistorical abandonment of human issues in institutional policy at the center of society, and they are highly evident of church-college panic actions. The "move to the margins" of society may be accompanied by a diminished attention of the ministry to professional studies and strategic decisions; and in their place amateur, eccentric, short-run decisions are accentuated.

In the vast majority of the large universities some form of co-operative interreligious councils of ministries (usually of the United Church of Christ, Presbyterians, U.S.A., Baptists, Disciples of Christ, and Episcopalians) have come into existence,[13] and as the funds become tighter these are represented by fewer and fewer staff. The Lutherans and the more conservative denominations have been increasingly reinforcing their pattern of local parish chaplain. In most of these ventures the obvious functions which embrace all groups—gathering religious census data, unified publicity about religious programs available to students, conduct of short-term social action projects—have become ecumenical.

But the more strategic questions are not as often faced. What professional and lay services are indispensable to ministry, and does the team represent them? What constituencies are reached, if specialization of ministry is practiced (for example, medical school)? How does this specialization fit regional or national plans for the educational life of all the churches? What do these ministries require of university intellectual and educational resources? These are professional and policy questions.

As Charles McCoy and William Kolb have noted,[14] many people in these ministries have been seeking to move toward professional competency and status in recent decades. The number and size of co-operative ventures have been an expression of greater individual specialization and search for standards of professional competence. What does not often get seriously asked in these developments is whether the Christian ministry is a mix of professional and amateur, rational and charismatic, attributes which distinguish it from other professions. How does it com-

---

13. Seymour Smith has reviewed the history of some of these groups in his *Religious Cooperation in State Universities* (Ann Arbor: University of Michigan, 1957); the ecumenical history of particular campuses is recorded in Austin, *op. cit.*, and Richard Henry Edwards, *Cooperative Religion at Cornell University* (Ithaca: Cornell Cooperative Society, 1939).

14. Charles S. McCoy and William Kolb, *The Campus Ministry in the Context of Higher Education* (St. Louis: Danforth Foundation, 1964, mimeographed).

pare with other professions in attention to selfhood, corporate policy, theoretical discipline? What do attempts to combine leadership of a religious movement or community with specialized skills do to professional images of success and failure?

The governance of an institution, including the church, involves, as Phillip Hammond notes, the formulation of expected, complementary roles. They may be separately identifiable and specialized, but together they achieve the essential objectives of the organization. Governance also involves the provision of resources for training people in these competencies and the evaluation of their capacity to carry them out.[15] The campus ministry, as we have noted, during its history developed fairly stabilized roles of pastor-counselor, preacher-priest, teacher-inquirer, and administrator-enabler in the adaptation of historic modes of service to actualities of American education. By 1887 a college Christian movement had emerged out of local societies. Charismatic figures such as Mott and Baker led the way to professional leaders with official, campus-wide responsibilities for religious programs.

The current and varied names of positions or offices (counselor to religious associations, chaplain or dean of the chapel, teaching elder, co-ordinator of religious affairs) as well as the names of professional organizations (Young Women's Christian Association and University Christian Movement; National Association of College and University Chaplains; National Campus Ministers' Association; Association for the Coordination of University Religious Affairs)[16] attest to the fact that the ministry has been institutionalized as separate interpretations of specializations.

The evidence is strong that these specialties and associations reinforce different interpretations of religious commitment and that they have assumed little initiative in trying to see what co-operation between them would produce in a functioning campus ministry in a city or re-

---

15. Phillip E. Hammond, *The Campus Clergyman* (New York: Basic Books, 1966), pp. 111–131.

16. A co-ordinator of religious affairs is not usually a chaplain, in the sense that he is willing to be identified in the university as one who preaches or confesses a particular faith. But is he a co-ordinator or maker of policy in the sense that he works to have the historic modalities of ministry fully, consciously, and effectively represented in a university? If the co-ordinators do not govern in the influencing of a balanced personnel staff in campus religion, who assumes this responsibility?

gion. The chief professional issue is whether these associations provide for the development of models of ministry and evaluate causes in order to help men reinterpret their work or relocate, or whether they see that church and university organizations are provided to do this if they cannot. Having done this for their own specialized group, do they bring themselves into effective collaborative discussion with the other associations? Evidence of such professional developments is meager.

Most of these issues are caught up in the images of leadership of any campus minister whose work has brought him into a position of professional responsibility beyond a specific denominational constituency. This can be seen in the career of Robert Bottomley.

Robert Bottomley is the new dean of the chapel of one of the most prestigious and influential private universities in the South. This man's early Southern Baptist nurture came under serious review in his theological education at an eastern interdenominational seminary. But his ties with the South remained. He took as his first parish a church in a textile town not unlike the Gastonia of Liston Pope's *Millhands and Preachers*. In time he was brought before the local Baptist association under charges of religious heresy; the real issue, however, was that for some businessmen his emphasis on the social and ethical implications of his faith was an impediment to the economic growth of the town.

His next two parishes were in college communities in the Midwest. In each of these places he led a community church and sought to create an independent and constructive criticism of the intellectual, spiritual, and social life of the local college. He also served the parish needs of the families of varied professional and vocational background in his congregation.

By the time he accepted the position in the church-related university, he had begun to have serious doubts that he was significantly influencing the life of the colleges in his community. In the first year as dean of the chapel, he told the chancellor in very direct terms what he intended to do and won his full support. He spent three months studying the university and the area surrounding it. He dropped in on classes in law, medicine, and city planning and talked to the major leaders of business, secondary education, and dissident Negro groups in the city.

Bottomley made the chapel a place of preaching and worship which it had never been. At first the attendance was small, but he gradually began to attract the faculty of professional and graduate schools and a few key professional and business leaders and artists who had given up on the local churches.

Then he began to invite at these Sunday services faculty, students, and business and public leaders to discussions of the issues his sermons and prayers raised. When they wished to pursue issues with more care, he organized small groups.

Further, Bottomley tried to obtain by fairly rigorous study of existing university data some picture of where the region was headed in its social and economic development. He invited the leaders of the national denominational center in the city to consultations with university faculty on some of these data, asking them what they made of such studies. He discovered they had never initiated such sessions in the university, that many were highly disturbed by the shift of some of their functions to the university, and that the divinity school of the same denomination had never encouraged such consultations.

Finally, he met regularly with the campus ministers in the area. He hired an ecclesiastically sophisticated associate minister, and together they began to call on and observe each minister, trying to find out what each thought he was doing, who evaluated his work and hired him. They hoped to begin to exercise some influence over future appointments in a way that did not violate denominational traditions, but built a functioning, balanced ministerial team.

This whole procedure impressed his seminary, which put him on a committee to evaluate its education. He serves on crucial Danforth Foundation committees. He returned to his alma mater to tell the students why some of the major national pulpits were now emerging in university centers.

His work also impressed the staff of this study. But as the national trends of education became clearer to the staff, they hoped that Bottomley would be invited to lead the reconstituting of church work at Berkeley or Madison or New York or Boston, or some place outside the Protestant culture and chaplaincy of the southland. The centers where most educational work now goes on are not where Bob works. Once these places are described, the questions of where Bottomley would find a worshiping, proclaiming constituency, what organizations he could use to build teams of ministers, and so on, become quite different from those in his present post. The Robert Bottomleys and other leaders of the church are now entering a new phase of ministry in which church-university-social policy becomes a major component of action in the principal metropolitan areas.

The new occasion the churches confront might best be characterized as a time in which all historic, primary modes of ministry are now mandatory wherever the church exists in full witness to the work of its Lord—mandatory not in the actions of individual pastors, but in full consort. The next decade may be chiefly a struggle to go beyond the most debilitating marks of secularization—a technically and denomination-ally fragmented ministry—to social policies of the churches that imaginatively and compassionately bring all the resources of ministry to bear on the spiritual and moral problems of particular constituencies and institutions in the society. These are long-range programs which combine religious belief, technical data, and the personal skills and institutional resources of all basic modes of ministry in a field of Christian actuality. This study is an attempt to describe and understand this field as it has been engaged in or avoided in the campus ministries. The field of Christian action in higher education is the exclusive province of no one ministry, though that ministry has important and special responsibilities.

The task the churches confront can be seen simply in bare statistical data. After World War II, with an upsurge of lay financial support and religious interest, the churches rapidly expanded their work on the campuses of nonchurch-related colleges and universities. In the period from 1953 to 1963 the number of full-time campus clergy in eight major denominations almost doubled, while the total of all ordained clergy advanced but 15 per cent.[17] Yet this period of growth was less expansive than the decade from 1943 to 1953, the 1960's having become for leaders of most denominations a time of reassessment. *Full-time* professional leadership involved in the work of campus ministry at the start of our inquiry in 1963 was about 3,000 staff persons.[18]

---

17. These data are based on reports made to the Danforth study by the American Baptists, the Christian Church (Disciples of Christ), Episcopalians, Evangelical United Brethren Church, Missouri Synod Lutheran, Methodists, Presbyterian Church in the U.S., United Presbyterians in the U.S.A., and YMCA and YWCA. Estimates of a more impressionistic nature were made of the Southern Baptists, Church of God, and other groups less given to co-operation in statistical surveys.

18. This estimate is based on the following sources: (*a*) questionnaires to denominational officials; (*b*) study of rosters and records of the denominations and

These tended to be concentrated in the academically strong private and church-related colleges and in the large public universities. The more recently established community colleges and urban universities and the technical and professional schools had the least representation. About 350 were YMCA and YWCA secretaries. About 450 of the professional assignments were designated by their sponsoring agencies as college chaplains and deans of the chapel; persons in these positions were usually employed officially by the college or university. Most of them taught part time in the formal curriculum of the school which they serve. There were an estimated 400 evangelists, chaplains, pastors of more conservative denominations, who visited campuses seeking to set up special meetings and associations.

The largest number of campus ministers, about 1,500, included university pastors, leaders of denominational foundations, and associate pastors of large college or university town churches which had developed specific programs for students. Most of these were participants in the United Ministries in Higher Education under sponsorship of several denominations and are members now of the National Campus Ministers' Association.

Approximately fifty Bible chairs were sponsored mainly by the Disciples of Christ churches and offered university courses in Christian Scriptures and doctrine. About seventy-five co-ordinators of religious affairs were employed by the universities in student personnel offices. A small but influential group of about one hundred professionals directed more specialized ministries, such as institutes specializing in policy research and leadership education, faith-and-life communities, coffeehouses, experimental programs with graduate or professional students, and so on.[19] Seventy-five administrators, field supervisors, directors of

the professional associations, such as the National Association of College and University Chaplains, the National Campus Ministers' Association, and the Association for the Coordination of University Religious Affairs. These figures do not include pastors of churches near college campuses and those who participate informally during less than half of their time in college chaplaincy responsibilities.

19. Most of these professional ministries on campus have been the subject of special study. On all types of campus ministry, see George L. Earnshaw (ed.), *The Campus Ministry* (Valley Forge: Judson, 1964). On the college chaplain, Seymour Smith, *The American College Chaplaincy* (New York: Association Press, 1954); James C. Windsor, "The American Higher Educational Chaplaincy," *Chapel and College* (Spring 1963), pp. 18–35. On the denominational worker, Stuart D. McLean, *The Campus Ministry* (New York: United Church, 1962, mimeographed);

denominational and interdenominational agencies and national evangelical organizations (such as Inter-Varsity Fellowship), completed the professional personnel.

The leaders of the YWCA and YMCA were among the first to indicate publicly that the rapid growth and complexity of higher education and the leveling off of particular sectors of financial support were factors in their giving increased attention to strategic centers of ecumenical work and leadership training and to the role of part-time lay staffs and local parish ministries in higher education. What did the addition to the professional ranks of 555 campus clergy from 1953 to 1963 mean in a period when the nation's colleges and universities had added several million students, plus hundreds of new community colleges and urban universities, and the major centers of professional, technical, and continuing education had extended their research teaching beyond the comprehension of even the administrative officers who directed them?

In the light of these trends, the leaders in the ecumenical and denominational boards increasingly in the 1960's asked questions such as these: Where should the best of the limited professional leadership of the churches be concentrated? What are they to do that will enhance not only the life of a few students but the education, worship, and community action of many churches? Do present and proposed allocations of budget and personnel have a radical or comprehensive enough strategic rationale in terms of what is happening in the broad movements of higher education and the lives and work of the laity in the modern world? Does the whole church take its university relations seriously? Does church leadership have the kind of relation to university research to obtain help in finding answers to such questions?

These questions are clearly moving toward attempts to see the problems of the campus ministry as a function of the church's capacity to

------

Parker Rossman, "The Denominational Chaplain in the State University," *Religious Education*, Vol. LV (1960); Parker Rossman and William Baker, "The Worldly Ministry," unpublished manuscript, Yale University Divinity School archives on campus ministry; Don Fleming, "The University Parish Pastor" (Th.D. dissertation, Pacific School of Religion, 1961). On college-town pastors, J. Gordon Chamberlain, *Churches and the Campus* (Philadelphia: Westminster, 1963). On experimental ministries, John Perry, *The Coffee House Ministries* (Richmond: John Knox, 1966); John E. Cantelon, *A Protestant Approach to the Campus Ministry* (Philadelphia: Westminster, 1964). On co-ordinators of religion, John Paul Eddy, "Public School Directors of Religious Affairs," Ph.D. dissertation, Southern Illinois University, 1968.

understand the part that education now plays in the development of the whole society. The leaders of the Christian church and the university, whether they know it or not, are dealing with the same realities: struggles for personal meaning in the midst of despair and decisions about the direction society should take and about how and where and for what purposes the awesome power of the various sectors of our nation should be used. They are responding to these realities in different ways, however, because of different assumptions about their essential nature.

The initiative of well-informed, dedicated leaders becomes crucial. It can hardly be said that the campus ministers appear to the church at large as having persistent, unavoidable questions of policy priorities. There are significant exceptions. For example, the California campus ministers of Methodism challenge key denominational leaders with policy statements which set priorities for the church as a whole. But these exceptions have been too few to affect national policy significantly.

The campus ministry has reached a position in its history when policies toward it can be formulated only within the context of the church's whole ministry to the society. These policies, further, can be formulated only through a view of higher education as a part of a whole system of primary and secondary education, head-start programs, research and development, universities and colleges. Higher education itself can no longer be thought of in terms of what happens on a certain campus. It involves such things as the quality of intellectual inquiry in a research institute on Route 128 outside Boston and the subjects and approach of informal "research seminars" arranged for juvenile court staffs, as in Denver. Significant influence in such affairs is manageable by individuals of commitment. They are the stuff out of which just social policies emerge. They are the testing grounds of the ministry of the contemporary church, not to say the education of the university.

❧ 6 ❧

PRIMARY MODES OF MINISTRY

AND SOCIAL POLICY

RELIGIOUS institutions which have survived for centuries have obviously been able to adapt themselves to the environment of many ages and peoples and yet retain sufficient loyalty to their originating commitments and forms of ministry so as not to lose their integrity and identity. Understanding a movement's endurance and change is required to see stable patterns created by individuals and groups meeting new human situations and needs.[1]

Do campus ministries have patterns of identity in the Protestant churches which have endured through time as an achievement of value? Phillip Hammond concludes that the campus ministries represent a "radical" break from "undifferentiated conceptions" of the ministry traditionally held. Thus the mark of the campus clergy is not overspecialization, as popularly supposed, but the *range* of its use of varied types of ministry.[2] Conceptions of parish ministry have historically had

---

1. Our inquiries into the subject matter of this chapter were aided greatly by the fact that the office of the study was located, after the first year, at Yale University Divinity School, and a research colloquium of Yale and Wesleyan faculty began to discuss working papers and reports from the other colloquia and from the staff. Out of this experience came many leads into theological and social ethics studies that helped the director develop his own pattern of interpretation and provide knowledge of graduate students whose Ph.D. dissertation work might be related to or inform the Danforth study. Actually, three dissertations (by Wayne Meeks, Hoyt Oliver, and Elden Jacobson) were of considerable influence in this study, as will be indicated at appropriate points.

2. Phillip E. Hammond, *The Campus Clergyman* (New York: Basic Books, 1966), p. 50. See also Hammond, "The Radical Ministry," in Volume II of this report.

to do with roles that concentrated on preparing members for participation in the church and rebuilding shaken religious commitments. Most campus clergymen are willing to carry these roles out, Hammond concludes. But their greatest identification, in contrast to the parish clergy, is with a variety of "differentiated" goals facilitating religious and human development of members. This is true even if some of the traditional activities of the institutional church are jeopardized and even if the minister needs to engage in tasks other than that of preacher, priest, and evangelist. Hammond's study also identifies this flexibility with comparatively liberal positions on various social and educational issues.

From Hammond's data, it appears that the campus ministries represent an organized and conscious effort to widen the range and viability of modes of action available to the ministry. One might even say they recovered neglected historic modes, since local parish forms and skills have become too limited. This achievement could not have been possible without, in Hammond's judgment, the church finding room for "radicals" who threatened traditional organizational practices. This was done by "segmenting them, thereby minimizing disruption without sacrificing their potential insight" but excluding them altogether from the ongoing life of the rest of the church. The campus ministers in response should, in his judgment, maintain and deepen their character as segmented radicals by becoming even more institutionally developed. This would be achieved through improvement of their own standards of performance, by clustering colleagues in small communities for mutual reinforcement, by assuming greater freedom from routine duties such as worship and visitation. Thus the campus ministry could be a "safety valve for dissidents" and a "learning" influence through the "circulation of radicals" and their "clients."

We can be grateful to Hammond for helping us see that the radical thrust of the campus ministry generally is not toward a narrowing of ministerial roles and responsibilities, but rather toward an attempt to break out of the confines of too specialized attention to pastoral concerns for existing church membership in the local congregation. And Hammond may be right in saying that reformers need to band together to seek leadership in the whole church for expanding the modes of ministry and achieving an intimacy of relationship between persons and community action, data-gathering and proclamation. But the direction of reform and service should be toward the confrontation of the church with the realities of its primary ministry and the centrality of the university to that ministry. The basic question is whether the roles of campus ministry represent a recovery of historic ones and whether the present situation permits any longer a basic strategy of "radical segmentation."

The Present Transitional Period for Modes of Ministry

The ministries of the Protestant churches are now going through a particularly painful and controversial period of transition. In this period the issue over the relation of the "general parish" ministries to specialized ministries, such as to the campus, is a crucial one. Many seminaries and denominations are confronted with a majority of students or ministers who wish to be in ministries other than in a local parish. Yet in the literature of the church and university and in the minds of the laity dominating church policy, the parish congregation remains the normative model for ministry and one without the possibility of specialization. The diversification of ministerial form is now forcing serious reconsideration of the relation of religious experience to organization and of innovative service to historic theological convictions.[3]

For example, historically one of the major dialogues of Protestants with Catholics has been over the question whether or not God is immanent in a ministry (as in the perfect, full substance present in a cultic act, in an infallible doctrine or a high-level ecclesiastical judgment). The main-stream Protestant witness has been that each mode of ministry, whether in a local parish or university center, is to be viewed as having a partial witness. It represents a segment of the Gospel, a concrete but limited vision of the character of God's ways of acting in the world. There is no way for the Protestant to extract from this act something that is in itself holy.[4] Division over this point today, in contrast to

---

3. For example, James B. Ashbrook, "Ministerial Leadership in Church Organization," *Ministry Studies*, Vol. I, No. 1 (May 1967).

4. The influence of this principle on the life of one American city is explored in Kenneth Underwood, *Protestant and Catholic* (Boston: Beacon, 1957). See also Paul Tillich, *The Protestant Era* (Chicago: University of Chicago Press, 1948); Claude Welch and John Dillenberger, *Protestant Christianity* (New York: Scribner, 1954); George W. Forell, *The Protestant Faith* (New York: Prentice-Hall, 1960).

earlier times, now seems increasingly to cross formal Protestant and Catholic affiliations.[5] Educated Catholics, as we shall see in the Berkeley student survey, may more generally resist identification of the holy with particular modes of knowledge, but not with church forms, than Protestants of the same academic level.

The issue of the holiness of particular church forms is where the radical Christian chiefly splits with the conservative. How is the Gospel of the one high God in and beyond the many to be conveyed? Could any organized religion have been possible, the conservative asks, if there had not been convictions that particular modes of ministry more than other acts indicated what God willed them to be and do? From these enduring modes men infer the nature of the God loved and worshiped.

Yet this doctrine is always under suspicion in radical Protestantism. How is Jesus Christ as Lord to be made known? This is not done simply by preaching a logical, coherent theology, nor is it done exclusively by the courageous organization of public resources to serve the poor and ignorant. Christ is not made known simply by inquiring into the human adequacy of plans for urban reconstruction. Rather, says the moderate, the Gospel is presented by thinking and acting out ministerial modes in their essential relationship to each other in a special kind of personal responsibility in society. Essential relationship of these modes is not merely in the self but in social policy.

The historic phrases used in the church for showing the essential relationship of these are many: for example, pastor-director, prophet-king. In past ages more than our own these terms drew upon historic images and experiences of the church. Today the favorite image to mediate the essential relation of all these modes is probably the moral self. A new generation of scholars in the universities and seminaries senses that the American movement of Christianity has assumed a particular responsibility to work out in images of selfhood the moral and political implications of its faith.[6] The Kingdom of God and social self-

---

5. Examples of Catholic authors who have positions similar to the Protestants previously cited: Thomas F. O'Dea, *American Catholic Dilemma: An Inquiry into the Intellectual Life* (New York: Sheed and Ward, 1958); Gordon Zahn, *In Solitary Witness* (New York: Holt, Rinehart, and Winston, 1964); Albert Dondeyne, *Faith and the World* (Pittsburgh: Duquesne University Press, 1963).

6. See Dean Peerman (ed.), *Frontline Theology* (Richmond: John Knox, 1967); William R. Miller, *The New Christianity* (New York: Delacorte, 1967); David H. Kelsey, *The Fabric of Paul Tillich's Theology* (New Haven: Yale University Press,

motifs, so central to H. Richard Niebuhr's thought and recurrent in American theology, carry a vision of effective personal and corporate agency. They describe men who understand that they represent limited interests, talents, and beliefs which if used in proper relationship might serve the common good. The leaders of churches are to recognize that they support special interests in the world. They are not to claim for their judgments on public issues universality or other attributes of divinity. Each special service and ministry is to be performed in an essentially interdependent mode. The special and partial nature of each basic function persists, but in a way that can show its interdependence with other ministries.

The Modes of Jesus' Ministry

The Johannine understanding of the essential way Christ had of relating the prophetic and kingly offices has been explored in an important study by Wayne Meeks.[7] In the Gospel of John the church was chiefly concerned to reinterpret to a hostile Jewish community a moral and political explanation of the Christ's view of his way of doing God's work in the world. The principal motifs used were prominent in Jewish literature about Moses: that is, the kingly and prophetic functions. But a significant change occurs in the manner in which these modes of action are interpreted and related. The change always has to do with the issue of fulfillment of suffering service; that is, of ministry as it is to be practiced and thought about by human beings.

The meaning of the terms "king" and "prophet" depends on their essential interrelationship. For Meeks this is always an ironic (not an irenic) relationship; Christ always used these terms so that their mutual relationship is understood. When Christ is pressed to identify himself with a kingly, governing ministry, he speaks of the teaching, rabbinic offices. The opposite is true also. King and prophet are not separate functions, as if each is to be done at a particular place and time in one's

---

1967); James T. Laney, "A Critique of the Ethics of the Radical Contextualists" (Ph.D. diss., Yale University, 1966); Richard R. Niebuhr, *Schleiermacher on Christ and Religion: A New Introduction* (New York: Scribner, 1964); James M. Gustafson, "Christian Ethics," in Paul Ramsey (ed.), *Religion* (Englewood Cliffs: Prentice-Hall, 1965).

7. Wayne A. Meeks, *Jesus as King and Prophet in the Fourth Gospel* (Leiden: Brill, 1967).

life and in a kind of simple moderation. Jesus' kingship is related throughout the gospel (see John 18:33–38) to the mission of the prophet who speaks and teaches the truth; and the prophetic mode is described in terms of the acts of mercy and love in which the blind are given sight and the hungry are fed (John 9:24–28). The theme of the gospel reaches its climax in Pilate's confrontation of Christ with the question, "So you are a king." And Jesus answers, "You say that I am a king. For this I was born, and for this I have come into the world, to bear witness to the truth." In the crucial encounter only those who rule in obedience to God's will are those who can speak the truth.

The kingly and prophetic roles are, in Johannine Christology and in much of the literature of the first-century church, related at every crucial point to the symbol of the good shepherd (John 10:12–13) who "lays down his life for the sheep. He who is a hireling and not a shepherd, whose own the sheep are not, sees the wolf coming and leaves the sheep and flees; and the wolf snatches them and scatters. He flees because he is a hireling and cares nothing for the sheep." In the biblical world, the shepherd is a royal figure of serving, selfless leadership who guides and safeguards the lives of those entrusted to his care. The shepherd is also a prophetic figure in the Gospel of John: judgment, intercession, admonition, are in his voice and manner. What is so often revealed as the true ruler, governor, or teacher is not what is expected or seemingly expressed, for the meaning persists in the essential relation of the other basic roles. In this case the language is not literal, but ironic.

This biblical view of primary ministerial functions requires, then, a heightened consciousness of the relation of oneself to the various ways he can help others. It requires a community of persons pervaded by a common spirit and by a rationale for fitting their particular talents into programs and resources which serve all the historic brotherhoods of the church: the fellowship of Christians, the needy and forsaken, the whole body of mankind. The picture of Christ and the church emerging in the contemporary biblical scholarship of both Protestants and Catholics makes these matters quite unavoidable.

Among biblical scholars there would appear to be considerable agreement that Christ identified his person with at least the traditional offices of king, prophet, and priest (the pastoral mode was included in the latter) and that the insistence on their essential interrelationship in a creative new way was not a peculiarly Johannine interpretation of the historical Jesus. The mode of Christ's fulfillment of these roles, Harold Riesenfeld notes,

> is not only that He does not assume His official functions openly; that is in keeping with the mystery that surrounds the whole earthly life of the Messiah. Rather, according to the unanimous testimony of the New Testament, the difference is that Christ is King in a higher degree than any mortal ruler; He is the perfect King, who refuses to follow the pattern of the rulers of the world. (Matt. iv. 3ff; cp. Luke xxii. 25f; John xviii. 36ff.)[8]

The same is true, says Riesenfeld, for all the other offices. Their fullness and unity in Christ are made evident in the fact that he is the real High Priest and the last and greatest Prophet (Hebrews; John 1:45; Acts 3:22 ff.) and that it is not possible in Christ's person and work to separate the offices.

Modes of Ministry in the Church

When biblical study proceeds to the question of relationship between ministries performed in the circle of Christ's followers, traditional religious offices are used in creating a central ministry in a community of people of God, an essential sign, promise, forerunner of the Kingdom.

The ministry of an apostle (1 Cor. 3:6, 9; 2 Cor. 11:2) is an extension of Christ's own work. It is but a visible and partial attempt at continuation of the offices which Christ fulfilled and united in his person and work. In the sweep of Christian history there appears to be some continuity in the persistent presence and mutuality of these basic functions and ministrations in the structure of the church.

Justin Martyr is the first Christian writer who expressly mentions that Christ held the three ancient Jewish charismatic offices of king, priest, and prophet. From them he sought to develop a view of leadership in the church.[9]

As the church sought to interpret these offices, the kingly governance which God intends to exercise over the world in all its aspects was destined to be the instrument for putting into force the terms of relations between God and man, and man and man, which God had revealed in

---

8. Harold Riesenfeld, "The Ministry in the New Testament," in Anton Fridrichsen, *The Root of the Vine: Essays in Biblical Theology* (London: Dacre Press, Black, Ltd., 1953), p. 105.

9. *Ibid.*

Jesus Christ.[10] Power, influence, greatness, are not for the true ruler ends in themselves, but are essential, transformed means for the achievement of the Kingdom of God.

The *prophet* is the man in whose mouth the Lord puts His words. By teaching and inquiry he freshly recalls the promise and the demand contained in the Kingdom of God and seeks its meaning for future actions. The prophet is, in Jean Bosc's words, the "sentinel who announced the judgment, but also the sunrise."

The *priest* is the public person who performs acts of worship in behalf of persons seeking to re-establish a broken relation with God. In the affectionate care for persons, he reconciles man to himself and to others. The priest reminds men of what God has done for them in restoring fellowship with man and of what man can do in response.

These functional motifs have been the basic ones in the Christian ministry. And the single purpose of these offices and the community Christ gathered around him is, as he stated it, to increase the love of God and neighbor among men.[11] The question which must be asked of any specialized ministry, including the *campus* ministry, is whether it can abrogate or fail to carry out these works and still be a Christian ministry. What might these modalities look like in the major structures of higher education? What are the consequences when men and women cannot decide whether or not they are in the full ministry of the church and are confused as to whether a specialized work demands this decision of them? These questions recur at every stage of our inquiry.

In the history of the church, the meaning and purpose of these *master* offices and of their interrelationship have undergone profoundly new elaboration and reconstruction. This has not necessarily been a gain. They have been broken up into specialized subfunctions or have been reduced to services performed by clergy and laity accommodating themselves to the divisions of labor and sociological illusions of the wider culture. There have been, for example, specialties such as personal counseling without a point of view, evangelism without justice, teaching without intellectual curiosity and passion, administration with-

---

10. Jean Bosc, *The Kingly Office of the Lord Jesus Christ* (London: Oliver and Boyd, 1959).

11. H. Richard Niebuhr observed rightly in *The Purpose of the Church and Its Ministry* (New York: Harper, 1956) that "no substitute can be found for [this] definition of the goal of the church" (p. 31).

out community vision. Perhaps the most profound problem for the church has been to present these ministrations so that the Lordship of Christ was witnessed to in loving service to the society outside the churchly fellowship. The problem that pervaded the Johannine Christology has been the persistent one; that is, the relationship of the prophetic and kingly office to the suffering care of people.

The priority of these primary and essentially interdependent ministries has continually been the occasion for division in the church. At one extreme have usually been those seeking in some kind of personal piety to escape the temporal, kingly complexities that the Christian ministry represents. They wish to "meet Jesus" or "find God" in some direct, individual way. And at the other extreme have been those seeking to evade the institutional history and forms of office and ministration in the church. They may even try to gain for their own particular specialization an autonomy which would deprive the ministry of its meaning and capacity to help others. Often these polarities find curious reinforcing, self-serving accommodation to one another in the church.

Until the modern period the restatement of the essential relationship of these offices was often in terms of the pastoral-parish image. St. Gregory the Great's famous *Liber pastoralis curiae* (c. 591), later called in English *The Book of Pastoral Care*, was principally an attempt to state the responsibilities of church leaders to minister to all the people in a special area: the parish. The kingly, governing images were stressed, so that the principal work of a pastor was supervisory and administrative. But still Gregory saw all the offices related to this rule, and this was a major achievement.

In the sixteenth century, the church was shaken by the Reformation. Luther's cry of justification by faith alone was a protest from the depths of human consciousness against the reduction of pastoral management to a third-rate Gregorian model which determined salvation by dispensing churchly and other worldly rewards. Luther sought a recovery of the personal and historical meaning of what was professed, of freedom to love those who did not merit it by traditional church standards, and the reconciliation of persons in the community of the faithful.[12] In this sense he was a precursor of Protestant evangelical emphasis on

12. See Kenneth Underwood, "Protestant Political Thought," *International Encyclopedia of the Social Sciences* (New York: Macmillan and Free Press, 1968), for a review of scholarship on the reformation in social sciences and Christian ethics.

pastoral care which stressed personal and familial love and the winning of a decisive commitment to the Gospel.

The Calvinist phase of the Reformation, more than the Lutheran, sensed that the church was dependent for its ministry on the participation of the laity in a variety of emerging associations in the society. In the first book of *The Institutes,* John Calvin notes, "For knowing to what end Jesus Christ was sent to us by the Father and what He has conferred upon us, it is chiefly necessary to consider three things about Him: His office of prophet, His kingship, and His priesthood."[13] The priority of the essential offices has shifted; the prophetic-teaching mode is singled out for special analysis not present in many Catholic manuals of ministry.[14] And the Calvinist churches gave new importance in their polity to the teaching elder or informed layman. These developments were related to the emergence of a society in which traditional ecclesiastical and political regimes were being challenged to express in their public actions the increasingly diverse interests and concerns of the people.

But the most significant contribution by Calvin and his followers to the understanding of the ministry is that the three major offices are identified not only with services or obligations of individual believers but also with the "unctions" of specific institutions. The prophetic office is for Calvin chiefly identified with and dependent on the work of the academies of higher learning. The offices of kingship and priesthood are principally manifested in the state and the church, respectively. But all these modalities are aspects of God's work in the world, as Christ has made these known to us, and each office has its Christian representation and meaning in the services of the church.

Modes of Ministry and Social Policy

The shifting structures of ministry may be one of the most significant clues within the churches to developments in the larger society. These structures mediate between religious beliefs and public policy. Van Harvey notes that in the historic church of active believers, "Jesus Christ is the key image in a parable which the Christian uses to inter-

---

13. John Calvin, *The Institutes of the Christian Religion* (Philadelphia: Westminster, 1936), Vol. I.

14. Jan A. Muirhead, *Education in the New Testament* (New York: Association Press, 1965), p. 66.

pret the more inclusive reality with which all men are confronted and of which they try to make some sense."[15] The work of ministry, then, is not that of performing some sacred-cultic act in which God presents himself to men; rather it is representing Christ through the acting out of the interdependent relations of the essential ministries. In our age the restatement of ministerial modes is principally in terms of social policy.

The search for such a viable expression of the essential ministries is made anew in each generation. The contemporary church confronts its own distinctive occasion permitting no simple recourse to history or Scripture. The American churches have, for example, made the pastoral care and counseling movement, the search for personal identity and integrity, into a fourth and separate office of the ministry. The movement seemed for a while to offer an intellectually respectable reformulation of evangelical concern with the familial and personal meaning of faith. This movement offered a reinterpretation of the other ministerial modes and a radical political disassociation from major policy issues. Devotees saw the church discovering that its distinctive mission among the other major institutions of the society was an overwhelming concern for the whole person, for what happens in the cumulative impact of education, politics, business, and medicine on each individual.

American Protestantism seems at present to occupy a halfway house in which no satisfactory relationship between its deep concern for the whole person and for the public order has been found. We prefer to talk in terms of social policy as the focal point in analysis of ministerial careers, lay resources, and church actions because the religious crisis is not a phenomenon that can be confronted by single persons. The needs of human beings to be served require the resources and talents (religious, political, social, and psychological insight) of more than one minister—lay or cleric—and of more than one parish or congregation, and of more than one specialized ministry.

In the first year of the study the director made a "preliminary evaluation of Danforth programs in the Campus Ministry." The offices of the ministry we have been describing were used to ask some evaluative questions. An excerpt from this report may indicate the way in which the theoretical and operational significance of these modes of service

---

15. Van Harvey, *The Historian and the Believer: The Morality of Historical Knowledge and Christian Belief* (New York: Macmillan, 1966), p. 238.

had begun to be seen as a clue to basic policies of the church toward higher education.

If the concern of the Danforth inquiry is to determine whether the work done on campuses by the Protestant clergy and programs to aid them in this work have in fact been that of a ministry containing the marks of Christ's person and his work, then the full meaning of these offices needs to be explored for the contemporary church. . . . Any recommendation of a shift in program priorities or emphasis is then not a fad or gimmick of the moment, but action related to a rational model of the campus ministry.

The kingly office, for example, gives attention to established institutions or organizations in the ministry and society and the fundamental changes occurring in them. . . . Any appraisal of the campus ministries from the perspective of the kingly work of Christ must note the extent to which this ministry serves the major structures and constituencies in higher education, as well as undergraduates, and the dissenters as well as the conventionally committed.

If we emphasize the prophetic and teaching office, then we shall need to see to what extent the full intellectual and moral resources of the universities and of the laity of the churches are being utilized in the development of critiques of actions in major areas of public life and in encouragement of serious moral inquiry in the learning experience of students. Does the campus minister who stresses the prophetic office lose sight of the reality of the institutional church and develop few responsible relations to parish congregations whose programs of adult education might be greatly enhanced by knowledge the campus minister has gained from the university?

Does the minister who stresses the priestly function tend to conceive of the Kingdom of God in magical fashion, and neglect specific judgments about lay responsibilities in new, emerging organizations? Do the ministers who minimize the governing office lose sight of the reality of the church and develop few institutional implications from their theology, relying heavily on pastoral activities, such as counselling, which do not explore the social and moral dimensions of the problems the laity bring to them? As to the exclusion of the priestly function, have some ministers by their neglect of worship and the historic meaning of the Sabbath been led to an over-emphasis on experimental forms of teaching and the cognitive content of Christianity?

The pattern of selection of interns wishing field experience and of campus ministers wishing additional study needs to find the connections between concern for self-discovery and particular work in the ministry they hope to undertake. The applicant's reading of the situation in higher education or the church to which he wishes to direct his ministerial training might all have a bearing on the place in which he is located, the varieties of supervision to be given, the consequences of his training and ministry. Attention to the specific talents and gifts of men are crucial—their major and minors in college, their predispositions toward organization and roles, etc. David Byers calls prophetic work "the critical mind with constructive intent," a phrase fusing nicely the liberal and technical concerns of ministry and its education.

One development in self-consciousness about primary ministries is a comparatively greater fluidity and mobility in career patterns. Another development is the increasing search for ways of cooperatively using resources in parish and campus ministries, in order to participate in the actual world and faith of laymen. The influence of higher education is so pervasive now in the best ministries and churches that men move in and out of different specializations of work with increasing ease and power. Church and foundation programs have been too little used to encourage work which breaks through the fragmentation of professions and disciplines to new spiritual and intellectual concerns. Are there provisions in ministry educational grants for study at a business school to develop a new program of adult education? Can campus ministries make use of parish ministers who have been exposed to questions of inner city disorganization and wish to encourage students of social science and the arts to explore the implications of their study for the kinds of urban tragedies they know so well?

The questions asked the Danforth Foundation in the statement above are primarily social policy questions. They have to do with the intellectual, moral, and spiritual quality of personal and corporate decisions made in the major organizations and institutions of our society and affecting great numbers of people in the body politic. The focus of attention is the responsible self engaged in shaping *social policy*. By *policy* we mean the projection of a pattern of action over time within and between such realms as business, government, politics, medicine, social welfare, and mass communications. These are questions, then, which cannot be handled by private arrangements in the layman's or clergyman's career. They are not to be viewed simply as questions of style of a man's life. But neither are they merely sociological questions of the role a man is to assume in life.

The questions we have been raising about the primary offices of ministry and their interdependency in the church have to do fundamentally with the way and direction an institution is moving, with issues about how, where, and for what purposes the power of the church and associated organizations are to be used in the future. These are all at once theological, moral, sociological, political, and psychological questions. What have to be decided in order to give opportunity and range to a career are policies that make or break whole groups of men and women, activate and redirect church resources on major university campuses, give greater powers to some interests and reduce others. These are social-political-religious decisions that are not final, neat, or systematic; they represent the compromise and bargaining of a complex of competing goals and interests. Social policy discussions force people both inward toward institutional survival and outward toward the new needs of others.

One of the most important things in a person's life and faith is not just seeing a city, an institution, an organization, as it is, but being able to see new possibilities in it, being able to participate in shaping a corporate enterprise into becoming something important in the hopes and expectations of others. To talk of social policy is to talk of projecting oneself and others into the future, of being able to achieve goals with others, of being effective organizationally. To teach, to lead worship, to preach in such a way as to enhance the powers of others to participate in the formation of social policy, is seen as one of the most important aspects of being human and being Christian. To claim to be a Christian who loves God and neighbor and not to attempt to be an effective person in the formation of just social policies is to talk nonsense in the modern world. The purpose of education in the church and university, or better, the best test of its quality, is that it enhances the capacity of laymen to achieve just social policies.

The term "social policy" is used rather than the vaguer terms of "servant role," "mission," "the building of the earthly city," and the like in the ecumenical literature in order to express the intention to deal with all the technical and bureaucratic powers and problems that need to be faced for effective action in changing the direction and quality of impact of various major institutions. The term is expressive also of an awareness that the strategies to achieve such objectives are not the product of a simple role (servant) or tactic (protest action). Social policy connotes a commitment of the self over time to achieve the competencies which will affect changes in the training of personnel and the allocation of financial resources of key institutions. The term does not, as that, for example, of "earthly city" (a Vatican Council phrase), imply that the actions taken have only a secular, nonreligious aspect to them, that some other purer, higher realm exists where men do not build cities.

So, too, the more historic term "Kingdom of God" has its use for these ministries in designating God's guidance of all that happens toward a final transformation. It is an image embracing everything that is honorable and of true report in the world, whether within the church or outside it, whether overtly religious or appropriately secular. But the term "social policy" helps to indicate the realm of actuality which most tests faith and compassion in our time; it directs the talk of serving the world toward questions of what corporate actions do to people and what produces them without in any way assuming that the questions of traditional Christianity about the mystery and transcendence of God are now by-passed.

At issue is not whether elite, policy-making, professional groups are to be the only recipients of Christian ministry or whether the lonely, depressed, poverty-stricken, and forgotten of the inner city are to be the focus of the church's leadership. At issue is whether the actions of the former are being critically and constructively reflected on in the church for their effects on the latter and vice versa. The issue is not whether the church's best-educated, most professionally minded clergy are now in suburban churches rather than in the big cities, but what provisions are being made in the university and church for new literature, leadership training, and educational settings that open up the realities of social influence of these suburban constituencies on the body politic, on professional services, on new careers for the poor, and in turn bring the needs and experiences of the poor and forgotten in all areas of the city to the attention of those who can act to help them.

The crucial issue in the life of the church today can be simply put in terms of whether it is going to face consciously the questions of ministry and theology tested in policies or whether it is going to become a place of escape from the world of corporate action, from the arena we call history and politics, or in religious terms, the place where God acts and where His action is to be seen.

In Hebrews 11 and 12 the task of the people of God is to see where God is acting in history and then to move to join God in His activity. This activity, for the founding fathers of our nation, was to build a "Godly Commonwealth" which would encompass the whole of their existence. And the church was to be an energizing, reflecting, directing center for this work. The historic modes of ministry were to provide some clue, some symbolic disclosure of the Kingdom of God, the Godly Commonwealth.

In being such, the ministry in our day does not draw near the university as a matter of status or even primarily to remind it of its mission. It does so because it needs the knowledge and wisdom of the university to do the proper work of the church. The church is to speak and act in a way which shows the nature of human need and service in the orders of society which most often control the lives of people; the church is to contribute by its social policies to the building of a just, peaceable, and beautiful commonwealth.

PART III

The Pastoral Structures of Faith and Ministry

≥ 7 ≤

PASTORAL CARE, RESPONSIBLE KNOWING, AND

STUDENT RELIGIOUS COMMITMENT

(San Francisco Bay Area)

T HE title of this chapter conveys the major realities to which the campus ministers of the San Francisco Bay area are trying to respond: (1) the increasing concern with the personal dimensions of ministry and learning in the university; (2) the centrality of epistemological issues in education; (3) the changing and varied nature of student religious commitment. The relationship of these factors has become the ministers' major personal and corporate problem.

The San Francisco Bay area was the site of our first attempt at understanding the factors that have influenced past actions of church leaders in a specific metropolitan area and may shape future policies. We brought to bear on the area more research resources than on any other place studied. We began with the establishment of a research colloquium of scholars and clergy to prepare trial survey instruments and interview questions for the study of student religious commitments and values and for reviewing data developed in special studies by the national staff.

We were aware that much of the thought and action of campus clergy emphasized the strictly personal, subjective, or incommunicably "I" aspects of faith, rather than traditional church organizations or formal course teaching and systematic research in the university. Such clergy often saw their own ministry as reconstituting the traditional pastoral care of the church. Under the influence of modern existential and romantic thought (theological, social, psychological), their pastoral concern focused on a realm of reality belonging profoundly to personal or innermost being.[1] They wished, above all else, to discover and deal with the problems that confronted persons. Such problems could be examined in counseling or in informal discussion, usually from a variety of perspectives, including one's own experience and feelings. Only if such mysterious, human, at once subjective and objective problems were put at the center of the university and the church, they argued, could education and faith be meaningful. For them, learning and the formation of belief took place only when a problem forced a person to know himself, to grow spiritually or to fail miserably, to take certain attitudes with regard to good or evil, to open himself to his neighbor and God, or to be shut off in pride and selfishness.

This image of pastoral care, whatever else it has meant in American religious life, symbolizes the one-to-one relationship of Christian love. For the clerical mode we are describing, the church in its most generally acceptable form is to be an affectionate fellowship of people concerned to sustain a man or woman in his or her search for integrity and meaning in life.

Given the importance of this mode of ministry in the church, we knew that we needed to establish an inquiry which would seek to understand and test the realities of this kind of thinking and acting. We concluded from several meetings with the Bay area campus clergy and a number of interviews that the ethos of the professional church leaders there strongly reflected this type of personalistic-existential-pastoral care. We could study in the Bay area the pattern of actions of a group of ministers strongly influenced by a particular mode of service but also representative of a variety of other modes. In the Bay area, therefore, we had an opportunity to gain an understanding of an influential mode of ministry, while seeing it in the context of the whole ministry to a complex educational system.

Consultations with some ministers representing this approach revealed serious anxieties as to whether they now adequately represent their own faith's traditions and resources for ministry and whether they interpret truthfully major developments in the intellectual life of

---

1. The references to personalistic-existential-romantic theology are to designate a configuration of ideas: the revelation of God in the person of Jesus Christ, and hence the primacy of personal reality over laws, principles, or social policies; the limits of rational analysis and scientific objectivity in exploring selfhood with its mystery, uniqueness, and radical freedom; the consequences of revelation as the capacity to respond to a situation rather than simply be determined by it.

the university. They and their student constituencies believed they were confronting in the powers and policies of the universities a growing commitment to the sociotechnical aspects of education and to the dreams for American society they represent.

The problem which Christians with a personalistic faith and ministry confront is the relation of their world of dialogue and intimate encounter to the university world of responsible knowing. The latter is made up of people who see the epistemologies of science and technology not as ideologies, but as perspectives and skills to be appropriated creatively in personal and corporate acts for the achievement of the public good. Only ministers considerably isolated from enormous developments in scientific and technological research on the campuses could continue to describe this world as impersonal and inhuman.

Bureaucratic behavior can violate human dignity. But these problems are to be dealt with mainly by those who share responsibility in the network of systems of knowing which are the "multiversity" and provide the technical skills making possible the major healing, helping, managing, inquiring professions and vocations of modern society.

The problem of relating a personalistic morality to this technical, professional world is not confined to the Protestant churches. The universities themselves are shaken by the problem. Many of their leaders have been slow to understand student protests against individualistic, narrowly specialized, faculty-career-oriented intellectual inquiry which does not give students an opportunity for participation as persons of dignity in corporate research on pressing public problems. Such leaders see educational institutions organized for learning that enhances private leisure and personal arts, but not for helping the student relate himself to the major organizations and professions of contemporary culture in a creative, constructive, and influential way.

The traditional motifs of pastoral care in the campus ministry were formed under the church's experience with the voluntary associations and chaplaincies of the small private colleges of the eighteenth and nineteenth centuries. In these colleges, as we noted in our historical survey, the faculty and administrators, as well as clergymen, were assumed to be responsible for the pastoral care of students, so that education contributed to their character and personal development. In the contemporary university a differentiation and specialization of concern for the "pastoral" dimensions of education has taken place; this is evidenced in the expansion of the student personnel work and its association in the minds of many administrators and faculty with the development of a professional campus ministry operating out of denominationally sponsored "houses," "fellowships," and student "centers" and providing a "home away from home," counsel on difficulties of maintaining private moral standards, and conferences to help students be whole persons; that is, see the relations of their studies to life and work.

Campus ministers, like student personnel officers, are now facing a situation in which the specialized care they have offered in the past is less and less welcomed by students seeking freedom to direct their own lives and to find opportunities to discover the personal meaning and public significance of technical knowledge. *The question for the future has become how to organize the varied skills and historic convictions of individual clergy into an ecumenical ministry that offers respected, recognizable, associated pastoral services in a vast system of personnel workers, counselors, faculty research, student organizations, and continuing and adult education.* Can a pastoral ministry be developed which effectively helps the complex academic and research structures of the university better serve the personal needs of students and helps students share responsibility in meeting the epistemological and learning problems of the modern university? Can the campus minister move from moralistic shepherd to member of an ecumenical team able to think and act in response to the distinctive problems of bureaucratic impersonality that academic institutions confront?

All these perplexing questions led to a more basic one: the nature of student religious commitment in the varied environments of higher education. Some clergy told us in our first consultation that they "were no longer sure what distinguished the religious from the nonreligious person, the Christian from the unbeliever" in the college or university. Who "welcomes our care," and who is to be considered "a member of our parish or community"? As one clergyman noted, "I often find myself in theology and ethics closer to the dissenters than to the kids who show up regularly at our center."

One scholar in the Bay area research colloquium who opposed the "personalistic" model of religious commitment argued that the public atheism of many students stemmed from their inability to believe any longer in a God who is an individual person and who interacts with the world only in personal encounters or intimate conversations. Such students, he said, were deeply aware of the interpersonal dimensions of existence, but found that "ministers who were most preoccupied with pastoral care and counseling as a way of legitimizing their work were also most neglectful of the new truths, injustices and epistemological problems that dominated the intellectual life of the university."

The national staff, therefore, encouraged the colloquium to develop a survey instrument which gave students an opportunity to identify their religious commitment in terms of its power to unite varied cultural perspectives and ways of knowing in a responsible personal and corporate act, and not merely in traditional doctrinal terms.

These, then, were the chief actualities and problems which influenced our inquiries in the San Francisco Bay area. We hoped to illumine them by study of research in the behavioral and social sciences on trends in higher education and religion.[2] Our surveys were developed by a Bay area research colloquium composed of scholars who had been involved in these research enterprises, of campus ministers from the major colleges and universities in the area, and a number of other persons whose work and institutional backgrounds were to be important in future studies.[3] The research director of the colloquium was Parker Palmer, a young scholar whose graduate studies were both in sociology at the University of California and in theology at the Pacific School of

---

2. For example, the work of Nevitt Sanford, Joseph Katz, and their associates on the relationship of character, personality, and college education; the study of different educational environments and their influence on student attitudes and values at the Center for Study of Higher Education; the studies of educational axiology by W. H. Cowley at the School of Education, Stanford; the Survey Research Center, University of California; the theological studies of religion and higher education at the Pacific School of Religion under Charles S. McCoy; the Bureau of Community Research at PSR.

3. The Bay Area Research Colloquium, formed in December 1963, consisted of the following persons: W. H. Cowley, Professor, School of Education, Stanford University; A. Hunter Dupree, Professor, Department of History, University of California; Richard L. Gelwick, U.C.C. Campus Minister, Berkeley; John Hadsell, Presbyterian Campus Minister, Berkeley; William K. Laurie, Secretary for Campus Ministry, United Church Board for Homeland Ministries, San Francisco; Robert Minto, Chaplain, Stanford University; Shunji Mishi, Episcopal Campus Minister, Berkeley; Herbert Reinelt, Professor of Philosophy, University of the Pacific, Stockton; Mrs. Gertrude Selznick, Research Associate, Survey Research Center, University of California, Berkeley; Robert Wert, Vice-Provost and Dean of Undergraduate Education, Stanford University; Parker Palmer, Research Director; and Charles S. McCoy, chairman of the colloquium.

Religion and who had worked for the Survey Research Center and the Bureau of Community Research.[4]

The Survey of Student Religious Commitments

The Bay area colloquium took as its primary task the preparation of a survey instrument for discovering

> the . . . various types of personal commitments as they are found in the university context. Specifically, we are concerned to treat individual commitments as both independent and dependent variables, asking how they influence the environment of the academic institutions and how they are influenced by that environment.[5]

The colloquium viewed the strategy of campus ministries as heavily dependent on "an accurate assessment of commitments present in the academic community and a precise understanding of issues arising within them." Only after the conceptual problems of a survey of student belief and commitment had been solved and after data had been attained could the pastoral concerns and actions of the church be properly assessed.

The colloquium explored various meanings of commitment: how the individual relates himself to an idea or an ideal (Palmer); an act of entrusting, the acceptance of responsibility, an individual or group agreement to act in a specific way (McCoy).[6] The colloquium moved toward an understanding of religious commitments as those "final or ultimate commitments which permeate and shape decisions and actions of individuals and groups." In the language of the chairman of the colloquium, "the survey would need to look for an ordered field of human commitments, valuations and conceptions governing a context of action." In this realm of activity, religious commitment would be the

---

4. Parker Palmer's religious convictions were strongly influenced by Kierkegaard, Tillich, and Buber; he represented the critical struggle of a new generation of Christians to relate their theology to the scientific and technological scholarship of the university.

5. Parker Palmer, *Report of the First Meeting of the Bay Area Research Colloquium of the Danforth Study of Campus Ministries* (Berkeley: Pacific School of Religion, March 1964, mimeographed).

6. Charles S. McCoy and Parker Palmer, *Religious Commitment and Campus Ministry* (Berkeley: Pacific School of Religion, March 1965, mimeographed).

"pervasive element binding it into a whole, giving to it an overall form or style and defining its perimeter or horizon."[7]

Parker Palmer sought to interpret these broad directives of the colloquium in a way that would meet the elemental tests of science, such as the ability to discriminate analytically among phenomena. He treated religious commitment as a member of a class of world views by which people might integrate their experience, ground their values, or inform their social acts or policy decisions. By *world view*, Palmer was referring to an entire matrix of meaning, and not necessarily a systematic, unified view of things. His world-view terms convey feelings which influence various ways of knowing the world. Whether there was a consistency or a discernible connection between a world view and particular attitudes or judgments was treated as an empirical question. Palmer and the colloquium hoped to get beyond a naïve theological personality which simply assumed a disjunction between inward piety and technical knowledge and beyond a naïve realism which assumed that science grasped "things out there" in some definitive way removed from personal choice. Personal perceptions were seen as intimately bound with what science called "fact" or "datum."

The conceptualization of religious commitment that formed the survey instrument moved beyond the conventional notions of religiousness identifiable by indicators drawn from participation in churches or synagogues.[8] The instrument is not dependent on doctrinal formulations of a particular historical religion. Moreover, it does not assume, as does the instrument developed in the Danforth Study of Church Related Colleges, that an individual's knowledge of religion necessarily tells anything significant about its significance for him.[9]

The world-view scales developed by Palmer have two parameters for commitment, namely, "perceptions of ultimate reality" and "relations to ultimate reality." He points out that two types of ultimates might be perceived, the "holy" and the "nonholy." The holy is per-

---

7. Charles S. McCoy, "Religious Commitment and the Realms of Actuality," in Volume II of this report.

8. Parker Palmer, "A Typology of World Views," in Volume II of this report. Palmer's basic working paper on a typology of world views begins with an attack on both pastoral and sociological assumptions that correlate church attendance and the religious interests of laymen.

9. Manning M. Patillo, Jr., and Donald M. MacKenzie, *Church Sponsored Higher Education in the United States* (Washington, D.C.: American Council on Education, 1966), pp. 142–147.

ceived as a mystery, a power and urgency entering human life that is wholly other, transcending nature and history. (Items forming the H-scales included: With his proven ability to control the forces of nature, man is potentially the greatest power in the universe; There is nothing which science cannot eventually comprehend; There is no power in the universe which man theoretically cannot someday control; Science is capable of disproving religion, even though people may go on believing in it.) Nonholy ultimate reality is perceived as a problem, difficult but solvable, passive and nonactive in man's situation, and similar to the structures of nature and history. The instrument does not imply that these basic views are contradictory, but only that they can be qualitatively distinguished.

Three types of relation to ultimate reality might occur. These are "faithfulness," "identification," and "domination." "Faithfulness" included being grasped by a superior power, reflecting on the meaning of the power that held one, and being obedient to that meaning. "Domination" involved fully apprehending a perceived reality, shaping it to one's own ends, and making commitment dependent on what it produced for the achievement of those ends. The category of "identification" described a relation to ultimate reality in which that reality becomes identified with a particular social or psychological system. Items forming the faithfulness scale included: The thought of being at the mercy of forces beyond my control is intolerable to me; Faith is a poor substitute for assurance and knowledge. Items in the domination scale were: It's who you know rather than what you know that's important in getting ahead; Yoy can't blame people for taking all they can get.

Combinations of these dimensions go to make up types of world views. The "religious" world view is one which conveys a perception of a holy ultimate reality and a relation to it of faithfulness. The "magic" world view consists of unconscious, unsystematic attempts to conquer, control, or manipulate the powers of nature that seem to operate from without or beyond man's understanding. The "scientific" view, or "scientistic" ideology, as some members of the colloquium called it to indicate their awareness of its limited evocation of their own stance, shares with magic the desire to gain mastery and control over nature. But the scientific view is a conscious, critical effort of experimentation that is capable of recognizing perception of a nonholy ultimate and of domination over some areas of nature while precluding dominance over the whole. Social or religious ideology involves the identification of a holy ultimate with some social or ecclesiastical system. In this type, for example, biblical symbols may be used simply to induce an institution to adapt to certain aspects of the modern world: for instance, developments in technology and science are identified with a process of secularization initiated by a Christ who loves the world.

The acute problem in ideology is the maintenance of a critical and historically viable religious life. All profound religion in this typology is viewed as being able to distinguish between God (ultimate reality) and a particular system of knowledge or government. It is no accident, Palmer notes, that the Jews have been able to survive historical vicissitudes, because when their personal or social hopes failed, their God did not. In our own time, it is important, therefore, to know whether the university is having the effect of moving the commitments of students from religion to some kind of secular ideology and then to a fundamentally scientistic view of the world.

The colloquium members hypothesized that the main manipulation of symbols, power, and persons in the university takes place over epistemological issues. The questions of commitment to realms of action in the university will in the future have to do mainly with gathering, evaluating, and appropriating data. This is because the organization of work and many other areas of life, among faculty, administrators, and upper levels of students, goes on around modes of knowing. Therefore any survey of the nature of religious commitment in the university has to determine the presuppositions of the student in regard to competing epistemological claims; it must discover whether the students' way of dealing with these claims influenced the direction of their actions or the pattern of their involvements in groups outside the classroom or campus. People with access to data necessary for policy actions have tremendous power. The threatening questions in the university have to do with the legitimacy of data and their importance in shaping future actions.

After the questionnaire was pretested (it contained many other scales and items than those dealing simply with world views, as later chapters will indicate), it was mailed to a sample of the 1963 freshmen and seniors at a state school, the University of California, Berkeley, and a church-related college, the University of the Pacific, Stockton.[10]

Findings from the World-View Scales of the Survey

No evidence was obtained to show that the university was moving students toward a naïve rationalism and scientism, but the university was influencing attitudes toward world views of the students and toward a range of issues we might term as in the area of the morality of knowledge, or the quality of relationships between disciplines and the commitments they represent. There would seem to be no need to continue a war between the romantic-existential theological advocates and fanatical defenders of scientific and technological reason. Most students seem to know that rational faculties and scientific methods have their place in the competencies men must develop to serve one another, though small subcultures and groups may for a time fly the old banners of a pseudo conflict. An item analysis of the world-view instrument indicates strong rejection of basic elements in absolute rationalism or scientism and victory for an epistemological battle that has made for uneasy alliances between conservatism and neo-orthodox theologies. For example, 65 per cent of the students agreed that "there are many important things which will probably never be understood by the human mind," and only 10 per cent agreed with the statement, "There is nothing which science cannot eventually comprehend."

In all groups of students surveyed, the scores on the holy dimension scales were significantly higher than those on the domination dimensions. Thus, of all the possible world views speculated about in Palmer's working paper, the largest group of students fall in the "religious" category. There is comfort in the data also for the theological liberals and secular theologians, for the great majority of students know that scientific and technical methods seeking heuristic control of an environment or a problem have their place in the world and are not coterminous with the boundaries of man's intellectual and experiential life. The issues held to be very important are those surrounding the claims one way of thinking makes on another in enhancing man's power to act.

---

10. The total sample numbered about one thousand students, with a return of 60 per cent at Berkeley and 65 per cent at Stockton. The major parts of the Bay area questionnaire and the revised questionnaire, more generally used in our study, as finally developed at the University of Wisconsin, are reproduced in the Appendix of this volume.

But the one-third of the students who had disagreed with the H-scale or were uncertain about their position tended to regard these items as not very important.[11]

One of the significant implications which the Bay area colloquium drew from these findings was that most students with whom the campus ministries work are at a point in their development where they are much more interested in pursuing the specific potentialities of scientific and technical epistemologies for understanding the world and for meeting human need than they are in pursuing the more general and now conventional theological critiques of scientism. Admittedly a minority of students still need to be alerted to the wider implications of the religion-science debate, but the future frontiers of discussion will be in terms of the kind of issue with which students and laymen such as Parker Palmer are struggling: the choices they face in making use of the skills of survey research to probe more fully religious phenomena in the contemporary society; the implications of these findings for social policy; the relation of research in one discipline to other courts of appeal in verifying fundamental concepts and beliefs.

As to church influences on world views, the survey revealed that the more frequently one attends church, the greater the chance of his having a religious world view; and the less frequently he attends, the more likely he is to be classified as scientistic. But it is equally clear that classifying the parish of one's pastoral care on the basis of church attendance ignores a variety of religious interests and views of the world. One-fifth of the frequent attenders are classified as scientistic, and one-fifth of the infrequent attenders are classified as religious in the Bay area survey.

The most important leads for the campus ministry appear in the survey data on the possible impact of varied structures of academic training and vocation orientation on world views and epistemological consciousness. The data reveal the degree of alienation from certain academic majors or vocational fields which those holding the kind of religious world view described in this survey represent. The physical and natural science students are found to be less scientistic than those in social science, business, engineering, or the humanities. Is this because they have learned the limits and possibilities of the scientific method better than students in other fields? On the other hand, business

---

11. Students were given an opportunity in the Bay area questionnaire to rate the importance of the principal items to them.

and engineering students seem to be increasingly manipulative toward reality the longer they are in their major academic fields. The seniors in physical and natural sciences are more scientistic than the freshmen.

But what are church leaders to make of the data that when the major academic fields are ranked by their church attendance and their holding of a religious world view, an inverse correlation of —.70 results? And what is the meaning of the fact that seniors generally tended to be more alienated from the religious institutions than freshmen and much more impressed by the importance of the epistemological issues represented in the world-view items than freshmen? To answer these questions, we must go beyond the survey data.

The colloquium and the national study staff concluded that the churches and ministers need to be aware that their potential laity increasingly work out problems of faith in relation to issues in the morality of knowledge. The college/university-educated laymen are likely to find the level of much theological reflection on these issues (such as the existential-conservative-romantic critiques of rationalism and the vague celebration of technology and science by the secular theologians) amusingly polemical and ill informed as to the choices in the vocational realms of the university in which they seek a humane and significant calling.

It would seem from the survey data and from the intellectual history of the Bay area colloquium that many laymen deeply involved in both the university and the church are trying to articulate a religious world view which represents: (1) a positive affirmation of the world of science and technology; (2) an epistemological rigor and self-consciousness which expresses appreciation of the limitations and uses of various methods of inquiry; (3) a transcendent religious foundation for opposing stagnant and dogmatic authorities wherever they deny open debate and fear social change. They do not see the methodological battles in which they engage as evil, to be avoided by good church people, but as the scene where some of their most difficult and influential choices are being made in love of God and neighbor.

Religious World-View "Cases"

Perhaps these conclusions can now be made meaningful if we turn from survey data to the relations which the chief formulator of the Bay area survey had with individual students in his own research and teaching career. We asked Parker Palmer to describe some kinds of student problem involving the relation of their religious commitments to their studies and to their group activities outside the classroom. He reported to us on three types of student: a conservative in tension, an orthodox rebel, and a normal Christian. His reports follow.

Lynn Adams: a conservative in tension

I have known Lynn Adams for a year and a half, ever since she entered the College as a freshman. As adviser to a group of students with religious interests (mainly of the *avant-garde* variety) I came to know her as a quiet person, struggling somewhat to reconcile an orthodox religious history with the challenges presented by the other students in the group. She seemed willing and eager to learn from the others and spent much time probing their minds.

Then, bit by bit, she began to drift away from the group. I didn't think much about this at first, except to be concerned about the fact that this group was her only visible place of social involvement on the campus. She is not an attractive person—overweight, a little homely, compounded by lack of knowledge or desire about good grooming—and I feared that she was drifting into real isolation from her peers. But about this time she left for vacation, and my attention turned elsewhere.

After vacation she turned up as a student in my course on classical social theory. I began my gamut of lectures (from Machiavelli to Marx) and became aware of her again as a student who was willing to raise questions, doubts, and claims about the material we were discussing in class. After a few weeks, however, she lapsed into silence (a retreat similar to the one she made from the religious group, but made much more quickly), and I finally asked her why, telling her that I missed her contribution.

She responded by indicating that she had decided (and she made it sound like a decision at the end of a long quest) that she had nothing to learn from the theorists under discussion. She very baldly stated that she knew what Truth was (the capital "T" was unmistakable in her voice) and that there was little Machiavelli, Marx, Durkheim, Weber, and the rest could add to her knowledge. She appreciated the points at which these theorists conformed to her understanding of Truth, but her mind turned off at points where they diverged.

I asked her to name the source of this assurance she had, and the answer she gave was "God, as revealed in Jesus Christ through the Scriptures."

This discussion was taking place after class, and by this time several other students had gathered around to listen. It was an awkward time to probe Lynn on this matter, but I felt I should, even though we couldn't discuss the issue in depth as we might privately. I began by indicating that I had deep respect for varying conceptions of the nature and source of Truth—that when one was engaged in the quest for Truth, as I felt myself to be, one could not afford to turn one's back on any ideas. I indicated that I (as Lynn knew) regarded myself as a Christian, but did not feel that my Christian belief necessitated my rejecting other perspectives. On the contrary, I suggested that the doctrine of creation impels the Christian to study the world in all its dimensions; in an ultimate sense, such a study seeks knowledge of God. And I proposed that the Christian might see Jesus Christ as normative Truth (singular) without having to see Him as all descriptive truths (plural).

Lynn listened attentively (as did the other students—largely non-Christians) and with no embarrassment whatsoever. She replied that she remained committed to her rejection of all Truth but Jesus Christ and implied (or perhaps I inferred) that any other conception of Christianity was not worthy of the name. She suggested this latter without the slightest trace of emotion or, I felt, of rejection of me. She was simply affirming her belief, looking the world squarely in the eye, and betting that the other guy would blink first.

I entered a feeble rejoinder—something to the effect that we must discuss this matter further—and the group broke up. I have no idea how the other students felt, except to guess that they probably took this to be a unique occasion in their college experience.

Lynn said little in class after this episode, although she continued to attend regularly and exhibited no hostility or tension. She seemed to be simply accepting the world as she had defined it with no animosity toward those who did not share her definition.

The last word I had from her was on the final examination. I first asked the students to make a systematic statement of the criteria by which they might judge a social theory; I had in mind the classical tests of coherence and correspondence and a discussion of the philosophical issues lying behind them. Some quotations from Lynn's examination paper will be revealing at this point:

My Authority for any judgment of "good" or "bad" social theory is my personal belief of what is truth. I read a theorist as a *person* making a statement about what Truth (Reality) is. A "good" theory is one I agree with.

In one sense, this statement could have been written by Michael Polanyi (*Personal Knowledge*) when he was a college freshman. But in the context, Lynn is not a Michael Polanyi. This comes out clearly as her examination proceeds:

Whenever I make a stand for something it is to [be] read as a statement of my understanding of truth as revealed to me by God in my faith.

As Lynn's examination proceeds, it seems clear that she was recalling our conversation in class some weeks earlier. On the examination, I had noted that the students' answers would be strengthened by specific references to the term's readings. Lynn has this to say on her last page:

In criticism of this paper I feel I have not fulfilled adequately the suggestion that use of ". . . illustrations drawn from this term's readings . . ." will strengthen my paper. My response is that my knowledge and exercise in criticizing social theorists has become greater in amount and more adept in technique. But the two factors of my "human condition" have allowed my paper to perhaps lack a satisfactory amount of illustrations for the reader. Time and what my faith honestly lets me write down have both limited and strengthened this paper. Not in apology do I say that this "theory" is incomplete, but in recognition of the performance I have done.

It is tempting to see Lynn simply as a hard-shell fundamentalist who gives every indication of being driven to that religious position by symptoms of deprivation and an authoritarian personality in the classic mold. I think there is some truth in that analysis—I am sure that there is a psychodynamic dimension to her religious situation especially because of occasional information she gave me about her consultations with a psychiatrist. But I do not believe that this analysis does full justice to her dilemma; it too easily reduces a profound religious quest to the variables of Freud and/or Skinner.

I would like to suggest additionally that Lynn Adams finds herself caught in the classic dilemma of the Christian intellectual and even the Christian college: can this commitment mean anything if one is also committed to the unfettered quest for truth, and vice versa? Most Christian intellectuals (and even more Christian colleges) resolve this dilemma by ignoring it or being schizophrenic, but neither of these solutions is very admirable. Lynn Adams seems to believe that there are only two other options: first, cling fast to Christianity and let the life of intellect influence you only where it fits your faith, or, second, reject the faith and become a secular intellectual. For a number of reasons, she has chosen the former, I think primarily because the latter would leave her too rootless, too friendless, to survive. For some people, clearly, the latter would be the more viable option; indeed, I have known graduate students in sociology whose rejection of traditional religion and loyalty to unvarnished secularism excelled in piety and devotion the converse attitudes in Lynn.

One would hope that the Lynns of this world might be posed with a better option than those discussed above, and one would especially hope that the campus ministry would take it upon itself to articulate such an option.

JIM SMITH: AN ORTHODOX REBEL

Jim Smith is twenty-four years old, two years older than a senior at his college should be. He is doubtless paying a price for this in terms of lack of contact with his presumed senior "peers" and in terms of embarrassment at watching his friends from the first two years of college forge ahead with their vocational and family plans. But he conceals well any pain he may be feeling, probably because the two-year lag in his college education is explainable (although he isn't defensive enough to have to do so) and because the events that explain it have given him a perspective on life which makes his tardiness in getting a degree rather inconsequential.

One of these years was spent working for a government agency in Washington, observing at first hand and, on occasion, participating in the highest level of political activity in the country. The other year was spent participating in, and on occasion observing, the civil rights movement in Mississippi. Neither of these "time outs" was motivated by an escapist desire to shake off the strictures of academia, but both were precipitated by the fact that Jim saw a job to be done and felt ripe to do it.

Jim's grades are not the best in the world—he is running a B-minus average going into his penultimate term—and not a few professors at his college feel his involvement in the "world" at a premature stage has limited what might have been a brilliant academic career. He is widely regarded as a young man with great intellectual potential, but one who was incapable of the four-year monasticism which is needed to bring that potential to fruition. Jim is aware of this assessment, but—as is the case with his apparent social deprivation—harbors no grudge about it (at least not visibly). He has, however, developed an ironic twist of mind about an educational system which insists on the relevance of ideas to the world and a life of personal commitment to action in the world—and then fails to reward a student who interrupts an arbitrary scheme of education in order to respond to that insistence.

Some of his hang-loose attitudes about this matter are beginning to tighten up as he faces his prospects for admission to graduate school. Typically, he faced these prospects late—perhaps too late for even a mathematical chance for admission to the better schools. Part of the reason for his being late, again, was his indecision about what kind of experience to pursue next. For a while he thought about accepting an excellent job offer with a civil rights organization in his home state. But, perhaps having learned something from his two sabbaticals, he decided on more schooling as the best next step.

Seminary was a possibility for him at one point, but perhaps because of his negative feelings about the institutional church, perhaps because of the fact that his father is a minister, perhaps because one of his best friends failed to get a Rockefeller, he has not pursued this option very far. Right now he is divided between law school and graduate work in sociology. He says he will go wherever he is accepted, so lacking is he in a rationale for his future.

He came late to sociology, having completed a political science major in the early part of his senior year. He decided to double-major largely because he was "inspired" by several professors of sociology who seemed to speak to him in ways that the older Establishment types in political science never had. And, typically, he double-majored simply because it felt right to him, despite the fact that the decision will delay his graduation yet another term. The sociology department is rather proud of him, and, after only two terms of study in the field, he has been made a teaching assistant in one of the introductory courses.

Despite his feelings about seminary and the church, Smith understands himself as a Christian, and in some way that he either cannot or will not articulate, one has the impression that this self-understanding is behind much of the behavior described above. It is likely that he will not articulate this motivation rather than being unable to; he, like so many young Christians who have coped with the world, is schooled in the tactic of being a crypto-Christian. And it is just a *tactic* for them; they believe very deeply in dialogue with the world and that their part of the dialogue has to be communicated in action since adequate words have yet to be provided.

There is a danger that this tactic may produce a variety of anti-intellectualism, that an initial recognition that one acts because the words are temporarily absent may lead to a total bias against discursive communication. But Smith exhibits none of this. Despite the fact that his deepest commitments and quests have been acted out rather than simply verbalized, he is willing and increasingly able to engage in penetrating analysis of that action. I think he is able to do so largely because he takes himself much less seriously than those who can't.

Jim's inability to take himself seriously is one of his most significant characteristics; his life is permeated by a kind of playfulness and humor which do not characterize the younger "serious generation." You have the feeling that here is a human being whose gaiety does not come cheap—who is not fooling himself about death—but who has faced death squarely and is able to laugh at it, or at the comic creatures it makes of man. I think a concrete example of this trait might help.

Several years ago, I had the experience of spending a week end with a group of Mississippi civil rights returnees of college age. I asked them, in various ways and at various times, what they could tell me about their experiences in the South—what "message" they had for those of us who had not gone. To a man they told me that my request was impossible and even arrogant; that they would be prostituting themselves if they tried to verbalize things one could only experience; that they brought back plenty in their "guts," but nothing in their minds, and it was the effete educational establishment that was wrong, not them, if we could not understand this.

I often use this story with students to illustrate the failure of intellect among the "hippies" and the ways in which the irrelevance of education is coming home to roost. I once used the story in Smith's presence, not realizing that he was a Mississippi veteran. He agreed with my point at once and then provided me with reams of material illustrations out of his own life, regaling the group for an hour with stories of how he had followed the same anti-intellectual path I had described (and had taken money for doing so in front of church groups!).

In a day when every college student in the country would give his left arm for a Meritorious Mississippi Service badge, this kind of honesty is refreshing. And it is Jim Smith's most salient characteristic, rooted I am sure in his religious conviction (or perhaps it *is* his religious conviction). Somehow, Smith has achieved that happy state of trusting the world, but not really; of taking other people seriously, but not himself; of seeing life as a game, but not playing around. His is the "hang-loose" ethic in the best possible sense, but it is not a rootless ethic as so many humanisms tend to be (humanisms which all too often die for want of roots). Instead, Smith's ethic seems to be grounded in some kind of comic, not cosmic, ontology, one which brings to mind a favorite quote of John F. Kennedy:

> There are three things that are real—
> God, human folly and laughter.
> The first two are beyond our comprehension.
> So we must do what we can with the third.

FRED GARDNER: A NORMAL CHRISTIAN

Fred Gardner is a senior who recently ran for class office as a lark—and won. His platform was a careful mixture of fraternity–bourgeoisie–good-guy elements (spiced, perhaps, with a little bit of tongue in cheek) and was highlighted by the campaign of his opponent who was an independent-beatnik-libertine type. Even though this encounter is one that Fred and the rest of the world will soon forget, it stands as a symbol of Fred's life style and—of greatest interest to us here—his religious commitment.

I first met Fred early in his sophomore year. He had been roped into a religious activities group of which I was faculty sponsor, and the prime mover behind his involvement in this group was a sweet little sorority girl. At that time Fred was "joe-college" fraternity boy, slouching in his chair at meetings in faculty homes, chewing gum both visibly and audibly, delivering himself in cool and decidedly anti-intellectual pronouncements when the spirit moved him, and suggesting that the best way to improve faculty-student relations would be to show football films to the professors while some student "jocks" instructed them in the intricacies of that sport. He came on like a super-Greek.

Fred left campus shortly after this to go on an overseas work experience. It is significant that he had told me he was going overseas, but not that his work would be with a Protestant missionary society. I do not know what motivated Fred toward this kind of work: it seemed so out of character for him. But it was consistent with the fact (as I learned later) that by this time Fred was taking a great number of courses dealing with religion and beginning to think about a career in the church. It may have been his fraternity involvement and the vacuous life style associated with it that moved Fred in this direction. It was certainly those factors that kept Fred from talking about what was happening to his life until some time after it happened.

Fred came back from his missionary work a new man—"in Christ." Something happened to him there—something by way of a "religious conversion." All traces of the happy-go-lucky fraternity Fred were gone, and in their place stood the marks of a committed Christian missioner, ready to take the Gospel to the world.

It was somewhat embarrassing to run into this part of the new Fred; to walk up to a fellow you hadn't seen for months, treating him as if he were still a rake, and finding a Christian in his place. But even more embarrassing—and worse—than that was the fact that a kind of seriousness, even gloominess, even morbidity, had invaded Fred's once shiny personality. He seemed unable to laugh any more.

Shortly after this encounter with the new Fred I saw him again, this time at his request. He was seeking my advice about transferring from his present school to one which is nationally known as a Bible-centered and very conservative institution. Fred believed he was wasting his time at an educational institution which took religion so lightly. He wanted the best possible preparation for the ministry and was sure he couldn't get it where he was.

I tried to convince Fred that he would get enough of the Gospel in seminary, that what he most needed as an undergraduate was a good exposure to the world. And Fred turned off. His growing distrust of me was a tangible thing during that counseling session, and this was the same Fred who four months earlier would have drunk me under the table if I had given him the chance.

Perhaps the most significant theme of our conversation that day was Fred's feeling that he had to transfer in order to retain the life style and sense of personal discipline which he had so recently achieved. Fred believed (and, as it turned out, rightly so) that he was largely at the mercy of his environment in this regard and that only a permanent change in environment would save him.

One could not help but feel that his commitment to the ministry was based on the same kind of fear.

Up to this point Fred sounds much like Lynn Adams, the "conservative in tension." But there is a significant difference: Fred's tension was a passing thing. It wasn't six weeks after this conversation with Fred that he had decided not to transfer, that his old personality was beginning to emerge again (gum and all), and that he was barely distinguishable from himself of two years earlier.

Barely distinguishable—with one exception: he retained his commitment to the ministry from his "conversion experience," was laying plans to go to seminary, and was quite public and vocal about the whole thing. But his style of announcing his intentions had changed from his immediate postmissionary days. Instead of cloaking himself in great bolts of piosity, he now talked about the ministry with all the college-boy coolness with which he had once discussed showing the faculty football films.

There is a sense in which Fred's story might be read as a saga of success. Here, after all, is a young man whose life was saved from super-coolness (which Americans in their better moments don't really like) by an experience with God and poverty and (better yet) whose life was also saved from piosity (which Americans at any moment don't really like) by another experience with the middle-class world. Isn't this simply an instance of a boy who has learned to accommodate his religious beliefs to the style and language of the world and will be a much more effective minister for it?

Maybe. But I don't think so. I am, instead, inclined to read this story of "normal Christianity" as a real failure—a failure of courage to live on the far edges of life rather than in the comfortable middle. Fred will doubtless be a "success" in a parish (probably suburban) church. He has the conversion credentials (which puts him a jump ahead of most ministers), and they do not show too badly. But he has lost the sharp edges he possessed immediately before and after his conversion—edges he will probably never recover.

It is too easy to see Fred showering after eighteen holes of golf with his parishioners at the local country club, slipping into his clerical collar and suit, and despite his means of visible identification, getting lost in the crowd.

Would each of the three students described in these observations place himself within the religious world view of the Bay area survey? Would Lynn Adams more so than Jim or Fred? We doubt it. From these reports we can see something of the personal anguish and concern behind the aggregate data. We can also understand more adequately the strength and limitations of our measurement of student commitments. We are dealing in surveys with broad cultural trends and historic types, and they differentiate only grossly between individuals within a trend.

One of the major gains of the world-view scales, it now appears, is that they help us to identify students who have a religious concern to redeem each method of inquiry from its peculiar demonic bent toward idolatry. They want to prevent it from becoming a method that excludes by implication other ways to responsible knowledge. This was a helpful achievement in our search for the truth about the situation of campus ministries. We probed a bit the religious ground for open and conscious appropriation of a great variety of knowledge in the responsible act. The person with a nonholy view of the world comes to think and act as if reality existed only for a particular method of knowing and could be manipulated at will; the person with a religious view is seeking to keep the world open to God and to avoid a church or university which acts as if reality is exhausted by a single method of faith or inquiry. The problem of the "conservative in tension" is that the ultimate reality in which she believes is not a power that makes her metacritical. Her belief does not help her take the other ways of knowing as means to the achievement of personal acts and social policies that glorify God and fulfill the purposes of His creation.

But it can also be said of the other students with whom this teaching-research minister interacts that they are having difficulty in relating their and his concept of holiness to the shaping of corporate structures in the world. The orthodox radical has found a cosmic comedy which helps him in his private frustrations with past efforts at reform. But his perception does not throw much light on ways in which he is to distinguish the forces with which he will work and against which he will fight in the institutional structures of contemporary society.

Perhaps the view of holiness we had arrived at thus far tended to stress too heavily the discontinuity between God and the world and too little the possibilities of man's communion with or discrimination between the holy and nonholy in the world. But what the colloquium had been seeking was the students' consciousness of the dignity and glory of God, the importance proper to His being which made Him God. The sense of dignity or glory of God gave weight to the experience of the "normal Christian" among Palmer's students, and it was this dignity and glory which Palmer thought Fred Gardner had later lost, and with it a sense of the comedy and tragedy in life that Lynn and Jim had grasped.

The Bay area world-view scales were most helpful in opening to our study at an early stage the cleavages of epistemological proportions at the foundations of the university and the culture. The scales were least helpful in discerning the power of ultimate reality to evoke human initiative for reshaping professions and institutions to meet new human needs.

Campus Ministers' Response to Morality of Knowledge Issues

Having made some assessment of our survey data, the national staff turned to the campus clergy in the Bay area. We did not seek to describe and assess their reaction to the survey data (this was not yet available to them). Rather, we wished to see how sensitive their work had been thus far to the actualities of religious life which the scholars in the university were studying.

It became clear early in the discussions that for all the writing and talking which the campus clergy had done about their "ministry to the faculty," their role "to enable scholars to understand the Christian significance of their work," and the need to present to "the key leaders in the university structure (faculty) the importance of the religious dimensions of existence," they had little or no knowledge of the research being done by scholars into the nature of student values and commitments, comparing campus cultures, or the influence on personality growth of formal learning experience in higher education.

The Center for Study of Higher Education at the University of California had been for years conducting extensive surveys of students in a whole variety of academic environments. They had used scales which ministers, once they studied them in the colloquium, regarded as reflecting great theological naïveté and as having the effect of producing typologies that primarily set anti-intellectual, antiscientific, parochial, rural, orthodox Protestants over against intellectual, scientific, cosmopolitan, secular liberal students. Yet the campus clergy had never studied these instruments, or made a responsible critique of them, or suggested alternative scales.

Joseph Katz and his associates had been interviewing at length and frequently a great variety of students to see what they believed was happening to them in their whole academic careers: undergraduate, graduate, professional, and postdegree schooling.[12] No campus ministers that we could find in the Bay area had a "beat" in the university which informed him of such studies and got them used in discussions at staff meetings to objectify and enrich their knowledge of the kind of people and problem they faced in pastoral care.

The second characteristic we noted of the campus clergy's approach to these morality of knowledge issues was that they sought to approach them as a specialized problem of a particular constituency to be met by a "new" or "experimental" program. For example, Walt Herbert was employed in 1963–1964 to establish an "experimental" and "specialized" ministry with graduate students. His constituency was, potentially, the 8,000 graduate students at the University of California. In hiring him and defining his relationship to the other campus ministers, no effort was made to define his constituency in epistemological terms.

One fruitful way of doing so, Palmer suggests, would have been to organize his movements about the campus in terms of work with graduate students interested in studying religious commitments and values

---

12. The studies include, for example, the poignant reports by a Methodist student to researchers over a period of six years (and in over 300 pages of interview transcripts) on what it meant to him to break from a narrowly moralistic and pietistic family background through his studies in intellectual history, to decide to enter medical school in emulation of his brother and at the insistence of his parents; to discover his ignorance of what medical education and practice were about; to face his inability to keep alive in medical school other interests than the pursuit of the technical and scientific wonders of molecular biology; to "drop out" of the medical school and to search for a counselor who would help him with his vocational problem and not reduce it to a "mental health" or neuroses issue; to feel that he was a failure in personal ethics and faith because he could not discipline himself to learn a skill that would serve others and pay well.

in the university from (1) a phenomenological approach (students probably in the social science departments), (2) a theocentric or Christological approach (students probably in the seminaries), and (3) an anthropological-existential approach (students in the free university movement interested less in questions of whether God is dead than in questions of whether man is alive).

But instead Herbert tried to find his constituency in terms of categories then current in the literature on "presence," on "authentic, intimate dialogue" in an I-Thou world. He notes in a report on his first year:

So I set about this business of moving around trying to find the places where people would be engaging in the kind of conversation about themselves and the world toward which a Christian presence would have some kind of relevance, into which one could speak, and I was really surprised to find that this didn't seem to be going on.

In his "moving around" Herbert discovered "The Silence":

The absence of basic dialogue on matters of value and meaning, the absence of significant discourse on how one makes sense out of life, the absence of philosophizing on questions concerning man's place in the cosmos, concerning how man's life is to be governed with regard to the truth about man, concerning what it means to follow the good, concerning what it means to be a human being: that is the silence of which I speak.

Where did Herbert go to hear the university in conversation? Did he hear social scientists debating what would go into survey instruments? Did he see architects trying to learn about ethnic ways of living in order to express them in their plans? Did he talk to moral philosophers in the business school seeking to clarify the assumptions of businessmen about the values of a society? Or was he listening for a "basic dialogue" that fitted his particular humanities, liberal arts, personalistic images of concern?

Herbert sees himself as "an evangelist offering an invitation to a kind of struggle" for "personal meaning" in an atmosphere of "openness and common concern" and not "bound to any particular language or set of phrases." But his reports about the university's "silence" are bound up with a kind of language which assumes that efforts by teams of specialists to control the environment, or the practice of a profession, both dehumanize people. The university books are not read and the conversations not heard that deal with human experiences in the sharing of a creative corporate enterprise using special skills to meet pressing social problems. Hence "The Silence." There is a silence in this kind of ministry about the range of personal choice made possible by collective technology and research.

Herbert's reports speak of an "invisible parish," a "complex of relationships between me and certain individuals and groups of individuals, some of whom are acquainted with each other, some of whom are not." He sought in this parish "intense personal relationships, primary confrontations where a new sense of fellowship and community" might be realized. One of these confrontations, in which Parker Palmer was involved, brought together for a few evenings graduate students from a variety of fields who were asked to tell each other why they had decided to make a career of scholarship in their particular discipline, what developments excited them in their field and seemed to offer some significant service to others. These young scholars had never been asked to do this by the senior faculty; and in the spontaneous and varied mix of people Herbert's style had produced they learned a great deal about their own motivations for and methods of work and the difficulties of getting fuller debate about different career patterns in scholarship.

A student's participation in research and scholarship and in interpretation of its significance for actions taken in society provides his major avenue of influence in the lives of others. Pastoral care for persons in the university, therefore, begins with the church's capacity to reveal the sources of its belief, as Richard Gelwick has put it, "in the pursuit of truth which is always beyond the current consensus" and the achievements of a particular methodology.[13]

The basic goals of education and the condition for their achievement as seen by campus ministers throughout the nation might best be caught up in the phrase, "the freedom to discover the truth in order to serve." The Herberts as well as the Gelwicks tried to judge their own work in terms of their support of this mission shared by the church and university. Note two statements from leaders of this ministry outside the Bay area:

Generally considered, religion is the quest for that meaning which has power to give shape to experience, purpose to existence, and motivation

---

13. Richard L. Gelwick, "A Paradigm of Freedom" (Sermon, Danforth Associates Conference, Ojai, California, March 1966).

and moral energy to the human enterprise. Its coordinates are intimacy and ultimacy, finitude and transcendence, nature and history, good and evil, the self and the other, faith and doubt, despair and hope, life and death. And it is precisely these things that we have excluded from the learning situation, and it is their absence, rather than the absence of an intellectual synthesis of world-views, that has generated the loss of religious depth.[14]

It is not so much the case that the world has come of age, but it is the case that Yahweh has set the world free. Thus, all the men in it in all their several institutions are free to find their life in covenant together, each one as a servant to the other. In the university, for example, a student is free to pursue the truth that enables him to develop his personal capacities without hindrance so that he may enhance the public good. Once any man, Christian or not, makes a commitment of this sort, he is of all men most free. He has made the last commitment, namely the commitment to serve. In making this last commitment he realizes that he is utterly free from all other commitments. In fact, he has been liberated into a new order of humanity.[15]

The campus ministers regard the mutual pursuit of knowledge which will inform just public policies as a response to One to whom all knowledge and being are related; at their best these campus ministers know the principles of value and being. But talk about such matters is pompous piosity without attention to the structures of group involvements and power in the university.

---

14. Lloyd J. Averell, "Christian Values in the Student Personnel Program," *Liberal Education,* Vol. XLIX, No. 1 (March 1963). Averell is now president of the Association of Protestant Colleges and Universities.

15. Jack Harrison, "Dwelling with Man" (unpublished paper, March 4, 1967). Harrison is director of the Christian Faith and Higher Education Institute, East Lansing, Michigan.

❧ 8 ❧

STUDENT GROUP INVOLVEMENTS AND CHURCH

CONCERN FOR THE SOCIAL SELF

In the Bay area colloquium, student commitments were seen to revolve not only around the pole of the individual's relation to ideas (for example, his openness to new insights and methods in inquiry) but also around the individual's relation to people. Crucial to the educational process, one paper of the colloquium observed, is the student's capacity for interpersonal knowing, his ability to see the idea content of interpersonal relations and the interpersonal implications of knowledge and learning.[1] Of particular interest in the Bay area colloquium was the way in which the student's intellectual life was tied up with various communities which have some claim on him and to which he gives his time and energy. One of the major themes of H. Richard Niebuhr's *The Responsible Self* was particularly relevant to the inquiries at this point:

> Without obscuring the fact that the self exists as rational being in the presence of ideas, this view holds in the center of attention the fundamentally social character of selfhood. To be a self in the presence of other selves is not a derivative experience but primordial. To be able to say that I am I is not an inference from the statement that I think thoughts nor from the statement that I have a law-acknowledging conscience. It is, rather, the acknowledgement of my existence as the counterpart of another self. . . . Many lines of inquiry have converged on the recognition that the self is fundamentally social, in the sense that it is a being which not only knows itself in relation to other selves but exists as self only in that relation.[2]

1. See Parker Palmer, *Studying Commitments on Campus* (San Francisco Bay Area Colloquium, Berkeley: Pacific School of Religion, April 1964, mimeographed).
2. H. Richard Niebuhr, *The Responsible Self* (New York: Harper, 1963), p. 71.

Among the lines of inquiry that have converged in the concept of the social self are studies of personality development and growth in psychology and education.[3] They report as the essential ingredient for the development of intellectual capacities, or capacities in any other sphere, the need of a person for loving care and attention from his elders. The reciprocal interaction necessary to the development of the child or adolescent in an educational institution need be only the most ordinary kind on the part of the teacher and the student: listening carefully to what a student says and evaluating his mastery of a point of view or method of inquiry; providing the student with an opportunity to help contribute to serious academic work of the university; encouraging his speculation about the implications of his new-found knowledge for decisions that matter to him, such as the choice of a vocation.

This inextricable relation between ideas and communities of selves is one which many empirical studies of the processes of learning and of belief formation have neglected. There has been a tendency to analyze separately the impact of the course content on student commitments and the influence of peer groups or charismatic professors. The academic, the social, and the personal have been treated as totally separate phenomena in the collection and analysis of data, with the result that the committing self, who is both intellectual and social, has eluded the research.[4]

Thus the key to significant religious and value changes, which the Bay area colloquium pressed the Danforth study to test empirically, was the learning situation in which an imaginative integration was achieved among knowledge developed in the formal curriculum, the personal meaning and experience of the student in groups outside the classroom, and the creative formulation of new social policies.[5]

---

3. See, for example, Joseph Katz *et al.*, *Growth and Constraint in the College Years* (New York: Oxford University Press, 1967); Martin Tarcher, *Leadership and the Power of Ideas* (New York: Harper, 1966).

4. For example, Edward D. Eddy, Jr., *The College Influence on Student Character* (Washington, D.C.: American Council on Education, 1959).

5. This is the direction of Philip Jacob's thought when he comments on the minority of student cases in which value changes were significant: "Potency to affect student values is found in the distinctive climate of a few institutions, the individual and personal recognition of a sensitive teacher with strong value commitments of his own, or *the value-laden personal experiences of students imaginatively integrated with their intellectual development.*" Philip Jacob, *Changing Values in College* (New York: Harper, 1957), p. 11 (emphasis added).

The concept of God which informs this kind of research thrust is neither that of the traditional personalistic being who undergirds the freedom of the individual to discover and pursue his own unique and independent life style nor the sociotechnocratic God busily creating a new environment to which man must adjust as quickly as possible. The God of this vision of education is the unifying object of loyalty in an encompassing system of disciplines and perspectives appropriated by the person whose life vocation can be achieved only through his critical and conscious involvement in a family, continuing education, politics, and work. Ministry to others is to be understood only in terms of personal and corporate accountability within these systems of knowledge and power. The Bay area colloquium conceived of learning as taking place within a network of interpersonal trusts. It viewed the ministry by teachers and students in the university as a matter having to do at least with the quality of relations between whole persons. Relations of students to faculty were presumed to be the most important interactions to be studied in the university.

Data on Faculty-Student Relations and Implication for Campus Ministers

It is significant that at the University of California, 75 per cent of the freshmen and 63 per cent of the seniors indicated that there was no faculty member who they felt was particularly responsible to or for them. Further light was thrown on the question of whether an intellectual community existed in the university consisting of persons who believed they were engaged in helping and caring for one another's intellectual and educational needs by the fact that 88 per cent of the freshmen and 67 per cent of the seniors at Berkeley reported that they had never had a faculty person single them out for special academic work or ask their help in an academic project. Thirty per cent of the seniors at the University of California felt that very few or no faculty members were really interested in students and their problems, whereas only 15 per cent of the freshmen saw the situation this way.

The matter of faculty-student relations is not simply one of an easy camaraderie which makes the collegiate years socially more palatable. The relations may reflect a deep split in some educational institutions between faculty and students at points of serious academic concern.

When asked how they felt about their own intellectual capacity and potential in comparison to that of their professors, roughly 25 per cent of the students at Berkeley indicated they felt they were viewed as equals, 15 per cent as inferior; 60 per cent said they had no idea how their professors saw them in this regard. This may reveal an uneasiness about academic capacities. It is an anxiety enforced by many mechanics of education, not the least of which is the lack of experience by faculty of the student's use of concepts and data in nonacademic involvements. Here the student's experience and commitment may be crucial factors in providing new knowledge and a passion for learning.

Given this situation, it is understandable why about 70 per cent of the students could think of no individual faculty person after whom they would want to model a career. Thirty per cent of the students were unable to think of a course which they felt had been particularly influential in their lives. Of those who were able to recall such an experience, very few attributed its importance to contact with a particular professor. Interpersonal relations, either between students or professors or among the students themselves, received very little mention.[6]

The colloquium and the national staff speculated about the significance of these data for the campus ministries. The quantity and quality of interpersonal relations in the environment of many universities is so low that an active ministerial effort is needed. Yet this ministry cannot be satisfied to provide a home away from home for the students. It must enter vigorously into the main life of the university—the life of discovery of knowledge, its transmission and use. This means that the professional campus ministry must be aimed more directly at exploration with concerned faculty and other leaders into the interpersonal, noncognitive, emotional, and affectional dimensions of learning. The faculty are the people who ride herd on most of the students' learning experience; if they cannot be bearers of interpersonal concerns in the midst of academia, there would seem to be little hope

---

6. One interesting reflection of the lack of personalized student-faculty relations is contained in the extreme idealization of the professor by students. Compared to businessmen, for example, professors are seen by students as having much less intense competition, more leisure, much more freedom of expression, significantly greater creative opportunities, a much more secure future, much less high-pressure work. Is this an accurate notion of the professorial life or simply a reflection of the lack of real interpersonal knowledge which exists between students and their mentors?

that the pastoral dimensions of learning will be developed in mass education.

In this situation, the campus ministries will need to give priority to providing opportunities for students to form task forces that use their developing academic competence to explore actions of the churches in areas where significant influence is widest: the expenditure of funds for architecture, the preparation of study guides for young people and adults on contemporary public matters, the provision of pensions and retirement facilities for the aged, and so on. After the churches have demonstrated their respect for the students' competencies in the reform of their own institutional life, they can with more authority and grace encourage students to propose greater collaboration with faculty in the study of public problems.

The ministry of John Hadsell at Westminster House in Berkeley represented during our period of study a beginning in this direction. He had engaged a few law students in reflection on how their studies influenced their career styles, but he had not yet been able to give them experience in using their knowledge in a constructive critique of the church. Nor had he been able to inform them of developments at other schools that were expressive of purposes and policies emerging in his own ministry.[7] Hadsell had not been able to bring the other campus ministers into enough common action on such concerns to have a chance of influencing faculty and student positions on academic policy in any sector of the university.

The ministry of Norm Gustaveson in the YMCA at the University of the Pacific was directed much more than any at Berkeley toward the encouragement of a group of young faculty and students to envision the reorganization of the campus (for instance "clusters of students, faculty, and guest public leaders into new colleges"). The YMCA during

---

7. In Chicago, for example, ministers and lawyers co-operate to provide voluntary legal counsel to people in trouble with the law and without the means to obtain professional help. Out of this experience have come several innovations in the teaching of law and reinterpretation of the work of the lawyer in the community. Such programs provide students with models of work which take a whole lifetime to accomplish or of a calling so richly expressive of their gifts and talents as to require their involvement in a variety of new roles and institutions in the university that they had not taken seriously before their new, voluntary legal experience.

Gustaveson's years at Stockton became an informal but important place for exploring ideas for educational reforms and for rallying support to achieve these reforms.

A special report from one of these new clusters, Raymond College, indicates that such colleges do influence student experience, reducing their sense of alienation from faculty, academic work, and evaluation of them; and the new colleges attract to them students who have different views of religious commitment (for example, they are more likely to regard traditional church involvement as discouraging the student's appreciation of the options and opportunities for use of scientific and technical knowledge and methods).[8]

What both Hadsell's and Gustaveson's ministries have opposed is the assumption by lay faculty and students that the university has no responsibility for the personal dimensions of education. They have not been willing to accept the view that the faculty are not responsible for seeing that the student has adequate opportunity to explore the personal implications of his academic proficiency. They have discovered that faculty who assume they have responsibility only to develop new data in their specializations, and to present it objectively, usually hold false expectations about the student's power to integrate and apply what he learns. Hadsell and Gustaveson have wanted their ministries to provide faculty and administrators with some experience of student attempts to engage in this integration and application of knowledge to personal and group life outside the classroom, so that they would see the hazards, difficulties, and possibilities.

Data on Student Experience in Groups Outside the Classroom

The convictions of ministers such as Hadsell and Gustafson have some grounding in the data from the Bay area survey. The personal and social identification scales of the survey were the only ones on which a majority of students consistently indicated that the issues dealt with were of great importance to them. These scales dealt with the whole network of intergroup relationships in the students' life. For example

---

8. Jerry G. Goff, *A Report to the University of the Pacific Commenting on the Danforth Study of Campus Ministries* (October 1965, mimeographed).

the students were asked whether they agreed, were undecided, or disagreed with the statement, "As a rule, the interests of the group should take precedence over the interests of the individual." The students at Berkeley split into three almost equal segments on this question. But in every category of response they saw the issue as an important one. An almost identical breakdown was found in response to the statement, "Personal survival is generally less important than the survival of the group."

On the statement, "There are certain groups in my life without which I could not get along," over 40 per cent of the students were in agreement, and of these 80 per cent saw the statement as very important. Of the 35 per cent who disagreed with the assertion, 70 per cent saw the issue as not very important. The same pattern emerges from responses to the question, "I am involved in at least one group for which I would give up a great deal." Over 55 per cent of the students agreed with this, and 95 per cent of these found the issue very important. Of the 30 per cent who disagreed with the statement, about 85 per cent found it "not too important."

On the statement, "A person should be prepared to give up his personal goals for the sake of an ideal," almost 50 per cent of the students indicated they were undecided, with 30 per cent agreeing and 20 per cent disagreeing. Again, those who considered the issue "very important" far outweighed those who did not. Forty-five per cent of the students agreed that "Its only natural that a person should take advantage of every opportunity to promote his own welfare." Twenty-five per cent of them were undecided, and 35 per cent disagreed. In every category there were more students who indicated the issue was very important to them than who regarded it as "not too important."

It would appear from these data that the fundamental life problems of students revolve around the tension between an egocentric world view, in which everything is aimed at self-enhancement, and a world view in which social responsibilities are seen as basic and intrinsic to the nature of the self. Campus ministry programs would be well advised to center their theological reflections and inquiries on the nature of the self and the images of man and God which dominate the various positions they are exposed to most regularly in American education and culture. It may be that the most telling critiques of the self for the present and foreseeable future generations of students will be those that explore the inextricable way in which the lives of concrete selves are interwoven with the existence of other selves.[9]

The need for settings, such as the church, in which the motivations and expectations of group involvement can be explored critically and sympathetically is evidenced by data that students who do not think group relations demand anything from them tend to downgrade the salience of the issue for their lives. It would seem that a certain amount of compensatory activity is going on, with a deprivation of certain social contacts and a devaluation of them for human life. Probably the most acceptable and important way to talk about the meaning of religious commitment in our time is to explore with laymen the ranking they give various interpersonal activities, interests, and needs of the self which they regard as of greatest importance. If faith has to do with the loyalties and values which order the whole network of associations and expenditure of life energies, a high order of priority needs to be given to the kinds of issue the Bay area colloquium dealt with as group and personal involvements.

The universities are now the sources of studies pertinent to these matters. Yet the Bay area campus ministers had done almost nothing to encourage the church to ponder the meaning of such data. For example, the six years of detailed study under the direction of Joseph Katz of the "total" educational experience of 3,000 students indicated that most students are not primarily oriented toward academic curiosity and knowledge, achievement, fame, and recognition of wealth; rather they are involved in a much more complex problem of relating work and personal fulfillment. They are much more deeply concerned with the emotional aspects of their lives than most educators recognize. In terms of *group* involvements, the males see their career as most important. Both sexes give chief importance after work to relations and activities with future family, love and affection, and developing a personal identity. Their participation in activities directed toward the public good, religious activities, and sexual needs all rank lower than what might be

---

9. The church has encouraged little systematic inquiry by students and faculty into the activities of the social self in the varied technical and professional structures of American society. Theology had tended to surrender this field to the empirical sciences, such as anthropology, psychology, and sociology. Many of these studies have reduced human behavior to self-seeking or the determinacy of institutional structures on selfhood. Faculties of theology and religion have not sought alliances with these disciplines in planning studies.

termed in the pastoral tradition a search for an affectionate community and personal integrity.

The data of the Bay area colloquium, although not as detailed as the Katz studies, present a similar picture. It is hard to conceive of stronger justification for the resurgence of concern in both Protestant and Catholic churches with the pastoral dimensions of ministry. The real issue is whether this need is to be met by the churches, universities, businesses, welfare agencies, and so on within the power structures of the controlling specialists and governors.

Joseph Katz has noted that in his data the question urgently presents itself as to what extent these personal needs (for example, for an affectionate community in which to achieve autonomy and to develop initiative) are encouraged in the didactic and directive climate of many colleges. They do not offer enough opportunity for the student to exercise caretaking responsibilities toward others or to be in charge of projects connected vitally with his own motivations and purposes.[10] If the student should be given varied opportunities to enhance his formal academic experience, the question then presents itself, says Katz, why the scholar, with his stress on cognitive factors, has been put into leading, policy-making positions and the student excluded from significant influence on educational policy. His training is as a specialist in a subject matter or discipline rather than in the understanding of human personality or of the educational processes, curricular or extracurricular. Therefore he needs help from other professors and institutions with information about the attitudes and problems of students, including campus ministries.

Our survey data also lead us to conclude that the larger majority of students are involved in groups which are hardly supportive of the dominant intellectual values of academia. The students make a fairly radical separation of areas of their life. Indeed, many of these groups are organized in disdain of, if not outright hostility to, the professed goals of the academic community. The shape of group involvements reflects basic student dilemmas between concern for affectionate commitments and for formal mastery of cognitive skills, between search for personal identity and the fearful drift into a vocation they know little about ex-

---

10. Joseph Katz, "The Role of the Student Dean in Educational Innovation" (paper at the Annual Conference, College Student Personnel Institute, Claremont, California, November 2, 1965).

cept that it pays well. If one of the focuses of work of the campus ministry is the morality of knowledge, it seems equally clear that another is the shape of the student's group involvements. And the significant question is that of the connections or discontinuities students make among religious commitment, learning experience, and other group involvements.

The Bay area survey asked students to think about both their formal and informal group involvements and then indicate which group was most important to them. Eighty-five per cent of the students signified that they were involved in at least one informal group of friends with whom they spent a fair amount of time. This was primarily a form of social life; fraternities and sororities were the most frequently mentioned examples. Only 10 per cent of the students indicated that their informal groups were characterized by common intellectual concerns. Students were asked to indicate why the group they would call most important to them occupied this status. The most frequent responses recall Katz's findings on the importance of self and social identities; the students stressed, "In it I can be myself," "It gives me support in facing problems," and "It gives me a feeling of belonging."

Most students are not talking about denominational groups in these terms. Roughly 15 per cent of the students indicated some form of involvement with religious groups; normally this meant attendance at a service or meeting a few times each month. For 7 per cent of the students, involvement in religious organizations and activities on campus is regarded as most important in their lives.

Academic groups per se are not those most cherished in interpersonal terms or in terms of providing help in facing problems of personal life. Almost 50 per cent of the students agreed that attending classes is often a waste of time, but 65 per cent of these regarded this fact as "not very important." Eighty per cent of the students disagreed that "the person who lacks a college education is not adequately prepared for living a broad, well-rounded life." This view may indicate a recognition that wisdom is not a monopoly of the formally educated, but it also reveals that students do not see themselves as receiving any *special* life prerogatives by virtue of higher education. There is nothing intrinsic to higher education which they regard as of special importance to their style of living.

The churches and ministers need to face the fact that what most students actually hold in highest regard in their university life is their peer-group culture. Much more attention needs to be given to the internal dynamics of the peer-group social life of young people. Most of the psychological-theological literature on pastoral care or on the interpersonal aspects of religious commitment concentrates on parent-child relations and on the quality of relationship within church groups. It deals little with the influence of the peer culture on the adolescent. What little comprehensive research we now have in this area indicates that from the seventh grade of secondary school on, the majority of young people look mainly not to their parents as models, companions, and guides to behavior, but to their peers.[11]

This is one reason why faculty and administrators have been giving increasing attention to proposals for the reorganization of large universities around "college clusters" or plans that envision a closer relationship between social, personal, and academic activities (for example, a college of religious studies). The concern is to offer alternative peer cultures.[12]

The denominational centers, for all their attempts to mix serious religious study with the recreational and affectional interests of students (through covenant communities and week-end conferences promising "Sun, Fun, Food," and even something the University Christian Church at Berkeley calls "Singspirations"), have had little effect on the peer cultures of a large campus. They cannot and do not supply the peer culture base for most students and should not entertain the illusions of doing so in the future. Most of them merely isolate religiously oriented students further from the world of the campus. A more realistic possibility is that by careful study of the peer cultures and of the influence of dissenters within them, the centers may prepare Christians for a significant role in the internal group life of the campus. The peer group, several studies now document, can propel members toward destructive,

11. See Theodore M. Newcomb, "Student Peer-group Influence," in Nevitt Sanford and Associates, *The American College* (New York: Wiley, 1962), pp. 469–488.

12. This concern helps explain why Browne Barr, pastor of the First Congregational Church in Berkeley, and Richard Gelwick, his associate, have explored the possibility of establishing in the parish a "free college," without academic accreditation but operating alongside the University of California with the resources of several hundred faculty and graduate students who are members of the church, if the University of California offers at most a department of religious studies in the next decade.

anti-intellectual acts; but it can also have the opposite possibility. Experiments in response to group pressures have shown that the presence of a single dissenter can sometimes be enough to break the spell of a group so that its participants have to consider the consequences and varied interpretations of their intended acts.[13]

This experience of dissent appears to be rare in most campus peer groups. Students were asked in the Bay area survey if they were involved in groups where members held diverse points of view and enjoyed arguing them. Less than 5 per cent mentioned such an experience.

Students, Their Families, and Religious Commitment

Primary among all group involvements of the student are those of his family. The Bay area survey sought not simply "objective" factors such as the income and occupation level of the student's parents but the individual's perception of his relation to his parents. We wanted to know whether they established the experience of responsible knowing in the family, so that the child would face the epistemological problems of collegiate life with some security.

Did the parents encourage a kind of openness about difficult and basic questions of value which made exploring them appropriate? Did they admit to a certain ambiguity about ultimate questions and encourage a quest for answers? Does the student remember his home as helping him to face the important questions of faith, value, and fact? To what extent does the student feel that his family is currently appreciative of what he is doing? Do students feel that they have to totally reject familial ways of decision and styles of life in order to find a responsible morality of their own?

These were the kinds of question which the Bay area colloquium knew it could not answer simply in a student survey; but it used such questions in working papers as clues to what church and community leaders should be exploring with the families of college students and with student personnel workers.[14]

---

13. Urie Bronfenbrenner, "The Split-Level American Family," *Saturday Review of Literature*, October 7, 1967.

14. Whenever campus clergy have consulted with the student health and psychiatric services, these are the kinds of question raised. Psychologists working with students in the Bay area report that they counsel with an increasing number of college students who complain of vague feelings of apathy, boredom, meaningless-

Our survey data indicate that most students' religious world views and approaches to a morality of knowledge are strongly correlated with those they perceive in their parents. Though they regard themselves as searching for a morality of their own, they are strongly influenced by the expectations of their parents. Most do not regard where they are coming out on sexual behavior, vocational choice, and a variety of other issues as widely different from the decisions their parents made. There would seem to be in these data the basis for much greater exploration between generations, and between campus and parish ministers, of continuing problems in character and personality development.

Pastoral care in the churches might focus for a while on a study of data from surveys, interviews, and case records of the universities in the Bay area and elsewhere on minority and majority student trends in group and public involvement. The shepherd has concern both with the flock and with the sheep moving out from the fold.

The rebellious students of the left may reveal to us in part, as George Kennan says, "our own ugly and decadent face that we see in this distorted mirror."[15] According to several studies, a significant percentage of the students estranged from the values of their families and of society come from middle-class, permissive parents whose own values and religious convictions have crumbled.[16]

---

ness, and chronic unhappiness. They are anxious that data and perspectives on these problems be shared with the clergy, the faculty, and other agents of personal care, since the factors and conditions involved are not the sole province of specialists in psychotherapy and psychiatry. Similar questions were also suggested by sociologists consulted in the colloquium who study subcultures of students.

Chancellor Roger W. Heyns, of the University of California, has told campus ministers that he looks hopefully to them for "models of moral action in a new age." He requests them to report to the university and to parents what they have been able to learn about the intentions and expectations of young people. Faculty and parents alike, he says, need to know why the university cannot escape obligations to see that standards of character are developed and also freedom to conduct inquiry into the various options and meanings of human conduct.

15. George Kennan, "Rebels without a Program," *New York Times Magazine*, January 21, 1968.

16. Such parents are reluctant to make use of physical, economic, or legal power available to them to help students face obligations of generations toward one another. They have left their children free to challenge their rules and standards and soon found it impossible to arrive at any consensus as to sensible and just use of the families' resources and time. Parents and children have been caught up in a number of historic value shifts external to the family: lengthening the period of childhood and adolescence, increasing formal educational requirements to qualify for professional work, diminishing opportunity to participate in adult household ac-

Yet more main-stream youth culture has emerged that does not pursue total personal permissiveness. But it has broken from certain parental standards of success and morality. Its participants will not delay sexual intercourse if they find the "right relationship" or marriage through all of education. They seek some significant participation in the shaping of educational policies. They seek summer employment and social action in a real world which enlarges their educational experience. These are all expressions of persons wanting to be mature, to attempt judgment, to be honest about feelings, to take public responsibilities. They are often expressions of adolescents emerging into a larger society with little experience of authority or power structures, legal, political, or economic. Much more attention needs to be paid to this "moderate" youth culture than to the extreme or radical subcultures.[17] (Our Wisconsin analysis begins with an intensive look at this "moderate" youth culture both inside and outside church organizations.)

But no sustained effort was being made to bring student and parents from campus and parish churches into study and reflection on what this research of the university was discovering about youth. What is not happening in the campus ministry is the organization of consultations with parish church leaders who have access to the family and secondary-school cultures out of which many of these students come. Hence no careful, informed plans are developed for adult church activities that reflect what campus ministries are learning in their contacts with faculty and student personnel workers. There is little evidence that campus ministers in the Bay area have mobilized the resources of their own environment to help the parish churches in this regard. They could undertake a serious look at Christian models of high schools preparing students for responsible judgments on issues such as sexual morality and drug addiction. They could inquire into what parents know about their children's leisure time and peer-group activities or about significant studies of family life such as John F. Cuber's *Sex and the Significant Americans*.[18]

---

tivities, setting "minimal" standards of living that cannot be achieved in an early marriage.

17. Seymore L. Halleck, "The Source of Student Alienation" (paper before the American Psychiatric Association, reproduced in full, *New York Times,* May 12, 1967).

18. John Hadsell, of the Berkeley Westminster House, and other campus ministers have been involved in major attempts by the parish churches in the Bay area to establish experiments in raising the intellectual level of adult education.

Default of attention to the relations of self, education, and social policy is not represented by omission of some "social action" program or better "public relations of campus clergy with the parish churches." What is at stake is a Christian understanding of the processes and crises that make human personality possible. Christian parents need to see their children and themselves in terms of their potentiality in a learning process by which they become men rather than animals.

There are many points of departure for serious dialogue in the Bay area between people in the churches and the universities; it would appear that one of the most promising proposals would be to examine the shift in clerical and academic thinking about the person as fundamentally estranged from his culture to that of his coming into being as a participant in the lives of others. The social-existential motifs of psychology are coming to the fore in many students; they have their profound counterparts in theological discourse. The Judeo-Christian faith fosters the hope that man can become an actor, capable of deciding and feeling. The most certain mark of his having been touched by God's revelation is in his renewed faith that he can live in the world as a person of integrity and that he can find some meaningful pattern in his public actions. The fundamental striving of the person is for the actualization of his potential as a human being.

If development and growth are like this, what is implied for churches trying to think in terms of the relationship of their ministry to education, parish involvement, and other urban organization? Do they plan to know men of faith through a whole life cycle?[19] Do they place their work in this cycle?

These programs use faculty in biblical and religious studies, Christian and social ethics, but they do not bring these resources to bear in a concerted way on problems which are public and personal for all the families involved, which have been the object of sustained research by the behavioral and social sciences, and involve pastoral care by the colleges and universities. The study by John F. Cuber is fully titled, *Sex and the Significant Americans: A Study of Sexual Behavior Among the Affluent* (Baltimore, Md.: Penguin, 1967).

19. See, for example, Erik H. Erikson, *Identity and the Life Cycle, Psychological Issues Monograph* 1:1 (New York: International Universities Press, 1959).

≈ 9 ≈

COUNSELING, REBELLION, AND POLICY FORMATION

W HEN the Bay area colloquium had completed its studies, the national staff was convinced that it had not yet done the kind of research which revealed the concrete ways the clergy actually performed specific pastoral functions. We had not found the realistic limits of power by campus clergy to initiate new policies in the church and university, and we could not envision where policy alternatives were going to originate.

The next stage of our research, therefore, took three directions. We arranged for intensive interviews with a sample of clergy in the Bay area as to their approach to student counseling, believing that this probably represented the most intimate and sensitive area in which pastoral care was exercised. We also interviewed a sample of student personnel workers and administrators as to their understanding of pastoral and other responsibilities of campus clergy. Second, since the Berkeley student rebellion had taken place, Elden Jacobson was assigned to the national staff to investigate the response of the campus clergy to this event. And third, we planned a field survey by Clarence P. Shedd of the religious developments in California's community and junior college system and of the relations of the Bay area campus church leadership to these developments.

Pastoral Counseling in the University

The counseling activities of the campus clergy represent the most intimate relationships to students by a professional religious leader. Here perhaps more than in any other role the connections can be traced among the academic life of the student, his peer group and family, his

future hopes for a vocation, and the resources of the church for exploring the significance of his religious commitments.

Our student survey instrument had not probed the students' version
of what happened when they sought religious counsel, except to note to
whom they most frequently turned in "time of personal need." The
clergy, we discovered, stood high in this regard, even though only a small
minority of students participated in any church activities. This fact
raises some important questions at once as to whether the students, with
their tangential relation to the churches, knew anything concretely
about the varied perspectives and resources represented in the clergy's
approach to their problems. It was a question, too, whether the campus
ministers themselves viewed their counseling activities simply as an
individual enterprise or as part of a conscious team effort. The questions
of what happens to the student in his counseling relations to a clergyman, the minister's operative psychological, social, and theological assumptions, and the counseling policies of a united ministry were being
pressed increasingly upon the clergy by the professionalization of student personnel work and its close ties to the educational and psychological research being conducted by the faculties.

The interviewers sought to give clergy the opportunity to explain
the relation of their pastoral care to that of other student personnel
workers. The campus minister was asked to place his counseling duties
in the context of his other roles, to explain the types of counseling he engaged in (giving the interviewer his own typology), and to illustrate
his approach in terms of recent "cases" in counseling. He was encouraged to contrast and compare himself to other pastors, to indicate to what
extent he thought students were made aware in the church of the varied
approaches to counseling available to them, and to describe the sources
of their chief images of counseling. He was asked to describe the structures and associations which supported and expressed his work as counselor and what occasions there had been for review of his approach
with other ministers and with people having important, though different,
competencies in the field.[1]

---

1. These interviews were viewed as highly confidential, and therefore all reference to specific persons or campuses are omitted in our public use of the information. Interviews were conducted in counseling in every city or campus that was a
subject of intensive study in the general design. These were conducted by a number
of people: Ray Rymph, James Glen, William Horvath, Hoyt Oliver, Elden Jacobson, Audrey Clapham, and Kenneth Underwood. Data from these interviews will
be used at other points in the report of this study.

The campus ministers generally report that the most common kinds of problem to which they are explicitly asked to give counsel have to do with disagreements with parents or student associates over standards of sexual conduct, the use of alcohol and drugs, and the meaning and purpose of life. These problems are often intimately tied up with questions about the values dominating various "leisure and peer-group syndromes," with decisions about the wisdom of marrying "now" and the extent to which campus experience has given the student an adequate basis for choosing a suitable mate. Most of the clergy do not find students seeking help from them when they perceive their problem as having to do with academic matters.[2]

Eighty-five per cent of the students at Berkeley say they do not know any campus minister personally. The impressions of counseling interests and competencies rely heavily on information in the popular press and on local parish experience. Most students do not perceive that clergy have an interest or competency in areas outside personal morals and traditional religious beliefs or that some academic problems would be illumined by discussion of the religious and value commitments which inform decisions in these areas. It is also clear from our interviews with student personnel workers in the Bay area that most of them, like the students, look upon the counseling concerns of the clergy as having to do with a limited range of interpersonal or private moral and religious problems.

Given these public images, the question was pursued in our interviews as to whether they accurately reflected ministerial approaches to counseling; if not, we wished to know what efforts had been made by the clergy to correct these public images. The most general conclusion to which our interviews led was that the campus clergy represent a vast variety of interests and approaches to counseling. The subjects thought to be of least interest to the clergy by students are for some clergy the areas where they wish most to provide counsel. However, the students

---

2. This impression is strengthened by a study of female students and counseling conducted by Mary Kinnane in six colleges and universities and reported in "The Chaplain: Perceptions of His Role; A Comparison by College Staff Members and Undergraduates," *Humanity* (Spring 1966). Dean Kinnane found that most clerical counseling focused around parental rules and regulations over female and male relationships, honesty in course work, personal despair or anguish over loss of belief in God, and the use of traditional sacramental acts of the church, such as marriage.

are generally realistic as to the kinds of problem with which most of the ministers believe they deal with competence.

The campus clergy has made very little effort to bring into open consciousness its approaches to counseling or to discuss together varied interpretations of objective "cases." Clergymen have not sought to inform students and student personnel workers, through carefully formulated statements and consultations, of the varied kinds of counseling resource which the churches offer the university. There were, however, signs at the close of our studies that more regular consultations in this regard were taking place and that some church policies toward counseling were emerging.

This development is important in light of the students' increasingly sophisticated appropriation of psychological and social theories that govern relations to themselves. It is particularly significant in terms of the students' general interpretation of religious commitment (see Chapter 7) as freeing them to resist attempts at a manipulative control of human personality or at comprehension of ultimate reality from one particular way of knowing. Also, counseling activity quite clearly, our interviews show, has become one of the major ways by which campus clergy seek to legitimize their presence on campus. They generally spend at least a fourth of their time in counseling—some as much as 40 or 50 per cent—and they estimate that the pressures on them for additional help are growing.

Our interviews discerned at least four major approaches to counseling among the campus clergy.

First, there were campus ministers who saw the students as grappling with irrational forces within themselves which kept them from relating effectively to other persons. The task, then, was to bring these forces into the open by the creation of a nondirective atmosphere that would permit the student to "open up." Counseling sessions of these pastors are punctuated with questions such as "Why are you afraid to come out in the open," "Why don't you level with me?" The role model appears to be the professional therapist who accepts students for their intrinsic value as persons. For these ministers, counsel and discussion in the church should convey an atmosphere conducive to leisurely contemplation and to delving into the fundamentals of personal living, but not solving any career problems, developing any policies, or meeting any agenda.

The problems which these pastors reported to us project a world of family and covenanting fellowship as the center of a personalistic society. They approach urban, career, or academic problems as an extension of their kind of concern with existential, interpersonal situations. They talk much of "freeing the person" by loving counsel and authentic encounter from "passing moralities" and "social fictions" and the bureaucratic structures of the university. This counseling assumes the counselor's and counselee's need for a continuing "home" in some community of affection and acceptance.

At the other extreme is a second type of campus minister-counselor, who sees students as passive recipients of social pressure from established bureaucracies and "power elites." When asked to identify these, they talk about the views of C. Wright Mills, Peter Berger, and other favorite social scientists. These ministers often reject counseling as a form of action for themselves. What they have to do of it usually takes place in small groups and is directed toward heightening the students' awareness of their own ways of thinking and of the factors influencing other people's images of them. They do not want the student to escape from thinking for themselves about what their responsibilities are in the society and what resources are available to them for making a judgment. They wish the ministry to help people see the structural situation and various ways of looking at themselves and at what they can do with others in that situation.

These men do not deny the validity of counseling, but they tend to think of it as relatively unimportant and unsuccessful in the church's care for persons. They do not regard counseling as a technical activity to be professionalized, particularly with principles borrowed without criticism from psychoanalytic or psychotherapeutic writers. For them, what should go on in most counseling in the church is what goes on in good conversation with informed, publicly involved people.

This kind of counselor holds strongly to the position that much of psychiatry has perpetuated a myth and language of mental illness which is seized upon by the lonely, the downcast, and the alienated in hopes of getting their share of human love.[3] When the university and the church have organized their corporate life to clarify the problems and tasks of human beings in contemporary urban society, clerical personnel will be spending less time in vague, formless counseling.

A third type of counselor in the campus ministry is the theological

---

3. This position toward counseling is fully developed in Thomas S. Szasz, *The Myth of Mental Illness* (New York: Harper, 1961).

conservative who is waging a battle against "the permissive and relativistic ethic of psychotherapy which ignores the problems of guilt and faith" and the "social gospelers who would try to build the kingdom without redeemed men." These counselors have been strongly influenced by O. Hobart Mowrer and his interpreters, such as David Belgum. The latter acknowledges that there are many causes of mental illness and suffering besides guilt, but is persuaded that "where personal guilt is the crucial problem in diagnosis and therapy, there, religion and psychology meet."[4]

The main endeavor of counseling by pastors of this type is to discover the evasion of personal responsibilities and to uphold behavior for which they believe the traditional principles of the church give unmistakable guidance. They wish to provide supervision without short cuts of a whole process of reconciliation between the sinner and those done harm, a process involving contrition, confession, and satisfaction. There is in this counseling little or no attention to corporate or environmental factors affecting the situation of the actor and little potential for emancipation from conventions of a particular ethnic or sect culture in the service of a higher justice.

There is a fourth type of counselor in the ministry whom Charles McCoy terms "the professional campus minister." He is able to locate his own views of counseling in relation to those of his colleagues and to the academic formulations of these approaches. He may or may not spend considerable time in counseling; he considers it as a valid competence in the ministry, but one that must be intimately related to "intensive study, fellowship and worship in the church." His clientele mainly focuses on ideas and actions in his "home base" or center. He works extensively, chiefly with students who because of their interest in the problems of a community of faith and institution "have a frame of reference within which they feel they can start talking." He often develops what he calls "a weird capacity for sensing when someone is having difficulty," and will go to that person hoping to form a relationship that can lead to counseling.

His counseling is seldom, in contrast to types two and three, a "one-

---

4. For example: O. Hobart Mowrer, *The Uses of Psychiatry and Religion* (Princeton: Van Nostrand, 1961); David Belgum, *Guilt: Where Psychology and Religion Meet* (Englewood Cliffs: Prentice-Hall, 1963).

time affair." His work with a person involves neither a permissive relation without perspectives of his own nor a relation in which he renders a judgment quickly. Rather he helps the counselee explore his situation from a variety of perspectives. The hoped-for consequence is a person who arrives at his own discriminating judgment as to what he is to do and be in the future.

He does not see in the ethic of being honest, of knowing the structures that influence one's acts, or in neatly defining an area of personal influence what he would accept as an adequate grasp of the religious condition of man. His counseling has gone far beyond the writers on "normality," "adjustment," or "guilt and forgiveness" in seeking sophisticated answers appropriate to the complexity of human values and of the multiple group involvements of most Christians.

Most pastors of this type have had some exposure to clinical work in a hospital or other "healing" institutions. They have made their own common-sense modifications of Carl Rogers, Seward Hiltner, David Roberts, and others who have written thoughtfully on pastoral counseling and on the relation of Christian faith to psychology.

Their interpretation of the problems with which the student comes to the minister, and the processes of unfolding their Christian meaning, are well represented in this partial exchange from one of our interviews:

Q. What are the major themes or problems in your counseling?

A. Probably seven to eight out of ten students who sit and talk with me are extremely anxious about what it means to be a human being (including what it means to be a human being and accept your sexuality). Perhaps the next largest area of concentration is how do I do something relevant in my life? Where do I plug into society that is going to amount to something and be relevant? I suppose the next most prevalent area of concern is making some sort of accommodation to life in terms of what I have known in the past. And here you move into some of students' earlier religious training, family sociological background, etc.

Q. Do you find a number who came here because of family difficulties?

A. They don't necessarily. In fact I can only recall a few who would come because "of family difficulties." But as we talk, certain family difficulties play a part in the confusion and in the perplexities of the students. So, yes, family difficulties from one extremity to another do enter in.

Q. How about peer relations in the sense of not being socially accepted?

A. These enter in, but these frequently find expression in the earlier categories. This is one of the main areas that frequently stir up difficulties, mainly for men, but sometimes for girls. I find that acceptance by your peer group has to have a certain sexual connotation.

Q. Why do these people come to you?

A. Well, I don't know.

Q. Perhaps I could rephrase it. Why do some of these students go through the subterfuge of talking with a religious counselor when a faith problem is not really the main problem?

A. First, perhaps in their own naïveté and being religiously oriented, they think that if they are disturbed they have something religious as a problem. This is a part of our culture, but it's not necessarily good. The second thing is that sometimes the only way a person can engage in an encounter is to begin to engage at a more elementary level. And the level at which they feel free to engage is to say, "Something you said in a discussion disturbed me" or "I heard something in a sermon which I'd like to talk with you about." This becomes the jumping-off point. This truly becomes a bridge, but they don't realize it is a bridge. The third thing is that for the most part the person who comes in with this approach is not too aware how much he or she is groping for something in the way of a listener and a responder. But for some peculiar, inexplicable, and perhaps essential reason they do follow through on the basis of a question about their faith. This becomes a doorway through which we pass into other events.

Q. When students come to you, do you think they see you as a counseling expert, as an older brother, a priest? Is this a Protestant confessional? What definition do they bring?

A. Everybody brings a different definition. Whether we think it is professionally dignified or not, one of the things we do is meet in these experiences a substitute father image or an older brother image or something of this sort. This is bound to happen. I think for some we are the teacher. I think for some we are persons who have thought through various aspects of life and various problems of life and have come up with some answers, and they want to hear what these answers are. They don't want to be told that these are their answers, but they want to hear what our answers are. There are some who need exactly what you said—the Protestant confessional. Absolution, and this is a priestly function. I would be hard-pressed unless I did a careful analysis of my records to tell you where these fit in a numerical breakdown. At different times of the relationship these may be cross-referenced.

Q. Do you have a favorite style as a counselor?

A. Yes, if you wish, I have a gimmick I use. I try to listen to what people say, having cut my academic teeth on Carl Rogers. This is partially influential. Another influence: in my background of people who were helpful to me were those who were genuinely interested in me as a human being, responding to me and then letting me accept them as a human being. This is essentially the role I try to play. When I have a student come into my office I generally feel around and try to find out something about the individual: "Tell me something about mother and dad," etc. I get the person talking about himself within the context that is very familiar to him. From there I move into the areas which seem a logical point of interest from things which he raises himself in conversation. This is so in a more general case. If a person comes in with a more specific problem I still try to get acquainted by going through the family and childhood experiences to put the person at ease and to show him that I am interested in him as a person. Then we can get to a place where we can talk honestly about specific things, and this usually unfolds.

Q. Do you think healing takes place in your counseling sessions?

A. In some instances yes, and in some no, because I'm not a miracle worker. Sometimes I just can't say what I think needs saying in a way that breaks through to the heart of the problem.

Q. Do you reach a point in your counseling where you prescribe behavior for a person that you think might be helpful?

A. Yes, I think there must come that point. I don't think there is any excuse for a person coming to me unless he thinks that somewhere along the line what I am or where I am or what I do has some relevance. I find revealing this is not the first thing I do. I have to find out who this person is and how he is. And I try to be relevant to him where he is. I think the Christian faith has something to say about all of life and that's why I'm here. I'm not here to twist them into being members of the "God-squad," but I am here to try to make any relevant comments I can insofar as I understand life within the Judeo-Christian perspective.

Q. Does your counseling have a theological basis? Do you see it as part of your religious function as a minister of the gospel? Do you find it an outgrowth of the teachings of Jesus? Where does this work fit into the Christian ministry as you see it?

A. There certainly is a theological perspective through which I enter the counseling relationship, but I do not think it is a perspective that was there originally. I think it has evolved and unfolded and become clearer to me as time went on. My formal seminary training lacked very greatly two crucial areas—the area of Old Testament and its relevance to life; and a broad, rich, contemporary, theological orientation. As a counselor I relate as a Christian person to another person, and most often to another Christian. This says something of what I am doing in relationship with this person. I am speaking from the perspective of my own acceptability and acceptance as far as my understanding of the acceptability and acceptance of the person to whom I am speaking, as far as I am concerned, and also as far as God is concerned. I am in no sense of the word sitting there as a prosecuting attorney, judge, or jury, and much of the time I have to convince the student that he is not to play the role in his own life of prosecuting attorney, judge, and jury, but that his role is to accept his acceptance because this is the basic meaning of the Christian faith, and then respond to that acceptance affirmatively in his living experiences. As I understand the Christian faith in terms of what it says about man being aware of his shortcomings— a sinner; man despite his shortcomings, being involved in a divine-human encounter—that God is concerned with His creation and involved with it and seeking continually to be related to it and have a transforming relationship; human relationships are meant to be responsive, responsible relationships, not exploited. I spend much of my time trying to tell students, when they apologize for taking my time, that they don't need to apologize because time is for people and he happens to be a person. The only reason we exist on the face of the earth is to be relevant and of assistance and supportive of one another. I can't find any other excuse for human existence.

As this exchange indicates, for the professional, informed pastor the initial "problem" with which the student comes is not a crucial clue to what goes on in his relationship to the student. In that relationship the student is helped to look at his situation theologically, socially, economically, legally, psychologically, and in this he is liberated to act responsibly. It is also apparent that technical knowledge of these perspectives is not the key to the pastor's authority for the student. It lies in the quality of his caring for another as an expression of what he believes the power that created the world wills him to do in it.

There is no evidence that the clergyman in this interview seeks to make each counseling session an eyeball-to-eyeball confrontation of belief in the Christian faith, or that he has to prove his courage to speak authentically or his power to strip away the social roles of the man to reach the inner core. He may speak critically and compassionately. The roles and offices in family, work, and academic life are all relevant and an expression of the self. It is as if Christ's own understanding of the love of God and man is a readiness to learn what is really happening to people in their lives and to give of one's best, whether it be technical or theological skill, political influence, or spontaneous affection. This type of counselor keeps files of what a student and he talk about, not to make him a case in a study, but to maintain some record of progress and growth of mutual understanding in a sequence of sessions.

He is the type who has taken the initiative to bring campus ministers to a greater awareness of their separate approaches to pastoral care. He studies the data of the relevant health services and sciences and communicates directly with student deans and health center officials about common problems and concerns. The chief resistance to his activities in ministerial association comes from the second and third types of pastor-counselor.

If the data from the student survey are accurate, this fourth type of counselor in the church is going to have growing support in the future from the educated laity of the church. A substantial proportion of students are sensitive to efforts to force a particular point of view upon them or to avoid judgments on matters from a reasoned point of view. Whatever the issue, counseling goes on best in the context of an institution or community that has organized itself to conduct a full and frank discussion that brings varying points of view to bear on an issue, makes use of the technical wisdom of varied disciplines, hears from people who have used these in different contexts, and encourages movement to personal decisions.[5]

Student awareness of the variety of approaches to counseling in any particular area of human behavior by the churches is going to increase with research by the university into such practices. All church leaders operate from some kind of value and faith position and with some impressions of behavioral data in a field. The student needs to be aware of what is being presented as a religious perspective and as "objective facts." Immaturity, ignorance, and manipulation are perhaps most common in the counseling care of persons. As the campus clergy move in the direction of seeking data as to the bases of practice in this area, they will find strong support from student personnel administrators, many of whom tend to view the work of the clergy in their area as "untouchable," but bordering on "chaos."

The data and faithful concerns of this study indicate a staff preference for this fourth kind of pastoral care, but it need not be the only faith context in which responsible counseling is developed. What ever else pastoral care has meant in the history of the church, it has carried the image of the "good shepherd" willing to "lay down his life for the

---

5. These conclusions will be explored in greater detail in the chapters on "governing" in the campus ministry (chapters 16–18). The Danforth study does not draw these conclusions simply from the Bay area. For example, it participated in a two-year colloquium initiated by campus ministers and student personnel leaders in six colleges on the east coast. The papers of this colloquium are available: John A. Buerk (ed.), *Personnel Services and The Campus Ministry* (Buffalo, N.Y.: Department of Campus Ministries, Council of Churches, 1968).

sheep." All four types of counselor accept this image as their own. The image, shorn of its rural overtones, conveys the sense that Christians will be those who care what is happening to each student in the concrete structures of the university, where he is going in his work, and what he is doing with his knowledge. They are concerned with the student's developing capacity to care for others as for himself and to do so in terms of the discipline and control of one who has learned to care.

The Berkeley Student Rebellion and the Campus Ministries

The free speech crisis at Berkeley in the fall of 1964 provided the campus ministries with a time for testing their professional spirit and discipline in the midst of a radical breakdown of communication between members of the student body and the administration. In this crisis, fundamental factors in the actions and interactions of people in the church, the university, and the larger society were laid bare.

The Berkeley crisis began with student protest against a ruling which stated that the Regents' policies specifically forbid use of university facilities for "supporting or opposing particular candidates in national elections."[6] This had the effect of closing a strip of sidewalk immediately adjacent to the campus which had for many years served as a "Hyde Park" kind of forum from which student opinions might issue and funds be solicited for a variety of causes. Students such as Mario Savio, who had worked to secure civil rights for Negroes, saw the ruling as a curb to increasing student political involvement in reform movements.

At first most campus clergy did not see the order as an infringement on activities in which religious groups normally participated. But as the opposition spread and became articulated in terms of a violation not only of civil rights but of free pursuit of truth in the university, most campus clergy were drawn in some way into the conflict.

The Jacobson report to the Danforth study is in the form of a Yale University Ph.D. dissertation, in which he describes the action of six Protestant campus ministers at the University of California as they

---

6. Seymour Martin Lipset and Sheldon S. Wolin (eds.), *The Berkeley Student Revolt* (Garden City, N.Y.: Doubleday, 1965), and Michael V. Miller and Susan Gilmore, *Revolution at Berkeley* (New York: Dell, 1965), are sources of both fact and interpretation of the issues.

participated in the crisis. It seeks to describe what these men did, what they thought and said, and the aspects of Christian faith and situational factors which might account for their action.[7] The study constructs a threefold typology of response:

1. *reactive:* those who refused to support the Free Speech Movement;

2. *middle range:* those who offered selective support;

3. *supportive:* those who provided considerable support and identified strongly with the movement.

The campus ministers were found to have played a part of some importance in the events; the supportive clergy, such as Walt Herbert, acted at several points as chief liaison figures between the university administration and the student leaders. Herbert contributed to the formulation and public statement of concerns of the student movement. The middle-range clergy, such as Richard Gelwick, were critical of certain "illusions" the Free Speech Movement had about the university and of its inability to formulate concrete and constructive proposals for educational reforms. He was active in trying to bring the campus clergy to some position on the leadership they expected from the faculty. The reactive clergy were represented by Teman Johnson, of the Southern Baptist Center, and by Shunji Nishi, pastor in St. Mark's Episcopal Church, who saw his ministerial work primarily in terms of an identification "with the essential intellectual aspects" of university life.

Jacobson's study finds the religious world view and value orientations of these clergy more crucial than situational factors in exploring their actions in the crisis. He does not describe these orientations in relation to all their other pastoral roles, such as counseling. And Jacobson's sample is not identifiable with our counseling one. However, it is our observation that types one and two of the counselors tended to be supportive of the Free Speech Movement, type three to be reactive, and type four to be in the middle range. We do not wish to make too much of these general convergences, but merely to indicate that fundamental modes of ministry and views of society and the self operate through all these pastoral activities.

Perhaps the most widely quoted interpretation by Mario Savio of the Berkeley rebellion was recorded on tape by Richard Gelwick.

---

7. Elden E. Jacobson, *The Berkeley Crisis: A Case Study of Protestant Campus Ministers* (Ph.D. dissertation, Yale University, 1967, mimeographed).

In our free speech fight at the University of California, we have come up against what may emerge as the greatest problem of our nation— depersonalized, unresponsive bureaucracy. . . . As bureaucrat, an administrator believes that nothing new happens. He occupies an a-historical point of view. In September, to get the attention of this bureaucracy which had issued arbirary edicts suppressing student political expression and refused to discuss its action, we held a sit-in on the campus. We sat around a police car and kept it immobilized for over thirty-two hours. At last, the administrative bureaucracy agreed to negotiate. But instead, on the following Monday, we discovered that a committee had been appointed, in accordance with usual regulations, to resolve the dispute. Our attempt to convince any of the administrators that an event had occurred, that something new had happened, failed. They saw this simply as something to be handled by normal University procedures. . . . Here is the real contradiction: the bureaucrats hold history as ended. As a result significant parts of the population both on campus and off are dispossessed, and these dispossessed are not about to accept this a-historical point of view. It is out of this that the conflict has occurred with the University bureaucracy and will continue to occur until that bureaucracy becomes responsive or until it is clear the University can not function.[8]

Gelwick later came to regard this as the clue to the meaning of the entire crisis; he saw the students as protesting against university leaders who had become imprisoned within a particular method and procedure of knowing. The issue for Gelwick was not simply "commitment to free speech, dissemination and advancement of knowledge" but a more fundamental "center of commitment"; namely, a "belief in the pursuit of truth" which was always "beyond the current consensus" and beyond the achievements of a particular methodology.

Gelwick tried both to support the students' protest against the denial of freedoms of inquiry and political involvement and to make the student movement self-critical. He sought to make it capable of offering concrete proposals for reform, able to listen with tolerance to faculty and administrative figures trying to understand the realities of student life, and prepared to test convictions in the long battles for policy change. Gelwick tried to work with the campus clergy in the same way, seeking consensus among them on concrete proposals to be presented at public meetings (the occasion for this was never found) and designation of faculty who could moderate between the administration and student concerns.

---

8. Mario Savio, "An End to History," *Humanity* (December 1964), p. 1.

He had throughout the crisis a growing sense that the clergy were "just almost not making the scene at all." There was now as in the past no development of a common way of thinking, no standards of professional competency. The clergy, like the other university actors, could take only a series of *ad hoc* actions that were mostly ineffectual and irrelevant. Hence the absurd situation developed that for a short while in this major university, Herbert was the only tenuous line of communication of students with the administration. Gelwick and his kind of mediating figure does not appear at the center of activity in the crisis, but only in reflections and actions to come in its long-range implications. A few months after the crisis he moved to an administrative position in a university outside the Bay area.

In a sermon reflecting on the meaning of the crisis he chose the text, "You shall know the truth and the truth will make you free." Gelwick noted that Berkeley's struggle had helped him to see that

> we live in a time when we are threatened not by the lack of moral passion but by the excess of it. Our age is concerned with moral fervor. The ideal of a society that is just, free from poverty, ignorance, and servitude is universal. Men everywhere and especially this student generation, are concerned that these goals shall be immediately realized. This very ability to want passionately the good society has become a form of tyranny.

He observed that there was in the moral revolutionary such as Savio the potentiality for rigidity and dogmatism that could be as dangerous to the pursuit of truth as the rule-ridden bureaucrat. He notes:

> The way of the reformer today is the ruthless, blunt, tactless, straightforward personality. To be radical is to expose all to a kind of naked honesty. This toughness represents the tyranny of a freedom without the source of self-criticism and restraint, the loss of truth that is beyond us.

The campus minister closest in fundamental conviction and style of action to the leaders of the student rebellion was Walt Herbert. But Jacobson's close look at his career, and his reflections on what his experience in "the movement of a whole generation" toward social reform had taught him, does not make him a man of "inordinate moral passion" so much as a minister finding his way into a new pastoral mode that will not give up its intense theological concern for the affectional and personal dimensions of life, but hopes to find their expression in a "nonpolitical idealism." This idealism simply does not understand the forces which make the faculty-administrative power structure insensitive to the social conditions that promote care and affection. Herbert is also full of great illusions during the crisis as to the power of student rebellion to affect these forces in a way that provides faculty and administrators with viable sociological-humanistic models for future campuses.

Jacobson's picture of Walt Herbert after his exciting participation in the FSM rebellion is one of "increasing despair and pessimism, a sense that nothing has really been significantly restructured." Herbert notes, "There was a fundamental miscalculation [by FSM leaders] about what had been accomplished among the students." He had watched the FSM "cut to bits in the course of the spring. . . . People whose power should rightly have been theirs [FSM's], found their power taken back." This was done by the faculty and the administration.

Herbert prophetically saw that what was missing was a society or community that could infuse the academic world with saving elements of "personal encounter" and "human caring." He was aware that a humane social situation must be continuously fought for by students and planned for and worked at by faculty and administration. He sensed that the crucial aspect of reform in American higher education is to devise the substructures of community on the large campus that promote informal influences and a sense of personal contact instead of substructures that build arbitrary, authoritarian, formal relations.

The tragedy in Herbert's ministry (which he abandoned for further graduate study soon after the FSM rebellion) was that his vision of needed reform had no chance of being critically studied and acted on by the campus ministers. The structures for this were simply not there.

From the data of the Jacobson study we begin to sense that the American university may be working its way into a state not unlike the American city at large. The old images of the university as a "community of scholars," of "dialogue" and "encounter" between student and faculty —dear to images of the church itself—no longer apply descriptively to either the church or the university. And no one knows their normative function.

For the city, as for the university, there had been the hope that the interplay of dominant economic, political, and educational interests would provide a viable society. But the social ineffectiveness is staggering in institutions that cannot or will not plan for the future, will not choose priorities, will not give attention to the structures that put various people together. Unless the churches and universities learn to ask about the quality of interaction of laymen and clergy, students and faculty, specialists and nonspecialists, they will follow the American city into mindless cruelty because the structures of caring for other persons so necessary to freedom and order are not there.[9]

The Junior College System and the Campus Ministry

When the Danforth study turned its attention to developments in the whole system of public colleges and universities in California, the same problems and possibilities were soon discovered as have been analyzed in depth at Berkeley.[10] The junior college system, which is rapidly expanding in size and significance in the state, is making even more imperative the development by the churches of some center for continuing inquiry into the kinds of action being taken.

With certain notable exceptions, these community colleges are at the point in their religious activities where the large state universities were three or four decades ago. They do not have full-time ministry personnel, but rather rely on interested faculty to sponsor voluntary religious associations and conferences and on students to keep alive the connection between their local parish experience and their academic life. The rapid expansion of these colleges now confronts the churches with the question of whether there is a primary ministry that a small staff of professional clergy can perform in them which is integral to both the colleges and the local churches and therefore supportable with enthusiasm by religiously committed faculty, students, and local parishes. Churches are also confronted by the question of whether some team

9. See Burton R. Clark, "The New University," *American Behavioral Scientist* (May 1968), for an excellent description of the forces leading American universities to becoming primarily "examining and degree-granting institutions."

10. We are relying strongly for this conclusion on the unpublished report made for the study in 1966 by Clarence P. Shedd, comparing the Bay area findings with his observations of the situation for religious work at seven California junior colleges: American River Junior College, Sacramento; Shasta College, Redding; College of Marin, San Francisco Bay Area; Los Angeles City College and Palomar in the Los Angeles area; and in central California, Modesto Junior College and Bakersfield College. Mr. Shedd has been studying the junior college developments intensively since his participation in the creation of the Moral and Spiritual Values Committee in 1956 with offices at the Pacific School of Religion, Berkeley.

ministries on the larger campuses can provide training centers for the development of lay leadership capable of exploring the kind of religious commitment we have found to be at the center of student and faculty life. The personnel or financial resources in the church are not present, and the college administrators are not willing, to bring into existence a variety of denominational ministries which lack consciousness of whether they express the primary modes of commitment and service of the church. Such basic questions cannot be ignored in developing models of ministry for an entire state.

The surveys, publications, and conferences of the Moral and Spiritual Values Committee, located at the Pacific School of Religion, have been indicated for the past decade that the obstacles to ministries in the public junior colleges are no longer legal or administrative. The colleges are generally aware that there are no constitutional or legal grounds against the establishment of religious associations or activities on campus so long as they do not engage in sectarian proselytizing. Administrators see that it is politically, financially, and academically possible for them to offer courses that study the thought and actions of the major religions of the world, including the Judeo-Christian traditions that have most informed American culture.[11] And the key administrative leaders in these colleges have again and again displayed their willingness to sponsor or attend meetings to explore proposals of the church as to what they regard as the best relations of the colleges and religion.

Student, faculty, and administrative leaders are predisposed by religious commitment, intellectual interest, and organizational wisdom to new alternatives of campus ministry. The students surveyed by their departments of psychology and sociology generally evidence an even stronger interest than that found at Berkeley or the University of the Pacific in exploring the connection between their religious commitments, course work, and vocational and community organizational involvements. Symposia and conferences initiated by students and faculty for "religious or ethical emphasis" weeks on these campuses have in recent years investigated the views of man and God involved in medical education and practice (for instance, American River Junior College), in counseling on sex in the college and church (as at Fort Hill College),

---

11. In 1955 only eight community colleges in California offered courses to students in religion, but in 1966 thirty-three out of seventy-nine colleges offered such courses; these tended more often to be studies of "world religion" than intensive inquiries into developments in Jewish and Christian thought and action.

the civil rights of students (Diablo Valley College), urban planning (Los Angeles City College). Most of the colleges have elaborate student centers. These could be used for all kinds of community educational activity initiated by local churches.

The faculty who would be most readily available as advisers to religious activities groups are not interested in theological study per se, as indicated in the essays written for the Moral and Spiritual Values Committee of the California Junior College Association. They are chiefly interested in the kinds of phenomenological and epistemological problem that the Bay area colloquium was exploring. They want more data on the relation of religious and ethical views to educational processes and philosophies, to aesthetic activity in urban areas, to research in the life and social sciences. Many of them regard the educational process as a "free inquiry" into perceptions of the world and their consequences for personal and social action. They reflect not a traditional, residential, liberal arts setting, but one highly conscious of the closeness of the student's life to his family, to part-time work, and to a city environment. Thus far there has been almost no response from the local churches to these developments.

Social Policy and Campus Ministries

What would seem to be the greatest need in the future of California campus ministries is the creation, probably in the Bay area, of an organization capable of continuing policy research and advanced learning for laymen and clergymen. It would need to bring together the complex factors we have seen influencing religious commitments and public ministries in the California colleges and universities. This organization would perhaps need to be separately incorporated at the initiative of the churches to appropriate the resources of the professional campus ministries in the state; the university and seminary scholars engaged in the studies (such as the Graduate Theological Union in the Bay area); the faculties of religious studies, education, personality growth, outside the seminaries; and particularly those administrative leaders engaged in student personnel work. This new organization would interpret and evaluate the actions of all Christian leadership seeking to minister to the people in the colleges and universities in the state and would relate these ministers to the activities of the parish churches of the area.

The denominational agencies of united campus ministries have shown no power to develop such an organization, despite much talk of collaborative, ecumenical action. Nor have the seminary faculties produced significant models for corporative ministry or centers for policy research. Perhaps the initiative of foundations, of national denominational church staff, and of concerned lay administrative leadership is the only hope that the anarchy and frustrations of organized individualism in the church's approach to education will come to an end in California.

In summing up our finding in California we can say that our survey data have revealed the tremendous forces at work in the university toward making the educational intent of the student more and more degree-centered, his participation in the academic process more segmented, and his achievement of graduation chiefly the accumulation of course grades and examination results. The trends in our society toward large-size and greater complexity of formal organization are becoming ever more apparent in higher education. The large urban, public universities where most of our population is provided higher education are settings for several hundred distinctive clusters of experts. The urbanization of education is producing a commuting, very segmental involvement in the university, accompanied by part-time work and off-campus living. The traditional collegiate forms of campus governance have lost their effectiveness, and students are confused and frustrated as to how to exercise influence on educational policies.

The central interests of the administrators and faculty are no longer to be equated necessarily with the interests of students. The administrators, in response to public and legislative pressure, may be concerned chiefly with institutional growth necessary to satisfy public and faculty demands—a growth that is complicated as little as possible by diverse educational standards and innovative clusterings of faculty and students in the system. The dormitory arrangements of many large campuses reflect the connected logics of growth and cost efficiency and hence are cultural disasters, affronts to educational processes and to human privacy and sensitivity. The exceptions to these developments in a state such as California need public church support and understanding.

Many faculty interests and ideologies also present powerful structures that offend the pastoral concerns of church leaders we have been exploring. Burton Clark notes that what all faculty have in common "is a logic of career in which a man gets ahead by a combination of personal publication and departmental aggrandizement." Career orientation means devotion to one's scholarly labor and to the disciplinary rank of one's department. Such an orientation, our survey indicated, is not automatically good for the learning processes of the student.

Given these formidable structures in any consideration of the fate of pastoral concerns in the university, it can hardly be said that the churches of the Bay area have as yet mounted any serious effort to face the situation of their campus clergy or to influence significantly the interests of the modern university toward care for persons. The campus clergy soon learned that the multiversity has become for thousands of students an alienating and suffering agency of major proportions in a technological society. They learned that because of this the new university is an increasingly conflict-prone society. They learned how to identify Christian hopes with student expectations, often illusory, of participation in a community of scholars. They learned that the loose, bureaucratic structure of the new university contributes to crowd behavior and rebellion and the polarities of tightly organized blocs. But they have not learned whether the work of Christians in them helps produce effective policy changes.

What church leadership seems not yet to have learned in the Bay area is how the structures of pastoral caring are incorporated into the daily life of churches and universities, thus providing some balanced and integral experience of their deepest historic functions and services. They provide little islands of sympathetic and friendly meetings for 5 to 7 per cent or so of the student population. But the approaches to specific functions—counseling, theological inquiry, and so on—are so varied and dependent on the interests of a particular minister (usually of short duration in his position) that the categories of profession or of social and religious policy can be applied only in terms of hopes for the future of the work.

PART IV

The Priestly and Preaching Structures

of Faith and Ministry

≫ 10 ≪

THE STUDENT PARISHIONER AND

MAINTENANCE OF THE FUTURE CHURCH

The next mode of ministry which we explored in depth, and the one which dominates the religious organizations at the University of Wisconsin, seeks the maintenance of church traditions chiefly through the priestly and preaching ministries. The proclamation of the faith and the administration of the sacraments are the chief expressions of this kind of leadership. Those most deeply involved in the churches' activities and most conventional in religious belief are those most dedicated to the maintenance of the traditional patterns.

This mode of ministry may not be the manifest purpose of many clergy at the University of Wisconsin who share with enthusiasm the liberal and progressive values of political and social reform and intellectual inquiry. But it is their latent function. The selection of our key researchers, Jay Demerath and Kenneth Lutterman, and their establishment of an informal colloquium with Madison campus clergy and graduate students led at an early stage of discussion to this basic hypothesis: various movements for reform of the structure of church constituencies and attempts to carry out ministerial modes other than those of conventional priest and preacher have had little fundamental influence on the dominant patterns of church life and thought of the Wisconsin campus.

We thought it highly important to test this hypothesis. We sought to probe the characteristics of these established patterns of institutional life and belief, what needs they serve in the lives of students, what changes may be taking place in their saliency and support among students, and the nature and source of dissent from traditional religion that is occurring. We were anxious to know just what power clergy and other church leaders have in producing religious change and what factors are crucial for reinforcement of and significant change in traditional institutional patterns.

The Priestly-Preaching Mode of Maintaining the Institutional Church

The pattern-maintenance type of leader is not hard to identify. In describing their dominant roles, most Lutheran (Missouri and Wisconsin, not United), Catholic, Southern Baptist, and Evangelical United Brethren leaders begin with the assumption that for a ministry on campus to exist "there's got to be a religious institution or organization that you work to have grow in size and support." Whether you like it or not "you've got an identification among the rank and file student body and faculty with a church, and you have to make something of that identification." The only bona fide basis on which a minister is on campus, in the eyes of most administrators and faculty, one Wisconsin Lutheran pastor noted, is "that you represent an historical community of believers in the gospel, a particular constituency of people, and you had better know who that constituency is, what it stands for and how strongly."

The second thing usually asserted is that preaching of the Word, attention to what and how beliefs are articulated, administering the sacraments and liturgies, public covenanting as to future communal hopes and intentions, remain the primary ministries without which there is no church or other occasion for service. These people hear significant religious utterances in ordinary daily speech at academic work and in bedside visits with a patient in a student infirmary, and they can envision the need for men to confess or to proclaim to one another their deepest loyalties and trusts. But the mode of a declarative, confessional tradition in which a man speaks about what has been given him in a revelatory, historic event, in memories of it and in a search for its meanings among a community of believing men, and in certain liturgical, ritualistic forms—this mode belongs above all others to a particular institution, the Church of Jesus Christ.

The issue raised by the pattern-maintenance ministries is not whether the faith is to be proclaimed, but what is its content and to whom and how is it to be preached. Men who are not fundamentalists wish to ask about whether the *whole* tradition of the faith is being taken seriously by the young people, whether the major constituencies of Christain people—or at least people once or potentially interested in religion—are being served in the university. These are questions which have as much to do with the maintenance of institutional patterns and the nature and context of the priestly and preaching modes of ministry as those asked by the conservatives and fundamentalists.

In its most parochial forms this conservative priestly-preaching syndrome could be identified with the forms of magical manipulation of God that Charles Glock[1] has correlated so strongly with anti-Semitism and other forms of particularism and prejudice. But the dominant institutions and belief patterns of the University of Wisconsin are much more complex and multidimensional than seen in most current sociological and psychological studies. Significant shifts in belief and action styles are taking place internally under these denominational labels during college years. Distinctions are emerging in intensity of conviction on beliefs; this makes habitual adherence to many traditional doctrines much less important than many studies have thought. Appreciation of the limits of human powers and of the presence of tragedy and sin in the midst of promise and freedom adds to the rich intellectual-religious interactions of student life; this, too, makes old liberal-conservative labels misleading.

There are, however, students who are precursors of a new style of church life. Taking seriously the traditional aspects of faith having to do with fidelity in interpersonal relations and with the ethical demands of faith in public life, these students can produce minority movements for social and religious change that burst the bonds of conservative congregations.

The questions which the pattern-maintenance clergy raise cannot be avoided by any ministry. They have to do with whether particular institutional forms of the church have an integral or necessary part in the formulation and nurture of religious commitment. The priest or preacher usually begins his discussions of the church in terms of how its visible marks are to be identified; then he moves to what tasks the church and the parishioner need to do in response to the world. He wants to argue for some type of institution that is now in existence and

1. Charles Glock and Rodney Stark, *Christian Beliefs and Anti-Semitism* (New York: Harper and Row, 1966).

can be seen, that people will know as having a structure of belief and thought that will influence what his response will be to whatever happens in the world tomorrow.

This insistence on the latent, habitual forms of identification and action with the institutional church is not to be denied its validity in this study. After all, are not some institutional, organized ways of symbolizing the gospel and celebrating its meaning more helpful than others to keep alive the world view, the values, the ultimate commitment, of Christianity? If so, what are they as seen by the various major bodies of laity? How is the gospel to be shared in unity amid diversity by members of a community, and continued through time, if particular historic symbols and central ministries are not given a controlling significance in the church? What are the functions of major symbols in the church? Are many old doctrines still "agreed to," but have no driving force for action? Is not the message of the church, as in any institution or movement, conveyed principally in its routine activities? If so, what do laymen conceive these to be, and where do they take place? Are church leaders, despite all the talk of reform, supportive of fundamental shifts in these day-to-day activities and of the places where they are to go on? If an institutionally centered ministry is taken seriously, these are the kinds of question the church finds itself asking.

Clergy Expectations of the Laity with Whom They Work

The survey instrument used at Wisconsin and subsequently at a variety of other institutions made use of the California instrument, but went considerably beyond it in providing laymen with opportunity to show their perspectives on the institutional church, its traditional beliefs, and the activities of the campus clergy.[2] The devisers of the instrument knew that at the heart of the controversy over the validity of the priestly-preaching ministry was the awareness that the clergy and laity themselves were deeply estranged from each other on these issues. They were without concrete knowledge, moreover, of what other participants really thought of the activities in the church and of the belief context in which these were carried on.

It seemed highly important, therefore, that the campus clergy answer

---

2. See Appendix for Wisconsin Survey Instrument on University and Society: Student Perspectives.

the survey instruments devised for the students and from two perspectives: (1) what their own position was on the varied items; (2) what they thought was the position taken by the students in their constituency.

The report on the student parishioner at Madison[3] reaches the general conclusion that the campus religious organizations are bastions of orthodoxy (see Table 10–1).[4] The students most involved in campus ministry programs are also most conservative in religious belief and social and academic attitude. They do not come near the student averages in many items and scales. The chief differences are often to be found in the varied levels of involvement in campus religious groups, and not in comparisons between the various denominational groupings generally. In 26 of 30 comparisons on key scales in the study, Demerath and Lutterman find that the differences between the highly involved students and the somewhat involved (usually those who attend the more standardized services taking at most two or three hours of their time) are greater than differences between students somewhat involved and those not at all involved.

The more involved a student becomes in campus religious organizations, the more emphasis he puts on an ethic governed by a few basic religious and moral principles. He is more apt to discount the importance of other perspectives in his judgment about an issue; he is attracted most to a faith that is not involved in doubt and ambiguity over the meaning of belief or in discussions with those who have such problems; he desires a faith that gives its chief attention to assurances of salvation from the hell of otherworldly judgment, the removal of guilt for present transgressions of the moral law, and the promises of life after death, rather than to discerning the creative activity of God in the solution of contemporary public problems; if he belongs to a conservative or moderate religious group, he is less sympathetic to government welfare activities and to social action in civil rights (in the liberal groups the more involved he is, the more radical he is politically).

This gives an idea of the mind-set of the students who are the most

3. See N. J. Demerath III, and Kenneth Lutterman, "The Student Parishioner: Radical Rhetoric and Traditional Reality," in Volume II of this report.

4. Study of this table will indicate the major relationships between types of participating students and religious attitudes, between the theological beliefs and social educational attitudes considered in the next two chapters. The principal items and scales in the survey are described and analyzed in the chapters by Demerath and Lutterman in Volume II.

TABLE 10-1. Religious Group Differences on Basic Scales University of Wisconsin

	Group					
	Not Involved in Campus Religion	Roman Catholic	Hillel	Liberal Protestant	Moderate Protestant	Conservative Protestant
% Disagree with Organized Religion	37	9	42	20	18	5
% Orthodox on Heaven and Hell	13	48	3	12	13	63
% Orthodox on Sin, Devil, and Evil	27	64	13	38	36	82
% Tend to Identify Christianity with American Culture	34	53	10	33	42	77
% Moral Absolutism Opposed to Radical Contextualism	59	76	61	68	72	83
% Highly Involved in Religious Institutions—Opposed Radcial Contextualism	—	93	74	74	79	90
% Permissive-Contextual on Sex	26	7	31	14	11	5
% Very Uncertain about Religious Belief; Strong Doubts	29	11	37	25	18	4
% Support Teaching of Theology in Public University	11	69	7	41	43	27
% Perceive Need for Serious Discussion between Believer and Unbeliever in Church and University	—	21	30	52	33	5

TABLE 10-1 (*Continued*)

	Group					
	Not Involved in Campus Religion	Roman Catholic	Hillel	Liberal Protestant	Moderate Protestant	Conservative Protestant
% Not members of fraternities and sororities	77	79	79	78	75	83
% Highly involved in fraternities and sororities	11	12	9	12	13	8
% Highly involved in fraternities and sororities of those highly involved in religious groups	—	9	9	12	11	7
% Have no friends in religious groups	60	28	49	27	21	15
% See research at university more important than quality of faculty relations to students	24	19	23	23	22	25
% Find university not relevant to public issues and withdrawn from world	21	23	18	24	20	27
% Perceive great change and ferment in society and church	—	21	29	36	20	2
% Radical on politics	29	25	30	24	21	25
% Radical on Negroes and civil rights	21	16	30	20	17	11
% High on pattern-maintenance function for clergy	—	28	14	9	15	42
% High on social action in Church	—	19	31	33	23	9

ready volunteers for work in the general run of student religious activities and who represent the core audience for those activities. The issue, in policy terms, is whether they are going to set the day-to-day tone of student religious affairs, determine the allocations of funds for programs, and choose leaders to run them.

The clergy's estimates of the laity's religious commitments were carefully compared with the varied types of student parishioner that emerge from our general survey (see Table 10–2).[5] The clergy's views are con-

TABLE 2. Number of Ministers Who Are More or Less Liberal than Their Students on View of the Campus Ministry and the Number of Ministers' Estimates Which Are More Liberal than the Students'

		All Groups			Conservative Group			Moderate Group			Liberal Group		
		More	Same	Less	More	Same	Less	More	Same	Less	More	Same	Less
Minister's Own Score	Total	4	4		2			2	1		3		
	High Inv.	3	5		2			1	2		3		
	Somewhat	4	3	1	2			2	1		2		1
	No Inv.	5	3		2			2	1			1	2
Minister's Estimate	Total	1	6	2	3			1	2		1		2
	High Inv.	1	5	3	3			1	1	1	1		2
	Somewhat	1	5	3	2	1		1	2		1		2
	No Inv.	2	5	2	2	1		1	2		1	1	1

siderably different. They hide by their illusions the fact that their time and energies are captured by a minority of students, many of whom would probably find religious homes in existing parish organizations in the city if the campus religious organizations were not around. The ministers are also torn between the demands of those who want to hold onto the traditional roles of the preaching ministry and those who discern considerable changes in student convictions and ways of testing these and who particularly sense the demand for more open inquiry in the church. Irresolution as to which is the more important demand to serve and the corollaries of belief in these demands leads to lassitude, inaction, dissembling. Some have made a forthright choice, but the data expose the illusions and frustrations of a liberal clergy who

---

5. These data were developed and interpreted in a paper by Daniel E. Moore, "The Campus Clergyman and His Student Parishioner: A Comparison" (University of Wisconsin, 1968).

thought they could attract a basically new constituency by imaginative programs and roles.

These illusions exist for conservative, liberal, and middle-of-the-road type clergy. The ministers generally do not have good information on who their constituencies are and what they believe. Their views in many crucial areas (such as educational issues and how students view their ministry) are quite random and more usually wrong than right. A significant number of the pastors appear as men less determined to be intolerable to some laity for the sake of the church and the world than as men vaguely aware of divisions between their own position and that of many of their constituency. They do not have the ability to define what the really important lines of agreement and disagreement are.

Such data account for the inability of a group of the campus clergy to get together on any significant strategic acts. Such actions would be based on hypotheses as to: what are the major shifts in belief and action in the whole campus scene, the chief sources of alienation between clergy and laity, the new constituencies emerging that could be attracted in an ecumenical thrust or educational mission. Furthermore, there is the more dangerous crisis in the church: the inability of leaders to perform the historic function of prophetic proclamation, they are unable to bring to the surface the underlying hatreds, ignorance, and indifference in the fabric of student-faculty life. All this is the prerequisite of policy action.

We are viewing here the chief source of frustration and cynicism among ministers about the power of dedicated leaders to change significantly the nature of an institution. The fact is that the clergy in all theological camps are generally more liberal than the students they most attract; they are more flexible in the relation of their religious views to their social and political opinions and more open to varied activities in the churches than are the students who participate most regularly in their services.

What the clergy do not see is that they have offered no significant alternative in public, institutional, religious involvement to the traditional structures. All they have offered is highly individualized informal discussions, covenant communities, occasional calls to a protest march, a coffeehouse, unstructured counseling.

Many attempts by the campus ministers were made to initiate new church activities and to participate in nonreligious activities in the interest of innovation for the trusty churchgoer: one man started a theatrical group doing plays the drama department would not do; another built up a colloquium of faculty and graduate students in science and religion; the Baptist faith-and-life community mixed atheists, Buddhists, and Christians needing cheap lodging and wondering what to make of their academic careers. But the leader of the theatrical group became ill, and the group dispersed. Mike Teske's science seminar meant much to a loyal few, an intellectual awakening to issues the university courses were not raising, but it was never understood by his Lutheran superiors, and this work was discouraged by crude administrative methods. The faith-and-life group was not a structure on which a well-educated gifted young minister could build a career. These were all outside the consideration of policy choices that are really available in Madison and offering some chance of affecting major structural changes.

There are some interesting data on how this failure to envision possible policy choices affects the clergy. The liberal and conservative clergy's expectations of support for new programs or for traditional functions are considerably closer to the realities of their situations than those of ministers in the moderate denominations. The leaders of these have not yet settled for the neat alternatives of programing, as have the conservative and liberal forces. In these main-line denominations there is a much more complex mix of students in the constituencies and much greater cynicism and doubt among the clergy about their ability to project new programmatic goals that will secure substantial support. They have the power in the potential student constituencies for larger, more decisive acts, but they do not know what they might be.

The survey had in it suggestions of new programs to test the range of potential student support and the willingness or competency of the moderate clergy to act. For example, the survey asked students if they preferred campus ministry goals, among other more traditional options, of "encouraging the student to bring his academic specialty to bear upon the church and his religious activity." A minister or student might grasp in this proposal the excitement of a group of students interviewing people in a church that has faced a recent racial or civil crisis. But in interviews by our study staff with these clergy, if an exciting picture of the future might be seen for a moment, the vision quietly faded. A minister feels he cannot carry it through "because of his special theological academic training," the "lack of ties to faculties who know how to organize such activities," or "other commitments of time." One minister told of an idea two or three students got in a discussion with him to unite their term paper work and find out some of the effects of dormitory expansion programs of the university on people living in an area. They asked if the church could help organize a study. They asked the questions: Does this have anything to do with the pastoral concerns of the church? What will be university official reaction to such an inquiry? But the realities of power and ethics face the pastors, and they become afraid of such projects.

Yet the fact is that over five hundred people in these main-line denominations on the University of Wisconsin's campus clearly in their questionnaires strongly want programs in the campus ministry that "further contacts between students, faculty, administrators, public leaders, and for more responsible action in all areas," as well as wanting to use their academic specialty to reflect critically on church activities in the region.

All this is to say that basic shifts in models and roles for clergy and laity are taking place in the university and larger culture. These are more subtle and complex than the popular polarities of conservative and "new breed" clergymen. These models are now beginning to be articulated, documented, and evaluated in speculation and debate on the church. The need for this is great when the choices in ministry become too parochial in value and method, the proponents cut off public communication with one another, and mutual trust, as well as freedom and creativity in the use of personal talents, disappears.

The problem of what to do about the serious differences in clergy and lay belief structures and church expectations is not one that simply involves the clergy of the "liberal" and "moderate" congregations. Profound differences in saliency of belief and meaning of faith and doctrine for action are showing up also in the traditional groups. The problem in most congregations is not that of getting everyone either to rally around a particular clergyman's theology or seek another church "home," but to give freedom to the clergyman within the institutional church to recognize his varied constituencies, to interpret them to one another, to help them where they are to explore their faith further in thought and action. These are issues of governance as much as preaching.

The priestly-preaching role is perhaps the most deeply affected of all roles by these tensions, illusions, and pretensions as to what beliefs are really held in a church. The minister's personal confession of faith has been thought by most clergy to be dependent for effectiveness on the existence of a congregation sharing his general beliefs, affirmed in public covenant and now engaged in inquiry into their meaning.

But the situation that most campus ministers confront is one in which they lead people who for the most part come out of parishes with patterns of religious and social commitment much more traditional than the clergyman's own convictions. The campus minister has little control over the composition of this constituency. It is given to him by the structures of parish life in his denomination. Is he going to tell them what he really believes today and not remake it for some image of a dominant constituency?

A positive answer may be aided by his knowledge that so far as we can discover, there are likely running through an influential, or potentially influential, element of his constituency—even in the conservative churches—all kinds of complex questions, doubts, shifts in ethical sensitivity, quests for new ways of expressing in action religious convictions that do not fit the tradition. These are close to the pastor's own deepest "hangups" and "doubts."

What most campus pastors are just discovering is a style of proclamation and worship that does not at this stage force simple choices between the old ways of formulating belief and the new, deepening polarities of doctrine. They are trying to bring into the open the genuine tensions and conflicts of belief and commitment that are now deep in the life of the church and their own existence as pastors, having been there before in occasions when a new cultural religion was coming into existence. This is not to say that in these complex denominational constituencies there are not choices to be made in the use of church resources or in the importance to be given certain aspects of the tradition in a contemporary situation. But these choices need to emerge out of a frank facing of issues and convictions that now divide Christians and a candid look at the bases on which these choices of belief and policy are to be made. Where priestly ritual and preaching discourage this context for confession and proclamation in the church, it is quite clear from our data that no significant communication on religious or ethical matters takes place.

The only honest response of a minister in any of the larger congregations of Madison is to see his constituency politically, intellectually, religiously, as offering the varied perspectives and experiences needed to explore the meaning of contemporary Christianity along with various other religious and ethical options now influential in the society. The educational problem is how to get these objectively into the open so they do not pose direct threats to individuals in the congregations and how to interpret resistance creatively and positively as a step toward change and reconciliation. Proclamation and worship in this context changes the whole role of priest and preacher from pleasant repetition of unquestioned truths to a role that is absolutely dependent on inquiry and governance.

Saliency of Belief

The crucial differences between persons in religious organizations is most apparent in the examination of the data on saliency of beliefs (the importance which they are given and the strong personal predisposition to act on them) and simple indication that certain beliefs are accepted as true. A third of a student body may identify their position as traditionally theistic (for example, "I have faith in God as a person who is concerned about me and all mankind and to whom I am accountable") in a range of alternative statements about God or ultimate reality (see Question 95, Part II, in the Wisconsin survey); but 60 per cent of these may sometimes or often have doubts about that belief. A substantial majority (76 to 85 per cent) of students in conservative denominations (such as Missouri Lutheran) may agree that "only in Christianity is the one true God revealed and confessed" or that "Christ vicariously atoned for our sins by his death and resurrection"; but an impressive minority—one-third of that group—do not indicate strong support of these items.

The most important bellwether group in the director's judgment for the moderates and liberals to study makes up a significant, fairly cohesive minority (approximately a third of the students with some indication of conscious religious interests). In the complex rotation of computer correlations and reciprocal relations, this group turns out to represent a religious factor that has the complex of beliefs on which new institutional structures can be built. The most obvious configuration of strong agreement, not just assent, among these students "somewhat involved" in religious activities shows up in their responses on the items that attest to a radical monotheism that makes the ethical dimensions of faith a test of one's religious seriousness. For example, there were items such as "A person's ethical concern and activity are the crucial measures of this religiousness and therefore even an avowed ethicist may be more religious than a devout churchgoer," or "If I felt strongly about a cause, I would be willing to participate in a public demonstration." Strong agreement on such items is accompanied by consistent expression of preference for campus ministries that use the institutional church creatively and critically; that are "exploring and ameliorating major social problems"; that are "furthering contacts between students, faculty and administrators, public leaders, and professionals for more responsible action in all areas." These students use varied intellectual resources of the university for making moral judgments and regard the Scriptures and theological studies as potential sources of positive insight into wise personal and public action.

This style of thought and action is probably willing to identify itself with many traditional beliefs. But these remain subjects of fascinating and important speculation for them in terms of whether the beliefs mean anything for the action of men in the world.

This crucial minority wants to give chief attention to statements which explore the possible relations of religious and ethical convictions to acts and programs in the society. They have been taught critical, linguistic analysis; they know words have varied meanings and they want to get on to those aspects of a survey or a proclamation or a discussion which are working out these meanings in personal involvement in the society.

This nonorthodox-ethicist type of student is undermining, with criticism or indifference, the student centers which display their indecision by offering a large round of activities. This influence is just beginning to be understood in the church at large. Students are insisting on *quality* of programmatic involvement and on a *fundamental shift* in theological-ethical emphasis that produces structural, institutional change worth fighting for.

This emerging minority can have a healthy effect in raising afresh the priorities of what is to be proclaimed, to be speculated about and confessed in the regular Sabbath services of the church as well as among assembled Christians and non-Christians. And when legitimate policy queries are ignored, students often feel forced to a more radical, dissenting stance. About twenty students, for example, felt so strongly that their pastors did not understand the question of policy priorities they were raising that they went around to a number of churches in Madison and stood up in silent protest at the irrelevancy of the sermons being preached and the narrow heritage drawn upon in liturgy. Two churches—Congregational and Methodist—welcomed the groups after the service, seeking to find out the basis of their actions. But in one Lutheran church near the university campus the ushers literally tossed two of the group down the steps and tore up their signs. After a few more attempts at protest and discussion in other churches, the activist group disbanded its effort at change.

Most of the students are not ready to narrow the agenda of theological proclamation and speculation as much as the radical activists or the "significant third" we have described. But there is a pronounced shift in the majoriy of students in the *whole* campus, not just the church participants, away from stereotypes that have dominated traditional preaching and worship. If church leaders are to think about what is happening to the religious convictions of a whole university people, and not just about the minority who now support their work, such facts are important. The scale most agreed on by *all* Wisconsin students as having the items which are the most urgent and central to them expresses the expectation and possibility of doubt in the midst of faith. This awareness of the variety and intensity of unbelief in the midst of hope and search for a compelling faith defines the only real context in which most students are willing to have faith proclaimed, confessed, or discussed.

This fact simply changes the whole conception of the "congregation" or "assembly" coming together in a university city. It will be composed of people some of whom once went to church, were baptized, and gave it up as not dealing with the questions of life's meaning they faced. It will include people intensely involved in the issues preached and prayed about; but they will weigh this experience with well-directed study of religion under competent faculty, with selective participation in certain activities of drama or social action which the church and university organizes. These people will never accept or expect an invitation from the pastor to make some formal commitment before a congregation. They expect to live in a continuing mode of inquiry and affirmation, to be selective and mobile participants in a variety of institutions, including religious organizations.

These interpretations of the nature of a functioning congregation break from narrowly orthodox and neo-orthodox images. Ranked in high importance with this "tolerance of doubt and ambiguity" among students generally was support of all items which provided in religious and educational institutions for open confrontation of people with different world views and counter perspectives. The context of belief formation for these students is to be comparative, controversial, speculative, experiential, as well as confessional and proclamatory.

The next most important scale of items in the Wisconsin survey[6] sought to detect a shift of emphasis from concern about divine judgment against one's own personal beliefs or action to the illumination of concrete actions to be taken for the betterment of human life in contemporary society. The willingness to accept the risk of involvement in complex events of the world was the point that seemed to be most strongly made against the identification of the church simply with issues of personal salvation.

The third most important scale for all students dealt with the meaning of Jesus Christ in God's creative and governing acts in the world. This figure still haunts, attracts, and repels most students, and they do not want the church to give up on the exploration of the Christological issues. This is true, even though they may reject all the present options offered them.

Enough has been said to warn against the premature closure, under the enthusiasm of the ethical activists, of many of the theological issues which have been historically important in the church. But an equal warning should be issued against the reduction of the Gospel to a narrow range of issues which do not provide for proclamation of faith in the midst of disputation over linguistic meaning, epistemological method, and social policy implication.

The real problem of proclamation lies in the competencies and convictions of the clergy which will enable them to respond with political realism and religious power to what the campus laity are saying and doing. The ability to turn the ineffectualities of the conservative search

---

6. This is so for all campuses, not just Madison's. The realities of Wisconsin are very close to those that turn up on all the campuses we studied, though significant variations will be noted later in this volume.

for reassurances and of the activist's amateur enthusiasm toward the larger issues that dominate the minds of the student body and faculty has to be today a test for each minister. If he cannot set limits as to how far he will represent the concerns and public symbols of a parish, his preaching will show his incapacity to govern.

New Structures That Will Significantly Influence Preaching and Worship

The fundamental point to be noted in the Demerath-Lutterman findings is that despite denominational differences the over-all structure of the campus ministry tends to pull each issue the students raise back into the traditional categories and programs. This process changes the substance of the issues and the commitment involved.

In their study, Demerath and Lutterman are raising policy questions. They are ready to grant that their survey data have revealed all kinds of cross currents of religious belief, that there are functioning enclaves of dissident religious groups in the total picture, and that the apparent intent of a significant number of the clergy is to produce sizable constituencies that at least meet the liberal standards of the student body as a whole and raise issues about university and political matters which go beyond the campus consensus. *But they are saying that these elements of expectation and constituency have not been organized to form any really significant alternative church structures in relation to emerging academic developments in the university and in the larger society.* This is a conclusion that must be taken with great seriousness.

Having allowed a great deal of their time to be taken up with a very small minority of the student body, the campus ministers have ignored or poorly served the wider cultural-religious movements discernible in the surveys. They have ignored or been unable to envision how to serve significant minorities of "somewhat involved" constituencies and of highly creative, noninvolved people who dissent consciously from past organizational religious activities.

The campus ministers and their executive leaders simply have to make some corporate decisions of their own as to whether they are going to create any institutional structures that rally and discipline forces within the church. The campus ministry has to think in broad terms about the creation of a well-established, major organization which will be responsive to the most vital commitments in both religious and university life. This would be a structure that took on these new, fruitful questions seriously, with the full resources of the university and church and with people who must exercise major responsibility in seeking answers. The action and structures to be envisioned must not be an aggressive break from the past of the church, but an expression of some continuity and interaction with these memories and traditions.

Yet such a new structure would express the reality that most people are caught up in doubts about both traditional and new beliefs. They wish at times to affirm their interpretation of past principles and at other times to bring them under intellectual scrutiny. They do not wish to be forced into a choice of old and new institutional expressions of faith. What kind of church structure would test afresh the claims of conservative and liberal, old guard and new breed ministries, bring them under the intellectual scrutiny and skepticism of the university, so that all are freed from absolute claims of finite beings?

The strategic decisions we are going to suggest in the next chapter are those we believe the data of our survey, and of our observations of the Madison campus, invite. They are likely to cause some withdrawal of support from people still predisposed to dogmatic, literalistic use of the Scriptures and the historic resources of the church. But they will attract the majority of the Christians and dissidents who see religion as faith for inquiry into the meaning of life and view theology as an emerging, living body of truth.

◈ 11 ◈

NEW CHURCH STRUCTURES FOR

PROCLAIMING FAITH

THE basic reality made available to us in Wisconsin survey data is that the over-all structures of clerical leadership, constituency participation, and property and programmatic fund allocation at Madison give forth a big message, an unforgettable image of what the church really wishes to emphasize as its stance in the academic world. Madison sends the message out over the area, since here three-fourths of the funds going into religion and higher education in the state are being spent. What is the big message? It is that the dominant structures have produced an enforcement of orthodoxy and conservatism by the maintenance of a traditional priestly-preaching ministry as the chief mode of action. Most of the campus clergy claim that the over-all structures of ministries and the constituencies they seem to attract are not representative of the religious direction to which these clergy say that they are committed. Nonetheless, student religious and ethical commitments that have great salience, expressing the hopes of thousands of students for the churches, are not being given adequate institutional expression; the relations between religion, serious academic work, and career expectations are not being made.[1]

---

1. These generalizations are made not simply from student survey data. Three men of the Danforth national staff spent two weeks in Madison interviewing clergy, students, faculty, university administrators, observing religious and educational activities, studying the programmatic and historical literature and materials of the ministries, and so on. The director in eight trips to the campus sought not only to gain an understanding of the research being conducted by the faculty team at the university under the direction of professors Demerath and Lutterman but to scan the larger trends in the educational and intellectual life of the university.

When church leaders see that forces within their own institution have locked them into postures and services that do not express their deepest and fullest convictions, they have to look for ways out, not simply through the internal mix of people and programs but through the external constituencies being formed and reformed by the university and by broad cultural-religious forces. What reinterpretations are taking place of the historic, basic functions of the university, such as in its extension and adult education responsibilities? President Fred Harvey Harrington says the business of the University of Wisconsin "is to grow. We believe in mass education; it is the very nature of our higher education." Where is the growth occurring? What new student masses are being added and for what educational and social purposes? The leaders need to make sure they understand these new constituencies; they must serve them and confront them in learning.

Division IV and Campus Ministries

Chancellor Don MacNeil administers Division IV, a section of the University of Wisconsin which he hopes will become the major center for extension education in the nation. Division IV will combine all activities previously done in extension education, TV, radio, county agent work, home demonstrations, experiments with inner-city ghetto children, adult education, and so on. For him Division IV is "the coming way the resources of the university are going to be related to society." The focus of mass public education, as he sees it, will be on solving community problems. Provisions for extension education are now written into all federal educational grants, from primary school through postdoctoral programs. This recognizes that in the future most education is probably not going to bring adults to the university to pursue courses primarily for individual enrichment (the liberal arts idea), but will take the university into the locality where corporate and human problems of living together are to be solved.

The full resources of the university will be drawn upon for this purpose; this will be a major departure from past extension education. The faculties that need to be motivated to participate in this kind of corporate enterprise are humanities and science scholars who have been accessible chiefly to resident students who seek competency in an academic specialty but see their professional and personal lives as enriched by confrontation with public problems. This wider resource is necessary because the extension faculties are too narrowly oriented to pragmatic solutions and avoid the deeper methodological and ethical problems which have to be faced now in the most common technological-urban confusions and conflicts. The task of clarifying the changing professional roles and values at issue has never been a subject of conversation between campus clergy and administrators of these new programs, we discovered. Indeed, 80 per cent of the campus ministers we interviewed could not see Division IV as having developments possibly affecting their responsibilities.

But men such as Chancellor MacNeil see that Division IV will soon require the leaders of most major institutions in the region to make some policy decisions. The division wishes to use the full resources of institutions for reflection, education, and action in major communities of the state to solve pressing public problems such as city design, school curriculum innovation, opening up of new job and housing opportunities to minorities, and the like. And it will be asking for the co-operation of church leaders as well as doctors, businessmen, and politicians. It will be asking not for the help of individuals as such, but for access to group and institutional resources.

The leaders of Division IV hope that institutional leaders, such as campus ministers, will relate these new programs to parish church life in the state, particularly where university adult education and research centers have already been well established. They would like to see faculty laymen who wish the theological, ethical, and historical dimensions of such problems explored to join with them in discovering how they may be a part of the expanding extension services.

Chancellor MacNeil, Wilbur Katz, one of the great authorities on church-state legal problems in education and a Wisconsin faculty member, and key staff members of the division can see no legal problems in the kind of teaching and research they envision nor in the development of special programs to train church leaders in extension problem-solving education. These people may differ on whether the university is ready to establish a department of religious studies; but they agree that where theology or religious belief or religious organization is studied in terms of solving problems in the society, pursuit of such knowledge is entirely acceptable in the university. If religious leaders were to insist on religious training or proselytizing or deepening a person's faith, rather than bringing religious insight and motivation to bear on solving a public problem, university-church co-operation would end at once.

There needs to be a spirit of speculative adventure in both the university and the church regarding proposals for programs of mutual interest.[2] Those involved readily confess that the university knows very little about how and what competencies are the most effective in educating community leaders to act on public issues. Therefore, reflections by the church on foreign and domestic experience in such learning are welcomed.

Division IV is now developing a Ph.D. and graduate program in extension education for leaders in all major community institutions— the professions of law, medicine, social work, ministry, the organizations of business and industry, science and technology, and so on—since all of these now are developing adult and continuing education programs that combine career and public issue concerns. Thus intern experience in all the major institutions in the principal cities of the state will be possible. Most of the leaders of Division IV believe that in the next two or three decades all institutions and professions, private and public, will be involved in extension education as they conceive of it and will have ties to universities and colleges that are willing to assume responsibility for such education. The extension education, in the Wisconsin view, is a "creative educational process directed toward making the University an integral and dynamic part of the life of the state." It looks to an

> intimate partnership between people and professors; to bring eager students, regardless of age or location, into contact with stimulating scholars and teachers; to help lift the life of both campus and commonwealth to higher planes. So Extension [education] functions as a two-way street: identifying public problems and public needs, interpreting these concerns

---

2. What in concrete terms would indicate that churchmen are ready to understand some of the potentialities of Division IV for solving the difficulties of proclaiming the faith in Madison? They might, for example, study the work of Wisconsin scholars, such as the historian Jurgen Herbst. He is an expert on the forces at work in American educational ideals. He thinks the religious images of the new man and the new, holy commonwealth have had considerable influence in American education. They might study the work of a Catholic historian, Edward T. Gargan, who has analyzed the religious factors in DeTocqueville's view of America. Such study might have a liberating, humanizing effect on the deliberations of Madison or Milwaukee educators as to what they want high-school learning to be.

to the University, and then translating University insights into educational programs and projects throughout Wisconsin.[3]

This is, in contemporary terms, the "Wisconsin idea" which has been the major contribution of the land-grant colleges to American higher education. It is now, in Chancellor MacNeil's judgment, the central thrust of American education on the world scene. One of the tasks of the churches, then, in a university such as Wisconsin is to get inside this movement, understand it, rethink its meaning for their own work, and give of their theological and ethical insight to its fullest development. This would entail taking a university's central mission seriously, and this is what the campus clergy and the state's religious leadership in their five decades at Wisconsin have not done.

There have been other developments in the campus ministry, led by LeRoy Oates, Jack Harrison, Harold Viehman, and others, that are making very extensive use of the adult education facilities of Michigan State, Notre Dame, University of Minnesota, and others. Special conferences are held to co-ordinate plans, and a literature is emerging, chiefly from the Christian Faith and Higher Education Institute, on various experiences in using these resources. But Wisconsin stands out as having tremendous resources of tradition and technical data on traditional church interests that need to be explored in depth. Such an exploration can illustrate the kind of analysis that needs to be made of other major educational centers.

The possibilities need to be surveyed on three levels: (1) the parish and region; (2) the national policy level for the church, the university, and the federal government; (3) the international missionary level.

The Parish and Regional Dimensions of a Relationship between Churches and Extension Education

During 1967–1968 the Methodist, United Church, Lutheran, and Baptist denominations have been engaged in negotiations as to whether some common building and ecumenical ministerial structure could be developed at Wisconsin. The discussions have occasionally touched on the curricular and educational structures of the university, but they have

---

3. "Education for Continuing Change" (Madison: University of Wisconsin Extension Division, 1962), p. 18.

chiefly turned internally to arrangements that will meet crucial ministerial needs of the denominations involved and serve the "university as
a whole."[4]

What has not been proposed, and what is closest to our recommendations, is that the churches think in a modest way of emulating
the model of a multipurpose, university-church-civic complex that the
Lutherans are promoting for the Twin Cities (near the University of
Minnesota) under the direction of Loren Halvorsen, associate director
of the American Lutheran college programs. The Twin Cities plan is
for an office complex with tenants from the churches, professions, urban
planning, universities, and colleges who wish a place where they can
meet easily during the day to talk over public problems that cut across
varied specializations. The office complex will have an organization for
an adult education program which alerts tenants to civic and professional problems and intellectual, ethical, and religious trends in the
region. Their rentals will include budgets for this program. The new
buildings will have conference, assembly, and eating facilities that make
possible use by any religious group. Already seven churches, a number
of private colleges and seminaries, and campus ministries have plans to
use the center as a major educational facility.

The Madison, Wisconsin, churches might well develop some less
complex but flexible structure close to the administrative-intellectual
center of Division IV, even if this means selling property and leasing
and financing arrangements with the university and private groups. The
latter would be groups who wish to have such a center to facilitate their
coming into the life of the university and who have social-ethical concerns that under the proper ministry could combine civic practicality,
epistemological sensitivity, and intellectual sophistication.

The center would have facilities for week-end conferences with
parish lay and clerical leaders, students, faculty, and public leaders
wishing to work on a problem not yet dealt with in the formal curriculum. It could be a place of orientation for interns on short-term leave
from local parishes. Unused space in some of the older denominational
centers might provide study facilities.

---

4. The Methodists have a model that is a sort of even bigger Wesley Foundation with a chapel large enough for ecumenical gatherings and adaptable to varied
denominational uses for worship. The large Lutheran Cathedral structure is likely
to be used little in a few years as a result of traffic routing that makes it extremely
difficult to reach.

The center would have a core staff of men well trained in theology and some other academic discipline who could teach in both the university and the center. The career choice of a man whether to be formally associated with the church or university in his teaching and inquiry would be based on possibilities the center offered of dealing with substantive issues and with the kinds of people working to learn about these issues and to act.

What is most essential is that this center not be interpreted as a substitute for, or as antagonistic toward, other kinds of church structures; rather it is a resource for their leaders. It is true that some personnel must be trained and relocated and some church property closed. But this is not to deny the feasibility of separate denominational establishments with distinctive programs reaching constituencies the center could not touch. The effect of this proposal would be to open up a wider range of programmatic possibilities. Let us look at some of the survey data which illumine these possibilities.

1. One of the difficulties of the younger radical campus ministers, such as Jim LaRue, is that they are trying to make too much of what can be done with eighteen or so faith-and-life community students. He, like many others on every campus, has not found a place in the church that has the complexity, the range, the action excitement, that will let him use his full powers. So he confesses his heart out to a few similarly frustrated young people. A young minister like this probably needs to go back for a while into the university as a student, working in both extension education and the more basic academic disciplines, trying with other students to see their connections. The center we propose could help make this possible by using him as a resource person. Some of the Danforth campus ministry grants, if they continue, should be for such men.

Many of these men operate best as spiritual leaders when they do not wear the clerical collar. Some will probably go into extension teaching in the university, in the inner city, and so on. Ministers from parishes and campus positions who are doing intern work in Division IV might make excellent advisers in graduate dormitories of the university. There they would have much more influence in the structures of education than they would as campus ministers and would emerge with a better basis for a decision as to whether the church or the university is the better place for their kind of ministry. Or perhaps such men may learn in their internships in ghetto education and organization whether this is what they do well and whether a church is the best organization for such social change.

2. One of the chief gains in the center such as we are proposing is that its focus is on public problems, and not on what to do about the church or clergy. The questions that the church is forced to ask by the terms of its admission to the enterprise have to do with whether it wishes to offer the university some genuine educational-intellectual-pastoral-governing services. For example, many of the people who need research grants, leave time, and travel money (and often not very much money) are graduate students and young faculty who wish to explore new intellectual departures in their academic work. The church center may have funds to help in this. Or, again, note the risks faculty see to their careers in combining extension education and classic professional research. The church center can initiate the taking of such risks by consultations on new, cross-disciplinary issues; people writing dissertations that do not fit the usual academic mold need the interest or attention of other institutions and foundations such as a church center can give. A student's time can be bought to do research for the church on attitudes of a people in trouble or in anger at local injustices. Therefore, the difference in religious and social gains between the $25,000 a year for such discretionary help in a center we envision and funds for support of a campus ministry that has lost its way, and so takes solace in the activities of a few isolated church people, may be great indeed. We are not talking in abstractions here. According to the figures, the average staff member at Madison is working, at the most, with about fifty students.

This kind of concrete involvement of the churches in the basic intellectual work of the university is a form of understandable proclamation to the students and faculty who have long dissented from irrelevant institutional forms, but not from many of its historical ministerial concerns.

3. Such dissenters to social policies may be the student volunteers for summer civil rights programs which we singled out as a special study in 1964–1965.[5] The data do not support the popular caricatures of these students who worked summers in the South to register Negro voters

5. Michael Aiken, N. J. Demerath III, and Gerald Marwell, *Conscience and Confrontation* (East Lansing: Christian Faith and Higher Education Institute, 1965).

for SCOPE (Summer Community Organization and Political Education) and CORE (Congress of Racial Equality). They are not alienated rebels who have broken ties with families, schools, churches, high occupational or professional aspirations, or political democracy. Nor are they single-issue reformers, more liberal on racial matters and civil rights per se than on other pressing public matters. Two-thirds of their parents supported their summer programs; some 58 per cent of the SCOPE volunteers had had some contact with campus religious groups in planning their participation; and 28 per cent cited their campus clergyman as a positive influence in their decision to participate in the civil rights movement.

What is most important for the churches to realize is that most of these young people who went South, with the complex of beliefs which Kenneth Lutterman has been able to identify as the basic core configuration of Christian belief in the Madison data,[6] came back still believing in the possibility of nonviolent solutions to racial injustices and with hope that there was enough health in the democratic process to solve these problems in this way. The students who went down to these regions without faith in any creative, redemptive processes at work in the relations of men came back resigned to the use of more and more violence, really hopeless and angry, without having anyone or a community to hear them out. They effected in public a kind of Rap Brown revolutionary image of a world reduced to black and white.

These students are now caught up in tremendous power controversies. The tensions between many leaders of the Southern Christian Leadership Conference and the more extreme left Black Power organizations symbolize the ideological and moral models at stake. But the bulk of the churches in the area are still trying to look away from these struggles of faith and ideology rather than open themselves to the frightful, nearly violent dissensions these young people are engaged in. Yet these students are the best sources of understanding and involvement

---

6. A technical paper will be published later by him on this involving a statistical manipulation of correlating scales to produce a religious factor with more complex components than show up in studies such as those by Glock and Stark. They include affirmation of a theistic position with appreciation of presence of ambiguity and doubt, a sense of ethical action and concern toward others as the most crucial test of seriousness of faith, a belief that God had created and is creating in the world for the positive enrichment of human life, that man is a mix of good and evil, but capable of support of groups that positively serve others needs, and so on.

for the churches in the controversies that are raging in the public schools, the professions, party politics, and the urban planning and design boards of every city in the country.

The crucial challenge to the churches is to nurture—not just preach to—these young people in all ways. The question is whether or not the churches can develop similar ethical concerns in a manner that is intellectually responsible. There are going to be many occasions when the issues student volunteers bring back to the church will need to be debated and analyzed first in private organizations, such as the center we are envisioning, before the issue can be picked up by a university department. These volunteers often are mixing, in their summer work, career choice and academic interests that go to the heart of a man's or woman's faith. The church centers we propose should have experts in this kind of nurture. These centers can become the crossroads of universities, the places where questions first get asked as to how a man can combine classic liberal arts and extension education, in order to test new relationships in theory and practice emerging in his mind.

Generally, from our data, it appears that the summer experience of student volunteers does not produce much change in their basic orientation. (We surveyed students before and after their summer experience.) It did help them to test the adequacy of a way of thinking and acting; this was important to them. All this is to say that men act in matters of courage and responsibility out of fairly well-established and deeply held patterns of commitment. Men and women are much less changeable (every act a new decision about who I am) than much of the rhetoric of existential literature and secular liberalism supposes. There is a constancy of factors in the socializing and resocializing process of persons that needs to be given much more serious attention by the churches.

The students are actually receptive only to fairly sober, carefully analyzed, strongly committed institutional acts and policies, made with the expectation that over time institutional habits, affections, and traditions will be established. The radical changes in institutional form which we are talking about must offer this kind of long-run restoration of balances in ministry and constituency. If the serious commitment on a large scale is not made, what results is proliferation of the kind of industrial missions, faith-and-life communities, ecumenical institutes, and so forth that often indicate the tentative, nonserious nature of the churches' involvement in the complex of intellectual, religious, and public problems with which we are dealing.

4. The leaders of the centers we envision will be out in front on most of the new educational reforms, clerical re-evaluations, and policy studies that are going to go on in a region. These centers will be places where change is conceived and introduced as response to vaguely articulated local problems; they will later review action on recommendations. They are going to encourage seminaries and other church agencies to fashion their own counterparts to these model operations as soon as possible.

But how does all this occur without polarizing further the university and the church? If the radicals capture such a center and use it as a power base to spread their kind of faith alone, they will soon find themselves without any institutional ties to the places where decisions are made on the issues that concern them.

In anticipation of this problem, we wish to explore some of the deep theological, ethical, social, and academic interests that have been traditional with many of the moderate and conservative denominations and could be fruitfully analyzed by a center such as we are describing.

(a) The data from our survey, and our discussions with Roman Catholic leaders at St. Paul's Student Center, in Madison, indicate that the latter would co-operate closely with the organization we are proposing, while retaining their own center. Their center is now being restructured so that lay influence, even control, of most of its operation will be the future pattern. The educational and preaching activity has shifted from a Newman club model—of providing social occasions and formal courses in Catholic doctrine and practice by the clergy, which no one would attend—to that of laymen exploring the components of responsible moral judgment on issues inviting review of traditional Catholic doctrine. Thus groups have been working intensively on Catholic thought on birth control and family life, parish organization, civil rights and uses of violence, for example. The student pressure for more ecumenical educational experiences is tremendous in this center.

Even though the Catholic center has with great care sought to get student and faculty representation from major areas of the curriculum, the leaders are discovering that they simply do not have the resources to carry the inquiries to the level of sophistication students expect out of other work they have done in the university.

It would be our prediction that the Roman Catholics would have much to gain from a center that made inquiry into the theological, ethical, and technical factors of action and moral judgment a focus of its work. The survey data support this. Roman Catholic students reveal rigid discontinuities in thought about religion and ethics, but great general convictions as to the importance of the issue. More than any other church group, Catholic students think all who live a good moral life are Christians (46 per cent agreed, as contrasted with 10 per cent of the Missouri and Wisconsin Lutherans); they are more cynical about human relations than the moderate or liberal Protestants on such items as "It's who you know rather than what you know that's important in getting ahead." Yet they are more supportive of a rigid, moralistic model of ethical judgment (for instance, strongest opposition of all groups to "What is right action in one situation may not be right in another"). They are the strongest believers in life after death and believe least that salvation refers to the capacity to live a fully human life in this world.

It is no wonder that the priests at the Catholic Student Center are fearful of opening up their discussion of theology and ethics to selected laymen and priests from the parish churches, as some students suggest. They see the disjunctions, confusions, and antagonisms emerging among students as being so great that they do not want their freedom to argue these issues hampered by the introduction of parish leaders. But a center such as we are talking about might begin to explore for the Catholics some of the connections of parish controversies and student intellectual inquiries without jeopardizing parish support for the Catholic Student Center. But more basically, the proposed center can provide intellectual leadership to meet student and clerical demands for increased sophistication in inquiry.

(b) The survey data on alignments of denominational constituencies with academic majors and careers provide one of the most forceful arguments for the need of some organizations to supervise the development of ecumenical strategy commensurate with fundamental social structures of the university. The Methodists, for example, need to go slowly in their allocations of funds for building or preaching or worship in relation to provisions for teaching and research. This recommendation follows from the fact that the Methodists have an impressive lead in the percentage of students who plan teaching and research as a career. Therefore, opportunities to explore different contexts of teaching and images of research which the center could provide might be of great importance. It is possible that in the future the most influential place where beliefs are formed will not be in the traditional church chapels. Rather, it will be in a variety of classrooms, workshops, storefront classrooms, and policy consultations participated in by students and teachers.

It should be noted also that the Wisconsin and Missouri Lutherans have the largest percentages of students majoring in business, engineering, and mathematics. In the moderate and liberal denominations, students involved in the campus religious activities place entrance into these areas significantly lower than the general student body. The Lutheran students place among the highest (with Roman Catholic) in viewing vocational training as the chief purpose of education. They expect their churches to develop meaning and values in life much more than students in most other denominations.

This situation invites the kind of delicate cross-denominational explorations that the campus ministry now has little room for, but that the proposed center might initiate. What are the motivations and expectations of the Lutherans going into these areas? Recall that the Parker Palmer studies of world-view correlations, like the Wisconsin studies, found a much higher mix of magic and scientism among these majors than others. What responsibilities are the Lutheran leaders actually assuming to encourage students to think about the relations of their academic majors to their church loyalties? What are the bases of objections which students in moderate and liberal denominations are making to business careers? Do these represent reactions against parental value systems? Do they know anything about different styles of life and work emerging in some areas of business? Who assumes responsibility in the university to open up these possibilities?[7]

The study staff, while in Wisconsin, tried to interest Donald Bossart, of the Wesley Foundation, to specialize in developing policies for the counseling situation of campus ministers. He was thwarted by a be-

---

7. A recent study by the Dean of Students office indicated that except for a very few technical schools, such as agriculture, the faculty showed least interest— among several academic responsibilities offered—in counseling or teaching students about career choices, and the students listed it as the area in which they most desired additional help from the faculty.

havioral-oriented psychology department that did not welcome his teaching with them and by very limited clientele. He was probably realistic in seeing that counseling needs, such as vocational choice, are eventually going to be taken on by the university faculty and administrative staffs. The church can enter the issue only if it has the facilities and leadership for encouraging the intellectual, administrative student, and public forces to take informed action. Our proposed center might provide such resources.

(c) The national staff also asked the campus clergy in Wisconsin if it might read, or talk with them about, the sermons which they had delivered in the past year dealing with the relation of the Christian faith to various burning educational issues. Our efforts produced very little. This helped us understand why our survey data indicated that campus religious organizations had had little or no influence on the kind of issues which our California study had found to be of considerable significance in the educational process.

What influences there are have to be looked for in very subtle, indirect connections of theology and educational attitude. For example, the members of campus religious organizations actually find depersonalization of education less an issue than the noninvolved student. This probably indicates that for them religious organizations provide a social group which reinforces deep interpersonal ties. The problem in some religious organizations is to break students out of overdependence on particular groups for their campus social and religious life.[8]

The differences in denominational scores on what students regard as important in university life can provide religious leaders with the basis for investigations of student motivations on campus. Of all the religious groups, the Missouri Lutherans give the least importance to classroom vitality. The Episcopalians are of all groups least interested in the relations of theory to action in education, while the Presbyterians put great stress on this. The Missouri and Wisconsin Lutherans put the least emphasis of the religious groups on the importance of the quality of interpersonal relations between faculty and student as a factor in learning, while the United Church of Christ and the Baptist faith-and-life groups, which have ministers with strong existential, personalistic convictions, put the highest premium on such an issue.

---

8. For example, the director's visit to the Wesley Foundation coffeehouse on a Sunday night revealed more campus ministers and wives present waiting for an opportunity at informal conversation with students than there were students.

Such views lead to different approaches as to what are priorities in educational reform. Generally, the average participant in campus religious activities tends to stress less than the noninvolved student the importance of research and pursuit of new knowledge in the university aspects of education. No student group or ministry has been known to proclaim that its moral-Christian reflections led it to demand greater allocations of faculty energy and time to study of a neglected area of social or intellectual need. A faculty committee has been at work devising plans for a department of religious studies which stresses research and new learning as well as traditional and historical approaches. But the committee has been slow in influencing faculty and has not had the general support of the campus ministries as a priority to be explored in all its alternative forms.

There is nothing in the preaching and worship functions of the clergy that would lead students to think that these activities had to do with the central university enterprise of discovery of knowledge and the use of it for meeting human problems. There is no evidence at the center of the traditional church—its Sabbath proclamation—of concerted efforts to direct corporate faculty and student intellectual efforts toward problems of organized religion in contemporary American culture or any other public issue affecting the spiritual and moral health of the nation.

The sermons do not reflect even a *Saturday Review of Literature* awareness of the controversies sweeping through education, let alone theological reflection on these. Therefore, the most urgent evaluation questions of a human enterprise such as the university are not raised at the very place where traditionally they have been raised; namely, in the church's priestly and proclaiming work. These questions have to do with the criteria of judgment, of justification, of evaluation of the goals of the various educational enterprises, including Division IV. Are technological, practical interests balanced with humanistic ones as to the loyalties and affections of the citizenry involved? These questions about the day-to-day pursuit of truth, the criticism of allocations of resources to discover and learn, have not been raised in the traditional roles of the ministry, and therefore the crisis of believing in truth that is both transcendent and empirical grows.

The center we talk about is not to destroy preaching or worship, but to provide some organization by which men can gain a vision of that critical task and the resources available.[9] These resources are most often

9. See, for example, the papers in Volume II of this report by Edward L. Long

to be found in a setting of learning where men in private and in affectionate, critical understanding find out what they have been doing in their attempts to save the church and what they can do to serve and save together. A church leader needs to know that most of the students he works with appear in careful social survey to have isolated the experience of exhilaration and joy in human life from religion and their own personal faith. But he needs to learn such data in more places than a book: in an institute or center or seminary that will help him grope toward an understanding of what happened to create such disjunctions in religious consciousness.

The center we envision can operate alongside a whole network of denominational foundations and houses spread over an entire campus and out into a complete city. The latter have their work to do, in reaching constituencies often very specialized (such as medicine, agriculture, inner-city Negroes). But the center we describe helps the whole ministry of an area learn what is going on or could go on in these places for the good of the entire work of the church. The center may or may not grow out of a reordering of urban survey and extension work, out of church councils, out of a new mission of a campus ministry and a department of religious studies. We offer no blueprints.

Madison may not move toward what we are describing as its ecumenical solution, but this is not important in national terms. We are simply delineating the forces that are moving religious leaders in scores of major educational and urban complexes toward consideration of the kind of organizational possibilities we have raised here.

National Policy Aspects of the Center

The people who get excited about this kind of center of religious affairs in Stony Brook, New York, in Philadelphia, or in Madison, Wisconsin—Presidents of the University, Chancellors of Divisions, national denominational executives, a core of ministers from campuses, urban and

---

Jr., "A Content Analysis of Study Materials in the Campus Ministries," and by Julian N. Hartt, "Liturgy and Politics." The prayers of a Robert MacAfee Brown for social science as well as hundreds of other successful worship aids are available in campus ministry programs (as at Yale). So, too, are academic critiques of the inward-turned existentialism of Malcolm Boyd's *Are You Running with Me, Jesus?* and other popular books used without much thought as to their basic promises and loyalties.

suburban ministries, faculty—do not want only a local or regional program. It must not fail on this level. But it should seek to be a model for centers in other areas and to train people to lead them. It should develop programs which offer alternatives to national actions in need of being stopped or reformed.

Thus, as the study staff explored the possibilities of such a center with national leaders, they came to see that it might in time have the resources, for example, to make a survey of federal policies toward the education of potential leaders in Latin American countries. To what extent is the training now conducted under military auspices designed to gain and keep power or to resist reform? Could the kind of education for orienting agricultural peoples to technological and urban changes—the specialty of Wisconsin throughout its history—be a possible part of this federally financed training?

The study staff was told by university scholars who have been studying intern programs for ministers and laymen in religious education, rural parish work, and inner-city missions that these might well be supplemented or replaced by special programs that could be developed at Wisconsin.

International Policy Aspects of the Center

Some of the most wide-ranging possibilities for the center could be in the strengthening of the work of the foreign missions of the churches. Many of the leaders in foreign missions will be trained in institutions which are moving away from traditional theological curriculums to much greater emphasis on the relation of Christian ministry to public problem-solving in areas confronted by social and cultural upheavals. The relations of these educational and religious traditions to the emerging new technological society are at the heart of Division IV's concerns.

It is possible to conceive, then, if the Wisconsin religious affairs center were intimately related to Division IV work, that the foreign missions of the church might find close ties slowly developing. Although six denominations now have a center at Stony Point, New York, for intensive training of missionaries going into the field or on leave, they might find occasion to grant special training fellowships at Wisconsin and exchange data emerging from that center. There are some denominational conference activities for missionaries near Madison which could facilitate explorations: the Lutheran Center in Chicago, the Baptist and Disciples of Christ conferences at Green Bay, Wisconsin. The Catholic Inter-American Cooperation Program in Davenport, Iowa, has great interest in seeing that both Roman Catholic and Protestant church programs in Latin America give greater attention to the relation of religious, social, economic, and political factors in their area of ministry.

A regional or metropolitan center capable of offering evaluative research on the policies of the churches and advanced learning in extension education that has some sensitivity to the missionary convictions of the churches could well be a crucial factor in a great many decisions facing the churches.

NEW WINE IN FRESH SKINS

A Theological Interlude

T HERE are certain biblical images of social change which we would prefer to dominate the church's thinking about the transformation of relations between religion and education being proposed in this study. Therefore, we would like to discuss their meaning in the early church and now.

In Mark 2:22, Matthew 9:17, and Luke 5:37 Christ communicates essentially the same message: that new wine should not be put in old wineskins because the new wine will ferment and expand, causing the old, stretched, dried skins to burst, spilling the wine. The Markan passage, probably the oldest version, reads: "And no one puts new wine in old wine skins, if he does, the wine will burst the skins, and the wine is lost, and so are the skins, but new wine is for fresh skins." The last phrase in Mark is offered as a logical conclusion: "New wine is for fresh skins." Luke adds one original sentence. It seems to recognize man's natural and often wistful clinging to what has been, to the old and secure ways.

It is important to look at the context in which this parable occurs. It is accompanied by the parable on patches of new material sewn on old garments. In both parables, Jesus appears to be saying that the new is a dangerous and even destructive force on the old. A new, unshrunk patch of material sewed on an old garment will cause the threads of the old to pull apart and tear even more when the garment is washed and the new patch shrinks. Luke adds another dimension by saying not only that the new is dangerous to or destructive of the old but that the two are so incompatible when placed together that both suffer destruction. In Luke the patch is not merely an unshrunk piece of new fabric but a piece torn from a new garment to patch an old garment. He points out that it is foolish to mutilate a new garment for the repair of an old one, for in the end both are made useless. Luke, therefore, is illustrating the consequences of incompatibility of structures and substances.

This point must be considered together with the parable about the new wine in old wineskins. The second parable clarifies the implications of the incompatibility motif. Either the new and the old are combined and due to their incompatibility are destroyed, or the new, to survive, must be conveyed in compatible vessels.

From what the new wine passage does not say, we might suggest the following logical steps: the new does not have to replace the old; the old does not necessarily have to be replaced to retain usefulness; new and old can continue, survive, and perhaps even flourish, so long as each is conveyed separately in an appropriate vessel; the old cannot be helped or improved by the new. No judgment is passed on the relative merits of old and new.

What does this understanding of the passage suggest to the Christian who faces the choice of which policies will best enable him to be the church today? If the Scripture is saying something here, it must be tied with this idea of the incompatibility of new forms with old contents. Perhaps it suggests that the introduction of new forms of ministry, worship, Christian education, into the life of the church must be accompanied by appropriate, new vehicles for their sustenance and development. The introduction of denominational literature on applying Christianity to career choices with the same deductive, exhortative ethic and the use of some up-to-date pictures of students in action on urban service fronts does not result in a new and vital teaching vehicle. Instead, it makes the old curriculum seem even more useless and inappropriate than before. New themes and new layout and even some new teaching techniques will not patch up an old and inappropriate epistemology and curriculum to give them new life. A thorough renovation is required. New ideas require the appropriate vessels or structures to carry and nurture them.

Suggestions for policy changes and new forms of ministry must be accompanied by concrete and appropriate means for implementing them. Appropriate vehicles must be offered to carry and develop the new ideas which we see as necessary to making the church a vital, genuine, and appropriate expression of God's love. Or, in the language of the parable on wineskins, we must provide the new wineskins as well as the new wine if this study is to offer more than inadequate patchwork to the church in the United States.

The conclusion to which our historical and contemporary research on the American scene has led us is that many of the church structures do not represent serious attempts to know and influence university life in its major centers. Other structures, such as parish worship and proclamation of the faith, carry traditions that are essential and irreplaceable to some people. The choice is not either one structure or the other. But there are inescapable decisions as to whether the church will make a commitment to needed new structures.

The Important Strategic Decision of the Church

The most important strategic decision in the next decade will be whether or not the churches are going to give ministry to higher education top priority as the chief avenue, properly carried out, to lay leadership of the church and to the understanding of the major structures of the world in which the church must serve. Granted all the failures and illusions of scholars and students in sensing the political and social realities of our times, the work going on in the university is the principal source of significant Christian education and action in the future. The failure of church leadership in major boards (decisions in departments of higher education have relatively little power or influence) to make this strategic decision in the next few years may mean that it will be generations before the church recovers its capacity to share in the lives and work of the modern world. Perhaps she will always bear the tragic scars of default on such a policy decision.

We are not talking here about the expansion of existing campus ministries; they are in need of the fundamental changes described in this study. Nor are we talking about the influx of parish ministers into campus organizations. There are existing and traditional programs to be maintained; there are programs and personnel to be dropped from the university scene; but there are new organizations to be established with great powers to initiate policy inquiries and adult learning.

The easiest course for the church will be to continue to dissipate its resources on a series of "experiments" where two or three men staffing industrial missions, ecumenical institutes, and the like, supposedly are en-

gaged in intimate dialogue and study with leaders of major institutions—
and these carried out alongside traditional parish structures that have
no relation to these specialized programs.

The alternative is to direct the most gifted professional and major
financial resources of the church to ministries of education. The purpose
will be to activate the university laity, to use their power to transform
the fundamental intellectual and learning experience of rank-and-file
churchmen. To do this, the closest possible collaboration with laymen
in professional, business, communications, and political leadership will
be necessary. The crucial point is that the chief source of new images
of, and data on, city design, of research and development, of personal
growth in our society, are in the university structures we are describing.
For example, the power to form the future curriculums of the churches is
shifting from denominational editors to the university. This power lies
in the educational standards being set, and the scholarship being used,
in university education and in the secondary and adult education it influences.

The churches' resources of leadership, property, and money are going to be so limited in our vast world that the decision of priority of concern we pose must be debated and faced. If it is not, surely the spirit of
Christ who saw the need for new wine in new skins, not the destruction
of the old, somehow, tragically, will have been lost.

PROPHECY AND GOVERNANCE

An Interpretive Interlude

I N the preceding chapters, we explored the capacities of campus ministries for care of persons and for institutional expression of religion in preaching and other acts of worship. We were much more concerned there with the internal church side of faith than in those that follow. Chapters 12–18 are a description and analysis of the relation of religious commitment to the processes of inquiry and learning and to functions of governance and political action. Chapters 19 and 20 are concerned with placing the campus ministry in the context of trends in the whole Protestant clergy, through use primarily of survey data. Chapters 21, 22 and the Conclusion fill out the policy implications of our analysis, indicating alternative lines of reforms and obstacles to them in institutional Christianity and the general culture.

Our investigation into the nature of prophetic inquiry in the church and university necessitated critical consideration of how the substance of a religious heritage is appropriated in our time and of attempts to form Christian faith by modes of ministry other than conversion and preaching, devotional and biblical study, in parish-centered activities. Prophetic inquiry has undergone radical transformation in meaning in recent decades of church life, while becoming a more prominent mode of ministry. We conjecture that this is chiefly because of the challenge of scientific and technological scholarship in the university and its influence on the whole culture. The challenge has come primarily to religious institutions relying on traditional methods of persuasion (like apologetic preaching and conversion of people by confession of personal faith).

The church has traditionally recognized its responsibility to teach and examine the faith in a systematic way. The Sunday school movement, adult Bible classes, and laymen's retreats and institutes have all been expressive of this concern. But most of these activities have been carried out with a particular image of learning: organizing the content of the faith into basic doctrines and principles which are then stated and illustrated by the teacher with some random or varied selections from his experiences or those of the class. The basic learning process had its counterparts in a theological discipline which saw itself as the basic discipline, if not the only necessary one, for informing the teacher of the content of the faith. Once the content was learned and its images were clearly established in the Christian's mind, the basic principles could be applied by the layman in his daily life. In the Roman Catholic and Protestant parochial schools—since the religious institution held the power to save souls—it was assumed that the more exposure to visible officially sanctioned religious objects and verbal symbols, the better the religious education.

What the churches are now experiencing is a widespread rebellion against these simplistic views of the learning process. An increasing attempt is made to combine in church-sponsored inquiry the freedom to hypothesize and examine varying perspectives of faith and to explore together aspects of religion which grow out of the personal experiences, talents, and social responsibilities of laymen. More attention is given to disciplined attacks on current problems of human welfare, to use of a combination of disciplines in seminary education, to examination of the values, knowledge, and commitments present in various educational programs. This kind of inquiry, termed "prophetic," combines informed value and theological judgments, academic investigation and social action. By insisting that the pursuit of the meaning of contemporary religious commitment is a complex process, intermingled with other factors and forces and tested by its consequences in achievement of long-range social goals, this mode of ministry emphasizes the interdependence of church and university. It struggles to establish new ecumenical agencies for inquiry. It ceases to be dependent on one-church staffs, on professional clerical leadership, and on evangelical patterns of learning.

The examination of this new emphasis in the ministry was undertaken principally in an area of rapid social change in the South. We had discerned in earlier stages of the study that many of the sharpest conflicts between the preaching and priestly and the teaching and inquiry modes of contemporary ministry were occurring here, since the churches of the area had been so dependent on preaching and confessional modes of learning. Some students of modernization have maintained that the process is best characterized as the embodiment in a culture of an attitude of questioning about choices men make; to be modern is to see life as offering alternatives, preferences, and choices.[1] The modernization process, if accompanied by no culture-transcending loyalties and commitments, can result, not in the "liberation of the human spirit," but in despair, confusion, alienation, and tyranny. This possibility is as near as new hope, new involvements, and new social service in technological and scientifically induced social change.

A social system may increase its capacity to receive and process information from within and without the system and still be disoriented as to what it wishes to do with this information. An institution can accept so much outside information that it loses its capacity to act, to identify its basic ordering of loyalties and convictions. Therefore, we have insisted that we are exploring prophetic inquiry which has loyalties to the church and to many of its basic historic beliefs. It also has ties to the university's pursuit of new knowledge, And we have insisted that institutional expressions of religion and critical thinking are to be put to the task of forming social policy.

In short, this section is greatly concerned to find the fruitful conjunctions of prophecy and governance in our society. Truth and wisdom need to be tested in the fires of politics and administration; politics and governance need truth and wisdom if they are to be great in service of human beings. These modes of ministry and action are often falsely separated in our world. The academician or intellectual, many say, seeks truth, apparently oblivious to the knowledge and insight of the university and other centers of inquiry. So, too, the pastor seeking to comfort and challenge his people with the ancient beliefs and wisdom of his faith is not to engage in judgments on social issues or organize community resources to do so.

But governance and politics do not conjure up in our minds simply the images of pursuit of power, protection of special interests, and reconciliation of conflicts between groups. Not only are we using governance, whether in the church, university, or elsewhere, as a method

---

1. David Apter, *Politics of Modernization* (Chicago: University of Chicago Press, 1965).

for arriving at decisions as to what goods are to be achieved and the means to achieve them but we are relating this function closely to responsibilities and methods of educating those who participate in the process and are affected by it.

We think of governance as involving relationships and forces which are part of a whole institution or socioeconomic system and the quality of life considered appropriate to them. We think of the effect of this quality on other institutions and the general welfare. The context in which a man administrates influences his actions and those led, while at the same time the mode of governance shapes the spirit and form of the institution he leads and its relations to the wider culture.

Most questions of governance in the church are recognized as having to do with qualitative judgments about the consequences of the use of various powers and techniques on the goals pursued and with winning commitment to certain objectives that the minister or other leaders have established. Governance has to do also with the relation of deep loyalties to technical data on what goes on in the world. These are not matters which the church, when it seeks to influence public leaders or other institutions, can reduce to simple interests and privileges to be negotiated. The politics of the church, the attempt to share in the formation of social policy, involves images of the community as a whole for which the church acts.

When the fourth primary role of the minister is seen as governing and engaging in politics, this breaks from views of the church as simply an adapter to a changing environment, or simply as an appropriator of the knowledge of the university better to accommodate itself to an "objectively given state of affairs," to use Talcott Parsons' phrase for an adaptive type of action. Such a view assumes society or a social system as an order of properties not dependent in any way on including the churches or religion in the system. Our images of governance and politics suggest the church as wishing and hoping to play its part in influencing the quality of the common life of a people, as being involved less in a system than a dynamic field of activity in which human beings influence one another.

There is a type of campus ministry which seems on the surface to honor this fourth master role. It is patterned on a type of rationality and cognitive learning believed to be associated with the scientific and technological enterprises of the university. It makes of teaching and preaching a kind of demonstration of the use of ideas in a purely cognitive or instrumental way; the personal and social dimensions of knowledge are discounted; the minister deals with theory and knowledge in a reasonable manner that does not make it a test of his personal convictions; he finds his authority primarily in his ability to interpret a situation in relation to the norms and commitments of himself and the community. This kind of campus minister tries to carry out the cognitive role of the scholar, teaching courses in religion, organizing conferences to enrich the individual's knowledge of religion.

Alternatives to this view of inquiry are not very clear in the behavior of ministers. The next section tries to open up alternative ways of religious inquiry by looking at what the secular theologians have suggested and at the varied types of formal religious studies in the university; and finally we look at extracurricular organizations in the campus ministry which have as their objective the investigation of usage of religious belief and ethical reasoning made by laymen in thinking about the reconstruction and design of a city.

Discussions of governance in ministry take on particular urgency because of the indications in public controversy and social survey[2] that lay opposition to clerical involvement in "secular affairs" and "social causes" seems to be growing in many denominations. Religious leaders have to decide whether differences in interpretation of the mission of the church can be reconciled and whether they have done enough to educate all their constituencies as to the factors which contribute to their decisions to engage in community organization and the like. The controversies affect the uses of church property, the sources of funds for church work, the distribution of professional personnel—all matters of great political significance and delicacy.

The campus ministries are involved in all these controversies, as our studies of church policy making on a regional and national level (Chapter 18) indicate. Not just the Catholic Church is being shaken by a "Memorandum of Priorities" which seeks the establishment of new departments, the consolidation or abandonment of old ones, the review of financial statements in terms of primary ministerial functions, the order

2. A Gallup poll conducted in the spring of 1968 indicated, for example, that 55 per cent of the persons interviewed felt that churches should avoid involvement in political and social issues, as compared with a similar poll in 1957 in which only 44 per cent wished to avoid such involvement. *The New York Times,* April 12, 1968.

of values assumed by clergy when various lay groups are not consulted (for example, faculty in social sciences).[3] The same attempt to limit and direct power by truth and to involve the discovery of truth in all exercise of power goes on in Protestantism.

The Hebrew prophets resisted making truth the servant of power, but they had no reservations about the power of religious wisdom to alert a nation or a king to the consequences of unjust acts. In Christ's view of the world, a profound revolution in personal and public values was going on with the break-through of the Kingdom of God into world history; and, by implication, any institution or leader of men seeking to fight this revolution and align with the status quo was destined to go down to defeat. What, then, does the Bible mean by "truth?" It means some thing or being which has been found to be enduring, dependable, and trustworthy; God and His ministers do what they say they will do.

In the modern world, the connections between prophecy and politics are obscure and uncertain for laymen and clergy alike. Even the seminaries, as we shall see, the traditional font of religious studies, are unsure whether they are professional schools, leaders of a movement for social change, or a residency for internship in the relation of theological learning to the university's discoveries of the nature of man and the world. In our time, the data of social surveys, as this volume shows, can display for all to see the polarities and differences of faith and morality in the clergy itself. But such studies can also adumbrate the structures of enduring and reformed ministry. And from all this knowledge can come fruitful speculation as to the policies to be pursued in the next few decades by church, educational, and public leaders.

---

3. In March, 1968, the priests of the Roman Catholic Archdiocese of New York presented such a memorandum to the Most Rev. Terence J. Cooke, Archbishop-designate. *The New York Times,* March 17, 1968.

PART V

The Structures of Teaching and Prophetic Inquiry

⫸ 12 ⫷

SCIENTIFIC INQUIRY AND THE SECULAR MINISTRY

(Chapel Hill)

In the past decade there has been a movement from extreme formulations of teaching and inquiry as a secular ministry to a more complex and fruitful attempt to discover the major components of learning that combine features of scientific inquiry, the prophetic tradition, and community organization and leadership.

The thrust toward a ministry of prophetic inquiry has been perhaps the major positive outcome of the theologies of secularization in this country (for example, see Harvey Cox, Dietrich Bonhoeffer, Friedrich Gogarten, R. Gregor Smith, J. C. Hochendijh). Many campus ministers believe that from the theologies of secularization they have been able to get a "new perspective on the university" which enables them to understand particularly the positive significance of scientific and technological inquiry for the Christian faith and the church. They believe that the kinds of questions asked by the theologians of secularization are in a sense more indigenous to the contemporary academic enterprise than the old questions asked about the nature of the university by many interpreters of religion and higher education they read in their seminary days, such as Arnold Nash, Walter Moberly, and John Coleman.

It is their conviction that over the past century a very dangerous separation of the intellectual and spiritual life of the churches from the scientific and technological inquiries of the university has occurred and that this came about principally because of theological and metaphysical preconceptions of Christian religion which could not appreciate the human and personal worth of the research enterprises of the university. Often the shrillness and extremity of the manifestoes on secularization are to be explained by the odds against which these ministers think they are fighting in bringing the Christian church once again into the center of issues which dominate the intellectual and political life of the nation.

At an early stage of the study the staff decided that these claims of campus ministries about the values of the theologies of secularization should be explored. A colloquium was organized at Chapel Hill, North Carolina, since Harry Smith, one of the most influential campus ministers in the environs of the University of North Carolina, North Carolina State, and Duke University, as well as in the nation, and a number of his faculty and ministerial colleagues were highly interested in exploring this theme.[1] The Chapel Hill colloquium, more than the others, became a dialogue between Smith and the participants, since the chief responsibility for presenting the position of a theology of secularization was undertaken by him. We saw the work of the colloquium, however, in relation to a broader issue: the nature of prophetic inquiry, a third basic mode of ministry emerging with new clarity and influence in the nation. This chapter intends to explore three major aspects of this mode brought out in our explorations at Chapel Hill.

In order to make this exploration more multifaceted, we arranged with Donald Shriver, a campus minister at North Carolina State University (who was conducting a three-year experimental study and observation program on "religion and society" with scientists, politicians, businessmen, theologians, and ministers) to have reporters and interpreters for the Danforth Study present at meetings he was conducting. Shriver's program planned to investigate the meaning of the Christian faith held by a number of southern leaders for their present work and thus differed in emphasis from the Chapel Hill colloquium.

The Danforth Study staff also set up a colloquium of faculty, ministers, and public leaders in Pittsburgh that would seek to learn the factors which contributed to serious ethical inquiry by the churches and universities into the priorities and possibilities of urban reform and design. Pittsburgh has been the scene of vast inner-city reconstruction, and we found a group that wished to study the power of the church and universities to mount a critique of their own role and values in this urban

---

1. The initial members of the Chapel Hill colloquium were the following: Waldo Beach, Barbara Benedict, William Bush, Jackson Carroll, Raymond Dawson, John Dixon, E. P. Douglass, John Graham, Anne Green, John Hallowell, Robert Mill, William Poteat, John Schnorrenberg, Harry Smith, and W. D. White. In 1968 Smith became a vice-chancellor of the University of North Carolina with responsibility for a residential college in the university's new college system.

reconstruction. These colloquia were supplemented by a week-long consultation of national leaders in community organization, city planning, and religion at Massachusetts Institute of Technology.

This chapter deals only with what we learned from the Chapel Hill colloquium about the churches' and universities' ways of engaging in learning and inquiry. Chief attention is given to the empirical, technical aspects of higher learning which, in the view of the theologians of secularization, dominate the context in which the religious beliefs are now formed in our culture.

An Inquiring Style of Belief and the Processes of Learning

Campus ministers such as Harry Smith and scholars such as Edward Long and David Duncombe[2] are seeking to create in the churches an inquiring style of belief which is inextricably tied to processes of instruction that draw heavily upon sectors of the university which hold beliefs in relation to their grounding in reason, empirical evidence, or response to the environment. They see this style as of great significance in distinguishing themselves from an evangelical, pietistic, orthodox Christianity which they believe still dominates the churches and people with whom they work.

A noninquiring, nonevidential style of belief, they argue, has little interest in understanding the processes by which belief is formed, the options of learning processes emerging in the university, particularly in behavioral and social studies, because it sees belief as conceptually independent of the processes by which it is acquired. Belief is given in an act of grace, and religious truth is given in the historic revelation by God of His will and nature in Jesus Christ. Belief is held quite apart from any empirical data or canon of epistemology and reason. The more conservative Christians, the "pattern-maintenance religious people," as Talcott Parsons calls them, have reduced Christian faith to a dogmatic and scriptural essence, which they presume, if accepted, will bind men together in community and assure their salvation. This is fundamentally a legalistic mentality which believes that principles inculcated in youth

2. Two chapters in Volume II are especially relevant to this section on an Inquiring Style of Belief: one is David Duncombe's "Toward a Scientific Theory of Experimental Learning for the Churches," and the other is Edward L. Long's "A Content Analysis of Study Materials in the Campus Ministries."

are separate from political life and, indeed, that such inculcation is a mode of action superior to mere politics. The picture of children reciting scriptural passages learned by rote in Sunday school comes most readily to mind. But we are talking even about seminaries where theologians and ethicists are dedicated primarily to keeping alive the memories and events given in the Scriptures, with lectures and sermons full of personal or random illustrations.

The exposure of campuses dominated by such an ethos to the pluralism and variety of commitment and conviction in contemporary society threatens this learning process. So a subtle reinforcement goes on in selection of guest speakers for chapel programs, honored donors, and reiterated values. Thus, the meaning of the Christian tradition is gradually reduced and solidified. The universal values of individual accountability and love of neighbor take on the connotations of special institutional, class, racial, ethnic, and professional interests. Technological, urban, scientific developments are distorted to fit the caricatures of an embattled Christian college—and a whole syndrome is complete. The importance of this syndrome does not derive so much from the strength and numbers of institutions of education in which it is present. Its significance derives more from the kind of rebellion its excessive rigidity and reductionism have produced. It is against this value context that the polemical style of many theologians of secularization is to be understood.

In the major inquiries of the university, Harry Smith argues, belief is held always in relation to the processes by which it has come to be held. Therefore, distortions between inquiry and indoctrination become significant. Inquiry is a peculiar, unique kind of activity which Harry Smith sees as centered now in the big universities, but it need not, if secularity is rightly understood, be simply an activity of higher education; it can inform the processes of belief formation in the church. Inquiry is distinct in that the process does not terminate in a comprehensive system of finalized truth which will command universal assent. Insofar as members of a church believe that they have been given in Jesus Christ and the Scriptures universal, final truth about what genuine humanness and divinity are like, they begin with intellectual assumptions different from most of the university leaders.

The advocates of a theology of secularization in the colloquium stressed that a basic aspect of inquiry is that it accepts a major point of empiricism: study of faith and morality should plunge at once into the facts we have about concrete things and human relationships in religious organizations. Inquiring, represented in the biblical acts of the prophets or of Jesus, has no use for some theoretic freedom or absolute value. Words and deeds are always related to something finite, which has operational boundaries, and a frame of reference permitting a person to set goals of inquiry with some chance of achievement.

What is understood today in most scientific circles is that the inquirer has contributed to the shaping of "facts" and "objects." Harry Smith noted that recognition of this situation provided a basis for trying different ways of ordering data about the world and for envisioning different social policies. The inquirer has contributed to making new possibilities for humane communities. What he knows about the world and what he plans to do in it are a constant and creative relationship.

William F. Lynch, in his book *Images of Hope*[3] (referred to by several members of the colloquium), observes that a wise poet (unidentified) once said that "the highest test of civilization is its sense of fact." A fact, a situation, a context, a realm of reality, is a necessary beginning to prophetic inquiry. One begins with the truth that is known about a particular situation, a real external part of the world, which dissatisfies or excites people either as a restraint on their humanness or as an offer of some hope to those involved. If the discussion begins with the introduction into public consciousness of what first outraged people, because it blocks hope for more meaning and significance to life, an important act of healing of the body politic has taken place. The act marks an end to private fantasies. Men and women are able consciously to look at what problems and realities they may be able to handle and no longer see the area as full of mystery. This reduces fear and hostility toward the situation under inquiry. The deeper a group probes the concrete realities of a situation, the more options for action can be envisioned. The prophetic-ethical imagination feeds on reality.

One of the basic realms of reality involved in such inquiry is that of academic disciplines and departments in the university. Harry Smith argues that "the church has to grant a certain independence and freedom to these disciplines." If truth is pluralistic, and if there is particular truth that cannot be usurped by theology, religious leaders have "to re-

---

3. William F. Lynch, S.J., *Images of Hope: Imagination as a Healer of the Hopeless* (Baltimore-Dublin: Helicon, 1965), p. 195.

spect the autonomy of disciplines in the university." Knowledge by Christians of these disciplines, he argues, is not best learned when filtered through a theology of culture, picking and choosing ideas to fit the purposes of a particular discipline, but is acquired through direct study of them.

It has been the experience of many campus ministers seeking to involve faculty in church-sponsored studies or instruction that they will usually resist participation in such an arrangement unless they see it as contributing to the basic theoretical concerns of their discipline and as part of a process which induces further inquiry. Inquiry for them is a continuing life style in which each stage of inquiry begins a new line of investigation and is related to an accumulating fund of knowledge. It is best, then, that church leaders, whenever they seek arrangements for study with the university, think of dealing with people who see inquiry as a state of thinking about the world which has certain canons of method, but no end in view of arriving at a set of absolute propositions, a system of belief, or a final solution of a public problem.

Prophetic inquiry is to be seen by the church, then, as not aimed at arrival at a systematic theological content to be transmitted to members; this belongs more to the preaching and priestly modes of ministry. The formal principle of inquiry and the environmental contexts of decision are not true or false in an absolute sense; they are appropriate or inappropriate, justified or not, in terms of the object of study, whether this be God, man, or society.

The results of inquiry ideally, then, belong finally to a community of scholars, not to an individual inquirer, or client. Hence most university faculty expect to participate in an arrangement with the church in which what is learned moves out through the academic and technical channels of communication. Without this, the discovery of relationships or connections among phenomena is not possible, and a crucial criterion of academic disciplines is violated.

Prophetic inquiry, in the view of most "secular ministers," will not give up imagining and hypothesizing about the factors that have brought about a human problem, about ways out of difficulties, or about different perspectives from which a life situation can be viewed. This is the point at which, they observe, art and science come to a mutuality of cultures. The life of the creative, artistic imagination is united with the whole scientific enterprise of hypothesizing, ordering and reordering, dividing and redividing reality.

The chief difficulty which many scientists in the colloquium had with advocates of this view of intellectual inquiry was that it idealized scientific and technological studies to the point of distorting the actual tensions and dilemmas that most faculty face. They regarded this picture of university inquiry as undiscriminating in the diverse ways it proceeds in the university. The important questions about learning and discovery of facts in the university cannot be illumed, they argue, by the church's simply adapting to the scientific, technical culture which Harvey Cox or Harry Smith describes. The internal questioning in that culture is too vigorous and the doubts about its self-sufficiency to make policy judgments too great for this. As Waldo Beach, a Christian ethicist at Duke, observed, "Selectivity goes on even in the theologies of secularization, which often represent a very doctrinaire, sectarian and parochial view both of religion and science." The university curriculum expands constantly, the data grow in geometric proportions, new specializations evolve, and new alliances are formed between them; but these developments are not observed by many a campus minister, who, anxious about his own status and role in the university, becomes imitative of what he thinks the most influential or respected faculty do. He eulogizes the dominant sectors of the university in his attempt to restore science in the church to the family of human aspirations and ignores the imbalances in research allocation in the economics of higher education. He becomes overfond of setting up conferences for parish ministers that simply expose them to social and physical science lectures on cybernetics, technology, social change, and so on.

W. D. White, a professor in religious studies at Duke University, argued in the colloquium that the secular theologians distorted not only the work and ethical dilemmas of the scientific community but that of theologians and ethicists in the university, such as Richard R. Niebuhr and James Gustafson. These men are in steady and disciplined dialogue with members of various professional and technical schools. Out of such scholarship is emerging, not the "secular city" of popular journalism, but a complex mix of religious and secular forces. The religious commitment of leaders in politics, business, and education appears as a field marked by inner tension and release, doubt and trust, flexibility and form, specialization and imaginative association, with a variety of professional technicians. In most of their action fields, people and institutions are continually being challenged to accept or reject obligations and promises to use their resources and skills to meet human need. Men continually seek a pattern of conduct which preserves life and enhances well-being. Their serious explorations of religion seek the pervasive elements affecting our total being. Faith for Richard R. Niebuhr, for example, is the apprehension of the power and goodness that is God as the Power and Goodness in the field of energies and vitalities that encompasses us. "The Christian life," he notes, is "the perceptual endeavor to bring into a single focus our understanding of Christ as the pioneer of our humanity and as the infantryman who has advanced the farthest into the region where the power and goodness of God meet and are one."[4]

The relation between traditional Christianity and modern Western culture is much more ambiguous and complex than the secularization process indicates. The thought of secular ministers seems mainly to be characterized by a shift from emphasis on preservation and transmission of a cultural and religious heritage to discovery of new knowledge and technologies through experimentation. The "secular city" types are so impressed with the recent achievements of influence on the human and natural environment through this knowledge that they are unable to see the continuities between past and present culture. The future is left wholly open, so no drama of human action involving suffering, mystery, or evil is possible. The gospel of "freedom toward others" seems to assume that once secular man is free of the bonds of religious community, he will be truly free. This freedom apparently for many of the secular ministers supersedes that of Christ, since he believed in God, the Creator, Judge, and Redeemer of the human family.

Once the discussion of religious phenomena moves to the level of the specific data new inquiry is producing, the scholar discovers he needs a more adequate set of interpretative tools than the theologies of secularization provide. Sociologists of religion are just beginning to understand (a graduate student in the colloquium noted) what limiting effect the technological, empirical mind has on the worship and pastoral life of the churches. With such problems, a kind of baptism of the secularist's and technician's role is not the contribution to university life needed in the future. The secular theologian's point has been made that the churches must be aware that theology and worship of the future will speculate on the consequences to human beings of the technological and scientific patterns of development in the world. But it is time to move on from there, the colloquium concluded.

---

4. Richard R. Niebuhr, "A Power and a Goodness," *The Christian Century* (1 December 1965), p. 1474f.

Waldo Beach observed that many churches had already moved on. They view the process of secularization as going on regularly as an ordinary experience in congregations which rightly seek "to translate Christian faith into the idiom of the world." The Scriptures and history of the church have "prepared many Christians for the appearance of God's grace in the secular realm more than in the church. The scandal of Christendom, now public knowledge [Beach noted], is that Christ has been in recent years turning over the workplaces of the priests and scattering them in the world as much as he had been judging the practices in the market place outside the temple. The same scandal precipitated the Protestant Reformation; today's reformation strikes every church, Catholic and evangelical."

What is lacking in the major thrust of the secular church, as Beach viewed it, is the power to deal as rigorously with the forms of secularism in the university and mass media as has been done in the church. The use of powers of intellectual inquiry to fashion education around the values and interests of narrow and overspecialized concerns of scholarship needs to be criticized by the church so that the powers of students to act with compassion and wisdom in the modern world are developed. This he saw as the basic problem of the university. The university did not need celebration of its powers so much as it needed to be called prophetically to its servant role as an inquirer after the truth that humanizes and liberates men in the world.

Prophetic Inquiry as the Posing of Ethical and Theological Questions for the University and Society

The second characteristic of prophetic inquiry which emerged from the colloquium's discussions stresses the meaning of prophecy as it relates to learning and the discovery of new knowledge in the church and university.[5] Prophecy in the biblical tradition is the interpretation in clear and intelligible language of the will of God—an interpretation developed, not by some lonely idealist cut off from religious and educational communities, but by leaders who are deeply involved in the future actions of governors and landholders, peasants and housewives, and who speak afresh of the loyalties that have created a people. This prophet's interpretation is always warning or foretelling what are likely

---

5. The most relevant chapter in Volume II in conjunction with this section is Albert Rasmussen's "Religion and Education in Secular Society."

to be the consequences of the actions of the leaders of a people and the discernment of divine imperatives for the people's action in response. The biblical prophets never sought the ground of their insight in the popular will or in present events, but in resources of their own personal faith and community of belief. Therefore, prophetic inquiry, as the director of the study came to conceive it, will have as one basic component the serious search for the divine will and purpose in a situation through the resources of a historic and free association of believers. Theological and ethical attempts to discern what are for them binding expressions of the meaning of the Scriptures and the teachings of the church will be a legitimate part of any study enterprise the church conducts with the co-operation of the university.

Thus, Daniel D. Williams notes in a paper referred to by a member of the colloquium that the theological dimensions of public inquiry are as follows:

> The ideas of sin as misplaced allegiance, as ruptured fidelity, as pretension and pride, are not at first evoked in casual conversation (in technological and scientific inquiry). With its category of sin, theological inquiry takes the normal categories of ethical experience—standards and then violations —and unfolds a new set of meanings. These meanings are not necessarily discontinuous with ordinary experience, nor are they confined to the specific experiences that are to be had within ecclesiastical structure. They are meanings which are explored with the aid of theological discourse, as it seeks to understand the commitment it professes to a particular world view. They are meanings which are relevant to the analysis of loyalty-configurations, and the description of the quality of human relationships in interaction with what is held to be of surpassing worth.[6]

Prophetic inquiry raises the explicit, concrete questions of what men are seeking to do with their energies and resources and what ought to be done with them. The ethical questions that have been so long neglected in sciences concerned only with the means of achieving certain "given" or "assumed" ends are raised afresh.

This characteristic of inquiry was impressed on the colloquium less by the advocates of a theology of secularization than by those who were its chief critics. A paper written by W. D. White argued, for example, that "with the dissipation of the religious spirit, the ontological

---

6. Daniel D. Williams, unpublished paper on the "Metaphysics of Love," Union Theological Seminary, April 1967.

bent of the mind is refused, that is the inner imperative of the intellect to grasp reality, to be immersed in Being." Beauty and goodness are "made matters of subjective taste, concerning which there can be endless disputing, but not significant agreement or disagreement, and no really ultimate significance."[7]

Harry Smith, in reply, indicated that the university could be a moral commonwealth given to ethical reflection only on the condition that the church accepts it first as an intellectual commonwealth; that is, its moral role of finding out what is good in reality or of providing a critique on society has to have an intellectually justified function. Such work is done by the university in affirmation of its concerns for ideas that reveal what is real. The theology of secularization, Smith noted, frees man "from the clergy's efforts to impose a theological meaning or category on what men are able to do on their own without the systems and codes of institutional religion." In a doctoral dissertation he writes that the process of secularization is

> the movement from a view of the world as mysterious and demon-filled nature or substantial and self-explanatory cosmos to a view of the world as the realm of historical existence, to be studied, explored and experienced. Although this is a process traceable to the Biblical understanding of creation and Incarnation and the notion of worldly responsibility . . . it has prompted scientific research, technological development and political and economic reforms which do not necessarily acknowledge their debt to these insights. Wherever men no longer worship the world, neither living in fear of it nor ascribing a mysterious divine power to it, and wherever men accept responsibility for studying, understanding and preserving the order of the world—there secularization, thus conceived, has taken place. Wherever men have assumed that the world is their natural possession and depends upon human effort for ultimate wholeness and purpose, or have opposed the development of experimental science, belittled the penultimate in behalf of the "ultimate," and felt their faith threatened by the discovery of new truth—there the process of secularization has been short-circuited by the absolutizing of the relative on the one hand, or by the secularizing of the secular and the perversion of faith into ideology on the other.[8]

The world is not to be viewed now as a "thing" opposed to human

7. W. D. White, "The Study of Religion and the Liberal Arts," unpublished paper, Danforth Study Chapel Hill Colloquium, October, 1967.

8. Harry Smith, "The Secular Theologians and Higher Education in the United States," Ph.D. dissertation, Drew University, 1967, p. 81.

existence, eternal and alien. Man has a coresponsibility with God for the world; he is involved in it in a way which makes possible some understanding and control of it without full comprehension of its mysteries or destiny. There is in the secular theology, as Smith views it, a new sense of humanness, of man's potential powers to control his environment, as a corrective on doctrines of previous decades which have stressed his limitations and sin.

In the colloquium, the critics of this theology noted that overoptimism about the social capacities of human beings had been challenged by our failure to discern the sources of civil disorders, the inability to impress the meaning of dissent against the Vietnam war on party leaders, the incoherence of governmental attempts at meeting urban problems. The experience of profound misreadings of national and group aspirations in places where Americans have tried to shape the environment to new ends (as in Vietnam and Africa) had brought a renewed awareness of the continuing structures and processes in the varied histories and cultures of peoples.

Waldo Beach and W. D. White observed, for example, that it is difficult logically for the secular ministers to claim to see Christian meaning in the developments of secularization and still disavow a religious or unifying perspective. How is the latter essentially different from the *Weltanschauung* deplored? The secular ministers observed in response that they reject theologies that claim that Christ, as any of us know him, is a synthesis of all truth, that theology or any other discipline in the service of truth can make coherent order out of human existence, relating all parts to one another. Rather, they see the first task of faith and theology as protecting against false universalities.

The common ground that seemed to be reached in the reflections of the colloquium was that each man may, at a point in time, find it is possible to say that for oneself Jesus Christ and the images of life and the world associated with him have become the most meaningful perspective on life, and this makes one a member of a historic church. But the working out of the meaning of this faith in some kind of metaphysics and ethic does not necessitate projecting a static, total system of belief for others to adopt as their own. Rather, the logic of belief tries simply to point to where the processes and structures of reality, growth, life, and change in the world are to be found, so one can more fully participate in them.

To understand, then, the signs of the profane and of grace in the secular university, the lay student, faculty, and administrator have to achieve some theological literacy. This assumes much greater attention by the churches to lay inquiry into the relation of theology to secular responsibilities. Waldo Beach stressed that campus ministers could explore with social science students and faculty the meaning of their evaluative terms for action, such as the "degradation of man," "alienation," "depersonalization." He thought this exploration would soon discover that these terms made little sense apart from a Christian view of man as capable with modern technologies of giving new shape to human communities and institutions, but also as a man "fallen and separated" from God and his fellow man.

The response of the theologian of secularization to this statement was that it assumed the Christian could carry in his mind certain doctrines or images of Christian faith and use these to explain to the social scientists what they really meant by "alienation" and other concepts. In this way faith supposedly becomes embodied in the world or is used to explain what the world is really like. Many of the students who come to the student religious centers believe that God, temporarily way back there, occupied the mind and body of Jesus Christ, to show what He and the world were really like, and then pulled out. Campus ministers inviting lay scholars to the church would operate in the same way if they followed Beach's advice: use sociology to illustrate the meaning of Christian faith and then get out of the struggle for new knowledge of the society. The theologians of secularization say that this procedure belittles the world. Such a minister or church is really interested, not in what the social scientist does or says, but in what he does for religion, in what he conveys of the essence of the Christian faith. "The question I am asking," said one secular minister, "of the professional theologian and the dependable, stalwart laymen of the church is this: what is the essence of the Gospel which can exist apart from the world? I don't know of any." Yet, he argued, the questions being raised by most seminary-trained theologians and ministers depend on faculty belief that some divinely ordained system of behavior was revealed to man at one point in history and is preserved through the churches' memory of that event.

Look, for example, Smith noted, at how the Christian student movement circles of the 1950's formulated the "university question." The problem of the university was seen as the fragmentation of knowledge and overspecialization epitomized in scientific research and experimentation. Many Christian critics (Nash, Moberly, and others) presumed there was one truth, one language, one purpose, one way of learning that was Christian—a oneness held together by a metaphysical structure inherited from the Middle Ages and making possible the definition of the distinctive essence of each human institution.

This encourages the minister to reduce a sociological study or a novel to his own favorite theological categories. "This was what Waldo was really doing," noted Smith. "He was acting as if he could put the truth of the social scientists' study of alienation into propositions and show where it had failed to come up to the essence of the Christian faith. The whole picture of the minister is that all he has to do in encouraging the university inquiry is to translate its work into 'okay' theological language."

The secular man informed by a Bonhoefferian kind of Christian faith, Smith argued, perceives that the truth he experiences cannot be talked about in a "holistic" or "substantialistic" way, as one does in metaphysics. Rather, he perceives truth in a much more functional, pragmatic light. This is the way modern science and technology now view truth, he observes, and this is the way the theologian should view the truth, he holds. Smith wrote in a memorandum to the colloquium,

> The good works of men are (to be viewed as) no longer necessary for the realization of salvation, but as expression of man's responsibility for the world. Included in this freedom are the autonomous decisions of the human reason, as well as the establishment and maintenance of law and order, in the world. When the Apostle Paul said, "All is permitted" (I Cor. 10:23), this is truly a word of faith in that it recognizes the differences between the divine reality or salvation and man's efforts, preserving the secularity of the latter.[9]

What happens, then, to the work of the campus minister in the eyes of the advocates of a theology of secularization? Much of his traditional advocacy of theological meaning in world events is forsaken. What is retained, they are not sure. Most of what goes on in university inquiry is to be regarded as a "sphere of things indifferent" toward which the

---

9. Harry Smith, "Toward a Definition of Secularization," Paper for Chapel Hill-Durham Colloquium of the Danforth Study, January 21, 1964.

Christian faith has no decisive word to speak. The campus minister is not obligated to try to discover Christian presuppositions in the work of social science and humanities or to devise theological interpretations legitimizing their findings. He does not discover deeper realities "behind" the empirical facts of science. The structures discovered in empirical research and experiments are not the expression of a priori patterns or orders that God set up in the past and are now being maintained. They are expressive of man's autonomous (freed from religion) work in science and technology.

Harry Smith notes that theologies of secularization (such as Gogarten's), "by limiting the realm in which faith operates to the relationship of God to salvation, and hence repudiating the Church's claim to sovereignty over all the areas of the world," state a giant truth. This truth is that autonomy is granted to man's existence in the world and to the orders of life there, and a moral self-determination in which man is responsible now for himself is affirmed.

In such a context of "de-divinization" of academic disciplines, the faculty member does not claim that his theories save, that they are a part of cultic or worshipful acts, or that his personal meaning in life is dependent on them. Students and other scholars are free to try out various theories in understanding a situation and to exercise their intellectual powers on the academic work of faculty members. Such action need not destroy the faith of men in ultimate reality, in some final unity to the truth they partially perceive. But "such unity is given by God," and it can best be spoken of in the parables and stories of Jesus Christ and in the worship of the church.

If this is where the secular minister comes out, no one need be surprised that he in time abandons leadership in the church as offering too narrow a range of activities, and his church constituency moves on to an ethical humanism, regarding the church's teaching as a duplication of what can be learned elsewhere. A great many exponents of such a position leave clergy ranks for administrative or faculty positions in the university or in community organizations. The theology of secularization represents a renouncement of the images of neo-orthodoxy in which the Christian, by his loyalty to Jesus Christ and the depth of his theological training, stands in aggressive judgment on the American way of life and the technical-scientific methods of inquiry of the university. These campus ministers do not see themselves in polemical disputation with the university, trying to lift it up to some ideal level of existence. They talk more about "understanding the structures" of the university and "enabling" faculty and students to carry out the legitimate purposes of higher education. The Christian does not by his superior morality bring order and justice to a formless, evil world. The Christian is present in structures which already represent in great part responsible action and social analysis.

Opposition to this position in the colloquium came not simply from theologians but from social and natural scientists. They observed that the old questions of the unity of knowledge and the ultimate meaning of education have come back into the university and church, but they are asked in a new context and out of a new experience of reality. This comes to the surface in the places where men are trying to see the relation of science, technology, politics, human passion, and commitments in public affairs.

Every educational system, whether in church or school, involves a technology, procedures, and techniques, a specialized vocabulary as well as world views and ultimate loyalties. What is to be avoided is not technology, procedures, and techniques, a specialized vocabulary as intolerance of ambiguity, complexity, and serious involvement in the world. All branches of knowledge can produce narrow pockets of men who have plenty of information, but no cosmic and human range of concerns. Such men focus on career security, rather than adventure and change. They deify procedures which turn out a standard product; they want education that teaches procedures quickly and ignores the hard questions of the purposes of the techniques and the quality of interpersonal relations involved. The technique-oriented person makes God into a category or member of a class (for example, religious activity) and sees churchmen as members of it. What is missed is the symbols of religion which organize and co-ordinate the affairs of society and personal life and the spirit, intensity, and direction of commitment which direct a life.

Most faculty of the colloquium viewed Harry Smith's "empirical," "nonmetaphysical" approach as a distortion of the methods of science as many self-conscious practitioners of these disciplines see their work—men like Michael Polanyi and J. Bronowski. Certainly it was a distortion, Beach argued, of what most Christian theologians have meant by a "sacred realm" as distinct from the "secular." As he stated in the colloquium, the sacred realm for him was a definite body of doctrine expressing

> the historical, ecumenical consensus of the faith about the universe and man's place in it, about the nature of God as a holy, mysterious, omniscient power, and of man's relation to this ultimate reality as one of obedience and love, of recognition of man's creativeness and sinfulness, and of history as an area of fulfillment of divine purpose. This sacred realm is revealed and made incarnate in the figure of Jesus Christ so that men may know the terms of their authentic existence.

That this sacred realm is perverted into idolatry in the church, in the worship of the Bible, in the reduction of faith to certain religious practices, metaphysical concepts, or doctrines, Waldo Beach was quite willing to concede. But to claim that there was a way of thinking and acting faithfully without "religion" or "metaphysics," without cognitive commitments and mental images, struck Beach as a doctrinaire tenet of a theology that had itself lost touch with the work of the university and with human nature generally.

A scientific, secular university ethos may become the central focus of hope, the chief dispenser of soteriological images of a contemporary culture. The salvation the university offers is an escape from self-absorption in the objects of research and a creative openness between man and the world. But for the Christian, White noted, faith, loyalty, commitment, are decisive in human existence, not learning and teaching. Christian Truth cannot be completed in the intellectual activity of the human mind, but in the acceptance of Jesus Christ as Lord of one's life and the world and in an intelligible, dedicated witness to this truth. As White noted, the campus minister's inability to develop a critical distance between himself, his church, and the university is but part of wider cultural developments in which the biblical view of man has been replaced by the assumption that if men know, they will be and do.

If, therefore, university leaders come to understand themselves as offering a definite salvation once the world is pervaded by order and endowed with intelligence, it constitutes for the Christian a community of unbelief. The "secular realm" and "secularism," as Albert Rasmussen points out,[10] should be understood as the insular, overspecialized conditions of man. He is a man preoccupied with his own small saeculum

---

10. Rasmussen, *op. cit.*

or slot in an institution, so that he is not concerned with social policy. He does not really live in the world, but in special, technical pieces of it. He cannot, therefore, as Waldo Beach noted in a paper on "the secular and the whole," see that the "whole earth is full of God's glory." The holiness of a God who seeks the welfare of all mankind and the integrity and wholeness of each person is foreign to him. Jesus Christ is to be seen by the Christian as the most human of men, who attributed goodness and holiness to God alone. He lived in the area of "life between the religious and irreligious activities of his time," between the orthodox Jew and everyone else. And so a reconciliation of men and God began to take place, a world of human community began to replace the saecula, and some people experienced a kind of wholeness in social and personal being.

Prophetic Inquiry and Mutual Participation

Prophetic inquiry has a third characteristic, as seen in the discussion of the Chapel Hill colloquium. It insists that the attempts to envision or imagine what is possible in the future be an act of mutual participation or collaboration carried out by at least three forces of people in the society: religious leaders, university leaders, and public affairs leaders capable of making or influencing social policy.[11] The church is used to conceiving acts of piety as private devotions. The liberal arts or humanities sections of the university, with which religious studies have been traditionally associated, are also habituated to thinking of scholarly inquiry as an act carried on by individuals in their studies. Therefore, campus ministers with a strong sense of the social implications of their faith find they need to do a lot of reinterpreting of the prophetic tradition. Many of the members of these institutions have never conceived of organizing their corporate resources to engage in a common act of inquiry into the meaning of contemporary religious belief. But panic, despair, or hopelessness about what a person, an institution, or a community can do is rooted in the constrictions and fantasies of private searching for a "way out," for a definition of a problem, for a way of discovering a manageable area that will respond to one's actions.

---

11. The chapter by Thomas F. Green, "Toward an Action Theory of Learning for the Churches," Volume II, develops this and other themes and relates them explicitly to biblical theology.

The ministers representing the theologies of secularization stressed these aspects of inquiry more than the others, but a general consensus emerged on the issue we are describing. At the last session of the colloquium there was introduced into the "record" a paper by a campus minister in East Lansing, Michigan: Jack Harrison, director of the Institute of Christian Faith and Higher Education. In this paper Harrison noted that

massive social problems demand the concentration of massive resources just for their study, to say nothing of their resolution. There is no easy order in which these may be approached; they exist simultaneously and must be worked upon at once, not one at a time. The universities have the resources at their disposal for a beginning. If universities respond to their social responsibilities cast in the light of man's universal problems, a radical reform of universities is required.

Higher education must develop a way to bring all its available resources to bear on the human problems. These resources would include every administrator, every faculty member and every student in the university. They would also include every organization or political body, every practitioner and every kind of group or person affected by the problems of the society outside the university.

As Harrison notes, decisions would be required by the universities affecting the organization of academic disciplines, curriculum, and extracurricular activities. None of the major social problems can be approached simply by educating individuals and engaging in departmental research. An interdisciplinary way is required, as well as the organization of the curriculum around issues and problems to be solved. Specialties and disciplines need to be learned not only for their own truth but for the sake of the central curriculum and the social responsibilities of the participants in university life.

In the colloquium, faculty members indicated that many disciplines and specialties have reached dead ends in their dominant and present trends of scholarship; they show little sign of having inward resources of renewal. They need the stimulation of inquiry shared with another discipline, of participation in formation of social policy, if they are to find stimulating new lines of investigation and imagination. They need help, which campus ministers can supply, in envisioning new human problems and needs, new ways of conceiving their basic work. This help need not go on within the rigidities of traditional academic courses, schools, or departments, but can take place in newly created organizations: task force groups, institutes, special seminars, and the like. The purpose is not to replace an academic discipline, but to give it the chance to participate in a public act of community in order to renew itself. Prophetic inquiry goes on between persons seeking to use the resources of their disciplines and their common humanness for the maintenance or forging of a just social order, a beautiful commonwealth, a peaceful, humane society.

The act of prophetic inquiry in the church or university signifies, from the study director's point of view, that people have found it possible to trust one another and their work so as to act together in the service of others. Every act of a person asserting his judgment and responsibility in the world is a sign of confidence that the world will respond. When its object of study is social policy, prophetic inquiry looks with particular skepticism at situations in which men are claiming that people must choose between one absolute human value and all others. One human value is not always achieved at the expense of another. In social policy the public or institutional good is seldom dominated by one single mode or goal. Many factors, interests, and values enter into a situation, and the policy achieved is a discovery of where a number of these converge, feed back, and reinforce one another.

Prophetic inquiry, then, is the bringing to bear on a situation the sum total of perspectives, disciplines, and facilities available to men to form an adequate understanding of what they may do in it. The various images of a situation held by the church and university are not left scattered about in an array of courses, majors, institutes, and so on, but are brought to bear on a manageable part of the world or society.

Prophetic inquiry differs from evangelical forms of persuasion; it does not see its work as done in week-end conferences on massive themes of technology and faith, in quick shock exposures to urban social realities, in all the modern adaptations of nineteenth-century evangelistic assumptions about learning. Prophetic inquiry is developed in organizations of the church which are not asking for the quick decision or solution of communication about a social problem, but rather for ways of participating in a continuing process of learning that reflects the complexity and depth of division between racial groups, specializations, and professions in our society and the cost of nurturing healing action in whole systems and institutions of modern society.

So prophetic inquiry combines waiting, investigation, and confrontation. The capacity to let positions be heard out, to rearrange agenda, to make detours around obstacles of understanding, to keep in sight long-range expectations of an inquiry, to resist "short cuts" that ignore the basic forces at work in a situation—and to do so without despair or panic—comes only from extended experience in this work of ministry.

Some campus ministers talk loosely and irresponsibly about the "rigidity of outmoded academic disciplines," about setting up universities that can solve crisis situations without attention to all the intermediate steps of scholarship apparatus now used by the faculty. Much of this talk is ignorant of what means are necessary for the achievement of data in various fields and of the richness of the history of peoples and groups involved in social crisis. It is talk which always assumes that the present is the time to act, when it may be the future that provides the occasion for a convergence of forces and convictions capable of changes in the magnitude necessary to reconstruct a society.

For most faculty in the colloquium, the theology of secularization had no important new or constructive contribution to make to the kinds of decisions and actions they confronted in their special work in the university and in public policy controversies. They saw it chiefly as symptomatic of the extent to which church leadership had lost an understanding of, or belief in, their most fundamental historic convictions and had sought almost desperately for some kind of acceptance and respect in the major structures of society. As a paper by theologian John W. Dixon comments, "To the assertion that God created the secular order, I want to ask only, who else? I can rejoice that theologians have decided to take seriously the first chapter of Genesis and have arrived at the conclusion that the rest of the world will live its own life without their direction."

What has to be asked now is whether campus and parish ministries are going to enable the church to institute fundamental policy changes providing continuing critical reflection in the seminaries, the church-related colleges, and special institutes for continuing education. Such policy changes should not reduce the work of scholars to educational gimmicks or fad solutions, but rather invite participation of religious leaders with other informed people in assessing responsibilities in public processes and in the changing orientations of key leaders.

⊱ 13 ⊰

RELIGIOUS STUDIES AND CAMPUS MINISTRIES

THE Commission on Higher Education of the National Council of Churches convened in 1967 in New York a conference of the leaders of departments of religious studies in the United States. They gave almost no attention in their discussions or papers to the extracurricular aspects of religious studies, which indicates how little they regarded campus ministries as partners or resources in the teaching of religion in the university. In the same year, the National Association of Campus Ministries met at East Lansing, Michigan, and though they organized discussion groups and panels on urban ministries, student personnel problems, and so forth, they gave no attention to the development of research and teaching in departments of religious studies. Yet it would seem to the outsider that these should be complementary aspects of a common program in learning the nature of religious phenomena and practice.

It is our concern in this chapter to open up to discussion the questions which have to do with evaluation of the relation of campus ministries to formal departments of religious studies and to all other forms of learning about or in religion. We intend to look at a specific program of religious inquiry outside the classroom—Donald Shriver's exploration with laymen of the relations of religion and society—to examine its theories of learning and ethical content.

We begin with a simple fact discovered in our surveys.

Extracurricular Learning

There is a kind of teaching being developed by campus ministers which neither seeks "certification status," nor emulates faculty courses.

It seeks rather to develop its own criteria of learning which draws upon experiences in the church and universities in running academies, institutes, free universities, continuing education programs, dialogic seminars, and so on. These lie outside the usual formal course instruction with its heavy reliance on texts, a series of lectures by faculty, graded exams, and the passing on of faculty-dominated wisdom to recipient students.

The campus ministers who have been the chief explorers of this extracurricular or cocurricular development do not assume that they teach only about religion; they are actually exploring with students their practice of religion in the collective technologies and organizations of the society. This teaching probes the conscience of the participant as to how he has dealt in the past with relational problems of self-identity and social policy, cutting across and appropriating for a particular situation the work of a number of disciplines. It invites imaginative judgments about what to do in the world, as much as perceptive judgments seeking to understand the factors involved.

Planned relations between religious studies departments and the extra-activities curriculum are often nonexistent, because the faculty of of the former are anxious to avoid identification with practices of institutional religion and the stigma of "nonprofessional," "nonacademic" standards for successful teaching and research. It has been possible, however, in an increasing number of universities, for the relations to become mutual and creative. Thought and data originating in the religious center can provide opportunities for sensitive and revolutionary sources of new ideas for faculty research and course work: for example, in the reaction of public leaders and students in different departments to theories of the religion department. The extracurricular colloquia and task forces can represent opportunities for students and faculty to be more experimental, exploratory, multidimensional, and confessionally permissive in the teaching of religious thought and action. The positive aspects of a plurality of approaches to learning the nature of religious life and thought need to be more adequately and publicly understood among faculty, administrators, ministers, and students. The kinds of faith styles represented not only in the formal curriculum but in religious activities on campus are a subject, as we have seen, of immense empirical richness and complexity.

Today a number of campuses are the scenes of "listening faculties"

(West Virginia University) where informal discussion of career, influence of family and community background, changes in values and commitments, go on with a mix of academic research faculty, ministers, extension agents, and others. Brandeis University, under the encouragement of Rabbi Leonard Zion, has urged students first to organize courses and learning innovations outside the formal curriculum in service projects and then to assess them for use in the formal work of the university. The informal institutes, continuing consultations on religion and society or theology, ethics, and public affairs, are growing in numbers on American campuses as instruments of both the chapel and religion departments.

Hence, the understanding of what such pastors as Donald Shriver do in their work is important to this study. They are essentially trying to find out what settings and styles of learning are most conducive to critical reflection on the normative images, theories, technical data, and skills which have informed past actions and will influence future public acts of people in churches, businesses, parties, and so on in their region.[1] Examples, other than Don Shriver's program, are the Christian Faith and Higher Education Institute, East Lansing, Michigan; the Church and the World Institute, Philadelphia; the Ecumenical Associates, New Haven. These organizations have been influential in development not only of campus ministries but also of inner-city and suburban ministries as well, for they open up renewed association with university life.

These organizations are in most cases an evolution of ideas from the evangelical academies and covenant communities of Europe, but with an American twist. A much greater attention is paid to the mix of church, university, and public affairs people in the educational programs and to contact with continuing structures of research and inquiry.

Who in these organizations are campus ministers? They may be the victims of politicians running decadent party machinery in the inner city or challengers of the indifference of doctors and nurses to the special medical problems of the poor in a major medical center. They may be

---

1. Among a number of useful discussions of the ideas that inform this kind of inquiry are John Bennett, *Christian Ethics and Social Policy* (New York: Scribner, 1946); James Gustafson, "Christian Faith and Social Policy," in Paul Ramsey, ed., *Faith and Ethics* (New York: Peter Smith, 1959); Edward L. Long, Jr., *A Survey of Christian Ethics* (New York: Oxford University Press, 1967). See also Volume II, paper by Kenneth Underwood, "An Experiment in Critical Inquiry Into the Ethics and Religion of Public Leaders, Wesleyan University."

community planners with some questions to ask of students in architecture, sociology, and political science—questions that do not seem to be the technical responsibility of any one discipline in the university. The man who ministers may be a visiting juvenile court judge, discovered by a campus clergyman to have begun a staff research colloquium that makes an interesting use of university students from social work, law, psychology, and theology in understanding first offenders. The campus minister may be, more conventionally, a clergyman seeking to open up the human consequences of past social policies by the churches as they have built churches and retirement homes or raised money for pensions. This man asks of church administrators what they see to be the interconnections for future actions of the thought of church, university, and public leaders. The campus minister who does this has in the emerging literature of this mode of ministry the marks of "grace under pressure," of "historical consciousness," of the real "pro" on contemporary ethical problems of professional people about him.

What is being described is a way of action that cannot be envisioned apart from the developments already reported in previous chapters. These ministers are holding conferences and consultations which they regard as a contribution to learning and inquiry in the university and the church. They do not see them as one-shot, week-end attempts to change whole world views, but they work overtime with a carefully selected constituency. These activities take a certain expertness in defining social policies that will be brought under critical examination and discussion. They require decisions as to what mix of people and professions will be brought together. The talents of reporting and interpreting are often displayed. A substantive, disciplined content is supplied in describing the issues which seem to involve a college, a church, and a corporation.

With this noncurricular inquiry often comes a new status for a minister. It does not attain that of a scholar or a preacher in the university chapel. But such ministers earn the respect of laymen for bearing the risk of setting up conferences and consultations that will begin to conceptualize the responsibilities for research, learning, and public action in new, nebulous areas of human need not yet at the forefront of the specialist's attention.

The imagination and care involved in such "enabling" ministry can be seen in the literature of the Christian Faith and Higher Education

Institute: an intensive case study of a San Jose, Texas, church in a college town; report of queries put to a seminary faculty invited by the institute to learn about the research of the faculty in education at Michigan State; the investigation of ethical problems in agricultural economics; and so forth. They enable the faculty and students to discuss those issues in higher education they know have public consequence, but which none of the academic disciplines see yet as involving their academic status and competence.

These ministries are trying to carry out the charge of one of their professional organizations (National Campus Ministers Association). The following statement is from a working report of the Association, "Recommendations for 1966:"

> to be continuously involved in the study of the changing nature, philosophy and practice of higher education in our time in order that they may become more sensitive to the directions of change, aware of and informed concerning the significant problems, and competent to be engaged with persons both in higher education and the public domain, including the church at large, in seeking for solutions.

In short, we are reporting that the relations of students and faculty are characterized by an increasingly complex and dynamic pattern of extracurricular engagement in special lectures, consultations, action and work projects, internships, and covenant communities alternating with college study. Furthermore, in many administrative and faculty circles, the problems of organizing the educational experience of the student so that the relations of classroom to extracurricular learning and experience become more explicit have been recognized at last as worthy of intensive exploration. Policies are informed by new learning experiences, and freedom is granted to initiate programs responsive to surprising changes in student life and environment. The campus ministry has, of course, a great stake in these explorations.

By nature of their specialized role in a discipline, faculty may wish to explore only certain kinds of intellectual problems in their classrooms. But they will encourage the relational, speculative moral questions which their disciplines raise if these are taken up in noncurricular settings, such as in the churches. However, there are grave difficulties in such trends toward separation and specialization for church and university alike. Some professional schools now confine to the noncurricular areas the questions of responsibilities toward public policy or the relation of various world views to professional actions (as, in medical school, questions such as financing preventive medicine, manipulation of persons in research, group practice). Church leaders must continue to work toward having these matters be given sustained, disciplined thought and research in the formal studies of education and ensuring that many programs and issues first explored extracurricularly will be taken up by the research and learning agencies of the faculty.

The issue at stake in the growth of much of the "extra-activities curriculum," as Christopher Jencks calls it, may be that students are not getting in the existing university system what they need and want. Teachers need to be taught to teach—to relate research and action. Teachers and students need to know when they must leave people alone to order knowledge and data in their own ways and when they also have definable responsibilities for creating policies that deal with credits, tenure, rank, and size as well as course content, for these influence greatly the substance of education. Few faculty and students are prepared adequately for the tasks that need to be done. The church, as well as the family, the university, the government, has its role to play in this preparation. But thus far, as we noted in our student survey, only a small minority (10 to 14 percent) who participate in campus religious activities take part in discussion and study of educational policy and religion.

The question of the quality of the relationship between the university and special interest groups, research and industrial park programs,[2] government requests for scholarships directed toward meeting public crises, is all tied up now with the extracurricular learning process. All nationally known universities are deeply involved in efforts to serve these pressures for information and perspective on a changing world. These nonacademic institutions, like the churches, now have their own professional and vocational concerns built into the vast formal structures of higher education—in the definition of faculty disciplines, course offerings, and research resources for schools of agriculture, restaurant

2. John W. Daly, "Results of Survey to Determine Characteristics of Existing University Related Research and Industrial Park Programs," Albuquerque Industrial Development Service, 1966.

management, forestry, business, mass communications, foreign policy, area studies, and the like. And all have complex programs of extracurricular, noncredit education.

Among at least a significant minority of the faculty, the relationship increasingly sought is dialogic, one in which the university faculty and students seek to define their own particular mission in the society—that is, the kind of research and learning which is their forte—and to invite exploration of the significance of this work for the actions of various leaders in the society. The dominant concern now of many faculty primarily devoted to teaching is that these other encounters enhance the legitimate, long-run scholarly concerns of the faculty in the key historic disciplines and that they do not simply become the province of the "field work" office, the extension, or adult education, or deans who still wish to "teach a little." But the connections take time, imagination, and hard work to discover. And the method being explored is that of making the encounter an occasion for clarification of the theory or hypothesis under exploration in the undergraduate and graduate programs: the student has an opportunity to observe the reaction of responsible leadership to academic perspectives on his situation, to see how he appropriates a particular discipline's view and data into a larger frame of action.

Happily, also, we are now seeing in the social and behavioral sciences a growing sophistication and interest in the relations between the individual's orientation toward reality and his overt actions in the various structures of society.[3]

An Experimental Program in Religion and Society

One of the pioneers of the possibilities for the church in extracurricular education is Donald W. Shriver, Jr., minister for a decade to the Raleigh, North Carolina, State University, a school with a long tradition

---

3. Maurice Natanson's *Philosophy in the Social Sciences* (New York: Random House, 1963), Michael Polanyi's *Personal Knowledge* (Chicago: University of Chicago Press, 1958), and Glenn Tinder's *The Crisis of Political Imagination* (New York: Charles Scribners Sons, 1964), are but three reports on the widespread questioning of past disjunctions and discontinuities which social science and theology have established or assumed for all people between perceptions of ultimate reality and professional mission, between person and knowledge, between inward belief and public act.

of agricultural and technical education combined with liberal arts. His "Experimental Program in Religion and Society" draws upon the earlier experience of a number of American experiences, but enriches and extends their application. He indicates that his program follows the same "three-cornered dialogue" as the Wesleyan experiment, combining people from the church, university, and the civic community.[4] He is chiefly dealing with leaders in the white middle class: administrators, teachers, technicians, and scientists. In all, he has involved 17 businessmen, 12 politicians, 15 theologians, 12 scientists, and 16 other university professors over a period of three years' concentrated study, including a fresh look at Gastonia, North Carolina, site of Liston Pope's *Millhands and Preachers*.[5]

He reports that his initial problem is to get church, university, and community leaders to understand how the realities of their lives transcend their "institutional niches." In a sermon on "The Holy and the Secular," he pictures secular men as entrapped by narrow loyalties in slots and pockets of the society such as class, caste, and technical or guild divisions. He seeks to explore with them common social and public problems and the problems of adaptation and legitimatization of their own professional careers. He is particularly interested in their roles in new, informally structured communities of persuasion and voluntary association such as church and university groups for adult reflection and criticism of the pervading society. He finds abundant evidence that many experts are not satisfied with their way of existence and "welcome a chance to square [their] thinking as a scientist with that of the church," or "to reflect on long-range goals, not tomorrow's lectures," or "to hear in surprise what a man in another walk of life says about public issues or reactions to treatment by the specialists."[6]

The reservations the Danforth Study staff had about this aspect of the program had to do principally with the definition of constituencies sampled. Representation of student power, Black Power, and women's rights leadership was not included, so that many of the new social forces

---

4. See Kenneth Underwood, Volume II, op. cit.

5. Liston Pope, *Millhands and Preachers* (New Haven: Yale University Press, 1942).

6. These quotes are taken from reports sent to the Danforth Study by graduate student interpreters of the meeting, and sponsored by our study of campus ministers. They are in the Campus Ministry Archives at Yale University Divinity School Library as "Donald Shriver Program Reports."

influencing the Raleigh–Chapel Hill area were not brought into the discussions.[7] These groups need the encouragement and legitimacy which inclusion in such projects can provide; the seminars provide an access to the establishment structures where personal association and confrontation can go beyond marches and demonstrations. Shriver reached similar conclusions in criticism of his own program.[8]

The second conclusion Shriver came to was that "inter-personal communication is as difficult and time-consuming as it is important."[9] We live in a society, he argues, increasingly vexed by decisions that exceed the competence of any particular specialist. Therefore the problem of finding models of discussion and action that are fruitful is exceedingly difficult.

Shriver's consultation reveals that the professional ministry, as well as the most profoundly devout laity, have reached in many congregations an almost incapacitating cynicism of doubt as to whether the images and principles which pervade the language of the pulpit and theologian have empirical reference outside the mind of the speakers. For an institution whose Scriptures reveal the unity of word and deed in the relations of God and man ("God said, Let there be light, and there was light"), the situation is fraught with anxiety. The churchgoer and minister are often caught up in a relation of empty roles and bad faith where people think one thing and do another. Experts in religious studies see that much pietistic, fundamentalist, neo-orthodox language of the faith provides an escape for the churchgoer from the real world of social change, racial evil, and moral ambiguity.

One of the greatest blocks to interpersonal communication in Shriver's seminars is the inadequacy of existing models of moral inquiry and action in the academic world. Shriver is aware that the great giants of European and American Protestant ethical thought in the 1930's and 1940's, such as Emil Brunner and Reinhold Niebuhr, worked out tremendous motifs appreciating the influence of the created orders on action (Brunner) and the manipulative-power dimensions of moral behavior (Niebuhr). But these ethics are now unequal to the task of

---

7. The book, Robert McNeill, *God Wills Us Free; The Ordeal of a Southern Minister* (New York: Hill and Wang, 1965) in Chapel Hill indicates the existence of these forces in the area. So also does Anne Scott's chapter on "Women and Men" in Volume II.

8. Shriver, *op. cit.*

9. *Ibid.*, p. 31.

giving guidance in the creative transformation of the established, technical organizations Shriver deals with. Brunner certainly perceived that the scenes of most responsible action are in the created orders of society, but he was not able to bring to the analysis of specific orders the insight that could help men distinguish between viable patterns of authority and innovation in a company, a government, or a church bureau. On the other hand, Reinhold Niebuhr has been able to see in the relations of men within and between institutions the dynamic forces of power, influence, interest, coercion, and manipulation which an ethics of order and structure had not. His theories of countervailing power in the interest of justice in a sinful world need now, Shriver believes, to be brought up to date with analyses of Black Power, student power, and other developing structures necessary to a free, integrated society. And these motifs need to be handled so that the significance of the radical selfhood of contemporary existentialist thought is fully appreciated.

Students' views recorded in the Shriver project show their desire for more opportunity to participate personally in social movements of our time and to contribute a voice to the forming of policies of the institutions in which they work and live. But their ethical wisdom includes little knowledge and experience of listening and *being heard* in the established relations of authorities and officials in the university and other orders. They do exhibit a Niebuhrian awareness of the elements of violence and coercion in society and of the necessity of forming new political forces to achieve justice. Having learned the techniques and excitement of civil disobedience and protest, will they also be given opportunity to learn the techniques of responsible change and renewal in the "persuasive societies" of the established institutions and leaders of the society? Will they have the chance to learn in associations such as Shriver's seminars some of the options in exercise of authority in corporate life, the power of charismatic personal gifts to give new direction and mission to institutions and to humanize formal functions, the ability to find communities outside the formal organizational charts to judge and sustain their acts?

In the popular jargon of the day, Shriver is trying to understand and create the conditions where dialogue can take place, rather than simply confrontation in settings of violence and protest. Shriver has been part of a movement in campus ministry and other church groups toward what is termed "dialogic education." The University Christian Movement has in recent years been perhaps its chief spokesman, but the way of learning is shared by innumerable publications and agencies among church-sponsored organizations on campus. As Richard Kean, coeditor of *Campus Dialogue*, an intercampus publication devoted to an "interdisciplinary study of the future," has noted, "Critique and optimism are the raw materials for an old but presently unexercised art!" For dialogue to occur, "both the trust implied in optimism and the honesty inherent in a critique must be present. They make the difference between talking at and speaking with an individual or a group, and thus draw the distinction between an authoritarian and an authentic relationship."[10]

The promoters of dialogic education in campus ministry circles are not opponents of technological communication innovations in higher education. They see closed-circuit television, teaching machines, and computers, for example, as increasing the opportunities for face-to-face conversation between students, faculty, and public leaders, since these can help in reducing the class load of teachers and can facilitate the transmission of specialized data.

In the contemporary educational situation, the professor's essential role is that of a human catalyst and responsible agent seeking to relate his special discipline to other knowledge in reaching judgments as to what is happening in the world. The professor in a dialogic situation is freed from an authoritarian role. He is not expected to structure the conversation so that concepts of his discipline always determine the direction of the inquiry. In less structured but responsible conversation, human concerns are foremost and need not follow traditional disciplinary channels. The thinking is action-oriented and therefore reflects on relationships of persons, groups, and disciplines, rather than a set of categories favored by the instructor.

The dialogic model of learning, as Don Shriver, Paul Schrading, Robert Theobald, and others developed it in preparation for the 1968 conference of the University Christian Movement, was intended not simply for higher education but for most organizations in a community or city. "There is every possibility that the dialogic community might become the basis for a new civilization," one enthusiastic participant in the UCM consultations observed. What the dialogic model stresses is that the need for conversation springs from a communal concern with

10. Richard Kean, "The University in a Cybernated Era," *Motive* (March–April 1967), p. 45.

a troublesome human problem and that the specialist can gauge his contribution in terms of its relevance to that common experience. The model also stresses the nonstructural nature of the processes of discussion, allowing for a shift in emphasis when something important happens that does not fit anyone's preconceptions of what ought to be discussed or studied. As the group develops and the discussion continues, the interrelated complexity of the subject of concern becomes clearer. The need for speculation by specialists about how to view the situation and shape it in the future is transcended.

The models of learning which have emerged from the experiences of ministers on campus over the past two decades are much more complex and rich than that envisioned by the images of dialogue drawn from the literature of existential theology and psychology. The dialogic education that these ministers have encouraged has been dependent on the continuing existence of structures of specialized research and instruction in the university and the governing orders of the society.

The third conviction to which Shriver has come is that the prophetic inquirer must always be on guard against his basic groups' developing into fairly comfortable, supportive centers of understanding in the lives of the participants who become reluctant to go beyond this experience to bring the resulting insights to bear in the rough, competitive gimmickry of the communication world outside. The familiar phenomenon of faith-and-life or covenant communities is that the ready participants in the atmosphere of dialogic education in time cut themselves off from people who do not share their rules of communication and inquiry.[11] The intensive work of scholarship in a particular discipline is ignored; the people who have given up on being heard by establishment leaders are excluded from the colloquia. The task of attracting a selected group of concerned, liberal, open-minded leaders is achieved, but little impact is made on the world outside the hallowed enterprise.

Late in the project Don Shriver began to correct this tendency by establishing formal ties with other institutions in order to use his leaders in their educational programs. His most notable experience in interinstitutional participation was with three regional theological schools, Duke Divinity School, Union Theological Seminary in Virginia, and Virginia Theological Seminary. The impact of the task forces produced

---

11. David Duncombe, "An Experiment in Evaluation of Faith and Life Communities," in Volume II, explains the realities of this phenomenon in detail.

a program of internships for theological students in industrial, political, and technological organizations in Washington, Richmond, and the Raleigh-Durham area. Relations to the universities themselves have been much less developed in Shriver's extracurricular program. We turn next to this problem.

Campus Ministries and Departments of Religious Studies

The number of legitimate models for study of religion in private and public universities has greatly expanded, along with the controversies.[12] An administrator in a state university, for example, may have become aware of a clarified legal situation, making it quite possible to provide academic study of religion, free of sectarian objectives. But he may need help in understanding the options available in the organization of such studies and the intellectual and religious interests involved.

From whom does he seek objective advice in establishing new departments or expanding established departments? Largely from the academic community, for he is fearful of sectarian divisiveness among the church leaders. The models being developed in the public universities are particularly important in freeing the study of religion from the control of the seminary or church.[13]

Until a couple of decades ago, there was a dominant, basic curriculum structure developed in the seminaries; Bible, History of Christianity, Theology, Christian Ethics, and History of Religion. This is a structure of curriculum and scholarship in religion rooted in a period when the humanities were seen as the chief carriers of religiously informed culture, when higher education was thought to be concerned primarily with liberalizing the individual student so he could develop his own style of life, and the task of the orthodox Christian church was an evangelical one of saving individual souls from the world.

---

12. Robert Michaelsen, *The Study of Religion in American Universities* (New Haven: Society for Religion and Higher Education, 1965); Clyde Holbrook, *Religion as a Humanistic Discipline* (Englewood Cliffs: Prentice-Hall, 1963); Paul Ramsey, ed., *Religion* (Englewood Cliffs: Prentice-Hall, 1965); Christain Gauss, ed., *The Teaching of Religion in American Higher Education* (New York: Ronald Press, 1951); Milton D. McLean and Harry H. Kimler, *The Teaching of Religion in State Universities* (Ann Arbor: University of Michigan Press, 1960).

13. The Consultation of the Study of Religion arranged by the Department of Higher Education, National Council of Churches, January, 1967, explored many of the options. Working papers were prepared by Paul Harrison, Luther Harshbarger, Wesley A. Hotchkiss, and Robert Michaelsen.

The study of religion in the university is now breaking from this seminary-dominated structure toward a much wider involvement of the scientific disciplines, greater attention to the relation of selfhood to corporate and public life, and religious commitment as a multidimensional phenomenon ordering and pervading the whole realm of action in a person's life. The scientific disciplines such as sociology, anthropology, economics, psychology, archeology, and philosophy have greatly expanded their study of religion. Academic and public interpretations of the relation of religious commitments to values, social attitudes, intellectual inquiry, and personality development are no longer formed chiefly by people trained in theology, history, literary criticism, and philosophy.

Faculty, administrators, and ministers are just beginning to understand the implications of this shift in academic structure. Apparently laymen and clergy alike are searching for more discriminating criteria for identifying religious world views from nonreligious ones, for distinguishing church activities that can be supported in good conscience and serious reflection from others that should be opposed or abandoned. In the eyes of students who take work in religion departments, the rapid growth of these departments is an important factor in developing a body of liberal arts graduates well grounded in the history and theology of all major religions and in the emergence of a liberal, ecumenical church leadership. Ninety per cent of the public universities and colleges now offer some courses in religion; increasing numbers of private universities and colleges are revamping their programs in religious studies. Meanwhile scores of seminaries are struggling to survive, and in the next decade perhaps as many as a hundred will be combined or merged into a few major ecumenical centers that have the resources of major universities available to them. Already university departments of religious studies are raising serious questions about the quality of the basic academic disciplines of the ministry as developed in the seminaries. Realignments are taking place between groups in the major denominations. Liberal Roman Catholics are combining forces with Presbyterians, Episcopalians, Methodists, and some Lutherans, while conservatives within these groups also seek some operative rapprochement.

In contrast to several decades ago, theology, sociology, and psychology of religion, intellectual and religious historical studies, are increasingly regarded in the general faculty as sound, growing, respected disciplines, and not as anachronistic throwbacks to another era. They are seen by their chief advocates (like Robert Michaelsen) as dealing with questions of the nature of the "total culture" and of integrative and dissident forces in it, with the relationship of disciplines in a morality of knowledge and so on—themes which have been neglected by other academic specialization. For example, the classic questions asked by Max Weber, Troeltsch, Tawney, and Durkheim about the relation of personal world views to the processes of modernization are coming again to the fore. There is a growing recognition that university scholarship has neglected the study of non-Christian, non-Jewish religions in their historical and cultural settings. These settings are now faced with the gravest problems of overpopulation, economic underdevelopment, racial strife, and tradition-frozen leadership. The questions of how to train or teach corps of administrators, teachers, and technicians now, so they can educate the younger generations, are being asked in missionary as well as university circles. The attempts to provide some basic theory and data on social dynamics guiding the United States' relations to these "have not" societies now involve a number of disciplines: psychology, economics, and political science as well as theology and ethics.

The initial problem of religious studies in the university is not that of adding a few more courses in non-Christian religions, but of an adequate definition of the field—its subject matter and epistemology. What are religious commitments, experiences, or world views, and how are they studied? What are the processes and forces in the university and all other associations which people regard as most influential in the formation of their beliefs? Do people with great doubts about the meaning of their parents' faith prefer the university classroom to the chapel for exploring developments in contemporary theology? Do they have an opportunity to test-practice their faithful conclusions in the classroom? Indeed, it seems likely that the problems of co-ordinating formal academic study of religion with social action efforts, and the reinterpretation of traditional dogma in relation to processes of secularization and political renewal, will dominate the next two decades of religious studies.

These are developments around which we might expect a great deal of study and reflection to center in denominational campus work, chaplaincies, and church-sponsored institutes. Both faculty academic-research interests and professional clerical concerns might converge in such questions. If the campus clergy have an academic expertise to distinguish them, would it not have to do with these questions: What resources of the university have actually been used by laymen and clergy involved in campus ministries to evaluate their work, to discover the variety of belief and unbelief among their present and potential constituencies? What methods of inquiry would people involved in the life of the churches near or on campuses prefer? What do they know about the research of sociologists and psychologists into religious commitments in their own academic institutions, and what critique do they make? The clergy on campus have considerable stake in the quality and nature of the religious studies which the administration and faculty provide.

In our society, we may be reaching the point where the only process by which belief is formed and acted on for most people is that of genuine inquiry in a college or university setting, and the testing of it in relation to the policies of institutions most influencing their lives. Yet inquiries into personal allegiances and loyalties seem to gain faculty and student support only when placed in a context of comparison with other viable world views and commitments. Students are looking for typologies of religious commitment which make possible comparative studies of religious life and its social influence in non-Western as well as Western countries, permitting the study on a world-wide basis of major options of belief. Such studies are conducted in terms of the internal integrity of each option and do not make a particular theistic faith the standard against which all other commitments are measured. The patterns of thought and action of a particular religion will need to be looked at both internally, as seen by participants, and externally, by those who view it from other perspectives. Students increasingly expect that no matter where they go to college, serious, "no nonsense" departments of religious studies will give them the opportunity to compare particular Protestant denominational traditions with others in the movement and with Catholic and Judaic thought—in short, that the ecumenical realities of contemporary Christianity will be represented on campus.

The criteria of objective, nonsectarian study are being worked out for primary and secondary schools as well as colleges. The resources of federal and state funding may in time be drawn upon in ways that will transform our knowledge of the relations of belief and action to the modern world and of the consequences of parish-sponsored religious education. Models of college and university departments of religious studies and of urban adult education in churches assume that theologians will be engaged in close co-operative research with men who use social science survey methods; with historians not only of ecclesiastical institutions but of cultural and intellectual movements, and with psychologists who probe the personal depths of ultimate commitment.

Too often the traditional pattern-maintenance institutions have tended to identify moral and religious concern with the realities explored only by the minister or by classical liberal arts disciplines. As a consequence, new, fruitful meanings of faith now being explored by empirical and technical disciplines outside the humanities have been neglected.

For example, our consultations with the medical educators gave priority to the placement of competent faculty in medical schools capable of bringing disciplined theological and ethical insight to bear in clinical, diagnostic situations. These new faculty also will have mastered the traditional academic discipline of the institution. Indeed, these new people may be the key agents for relating the churches more adequately to the professional world. Furthermore, clerical ministries on the boundaries of such institutions may depend on this strategic development. Provision should be made as well for these clerics' training by the new faculty in the life and work of a hospital, a computer-knowledge bank, a center for study of urban education, so they can minister better to the people in their parishes involved in such institutions.

The student population represents the most readily available, willing, and diverse subject of intensive inquiry into the changing nature of religious commitment in contemporary society. Forty per cent of the college-age group in our country is in some form of higher education—six million at present—and it is predicted that by 1975 one in two of all college-age young people will be in some form of higher education. Over 100,000 of these students are potential leaders from foreign countries (faced with problems of the relations of religion and technology). A campus ministry's concern with students is not an escape from the world, but knowledge about the faith and life of most of that half of our population which is under twenty-six years of age. Moreover, a large sector of adult population is engaged in some form of continuing education, putting increasing pressure on the colleges and universities to enlarge all kinds of liberal arts, postprofessional, and public problem-solving education. The proportion of commuting, as distinguished from residential, students in most cities represents the majority of college students. The spread of education is so rapid geographically that within a decade it is unlikely that any parish church will be more than a few easy-commuting miles from a college or university. So churches come into a vital part of their potential constituency by encouraging the university to make free and full use of its resources for study of student religious life and activity. In turn, the churches have opportunity to open up questions as to whether academic disciplines have made adequate use of the theological and historical resources of the church.

Thus, a statement of James Perkins, president of Cornell, that the most significant academic progress is traceable to the interplay and tension connected with the acquisition, transmission, and application of knowledge has particular meaning here. "It is this interaction that creates needs for new knowledge, that brings inaccurate teaching to account, that shows the world what could be rather than what is. Taken separately the three aspects of knowledge lead nowhere; together they can and have produced an explosion that has changed the world."[14] Following President Perkins' lead, the activities of campus ministries and departments of religion might well be studied in each institution in terms of the attention they give to major types of research, historical scholarship, and teaching and to their integration.

Campus ministries and departments of religion both have their strong points and their weaknesses in actual influence on the religious commitments of those they teach. The task is too formidable—with too many counterinfluences—for the religious leadership to fail to co-ordinate their resources. The answers to our interview questions to campus ministers and teachers about developments in departments of religious studies lead us to conclude that many of the "new breed" of antiestablishment, existential, and personalistic campus ministers on the "left" are as out of touch with the research and teaching life of the university as are the fundamentalist and conservative forces. The "liberation" from a religious world view, symbolized in Harry Smith's position in contrast to that of Donald Shriver, has produced a dangerous indifference to developments in religious studies. Where for example, is the research into religious commitment in the larger society to go on? The churches should not be left with only the alternative of the abstract, popular

---

14. James A. Perkins, *The University in Transition* (Princeton: Princeton University Press, 1966), pp. 7, 8.

polemics of the new secular piety and the cruder know-nothingism of the fundamentalists. The day-to-day personal relations of campus clergy and scholars in religious studies may turn out to be as important to the health of the church and university as the establishment of ecumenical institutes and other organizations aimed to bridge the gap between study and practice of religion.

The departments of religious studies have much to gain, also, from this relationship, for there are abundant data to indicate that to most students and faculty, it is quite problematic that study of religion will affect the day-to-day morality and religious practice of a student's life. In both student and faculty surveys the ambivalence and confusions about the relation of religious thought to action are pronounced. In our student surveys, most of the students are not conscious of clear faculty support of or opposition to religious commitment. The faculty are seen rather as neutral in intent. Parents, campus clergy, and knowledge of other religions are seen by most students as having an influence toward inducing religious loyalties, but not the faculty (see Table 13–1). A

TABLE 13–1.   Factors Influencing Campus Religious Faith at University of Wisconsin*

	Influence toward Religion	No Effect	Strongly Away
Science	136	334	975
Parents	785	250	204
Campus Clergy	663	525	59
Knowledge of Other Religions	590	338	317
Faculty	81	724	439

*Absolute number of students in total sample.

scientific, moral view is seen as the chief dynamic factor moving students away from religion. This is why sophisticated study of the relations of theology and ethics of science and the technology it produces, rather than the old juxtaposition of the two, seems so pressing to students.

Yet a special study of faculty views of religion and action among North Carolina State University faculty[15] discovered that the teachers

15. Edward C. Lehman, Jr., "Religion and the North Carolina State University Faculty," presented to Science and Theology Discussion Group, Study of Religion and Society, North Carolina State University (mimeographed), 1966.

of religion are among the most doubtful of the faculty as to whether there is any significant connection between religious belief and social or public acts. This survey followed the five-dimensional paradigm of religious involvement developed by Charles Glock and Rodney Stark. It included study of the beliefs followers of a religion were supposed to share (ideological), religious feelings and experiences (experiential), practices such as worship and praying (ritualistic), religious knowledge of sacred literature and theology (intellectual), and application of norms and values to secular affairs, the relevance of religion to modern decision-making situations of automation, use of food surplus, research usable for evil purposes, military decisions, or manipulation of people by the state (consequential). Lehman divided the probability sample (100 faculty) of those interviewed in these matters into three groups: agriculturally connected natural sciences, nonagricultural natural sciences, and social science–humanities. Those who taught religious studies were differentiated in the last group.

TABLE 13–2. Relations Between Dimensions of Religiosity

	Intellectual	Ritual	Experiential	Relevance	View of Bible
Ideological	−.03	.68	.36	.61	.84
Intellectual		.04	−.04	−.11	−.24
Ritual			.42	.55	.80
Experiential				.42	.60
Relevance					.68

Lehman found on the ideological level that over one-half of the faculty accepted the Judaeo-Christian beliefs without reservations, 31 per cent had reservations, and only 3 per cent rejected them outright. On the experiential level only 6 per cent received the highest score, in comparison with over half in ideological agreement. On the ritual dimension 22 per cent received the highest possible score with wide distribution; 55 per cent attend church weekly, as compared to 32 per cent of the national population. On the intellectual scores, 57 per cent of the groups were below 7 on a 10-point scale.

The most significant data are on the relevance or consequences of religion. Only 30 per cent of the faculty perceived Christian religion as being relevant to all five of the decision-making situations. Eighteen per cent saw no guidance from religion for any of the issues; 63 per cent perceived faith as relevant in three or more situations. The more the respondents know about their tradition's essential beliefs, the more they tend to view it as irrelevant to modern life.

Faculty raised in the faith tend to hold more traditional beliefs and view religion as relevant to modern problems. The higher the class status, the less relevant religion seems and the less knowledge of it. The faculty raised in religious homes score higher in all dimensions. The better the academic rating of the undergraduate college attended, the less likely that the faculty member accepts the Christian tradition. The more faculty identify with their own discipline, the less religious involvement.

As to correlates in type of discipline, the nonscientist (humanist-social scientist) tends to have the lower score of involvement religiously. Those who objectively study religion as a part of their professional activity have greater doubts about the relevance of Christianity to modern problems than those who study it less professionally. This is to say that the optimism of the promoters of religious studies in the university that their growth in size and complexity can be correlated with acceptance and relevance of faith may not be firmly established. Questions have to be asked as to what kind of faith, epistemologies, and morality of knowledge are being talked about. We are back with the issues of our first chapter on California ministries. Sociologists, historians, and psychologists who see religion as a dependent variable tend toward a naturalistic explanation of Christianity. Academic disciplines and majors do affect religious behavior, often in ways not understood or envisioned by those who enter into them. It is possible to take theological stances which assume irrelevance of religion or evade the issue.

This leads us to advocate in policy terms that choices of scholars for departments not only rest on whether they have done their work in a particular discipline but consider also what epistemologies and modalities of action govern their work. It is important, as a complement to the present men in many departments, that additional appointments bring to the campus men who see their own professional specialized competence as requiring dialogic-academic structures in which a world view and the ideational aspects of a number of basic disciplines are speculated about in terms of their operational significance in some major contemporary institutions of the society. These may be campus ministers as well as faculty. Most religion departments have thus far given their chief attention to existential, individual questions intrinsic and standard in their specialization as now practiced. The departments do not yet represent to the faculty and students a serious exploration of the relations of personal religious commitment to significant cultural events and public policies in the nation or to other careers than in the church or scholarship.

The larger structures of professional scholarship and teaching of the faculty are as important to the students' knowledge of what it is like for a person or a corporate enterprise to be religious as are the activities of a particular department.

There is no reason why the faculty and students cannot with great flexibility cluster and recluster, fight and make up, in the pursuit of knowledge about how various academic disciplines view the situations confronting actors in urban affairs, in struggles for church renewal, in professional education crises in law, medicine, and the ministry. An expensive college plant with residential buildings for a college to do this is not needed. But religion departments need to provide at least a theologian and a biblical scholar for a cluster of faculty working with students trying to understand the actions of people in careers they are considering and in facing problems they are soon to confront. If this does not happen, the students who are least reflective about their faith, are most given to an uncritical choice of a religiously meaningful career (in the church), and are most dissident and skeptical about religion are likely not to confront one another effectively. The effective setting is with scholars trying to discern what religious commitment or experience is like in the technical, public orders of contemporary society or in the whole life and career style of the student five, ten, fifteen years out in the world. Often students are found in a small-college religion department because they are trying to solve problems of their own worth and identity through their religious studies, or thew are entering a church-related vocation, or they are from a minister's family. Much more attention needs to be given with them to the connections of science and theology and of their concern for the quality of interpersonal relations to the policies of the bureaucracies of our society.

As to the relation of undergraduate religion department students to the graduate and professional schools, we can say this: the leaders of post-A.B. education are opening up a bit in their relations to undergraduate studies in religion. This has to do with their awareness of the increasing variety of legitimate options for religious studies available to the colleges and universities. The departmental choice is not a hard, clear one between preparing students for rigorous, specialized graduate or professional study and "liberating," "undisciplined" joys of general education. The opportunity for the student to test the full implications for personal and social action of a few basic images and theories may be more important than a department trying to offer a comparatively wide variety of courses. The opportunity to major in religious and historical studies or other combinations and to participate in an institute or a research colloquium, such as Shriver's, may give the richest undergraduate experience and provide what will be lacking most in the specialized work of graduate or professional school.

≫ 14 ≪

THINKING ABOUT A CITY IN ORDER TO REFORM IT:

THE PROCESS OF SELF-ANALYSIS AND OF

ETHICAL REFLECTION

(Pittsburgh)

W E have in this study examined three of the primary modes
adopted by campus ministers as they have sought to work meaningfully
in the highly varied, ambiguous contexts of the university. And we have
also observed the extent to which definitional uncertainties, the casting
about for roles that are useful to fundamental purposes, occur amidst
such student unrest and institutional confusion, generated by extraordinary social, technical change. This is change which is derived and
sustained in fundamental measure by the university's own scientific
inquiries, which in turn exert profound influence on the rest of the
university.

As Clark Kerr has rather vividly illustrated, national defense, health,
and space exploration, to suggest but three societal concerns, have
offered manifold technical questions which the modern university is
admirably suited to analyze and solve in patterns of involvement as old
as the Morrill Act. To these now must be adjoined a deeply mutual uni-
versity-society concern for the complex issues of urbanization and the
social disorders that flow from them. Involvement of academicians in
study of urban problems and processes, and in the formulation of policy
for their amelioration, now seems in the popular mind to be legitimately

This chapter and the following one were written in collaboration with Dr.
Elden Jacobson, a Fellow of The Washington Center for Metropolitan Studies,
Washington, D.C.

subsumed under such statements as Mayor Lindsay's: "The universities are emerging as one of the largest and most interesting employee groups in the city, and we should make sure they are used to full advantage."[1]

What is prophetic inquiry in such settings? What learning is to be mastered by campus ministers who seek to influence the normative choices confronting those possessors of competence and knowledge so eagerly pursued by government and business? Can Roman Catholic and Protestant leadership provide a constructive critique of the role of higher education in the renewal of urban environments? These were the questions and issues at stake in the Pittsburgh colloquium, established to explore what a special ministry to people in the institutions of higher learning of the region might be like.

Pittsburgh seemed a logical place for such an inquiry. The Roman Catholic bishop of the Pittsburgh Diocese established in the early 1960's an Oratory with a concentration of lay and clerical intellectual leadership and with assumptions for campus work significantly different from those of the Newman Club. Likewise, Protestant churches had established in the past few decades a number of centers for denominational and interdenominational work, marked by considerable conversation with Catholics and by experiments in lay theological studies of urban problems. Of equal importance, the situation which campus ministers confronted in the Pittsburgh area was characterized by the vigorous cooperative efforts, in the postwar period, of educational and business leaders in the reconstruction of the city. Too, the University of Pittsburgh was just emerging from a period of tremendous stress and divisiveness as it consciously bid for first-rank scientific and technical academic personnel. This action was strongly supported by the business and industrial community, recognizing the profound mutual connections between strong graduate and professional schools and the economic prosperity of the region.

The Pittsburgh area represents a vast complex system of educational institutions whose particular relations and missions, internal and external, to diverse, often contradictory publics are even now only partially understood by churchmen, citizens, and educators alike. In short, the convictions of all Christian leaders are being tested by the changes

---

1. Quoted in *The New York Times,* July 16, 1967.

taking place in higher education, which are in turn responses to developments in the larger urban scene.

A working group of ministers, academicians, and laymen was drawn together, representing among them the University of Pittsburgh, Carnegie Institute of Technology, Mount Mercy College, Chatham College, and Bethany College, in West Virginia. The participants were charged to lay bare the roots and the fundamental character of the relations of the principal moral agents in the churches, the institutions of higher education, and the larger urban society and to suggest implications of these relations for the campus ministry.

The colloquium would, it was expected, move through a series of explorations designed to establish a mode of self-critical reflection by campus ministers on their capacities to discern the significance of faith and morals for concrete problems and issues in the civic life of the area; they would examine the role of the city's universities in the processes of urban development and the churches' response in their own educational programs; they would think systematically about the present nature of those constituencies they presently invited to think critically about their roles in urban reform; and finally, they would seek to expose the bases of ethical inquiry in the church and university, the manifold principles and presuppositions which enable or thwart such inquiry. This chapter discusses the processes of self-analysis, particularly when turning to questions about which they professed no competence save as men and women seeking to understand the technical, urbanized scene of which they were a part.

As we have indicated in previous chapters, critical discussion and evaluation of what men did and thought in the recent past (1964–1965) risks distortion of the processes set in motion by the colloquium itself. As recent conversations with several of the colloquium's participants dramatically indicate, they are themselves highly critical of the narrow fields of vision and understanding revealed in the papers they wrote and in the responses they offered to those papers. Nonetheless, fundamental problems are evident in the Pittsburgh data that reside generally throughout the campus ministry, church, and university—fundamental questions of understanding and response in an overwhelming urban environment.

It is possible and useful to discern, with minimum violence to the materials, three significant areas of concern throughout the colloquium's deliberations. These men began, in response to the study's mandate, by reflecting on their own recent history, on themes and trends observable in their own study and teaching in relation to other modes of ministry. This moved, secondly, into more intensive reflection on the modes of ethical thought by which value judgments might be systematically formed in relation to major social institutions influencing urban change. The colloquium then considered, thirdly, the processes of renewal in the urban environment in which they sought to minister and the university role in those processes.

The Process of Self-direction in Corporate Inquiry

It is perhaps predictable that the colloquium's reflections are not unlike those of numerous colleagues elsewhere; Clarence Shedd's book title, *The Church Follows the Student,* translates and compresses into briefest compass a ministerial model which these men acknowledge as descriptive of, even normative for, much of their own previous work and understanding and deeply flawed as a useful concept now. As one campus minister observed in describing the Pittsburgh scene "before 1960":

> The Church Follows the Student . . . became a model for Pittsburgh. This was a distinct image of the church's understanding of its ministry through the various denominations. The function of the campus ministry in light of this image was to establish links among students of a given denomination in order that they might find their continuing life in the denominational setting and also to avoid their transfer to other denominations or away from any denomination during the college experience.[2]

The obvious corollary to denominational identification is "group orientation": emphasis on small groups of students meeting on some regular basis for, ostensibly, fellowship, worship, study, and discussion. Judgmental criteria are simple: "The success or failure of the campus ministry was determined by the size and effectiveness of the group"; and the recognized insufficiency of such thinking pervades the collo-

---

2. Quotations of colloquium members are taken either from questionnaire answers or from papers prepared by them and are on file as materials of the Pittsburgh Colloquium of the Danforth Foundation Study of Campus Ministries, Campus Ministry Archives, Yale University Divinity School Library, New Haven, Connecticut.

quium's deliberations. These men perceive with clarity the peripheral relationships of denominational-centered, group-type forms of ministry to the vital processes they discern in the university and city. Their discussions are permeated with the language of alternatives which seldom make sustained ethical inquiry a high priority: for instance, the freedom to wander, to engage, to talk, to challenge, to assist, to influence, unfettered by the institutional trappings and organizational detail of the denominational focus and center. It is true that these expressions of hope are themselves embodied in newly discovered means and possibilities partaking of learning—"floating" or "scouting" ministries, "faculty involvement," ecumenical and multiple ministries, "constructs for community," and, wistfully, an "impact on the total life and thought of the institutions of higher learning in Pittsburgh"—but the concrete modes of inquiry are not described.

There inheres within the disavowal of traditional ministerial modes the lack of conceptual clarity, observed throughout the study generally, as to new hopes and possibilities. The indistinct outlines of divergent images suggest again the ambiguities and indecisiveness of purpose with which they live. These images are crucial; in one will be found the personal, the freedom of direct and individual response to events, to the university, and to society, while another speaks of community, of mutual enhancement, of covenanting together in common purpose and tradition. They are not, of course, mutually exclusive, even as analytical constructs. But neither are they readily synthesized, and they coexist in the colloquium's thought, often unrecognized, always in uneasy tension in debates over the educational theories and practice of the ministry.

The first is perhaps most apparent in the frequently stated objective of "faculty involvement" in campus ministries. Both normative hope and sober actuality are conveyed in the following comments of colloquium participants.

It seems to me that both students and faculty, but particularly faculty, must be involved and recognized as responsible carriers of the campus ministry.

The sharpest critique of all, however, came when we realized that, except for a few beginnings of contact and rapport with faculty as such, the campus ministries were content to involve faculty occasionally as members of our Boards or as speakers in programs. The harder job of scouting out faculty interest in questions of epistemology or a theology of education was hardly begun.

"Responsible carriers": that is a suggestive phrase, and the colloquium actively sought to give it life and meaning. Thus, one participant asserts, concern for faculty resides in several observations of a "crucial nature":

> The faculty spends more time than any other member of the adult community in the college setting. . . . The faculty also shapes the values and attitudes of the students. . . . The average faculty is not aware of the role of the personal example he gives or of the meaning of personal relationships.

Faculty are, thus, channels of influence, but the dispiriting sequence of reasoning suggested—campus ministers desire influence over student values; faculty are large consumers of student time; therefore, to influence students, we must relate to faculty—exhibits again the extraordinary problems of men seeking new modes of thought and action for which previous training and perceptions are inadequate. The use of the term "faculty," for example, as a unity does not properly differentiate the diversity of involvement in urban problems, the complexities of values and perspectives observable in all but the most parochial of universities and colleges; and we know of no study which supports the quantitative relationship of time to influence offered here. Also, few faculty, we suspect, will accept the basic premise that they are "not aware of the meaning of personal relationships" to the extent that campus ministers must be employed to correct such deficiencies. Other responses in the colloquium sought to resolve these questions in more explicit terms. One by a Roman Catholic layman declared:

> One reason for the positivism and/or religious diffidence of faculty members is the fact that for most of them their level of religious comprehension is distressingly below that of their particular professional and general cultural sophistication. The campus minister, even as he is learning from the faculty, *must be prepared to teach them theology.* [Emphasis in the original.]

The romance and liberating spirit of such imagery leaps to the fore here. Campus ministers have transcended their peripheral position and limited concerns of the past for a heady equality with faculty in the future, a partnership through which shared competencies enhance the educational process. As one Protestant campus minister militantly asserts:

> The campus ministry must become relevant. To become relevant it must divest itself of this inexcusable image it has begotten of itself and which it pietistically portrays. It must throw off the notion that it is a moon to the academic sun. To carry this out it must prove itself to the academy academically. . . . If this is carried through then it should follow that the ministry will be instead of a service station, a partner in intellectual pursuits.

Hence, we are not surprised when the colloquium's deliberations frequently center on the campus minister's legitimation in the university context and the extent to which the standard accouterments in specialized graduate training are necessary requisites to the ministry they envisage for the future.

Thus it is freedom, independence, and equality of academic relationships, the personal, the unfettered "engagement with the academic and administrative factors of a great university center," that bespeak the awareness of God's action in higher learning. As one member of the colloquium later ruefully observed, "We were still entranced [in 1964] with a new sense of freedom. Some of us thought that was enough."

It is not, of course. And as the colloquium attempted to grapple with the manifold implications and potentialities of ideas introduced, and of action through which they might visibly affirm faith's stake in university and city life, the communal image came into view. The problems of mutual support had already resulted, during the early 1960's, in various attempts to "speak of co-operative efforts, divisions of labor in our ministry, worship, seminar leadership, and even efforts at combining office facilities," discussion which was clearly accelerated by the colloquium. Even as the heady language of relevance and influence pervaded their thought, they also expressed the more sober recognition that sustaining roots of tradition, of Christian belief and concern, are also crucial. "Community," "ecumenical efforts," "multiple ministries"—each bespeaks the groping for group awareness and identity that outlines this second image.

To what end, this "community"? Several papers sought to explicate the meaning and substance of this ethereal idea. "Community" is a "place of genuine meeting, of trust and of training"; it has the " 'style of life' or 'character' which is consistent with or reflects its commonly held goals, values, and loyalties" which "may or may not be consciously declared." Or, again, as another participant wrote: "Community would describe the rich fabric of association within a ministry; the mutual up-building of the saints, the conveying of the Christian witness, and the joy of discovery of God's truth in the university."

It need not, however, be limited to campus ministers. An examination of "community" among the faculty at Carnegie Tech suggested that this concept includes "a fairly high degree of interpersonal action and concern, as well as a shared sense that its members' individual purposes are mutually intelligible and commonly valued"; but this study began by concluding that "I must almost exclusively describe and explain the *absence* [emphasis in the original] of community on the Carnegie Tech campus."

A member of the Catholic Oratory feelingly declares: "As a further attack upon artificial and pernicious compartmentalization of Christian reality in the university, there ought to be developed a kind of community within the campus in which the work of education and the activity of worship are organically associated."

Yet, as the colloquium's deliberations were concluded, and participants reflected on its meaning and significance, a codirector depressingly observed that "the most serious deficiency found in this study is the lack of an identifiable community of persons involved in and concerned for the campus ministry."

How are we to account for the colloquium's inability to discover or create means by which this deficiency might be alleviated? Quite clearly, these men and women confront many of the forces we have observed throughout the campus ministry generally. Denominational pressures and expectations are evident, confusions exist regarding relationships with university administrations, and traditional student-oriented programing is no longer believed satisfactory. And opting for the imagery of "total involvement" has placed in bold relief the campus ministry's marginality to academic processes. They are surprised when a university department does not exhibit the characteristics of camaraderie they have defined "community" to contain, and they speak angrily, or for effect, of the "artificial and pernicious compartmentalization" which is the university's departmental system—understandable reactions to frequently encountered abuses. Efforts to translate these vivid perceptions into language meaningful in academic disciplinary debates, however, run afoul because they lack access to faculty and useful alternatives to difficult, highly complex institutional practices.

The Process of Thinking Ethically

Nor surprisingly, these images—the detached, "free-floating" scout in the institution and the self-conscious identification of a Christian "community"—occur throughout much of the colloquium's thought. Too, in the search to clarify the normative questions of act and influence in the university and the wider social order, corollary tensions between the personalistic-individual and social-institutional images become evident, setting in sharp contrast the crucial relationships between social awareness and technical competence.

The colloquium's major effort at systematic ethical reasoning was contained in a paper written for that purpose by a Catholic moral philosopher. It is a useful, often constructive endeavor, which begins with the observation that "the question of ethic and ethos is one so profoundly relevant for any Christian ministry that one suspects that its very centrality of import is involved with its frequent neglect." The paper moves easily, if briefly, through historical factors seen as vitiating the "ethical viability in our churches"; three receive explicit attention —the "fusion of religious faith and culturation," rejection of "credo in the name of mythos," and the "tendency to deprecate subjectivity" and to stand aghast at "value judgments"—from which derives the following conclusion: "This problem suggests, among other things, that the campus minister is not well advised to attempt philosophical neutrality, and that he has perhaps some serious educational work to get done with faculty collaborators."

And in what does such "educational work" consist? Four facets of campus minister–faculty "collaboration" are explicitly offered:

1. Fusion of their respective "problems and insights . . . should be realistically faced and concretely applied"; curriculum formation "ought not be excluded here."

2. Campus ministers must learn from faculty, who "supply a fund of empirical awareness which should in turn prevent the ministry from

developing circular habits of language and neoquietistic patterns of irrelevance."

3. Concomitantly, however, "theological teaching in depth" for faculty by campus ministers must be developed as a corrective balance to the "positivism and/or religious diffidence of faculty members."

4. There must be, as we have noted above, "as a further attack upon artificial and pernicious compartmentalization of Christian reality in the university" a form of "community" in which "the work of education and the activity of worship are organically associated."

How shall such considerations be implemented? Two "areas" require explicit attention: the achievement of Christian community in the university, and the theological formulation of that community, both of which are "joined" by the "vital structural concept of the *campus* ministry faculty conference," in which, again, the campus minister "works out a program of kerygmatic theological formation." The image here— buttressed with appeals to "the *central theological data of Christian faith*" as "taught and studied on a level proportionate to levels of investigation to which university professors are accustomed"—remains that of shared competencies, of Christian faculty and campus ministers who mutually learn through the confrontation of disciplinary expertise with carefully structured theology.

Also implicit in this image, however, and seemingly crucial to it, is the question of sequence; faculty must walk theologically before they may reasonably soar as ethically liberated spirits. To this end, therefore, campus ministers must develop a "dynamic criteriology of absolutism, as against tradition-directed, totally essentialist and natural laws of moral obligation," an ethic which transcends the existential posture of doubt and ambiguity from which we often "despair of achieving truth with any clarity." Such despair, deriving as it does from the pervasive forces of positivism in the academic world, is believed to characterize university faculty generally. Offered as a theologically grounded ethical alternative is, therefore, the distinction of the "negative" and "positive" will:

> Relating among other things, to a dynamic and holistic theory of personality development and maturity, it may be observed that the acts of positive virtue we perform are distinguished by their uniqueness; two acts of love are never alike. Man, in the state of openness to the world, and also in the posture of responsibility to his neighbor, is able to make contact

with the world and it with him. The nurture of encounter enables him to grow, and to grow in a radically individual way. For arising out of a good, bad or mediocre past which is nevertheless his, the combination of acquired traits and achieved truths, accident and environment, comes the epiphany of the moment, the challenge of the unique present. And in this epiphany be it faceted aesthetically, morally, politically . . . "the will of God for me" is found.

This will of God which is *for me* is the positive will of God; and the positive will of God turns out to be uniquely directed. . . .

God's negative will, however—the "shalt not"—is for all of us in all circumstances. To betray a friend, to seduce a girl, to give way to vengeance; these are universal structures; their evil does not depend upon momentary configurations; God does not speak through them in time.

Thus, "God's positive will" may be thought of as that which comes to us in any given moment, tempered only by the confluence of circumstances"—"weather, the person, and all other circumstances." But do men act, actually, in the random fashion such formulations imply? Too, patterns of morality not only are discernible from one historical period to another but are typically characterized by widely fluctuating, often nearly disjunctive, emphases. The paper recognizes such facts and thus invokes the concept of "evolutionary development" as an explanation of historical change in perceptions of the morally "right" act.

I would suggest that in the case of a moral idea, we can speak of its progress through three basic states of evolutionary development. In the first stage, keeping slavery in view as our example, it may well have not only escaped moral condemnation on the part of anyone, but, as certain authorities will assert, actually constituted an actual socio-ethical advance. At this stage not only was slavery not morally questioned, but the epistemic and psychological levels of consciousness, due to the total complex of factors in the world, *would not permit such questioning to occur.*

I would next jump to the third stage (the present) in which e.g., slavery is generally seen as morally wrong, generally unnecessary, certainly not particularly pleasant, and hence, almost universally eschewed.

The problem thus resides at the "second stage," where to sense the impropriety of slavery is to be "forced outside the realm of *present* practicability, and in effect thrown, willy-nilly, into the function of prophet." Such stages are believed discernible for a wide variety of social problems; society had entered the third stage regarding slavery and capital punishment, the second respecting "the problem of war and killing."

Well, war is certainly a crucial social issue affecting the future of cities; and ethical approaches which promise to enhance our capacity to understand and contravene are obviously of considerable interest. Inexplicably, however, none of the examples offered is examined in any systematic manner in relation to urban reform beyond the assertions offered. Rather, in order to illustrate the guidance an evolutionary approach to positive-negative will is presumed to contain, the discussion turns to an extended consideration of premarital sexual relations, concluding with the not altogether surprising statement that "we must judge it to be sinful, and make an attempt to avoid doing it." We have, after all, as individuals and as a society moved into that third stage where the "sane man of our time" must recognize that "in 'making love' where there is not love, [he] objectifies the other in the language of [his] body, and [is] hence guilty of deception and/or brutality," which is to say, "sin."

The paper draws to a close by asking a series of questions which seek to address issues, particularly in the context of business and industry: "What is the ethic of spending beyond one's needs? . . . Does advertising attempt to foster psychological attachment to worldly goods . . . ?" "I believe that here as elsewhere if the campus ministry in its ethical investigations is going to be meaningful it must ask most meaningful questions possible and let the answers fall where they may."

What are we to say to such efforts? Technical questions clearly occur at numerous, often critical points in the sequence of reasoning. However, the critical fault lies elsewhere. Offered to campus ministers and interested faculty "as an example of the kind of problem and perhaps the level of debate which can be useful," it is finally something less than that. It illuminates again the maddening gulf between the rhetoric of "relevance," of "total university involvement," and the limited, almost pedestrian result such "relevance" so frequently calls forth.

Relevance, of course, is susceptible of several meanings. It is not, finally, a substantive or self-contained category, but rather a quality of relationship between such categories, the "pertinence" of one category to another. Hence the question, pertinent to and for whom? As an exercise by the colloquium, therefore, in "thinking ethically," the constituency is clearly stated: "students" who "like embarrassing questions"; campus ministers "seeking ways to escape a role, image . . . of functionary decoration," and the "university" which "badly needs a structure of ethical concern within it."

Two considerations obtain. In a institution of specialized learning one must ask: Is what one says heard? Do the categories of thought, the language and form, adequately transcend the speaking in tongues so characteristic of disciplinary growth? Clearly the colloquium wrestled with such matters. Yet those same habits of discipline and usage are not easily set aside, and the paper lapses into the esoteric language and issues of which Christian thought has too frequently been guilty. Consider the following:

> It is in fact the absence of the whispering of the *logos;* the awful silence at the heart of chaos, the silence of non-being, that is so fearful about sin. And it is precisely when we step into the realm of chaos that we enter also the realm of anonymity, since we have moved away from the subtle structuring of our uniqueness which occurs when we answer the call of God in situations, and we have entered into the realm of universal negative structures of action.

Nor is hyperbole limited to the theological. To speak, for example, of human growth and development as "radically individual," while consistent with much that is current in both theological and philosophical thought, does insufficient justice to the continuities of need and habit the social sciences have carefully examined for several decades and seems poorly couched as a basis for faculty conversation. Thus, we must finally question the meaning and utility of such phraseology, especially in view of stated purposes, viz.: dialogue with and influence in the university for the sake of the city.

Our second concern is with the problem of the framework in which morality is conceived. The paper sought theoretical constructs through which "structures themselves" might be "questioned." Yet illustrative instances of the ethic's utility and approach were chosen, not, as we might have anticipated, from the complex choices of institutional purpose and commitment in the academic world and urban reconstruction the author wished to understand, but from the traditional, moralistic image of religion as the guardian of sexual chastity. This is an area of considerable importance, to be sure, but likewise one almost certain to confirm widely shared stereotypes of religion's functions and presence. As the paper suggests, "Ethics tends to be a timid discipline." And we believe it is potentially true that "when in the work of the campus ministry, the concreteness of moral issues is met with depth of moral vision and learning . . . , a profound sense of relevance emerges, a sense greatly helpful to students." The questions of doubt and concern arise for us when the problems of sexuality are conceived only in terms of "should they—shouldn't they"; whatever the level of cognitive and intellectual sophistication, such a formulation seems unlikely to move students with its "moral vision and learning."

Thus, we confront again the societal dimensions of ethical discourse. The ethics of sex is usefully illustrative of the general neglect and imprecision of the church's appropriations of the technical and social revolutions wrought by new knowledge and human expectations. With notable exceptions, sex remains couched in the personalistic language of individual choice and individual consequence. Even in the areas of family planning which greatly influence city planning, thought has most frequently utilized the categories of personal well-being and individual responsibility. Alas, that is simply no longer possible. What has seemed the most private of matters has become overwhelmingly public in the matter of consequence; belatedly, inadequately, population increase is being recognized as a world crisis of immense dimensions. The war on poverty in the ghetto is intimately tied up with presence or absence of family planning among the poor and with differences in ethnic, religious, and racial approaches to the problem. Yet, although geometric change is obviously not indefinitely possible in a finite space, and although population limitation has been encouraged by the federal government for "underdeveloped" areas of the world, such limitation remains outside the conscious consideration of nearly all Americans except in terms of private preference. Population pressures have demonstrably impinged on many of our traditional attitudes and values regarding privacy, independence, initiative, on the assumed right of men to live full and creative lives with minimum interference from society and government. What is fundamentally at issue is the basic values which Christians and Americans have long insisted inhere in the individual simply by virtue of his personhood.

Limitation in the numbers of children, however, is but the first of numerous problems which Christian sexual thought must embrace. We may reasonably suppose that the principles of heredity, of genetic transmission, will soon be sufficiently understood that various traits and characteristics, psychic and physical, may be enhanced or suppressed at will. And while such knowledge may finally illumine the often private, poorly understood world of the mentally ill, the possibility of basic

genetic manipulation and alteration of personality invokes images normally reserved for science fiction. On what basis, however, do we act
when future possibility becomes the actuality of today? Who will decide
which traits will be emphasized and in whom? And in a world of limited
children, with the possibility of particularized genetic selection, will
every potential father be permitted to exercise this option? Whatever
response we offer to such questions, they are not mere whims to be
dismissed as unreal; as Nobel Prize winner Joshua Lederberg asserts,
"We are very close to the ultimate scientific revolution: the precise
control of human development." And it is in the universities that this
"revolution" is, largely, being quietly waged.

We offer these comments only to indicate the social dimensions
inherent in the illustrative examples this paper chose to utilize. It seems
almost superfluous to indicate the potential proximity of campus
ministers to these extremely portentous events, or the possibilities for
a "moral vision" that comprehends and engages academicians in reasoned, searching dialogue. That seems minimally necessary if the church
is to speak with scholarship and sensitivity to those constituencies of
students, faculty, and laymen who must soon grapple with such
enormities.

In actuality, however, the data do not suggest that such understanding and anticipation are generally occurring, nor did the colloquium itself find it possible or necessary to ask such questions. But participants in the colloquium were not unaware of the limitations we have
here suggested. As one campus minister later reflected:

> This area of colloquium discussion was much more limited in scope than
> I expected. . . . How far can the university be the mentor for sex stan-
> dards of the campus—wherein lies this responsibility in the university
> milieu? How does the university train its graduates in the delicate process
> of decision-making in public life? How far is the university training for
> public responsibility? Little light was shed on these questions in our dis-
> cussions. I cannot assume, however, that they were not of interest to the
> participants in the colloquium. Rather, I can only conclude from our
> discussions that we were unprepared to consider these "large" questions
> because of our more parochial, personalistic view of campus ministry.

This is, indeed, a useful set of issues and questions. That they occurred
as the colloquium drew its work to a close, however, is a revealing insight
into the nature of the problems they faced.

≫ 15 ≪

THINKING ABOUT A CITY IN ORDER TO REFORM IT:

THE URBAN ECOSYSTEM AND CHURCH INQUIRY

(Pittsburgh)

T HE third major area and the intended culmination of the colloquium's deliberations reside in the complex issues of urbanization. Could
the campus ministry, reasoning in concert about the processes and
events which had already profound influence over the lives of the
diverse citizenry of a region, respond critically and creatively to the
pressing value questions such events and processes pose?

This question has, of course, significance far transcending any single
geographical or institutional location. Urbanization not only has rendered largely meaningless an old simplistic urban-rural dichotomy but
has likewise loosed forces, expectations, and problems from whose persistent presence institutions and persons can no longer turn, no matter
where they are located geographically. Concomitantly, however, effective redress has also seemed illusive, ill defined, and largely inadequate.
Indeed, even the questions have proved complex and difficult; where to
commence in meeting problems accompanying urbanization, and at
what level? Such circumstances account in part for the usually facile
and occasionally desperate assumption by much of society that institutions of higher learning contain both responsibility and resource to
find feasible alternatives to our present practices. These questions require further analysis here, not only because they did not fully emerge
in the Pittsburgh colloquium but also because they are integral to the
histories and policies of this country's larger academic institutions and
by implication set the university framework in which the campus
ministry moves.

What is the university's responsibility to the larger urban society, and how ought its resources to be most adequately utilized? By what criteria does the university (in its multiple parts) respond to and serve the interests of the diverse, frequently conflicting publics which compete for its knowledge and technical competencies in Pittsburgh, San Francisco, New York? Only fatuously is the question of an academic responsibility to society now cast in terms of "whether"; simple reference to the origins and subsequent history of land-grant universities bespeaks one of our powerful educational philosophies, and whatever the value judgment placed upon it, the fact remains that every major American university retains deep, occasionally devious, relationships with industry and government. Carnegie Tech and the University of Pittsburgh are not at all excepted, since the former received, in 1968, $9,428,000 from the Department of Defense for research, and the latter, $1,620,000. Such spokesmen as Robert Hutchins continue to plead eloquently for minimization of these entanglements, but their appeals appear rather quixotic to much of the "multiversity"; the maze of grants, subsidies, and research projects which accrue around the physical and mechanical disciplines, the pragmatic nature of decision making, and the selective imbalance of research funding have virtually foreclosed on dramatic change in present practice.

But genuine problems are inherent in this state of affairs, particularly at the point of "selective imbalance." For, unlike Buridan's ass, the university has often appeared all too willing to partake of every possibility when the price was right, or has been moved by what Kenneth Boulding calls "spurious saliency" in which the "dramatic quality of events" dictates university research and teaching, rather than their actual or intrinsic importance in the social system. If we are to be reasonably descriptive, then, the university appears as a most diverse creature where some have waged the "good fight" on behalf of a revered "academic freedom" and the "detached scholar" at a time when others of similar devotion have distended its boundaries to encompass areas of activity to the point where traditional definitions of higher education are remarkably tenuous.

Academic freedom remains, of course, the model. But the image of the solitary scholar and his students has little congruence with, for example, the large university-directed research laboratories, where contractual relationships with government and industry produce activities, many of which are classified "in the national interest" and hence not subject to scrutiny by academic peers, or in field situations where social research is undertaken for specific client-directed purposes, again not freely transmittable throughout the disciplines represented. In such instances, and they are many, the university's resources have been sold to special interest groups having sufficient capacity to pay; the essential, often beneficial nature of the resulting product does not vitiate the fundamental issue of whether the *major* issues of the society are being studied. And, while it participates voluntarily, the literature available (to say nothing of our personal experiences) is replete with the rationalizations and compromises frequently appealed to. As Kerr indicates, "A federal agency offers a project. A university need not accept—but, as a practical matter, it usually does."[1]

Nor do such projects bear, we have noted, any necessary relationship to crucial urban, social priorities, and if the study of urban problems is obviously an "in" thing to do at this time, the precise forms it should assume are not. Hence, while funds from foundations and government have begun to water the academic soil and urban centers have sprung up in eager response, Berkeley's Director of Urban and Regional Development, William Wheaton, has laconically concluded that "the sum of these efforts is trifling." He further states: "As a nation we are moving belatedly, haltingly, and in my judgment ineptly, toward any fruitful coupling of our scientific and educational resources with our most pressing problems of urban growth and development."[2]

Yet universities continue to acquire and expand, often in mindless unawareness of larger community considerations; departments of business administration and engineering provide the technical expertise by which economic considerations in urban redevelopment and design are maximized. Such, in brief, is the nature of a crucial, increasingly vocal and acrimonious debate being waged in nearly every major institution of higher learning. The irony is depressing: parts of the university are now attempting to examine what other parts have abetted for many years. And no one has a better view, potentially, than the campus minister.

---

1. Clark Kerr, *The Uses of the University* (Cambridge: Harvard University Press, 1963).
2. William L. C. Wheaton, "The Role of the University in Urban Affairs," paper delivered at Arlington State College, October, 1966.

Significantly, the city of Pittsburgh not only reflects many of these patterns and trends but is, in many respects, their prototype. Although urban renewal is commonly associated with the 1949 Federal Housing Act as amended in 1954, Pittsburgh's metamorphosis antedates federal renewal programs by more than a decade. Called into being by a small group of Pittsburgh industrialists in 1943, the Allegheny Conference on Community Development set out systematically to reverse the pervasive blight and polluted skies which were then slowly strangling the city's economic, physical, and social life. By 1945, the conference had grown to more than one hundred representatives from, according to *Engineering News-Record*, "industry, commerce, finance, labor, education, public administration and civic affairs" and had hired an executive director. Smoke control began in 1946; so, too, did planning for the now famous "Golden Triangle," that 330 acres of downtown Pittsburgh, wedged between the converging Allegheny and Monongahela rivers, on which has arisen an imaginative complex of office structures, freeways, parks, rehabilitated buildings, and multistoried garages. And through it all, the University of Pittsburgh, Carnegie Institute of Technology, and Duquesne University not only contributed the technical competence of their faculties to the many phases and problems which inhere in urban renewal but were directly involved as institutions through the acquisition of land for purposes of expansion—land which was first condemned, then razed, by the city's Urban Renewal Authority.

The end is nowhere visible. Although *Engineering News-Record* only mirrored a widely held, if superficial, optimism when it editorialized in 1959 that "Pittsburgh's progress is an accomplished fact" and is "the precedent all America needs to prove that any city worth its salt can find the way to rebuild, to fit itself to the future," that city's 1967 application for participation in the Model Cities program had to confess that "by and large, squalor and deterioration, both physical and spiritual, hold sway." Nor is the reference to obscure or isolated people and institutions; the University of Pittsburgh is located in the Model Cities program "target area." Thus it is that the campus ministers and local churches have witnessed, through 1968, twenty-five years of renewal activity.

University debate and urban renewal are two crucial aspects of unprecedented social change about which the colloquium was asked to reflect and to formulate patterns of thought and action potentially commensurate with the rhetoric of relevance and involvement. In order to facilitate these objectives, Clifford Ham, an urban sociologist of the University of Pittsburgh's Graduate School of Public and International Affairs, was retained to prepare a working paper that examined possible relationships between the campus ministry and Pittsburgh's urban renaissance. This paper, discussed at some length by the colloquium's membership, sets forth in brief the numerous developments that make, it is asserted, "the twentieth-century city . . . a totally different entity from its predecessor" in complexity, population and physical changes, mobility, complex social problems, and, significantly, the evolution of "urban experts." Pittsburgh's response to these conditions is described in terms of leadership strata discernible throughout the city's drive toward physical renewal, to which are adjoined the many and varied services provided by area university faculty. There follow (1) a critique of religious leadership's timidity and lack of involvement and (2) the justification for concern:

> Theologians are today pointing out that the city itself is a subject of vital concern for the church "the new creation as metropolis" sees the city as a joint enterprise of God and man. Man as creator has shared with God in the development and improvement of the city. Religious man has left the rural settlements in the past, and now is in the city to stay. The city, then, as an entity, is—or should be—his concern.

The paper concludes with an extended, often detailed and insightful program of possible action, comprising not only intimations of values to be preserved, and policies to be challenged, but structural arrangements through which campus ministers might more effectively be heard.

> If the campus minister is to function in a relevant manner and participate in the civic dialogue, major changes in his relationship, his role, and his own leadership must take place. The rather informal relationship of the campus minister . . . must be transformed into a more formal structure, that is, this program must be "institutionalized." . . . The status of the campus minister must be raised.

This brief accounting hardly does justice to the rich mix of theoretical base and practical outreach built into the Ham paper; although open to potential criticism in its use of the Floyd Hunter pyramid model of community power and in the emphasis placed on direct power confrontations, its general challenge and program offered the colloquium a useful basis from which to grapple with urban concerns. It found no means for doing so.

> The discussion we had on the Ham paper represented for all the participants, except Dr. Ham, an entirely new venture in implications for the campus ministry. Such seeming novelty in itself is indicative that the campus ministry in Pittsburgh was unaware of some of the powerful factors shaping not only the physical features of the city and university area, but was likewise unaware of the structures of decision-making in an urban complex which affects profoundly the living patterns of the city in which the university is set. It seems clear to me that as the campus ministry is confronted with the factors of urban and university renewal, it tends to fall back upon the "personalistic" domain. By this I mean that as we are confronted with a complex of factors which affect "big" decisions in the university and urban area, we are inclined to look upon our task in personalistic categories of counseling, preaching, and teaching.[3]

The participants seemed unable to move beyond a superficial awareness of the extensive relationships between major universities and large segments of the larger society, or of the political and sociological forces which account for the university's pervasive, but selective, social involvement. Nor had they perceived the extraordinary implications for ethical and theological theory which reside in university-based research and expertise. And they had not, by their own admission, given thought to, or sought to inform or be informed by, the complicated processes that are our "urban environment."

Perhaps the expectation should not have been otherwise. Trained in the traditional mold in American seminaries and theological schools, they brought to their deliberations neither professional training in nor extensive conversation with the methodologies and finding of the social sciences; placed by denominations in peripheral, student-oriented centers, they were without systematic access to their campuses, save through the dean of students. Indeed, as the data seem clearly to indi-

---

3. Quotations of colloquium members are taken either from questionnaire answers or from papers prepared by them, and are on file as materials of the Pittsburgh Colloquium, Campus Ministry Archives, Yale University Divinity School Library, New Haven, Conn.

cate, they are not unlike the clergy generally, accustomed to the categories in historical Christian thought which emphasize the personal, the covenanting community—the "folk" society now standard in sociological description. And from such imagery has come the attack on specialization and disciplinary emphasis, on "depersonalization" of the individual and the breakdown of "community" among scholars, climaxed in the Pittsburgh study by a paper urging abandonment of the "academic establishment's values." Authentic theological and philosophical concerns reside in such imagery, of course, and the campus ministry has often displayed a moral sensitivity notably lacking in important segments of the academy. But the impact is largely vitiated when the debate rises no further and when it seems quite unaware that what it perceives afresh from without has for some time been discussed vigorously from within.

What might such a group have said to the multiversity's technocrats? How might they have sought a synthesis of valuing the human need on the one hand and the ofttimes depressing quantitative technological mentality on the other? What is the mode of prophetic inquiry in the university and toward the urban scene? How, in fact, do we "think about the city in order to reform it?" There are, as yet, no definitive responses possible to such queries; nonetheless, the vast array of human need and demand contains a core of commonalities around which social discussion and remedial action have increasingly converged. Whether the campus ministry can effectively participate in this discussion and action remains an open question. That it must initially appropriate the requisite knowledge is not; for too long we have ignored H. Richard Niebuhr's insistence that "What is going on?" is antecedent to "What shall we do?"

What, then, *is* going on? We have already examined in brief the "selective imbalance" of social demand and university response and the colloquium's general unawareness, up to that point, of university participation in the urban processes. The debate was not really joined, for the basic issue of university autonomy is not exhausted in the simple recognition that numerous special interests compete for its attention. Much more crucial *is the nature of university response and its understanding of and acquiescence to externally offered definitions of given situations or problems.* As Frank Pinner asserts, "The business of the university is the advancement of knowledge. We do not advance knowledge measurably by passing out nostrums for various types of malaise. . . . Above all, we are gravely at fault if we accept the public's own definition of its problems and try to solve these as they are presented to us."[4]

What Is a Social Problem?

Yet the question seems more substantive than Pinner suggests and finally involves the power inherent in the very act of defining. What, after all, is a social problem? All human action is social; the power to define what shall be called "abnormal" or "a problem" is to direct, obviously, the structure and process of solution, which itself alters the larger social body. John Seeley sharply states the point:

> How legislative and consequential such definitions may and must be is illustrated by the alternatives, as for example, in defining delinquency (as against, say parental neglect or poverty) to be a "social problem," or unemployment (as against, say, idleness or vagabondage or vagrancy). Even before study, reporting, or recommendation of a "solution," the very cutting *out* of the problem in conversation, insofar as it reaches . . . a cut *in* and reorganization of the society.[5]

This question of the power to name and define assumes supreme importance in the area of urbanization where the study of intricate human relationships and of the values, attitudes, beliefs, and so on which sustain them constitutes the "stuff" of academic inquiry. "Everybody knows" the presence of a "Negro revolution" in this country, but the act of definition—poverty, lack of equal opportunity, substandard schools, discrimination, riots, denial of fundamental dignity, Black Power—from among the virtually infinite universe of possible variables has already set the modes of resolution. Belief that "riots" are a fundamental issue will almost assuredly suggest a course of corrective action at wide variance with a belief, and subsequent acts, that the root is "denial of human dignity."[6] Yet, these widely diverse perceptions and

---

4. Frank Pinner, "The Crisis of the State Universities: Analysis and Remedies," in Nevitt Sanford, ed., *The American College* (New York: John Wiley, 1966).

5. John R. Seeley *et al.*, "The Problem of Social Problems," in *Crestwood Heights: A Study of the Culture of Suburban Life* (Toronto: University of Toronto Press, 1963), p. 146.

6. "Hitler recently gave us a sufficiently graphic demonstration of the political motive and effect of his freedom to name, define and specify the solution of what he termed 'the Jewish problem.'" *Ibid.*, p. 147.

frames of understanding compete for attention. It is this maelstrom of conflicting voices in which we might expect the university, by virtue of its commitments to objectivity, rationality, and choice, to guide and modify the limited and/or self-serving definitions and perspectives of its publics. As Pinner argues, "Indeed, our responsibility to the community would be meaningless if we did not accept this burden."[7]

Problems of definition, however, are really explicable only as the urban context itself is adequately comprehended. What is seen as a problem will depend heavily on the richness of complexity and interrelationship the definer observes. Recent developments in the social sciences, therefore, seem as crucial in this regard as developments in theology, for our appreciation of urban complexity has deepened measurably. It has not always been so; one of the obvious features characterizing most traditional thought about, and study of, cities has been its piecemeal nature, the treating (at least for practical purposes) of individual urban phenomena as disparate, self-contained entities. (Housing, transportation, highways, health, schools, public health [usually], local government, urban renewal, minority problems [sometimes], and so on, are standard components in any city planner's vocabulary.) This procedure has a compelling plausibility, strengthened in large measure by inadequate knowledge and the practical necessities of limited objectives. Increasingly, however, such fragmented approaches to the study of cities and the people in them are recognized as insufficient. The following statements, from widely varying sources, stress the point:

> Urban problems are so interwoven, so interdependent, that scholars can only consider them together; in other words, it has been found necessary to consider the urban situation as a system in its own right, inescapably transcending the traditional disciplines.[8]

> Clearly, we cannot continue to experiment in bits. . . . The city is a completely interacting system.[9]

> If, as Lewis Mumford maintains, the purpose of a city is the care and

---

7. Pinner, *op. cit.*, p. 954.
8. John Bodine, "Liberal Education for Urban Responsibility," paper delivered to Danforth Foundation Workshop, 1964, p.6.
9. Athelstan Spilhaus, "The Experimental City," *Daedalus* (Fall, 1967), p. 1141.

nurture of human beings, each of the city's aggregate parts—every street, school, factory, and highway—must contribute to that care and nurture.[10]

The most critical problem facing humanity today is an ecological one of relating human societies harmoniously to their environments. . . . The knowledge of the humanities and the behavioral sciences, as well as the natural sciences, must be integrated.[11]

What each of these writers emphasizes is the intricate, interrelated nature of urban complexes; cities are "wholes" in which very large numbers of variables vary and interact, where situations or states of affairs in one sector or variable inexorably influence, condition, and alter states of affairs in other sectors, often in subtle and unexpected ways. Compounding the complexity of this conception of "wholeness" is the diverse nature of the variables involved: individuals, groups of structures, value systems, physical entities (natural and created), patterns of communication, bodies of knowledge, and the like, all of which are finally subsumed under the concept of "social system." And, as is evident, "social system" implies the concept of "environment," not only as physical but as social and cultural.

Another effort to convey this sense of totality may be observed in recent efforts to combine the traditional physical environment emphases of ecology with modern systems theory, from which derives the hybrid term "ecosystems." Whatever the terminology employed, however, the fundamental implication is clear and paramount; the broad issues which confront men in the urban setting must increasingly be understood by religious leaders from the perspectives of both the physical and the social sciences as well as theology—the relationships not only of man and man, and man and nature, but man and man through nature to God. One simple example may suffice: "The movement of radioactive particles or DDT through plants and non-human animals into man— who released these contaminants in the first place—is an ecosystem phenomenon."[12] And the phenomenon is freighted with religious-ethical issues of human responsibility.

---

10. Harold Gilliam, "The Fallacy of Single-Purpose Planning," *Daedalus* (Fall, 1967), p. 1142.

11. S. Dillon Ripley and Helmut K. Buechner, "Ecosystem Science as a Point of Synthesis," *Daedalus* (Fall, 1967), p. 1192.

12. *Ibid.*, p. 1195.

Concern for interdisciplinary understanding of human ecosystems is not, of course, "new," if by that one means its absence from previous thought in social science and theology. But the urgent nature of current "problems," the relative bankruptcy of policies and programs based on "single-purpose" planning, the desultory, depressing effects of Alfred Kahn's "tyranny of small decisions," have each, in their way, overwhelmingly dramatized the necessity for "holistic" approaches in which what is holy is not confined to a particular institution or set of principles. Too, only in the past decade has the prerequisite data-processing capability of computers been placed at the disposal of physical and social scientists, ethicists and theologians, providing an analytical tool of profound significance and usefulness. It seems reasonable to suppose, therefore, that the social sciences will vastly expand not only our understanding of social processes but our ability to predict and, presumably, control. How crucial this has become is drearily evident in society's capacity to create and disseminate its flood of technological affluence before analysis of social consequence is possible, the classic instance of which must surely be the giving over of Los Angeles as a hostage to the automobile only to discover that this same invention had trapped it in smog.

The crucial nature of this problem is further understood through the introduction of "time" and the meaning of "past" and "future" in a technological context. As John Wilkinson argues, much of what we continue to envisage as future is, for purposes of effective control, already "past." Points in time—"due dates"—constantly occur, beyond which rational prevision is no longer possible. No supersonic transport will fly in this country for another four years, but we have long since passed its "due date," the point at which fundamental questions of priority, of physical and psychic sonic damage, might have altered the outcome. As Bertrand de Jouvenal suggests, "There is a continual dying of possible futures. And two mistakes are common: to be unaware of them while they are, so to speak, alive, and to be unaware of their death when they have been killed off by lack of discovery."[13] Both of these questions —prediction and time—have immediate implication for the study of ecosystems, not the least of which are controlled, purposely planned social research and sophisticated attention to distinguishing, in effect,

---

13. John Wilkinson, "Futuribles: Innovation vs. Stability," *Center Diary*, XVII (March–April, 1967), 18. Published by the Center for the Study of Democratic Institutions, Santa Barbara, California.

between what is already "past" and what is amenable hopefully to control.

But what is the meaning, finally, of words like "control" and "problem" and "solution" when the city is understood as an intricate network in which, as Warren Weaver has indicated, "several quantities are all varying simultaneously and in subtly interconnected ways"? We have noted the extraordinary power which inheres in the authority to define disparate "problems," for which "solutions" may be devised and applied. A deceptive charm resides in such thinking, reinforcing a general technological disposition to believe that any problem is amenable to expertise and manipulation. Such conventional wisdom, however, is inadequate. We are required to utilize categories that take seriously the social reality we have briefly sketched; conceptions of "system" and "time" require social images of "process" and "influence" and religious images of commitment to action in the context of God's concern with the whole world, with neglected people, corrupted cities, and principalities. For we do not, in any meaningful fashion, "solve" the crucial questions of specific problems. But we can and must, within our collective abilities to do so, analyze and influence the processes and structures by which they are perpetuated.

The distinctions to be made here are crucial, for they move us beyond the facile assumption that social disorder is analogous in kind to, for example, the technical problems and concomitant resolutions of space research. As should be obvious, and most frequently is not, influence of social processes at any given point—say, urban renewal—sets in motion influences throughout each aspect of the system with which the original interacts—influences that often become manifest at points ostensibly far removed, actually or conceptually, from the original point of influence or alteration and that in turn exert pressure for change on that original point. The imagery is dynamic and relational, in which the very concept of "act" implies a reciprocal through which the act itself is no longer the same; God and man, man and man, man and nature, involved in indissolvable relationship at the heart of contemporary policy.

In Pittsburgh urban renewal, particular values and objectives were legislatively defined as though compatibility between them was a given; adequate housing and central city reconstruction could, it was anticipated, be served simultaneously in the same operational structure. But the pursuit of economic goals in this program—increased land values and tax bases—released forces and expectations that seriously impaired human values, such as housing, neighborhood and communal ties, and the like. Sensitive observers, of course, have been distressingly aware of such disruptions for nearly two decades; the resulting clashes of values, interests, and ideologies usefully illustrate the "stuff" around which ethical battles in Pittsburgh and other urban centers are joined and through which social process is influenced.

These various concepts—systems processes, due dates, definition, action, policy, and so on—emphasize the clash of interests, the often extraordinary latent consequences, and the limited vision of our goals that characterize most ethical thought and action of the churches and universities. As the "sex ethic" example attempted to demonstrate, even the most ostensibly private act now has extreme social significance, and the real ethical battles must now be fought at the level of social process and policy, where the potential for destruction is so complete. The "What do we do?" is a question of direction as influence is expressed and of the clash between human values and those of technology and efficiency.

The Life of an Ecosystem

Our intent here is to argue the principle that effective involvement in the life and processes of an ecosystem must of necessity embrace qualitative factors, the value judgments all humans make concerning goals and the methods of inquiring into their meaning for the means to be employed in achieving them. Several rather more specific aspects of the question of thinking about a city in order to reform it seem apparent, even though the campus ministers of Pittsburgh had nothing to say about them. One of these is that of ordering, cost analysis, and measurement. Most unfortunately, active contemplation of fundamental values and objectives, private or public, is a rare commodity, a fact made painfully abundant when Christians or elected civic representatives have tried to weight the moral and aesthetic intangibles inhering in a clear sky, clean rivers, pleasing architecture, or a vestige of wilderness. For some, of course, there is no apparent problem; such amenities simply have no particular meaning, and the question can be asked; What kind of public and religious education contributed to such narrow vision of the good life? Too, as a nation Americans have long been conditioned to draw disjunctions between public and private, the net result being continued growth and consumption in the private realm while aspects of our social and physical environment that we enjoy in common continue to suffer from abuse, indifference, and hostility. How to justify clean air? Aesthetically, direct visual response, sources of health, the abuse of God's gift?

Only the most primitive type of calculus currently exists for comparative analysis of "goods" or values and for determining (or balancing off) social and economic costs. Even so simple (seemingly) a problem in the ecosystem as pollution of the air invokes questions for which response is lacking. Having determined a basis for "how much pollution is tolerable?" (for which no scientific evidence presently exists), one must still resolve the issue of "who pays," who is accountable? And when our value questions are several levels removed, to the promised crises which leisure and work hold out for the near future, to the crises which segregation and prejudice will perpetuate into any foreseeable future, academicians, as well as ministers, are admittedly confused and lost.

Numerous individuals, it is true, have occasionally sought to devise formulas or methodologies through which the multitudinous variables might be weighted and related. Any such model for social calculus, however, inevitably is based on one or more "faith statements" or a priori assumptions, about which we are far from agreement.[14] And if we were, what of the variables presumed necessary? Hence, we are never quite sure whether to applaud such efforts on the basis of effort or to smile at their seeming inadequacy.[15] Yet the engineer, the physical planner, the sociologist, no less than the ethicist, theologian, or aestheticist, must surely face more forthrightly the demands placed on them by such dilemmas.[16] The fruits of technology and the skills necessary to their

14. Azrield Teller, for example, has worked out an ingenious series of graphs and tables, each of which is intended as assistance in balancing cost vs. clean air. He must, however, implicitly assume that everyone has equal rights of access to air, that the right to breathe clean air is logically equivalent to the right to foul it for monetary gain. "Air-Pollution Abatement," *Daedalus* (Fall, 1967), pp. 1082–1098. Alas, to ignore subjective aesthetic states or qualities, "things for their own sake," does not render them any less real or integral to the discussion. We have not, it would appear, notably advanced the problem by insisting on some natural right to utilize air or water as an open sewer.

15. See Constantine A. Doxiadis, "Anthropocosmos: The World of Man," paper delivered at the Aspen Institute, summer, 1966; Dennis Gabor, "An Ethical Quotient," *Technology and Human Values* (An Occasional Paper on the Role of Technology in the Free Society, Published by the Center for the Study of Democratic Institutions, 1966).

16. As J. Herbert Hollomon pointedly asserts, "Engineers must feel a sense of

utilization are requisite to many of our "urban crises." But until we have much more systematically examined the necessity to understand better and to mediate conflicts between attitudes and ideologies, and to bring them into an at least tolerable cost-benefit relationship, our efforts to think and act as responsible Christian or university leaders in the urban context will continue to sound like one hand clapping.

The chief question to ask of the university at this point seems almost trivially obvious: How shall men remain intelligently informed about the enormous urban change occurring around them? Not surprisingly, an impressive variety of university-conducted educational activities are presently much in evidence: extension courses, night-college classes, various seminars, institutes, and workshops, and so forth.[17] And in particular instances, universities have exercised leadership in controlling the physical decay lapping at their outer fringes. But Kerr's recent indictment—"They are in the urban setting but not of it"—seems generally to be right and no less true of most university urban research centers.[18] In light of the ecosystems concept indicated above, therefore, educational expressions for the urban context might now be significantly rethought. Research, particularly experimental in nature, is obviously vital; no other agency presently exists for sustained, theoretically oriented ecosystems analysis. The churches need the universities that will do such analysis; it can be generated, but not produced, by them.

But recognition that values, goals, and purpose are equally integral to the system and a commitment to resolution of the disharmonies which beset such systems now necessitate more carefully defined lines of communication and dissemination of knowledge, more adequate understanding of the university's ongoing concern for the "care and nurture" of minds.[19] Urban higher education can be understood as having at least

---

moral values through which they weigh the consequences for evil as well as the consequences for good of their work and make some judgments between them." "Literate Engineering," *Saturday Review*, July 1, 1967, p. 41.

17. An expansive, notable treatment of adult education will be found in John W. Johnstone and Ramone Ribers, *Volunteers for Learning: A Study of Educational Pursuits of American Adults,* National Opinion Research Center, Monographs in Social Research, No. 4 (Chicago: Aldine, 1965).

18. Quoted in Fred M. Hechinger, "A Call for the 'Urban Grant' College," *The New York Times*, October 22, 1967.

19. Review of the many centers presently operating throughout the country presents, as previously indicated, a wide variety of emphases. Most are research-oriented; nearly all have programing—usually in the form of seminars, lectures, and

three conceptually distinct "publics" (there is to be sure, overlap in actuality)—policy makers, the larger population, and full-time students—each of which must contend with "means" (information, research data, and so on) and "ends" (goals, priorities, preference of choice). Each comprises a significant subsystem within the ecosystem, acting and reacting, influencing and being influenced by other identifiable components of the ecosystem. This process is, in the parlance of system analysis, "feedback": any influence which impels a subsystem to action. And because particular subsystems demonstrably give rise to change throughout the ecosystem, feedback is consciously directed at these groups. As Monane states: "The important arbiter and judge of a new item [of change]—and its executioner or welcoming committee to the extent that it can—is the power component of a social system. Its thumbs up or down appears crucial. What it sees as implementive to its present direction of system line is received warmly. What it eyes as threatening is opposed."[20] This is why discussion of inquiry cannot be separated from issues of power and governance.

One obvious form of feedback is information about the ecosystem itself. Indeed, one observer of urban affairs insists that "perhaps the greatest single challenge in the cities is ignorance—not only the pervasive ignorance of city residents whose education has been limited and weak, but also the ignorance of well-educated people about the very

so on—designed to impart knowledge and give advice. Additionally, of course, centers provide channels for consultative relationships between professional (faculty) and client (usually city officials). Some, as the MIT-Harvard Joint Center, have no permanent staff; others, as the Institute of Government at the University of North Carolina (with which Donald Shriver's inquiries had some relation) report staffs approaching a hundred. For a useful summary of existing centers, see "An Institute for Urban Studies: A Preliminary Proposal," University of Texas, 1966, pp. 5–12. That many centers have a "ghostlike" quality seems beyond dispute, simply affording, as Peter Rossi observes, "convenient sally ports from which the professors can emerge to gather funds from foundations and government agencies." "Researchers, Scholars, and Policy Makers," Daedalus (Fall, 1964), p. 1151. Likewise, by virtue of metropolitan size and lack of funding (or inclination), most centers have been limited to highly particularized studies of disparate urban phenomena. In either case, the net result is similar: research is fragmented, performed on a piecemeal basis, dictated by sources of funding or private professorial interest (or both), and, it frequently appears, more closely meshed to the academic reward system and guild requirements than to oft-termed "external" considerations. In few instances do there appear to be clearly developed rationales for relating research findings to wide segments of the larger population, apart from "ability to pay."

20. Joseph Monane, Sociology of Human Systems (New York: Appleton, 1967).

urban problems they would hope to solve."[21] A seductive simplicity resides in statements such as this, for they frequently, perhaps unknowingly, assume the Socratic dictum that to know the good is to do it. But information, as such, has little significance until selectively filtered and ordered in our individual "frames of reference" or "ways of thinking." Hence, the university provides the data accumulated through quantitative research, but it cannot assume its "publics" will perceive with either accuracy or understanding. Much university instruction, we think, commits this fallacy on the misassumption that information is logically and epistemologically equivalent to wisdom.

The task, therefore, involves the fusion of our information into patterns of coherence, meaning, and loyalty. It is what de Jouvenal has called "education in wiser preferences"; Burney, "updating the intellectual framework"; Van Harvey, "perspectives of faith" and "moralities of knowledge." These are suggestive phrases, imploring serious concern for fundamental reconsideration of basic orientations to the world, for openness to creative possibility. The university does not so much solicit what people "want" as call them into increased understanding of a potential world "aesthetically and ecologically more satisfying than the one present trends promise."[22] As William Goode argues (on behalf of sociologists), "We can, I believe . . . demonstrate . . . that many desirable but presently non-existent arrangements are also possible."[23]

As repository for much of humanity's collected wisdom, one could presume the university's deep and sustained endeavors toward clarification and discussion of the options we confront as a society. But as a practical matter, this has not happened. Here, as elsewhere, we seem to have been at least partially victimized by the specious "public" vs. "private." Thus, university offerings to adults are overwhelmingly "private" in their rationale, emphasizing vocation training, personal enhancement, or leisure time enjoyment; they are premised on the client's own definition of preference and needs and on ability to pay. A trifling 4 per cent, for example, of all adults now engaged in "educational pur-

21. Robert L. Jacobson, "The Role of Higher Education in Solving the Urban Crisis," published proceedings of the 1967 Morgan State College Conference on Higher Education and the Challenge of the Urban Crisis, p. 7.

22. Nathaniel Wollman, "The New Economics of Resources," *Daedalus* (Fall, 1967), p. 1108.

23. William J. Goode, "The Protection of the Inept," *American Sociological Review* (February, 1967), p. 19.

suits" at the university level are confronting subject matter which could be termed "public affairs."[24] But this is precisely the dilemma; personal freedom has become so inexorably entwined with the corporate "public" decisions, activities, and effects of technologically oriented industry and government that private decision is reduced to inconsequential minutiae. Crucial decisions affecting the most fundamental and qualitative aspects of our social and physical environment are presently almost not at all influenced by the wider citizenry.

The implications seem almost self-evident. Within the ecosystem, "power components"—individuals and groups who control the political and economic decision-making processes—must be actively sought out and engaged by urban centers of the university and church and drawn into dialogue which enhances and broadens the recognition of alternatives, of restructured possibilities. We use the adverb "actively" with intent. Both religious and academic educators have been content, as a general rule, to imagine that learning is largely synonymous with physical presence in a classroom, on a campus, or in a church. Workshops, field service and observation, and the like, it is true, have been sporadically fostered in certain limited settings; but sustained efforts over time, in which effectiveness of program design is constantly evaluated and feedback introduced, are rare, indeed.

The principle for which we argue is actually little more than a recognition that in the urban context, the university and church should much more vigorously pursue the implications of "continuing education and inquiry," of ethical, religious, and social developments for varied influential "publics." If the city is a system in its own right, the arguments which seek "a new breed of ministry" aware of this system have the virtue of logic in their favor. But describing this "breed" in terms of competencies and sensitivities required (or even desirable), and the most advantageous means by which they might be imparted, undoubtedly must also be a subject of much more debate as to what responsible power and governance are like in a city system.

The Pittsburgh colloquium is representative of where most campus ministries are at the present time in their ability to understand and inquire into the city. There are urban areas, however, where the churches are much farther along in their development of leadership. As *Manpower*

---

24. Jerome M. Zeigler, "Continuing Education in the University," *Daedalus*, (Fall, 1964), p. 1175.

for Mission notes, Chicago has "become the focal point of invigorated innovation in American church life."[25] The campus ministries have had their ways of thinking about the city challenged by Chicago's civil rights movement, the establishment of the Urban Training Center for Christian Mission, the new four-year professional degree program of the University of Chicago Divinity School, the growth in student and adult education activities of the Ecumenical Institute, and the reconstituted work of the older, established organizations of the churches such as the Chicago City Missionary Society and the Church Federation of Greater Chicago under the leadership of such professionals at reform as Stanley J. Hallett, Don Benedict, Stephen C. Rose, and J. Archie Hargraves.

The most significant aspect of the Chicago church scene is that the leaders in each of these programs are thinking in common terms about the issues and conditions confronting people, the structures of power and decision processes at work in the socioecosystem of their city. Whatever the language, there runs through these programs the awareness that personal care and need, religious symbols and beliefs, cultural and epistemological patterns, policy-making powers and responsibilities, are all integral to the sytsems and processes which shape their lives in Chicago. They are trying to understand the relation of these basic perspectives to particular ministerial settings and roles. They know that if they cannot do this they are not competent, professional leaders of a ministry to whole Christian communities in the layman's contemporary world.

We can be critical of the too great dependence in many of the programs on the cultural-symbolic aspects and a neglect of the realities of power and policy. We can be critical of the proliferation of task forces and team ministries which have failed to think through with university and professional leaders the structures they seek to influence. But Chicago cannot be denied its achievement of church leadership which has broken from the individualistic-faith-dialogue images that bound the Pittsburgh leaders to a world of the past. In such a city as Chicago the campus ministries are challenged by the rest of the church to make of their denominational centers meeting places of students, faculty, church, and public leaders concerned with the universities' mission to the city

---

25. Henry Clark, ed., *Manpower for Mission*, Division of Christian Life and Mission, National Council of Churches of Christ (New York: Council Press, 1968).

and the institutions that have proved by actions that they are seeking to build a new commonwealth. The Westminster House, with its programs for the Chicago Medical Center, is called upon to envision the implications of what it learns for suburban churches where doctors and many other technical people related to the health and medical care system worship. And university pastors are called upon to expose the college and university to the ecological and environmental factors in health and leisure as they have come to know them. Significant models of ministry are emerging, and the churches will be immeasurably aided in their struggle to have laymen understand the limits and possibilities of these models if university scholars will turn their varied disciplines to the analysis of these developments and to the obstacles which change will encounter.

The campus ministers are increasingly being asked by the university to take positions in student personnel where the purpose of the work is to seek a more intimate relation between learning, community involvement, and personal talent. All the main figures in this part of our study—Smith, Shriver, Schrading—have been invited to head new residential colleges which have instructional and action programs planned to deal with the realities of systematic social and academic problems, to direct continuing educational programs that challenge large bodies of institutional leadership to critical reflection on their purposes and methods. Some of the campus ministries will work on these concerns from influential positions in the universities; some will continue to direct their ethical inquiries from a church base. But in either case, the necessity of prophetic inquiry in the life of persons, institutions, and urban systems is being recognized.

PART VI

The Structures of Administration and Governance in the Ministry

ᐅ 16 ᐊ

CHURCH POWER AND GOVERNANCE IN THE

METROPOLIS

THE analysis of the current sociopolitical situation of the church by *avant-garde* interpreters typically begins with the fact that man is achieving the power "to remake his environment in any way he chooses."[1] But their analysis seldom gives equal attention to the fact that man may be at the same time losing the power to give coherent and just order to the powers for change he now has and to involve people meaningfully in decisions that affect that order. The real crisis in our society is not the achievement of power to change man's environment; the problem is to govern in a way that directs knowledge to humane and just purposes shared and supported by members of the society.

There is no question about the powers of our nation to produce in abundance the physical goods and services that we want because of the ever increasing supply of energy, the ability of man to create new materials, the success of the university in training people who can do these things as well as computing their cost and storing vast amounts of information on how to induce change in the human as well as their technological environment. The question is whether we can control this power politically and socially so that new possibilities for a better world exist for those who share least in our present abundance and whether these visions of public hopes are fulfilled by vigorous action in the major governmental, cultural, and social institutions of the nation.

In the Christian and democratic traditions, governance is always distinguished from power simply to influence others "to get things done."

---

1. Robert Theobald, *An Alternative Future for America: Essays and Speeches,* edited by Kendall College (Chicago: Swallow Press, 1968).

Governance is the exercise of power in the structures and loyalties of a society or people; it is rooted in the statutes, functions, and authority of a society's organizations and associations. Thus Christ as King is worshiped in the church when men, already trying to govern humanely, perceive that the model of humanity by which motives and aspirations are to be appraised is love: the building up of the common life so that variety is not sacrificed to harmony or harmony to diversity. The requisite of love here is that fundamental humanity be guaranteed to all and this covenant be built into the major institutions and social processes. The promise is often violated; but in a deeper sense, it has not always been and will not be violated. The image of Christ the King governing his people is a perspective of hopefulness that the covenant is ultimate reality.

Power without such responsible governance becomes external force, unregulated by the need to gain the consent of the people that justice has been done. The ideology of power without the covenants of governance tends to blur distinctions in a pluralistic society. It reduces social and cultural factions to bland decisions of a controlling bureaucracy protecting itself from the realities of human conflict over the meaning of love and justice.

But the act of governance in a free society assumes the existence of diverse associations of men whose purposes cannot be expressed in simple slogans, neatly calculable gains, or existing social arrangements. The larger aims and purposes of policy must be envisioned that will encourage the sacrifice of lesser values and interests. The just governor, the responsible ruler, the president of a democracy, is occupied principally with giving shape to the social good, and this cannot be done with the issues that arise only from a particular interest group. His concern is with sensing the issues and conditions that cut across these divisions to express the style and spirit of a whole culture or age. Those who govern in the tradition of the Christian Lord as king never deal simply with a problem and its solution in some legislative act, but rather with involvements in a continual, changing process of interaction between government, churches, schools, and so on, with shifts in whole systems of a society.

Thus the significant battles in our kind of society are not those between labor, business, agriculture, and ethnic blocs, but between people who are capable and ready to govern and those who fear vast shifts in balances of power in the actions of groups such as blacks, students, intellectuals, professionals; who envision pervasive, demonic forces at work at the roots of the system of life they know and who have lost the confidence that they significantly influence their governors. The churches will have to aid people to discover ways, other than mere protests, of influencing the action of these professional, technical subcultures which govern. But any alternative must acknowledge both the need for disciplined competence in the society and the humanity of the expert. This means that the church's social action leadership should abandon its romance with the inner city, where white suburban people are increasingly unwelcome as leaders, and begin using its knowledge of conditions to influence the action of that professional, technical, and indigenous leadership representing most of the church's constituency. This means understanding the connections between professional, scientific experts and democratic participation in evaluating services rendered.

Knowledge of where and how community power is really exercised and effectively evaluated is not easy. Academe and church borrow simplified models, such as the elite power groups taken from the sociologists like C. Wright Mills or mass countervailing power structures taken from the theologians such as Reinhold Niebuhr. But religious and academic leaders still have not identified where decisions are made and where influence for reform is exerted in the institutions they claim to serve. This became increasingly clear to us as we studied the campus ministries in the vast metropolises of the Eastern Seaboard and Great Lakes— Boston, New York, Detroit, Cleveland.

With questions of what religious and academic leaders mean by power and governance as our chief concern, we arranged for an intensive investigation in three areas: Boston, New York, Michigan. We tried to simplify the analysis by looking at (1) the relations of governance to the goals the ministers sought to achieve, (2) the roles they preferred, and (3) the communications they maintained.

In New York, Robert Dentler and his associates in an Institute for Study of Urban Education sought to place campus ministry *roles and role definitions* in the context of a whole educational system in probably the most complex metropolitan area in America. This study is reported in Chapter 17.

In Michigan, the Danforth staff observed and evaluated the methods and patterns of communication between people in different hierarchical positions in the church and the manner and extent to which various types of behavior are rewarded. This study is reported in Chapter 18.

In Boston we principally sought to find out whom the campus ministers regarded as influential enough in the university and church to invite their understanding and support of their goals as campus ministers; what they told these people (such as administrators and faculty); what plans they shared with parish church structures, from which most of their constituency came and to which it returned; what critique they made of the goals of city institutions and professional groups closely related to the universities.

A city-wide colloquium with research responsibilities was established in Boston, as well as a special colloquium on Catholic educational and religious goals for clergy in the urban universities. The city-wide Boston colloquium was asked to examine the relation of campus ministry goal definitions to those held by other leaders of social systems of which they were a part. We wished to discover congruences and divergences of goals and how these were handled by the campus ministers. This concern was related to our view of governance as a process of enabling persons and associations wtih many different goals to interact effectively in achieving institutional and public purposes. We asked the participants to view power not as necessarily related to an ideology of force, but as a free expression by human beings of their need to develop their particular talents and objectives in an efficacious way. Governance, then, is an effort to channel and persuade this expression to serve viable and just social and public programs.[2]

---

2. The Boston colloquium had the following members: Paul Deats, Jr., Professor of Social Ethics, Boston University, Chairman; Sister Marie Auguste, Professor of Sociology, Emmanuel College; Dr. Robert Bellah, Associate Professor of Sociology, Harvard University; Rev. Mike Bloy, MIT Episcopal Chaplain; Rev. Newton Fowler, graduate student, Boston University; Dr. Philip Bosserman, instructor, College of Basic Studies, Boston University; Dean Robert Hammil, Marsh College, Boston University; Rev. Henry Horn, University Lutheran Church, Cambridge; Dr. W. A. Overholt, Protestant Chaplain, Boston University; Rev. Joseph B. Shannon, Church Society for College Work; Dr. John Walsh, Director of Education Research, Boston College; Rev. John A. Russell, MIT Methodist Chaplain; Rabbi Maurice Sigmond, Harvard-MIT Hillel Foundation; Dr. Herbert Stotts, Professor of Sociology, Boston University; Dr. A. Bertrand Warren, Professor of Psychology, Northeastern University; Robert Watson, Dean of Students, Harvard University; Rabbi Leonard Zion, Brandeis University.

One of the hypotheses that directed our data gathering in Boston was that campus ministers know governance as a mode of ministry less than any other mode. Another hypothesis was that campus ministers have more opportunity to function when they operate in institutions which (a) have complex and changing goals in respect to personal community inquiry and public service, (b) lack formal, hierarchical organization, and (c) permit a high differentiation of role and goal. Educational organizations with an ideal of easily obtainable harmony, with little diversity and tension between groups and little opportunity for informal groups, have a repressive effect on campus ministries. In short, different systems and atmospheres of governance strongly influence the goals and practices of campus ministers. Most of the conflicts between campus ministers and administrators are in protected, one-religion, one-class, one-race institutions, with narrowly defined, slow-changing intellectual and spiritual objectives.

The lack of attention to governance by campus ministers is partly attributable to the latters' alienation from the social and institutional structures which have traditionally been the channels through which power and influence flow. Often without experience on a campus, personal contact with leaders, and the exercise of power, the ministers tend to perpetuate student views of alienation toward the social order. They view the vast bureaucracies of the larger universities as remote, incomprehensible, often fraudulent, beyond hope or desire to change. They invite apathy and hostility, rather than a desire to know how one can give a part of oneself to a school or be closely and personally identified with it.

Alienation among ministers and those they attract is inevitably involved in problems of governance, for governance rests on the individual's concrete relation to social objectives, function, and authority. Leaders cannot govern if they do not believe they have a significant part in envisioning the objectives of major institutions which serve other people, in choosing the means for achieving these purposes, and in the selection and guiding of leaders. These are the requirements of societal or communal organization.

One theme pervades our analysis: governance is inextricably linked with prophecy, ruling with teaching, power with inquiry. The primary power the leader has in a democratic society is to assure full participation of citizens in learning the realities which confront them, the principles which guide a proposed course of action, and the limitations and costs of alternative courses. Conversely, the failure which stirs deepest popular resentment is to withhold or distort the resources for the governed to judge the rightness of a political course of action.

Do Campus Ministers Make Their Goals Clear to the Leaders of the University?

All governance is directed toward some envisioned goal by which the leader orients himself and others. The demands of goal achievement are for performance: for the spelling out of values in specific actions and using available institutional resources and personal skills to accomplish corporate purposes. The goal achiever is acutely aware of the competing designs of various actors in a social system and of the power they have relative to his own to achieve their goals.

The minister who stresses governance as a mode of ministry views the social system less in terms of its limits to power than as a reality that can be controlled or directed by individuals and groups who know what they want out of the system. Therefore, his is least alienated of all modes of ministry from the system; he constantly translates the latest theories and facts into mechanisms and plans for action; he values knowledge not for its own sake but for its help in achieving public goals. He sees that problems of personal identity cannot be solved simply by investigating subjective meaning. Rather, he knows that one's identity involves facing the meaning of his environment and achieving significant goals. Therefore, the moral and religious task of the administrative, executive ministry is that of making the church an expression and instrument of God's will, of their own and others' convictions as to the tasks they are called to do in a particular time and place. And one of these tasks is to see that the goals of other associations are humane and moral, the consequence of human covenants or willing acceptance of mutual obligations.

Like the other modes, the emphasis of the ministry on goal achievement can lead to extremes. These often appear as preoccupation with meeting one's own set of objectives accompanied by attempts to manipulate people or even God (for example, magic) so that organizational goals will be reached and deadlines met. Such people give inadequate attention to the process by which goals change through the participation of others and to the unintended by-products that often undermine central purposes of an institution.

Most of these general observations about the goal-achieving ministry were made by the early papers of the Boston colloquium. Dr. Stotts, in a paper on evaluation of institutional leadership, noted that in virtually all studies of the clergy, administrative activity is rated last in desirability, but first in time consumed. It was his hypothesis that the campus ministry might magnify this disjunction even more than parish ministers and fail to appreciate the "vacuity of institutions apart from leadership." It was his conviction that the denigration of the goal-achieving mode of ministry is related to a whole series of assumptions that are seldom examined critically in the church. For example, it is assumed that strong administrators are trying to control people and that this mode of action is unworthy. But the question needs to be asked whether a society or association can exist without controls' being exercised to give direction to social change so that humane goals are achieved. There is also the assumption that there is a mystery in the nondirected group and its happenings which is absent from the group that has strong leadership. This unpredictable element is held to be more religious than what can be seen and understood. But where is the biblical or theological basis for such assumptions? Did not Jesus talk usually of the meaning of what he had seen and of what could be acted upon? If he talked of mysteries, it was in relation to an unfolding future.

There is the assumption also that institutions cannot be modified, buried, or replaced. Yet many social scientists and theologians discern signs of vast innovations taking place in the patterns of our culture. The assumptions, furthermore, that human dialogue must always be unstructured, that no dialogue is possible in present formal association, leads ministers to disregard responsibilities to make clear to officials and leaders of the university what it is they are trying to accomplish in their work.

To test how operative these assumptions were in the campus ministries, the Boston colloquium arranged for a schedule of interviews among university leaders with whom the campus ministers would presumably discuss their goals.[3] This study revealed that the campus ministry in-

---

3. Mrs. Audrey Clapham, an interviewer trained in sociology and theology, was employed to interview a representative sample of deans of students, presidents, and church-involved faculty.

frequently spelled out in written memoranda, reports, and formal meetings its changing goals and activities. The nature of the governing structure of the host educational institution had much to do with this. No ministerial group had tried to arrange briefing sessions with people other than those on their advisory boards.

Consequently in every institution studied there was need for more communication between the campus ministry and university officials and faculty as to comparable objectives. Such communication usually has to be initiated by the ministry; it will not be done by the officials and faculty. "Every relationship with university officials," as one campus minister observed, "is a question of who are we and what do we do? If the minister is not sure of his answer to this question he avoids the contacts that will expose his confusion." The failure to initiate communications about church objectives is at heart often a failure at professional identity.

But there are also campus ministers who are quite certain about their mission to make the Christian Gospel known in campus intellectual life and social action and in raising critical questions about university policy. Their ministerial actions are always in need of interpretation because they often raise great problems for university leaders. For example, in many institutions the official expectations are that campus ministers will be supporters of the administration's efforts to hold the line against dropping of officially enforced dating restrictions and other parietal rules; officials are therefore confused and puzzled by the "new morality" by which the clergy back many student demands. They often prefer clergy who are less aggressive in their public actions and who do not highlight differences among religious groups, faculty, and students on sensitive campus issues. One dean of students with a reputation among campus ministers for taking quite personally ministerial criticism of university relations to students, and who saw their office chiefly as that of "moral guidance," when asked how he viewed the goals of chaplains, replied, "Frankly, I am confused as hell. The university is confronted by more moral and spiritual problems than ever before in its history, but I don't know what goals the chaplains are pursuing, will pursue, or want to pursue."

The problem of fulfilling ministerial goals in a university and of having these objectives understood, if not accepted by the academic power structure, is not one which can be explained simply as the outcome of individual clergy attention to keeping officials informed. The problem has to do with whether the clergy see their whole mission as being advanced in important ways by the work of an educational institution and as influenced by its ongoing changes and plans for the future.

This can best be indicated by a comparison of the relations of campus ministries to officials in two universities in the Boston area. One of these universities offers a fairly broad spectrum of traditional liberal arts majors and professional and graduate schools; it has had a historical connection to a Protestant denomination that feels threatened by many student demands. The other institution is secular in polity with principal emphasis in its work on engineering, technological growth, and applied sciences.

In the past few years the church-related university has been the scene of considerable student protest action and villain hunting on a wide front: college book store management, press censorship, civil rights, and so forth. The Protestant campus clergy have generally represented either outright support of these student actions, and participation in their organizational meetings, or public support of greater student participation in the university's consideration of future academic plans.

The relations between the campus ministers and the deans of students were strained and infrequent at the time of our study. One of the deans of students of the first university observed:

Social and university reforms are occupying too large a place in the campus ministry. If we have a pregnant girl who needs help, the chaplains give us support. But they are not concerned with the problems of drugs, cheating in academic work, or vandalism of university property, which are closer to home for most students. We have too many ministers at our university concerned with their popularity rating. They are afraid to be considered company men. Therefore, they haven't got the guts to investigate and talk about the relations of religious thinking to parietal rules and other issues I mentioned. I get little or no support from chaplains on moral problems. Meanwhile, the chaplains are advising some of the most irresponsible dissenters on campus. Much anti-university activity is emanating from one denominational student center. The whole ministry there is given to this role. I am critical, but confused. Is this a balanced, basic ministry we are getting?

The breakdown in mutual confidence and respect was widespread;

the position stated above was shared by many in the office of the dean of women, who had ceased to use campus clergy in meetings with resident leaders. Discussions of officials and the clergy never moved beyond the issues under agitation at the moment. The comments above indicate profound differences with the operative goals of most ministers at this university and need to be brought before the Council of Protestant Clergy and the association of deans of students and personnel workers at the school for thorough discussion. The issues raised should have to do with what moral inquiry is to be in the church and university, whether an adequate team ministry has emerged with all functions performed, what priorities of educational issues are established in the university, and so on.

One of the most obvious and pervasive problems in this institution was the expectation by highly placed university officials that the goals of the campus ministers would be set chiefly by "their communication with official and responsible university officers." The vice-president for student affairs noted that "as staff members they have a responsibility to follow university lines and policies. They do not help when they are part of a breakdown of communications, when they do not provide a linking function to appropriate people." In this official's view, the university had sought to encourage—through meeting with the Council of Protestant Ministers and through the university-designated sponsor of religion, the dean of the chapel—a more functional team ministry. The concern was that "pastoral care, such as counseling and visitation, relations to faculty teaching and scholarly study groups, and common worship" all be performed so that a given ministry not go off into tangents of social action or denominational programing. But in his judgment the team approach had not been carried out.

> I really don't know any more just what they [campus ministers] are doing; they are not acting in a way that indicates a clear focus of goals, but rather individually in dispersed contributions. There is a reluctance of the chaplains to report on their doings to the officials of the university. This creates problems. All of us have our work evaluated, through observation, reports, conferences, etc. But if information is withheld as to explicit goals and achievements or failures, we can only say with embarrassment, that we don't know what the campus ministers are doing.

When this official is asked about the rise of student power, he seems willing to acknowledge that the phenomenon represents a legitimate "complicating" of the decision-making processes of the university in which "regular and dependable communication in the revision of university policies is necessary." He sees student power as a complex development reflecting "the larger community currents" for social change and the attempt to bring it about "directly without taking recourse to the usual channels of responsibility." He sees the growth of "floating alienation" in the society against the impersonal demand that institutions place on people. The university, he acknowledges, is having to decide on its goals in a much more intricate power structure than a few years ago.

It is important to note that these observations are not applied to the situation of the campus minister. And there is no evidence that the campus ministers have tried to relate the change in their work to such forces in their talk with administrators. They have made little or not effort to explain why they cannot make loyalty to university policy their chief goal and why their functions have broadened to include concerns other than the traditional pastoral ones. For most of these ministers the student power structure is their chief focus, and they are just now beginning to sense with the students how much the issues the students fight for are tied up with powers in the whole metropolitan world, with professional organizations and training. Student Black Power action is reinforced by black community groups; protests over hospital care or book costs or housing services of the university take on the professional interests of doctors, businessmen, architects, and their academic accomplices.

In such a situation, the quality and success of ministry is directly related to the work it does in exploring its goals with those who have the power to effect their achievement. And these people turn out to be much more than student protest leaders, many of whom are uninterested in the basic adaptability of the major institutions of the society to social, moral, and intellectual challenges.

The second institution we studied in depth is ministered to by "religious counselors" (a name carried over from an earlier pastoral tradition), who have no formal ties to the university. But they have developed a consciousness among faculty and administrators of their goals which leaves no doubt in their minds that they are working with a group of professionals who have thought through their corporate responsibilities and have distributed them with an eye to bringing out the special talents of the persons involved. As to the pattern of authority in the school, the dean of students notes, the administration exercises its authority much like the ministry. It "rules by consent more than directive," by "faith in its objectives and allocation of its resources more than by control of the coercive powers to hire and fire." Objectives are achieved with the minimum of superstructure. The emphasis is on power of persuasion, rather than on formal status or hierarchy.

The campus ministry has responded to this ethos by arranging conferences for an advisory committee which "spell out in as concrete a way as possible the goals and philosophy of our work." They have responded also with a faculty seminar in technology and culture that provides a place for common discussion of many of the value problems implicit in the scholarship of the faculty and its impact on American society; they have established summer workshops for church leaders which explore the role of community organizations in urban reconstruction, in architectural and other aesthetic developments of an urban society. Both campus ministers and administrators look upon the clergy's position outside the formal power structure as offering students a freedom in counseling that produces more general information on student needs, dilemmas, and aspirations than that available to the official counselors. The campus ministers are seen by the administration as critical observers and supporters of reforms they also want in education: more flexibility in course arrangements to meet student interests, greater recognition of good teaching that helps the student contact, and the like.

The chief clue to the relationship between campus ministers and the power structures of the second university is that both parties sense they are learning from each other, that there is a mutuality of goals in the midst of frank and honest criticism. The campus clergy see in the institution's emphasis on problem solving, quantitative goal achievement, and technical discipline that remains sensitive to human values a strong challenge to the churches. As one minister said, "We are being forced into a new homiletical stance. The laity are ready to change, but we don't yet know where to lead them." The attempts of the faculty to explain the moral and spiritual dimensions of this kind of education to humanistic faculty and to churchmen expose new forces at work in the contemporary world. In short, these campus ministers think they are working in an institution on the frontiers of the intellectual and policy choices of our society; this kind of morale is not pervasively present in the first institution.

The problem of campus ministers' keeping the leaders of the institutions with which they work informed of their work is not, then, that of getting clergy to make some simple resolve to keep their lines of communication open. The problem has to do with the locus of significant educational change and reform and whether the church has been sensitive to the sources of public leadership and inquiry in assigning its professional leaders. Some colleges and universities are at the convergence of powerful forces, the centers of interaction between leaders of old and new power movements, and some are not. A minister may work his heart out trying to move a sluggish institution, but achieve nothing, for he does not work with complementary forces going his way. A minister may be part of a period of destruction of a long-established institution unable to reorient itself and frustrated in efforts at constructive action.

ᘊ 17 ᘕ

GOVERNANCE OF THE PROTESTANT CAMPUS MINISTRY

IN A NORTHERN METROPOLITAN AREA

G REATER New York—which economists have aptly described as a twenty-two-county area in the states of Connecticut, New Jersey, and New York[1]—contains some 180 institutions of higher education, almost 10 per cent of the national total. Here are to be found two of the largest and most prestigious graduate schools and producers of doctorates, the largest municipal system of free colleges, a rapidly increasing number of community colleges, and two federal military institutes. Here is *the* metropolis of the nation and a population aware of the struggle of minority groups for recognition in the American system.

The aim of this aspect of the Danforth Study was to build up an understanding of the total educational context in which the Protestant campus ministry of this metropolitan area manifests itself in various functions and roles, so that its actual power to affect the institutions and people it claimed to serve could be assessed. Verbal claims, written records, and observed behavior served as the indicators through which meanings could be grasped and interpretations reached.[2] Finally, in

---

1. Raymond Vernon and Edgar Malone Hoover, *Anatomy of a Metropolis* (Cambridge: Harvard University Press, 1959).

2. The chapter was written chiefly by Robert A. Dentler, Alan MacFarlane, and J. Russell Hale, with editing and revision by Kenneth Underwood. The data were gathered mostly from interviews with campus ministers, faculty members, administrators, students, and denominational executives. Parish ministers were also interviewed regarding their contacts with the campus ministry. Printed matter describing and publicizing campus programs, as well as the programs themselves, were studied.

Section II, we seek to relate these data to our knowledge of an even more complex context: the changing social and political ecology of this metropolitan region. For us, this broad backdrop is the only one from which the power to govern the allocation of personnel and the co-ordination of roles can be realistically studied.

General Findings

Our major discovery was that the full-time campus ministry of non-Jewish and non-Roman Catholic agencies in Greater New York is a minuscule operation scarcely aware of the problems of strategic action or the responsibilities of policy by their superiors. A constituency of some 400,000 students and 32,000 instructors was served by fewer than 48 full-time campus ministers; in New York City, only 14. Furthermore, these few agents were clustered at the older, private, "prestige" institutions. In one city borough, for example, one campus minister—a Y.M.C.A. appointee who happened to be ordained—allegedly represented Protestantism on eight nonsectarian campuses serving 50,000 students and more than 3,000 faculty members. (By contrast, *one* of these eight campuses employed 35 full-time and 90 part-time student personnel workers.)

In the five boroughs of New York City, eight major Protestant denominations and agencies sponsoring fourteen full-time campus ministers spent a total of $176,271 in 1963 on the ministry to higher education.[3] The mean expenditure per agency or denomination was thus $20,860, $700 less than the income of a single suburban cathedral parish in the twenty-two-county area of our study. Viewed in one light, the New York City campus ministry is a parish with 14 ministers, 220,000 parishioners, and an annual budget smaller than that of many Protestant parish establishments serving fewer than 1,000 church members.

The research focused on 80 of the 180 institutions in the Greater New York area: accredited, exclusive of Jewish, Roman Catholic, and specialized schools unaffiliated with a university. Included were large private universities, municipal colleges, denominational colleges, junior or community colleges, federal military institutes, and several new universities.

3. Earl Lowell and Eugene Monick, *Beginning Statements on Theology, Philosophy, Strategy, Structure and Budget Relative to the Proposed Ecumenical Foundation for Higher Education in New York* (New York: United Ministries in Higher Education, 1964, mimeographed).

Any discussion of the governance of campus pastors by denominational leaders must take into account the churches' adjustment to the major structural change in American higher education over the past century: the replacement of the private and denominational college by the university.

The personal touch supplied in the small college by dedicated faculty members has come to be provided for by new agents and ancillary organizations which safeguard the *in loco parentis* traditions long a part of collegiate life. The college dean, specialized faculty advisers, campus psychologist, campus pastor, were some of the agents. Among the "new" systems were freshman week, religious clubs, and denominational organizations.

The homogeneous undergraduate college with its official chaplain or director of religious activities has been totally overshadowed on the urban scene. The existence of vast graduate schools, professional schools, research institutes, and a 94.7 per cent commuter population of students indicates special ways of ministering and a largely different role for the campus pastor.[4]

In this context there has been a de-emphasis on the role of denominational associations at the colleges. One justification given was that they emphasized only student work; their outreach to faculty was chiefly in utilizing them as advisers. Another was the co-operative and ecumenical nature of the present-day campus pastorate. But the fact is that organizations and clubs are among the major tools employed in the pastoral ministry for which most campus pastors were trained. Therefore, in the urban university the campus minister, in laying down many of these ministerial tasks, often finds himself in a state of confusion. One respondent said he was "engaged in campus ministry without actually ministering." He stated that his work had no defined purpose and was neither worship nor mission-centered; he opposed clubs.

The fundamentalist Inter-Varsity Christian Fellowship differs from many Protestant campus ministries in that work with individuals and groups is still emphasized. As a spokesman stated it, "We are not for

---

4. The high percentage of commuters is not a new phenomenon. In 1941, 93% of the New York State students in the metropolis were commuters. For a discussion of this, see John W. Paige, "Commuting to New York Colleges," *University of the State of New York Bulletin,* July 1, 1946.

education for its own sake; our job is to save souls, to pluck them from Hell." The meetings of the movement are student-run, with staff members, mostly unordained, covering huge areas comprising many universities and colleges.

We found as many as fifteen students attending the regular Bible discussions on campuses, while an "area" meeting drew over ninety attendants. There was no debate or conflict of opinions. Commenting on the "well-attended meetings" of this group, one minister whose main work, incidentally, was with faculty said, "There's a lot of good in the fellowship of groups like this. We, on the other hand, have opposed programs and groups with worship, fellowships, etc. We appear to be suspicious of the type of solidarity these folks and the R.C.'s have. But has any alternative, successful thing been developed?"

WORSHIP ACTIVITIES

A close scrutiny of the leaflets announcing the programs and purposes of the Protestant student associations at the municipal four-year colleges revealed that little emphasis was placed on worship. Only at one campus was there a regular service. Of the day students' association, comprising 10,000 students, 500 of whom were Protestant, the campus pastor said: "The student who relates here most consistently is the one who is related also to his home church. . . . Wednesday is the program focal point of the association. We meet at the local Methodist church. Worship services first in the chapel—about 25 participate in this. Forty attend the lunch and meeting afterwards."

The evening students' association, in a division where over-all enrollment and Protestant preference is of the same order, draws about twenty-five to its biweekly services and meetings held at the church of a different denomination. The general pattern at these schools is to focus the worship experiences on Thanksgiving, Christmas, and Easter.

Predictably, at Protestant church-related colleges we found an emphasis on Christian worship and a well-arranged schedule, sometimes daily, of services and devotional meetings. These institutions—and there are very few in Greater New York—operate on a basis of one chaplain to an institution and often have other clergymen on the staff as well. Exclusive of a handful of fundamentalist colleges and junior colleges, nowhere was attendance at chapel compulsory. We found on these church-related campuses a somewhat clearer, if more rigid, view of the functions of the campus minister. The support of the administration, an official place on the college hierarchy, a largely undergraduate clientele, an atypically high percentage of residential students, a designated place and schedule for worship—all these factors make it easier for these campus ministers to fulfill the popularly conceived role tasks of the college chaplain or, indeed, of the Christian minister: "pastor of the church in this place." Yet one who attracted as many as thirty students and five faculty members to his daily services was nevertheless rather discouraged: "I teach because it is one of the few ways left to meet students —they don't come to chapel. Still, many of us are moving away from teaching and we're concentrating on worship—most of all on the Holy Communion. We need the church in the full sense of the church on the campus."

Another, who considered worship and "Christian Social Action" to be the most important tasks of the campus ministry and thought that many campus ministers neglected worship, pointed toward a ministry role:

> This is no midwestern church college; there's a lot of secularism here. Being chaplain at a church college is not the Heaven my colleagues think it is: we do meet with some hostility. A few weeks ago the librarian closed the library during one of my services. He did it on his own initiative because the kids were making noise. I didn't even know about it. But the kids were up in arms—"Freedom of religion and all that."

The largest private university in the metropolis has no Protestant chapel. In spite of the expressions of interest in worship which we encountered in the literature and from interviews with members of the staff, public worship or worship facilities are low on the list of priorities of the unified Protestant ministries on this campus. From a chaplain: "There used to be a Protestant Meditation Room—4 flights up—a crummy joint in the attic. 'You can't find God just anywhere,' motivated this effort, 'you have to go to a room like that.' No wonder nobody took the trouble to look Him up." From a student: "There were never regular Protestant services. Once Chaplain J. tried to hold services on a patio. It was to be weekly, but it only lasted eight weeks. About eight staff members and students came." A fundamentalist minister, not part of the staff, who does some student work on the campus, told us that "the main evidence of the weakness of their sort of ministry is the fact that they can't bring their little membership to *any* religious functions—only social."

By contrast, on the campus of the second largest private university in Greater New York stands a large chapel with several clergymen on the staff of the united ministry and three weekday services: Lutheran, Episcopalian, and a general Protestant service. On Sundays, there is a morning service. Attendance at all services was small in 1964 and 1965. The largest denominational service averaged fifteen attendants over the period of our concern. Other services had congregations of one, two, or three. An investigator describes one of these services: "It was a beautiful service. Bach chorales rendered by the excellent choir of six were a background for the majestic cadences of the Lutheran rite. The sermon was intellectual—suited for a college chapel. This observer was the only member of the congregation."

Nor were the official Sunday morning services indicators of widespread academic involvement in worship. Fifty to sixty worshipers were present, many of whom appeared to be older people living in the neighborhood, with no university connections.

The place of worship in the Protestant ministry at the United States government academies was clear: part of the training to be an officer and a gentleman is that one worship God on Sundays. One of these institutions described its program thus: "All cadets are provided a sound religious atmosphere. Each cadet must attend one of the weekly chapel services—Protestant, Catholic, or Jewish. . . . Protestant services are held in the cadet chapel every Sunday during the academic year and out of doors during the summer months."

While the Sunday 8:50 and 11:00 A.M. Protestant morning worship services are nondenominational, weekly Holy Communion services according to Episcopalian, Lutheran, and Presbyterian rites are also celebrated. Some 300 cadets are involved in either the cadet chapel or Sunday school teaching. Some also take part in daily morning devotions.

COUNSELING

Our investigations have not helped to clarify the role of the metropolitan campus minister as counselor. We found that *every* campus pastor conceived this work as part of his role; yet there was little definition involved. In a denominational college, where presumably some of the forces or urbanization and the large university socialization forces had not conquered, we found this estimate of counseling:

> That is always associated with the Chaplain's role. But with a wrinkle! The college looks upon the Chaplain (as in the army) as a morale officer. Keep the natives quiet—keep the peace—watch that the boat doesn't rock! Some of the men (chaplains) have gone into "psychological counseling" in a big way. They bring in the neighborhood psychiatrist, have a whole personnel set-up. We've got this here, too. A man could specialize and give all his time in this. But I don't think this is the "large thing" with most in our denomination.

A dean of students at a municipal college, well known for his sympathy for the campus ministry, commented:

> Rev. K. uses an office here once a week for counseling. The R.C.'s used to have the same privilege before they built their center. The main thing is: If a youngster is upset, is his religious counselor willing to have him seen by our psychologist? The churches have different teachings on moral matters—we respect them.

A campus minister's task, then, by this view, has been to add sectarian flavor to the main work of the counselor. No wonder that he could further comment thus: "The campus ministry in a set-up like this can't absorb the real needs. It is peripheral to the situation."

A pastor at a state university gave a "traditional" response: "My basic work is that of a pastor in the classical sense, a supportive person of religious identity. The reason we're here is theological."

MINISTRY BEYOND UNDERGRADUATES

At all but the four-year denominational colleges we found a belief that ministering to the university community meant a ministry to faculty and graduate students as well. Few pastors conceived of their task as "student work." Some were aware of a mission to higher education *in itself*. They were conscious of the rivalry between the various academic disciplines and felt that the campus ministry could serve as a meeting ground. One pastor put it this way: "I want to get the sociologist to speak to the physicist, and the English teacher to speak to the geologist."

Most of the "faculty work" is either informal or spasmodic. It must be recalled that few campuses boast even one full-time campus minister. At one of the colleges of the municipal university where there is no full-time pastor, the chief contact is through an *annual* student-faculty tea. At this institution some sixty faculty members are also on the mailing list of the Student Christian Association. At another of the city colleges, the full-time pastor said: "I have *some* contact with faculty. Some are on our board here. There is one faculty dinner a year . . . then we have two Disputations, fashioned after the medieval university ones." One staff member of one of the largest and best-staffed campus ministries, while conscious of the priority of the ministry to faculty, lamented the fact that little was being done. He wanted "individual Christian scholar-professors who would stand up and be counted. Some of them are scared stiff."

The public institutions appear to present as many possibilities as do the private schools. A pastor at a division of a state university describes one of his efforts:

> I had a faculty forum not long ago, and the President himself came and a lot of the top people. Some of them said they couldn't see what a parson was doing here because "parsons are sort of out of touch with life, aren't they?" Maybe everybody had a few too many drinks, but we had fun and people really relaxed and loosened up. One or two thought we had to "sum up"—they wanted to tidy up the discussion.

The dean of students at one large college of engineering (one of eight institutions served by a Y.M.C.A. minister only) would welcome a campus pastor, but not only for the "kids who have the blinkers and blinders of science and engineering": "A lot of faculty are the same. If a man could move around, get to know them, play pool in the faculty club, etc. he could do much to raise their sights."

The most highly institutionalized work we observed was a monthly faculty luncheon at a university in the city. This function draws forty to sixty faculty at every session and is believed by many to be a successful venture. At this school, one minister took faculty work as his major assignment and thus had the time to make contacts. We attended a session which had as its major program a speech on "The Problem of Free Speech in a Democracy." Forty persons were present, twenty-two of them academics.

Neither of the city technical colleges with which we specially concerned ourselves offered any credit courses in religion. One of the two "new" municipal universities listed no religion courses; the other, under its departments of Social Service and of Philosophy, respectively, listed one course in Comparative Religion and one in Comparative Religion and Philosophy of Religion.

Neither of the municipal colleges we observed had a Department of Religion. One offered three courses in the Department of Philosophy and two in the Department of Sociology and Anthropology. The other college offered one course in the Philosophy of Religion. Neither of the federal military institutes offered any courses in Religion or Philosophy of Religion.

At the denominational colleges, religion courses predictably occupied a major niche in the over-all curriculum. One of these listed ten courses offered under the Department of Philosophy and Religion. (Ten years earlier, in 1953, there had been eighteen courses and a Department of Christianity.) Another denominational college listed twenty-one courses, Both of these schools had three faculty members assigned as teachers of religion.

The prestige universities offered large numbers of courses in religion. One of these is formally affiliated with a major theological seminary, and, indeed, the seminary is in fact its graduate Department of Religion. Another, while having no Department of Religion, has an active Department of Religious Education.

We were impressed by the fairly uniform lack of co-ordination between faculty religion departments and less formal academic agencies such as the chaplaincy. In part, this results from the historic attempt of academic religionists to preserve their faculty respectability through studied dissociation from campus religious practice, especially in nonsectarian institutions. But that effort is a holdover. It bears little resemblance to the concerns, needs, and activities of students and university intellectuals in the metropolitan area community today.

SOCIAL ACTION

Every campus pastor we interviewed asserted an interest in social action, particularly in academic and religious involvement in the civil rights movement. Yet there were very few action programs initiated by full-time campus pastors or perpetuated by their identifiable constituents in religious associations.

This seems explainable by two facts which we have already explored: the small number of agents in the metropolitan campus ministry, and the tensions and difficulties surrounding the very existence of campus religious groups. On the positive side of the ledger must be recorded support for the work of the Student Christian Movement, personal involvement with, and assistance to, such civil rights groups as CORE, NAACP, and SNCC, and the scattered efforts of campus ministries to tutor underprivileged children. These somewhat successful efforts at campus ministerial involvement in social action in no instance became a primary channel of communication between the civil rights movement and the university community, however.

More direct social action on civil rights was generally not organized. We identified individual chaplains and professors who, through informal networks of communication, made common arrangements to travel to the deep South to take part in demonstrations, and we noted the participation of some of the same men in pickets and planning efforts inside New York City. But these seemed to be events generated through denominational and general Protestant affiliations and were not indicative of a group direction in the metropolitan area campus ministry. Campus ministerial investments in tutorial programs for low-income Negro and Puerto Rican children were neither innovative, initiatory, nor large. Moreover, investigation of the educational activities in five large Negro parishes revealed very little formalized involvement of the campus ministry. In one large parish where the pastor directs widespread educational activities—remedial reading classes run by college students, scholarships to deserving parishioners, supportive contacts with those actually enrolled in the university—we found no expression of need for the help of the campus ministry: "I avoid the chaplains. I go directly to the persons involved. I carry on my own private dialogue with key people. X college wants more Negro students. Dean P and others have approached me directly. They've promised that if I find the qualified boys and $500, they will do the rest."

The serious lack of man power and financial resources, coupled with the small number of students participating in campus ministry–sponsored societies, leads to the belief among the pastors that social action work should be done through secular student groups. Says an agent who works alone on two large campuses: "There are only 25 *really* concerned members on both campuses—what can we do? we can only work through existing groups *as Protestants. . . .* We're going to do some tutoring of kids after school. We back the student cabinet and other social action groups. We collected money for Mississippi."

Interviews showed that official or semiofficial recognition of the campus minister's status, while it *can* be useful in providing an audience for the prophetic call for justice, often led to administration interference and attempts to silence the prophet. There were real role conflicts. But the more serious difficulty was that the campus minister on occasion was confronted by a college or university administration which was confused over the limitation and possibility of university-based political action.

The Higher Educational Context

With the exception of the municipal colleges, most of the universities and related institutions common to higher education in Greater New York have only very recently come to "live *in*" the urban field. There is a vital difference between occupying space and being organized to behave in terms of it. Historically, the distinction was moot. In the years since the Great Depression, however, the urban environment has pressed inexorably upon the character of the university community, leaving increasingly indelible impressions.[5]

Rising building costs, extreme shortage of space for growth, the dispersion of faculty and student residential settlements, and the changing regulatory power of local and state agencies have constrained the urban university toward transformations which have little to do with the concerns of faculties. Inner-city colleges have begun to contend for space against the households and merchants who have surrounded them for decades. Changes in the scale of importance of the university as an institution have impelled changes in facilities, styles of academic life, and neighborhood relations.

---

5. Our remarks on higher urban education are informed by these sources: Oliver C. Carmichael, *Graduate Education* (New York: Harper, 1961); William C. De Vane, *Higher Education in Twentieth Century America* (Cambridge: Harvard University Press, 1965); Roger A. Freeman, *Crisis in College Finance* (Washington: Institute for Social Science Research, 1965); J. Martin Klotche, *The Urban University* (New York: Harper, 1966); Herbert Stroup, *Bureaucracy in Higher Education* (New York: The Free Press, 1966).

The new urban academic is cosmopolitan in nearly all respects. He is recruited from some remote location. When he arrives, he may elect to settle anywhere. In the years before World War II, for example, two-thirds of the faculty of Columbia University lived within a mile and a half of the central campus. At present, only half live within this radius. Most of them are younger instructors and assistant professors along with a cluster of the oldest, most senior professors.

The campus itself has more than one center. Increasingly, it fosters a network of subcampuses: professional schools, training and research and development centers and laboratories, which are dispersed across the urban field.

As the ecology of the urban university changes, and as its relations to the surrounding crush of community interests have begun to change, so has the urban university entered a period when its other functions are increasingly fluid and ambiguous. The old forms persist: the large introductory lecture course, the little liberal arts college buried inside burgeoning professional and graduate schools, the once-a-week seminar, and the emphasis on structured classroom procedures go on.

But they go on amid competing alternatives. Tool subjects are taught increasingly through self-instruction, travel, internships, and practical exposures. Research, even for the undergraduate term paper, becomes a tradition within, yet apart from, the classroom teaching tradition, for the student as for the teacher. Libraries changing into information retrieval systems and scientific experimentation changing into computor simulations suggest the alternatives.

Even as new interdisciplinary programs are created each year, departmental and disciplinary lines harden and differences are intensified through increased federal and foundation patronage. The result is an attenuation of informal relationships, the sociological core of institutional higher education. The gaps between administrators and faculties, between faculties and faculties, and between faculties and students stimulate new types of formal structures. The United Federation of Teachers is enjoying modest yet growing success in unionizing college teachers. Research faculties are devising separate forms. Mass student organizations are taking shape as instruments of protest and radical reform which are aimed only partially at campus *change*.

Interpersonal frustrations about objectives tend under these circumstances to fuse in a race against the exhilarating developments of new knowledge, new frontiers of inquiry, and new accomplishments in organizing scholarship and teaching to meet the requirements of the metropolitan society.

If this race were to be run by itself, the stimulation of the university community would be impressive, regardless of the outcome. But this race between confusion and achievement must be played out in the framework of an urbanizing polity. The pressure to accommodate the growing onrush of students in old and understaffed institutions, while new ones are built overnight, is nearly overwhelming.

Left to their own devices, most universities in the metropolis might meet the challenge of adapting. But they cannot survive through reliance on endowments, private patronage, and tuition. This has placed the urban university community in an open market of political choice. Scarce resources of space, equipment, talent, and autonomy of action must be reallocated. This reallocation is now mediated by a baffling array of local, state, and federal governmental agencies. These, together with pressure groups, power blocs, and divergent economic interests, are not only numerous but bewildering in their fragmentation of the authority to make decisions. The ability of the university to act is increasingly determined by the ability or inability of other urban institutions to act in concert.

In Greater New York, as elsewhere, the priority given to news about higher education has risen dramatically in the news media over the last ten years. Stories of mighty battles over control, "exclusives" about the contention for public resources, and feature articles about research grants and famous professors have become front-page news, where they went uncovered by the press only a few years earlier. Distinctions between private and public control have begun to disintegrate, as the prime resources to be gained come to be all but exclusively available from the state and federal government and as institutional prestige is built up more and more through media exposure and published indicators of stored competencies.

SPECULATIONS AND CONCLUSIONS

Viewed against this backdrop, failures to give some order and coherence to the Protestant campus ministry in metropolitan New York become much more intelligible. Dollar and manpower investments by the denominations have grown at a steady rate over the years, but the rate bears no correspondence whatever to the scale of change being experienced in secular sectors of the urban campus.

We felt at times during this research as if we were studying a "non-phenomenon," as if we were in search of program events that were nowhere to be found. This is not the case, to be sure. We met many able, productive campus ministers and some enthusiastically engaged academic laymen and students. Programs *were* under way, but their frequency and scope were partially obscured for the observer by the density of changing events in the larger context. Studied as a single case extension of the Protestant ministry into one mission field, the urban campus ministry we examined is not unimpressive. Studied in relation to the setting and its changes, however, this ministry seems ephemeral, lacking in relevant strategies and ideologies, and devoid of ultimate prospect.

We do not believe that our judgments are excessively absolute, unrealistic, or severe. They are based on an acquaintance with the surging, ambiguous, transformative nature of the urban university community. They assume that effectiveness depends on the ability to set goals to achieve, to order the competencies of personnel, to meet the institution's mission in society, and to command the attention of some portion of that community. Our empirical estimate is that this ability was missing—an estimate that was neither challenged nor contradicted by anyone among the many professionals and participants we encountered.

Of course, we agree with Gilbert E. Doan, Jr., Northeastern Secretary of the National Lutheran Council's Division of College and University Work, who commented on our first draft of this report:

> What is needed is a systematic attempt to define both the theological criterion for this kind of work and the actual expectations of those who legitimate it and then an attempt to measure performance by the employment of a method designed distinctly to deal with these expectations. . . . How do you measure, just for instance, the degree to which students accept basic responsibilities in mutual pastoral care for each other? . . . I am not at all persuaded that the campus ministry, least of all in New York, would come off any better, but until those who know about expectation and measurement . . . can supply us with methods, we are not likely to do anything but scare our legitimaters into giving us more money.

It is certainly true that deeper levels of behavior and meaning that obtain in the urban campus ministry have been ignored in this study and could not have been captured with the slight net of our role theory and methodology. To stretch the metaphor, however, we cannot accept the notion that we have missed the catch entirely.

Gilbert Doan also voiced a question that reached us from several quarters in the course of this study. He conveyed candidly his

> astonishment that New York City was chosen as a metropolis to be studied. Anyone who knows campus ministry in the east knows that, for five years at least, New York has been a mess in every respect. Those of us who are responsible for what goes on there are sick about it. But we have been utterly unable to find a constructive solution. . . . But why was not Providence chosen, or New Haven, Syracuse, or Philadelphia? In none of those places are we about to bring in the kingdom, exactly, but it would seem to me that to choose New York is to some degree to invalidate the study.

We were aware of this matter before undertaking the study, but we believe that New York may prove prophetic of developments in other metropolitan area communities. The chief difference between relative failure in New York and relative success in other northeastern communities is a difference in *scale of locality*: of subcultural differentiation, population density, higher educational proliferation, and technology. This difference can only diminish over the next two decades as other northeastern metropolitan area communities take their place in the evolution of urban fields and megalopolitan extensions. We may be overlooking vital differences from locality to locality in social and cultural structures, but we doubt it.

College youth and academic staff may be served religiously in the metropolitan areas of the near future by regular parishes which specialize somewhat in this activity. Locality specialization is now so advanced in the emerging *urban field* that it is increasingly difficult to extend the church by duplicating its full institutional apparatus inside other physically embodied institutions.

The vast bulk of metropolitan students, faculty, and staff are today full-time commuters. Even the faculty and some of the students housed around the great city universities and colleges behave primarily as commuters and not as residents in a total institution. That is to say, they put in their hours, draw their wages or credits, and retire to the privacy of home or friendship and secondary groups for the avocational life.

Ministry to this clientele can perhaps no longer be appended meaningfully to the interstices of the university establishment. Rather, it might be based in the local churches, which themselves now serve denominational organization, where co-ordination, program content, and leadership and training may be carried out resourcefully. One speculative conclusion is that the ends of the campus ministry may best be served in the future by redeploying to the very limit resources of that on-campus institution, by investing them in *parishes* that have substantial participation of university communicants, and by strengthening the vertical and co-ordinative functions of headquarters.

Of this approach, the Rev. John M. Scott, chaplain of the Episcopal Church at work on the campus of the University of Pennsylvania, commented:

> I find your conclusion to be most agreeable with my own observations after a four-year experience. . . . We see the commuter students at church on such dates as All Saints and Ash Wednesday, and Good Friday, but I must say that my ministry has been exercised principally among the students who do relate to the University parish. This is true even though I am part of the ecumenical staff of the Christian Association. Through that medium I have, for example, participated in three different seminar groups, each running from four to eight weeks involving some thirty students altogether. Through the parish, however, students have been led into community involvement as well as regular parish activities. . . . I do feel that such things indicate that the Church's primary role on the campus is pastoral although it must also be intellectual. We have had four students associated with the parish as undergraduates remain in Philadelphia and remain active in the parish after graduation, taking jobs here because the church's ministry became an integral part of their lives.

Many experienced respondents have pointed out to us two severe limitations on this speculative solution to the problem. They have noted that the ability of Protestant parishes adjacent to universities is extremely uneven when gauged against the need for parish involvement in the student and faculty communities. Some parishes are specialized around quite different groups: the aged, the sick-poor, the very rich, and so forth. Regardless of policy directives, parish "cultures" cannot be redesigned to serve students and professors merely by virtue of proximity.

In addition, our speculative solution is plainly regressive. It suggests a reversion to the pattern common to the scene prior to World War II and ignores the interim evolution of independent campus programs.

If a parish-centered solution could be designed that was sufficiently flexible and resourceful, the prospect of sacrificing what has evolved in the interim would not be more frustrating than the prospect of enlarging failures from within the campus ministry. But we found little in our field trips and interviews that would persuade us that flexibility could be induced or that additional resources could be secured on this basis. Too many other economic and social stresses are impinging on the inner-city parishes to allow for such adaptive absorption of this ancillary mission.

We can speculate, in closing, on the outline of what might work most effectively in governance of the campus ministry. It has its counterparts to what we saw as possibilities at Madison, Wisconsin, and elsewhere. New York City may present an ideal opportunity for experimentation with ecumenical consolidation. The presence of international and national headquarters of several denominations, and particularly the location of the headquarters of the National Council near Columbia University, could provide resources for establishing two University Religious Centers, one in midtown Manhattan and one at the periphery of the city, in Brooklyn or the Bronx. The purpose of each center would be identical; namely, to program for the campus ministry of the city as a whole. Founding of two centers would allow for better comparison and analysis of effects.

The University Religious Center would specialize in communications and encounters. As a communications resource unit, the center might take advantage of film production, film storage, closed- and open-circuit television, recording and radio production, as an intellectually oriented resource for the university community at large. Costs of these activities could be distributed nationally because the products could be perfected to serve national audiences. New York is undoubtedly the location from which to invest in the mass media and the storage of high culture.

As a setting for encounters, the center would offer very high-quality contact of a continuing and direct kind between religiously concerned students, academics, theologians, and religionists. The center could also plan and co-ordinate counseling as well as social action activities, as these require centralization for both quality and impact. Parish-campus co-operation could also be stimulated through center programing in this direction.

Such centers will not solve the problems of diffusion and decentralization which are central to the sprawling evolution of higher education across the urban field. On-campus efforts could not be closed down or substituted for by the introduction of these centers. But each local campus ministry might become more selective in initiating programs of its own. Each could build up its unique strengths, responding to unique local needs and capabilities.

The centers could also address the question of how to build enduring relations between selected parishes and selected university groups. This is a matter requiring co-ordination and consolidation. Part of center resources might be invested deliberately in selected local parish-campus undertakings, making that part of the center a distributor and holding company.

The concept of the religious center, while it does not close out alternative possibilities, also addresses one urgent requirement of the metropolitan area campus ministry. The thought, the art, and all facets of the activity of the campus ministry in the Greater New York area must, at selected times and places, offer the very finest qualities of skill, personality, and dialogue that contemporary Protestantism has in its vast preserve. Those who will come to participate are sophisticated, over-programed, even jaded; yet they hunger for highly meaningful integrations of their lives. To warrant a future, the urban campus ministry will have to bring forward programs that meet unrelenting demands for the highest quality of inquiry, communication, and governance.

The question that persists throughout this report is the following: How was it possible that young men and women could go through years of work in an anarchic, irrational, nonpolicy situation and never raise any significant, effective protest to their supervisors that their activity was ridiculous and ineffectual? They try to carry on as if a student conversation, a few dozen weekly discussion meetings, a Sunday service with a dozen people, were a significant work in their situation.

The fact of the matter is that these ministers had never been given the mental structures in their professional and leadership training to understand a university community in its total ecology, or in the nature of governance in the church. They learned some pastoral theology, some church and society general theory; but nobody ever gave them a way to comprehend a whole metropolitan system of education and how it was operated. So they did not really know how many others were at work as campus ministers and doing what, how many educational institutions there were in the area, why they were chosen to work where they worked, who evaluated them or decided that significant or no achievement had taken place. In short, they could not think in policy terms, and neither could their supervisors.

No one, not even the clergy themselves in these jobs, cared enough to do effective battle over the disorganized, spiritless, aimless body that the campus ministry was becoming under the relentless forces of their work. The campus ministry, able to politic and govern, can be an important independent force in the reform of the church and of education. Eighteen men and three administrators can change the definition of their functions. They can raise the painful questions of what their purpose is in the university and who cares. They can speculate about their place in a larger center of activity, with some rational division of specialization, and who they need and do not need for the work.

All they have to lose is salaries lower than they find in almost any related professional post as secondary-school teacher, in social work and community organization and a multitude of other fields now open to them. They can either ask that administrators of their area in church and university help them hammer out a rationale for their assignments with at least an awareness of the realities described by the Center for Urban Education or refuse to work any longer in these positions. There are places in the universities where their discussions can go on, such as the center. What is lacking is the simple awareness by people of what is happening to them in an institutional system. The ministerial function of good governance is to open the possibilities of power and policy before them.

PART VII

Social Policy and the Moving of Nations and Churches

❧ 18 ❧

ECUMENICAL AND DENOMINATIONAL ATTEMPTS

AT CHURCH POLICY IN EDUCATION

T HE antecedents to the denominational campus ministries that emerged in the American public and private universities in the first half of this century were described in Chapters 4 and 5. Born of churches well imbued with the values of the church-related college and fixed with the imagery drawn from parish models, the campus ministries relocated but did not change the familiar ministries of the churches. The apparent strategy of the churches was to release into new concentrations of students at public universities those clergy who would extend the ministry of Word and sacrament and provide supplemental religious instruction.

Having engaged earlier in a struggle against emergent public institutions of higher education, it is not surprising that the church fathers were not concerned with the character and substantive quality of the education being offered in these same universities to many of their own sons and daughters. They simply admonished the church "to take up as part of its regular work the provision of adequate means for furnishing religious culture to our young people at the state universities and safeguarding them in the church."[1] They sought a ministry by and for the churches, especially to insure educated church leadership for the future, both lay and clergy.

In more than fifty years such ministries have been extended as new public colleges and universities have been built. The essential church policy has not changed. The offices of preacher-priest, pastor-counselor, teacher-inquirer became normative models for the campus ministry.

---

1. *Minutes of the General Assembly, Presbyterian Church in the USA* (Philadelphia, 1904), pp. 161–164.

Recognizing this history, the campus ministry study attempted to inquire into the thinking and the struggles to evolve new patterns and new policies for the church's engagement with the university world. Meetings and conversations with national and regional church executives were coupled with more intensive explorations of a few experiments at new organization and management structures. Inquiry was made into the expansion of campus ministries in the decade 1954–1963. How were expansion decisions made? Who made the decisions? With what research? As new experiments had their development, what was learned about the initiatives and the patterns of support? What promise is there that more comprehensive church strategies may be developed?

While the evidences are not overwhelming and certainly not conclusive, one is encouraged by discovery of some breaks with a long history of limited policy assessment and planning. In a combination of circumstances that produce strain on old patterns and open questions of feasibility, some basic policy considerations are being brought forward.

This chapter attempts to record a few of these evidences and to note some of the problems that continue to plague church leaders as they seek to become open to new university relations for their churches.

Dilemmas in Expansion

The 1950's and early 1960's were years of expansion, not only for the universities but also for all forms of American church life. New church development enjoyed banner years. In the affluence of post-World War II America, the major denominations expanded their campus ministries along with all other church enterprise. A survey completed as a part of this campus ministries study revealed that in the decade 1954–1963 the churches began to invest a slightly larger percentage of their dollars and clergy leadership in this particular field. Table 18–1 shows growth figures presented by the communions.

The same ten-year period saw marked improvements in salary and manse provisions for campus ministers, new attention to living and working conditions, and a considerable investment in new student centers, campus churches, and general facilities for the conduct of campus ministries. In a few instances building developments were accomplished through co-operative efforts of several denominations. Generally, how-

TABLE 18–1.   Number of Ordained Clergy in Campus Ministry

Denomination	1953	1963
American Baptist	66	193
Disciples of Christ	15	34
Episcopal	98	153
Evangelical United Brethren	3	11
Missouri Synod Lutheran	25	46
American Lutheran Church &		
Lutheran Church in America	22	71
Methodist	236	443
Presbyterian U.S.	35	60
United Presbyterian Church, U.S.A.	116	160

ever, plans were made by each denomination along lines determined by an analysis of its own program, finances, and proximity to the parish church and to student living units on the campus. Only slight reference was made to the location or style of ministry being afforded by other denominations. As a result, many campuses were well equipped with a series of church buildings and campus religious centers along a major thoroughfare deemed to be in the main student traffic pattern, only to have church leaders discover that the development of new dormitories thrust a major portion of the students off into another direction. In very few instances did the church seek, or the university provide, a planned place in its campus development design for the campus ministry centers. Nor was the campus ministry so related to any of the major functions of most universities that faculty or administrative leaders were constrained to include them in their own planning for campus expansion.

The struggle to keep pace with the rapid redistribution of students and the seemingly limitless growth in sheer numbers of students concentrated on major campuses produced a growing frustration among the churches as they considered their campus ministry strategies. Few dared to believe that the familiar patterns would in fact maintain the contact with students so central to the purposes pursued for many years. The effort to expand campus ministries in much the same way that the church produced new congregations and new sanctuaries for worship in each major suburban housing development seemed fruitless and provided some of the first evidences that in the face of apparent changes on the campus, a different strategy of ministry might have to be conceived.

Additional Pressures

From within the campus ministries new questions of strategy were slowly emerging. With theological accents moving the church to face outward toward the world, with a larger number of more experienced and educationally prepared clergy being drawn to the campus ministry, it was inevitable that new questions of church and university involvement should arise.

The post-Sputnik student added to the incentive. Harassed and pressed by the intensive competition in studies which he had experienced in junior and senior high school, he carried his academic seriousness to the university. Student participation in all extracurricular activities, including those of student religious centers, showed a marked drop. In the expanded campus many new dormitory lounges and recreation and TV rooms changed the need for comfortable campus centers. All these new facilities were readily available at the student residence, where more and more time was spent on the unrelenting demands of the classroom and in the struggle to stay in school.

Campus ministers recognized that despite the enlarged enrollment in the university, their own ministries reflected no major growth in the number of students reached. As discouragement overtook them at the level of what they rightly believed most churches and local supporting boards expected, they began to envisage new dimensions of the ministry in the university. Could the ministry be seriously extended by the quality of the engagement with graduate students (often serving as instructors and enjoying the widest contacts with students) and with faculty? Was it possible to engender real dialogue concerning the substance of the various disciplines of learning? An attempt to separate Christian faculty into a self-conscious movement had already proved abortive. The engagement would need to be local and frequently with persons who expected little dialogue from the representatives of the churches. Most often the engagement was focused on the presuppositions and other philosophic premises of the various academic disciplines. Though somewhat esoteric, the approach did prove attractive to many faculty and had the distinct virtue of relating the church to the substance and character of the learning process. But this ministry was not prepared to meet directly the host of social policy questions being generated for the whole university world by the society and the abiding concerns of a new student generation.

In the new approach campus ministers made another discovery. Their ministry was clearly Christian, but one whose sectarian labels seemed totally irrelevant. Graduate students and faculty were not ready to be driven into the denominational categories which typical church life prepared for them. There was little that campus clergy sought to achieve that had a denominational ring to it. In this recognition were the seeds of a new collegiality in campus ministry which needed ecumenical church structures for real growth and flowering.

Harsh economic reality added further thrust to possibilities of change. In the early 1960's church receipts began to plateau, a warning of still more stringent times to come. Costs spiraled as the inflated economy called for added funds to continue centers of ministry already under way. Signs of crisis expressed in the civil rights movement and in a growing self-consciousness among the churches about urban problems (aggravated by a church as well as a population "flight to the suburbs") pressured a reallocation of available funds. Favored though the campus ministries had been for a decade, new areas now called for preferential attention.

As in the depression days of the 1930's, growing economic need became a distinct force for interdenominational co-operation. New strategies for the deployment of dollars and manpower were desperately needed. When added to the other dislocations of normative ministry already noted, the economic factor seemed to open doors for new ecumenical consideration by the churches.

Ecumenical Efforts at New Policy

In New York State, with a tradition of co-operation built round the New York Student Christian Movement, an organization born in the stringent thirties, representatives of governing boards of a number of communions explored together the provision of ministries at the many branches of the new state educational system. Commitments were made that none of the co-operating churches would move unilaterally toward new centers of operation. Joint assessments were made of the conditions and possibilities for ministry at the campuses. Discussion moved toward special centers and state-wide programs that would prepare the churches to make better use of all resources for ministries in higher education. New patterns were sought for local strategy boards that would strengthen and extend the impact on campuses long accustomed to highly individualized efforts by the churches.

After almost a decade of effort, there is considerable evidence that the New York program did find ways to improve communication and to enable the churches to extend their outreach to the expanded university system with a minimum of duplication and conflict. The efforts in the City of New York, already examined in Chapter 17, proved to be the last to feel the direct effect of such state-wide planning. There is little evidence, however, that resources of leadership and skill from the university world were adequately appropriated to open questions of church and university engagement in social policy developments. As evidenced in the study of New York City, these remain as new fields to be conquered.

Another intensive effort to move out in new directions was begun in 1964 when the Association for Ecumenical Ministries in Michigan Colleges and Universities was organized. As in New York, the new association was designed to assist in determining opportunities and priorities for new ministries and new forms of ministry in and with the institutions of higher education in Michigan.

Under the leadership of Lester L. Dobyns, the association developed with the endorsement and support of seven churches: American Lutheran, Episcopal (Diocese of Michigan), Evangelical United Brethren, Disciples of Christ, Lutheran Church of America, United Church of Christ, and United Presbyterian Church, U.S.A. Co-operation and various levels of participation with other church boards and councils in Michigan were also sought.

After several years of labor at clarifying its purpose and structure, the AEM records in its articles of association:

> The Association for Ministries in Higher Education is an Association of jurisdictional units bearing responsibility for ministry in higher education in the State of Michigan for churches which confess Jesus Christ as Divine Lord and Saviour. Church jurisdictional units may become full or consulting members of the Association under provisions of Article IV below.
>
> The purposes for which the Association is formed are as follows:

(1) To provide a channel of interpretation and communication among church boards and committees for ministry in higher education.

(2) To act as agency of cooperation and planning for Christian churches in their ecumenical ministries in and with institutions of higher education.

(3) To assist in the development of programs of training and continuing education for the churches in the strengthening of their total ministry in and with Michigan colleges and universities.

(4) To be an instrument of communication by which the resources of higher education are related to the life and needs of the churches.

(5) To be an agency of research and experimentation in the development of new forms of ministry related to the total area of higher education.

(6) To provide a structure for planning and for the coordination of the resources of finance and personnel for united ministries in Michigan institutions of higher education.

In the fulfillment of its purposes, the Association shall undertake three general functions:

(1) The responsibility of convening denominational Boards responsible for ministry in higher education in the state of Michigan in order to provide communication among these Boards, and to assist them both in an understanding of developments in higher education and in strengthening their separate and cooperative ministries in Michigan colleges and universities.

(2) The responsibility to provide an organization for research in new forms of ministry; for experimentation in specialized areas of higher education; for the development of new patterns of relationship and dialogue between the church and institutions of higher education; and for the development of processes of evaluation of ministries in higher education.

(3) The responsibility to provide state-wide structure for united ministries; coordinating budgets, finances, and personnel assignment and review.[2]

This Association for Ecumenical Ministries was given direct responsibility for supplementing existing ministries. It was not given supervisory powers for the long-established work, a division in planning and

---

2. See Lester L. Dobyns, Director, "A Report to the Churches from the Association for Ecumenical Ministries," Ann Arbor, mimeographed (Spring, 1967).

governance that was bound to prove troublesome for both the AEM and the various churches. Inevitably all new work tended to be in dollar competition with expanding needs of established ministries, and assessment of the relative merits of those needs rested with separated bodies. The AEM was also vexed with the long-standing problem of campus ministries' governing boards; namely, their representative character. Almost invariably the policy making and governance of campus ministries by the churches has been given to boards whose representative accountability was guaranteed; for example, representatives from the women's organization, from nearby churches, from ecclesiastical subunits, and so on. What tends to be neglected is the certain presence of persons so well informed about the life of the university that they give guidance and evaluation to the ministries being offered. In the composition of ecumenical boards, with a much wider church constituency, the problem is merely aggravated. From the outset, the AEM was not free of this problem.

Despite these handicaps it is instructive to note the enlarged areas in which the AEM soon found itself at work: a project in co-operation with the Center for Research and Conflict Resolution of the University of Michigan focused on the struggles to gain social and political power in a major urban area by the powerless and the poor; continuing education of campus ministers; consultation and involvement in problems related to the place of religion in the training of teachers for the public schools; and church involvement with the community colleges. Release into the open consideration of new needs had led the AEM into arenas for church engagement and policy making that were basic to the whole work of the church in higher education. The AEM needs to be watched to discover whether the tentative leads that have been opened will be permitted to flower into a new strategy and a new posture for the involved churches as they live out their lives with the universities of Michigan.

Another pattern for church-university venturing grew out of co-operation with the Christian Faith and Higher Education Institute located in East Lansing, Michigan, the extension division of Michigan State University and national staff operating in the midwest for major churches. Their combined efforts produced a consultation of the directors of continuing education and extension services of the major midwestern universities. The consultation was designed to explore ways by which these universities, through extension services widely utilized by education, agriculture, business, and industrial leaders, might be made to serve church leadership as well. It was hoped that such services might be used to prepare both lay and clergy in university communities to understand the internal movement and life of the academic world and then to design the services and ministries of their churches to make a larger contribution to real university needs. The single exploratory session proved most fruitful. The conversations were soon translated into offerings from several universities. Seminars developed by university staff persons in collaboration with church leaders were held at the University of North Dakota, Purdue University, Notre Dame University, University of Wisconsin, and others, opening possibilities for a type of church-university enocunter that could prove far-reaching in relating the two institutions.

In the Far West a San Francisco Bay community college exploration is worth noting. For almost a full year designated representatives of the administration of ten San Francisco area community colleges and ten carefully selected representatives of nearby churches held monthly meetings. In the course of dinner and an evening together, they examined ways by which through collaboration the community colleges and the churches might enhance the value content and the humane elements in the education of thousands of students enrolled in the commuter schools. After about ten months they prepared their findings for presentation at an invitational conference of persons drawn from throughout California. They urged that each of the community colleges in the state emulate the San Francisco experience, arranging church contacts in their own communities.

Each of the experiences cited is indicative of the struggling efforts of church leaders to establish new patterns for university ministries. Each indicates a reaching out to provide a more mature engagement with academic life. Each borders on, but does not quite fully enter, a developed inquiry into the meaning and consequences of religious and moral commitment or into full governance patterns in service to others. No one of the explorations enlisted the scientific and humanistic disciplines available in the universities to afford major designs for the exploration undertaken, and for follow-through in policy development. The churches seem, as yet, not to have arrived at a point where clear evaluations and policy controls have provided evaluated response and clear normative guides for the future. Yet there is considerable encouragement in the openness that is in evidence and the willingness to invest policy development in new and hopefully more capable boards and committees.

United Ministries in Higher Education

Many of the ventures already described received major support from four denominations generally committed to an ecumenical approach to the ministry in higher education. The four (Disciples of Christ, Evangelical United Brethren, United Church of Christ, and United Presbyterian Church, USA) had already supported their students in a unified United Campus Christian Fellowship. The experiences with the UCCF simply added pressures from students that the governing of campus ministry be brought into line so that it would truly support their unity rather than always threatening to tear it asunder by denominationally oriented interests and demands from the sponsoring and governing boards.

By 1964 responsible national staff of the four communions had found a way to "covenant" together, placing all staff and all national policy development in a single committee where decisions were made together. Administrative, fiscal, program, and publishing functions were united and assigned to the supervision of personnel contributed from the national staff of the participating churches. Field services to campus ministers and their governing boards, as well as interpretations of the work to the churches, was similarly divided. Basic to all was the determination of church leaders to support one another in a common search for new and more creative ministries in higher education.

The agreement among the churches was held open for negotiated participation by other denominations. By 1968 seven more churches had found their way into the organization: American Baptist, Church of the Brethren, Episcopal, Moravian Church (Northern Province), Presbyterian Church, U.S., Reformed Church in America, and the United Methodist Church. The merger of the Methodists with the Evangelical United Brethren brought the new total to ten and encompassed all major Protestant denominations engaged in campus ministries except three Lutheran Churches and the Southern Baptist Church.

National commitments by the denominations were assumed also to enhance similar developments by regional and local churches. In many instances such local and regional commitments were made far in advance of national policy. In a few areas local commitments and operating plans involve common planning and a pattern of team or collegiate-type ministry that includes Roman Catholic chaplains, Lutheran campus ministers, and others not fully involved in the new United Ministries in Higher Education.

The accession of several new denominations, and the learning out of four years of trial and error, led the U.M.H.E. to significant operational modifications in 1968.

1. A so called "tripartite" pattern of organization for the development and governance of the U.M.H.E. was created. The plan specifies that to the elected representatives of the ten sponsoring churches would be added an equal number of persons chosen from the university and public realms—chosen for their particular capacities to contribute to the strategy and development of ministries in higher education. The National Commission thus formed, it is hoped, will become a prototype for regional commissions and in measure local commissions across the nation. Participation beyond the churches was deemed necessary to the development of both strategy and support.

2. Within the operating structures certain selected areas were lifted into prominence as those to be given special attention, budget, and staff resources in order that the ministries throughout the country might be guided and informed. The areas marked for attention do include several which call for new social policy developments. In a listing that sounds a bit like the all too familiar church "program emphases" the following "task forces" were indicated:

Internationalization. To engage in analysis and study of the main trends in international education; to isolate the primary issues and concerns that UMHE should confront and to define priorities among the issues; to evaluate the ongoing international program of UMHE and to recommend new projects.

Urbanization. To relate UMHE to urban studies and ministries and to propose strategy for urban ministries in higher education.

Health and Human Values. To identify the new human problems in the context of the health professions and their services; to develop methods of clarifying and assisting in solving the problems and to develop change in both the professional attitude and public awareness in relation to the problems.

Generation Issues. To explore ways of working with alienated youth and to create "generational exposures" for commission members, campus ministers, national and regional staff.

Community Colleges. To develop resources for state commissions in reference to ministry and relationships with community colleges.

The United Ministries in Higher Education is a drawing-board strategy of the churches as this Danforth Study is being completed. The experience of the pioneering churches is impressive in the working agreements that bind them into a new ecumenical venture. This experience has proved sufficiently attractive and worthy to draw to the UMHE the major Protestant denominations engaged in campus ministries. It has promised to overcome debilitating divisions and sectarian characteristics that have been a problem to both the churches and the universities.

In its new expansion the UMHE must prove itself again. It must prove its capacity to meet the variety of perspectives, interests, and concern that mark the participating churches at every level of operation. It must prove that persons from both the university and public realms will take it seriously as a church agent intent on sharing with the universities the struggles to produce new accessions of meaning and order for modern life.

Most of all, the UMHE must prove that it can overcome the isolation from other dimensions of church life that has typified the campus ministries and draw the churches in all facets of ministry and mission into serious engagement with universities.

Continuing Problems

Despite evidences that out of desperation and amid vast confusion the churches have found new structures for the exploration of educational policy development, the evidences of movement toward change are filled with hope and promise. Change for major social institutions is always slow and agonizing. The churches prove no exception.

Policies in campus ministry now require formulation within the context of the church's whole ministry to the society. They require also a recognition that higher education can no longer be thought of in terms of what happens institutionally on a certain campus. For the churches this means that the isolation of campus ministries from other mission and ministry decision of the church must be overcome. The isolation is not merely a professional self-consciousness on the part of campus ministers but also an isolation of the boards, committees, and agencies fixed with policy and strategy considerations. Those who plan for urban ministries, those who guide the mission overseas, and those who develop new strategies for higher education need to be drawn into common consideration of their common tasks. To help reveal human values at stake in the great areas of life which need new ordering will take a conscious dedication by the churches of all the instrumentalities at their disposal. Each in turn needs the resources of skill and discipline which the universities can bring to social policy formulations.

Only in such wholeness of the life and ministries of the churches can the witness to God's Kingdom be set forward and just social policies approach realization.

PART VIII

National Survey of Campus Clergy and Parish Ministers

☙ 19 ❧

THE PARISH AND CAMPUS MINISTRIES:

A COMPARATIVE LOOK

by

Elden E. Jacobson, Hoyt P. Oliver,
and Lorna Jo Borgstrom

> The basic hypothesis and anticipated finding of this study is that in the midst of profound crisis and division over the direction and purpose of the ministry, the basic lines of march for fundamental reform are emerging. And they have emerged first in that most troubled and self-conscious of all ministries—the campus religious leaders.
>
> Kenneth Underwood, p. 44, Chapter 3 of this volume

How difficult it is," J. B. Priestly once lamented, "to make a beginning. . . . I will do anything but the work at hand." We understand. The death of Professor Underwood, depressing and untimely in the extreme, took a teacher, scholar, colleague, and friend. It also removed this study's center and prime mover, the source of its rich conceptualization; and its completion now rests in lesser hands. No small matters, these; for, invited by him to share the task and its urgency, we have strained to understand, to see what he saw, to find means by which it might be conveyed. And with Priestly, we admit "how difficult it is."

Our concerns in these two chapters have to do with the quantitative data. As has been obvious to the careful reader, Underwood entertained considerable expectations regarding the survey instrument and the insights derivable from it. As he wrote in the preface, it would seek "to measure theological view, social and educational attitudes, role, or preferences, and self-perceptions in the ministry and to discover their relation in aggregate trends in the parish as well as campus ministries."

Additionally, as he indicated in the Preface, analysis and discussion of the "empirical aggregate data" were to occur late in this volume, permitting the "reader (to) test other kinds of data . . . against the survey questions."

But the systematic analysis through which these many issues might have been clarified did not occur. That is to say, unlike those legions whose semantic wishfulness equates information with knowledge, Underwood was never certain that the data's interpretation had done adequate justice to the complex realities already observed through intensive examination of particular locations and the men who moved in them. The reasons for that uncertainty seem various. The study's general interpretive framework (utilizing the four ministerial modes: pastoral, priestly, inquiry, and governance) had not been finalized at the time of the survey's inception, and hence its design did not directly reflect that perspective. Too, additional technical manipulation of the data through which he had anticipated the emergence of much more sharply delineated images of varying ministerial "styles" has not even yet been performed. Time, or more precisely the lack of it, was equally crucial; the study's multifarious demands consumed his energies before these portions could be addressed by him in the manner he earlier envisioned.

We make these initial remarks not so much as apology for whatever inadequacies will follow, but as explanation of a most dispiriting circumstance. Our collaboration with Professor Underwood on these chapters did not really proceed beyond a commitment to do so before his illness foreclosed on such possibilities. Alternative arrangements were possible, we suppose, after his passing; certainly there are other scholars more technically competent than ourselves in the analysis of survey data. But when the Study Commission requested that at least a preliminary description of the data be attempted, we agreed to do so. In the brief span of time still available before established publication dates, we have sought, therefore, to understand the critical aspects of the study to this point and to discern the quantitative evidence that might further illumine what we understand the study's fundamental policy issues to be. Professor Jeffrey Hadden's earlier analysis of much of the parish data has been extremely beneficial.[1] And we have had

---

1. As Underwood states in Chapter 3, "major responsibility for the development and administration of this survey was that of Jeffrey Hadden," then of Purdue

complete access to Underwood's file drawers of fragmentary notes and inchoate commentary that now bear silent witness to the complex subtleties of his intellectual vision. But we do not—indeed, cannot—speak in his name; the errors we commit belong to us alone.

There are emerging, Underwood wrote in the paragraph with which this chapter began, "in the midst of profound crisis over the direction and purpose of the ministry, the basic lines of march for fundamental reform." That is, in many respects, a remarkable claim, born both of hope and of exceptional insight. For the less imaginative, nagging questions clearly obtain. The campus ministry is, in relative numbers, a small body of individuals. And much recent interpretation has placed it, not within the reforming center, but at the church's periphery, there to be viewed by laity and parish clergy with varying degrees of indifference or suspicion. Yet to the extent that Underwood's perception is indeed a harbinger, alternatives to such interpretation must finally be discernible.

Campus ministries, he had argued, have "reached a position in [their] histor[ies] when policies toward [them] can be formulated only within the context of the church's whole ministry to the society." And campus ministries share with others the necessity to hold in "creative balance" the four historic modes or styles of ministry around which the study is organized. But surely it is ridiculously apparent that a campus ministry integral to the "church's whole ministry" is critically dependent on the degree to which its beliefs, values, attitudes, styles of ministry, and so on are sufficiently congruent and convergent to permit and enhance such "wholeness." Campus ministers seem to provide unlikely models for vastly increased emulation if they are, in sum, but a means through which the activist minority is both retained in but isolated from the wider church today. That is the issue concerning us here.

In these two chapters we have sought, actually, two objectives, the first of which involves the comparison of campus and parish ministers regarding their theological beliefs, their social and educational attitudes, and their preferences of role. The second, to which the first is in significant measure ancillary, is more speculative and poses the question:

University's Department of Sociology. We have had brief conversation with Hadden regarding the survey, and we readily acknowledge our debt to him. He cannot, obviously, be held accountable for the manner in which we have interpreted the data here. For an imaginative treatment of the survey's central themes, see his *The Gathering Storm in the Churches* (Garden City: Doubleday, 1969).

Does the quantitative evidence support even inferentially Underwood's conviction that "ministries of inquiry" offer substantive possibility for renewal and wholeness throughout the church's contemporary ministry?

These are, we would argue, important issues, and we can only trust that the superficiality of our own tentative gesture is but a prelude to the deep and extended analysis such issues require.

One brief comment regarding the survey instrument itself. Without doubt its data have produced an embarrassment of riches. As has been stated previously in this volume, the survey contains eight major sections and a total of 524 questions ranging through religious beliefs, attitudes regarding science and religion, religion and higher education, counseling, and social issues. It solicits information regarding professional activities, personality, and background. And in nearly all cases, response is indicated on a Likert six-point scale moving from "definitely disagree" to "definitely agree." Of the nearly twelve thousand parish and campus ministers to whom the survey was sent, a surprising 70 per cent cooperated to the extent of completing what must surely have seemed an imposing, perhaps forbidding, document.[2]

But we have been served well. At no time previously have the complex interrelationships between campus and parish ministries been shown so completely and with such drama and implication.

Theological Beliefs

"Campus ministers," insists sociologist Phillip Hammond, "are not representative of all ministers."[3] Indeed they are not, as his own useful study demonstrates. The present data vividly indicate that they are more "liberal" than their parish counterparts on most social and political indices, and show the degree to which differences exist on matters of fundamental religious doctrine. Hadden offers a convenient introduction, beginning his analysis in *The Gathering Storm in the Churches* by examining in some detail parish responses to several questions historically central to Christian faith: the authority and sanctioned position of

---

2. For one account of the conceptualization and technical considerations underlying the survey, see Jeffrey K. Hadden, "A Study of the Protestant Ministry of America," *Journal for the Scientific Study of Religion,* Vol. V, No. 1 (1965), pp. 10–23.

3. Phillip E. Hammond, *The Campus Clergyman* (New York: Basic Books, 1966), p. 42.

Holy Writ. We, too, begin at that point. The three statements in Table 19–1 in particular appear to speak directly to issues of biblical interpretation, and to parish responses already discussed by Hadden we have added those by campus clergy with an indication of the degree to which denominational differences are evident.

We need scarcely point out the great variations among denominational parish ministers on the general issue of biblical authority. And as Hadden indicates, and the table above supports, even for clergy who hold to scriptural literalism, such literalism is not without limitation; fewer are prepared to extend this authority into matters outside the immediate faith.[4] Of particular note here is the general *rejection* of literalism as an operative principle by campus ministers, regardless of denomination, with the one notable exception of Missouri Synod Lutheran. And, as might be anticipated, they overwhelmingly acknowledge the range of expression that the language of "myth and symbol" implies. These very substantial differences become all the more apparent when the respective range of interdenominational parish and interdenominational campus response is noted.

As Table 19–2 illustrates (we have simply taken from Table 19–1 the two extreme responses for each statement), the range of belief within the parish regarding, for example, "literal interpretation of the Bible" are very wide indeed: forty percentage points separate the low (Episcopal) and the high (American Lutheran). This is simply not the case with campus ministers, where even the highest (again American Lutheran) remains very close to the low, in this case the Methodists. Taken compositely, campus ministers do not acknowledge traditional biblical interpretation.

Perhaps not surprisingly, much of this same pattern is equally evident when we turn to specific theological doctrines. (Table 19–3).

Again following Hadden, we observe immediately that rejection of a general literalism by no means forecloses on the retention of belief in a particular theological doctrine, a phenomenon most obvious in Episcopalian responses to *a* and *b* above but occurring generally in all denominations. It is also evident that less unanimity exists among campus ministers regarding these historical doctrines; consideration of the virgin birth evokes among campus pastors quite the range of belief it

---

4. Hadden, *The Gathering Storm*, p. 41.

TABLE 19-1

a. (I-7) "I believe in a literal or nearly literal interpretation of the Bible."

	Parish*		Campus		% Difference
		%		%	
Episcopal	N = (1261)	16	N = (106)	6	10
Methodist	N = (2516)	25	N = (227)	4	21
Presbyterian	N = (1198)	25	N = (113)	9	16
American Baptist	N = (654)	51	N = (68)	11	40
American Lutheran	N = (908)	56	N = (57)	12	44
Missouri Synod Lutheran	N = (895)	84	N = (34)	64	20

151 = 25.2%
average
difference

b. (I-46) "Scriptures are the inspired and inerrant Word of God not only in matters of faith but also in historical, geographical and other secular matters."

	Parish	Campus	% Difference
	%	%	
Episcopal	7	5	2
Methodist	18	1	17
Presbyterian	16	1	15
American Baptist	40	14	26
American Lutheran	29	4	25
Missouri Synod Lutheran	82	49	33

118 = 19.7%

c. (I-47) "An understanding of the language of myth and symbol are (*sic*) as important for interpreting biblical literature as history and archaeology."

	Parish	Campus	% Difference
	%	%	
Episcopal	95	95	0
Methodist	86	93	7
Presbyterian	84	99	15
American Baptist	74	91	17
American Lutheran	74	96	22
Missouri Synod Lutheran	48	74	26

87 = 14.5%

* In the tables utilized throughout this chapter and the next, each statement has been prefaced (in parentheses) by its number in the survey itself. Also, the percentages for parish minister responses differ somewhat from those reported for identical questions by Hadden; numbers 4, 5, and 6 on the Likert scale have been combined by us, while Hadden included responses 5 and 6 only. This

TABLE 19-2

	Parish		Campus
	%		%
a. Literal Interpretation:			
Episcopal	16	Methodist	4
Am. Lutheran*	56	Am. Lutheran	12
	40		8
b. Inspired Scriptures:			
Episcopal	7	Meth-Presby.	1
Am. Baptist	40	Am. Baptist	14
	33		13
c. Myth and Symbol:			
Episcopal	95	Presbyterian	99
Am. Baptist &			
Am. Lutheran	74	Am. Baptist	91
	21		8

* Unless otherwise noted, we have omitted Missouri Synod Lutherans from these discussions. The reasons are largely statistical; with an N of but 39 for campus ministers, and with this denomination's frequent and substantial deviations from the expressed views of the other five denominations, percentages permit disproportionate weight to such deviations. On the other hand, differences within the Missouri Synod Lutheran church between parish and campus remain highly germane to the questions at hand.

does in the parish. Methodists emerge as the most "liberal," Lutherans most "conservative," and for both parish and campus clergy, the degree of differentiation is 37 per cent. That is a curious finding; the relative unity apparent among campus ministers when responding to seemingly dogmatic and inflexible principles of interpretation has now been at least partially suspended when the issues involve individual doctrines traditionally central to Christian thought, as though protesting against dogmatism—but not just yet. They do so, however, very selectively; and whatever their diversity, they clearly remain at considerable distance from their parish brethren.

minor difference does not appear to have significantly influenced our respective and concurring conclusions.

In order to illustrate more forcefully the degree to which parish-campus differences do (or do not) exist, we have, for each statement, computed a "% Difference Score" that is simply the degree of differentiation, offered both as a total number and as the average percentage.

TABLE 19–3

a. (I-64) "I believe that the virgin birth of Jesus was a biological miracle."

	Parish	Campus	% Difference
	%	%	
Episcopal	69	41	28
Methodist	53	14	39
Presbyterian	64	15	49
American Baptist	73	30	43
American Lutheran	90	51	39
Missouri Synod Lutheran	97	95	2

$$200 = 33.3\%$$

b. (I-15) "I accept Jesus' physical resurrection as an objective historical fact in the same sense that Lincoln's physical death was a historical fact."

	Parish	Campus	% Difference
	%	%	
Episcopal	76	51	25
Methodist	57	24	33
Presbyterian	71	30	41
American Baptist	71	36	35
American Lutheran	89	63	26
Missouri Synod Lutheran	93	90	3

$$163 = 27.1\%$$

c. (I-80) "Adam and Eve were individual historical persons."

	Parish	Campus	% Difference
	%	%	
Episcopal	6	2	4
Methodist	26	2	24
Presbyterian	24	0	24
American Baptist	53	12	41
American Lutheran	65	5	60
Missouri Synod Lutheran	94	72	22

$$175 = 29.1\%$$

d. (I-89) "I expect to live after death."

	Parish	Campus	% Difference
	%	%	
Episcopal	97	90	7
Methodist	95	76	19
Presbyterian	96	75	21
American Baptist	97	82	15
American Lutheran	99	91	8
Missouri Synod Lutheran	100	100	0

$$70 = 11.7\%$$

Each of these four statements and those of Table 19–1 seem, in their individual fashions, to reflect the state of current theological debate, the critical scrutiny by learned, skeptical inquiry from which flow questioning, flux, and reinterpretation and to which all religious doctrine appears susceptible. And, given the complex histories and dramatically varying theological emphases in our present denominations, we are hardly surprised when these processes of reinterpretation fall variously and with differing result among them. If campus ministers show little unanimity regarding the precise nature of Christ's death, they close ranks again on the Adam and Eve issue, only to diverge somewhat on the matter of life after death. Parish also vary, as is obvious in Table 19–3, but do so "out of phase" with the campus. Considerable divergence regarding a literal "first family" gives way to near consensus when survival beyond death is at stake.

How shall we account for such phenomena? Several thoughts occur to us, none particularly startling. Perhaps "life after death" not only illustrates a pervasive historical motif in Christian belief but likewise an ego-derived wish that men not only should but will survive, if only in spirit. Even among the most skeptical of campus ministers, after all, three-quarters so believe. Another question speculating on the *nature* of life in the hereafter might have additionally clarified the issue.

There is another point, however. Even as campus pastors reject out of hand the dogmatism implied in the principle of literal biblical interpretation, so, too, do they appear to differ most dramatically from parish counterparts on questions for which there exists, at least ostensibly, the possibility of scientific evidence (or opinion). The Adam and Eve inquiry provides the most apparent instance, but the virgin birth and the resurrection of Jesus also fit this general pattern. In Table 19–3 *a, b,* and *c,* % Difference Averages are much higher than is true for faith statements (as in Table 19–3 *d*) less susceptible to inductive reasoning. Hence 19–3 *d* ("life and death") produces an Average Difference of 11.8 per cent; 19–3 *c* is 29 per cent. We have not carried this through all 115 responses on basic theological beliefs, but it appears to hold consistently and presumably reflects a selective influence by the university environment.

We note again that Missouri Synod Lutherans provide an interesting and unique exception to nearly every statement offered thus far, and for that perhaps we should be grateful; few canons in sociological writing seem quite so secure as the conservative-liberal continuum, and the data here initially support these polar types.

Two of the scales are of particular interest because they indicate something of the certainty with which clergy approach questions of religious orthodoxy. The first of these scales, labeled in this study as "Biblical Fundamentalism," contains most of the individual questions already presented in the tables above. The second, identified as "Toleration of Doubt," centers on the statement in Table 19-4.

TABLE 19-4

a.   (I-16) "I have greater admiration for an honest agnostic seeking truth than a man who is certain that he has the complete truth."

	Parish	Campus	% Difference
	%	%	
Episcopal	85	92	7
Methodist	85	94	9
Presbyterian	87	96	9
American Baptist	78	93	15
American Lutheran	67	86	19
Missouri Synod Lutheran	42	49	7
			66 = 11%

We suspect that a deceptive charm resides in a statement such as this, for it is general and noncommittal and permits the demonstration of tolerance. Campus ministers again reflect a remarkable unanimity of outlook, but so, too, do clergy generally; only with the Missouri Synod Lutheran Church are less than two-thirds willing to extend the benefit of doubt. The pattern changes somewhat when the general issue of "Seeking" is replaced by a particular (Table 19-5).

When that particular is recast in personal terms, however, the pattern shifts with unexpected abruptness (Table 19-6).

Several observations seem warranted here. Even allowing for our implied skepticism and the mildly pejorative phrase "certain . . . complete truth" (in Table 19-4 *a*), tolerance for nonbelieving "seekers" seems unusually high. Too, we note with some surprise, this pattern changes only slightly, even at what must surely be *the* critical theological presupposition: the belief in God's existence (Table 19-5a). Still, while the degree of difference is rather more pronounced in the latter

TABLE 19-5

a. (I-23) "I would expect a thinking Christian to have doubts about the existence of God."

	Parish	Campus	% Difference
	%	%	
Episcopal	77	85	8
Methodist	60	84	24
Presbyterian	72	93	21
American Baptist	54	85	31
American Lutheran	62	88	26
Missouri Synod Lutheran	49	69	20
			130 = 21.7%

TABLE 19-6

a. (I-94) "I find it increasingly difficult to believe in God."

	Parish	Campus	% Difference
	%	%	
Episcopal	6	17	11
Methodist	5	16	11
Presbyterian	6	20	14
American Baptist	3	19	16
American Lutheran	5	23	18
Missouri Synod Lutheran	3	10	7
			77 = 12.8%

question, in them both, two-thirds of all ministers (again excepting Missouri Synod Lutherans from the averages) profess this tolerance. How, then, to explain Table 19-6 and its seeming denial of the "doubts" readily accorded to "thinking Christians"? We do not really know, of course, except to speculate that the inconsistency is more apparent than actual. After all, these are overwhelmingly ordained clergy who presumably have grappled at considerable length with this problem's intellectual knots, and, having determined a workable, or at least tolerable, resolution (by whatever means), they appear now to be engaged in more immediate issues. Indeed, that fully one-fifth of the campus clergy harbor reservations about basic belief would itself appear rather remarkable and illustrates the critical point we read into these data: clergy, although personally professing decided views and opinions regarding basic theological doctrine and belief, are generally open to and tolerant of differing positions in others. To this point we shall return.

There are many other ways the data both could and should be manipulated. Age, for example, is imagined by some to portend a relative homogeneity of theological belief; for younger clergy, that is, denominational dogma is believed to be much less rigid than might be true for older warriors of the church's doctrinal wars. But as Hadden reports: *"Younger ministers tend to be about as close or closer to older ministers in their own denominations than they are to ministers of their own age in other denominations.* Thus denominationalism appears to be significant in determining what a minister actually believes about traditional theology."[5] [Emphasis in original]

Whether this will prove equally true for campus ministers we cannot assert with finality; the data have not, thus far, been correlated according to age for other than parish, and parish-campus combined, although strong inferences may certainly be obtained from the various tables throughout this chapter, where near unanimity of belief or attitude is many times observed. This may well occur in part because age differentials in ministries to the campus are not nearly so pronounced; proportionately fewer older men occupy campus positions. We do not really believe that to be sufficient explanation, given the frequency with which consensus seems independent of age *or* denomination. In any event, that question is lost in another; we see no reason to believe that age per se offers any significant possibility for achieving rapprochement of theological agreement between the institutional churches and those whose specialized claim is the campus. Hope must reside elsewhere.

Nor have we but introduced the richness contained in the 115-item Theological Belief section. Yet in each case, regardless of the manner of appropriating and manipulating the data, the conclusion remains consistent and persuasive: although the demythologizing process has fallen on these six denominations in very uneven fashion, campus ministers are relatively very much in revolt against traditional and orthodox modes of theological interpretation.

---

5. Hadden, *op. cit.*, p. 54.

Ethics—An Extension of Theological Belief?

It is hardly surprising, therefore, to discover such questioning and rejection deeply apparent in campus clergys' understanding of ethical thought and application. Here, too, the issues reside in questions of belief and the certitude with which they are expressed. But more: in what manner do faith statements translate into principles for informed action? Note, for example, as an interesting introduction to these matters, how even seeming agreement on theological belief (itself unusual) becomes mere gossamer when content is given to it (Table 19–7).

TABLE 19–7

a. (I-107) "Every area of man's life is corrupted by sin."

	Parish	Campus	% Difference*
	%	%	
Episcopal	81	83	2
Methodist	69	77	8
Presbyterian	88	89	1
American Baptist	82	84	2
American Lutheran	94	81	−13
Missouri Synod Lutheran	96	92	− 4
			− 4 = +.7%

b. (I-111) "Sin is primarily the infraction of God's law."

	Parish	Campus	% Difference
	%	%	
Episcopal	64	41	23
Methodist	68	34	34
Presbyterian	58	24	34
American Baptist	74	36	38
American Lutheran	68	39	29
Missouri Synod Lutheran	88	64	24
			182 = 30.3%

* We have utilized minus marks here and in other given statements merely to highlight the fact that differences between "Parish" and "Campus" did not move uniformly in a single direction. They have no other significance.

Perhaps the problem is in the phrase "God is law"; whatever, the dramatic differences separating campus and parish confront us with one of the more recent and pervasive (ofttimes acrimonious as well) arguments in the ranks of clergy and ethical theorists: principles vs. context. In their more extreme expressions, one observes a superficial scholasticism "in which rules for any and every situation could be found in the relevant manual"[6] countered by statements placing "radical obedience" in a contextual frame where decision and act must be left "to the man in his concrete situation," where "if a man really loves, he knows already what to do."[7] How do clergy mediate between such irreconcilable views? We do not presume to know with anything approaching finality, but the three statements in Table 19–8, each taken from the factor cluster we have labeled "Moral Absolutism," seem instructive.

TABLE 19–8

a. (I-9) "The most reliable way to judge whether a certain action is good or bad is to consider the consequences."

	Parish	Campus	% Difference
	%	%	
Episcopal	28	32	4
Methodist	40	43	3
Presbyterian	29	44	15
American Baptist	31	48	17
American Lutheran	20	44	24
Missouri Synod Lutheran	10	18	8
			71 = 11.8%

Well, all right. Christianity has for a very long time accorded the Ten Commandments, the Sermon on the Mount, and other normative passages of Scripture a paramount role in the formulation of prescribed or ethical action. To reject the compelling character of such doctrines and prohibitions would seem at least initially, therefore, to be a significant action, and we note with curiosity that nearly 50 per cent of campus ministers, having taken due note of the restrictive "most reliable," still expressed general agreement with the crucial importance of "consequence"—which we read to mean that judgmental referents are no longer otherworldly only but clearly reside in the observable. This impression is substantially reinforced with two additional statements (Table 19–9).

How is this possible? The first of these two statements clearly suggests that moral rightness has no necessary relationship to whatever

---

6. E. J. Egan, "Ethics and the Campus Ministry" (paper presented to the Pittsburgh Colloquium of the Danforth Study of Campus Ministries, 1964).

7. Rudolph Bultman, *Jesus and the Word* (New York: Charles Scribner's Sons, 1934), p. 94.

TABLE 19-9

a. (I-92) "People should do what is morally right without giving thought to the consequences."

	Parish	Campus	% Difference
	%	%	
Episcopal	60	37	23
Methodist	72	31	41
Presbyterian	62	21	41
American Baptist	77	46	31
American Lutheran	75	51	24
Missouri Synod Lutheran	85	69	16
			176 = 29.3%

b. (I-100) "An ethical decision which may be right in one situation may be wrong in another."

	Parish	Campus	% Difference
	%	%	
Episcopal	88	94	6
Methodist	82	96	14
Presbyterian	85	99	14
American Baptist	79	95	16
American Lutheran	78	96	18
Missouri Synod Lutheran	79	97	18
			86 = 14.3%

consequence(s) might derive from it; it is, in Max Weber's well-known dichotomy, an "ethic of ultimate concern." Too, the particular wording here utilized enhances, we speculate, an overly facile response. What could be more reasonable than doing what is "morally right?" Whether it be the precise wording or not, campus ministers again demonstrate significant differences when paired with parish clergy of their respective denominations, being far less willing to assert "moral rightness" as an adequate criterion for action. Is it, then, the academic environment, the traditional respect for empirical inquiry, for sensitivity to complexity and subtle causality, that helps "explain" campus-parish differences?

Such seemingly reasonable conjecture appears strengthened in the second statement, where the issue of consequence occurs in somewhat different form. No longer "moral rightness" as such, stress has been placed on the possibility of situational variation, on shifting contexts. Campus minister unanimity is nearly absolute, which does not really surprise us much. What is surprising is the very strong positive agreement among parish ministers, as well over four of five assert a flexibility of ethical principle. These questions, we immediately recognize, do not in any manner specify matters of content, any indication of *when* and under what *conditions* a previously right action might be reconsidered. They *do* suggest a disposition in principle toward resolutions of ethical dilemmas that are rooted at least partially in time and circumstance. Taken compositely, they suggest to us that appreciation of situational complexity and multiple consequence may be significantly present in the parish as well as the campus. Examination of the entire "Moral Absolutism" scale supports, we believe, this possibility.

There is another substantive aspect to this brief inquiry into the bases of ethical thought that must be introduced here. Thus far, analysis has been cast almost solidly in the language of personal disposition, of abstraction and belief. But ministers, parish and campus alike, can scarcely avoid the intricately structured, highly complex institutional arrangements of which they are a part and in which they "live and move." They are churchmen. They administer programs, however minimally. And they manipulate organizations. Thus the church as a structural entity would seem obviously fundamental to moral action, both shaping the belief systems of those within it and as an instrument for achieving agreed-upon moral objectives. Two of the factors—"Church in the World" and "Otherworldly Church"—address this question of institutional responsibility, offering some insight into ministerial perceptions of the church and the "world." From the first, these two statements are generally representative (Table 19–10).

In addition to the obvious support given these assertions by campus pastors, parish clergymen also profess their strong agreement. As was true in the discussion of ethical contextualism, so, too, here: four or five affirm the church's social role. We ought to note in passing two minor curiosities present in the "Humanity" issue, where Episcopalians appear in the generally unexpected role of "most conservative" and parish-campus Missouri Synod Lutherans have switched roles. The former results, we would suppose, from the particular wording utilized equating, as it were, an ecclesiastical "true nature" with something outside itself, a position that orthodox Episcopalian clergy could (and did) reject on doctrinal grounds. While we have become accustomed to the frequent wide variations that characterize Missouri Synod Lutheran–other denomination comparison, we are at a loss to explain the inversion noted.

TABLE 19–10

a. (I-5) "The Christian church can only be its true self as it exists for humanity."

	Parish	Campus	% Difference
	%	%	
Episcopal	69	76	7
Methodist	82	88	6
Presbyterian	78	94	16
American Baptist	84	96	12
American Lutheran	84	95	11
Missouri Synod Lutheran	81	69	−12
			40 = 6.7%

b. (I-21) "The church must speak to the great social issues of our day, or else its very existence is threatened."

	Parish	Campus	% Difference
	%	%	
Episcopal	87	93	6
Methodist	92	95	3
Presbyterian	91	93	2
American Baptist	87	96	9
American Lutheran	81	88	8
Missouri Synod Lutheran	73	82	9
			37 = 6.2%

It is atypical and may simply reflect the relatively small campus sample for that denomination.

The second factor, catalogued Otherworldly Church, appears at first blush to support the findings just noted (Table 19–11).

TABLE 19–11

a. (I-20) "The primary task of the church is to live the Christian life among its own membership and activities rather than to try and (sic) reform the world."

	Parish	Campus	% Difference
	%	%	
Episcopal	12	5	7
Methodist	12	7	5
Presbyterian	9	6	3
American Baptist	12	7	5
American Lutheran	17	5	12
Missouri Synod Lutheran	20	15	5
			37 = 6.2%

On few questions do we recall greater unanimity among the six denominations, both at the parish and campus levels, nor has the % Difference figure been (save for Table 19–7*a*) significantly lower. Without doubt, these denominations are, or believe they are, outgoing and responsive. But to what end? Alas, the symmetry again begins to flake at the edges. For "Christian Life" is another generality the content of which, being unspecified, resides in the mind of each individual respondent. And when supplied with one possible conception, the results in Table 19–12 were obtained.

TABLE 19–12

a. (1-4) "The Christian style of life is one of contentment with one's worldly possessions, forbearance toward others, and certainty of eternal life."

	Parish	Campus	% Difference
	%	%	
Episcopal	40	20	20
Methodist	43	12	31
Presbyterian	42	14	28
American Baptist	56	18	38
American Lutheran	72	35	37
Missouri Synod Lutheran	81	56	25
			179 = 29.8%

How does one account for this wide diversity, not only within the various denominations but with the preceding statement? It is not our task, nor do we intend, to "explain away" such issues. Nor is consistency necessarily a part of True Nature. But several comments may here be appropriate; others, no doubt, are also possible. One notes, for example, the obvious difficulty imposed when several relatively discrete ideas are incorporated into a single statement. Does the respondent then indicate disagreement only if all three components are unsatisfactory?[8] Or just

8. The problem of imagery has always proved extremely difficult in survey research. Complexity has often represented a deep desire to transcend the trivial or simple-minded, but the concomitant risk becomes lack of sufficient restrictiveness to suppose any continuity of meaning from one respondent to the next. G. D. Wiebe states it admirably: "Predictive opinion response is not only a symbolic representation of a personal state of mind; it is that plus a fantasy of a set of social circumstances plus a fantasy of interaction with those circumstances. . . . Having done his best, all of the vagaries of selective perception on the part of the respondent come into play. In spite of his best efforts, no researcher can vouch for the fantasies evoked in the minds of respondents by his carefully phrased item." "Some Implications of Separating Opinions from Attitudes," *Public Opinion Quarterly* (Fall, 1953), p. 343.

one? Or two? Any of these, of course, is possible. Had they been specified individually, response patterns might conceivably have varied quite differently; indeed, we have already seen that the vast majority of ministers, campus and other, expect to find life after death, which we take to mean "eternal life." We are compelled to conclude, it would seem, that relatively more parish ministers are saying, yes, the Christian style of life is probably this much; campus clergy, on the other hand, are insisting that the definition includes not nearly enough. In any event, once again we encounter that vexing split: statements of theological principle frequently bear unrecognizable offspring when translated into specific belief. We turn, hence, to the examination of these questions in rather more specific detail.

Social Beliefs

Summarizing his always useful and often interesting chapter on the relationship of theological belief and social issues, Hadden declared "that for clergy, rejection of orthodoxy is strongly associated with more liberal social and political ideologies."[9] Thus, as we have consistently noted the high degree of theological nonorthodoxy among campus ministers, one might reasonably anticipate increasing liberal manifestations; in his relatively brief comparative analysis of campus and parish, Hammond seems to demonstrate precisely such liberalism. And so it is in the data at hand. But the spectrum of "social beliefs" is broad in the extreme, and the degrees of liberality we find on it vary accordingly.

In this diversity, three particular areas of social distress immediately interest us as we attempt to clarify parish-campus relationships. We note, with depressing misgivings and without substantial fear of contradiction, the crisis proportions of white-black encounter throughout this land. And, for the reasons set forth below, we wish also to discuss the multifarious elements that now comprise the two factors categorized as "Responsibilities of Government" and "Sexual Morality." These, as is trivially obvious, do not begin to exhaust the rich possibilities and insights afforded by the data. But they may, we believe, more positively identify genuine issues of strain and distrust.

Because Hadden's own thorough and extended discussion of clergy and their relationship to the dispiriting problems of civil rights has be-

9. Hadden, *The Gathering Storm*, p. 98.

come readily available, only three of the Civil Rights items will be
utilized here (Table 19–13).[10]

TABLE 19–13

a. (V-7) "I basically disapprove of the Negro civil rights movement in
America."

	Parish	Campus	% Difference
	%	%	
Episcopal	6	2	4
Methodist	12	3	9
Presbyterian	6	4	2
American Baptist	10	4	6
American Lutheran	9	0	9
Missouri Synod Lutheran	14	3	11

41 = 6.8%

b. (V-14) "Negroes could solve many of their problems if they would not
be so irresponsible and carefree about life."

	Parish	Campus	% Difference
	%	%	
Episcopal	33	12	21
Methodist	45	18	27
Presbyterian	31	9	22
American Baptist	46	23	23
American Lutheran	42	18	24
Missouri Synod Lutheran	42	31	11

128 = 21.3%

c. (V-10) "I am in basic sympathy with northern ministers and students
who have gone to the South to work for civil rights."

	Parish	Campus	% Difference
	%	%	
Episcopal	69	86	17
Methodist	59	83	24
Presbyterian	78	97	19
American Baptist	70	89	19
American Lutheran	67	84	18
Missouri Synod Lutheran	49	61	12

109 = 18.1%

---

10. We also admit to some question regarding the adequacy of data that attempt clarity of these extremely volatile problems nearly four years after the fact.
It scarcely seems possible, in point of fact, to give any adequate systemization to
the myriad of riotous events, painful struggle, intensified emotions, and ragged
hostility that is now "civil rights."

We are scarcely surprised by now at the pattern which unfolds in these three questions. Ministers, whatever their theological conviction and regardless of parish or university, affirm almost totally the basic rightness of America's belated movement toward Negro equality. Indeed, we might well rather wonder that *any* minister of the Christian Gospel continues to "basically disapprove" of so fundamental a human right. Yet divergence appears immediately when statements of generality are replaced by such specifics as give them relevance for action. The first of these—"Negro irresponsibility"—contains evaluative difficulties, for like many similar shibboleths and capsule stereotypes, one may argue that sociological evidence (processes of accommodation, circumvention, situation adjustment, and the like) does in fact lend to it a minimal credibility (when carefully specified). We cannot, therefore, discount out of hand the possibility that respondents were simply registering their sophisticated grasp of sociological findings when addressing this statement. The more likely explanation would seem to suggest that traditional justifications of racial bigotry such as this are so recognized by most individuals capable of thought, including ministers.

The third statement—"basic sympathy"—would appear to lend support; fully two-thirds of all parish ministers at least verbally sustain such activities, a figure that increases to between eight and nine of every ten for campus clergy. Of interest, too, is the relatively low degree of difference between them, quite unlike several of our earlier observations. We acknowledge again the very limited fashion of this discussion (Hadden has already performed the task admirably) and would point simply to the one seeming fact we are seeking to establish: the general rejection of orthodox theological doctrine by campus ministers observed throughout appears to carry with it increased sensitivity to this nation's civil rights dilemmas.

Thus far in the survey data we have encountered with some consistency a rather rough pattern in which parish–campus differences have demonstrably broadened in transition from general propositions to statements about particulars. Though this is hardly startling as such, since this kind of pattern has been observed elsewhere many times previously, we are the more surprised when seeming anomalies emerge for which ready explanation is not available. Something akin to this has occurred in the cluster of items entitled Responsibilities of Government (Table 19–14). The factor's intrinsic importance, at least comparatively, is not especially compelling; numerous others derived from the data rank equally high on our mental list of priorities. But we make it explicit here because it tends to sharpen anew the fundamental conceptual problem implicit in all attitudinal research: the various linkages between ultimate beliefs and the means by which they become (if they do) operative principles and propositions in the lives we live. Or, again, how to move from first principles through values through attitudes to action? We raise this issue more fully in the following chapter.

TABLE 19–14

a. (V-23) "The government is providing too many services that should be left to private enterprise."

	Parish	Campus	% Difference
	%	%	
Episcopal	50	20	30
Methodist	57	19	38
Presbyterian	56	15	41
American Baptist	67	27	40
American Lutheran	77	38	39
Missouri Synod Lutheran	83	44	39
			227 = 37.8%

b. (V-25) "Adequate medical care for the aged through some kind of governmental program is badly needed."

	Parish	Campus	% Difference
	%	%	
Episcopal	84	95	11
Methodist	78	93	15
Presbyterian	78	95	17
American Baptist	73	86	13
American Lutheran	64	86	22
Missouri Synod Lutheran	58	72	14
			92 = 15.3%

c. (V-69) "I believe that a larger proportion of the federal government's budget should be allocated for public welfare expenditures such as schools, hospitals, parks, etc."

	Parish	Campus	% Difference
	%	%	
Episcopal	73	91	18
Methodist	73	89	16
Presbyterian	70	96	26
American Baptist	69	89	20
American Lutheran	62	84	22
Missouri Synod Lutheran	59	79	20
			122 = 20.3%

The first of the statements on government is, of course, the anomaly of which we spoke and it seems to pose, at first reading, a most peculiar contradiction to the latter two. Several comments are possible, however; the first directed at the statement itself. What kind of imagery, for example, is conveyed to the respondent by "services"? Partisans of the peace movement, or campus clergy identified with or sympathetic to SDS-type student organizations and protest, may quite conceivably have interpreted "services" to include federal military activity. At the other polarity reside those who, like the American Medical Association with its curious, intellectually immune theology, continue to belabor an ideology that never was. But generally we suppose that "services" conjures up for most respondents the welfare state, to which belongs most of the social legislation of the past three decades. Which is to say, a recognition that government, particularly at the federal level, is both morally and, increasingly, legally bound to provide agreed-upon basic social services to the segments in our citizenry unable to secure them without such assistance. And included would surely be medical care for the aged and more adequate schools, hospitals, parks, and so on.

We do notice, of course, that for all three statements, resistance to governmental activity is consistently related to degree of theological orthodoxy. In nearly all findings thus far, Methodists and Episcopalian parish ministers have been most "liberal" in their responses, followed closely by Presbyterian; Missouri Synod Lutherans have been found in nearly every instance to be most literal and dogmatic in their interpretation of biblical doctrine. Here, also, social beliefs seem closely correlated to religious belief. But all men are rich, often ambiguous complexes of many physical attributes, environmental influences, impulses, emotions, and intellectual belief systems, of which theology is one, but only one. That is, men are religious, political, social, and so on in intricate mixes still not at all fully and conceptually understood. Having made these self-evident remarks, introduction of data not thus far considered (Table 19–15) may clarify partially the table above.

An interesting table, this. One observes immediately what was predictable on the basis of our earlier data, but remains startling nonetheless; namely, the large percentages of campus Democrats amid an overwhelming Republican profession. This may provide a semblance of explanation for Table 19–15. That first statement—"government" and "too many services"—also contains the phrase "private enterprise"— a phrase whose descriptive neutrality long ago vanished on the sea of

TABLE 19–15

a. (VIII-18) "Do you usually consider yourself as Republican, Independent, or Democratic?"

		Parish	Campus	% Difference
Episcopal	Republican	35	22	−13
	Independent	26	16	−10
	Democratic	35	62	27
Methodist	Republican	36	14	−12
	Independent	28	19	− 9
	Democratic	36	67	31
Presbyterian	Republican	59	14	−45
	Independent	19	11	− 8
	Democratic	22	75	53
American Baptist	Republican	58	30	−28
	Independent	23	25	2
	Democratic	18	35	17
American Lutheran	Republican	60	33	−27
	Independent	24	19	− 5
	Democratic	15	48	33
Missouri Synod Lutheran	Republican	68	67	− 1
	Independent	22	15	− 7
	Democratic	9	18	9

conservative ideology. It is, as it were, a "trigger phrase" to which attaches and from which flows a wide variety of value assertions and commitments that presume to order and normatively set forth basic social arrangements. As such, "free enterprise" is quite as liable to heated rejection as it is to fond embrace, and we are inclined to speculate that this has occurred here. Younger, more liberal campus ministers who consider themselves Democratic and more conservative parish clergy who opt heavily for Republicanism have both responded in largely ideological terms. Yet, as they have increasingly confronted the tangled dilemmas embraced by the euphemistic "urban crises," recognition of government's crucial role is nearly inescapable. And it is parish ministers who must make the major adjustments between ideological principle and specific necessity.

One additional question ought to be introduced here, for it will provide another dimension that cannot long be ignored: persons vs. institutions (Table 19–16). Throughout the preceding chapters of this study,

TABLE 19–16

a. (V-24) "I am not nearly so concerned with the amount of power that the federal government has as I am with the irresponsibility of many government officials."

	Parish	Campus	% Difference
	%	%	
Episcopal	70	84	14
Methodist	76	81	5
Presbyterian	68	71	3
American Baptist	68	81	13
American Lutheran	65	74	9
Missouri Synod Lutheran	56	67	11
			$\overline{55} = 9.2\%$

and again in the data on role preference below, minimum sensitivity toward and technical understanding of the enormously varied institutions and bureaucracies comprising our social system remain a recurring theme. The identification and manipulation of community power, the analysis and control of structural influence on all forces and events that shape individual lives—these require competencies and training possessed by an insignificant number of parish or campus clergy. Prevailing themes overwhelmingly stress the mastery of ideas and the dialogue of persons, and these images are carried into ministerial perceptions of the ways in which social structures function.

In the statement above, emphasis again resides on the personal. We do not deny, of course, that malfeasance in public office has a long and glorious history in American politics, and clergy, like all citizens, ought quite properly to express their concern. The more fundamental problem here, however, involves the sophisticated recognition that bureaucratic structures and those who labor in them are very much less than coextensive, that formal organizations are entities in which, virtually by definition, role and performance are both prescribed and segmented. By intent, bureaucracies seek to minimize the idiosyncratic and the malfeasant, to standardize and enhance efficient achievement of articulated objectives. The point we wish to emphasize has simply to do with the fact, thus, that institutional power itself may be the much more critical dilemma here, an appreciation for the manner in which completely honorable and sincere men, functioning through governmental and industrial bureaucracies precisely as defined, may yet inflict untold suffering and despair. One need but cite the federal Bureau of Public Roads as one of many depressing examples, for the assault by highwaymen on central cities, park lands, and other "expendable" segments of our environment can scarcely be laid to the "irresponsibility" of individual officials. The Bureau of Public Roads is doing, after all, *precisely what the law mandates it to do*. Again, the fundamental questions reside in the very structures of the institutions by which we are governed.

The point need not be labored further. It seems possible that more recently collected data might reflect these perspectives, given the semipublic debate now taking place. But, as will be noted again below, the data continue to support our view of a whole profession that has consciously abstained from a general and purposive use of power.

The third major dimension of social beliefs we wish to introduce here has to do with the factor entitled Sexual Morality and its ancillary questions of Civil Liberties (Table 19–17).

As the chroniclers of these matters have so clearly demonstrated, the church's interest in things academic partakes of a sustained, often intriguing history, not the least part of which remains the varying forms of campus ministry. And while it seems certainly true, as this entire study so richly documents, that these campus ministries have in abundant measure appropriated the currently in vogue theology, language, and, to some extent, forms of "presence" and "servant," it seems equally evident that earlier expressions of religious concern reflected substantial uneasiness at the "alien" atmosphere into which "our young people" were moving with pressing urgency. While speaking for the YMCA, John Mott's statement appears generally descriptive: religion must "guard college men [and women] against the many temptations which assail them, not only in the body but also in the realm of the intellect." If the church then "followed its students" with "a home away from home," it seems quite certain that much of the result (and perhaps incentive) was to assist the university, in its *locus parentis* role, to preserve historical Christian values and encourage traditional norms of conduct. Whatever other functions they might seek to perform, campus ministries afforded an institutionalized means for monitoring and, to the degree possible, informing the dynamic turbulence of change and doubt that typically characterizes the college experience.

Central to such religious expression has undoubtedly been concern for sexual attitudes and behavior. And because sexual morality remains

TABLE 19–17

a. (V-46) "Women who engage in premarital sexual intercourse are almost certain to have serious emotional difficulties in marriage."

	Parish	Campus	% Difference
	%	%	
Episcopal	41	26	15
Methodist	59	37	22
Presbyterian	53	36	17
American Baptist	63	46	17
American Lutheran	61	33	28
Missouri Synod Lutheran	63	36	27
			126 = 21%

b. (V-49) "College teachers and counselors are too lenient in advising students about premarital sex."

	Parish	Campus	% Difference
	%	%	
Episcopal	61	41	20
Methodist	68	40	28
Presbyterian	60	27	33
American Baptist	72	43	29
American Lutheran	73	37	36
Missouri Synod Lutheran	80	69	11
			157 = 26.2%

c. (V-54) "It is conceivable that a particular situation could morally justify extramarital relations."

	Parish	Campus	% Difference
	%	%	
Episcopal	40	65	25
Methodist	27	65	38
Presbyterian	32	76	44
American Baptist	20	60	40
American Lutheran	16	63	47
Missouri Synod Lutheran	10	20	10
			204 = 34%

the focus on which are vented much frustration, ambiguity, and social unrest both inside the church and without, we introduce it here.

As was observed above, fundamentally differing perspectives continue to distinguish parish and campus ministers in the ethical debate on law vs. context. Too, nearly all research attempting to describe and explain intergenerational confrontation alludes to sharply varying sexual attitudes between younger and older age groupings (behavior appears to be yet another matter). Both of these facts contain important implications for our principal question.

The first of these statements—"serious emotional difficulties"—is really an empirical matter that, as far as we know, cannot presently be answered with any degree of certainty. Perhaps the continued centrality of traditional sexual ethics is therefore all the more in evidence when well over one-half of all parish clergy express their belief that "almost certain" damage will be incurred through premarital indiscretions. Likewise, with the campus; apart from Episcopalians (in both instances), over one-third so believe. The second statement—leniency of college teachers and counselors—supports the same general concern, although we cannot be certain what respondents had in mind when affirming "college teachers" as sexual advisers to students.

It is the third of these three statements that seems particularly illuminating, for here do the ethical cleavages become very pronounced, and predictably so. No longer an empirical issue, might ministers even *conceive* of an instance in which mitigating circumstances could "morally justify?" "Justify" does not precisely mean "condone," and to have disagreed with the statement most certainly cannot be understood as being "unforgiving" or "nonaccepting" (customarily invoked are the distinctions between, as they say, "sin" and "sinner"). Nonetheless, contextual grounds, as previously, are at least theoretically crucial for liberally disposed campus ministers; they are not for most parish, and the per cent of difference between them is as high as any yet encountered.

This flexibility, this commitment to contextual considerations, is further reflected in other, closely related areas (Table 19–18). There can be little doubt that censorship is, or is perceived to be, basically anathema to the academic enterprise, the life of open inquiry, and we suspect that campus ministers may well have responded quite as much to the specter of governmental or vigilante control as they did to tolerance for what passes as "obscene language." In any case, they do stand in sharp disagreement with parish representatives. And the rank order for the six denominations is remarkably consistent throughout each of the four statements used in Tables 19–17 and 19–18. One additional statement mildly supports our view of censorship (Table 19–19).

Here the emphasis has been placed, not on "sex" and "obscene lan-

TABLE 19-18

a. (V-17) "Publications that dwell on sex and use obscene language should be banned from the newsstand."

	Parish	Campus	% Difference
	%	%	
Episcopal	57	35	22
Methodist	72	37	35
Presbyterian	60	20	40
American Baptist	76	31	45
American Lutheran	76	25	51
Missouri Synod Lutheran	72	61	11
			204 = 34%

TABLE 19-19

a. (V-20) "Censorship is often necessary in order to protect the public."

	Parish	Campus	% Difference
	%	%	
Episcopal	48	30	18
Methodist	59	36	23
Presbyterian	47	18	29
American Baptist	60	31	29
American Lutheran	68	26	42
Missouri Synod Lutheran	70	72	−2
			139 = 23.2%

guage," but rather on censorship as such; no distracting specifics have been cited. That campus ministers appear to have seen these two questions largely as synonymous is suggested in the remarkably similar responses given to them. Without exception, it is parish ministers who react differentially to them, who are now not so prepared, at least on principle, to support the forces of moral control; "per cent of difference" has dropped by one-third. That well over half still find censorship acceptable may itself give pause for reflection.

Educational Attitudes and Belief

How does the parish generally comprehend and acknowledge the campus ministry that its financial largess has made possible these many decades? To what extent have the very substantial divisions of religious and social belief observed above been perceived in the parish, and to what result? What implications may be inferred as models of ministry are conceptualized that seek enhanced congruence between the wider church body and the special ministry it continues to support? We do not really know, of course, quite how such questions will finally be resolved, but the survey data offer tentative, sometimes provocative insights into them and may permit several not wholly inconsequential observations.

Perhaps no conviction has so forced itself upon us throughout these weeks of deliberation as has the recognition that parish-campus relationships must be seen in contexts more broadly conceived than many observers have been wont to do.[11] Parish attitudes toward the campus ministry seem surely to involve not only two relatively disparate ministerial forms, the larger body and a specialized extension of it. Campus ministries are by definition aspects of and within the world of higher education, however marginal they in fact may be. And because this appears obviously so, ministries to the world of higher education can scarcely be understood apart from prevailing parish attitudes about and reactions to that world, the exposure of number upon number of young people to its influence, the traditional controversies of a church beset by scientific discovery—indeed, the bases of knowledge itself and how we know.

Daniel Bell speaks for many competent observers in asserting that universities have become "one of the chief innovative forces . . . [and] the major focus of the intellectual . . . life" in this country.[12] Deeply committed, for example, to the primary research that makes technology possible, universities have exerted profound and not always admitted influence on our physical and social environments. As keepers of the degree-granting gate in S. M. Miller's "credentials society," universities have now become authenticating institutions, certifiers in the process of determining who shall do what and to what purpose. These are crucial issues that, again, not only at least partially define the context in which campus ministers reside but likewise inform parish reactions to it. And if parish clergy are found not to grasp and to comprehend the present centrality of academic endeavor, that itself is crucial data. Do

---

11. Which is simply to affirm what we understand Underwood's work to be about.

12. Daniel Bell, *The Reforming of General Education* (New York: Columbia University Press, 1966), p. 107.

clergy see, in short, beyond the immediacies of student protest and suspected sexual indiscretions to the revolutions in human learning and control being fought in the euphemistic ivory tower?

Such questions as these in significant measure account for the many statements designed to solicit clergy attitudes toward and knowledge about the academic world. Numerous factors emerge, hence, that usefully assist our progression here from general perceptions to specific reaction regarding the role of campus clergy in this immense complex.

Just how pivotal is the university imagined to be? Response to that inquiry is seen in Table 19–20. Unaccustomed as we now are to encoun-

TABLE 19–20

a. (III-13) "The universities have become major sources of national policy for the major institutions in our society."

	Parish	Campus	% Difference
	%	%	
Episcopal	71	87	16
Methodist	69	78	9
Presbyterian	70	75	5
American Baptist	74	78	4
American Lutheran	75	82	7
Missouri Synod Lutheran	73	72	−1
			40 = 6.7%

tering anything approaching unanimity, we are initially surprised at its relative occurrence here. Campus and parish not only, save for Episcopalians, speak nearly as one; the range of differences in each of these two groupings is strikingly narrow; for clergy in the parish, opinion falls between the low of 69 (Methodist) and the high of 75 (American Lutheran). And, taken compositely, full three of four ministers perceive the university in critical relationship to other "major institutions." But why, amid this unusual display of ministerial togetherness, did not higher percentages of campus ministers agree positively with the statement's assertion? Does nearly one-quarter of this select group, whose lives at least for a time are intimately bound to the academic milieu, sincerely believe it exercises no influence? Perhaps so; and therein may lie an issue of some importance. The data, we recall, collected in 1965, followed Berkeley's Free Speech Movement by about a year, during which period numerous campus ministers had already begun to analyze and question the university's presumed acquiescence and duplicity in matters of grave social importance. Universities were not, really, "sources" of "policy" in any direct and conscious fashion, but were, rather, merely purveyors of scientific knowledge and technically proficient "products" (students). Hence the statement above may well be indirectly reflecting this growing disenchantment by what we gather to be a sizable minority with the seeming reluctance of universities as corporate entities to actively espouse specific "national policy." In a word, numerous campus pastors are radically inclined.

Inferential support is found for such speculation in two additional statements, both directed at questions of social morality (Table 19–21).

TABLE 19–21

a. (III-30) "The universities are neglecting serious study of the moral choices which confront men in areas where we face major public problems."

	Parish	Campus	% Difference
	%	%	
Episcopal	73	72	−1
Methodist	71	81	10
Presbyterian	70	82	12
American Baptist	74	74	0
American Lutheran	73	67	−6
Missouri Synod Lutheran	64	64	0
			15 = 2.5%

b. (II-19) "There are serious limitations to the scientific method, particularly in respect to moral and religious questions."

	Parish	Campus	% Difference
	%	%	
Episcopal	90	92	2
Methodist	87	92	5
Presbyterian	90	92	2
American Baptist	91	86	−5
American Lutheran	93	88	−5
Missouri Synod Lutheran	96	95	−1
			−2 = −.33%

Again the remarkable unanimity. And the questions themselves seem self-evident enough; if universities be understood essentially as contexts for the pursuit of information and knowledge through the "scientific method," its inherent limitations would seem to virtually assure "neglect" of "moral choices." These reside, it would appear, outside the constricted purview of such methodology. Both of these statements can finally be resolved, obviously enough, into simple issues of fact, and it is entirely possible that these overwhelming responses have so resolved. Simply noted in passing is the rank order of campus clergy for the first statement—"neglecting serious study of the moral choices"—where respondents are less critical in the degree to which they are theologically conservative. As this mildly inverts the finding one might have anticipated, we can only speculate that theologically liberal ministers, more responsive to social questions generally, are equally cognizant of a yawning chasm between the university as perceived and the university as they define it normatively. Conservative ministers hold no such expectations. More distrustful of institutions, they have drawn fairly dichotomous distinctions between science and theology and seem indeed reluctant to permit the former a voice within the latter. One further example will suffice (Table 19–22). We think this statement requires no comment.

TABLE 19–22

a. (II-4) "The scientist's understanding of evolution is an important clue to the way God creates in the world."

	Parish	Campus	% Difference
	%	%	
Episcopal	95	93	−2
Methodist	84	92	8
Presbyterian	84	92	8
American Baptist	62	86	24
American Lutheran	63	97	34
Missouri Synod Lutheran	22	62	40
			112 = 18.7%

Perhaps these varying and not altogether consistent responses assist us in clarifying the ambiguity that seems to occur in further exploring ministerial perceptions of the university as a seat of social power and influence. For, as was observed in Table 19–20, clergy do believe that "major institutions" are in fact affected by an academic presence. But which institutions? A touch of uncertainty intrudes when "institution" is defined as meaning the church. Two statements, one descriptive, another normative, point to this ambiguity (Table 19–23). *Are* the halls

TABLE 19–23

a. (III-1) "Higher education in our society is the central place where Christians are engaged in study of and learning about the human needs and developments in all other institutions."

	Parish	Campus	% Difference
	%	%	
Episcopal	59	79	20
Methodist	63	85	22
Presbyterian	63	91	28
American Baptist	61	78	17
American Lutheran	71	93	22
Missouri Synod Lutheran	59	72	13

122 = 20.3%

b. (III-25) "Major programs and policies of the church in foreign missions, inner-city work, and adult education should now be significantly shaped by knowledge and research from the colleges and universities."

	Parish	Campus	% Difference
	%	%	
Episcopal	70	86	16
Methodist	67	87	20
Presbyterian	63	91	28
American Baptist	57	85	28
American Lutheran	58	95	37
Missouri Synod Lutheran	54	69	15

144 = 24%

of academe "the central place" for Christian engagement with and study about "other institutions?" As has so frequently been the case elsewhere, the data may here be interpreted rather variously. Fewer parish respondents are now willing to affirm this question of centrality when directed at the church, but key phrases in the statements themselves make it difficult to read significant meaning into the results. On the other hand, when the issues are phrased normatively, when the question is *should,* one notes a decided reluctance to agree that closely follows denominational conservatism. Yet—and this may be crucial for the discussion in the following chapter—substantially more than six of ten parish ministers support the desirability of integral church-university relationships. In a Presidential election, that would be classified as a landslide.

But what does it really appear to mean? Already in evidence is the near-complete conviction by parish and campus alike that the "scientific method" has grave deficiencies as a methodology in the religious and moral spheres. Yet the vast majority also perceive, and believe it desirable, that the university's knowledge inform the church's ongoing life and programing. We have, therefore, abstracted two more series of statements that seem not only to sharpen these basic distinctions but also suggest possible explanation (Table 19–24).

There was a time, we are told, when the queen of theology held sway over all lesser knowledge, reasonably secure in the exercise of divinely granted primacy. And while that period now principally belongs to antiquarians still immersed in such matters, we are swayed by the data to suggest that for clergy, at least, the abdication is by no means complete. In keeping with the earlier finding regarding the limitations of the "scientific method," the first three statements in Table 19–24 strongly reinforce an imagery of a limited, circumscribed social science—an imagery where the subtleties and ultimates of religious commitment and belief remain largely hidden, perhaps incomprehensible, to the empirical researcher. Ministers may, of course, be quite correct in their defense of religion's "essence," most especially in light of much past superficial sociological rhetoric masquerading as "religion explained." But we do the clergy no disservice to point out the self-serving, protective stance that seems inherent in responses to these statements. Whether "human behavior" is, "in the last analysis," "very unpredictable" remains essentially an empirical question, the preliminary evidence for which, assembled for decades in ofttimes forbiddingly exquisite detail by social investigators, seems largely on the side of regularity and order. What apparently has emerged again here is the personalistic, suspicious-of-institutions theological stance observed earlier and to which we return in the next chapter.

When the issues, however, no longer challenge the directly theological, the patterns of response become dramatically different. Indeed, when the imagery suggests the social and physical sciences as helpmates in explaining our present confusing, highly fluctuating environments, ministers again almost totally support such endeavors. And, it might be noted, campus clergy are in agreement virtually without regard to denominational affiliation, again excepting the consistent nonconformity of Missouri Synod Lutherans. Perhaps the case is stated not unfairly by remarking that ministers, campus and parish, exhibit relatively high degrees of suspicion when they infer or encounter persistent at-

TABLE 19–24

a. (II-18) "The views of psychology and sociology that hold that men are not responsible for their behavior are fundamentally at odds with the Christian view of guilt and personal accountability."

	Parish	Campus	% Difference
	%	%	
Episcopal	73	72	1
Methodist	78	76	2
Presbyterian	77	71	6
American Baptist	79	78	1
American Lutheran	84	74	10
Missouri Synod Lutheran	90	77	13
			33 = 5.5%

b. (II-22) "In the last analysis, human behavior is very unpredictable."

	Parish	Campus	% Difference
	%	%	
Episcopal	65	60	−5
Methodist	66	72	6
Presbyterian	65	63	−2
American Baptist	67	62	−5
American Lutheran	69	65	−4
Missouri Synod Lutheran	59	64	5
			−5 = .83%

c. (II-21) "It is impossible for the sociologist to fully comprehend the meaning and significance of religion unless he himself is a member of the faith."

	Parish	Campus	% Difference
	%	%	
Episcopal	79	73	6
Methodist	80	74	6
Presbyterian	80	67	13
American Baptist	81	81	0
American Lutheran	89	60	29
Missouri Synod Lutheran	88	80	8
			62 = 10.3%

BUT:

TABLE 19–24 cont'd

d. (II-14) "Various disciplines other than theological and biblical studies, such as sociology and psychology, may inform the Christian as to the nature of God's action in the world."

	Parish	Campus	% Difference
	%	%	
Episcopal	95	99	4
Methodist	91	98	7
Presbyterian	91	96	5
American Baptist	89	97	8
American Lutheran	83	95	12
Missouri Synod Lutheran	73	82	9
			45 = 7.5%

e. (II-13) "Science made it possible to turn away from preoccupation with mere survival toward issues of intellectual attainment, friendship, and participation in civic life."

	Parish	Campus	% Difference
	%	%	
Episcopal	67	75	8
Methodist	68	72	4
Presbyterian	66	71	5
American Baptist	70	71	1
American Lutheran	61	79	18
Missouri Synod Lutheran	63	67	4
			40 = 6.7%

f. (II-8) "If the church is going to express God's love for man in the modern world, it will need to make use of specialized knowledge developed by scientists."

	Parish	Campus	% Difference
	%	%	
Episcopal	86	96	10
Methodist	86	90	4
Presbyterian	84	96	12
American Baptist	76	92	16
American Lutheran	75	89	14
Missouri Synod Lutheran	60	77	17
			73 = 12.1%

tempts by social science to explain that which is finally seen only with "eyes of faith"; they are very much more willing to appropriate and utilize the competencies and findings of scientists in discerning the nature of God's creation and action with the world.

If, then, this suggests at least a tentative introduction to the perceptive framework in which both campus and parish clergy discern the house of intellect, we are led to inquire: How does the parish perceive the campus minister in relation to it? What functions ought he to perform? Where lies the minister's principal allegiance and clientele in the university context? Here, again, the data provide a number of interesting insights. One might well inquire, in light of findings to this point, as to whether, from the parish perspective, there really ought to be any ministry to the campus at all (Table 19–25)?

Two conclusions seem immediately apparent. Irrespective of denomination, campus ministries continue to enjoy almost total support; they are not a "waste," financially or otherwise, nor are they "frills," at least in the sense suggested. Second, parish clergy appear to recognize what the social scientist so laboriously seeks to discover: campus pastors are generally more "liberal" theologically and, presumably, in their social and political attitudes. This last statement above gains added significance when one makes allowance for the language it contains: "significantly distort" and "captured" are, after all, highly emotive phrases, virtually guaranteed to provoke feeling having no necessary direct relation to the central point about numbers. Hence one can well imagine numerous parish clergy who, disagreeing with the statement's basic premise, express disagreement with the statement in its entirety. Even so qualified, one minister in four purports to see a "liberal" takeover. Yet we are left with three in four who harbor no such feelings. These are, to us, important findings: regardless of its theological flavor, the campus ministry still commands considerable good will.

They are also, however, statements of generality. What ought this specialized ministry to do (Table 19–26)? As a "task," helping students "discover a new meaning of God that is relevant for the modern world" has a charming innocuousness that offends predictably few, and support for it nearly approaches a consensus among the campus-oriented. This statement contains, of course, the interesting assumption that such relevance is both comprehended by clergy and susceptible to communication. Whether all respondents fully recognize the significance of these assertions perforce must remain an open question. In any event, support of the statement remains very high for the more "liberal" denominational parish clergy, declining only somewhat among more conservative groups. This reflects, we would suppose, the continuing, often dichoto-

TABLE 19-25

a. (III-24) "For the most part, the campus ministry is a waste of time and denominational money."

	Parish	Campus	% Difference
	%	%	
Episcopal	10	10	0
Methodist	9	5	−4
Presbyterian	12	6	−6
American Baptist	9	11	2
American Lutheran	5	5	0
Missouri Synod Lutheran	4	5	1

$$-7 = -1.2\%$$

b. (III-39) "The campus ministry is in general a 'frill' in the church, a program designed for college students who are perhaps already the most pampered group in America."

	Parish	Campus	% Difference
	%	%	
Episcopal	10	5	—5
Methodist	10	4	−6
Presbyterian	8	4	−4
American Baptist	9	1	−8
American Lutheran	5	2	−3
Missouri Synod Lutheran	4	5	1

$$-25 = -4.2\%$$

c. (III-42) "Liberals, who significantly distort the meaning of the Christian faith, have captured a very large percentage of the campus ministry positions of my denomination."

	Parish	Campus	% Difference
	%	%	
Episcopal	20	11	9
Methodist	31	11	20
Presbyterian	27	7	20
American Baptist	35	16	19
American Lutheran	19	9	10
Missouri Synod Lutheran	16	10	6

$$84 = 14\%$$

mous distinctions still theologically drawn by such ministers between "secular"—hence suspect—and "otherworld"—or in but not really of. Even here, however, two-thirds of the most consistently withdrawn and

TABLE 19–26

a. (III-40) "A principal task of the campus ministry should be to help students discover a new meaning of God that is relevant for the modern world."

	Parish %	Campus %	% Difference
Episcopal	93	98	5
Methodist	94	99	5
Presbyterian	93	95	2
American Baptist	89	99	10
American Lutheran	80	97	17
Missouri Synod Lutheran	64	85	21
			60 = 10%

b. (III-44) "Campus ministers would be more effective if they were more concerned with evangelism and winning souls for Christ and less concerned with 'making religion relevant to the modern world.' "

	Parish %	Campus %	% Difference
Episcopal	22	10	12
Methodist	29	5	24
Presbyterian	34	4	30
American Baptist	40	10	30
American Lutheran	44	5	39
Missouri Synod Lutheran	59	38	21
			156 = 26%

c. (III-19) "A major purpose of campus ministry ought to be to keep students from being swept off their feet by the forces of secularization in the university."

	Parish %	Campus %	% Difference
Episcopal	69	39	30
Methodist	76	36	40
Presbyterian	69	19	50
American Baptist	78	42	36
American Lutheran	80	32	48
Missouri Synod Lutheran	82	72	10
			214 = 35.7%

literalist denomination represented in the data express recognition of a Christianity attuned to "the modern world."

The second and third of these three statements in Table 19–26 would seem to project this contemporary theological debate in full-blown terms. In the former, where traditional language speaks of "evangelism" and "winning souls for Christ," one finds once again convincing evidence that for all campus clergy save the Missouri Synod Lutherans these thought forms have been rejected out of hand. Not so for the parish; well over one-third agree to the "effectiveness" of these traditional emphases, although denominationally one notes the considerable variation in predictable directions.

Perhaps statement *c* is the most critically revealing. What these "forces of secularism" are perceived to be we cannot state with certainty, although we have already noted the degree of skepticism (however justified) expressed regarding the role of science and academicians in adequately comprehending, hence speaking causally and with definitiveness about, the fundamental nature of religious belief and act. And, as remarked previously, words like "secularization" have largely lost their neutral descriptive character throughout this past decade, serving now as symbols on which the Coxes and the Robinsons have constructed their "this-worldly" theologies. Thus we cannot be sure: are both campus and parish reacting to such symbols as opposed, say, to clearly delineated "forces" known to permeate university life? In either event, the result is disturbingly dichotomous to those who maintain the necessity for reconceptualized parish-campus co-operative ministries: *when the statement is phrased this way,* only the relatively narrow disagreement between Missouri Synod Lutherans restrains our per cent of difference from becoming the highest encountered thus far. Well over two-thirds of all parish ministers (again Missouri Synod Lutherans are a noticeable exception) reject it.

Three additional statements permit us to flesh out this crucial problem of parish perceptions and expectations (Table 19–27). Here, as has so frequently been the case elsewhere, the matter seems one of where to place our emphases. Parish ministers, in Table 19–27a, do believe—at least two of three—that "first responsibility" involves the students of their respective denominations. Given the various misgivings these men entertain regarding university life and thought, their evident concern for the sexual behavior of away-from-home young parishioners, and the fact that campus ministers are almost completely dependent on the local parish for financial support, these parish expectations appear fully understandable. But this desire for denominational loyalty is by no means

TABLE 19–27

a. (III-38) "The first responsibility of a campus minister is that of keeping in touch with the spiritual needs of students of his own denomination."

	Parish	Campus	% Difference
	%	%	
Episcopal	71	33	38
Methodist	70	40	30
Presbyterian	54	16	38
American Baptist	68	25	43
American Lutheran	84	72	12
Missouri Synod Lutheran	94	90	4

165 = 27.5%

b. (III-36) "The campus minister should be free from denominational restraints in developing his program."

	Parish	Campus	% Difference
	%	%	
Episcopal	41	63	22
Methodist	52	71	19
Presbyterian	55	75	20
American Baptist	58	71	13
American Lutheran	27	56	29
Missouri Synod Lutheran	14	20	6

109 = 18.2%

c. (III-16) "Assignments in campus ministry should increasingly follow functional (e.g. assignment to academic disciplines and professional schools) rather than denominational lines, so that ministries are provided to the major structures of the university or college."

	Parish	Campus	% Difference
	%	%	
Episcopal	56	80	24
Methodist	67	81	14
Presbyterian	76	95	19
American Baptist	69	82	13
American Lutheran	41	75	34
Missouri Synod Lutheran	21	21	0

104 = 17.3%

complete. Approximately half of these ministers also appear prepared to waive "denominational restraints" (in statement *b*), as campus ministers conceptualize and implement programing. More: parish clergy in the first four denominations acknowledge the need for "functional" approaches to academic ministries, to "structures" as opposed, we suppose, to individuals. And for campus ministers, such acknowledgment and support are devoutly to be wished. As the three statements clearly indicate, save for those in the Lutheran tradition, campus pastors at least verbally are deeply committed to ecumenical ministries that minimize denominations and, we note, denominational students. These findings give a widely based credence to Underwood's findings in each of the colloquia: considerable disposition exists among campus-oriented clergy for creating alternatives to denominational student centers. They also lead us to marvel a bit that parish ministers continue to express such warm feelings for a specialized ministry so seemingly bent upon minimizing parish influence, if not support.

There can be no doubting that in its ostensible thrust toward the university as a complex, multistructured entity with profound powers of fulfillment and debasing alienation, the campus ministry has rendered a crucially fundamental decision. Institutions are not individuals; they "live" in intricate detachment from those who inhabit the institution's functional slots and categories. And while we return to these questions at some length in the next chapter, it seems useful to address one additional inquiry to the data, for questions about training and competence in this reoriented calling seem obviously of central importance (Table 19–28).

That campus ministers should be well "trained" can hardly be questioned in light of the responses, and in this they have the overwhelming verbal support of the parish. But why the Th.D.? Does one minister to "major structures" from a background of professional, doctoral preparation in theology? Is ministry to be equated with the training and activity of other "disciplines" and "professors"? Both the Th.D. and theology as an academic field seem rather stock responses, and the substantial support for them—two thirds of the campus—at least initially belies the ministerial image that "structural" concerns evoke. Analysis of role preferences in the next chapter permits further discussion of this point.

As is evident, a curious inversion occurs between statements *a* and *b*. Having opted for doctoral preparations for campus ministers, parish clergy are noticeably unwilling to admit that anything less will suffice in the denominational parish church. Campus minister response, however, has risen; they appear quite prepared to perceive formal educa-

TABLE 19–28

a. (III-10) "Campus ministers should have a Th.D. and be as well trained in theology as professors in colleges and universities are in their own disciplines."

	Parish	Campus	% Difference
	%	%	
Episcopal	71	54	17
Methodist	83	75	8
Presbyterian	73	62	11
American Baptist	80	74	6
American Lutheran	77	72	5
Missouri Synod Lutheran	76	64	12
			59 = 9.8%

b. (III-20) "One needs more formal educational preparation to be a competent campus minister than to serve a resident parish or congregation."

	Parish	Campus	% Difference
	%	%	
Episcopal	67	78	11
Methodist	68	83	15
Presbyterian	63	62	−1
American Baptist	71	84	13
American Lutheran	72	86	14
Missouri Synod Lutheran	80	82	2
			54 = 9%

tional requirements not so evident to parish counterparts. Probably one ought not to read undue significance into these statements. Parish ministers might well be expected to support the most highly qualified, professionally trained ministry possible for the church's confrontation with the intellectual world of the university. At another point, and in a different context, when the issue reflects at least implicitly on one's personal worth and activity, should we be puzzled to discover significant numbers, both campus and parish, unwilling to admit the statement's basic premise? In either event, the problem is, as they say, somewhat academic: the Th.D. is possessed by only a minuscule number of clergymen, wherever they presently labor.

⪢ 20 ⪡

THE PARISH AND CAMPUS MINISTRIES:

A COMPARATIVE LOOK (CONTINUED)

W HERE to now? Beliefs, the values men profess as important in their thought and lives, the attitudes reflecting their vision of a social environment—these we have examined and speculated about throughout the preceding chapter, satisfying (to the extent that time, space, and competencies permit) our first objective in these pages: comparison of campus and parish clergy.

If, from this, summary statements are finally possible, we would offer only one: while generally in agreement on broad principles and commitment to humane values, parish and campus ministers verbally diverge, often startlingly, when specific implications or actions are suggested. We are left, however, with what for us are the more critical issues, viz., the action, the roles, the styles of ministry these beliefs and attitudes presumably inform. And there remains Underwood's vision of "ministries of inquiry," at once so usefully provocative and so difficult to clarify.

The Question of Roles

"Role" is a convenient concept, susceptible of various interpretation and usage; its constituent parts and their interrelationships still largely reside with the individual researcher. If we define "role," however, "as a set of expectations, or . . . a set of evaluative standards applied to an incumbent of a particular position," where "position" is "a location of an actor or class of actors in a system of social relationships,"[1] several con-

---

1. Neal Gross, Ward S. Mason, and Alexander W. McEachern, *Explorations in Role Analysis* (New York: John Wiley, 1958), p. 60.

siderations obtain. "Relation," for example, implies that roles not only are objectively given but also emerge in interaction with counterpositions, with other actors, thus introducing possible multiple sources of "expectations." With the modifier "social," situational factors enrich the concept. From what and where, we are then led to inquire, do parish and campus clergy derive, and recognize as legitimate, "evaluative standards" or "sets of expectations"?

The question is, of course, more complex than that. In the sense that such impositions or expectations are placed on an actor by others he perceives as having legitimate claims to do so, an actor is essentially passive, moved by demands seen emanating from without. But few roles demonstrate complete unity of definition and expectation; expectations flowing from any given counterposition may be diffuse and ill defined and the authority underwriting them simply denied. Or, although authority is acknowledged, it may be countered, modified, or negated by other counterpositions an actor perceives and acknowledges as primary or fundamental. In this process of selection, where questions of value and belief, where cognitive and evaluative considerations are brought to bear in the resolution of conflicting demand, authority, and pressure, an actor may indeed be active, a mover and shaper of the role he lives.

The conception receives added elaboration when the analytically amorphous terms "church" and "university" are more carefully delineated as sources of expectations and standards. To illustrate this point briefly, one notes the numerous denominational focuses that exist for campus ministers from which derive, at least potentially, conceptions of role having consequences for both attitude and behavior: national denominational offices concerned with the campus ministry, church boards which determine financial arrangements, local pastors who may or may not sit on policy-making or corporation boards for the various local foundations, and the peer group of colleagues who share in a particular religious worker's efforts. This same diversity is apparent in the university community, where, beyond the considerable variety existing between any two university settings, students, faculty, and administrators frequently define themselves (and each other) in terms often pointedly at odds with the other two; here, likewise, definition of role and function may vary widely within any one such grouping. Campus pastors who thus conceive of, in the argot, "ministries to the university" have, in actuality, specified attention to groupings (and a corporate structure) from which now cascade highly diverse, often hopelessly contradictory, visions, positions, and expectations. Yet from this rather remarkable mix of theological conviction and depressing practical realities, clergy must fashion patterns of tolerantly coherent and cohesive action.

No small task, this. As Underwood has demonstrated throughout the study, multiple and complex elements have always resided in the Christian faith from which derive normative tensions or, in our usage above, ambiguous "evaluative standards." *Faith and action,* or *self and others,* suggest but two of the manifold possibilities from which standards are forged. And these essentially personal categories become embodied in our guiding images of the church: holy institution, gathered community, social organization, "task force for action," and so on. These have consequences, as the organizing language of the study so vividly illustrates; pastoral, priestly, prophetic inquiry, and governance—each bespeaks roles and activities that are, as Underwood says, "freighted with theological and moral beliefs and commitments with skill competencies, with technical data and institutional resources." Ministers act out their role conceptions in concrete settings where God's reality is proclaimed, where men are called to the restored relationship made possible by Jesus Christ and charged to live in Christian community and openness.

What do these "modes of ministry" look like? In what fashion do ministers adjudicate and reconcile the many tensions and expectations to which they are heir, not only by virtue of time and circumstance but as inherently present in the Gospel statement? What kinds of action most typify these four historic modes? These are difficult questions, and we make, of course, no pretense at resolution. Even at that, however, the data are instructive, particularly at the point of those possibilities that seem present in the four modes.

1. *Pastoral* or *integrative* roles have been primarily individual-oriented and include such actions as prayer, spiritual counseling, pastoral calling, hospital visitation, conducting funerals—a deep concern for personal need and want: spiritual, social, and physical.

2. *Priestly* or *pattern-maintenance* roles seem symbolic and cultural and are characterized by preaching, interpretation of belief and doc-

trine, manipulation of persons and resources in conformity to institutional norms and laws, leadership in worship, and celebration through the sacraments.

3. *Prophetic* inquiry or *adaptive* roles, emphasizing the powers of rationality to affect adjustment of organizations, norms, and persons to a changing environment, bespeak action designed to train and educate, to appropriate from a perceived external social reality or situation such language and cognitive argumentation as will bring one's own institution and people into harmony with that defining external situation.

4. *Governance* or *goal-attainment* roles, essentially instrumental in nature, emphasize utilization of components—situational factors (physical and financial resources), other actors, organizations, and the like—for the achievement of particular goals. Advancing educational objectives, manipulation of finances, the construction of facilities, board and committee activity, represent obvious particulars, although the recognition of and competence for effective guidance and leadership as critical aspects of modern organizational life are also integral to governance roles.

We may also, additionally, distinguish an internal-external dimension, as it were, for each of these modes; as Talcott Parsons suggests with reasonable clarity,

> In analyzing the components of any particular action system, one must also consider the larger system within which that action system is embedded. The action system is related to the "external system" beyond it, which I refer to here as the environment of the system as distinguished from the situation of the acting unit.[2]

While we may hypothesize that the church provides this *internal* dimension for clergymen, the "situation of the acting unit," this is really an empirical question. With equal plausibility, the university may be discovered to be the internal, defining context in which the campus minister moves, the church and other social institutions being perceived by him as elements of the *external* "larger system" in which the university is "embedded." These are, for us, crucial distinctions. Men may well purport to minister to institutions of higher learning when in actuality "ministry" has been constricted to single modes or styles undifferentiated

---

2. Talcott Parsons, "Pattern Variables Revisited: A Response to Robert Dubin," *American Sociological Review* (August, 1960), p. 468.

from the traditional parish; others may ostensibly retain a religious identity and denominational affiliation when in fact their style or mode has so completely embraced the adaptive, has so identified with the university, as to foreclose upon a meaningful relation with the "external" church.

Such, then, is an introduction to what we understand Underwood to have been seeking in that section of the survey instrument which solicited Professional Activities and Missions; fifty-two activities or roles were evaluated by each respondent, again on the six-point Likert scale, from "Definitely Do not Enjoy" to "Definitely Enjoy." Underwood recognized, of course, that stated preference or enjoyment does not of necessity relate to what they in fact do; on the contrary, previous studies would seem to have established, on occasion, significant differentials between enjoyment of particular activities and amounts of time expended on them. Nonetheless, we believe it reasonable to suppose that enjoyment reflects individual perceptions of what one ought to do, what it is that would, at least ideally, define one's dominant style or mode of ministry. And as Hammond documents, "Persons differing in role conceptions do indeed behave in markedly different ways."[3]

In Table 20–1, we have arranged the nine most "enjoyed" roles, as indicated by parish clergy, on the basis of an "Enjoyment Score," the highest possible number of which is 300.[4] We have, likewise, sought to generally categorize these functions or activities in terms of the style or mode to which they seem integral.[5]

By way of revealing contrast, we indicate in Table 20–2 the roles or modes with which parish respondents express most discomfiture.

It is data such as this that, at first blush, so powerfully reinforce the radical's view of the Protestant parish as a bastion of inward-gazing support for established patterns and ways of doing. In these composite

---

3. Phillip E. Hammond, *The Campus Clergyman* (New York: Basic Books, 1966), p. 61.

4. The "scores" we have employed here are based on a system in which responses are weighted: the per cent of ministers indicating 4 (mildly enjoy) was multiplied by 1, 5 by 2, and 6 (most enjoy) by 3; these were then added. An "enjoyment score" of 300 would result if 100 per cent of all parish ministers in each of the six denominations chose 6 for a given statement.

5. As indicated in the previous chapter, the survey instrument was not originally formulated in response to the fourfold typology of ministry Underwood later adopted as the organizing and interpretive framework of this study; differing opinion as to the mode these statements illustrate is certainly possible.

TABLE 20-1

	Enjoyment Score	Ministerial Role or Mode*
Preaching sermons	253	L
Leading public worship	244	L
Administering Communion	231	L and I
Winning a lost soul to Christ	229	L and I
Helping a person or family resolve a serious problem, whether it be spiritual, social, psychological, or economic	223	A and I
Teaching and working directly with adults	214	A, L, and I
Reading the Holy Bible	214	L and I
Teaching young people	202	L and I
Conducting a baptismal service	202	L and I

* The following abbreviations have been employed here:
L = Pattern-Maintenance or Priestly
I = Integrative or Pastoral
A = Adaptive or Inquiry
G = Goal Attainment or Governance

TABLE 20-2

	Enjoyment Score	Ministerial Role or Mode
Participating in creating plans for improvement of city life	92 external	A–G
Influencing the policies of major organizations or institutions in my community	91 external	G
Maintaining harmony, handling troublemakers, averting or resolving problems	73	G–I
Giving theological interpretations of avant-garde movies and other art forms	67 external	A–L
Helping manage church finances	67	L–A–G
Managing the church office—records, correspondence, information centers, etc.	62	L–A–G
Organizing or administering local community projects	52 external	G
Raising money for special church projects	44	A–G

images, which we readily admit are gross and nondiscriminating, ministerial norms seem overwhelmingly ideational and individual-oriented; emphases that stress action, particularly corporate in nature, are nearly nonexistent. Indeed, no "goal-attainment" function requiring the exercise of active leadership appears in the data before the twenty-fourth item, and even here the statement seems relatively innocuous: "Taking a firm stand on some issue confronting the life of the church," where the "score" was 168. It is the *symbolic/theoretical*—worship and the sacraments—and the *symbolic/rational*—spiritual counseling—that pervade the imagery parish ministers describe, to the exclusion of functional action and institutional manipulation. Almost without exception, it is the pastoral and the priestly that here predominate. One notes, too, that none of these "most enjoyed" activities necessitates cognizance of or an expressed concern for that outside the church itself. Not until the thirty-fifth statement does there appear an activity that directs significant attention toward the external and beyond a congregational orientation: "Participating in a local ecumenical ministerial association"—112. And that, we observe, really has to do with the wider church.

Examination of Table 20–2 seems only to strengthen the portrait we have so sketchily drawn, as the problems of governance, the use of institutional authority and power in moving groups to action and change, finally emerge; it is here that the issues of "creating plans for improvement of city life" and "influencing community organizations" have dispiritingly appeared, as with an embarrassing afterthought. We must admit, of course, that our failure to distinguish among denominations does considerable injustice to large numbers of individual ministers, and one might plausibly argue that since the euphemistic "urban crisis" seems, in the jargon, to have "come of age," data collected now might well project quite different perspectives. In light of the consistency present here, however, we have no real reason for so believing. Parish ministers apparently enjoy most those functions in which they stand at the center, supported (perhaps elevated) by a theological doctrine of their position—preaching, leading worship, administering sacraments—or by their esoteric knowledge—counseling, discussing theology, teaching. Only minimally do they acknowledge activities in which, as member or leader, the group pursues specific goals and proximate outcomes.

What, then, of the campus ministry? Having already witnessed the substantial and often severe divergences of belief and attitude that separate campus and parish, differences in normative role conceptions ought also to be present. And indeed they are (Table 20–3).

At the other end of this professional continuum are the activities least enjoyed by the campus ministry (Table 20–4).

If initial examination of the data affirms parish-campus distinctions, they are not as immediately dramatic, perhaps, as might have been predicted. Four of the nine in each set of "most enjoyed" are shared in

TABLE 20–3

	Enjoyment Score	Ministerial Role or Mode
Teaching undergraduates and graduate students	252	A–L
Discussing contemporary theological issues and viewpoints with educated persons	238	A–L
Helping people come to grips with the problems involved in the relationship between the Christian heritage and the modern scientific world	225	A–L
Preaching sermons	222	L
Counseling with people facing the major decisions of life, such as marriage, vocation	218	A–I
Teaching and working directly with adults	217	A–L–I
Counseling with people about their moral and personal problems	214	L–I
Leading public worship	211	L
Helping a person or family resolve a serious problem, whether it be spiritual, social, psychological, or economic	204	A–I

TABLE 20–4

	Enjoyment Score	Ministerial Role or Mode
Visiting new residents and recruiting new members	77	I–G
Seeing a major building project to completion	73	G
Fostering fellowship at church gatherings	72	I–G
Working with congregational boards and committees	68	G
Organizing and administering local community projects	68 external	G
Promoting and creating enthusiasm for church activities	47	I–G
Participating in evangelistic meetings	39	L–I–G
Managing the church office	35	L–A–G
Helping manage church finances	26	L–A–G
Raising money for special church projects	15	A–G

common; the remainder for campus ministers reflect their peculiar situation and relationship with the academic world. And parish-campus dislikes are remarkably similar, both professing intense distaste for financial and administrative tasks. Most notable, of course, is the more evident concern for the adaptive, for the inquiring that characterizes the campus clergy, a finding that holds quite consistently through all fifty-two items.

It is certainly possible to argue, especially in light of this adaptive thrust, that campus ministers exhibit an "external" dimension and concern found absent in the parish, from which derives attention to a wider environment. If we understand the campus to be constituent of that larger whole, such does seem to be so. But it may be equally plausible to argue that in their adaptive emphases, significant numbers of campus ministers identify far more readily with the university than they do with the church and that their labors in the academy are quite as "internal" and inward-looking as is true of their ostensible parish colleagues. This receives additional support when we observe that none of the campus "most enjoyed" relate in any direct fashion to the wider community; "Organizing and helping groups who are victims of social neglect or injustice" and "Spotting the key places in the community where decisions influencing our common life are being made and informing church members of this" appear rather far down the list with scores of 145 and 140, respectively. To be sure, both of these are substantially higher than was true for the parish, and the combining of all ministers to the campuses smooths out significant points of denominational differentiation (especially Methodist and Presbyterian), but in light of the campus ministers' own literature in recent years stressing the radical nature of such ministries, these seeming facts give us pause.

We raise, therefore, simply as speculation our lingering doubts about whether the data finally support substantive differences between these two groups; or do we observe, simply, variations of familiar themes? Theological distinctions there certainly are, and they labor in differing vineyards, but they still seem to share a normative clergy image as one who relates ideas and the needs of people. The parish minister preaches and administers the sacraments; campus clergy teach theology (or desire to).[6] Men in the parish foster church fellowship; their campus counterparts establish coffeehouses or "situations for dialogue." And they all enjoy counseling. In a word: stress on and manipulation of ideas and cultic symbols, on individual and small-group relationships, on a teach-

6. They also enjoy preaching, as noted above. Interestingly enough, the following activities produced these curiously differing responses:
Enjoy preaching sermons: 98 per cent of parish; 94 per cent of campus
Enjoy preparing sermons: 85 per cent of parish; 81 per cent of campus
We leave to the reader whatever implications these data contain.

ing and advising that carry as corollaries an apparent insensitivity within their role images to the realities of power, corporate authority, and the demands of leadership that describe the goal-attainment or governance mode of ministry.

Perhaps we have misread the data. But consider just two additional statements of role, both of which have already been alluded to, when they are set forth in terms of percentages (Table 20–5).

TABLE 20–5

a. (VI-50) "Spotting the key places in the community where decisions influencing our common life are being made and informing church members of this."

	Parish	Campus	% Difference
	%	%	
Episcopal	71	75	4
Methodist	77	84	7
Presbyterian	77	88	11
American Baptist	77	85	8
American Lutheran	68	89	21
Missouri Synod Lutheran	55	56	1
			52 = 8.7%

b. (VI-35) "Organizing or administering local community projects."

	Parish	Campus	% Difference
	%	%	
Episcopal	37	40	3
Methodist	45	48	3
Presbyterian	45	49	4
American Baptist	47	55	8
American Lutheran	32	56	24
Missouri Synod Lutheran	30	46	16
			58 = 9.7%

Consistent with our usage throughout both of these chapters, the percentages utilized here are based on clergy response to any one of the three positive possibilities on the survey (number 4, 5, or 6). And because we have already indicated the relatively low "Enjoyment Score" given to "Spotting the key places . . ." (140), the large number of clergy marking 4's and 5's on this statement of role becomes immediately evident. No matter; when taken compositely, three out of four indicated at least *some* interest in these matters, whatever the intensity and its relationship to other roles "enjoyed." This appears entirely consistent with earlier observations that noted the overweening preference for activities and images in which ideas and their communication through teaching and counseling were centrally visible. One could, and probably ought, to at least suggest the wider implications of this claim, given the vigorous and by no means resolved debate regarding the dynamics of community power and decision making presently current among sociologists and political scientists;[7] oriented principally to internal maintenance and organization and, as we shall presently notice, related to political processes only tangentially, clergy seem unlikely sources of the information and insights this "spotting" role assumes and requires.

But let that pass; the much more critical element we read into these two possibilities lies with the second, and the remarkable disjunction that now occurs between *seeing* and *doing*. Averaging both parish and campus for 20–5 *a* and *b*, the differences become:

	Parish	Campus
Spotting the key places	71%	80%
Administering and organizing	39%	49%
	32%	31%

This is, in the parlance, governance that is directed toward the external environment in which resides the church, governance that presumes to act on and in the structural arrangements now so determinative to human activity and its quality. But here, as elsewhere, clergy have generally eschewed such involvement, either by defining it as outside the purview of religious concern or by opting for a radical stance that denies the utility of sustained organizational endeavor. For campus and parish alike, organizational involvement in the external community securely resides in the "least enjoyed" possibilities offered to them and does not appear to be a significant source of role authority.

As we have already admitted, simple distinctions between parish and the academic world conceal quite as much as they illumine. Categories that fail to discriminate between, say, Presbyterian and Missouri Synod Lutheran do obvious injustices to both.[8] In the initial factor

7. For a recent installment, see Charles Kadushin, "Power, Influence and Social Circles: A New Methodology for Studying Opinion Makers," *American Sociological Review*, Vol. XXXIII, No. 5 (October, 1968), pp. 685–698.

8. By positing the "most enjoyed" activities of Missouri Synod Lutheran parish

analysis of the survey's data, this problem has been at least partially resolved, since it identified which of these fifty-two activities tended to cluster together in identifiable though differing role patterns in the all-embracing notice of "minister's role." Further analysis is required to determine denominational frequency and strength; too, we know not how many of these twelve may be collapsible into one another. Yet they are insightful even now, and their examination will indicate to the interested reader the varying percentages of ministers, both denominationally and parish-campus, who have responded positively to the individual possibilities that constitute the twelve role factors.[9] Perhaps of more immediate moment, however, is the correlation of these twelve factors to those of belief and attitude discussed in the preceding chapter, affording an indication of the degree to which particular patterns of theological doctrine and social attitude coalesce with identifiable ministerial styles. To this point we shall presently return.

Problems, we superfluously suggest, still remain. It is methodologically inadmissible, for example, to extrapolate from what clergy say they enjoy to what they in fact are doing. As other research has demonstrated, ministers often find it necessary or at least expedient to devote inordinate quantities of time to pursuits for which they have disdain or, comparatively, little interest. Too, it seems altogether possible that respondents to this survey have reported enjoying such activities as they believe ministers *ought* to enjoy. They were asked, after all, only to indicate, in the language of the questionnaire, "personal satisfaction . . . independent of the time you may devote to it." Hence, we now turn, in our progression from belief through attitudes through role conceptions, to statements regarding what they in fact *do* do.[10]

---

ministers beside those of Presbyterian campus clergy, the following diverse contrasts are obtained.

Lutheran Parish Ministers	Presbyterian USA Campus Ministers
(30) Winning a lost soul to Christ	(16) Teaching college students
(13) Preaching sermons	(44) Discussing contemporary theology
(2) Leading worship	(22) Teaching adults
(21) Administering Communion	(33) Relating Christian heritage to the modern scientific world

9. They have been descriptively labeled as Evangelist, Community Leader, Church Administrator, Denominational Leader, Counselor, Youth Teacher, Theologian in Residence, Trouble Shooter, Adult Teacher, Traditional Pastor, Priest, and Preacher. See pp., where each factor is given in full.

10. The problem is not actually resolved, as we remain dependent on verbal profession. But in the material about to be discussed, ministers were presented with

In the section soliciting background data, a series of statements inquired into political activity, with the results in Table 20–6.

"How is it," Hadden rhetorically inquires, "that clergy have managed to get involved in the civil rights struggle at all?" To which he replies: "The simple answer is that a large proportion of the activist clergy are structurally removed from the parish and as such do not often feel the direct weight of laymen's reprisals."[11]

As we have noticed previously and as Hadden's own analysis documents, perceived congregational disapproval (occasionally erupting into loss of pulpit and position) generally exercises a restraining, sometimes debilitating, influence on parish ministers whose beliefs would seem to call for far more vigorous social action than has recently occurred. As with civil rights, so, too, with political affiliation and act; the eight statements above (of the eleven that comprise the "Activism" factor) cast this pattern into sharp relief.

We can scarcely doubt from the data that politics is acceptable conversation. As Table 20–5 a so clearly indicates, nearly all apparently speak with relative ease among ministerial colleagues and friends, nor does such conversation have much to do with denomination, place of labor, or theology. That is hardly cause for wonderment; one of the great commonplaces in American life is, after all, the assumption that everyone has a right to political opinion. Whether that opinion need be informed or not is another matter, since one-third of parish ministers and one-fourth of those on the campus had read no "books about politics" during the preceding year. For both statements of activity we note that the percentage of difference is not at all large by previous example: "conversation" at 4.5 per cent and "reading" at 12 per cent.

What most impresses one regarding these first two activities is their essential passive and nonthreatening quality. The next several statements, however, are something else. To write a letter, commission a telegram, or sign a petition is an overt act and entails explicit intent; it carries a hoped-for consequence and, potentially, risks the possibility of public identification. Thus we would anticipate that, based on Hadden's analysis, percentages of involvement would decrease through these first

---

particular and discrete acts which they either did or did not do within a specified period of time. That prescribes, we would argue, a specificity quite unlike profession of enjoyment.

11. Hadden, *The Gathering Storm in the Churches* (Garden City: Doubleday, 1969), p. 207.

TABLE 20–6

a. (VIII-17) "I discussed political issues with friends."

	Parish	Campus	% Difference
	%	%	
Episcopal	95	99	4
Methodist	95	100	5
Presbyterian	96	100	4
American Baptist	92	99	7
American Lutheran	93	98	5
Missouri Synod Lutheran	94	95	1
			26 = 4.3%

b. (VIII-17) "I read one or more books about politics."

	Parish	Campus	% Difference
	%	%	
Episcopal	67	76	9
Methodist	61	72	11
Presbyterian	75	79	4
American Baptist	63	75	12
American Lutheran	51	77	26
Missouri Synod Lutheran	54	64	10
			72 = 12%

c. (VIII-17) "I wrote a letter or sent a telegram to a public official."

	Parish	Campus	% Difference
	%	%	
Episcopal	43	59	16
Methodist	59	70	11
Presbyterian	55	75	20
American Baptist	56	69	13
American Lutheran	34	53	19
Missouri Synod Lutheran	27	44	17
			96 = 16%

d. (VIII-17) "I signed a petition for or against some legislation."

	Parish	Campus	% Difference
	%	%	
Episcopal	44	72	28
Methodist	51	71	20
Presbyterian	50	81	31
American Baptist	61	73	12
American Lutheran	30	75	45
Missouri Synod Lutheran	23	36	13
			149 = 24.8%

e. (VIII-17) "I contributed money to some political cause or group."

	Parish %	Campus %	% Difference
Episcopal	38	62	24
Methodist	25	58	33
Presbyterian	37	79	42
American Baptist	27	63	36
American Lutheran	23	54	31
Missouri Synod Lutheran	22	39	17

$$183 = 30.5\%$$

f. (VIII-17) "I participated in the activities of a political group."

	Parish %	Campus %	% Difference
Episcopal	18	43	25
Methodist	14	43	29
Presbyterian	19	49	30
American Baptist	12	43	31
American Lutheran	7	40	33
Missouri Synod Lutheran	7	13	6

$$154 = 25.7\%$$

g. (VIII-17) "I collected money for some political cause or group."

	Parish %	Campus %	% Difference
Episcopal	6	18	12
Methodist	4	19	15
Presbyterian	4	27	23
American Baptist	4	18	14
American Lutheran	1	14	13
Missouri Synod Lutheran	1	3	2

$$79 = 13.2\%$$

h. (VIII-17) "I voted in the last national election."

	Parish %	Campus %	% Difference
Episcopal	94	93	−1
Methodist	94	98	4
Presbyterian	96	95	−1
American Baptist	95	97	2
American Lutheran	94	93	−1
Missouri Synod Lutheran	93	95	2

$$5 = .8\%$$

four statements (*a, b, c, and d*); and they do, for both parish *and* campus, although the latter is not nearly so pronounced. Actually statement *d* increases slightly for campus clergy, due, we would imagine, to the seemingly endless flow of petitions, agitating for or decrying against, that circulate in any university worthy of the name. Nor does the pattern of diminishing involvement significantly vary further on, with the result that statements progressing through personal and financial political commitments to the solicitation of funds for partisan activity lead to virtually no parish involvement and a subsequent very wide differentiation from campus counterparts. Only on the latter issue—collecting money—do parish and campus return within hailing distance of each other, and only because neither is so engaged.

But wait. Ninety-five per cent of all ministers report voting in the most recent federal election, a finding that must surely qualify them as the most politically conscientious professional group in recent history.

This series of statements suggests to us additional explication of our earlier speculations regarding the largely "internal" patterns that we believe characterize most parish and campus clergymen. National political activity, seemingly external to both, introduces a basic category not really integral to church or university. In Table 20–6 the first five statements invoke not only acts primarily personal in nature but acts that entail largely intellectual (or emotional) commitment. Discussion, reading, letters, affixing signatures, and contributing money—they are not, to us, commitments of self, the allocation of limited, often precious time, a physical presence and visible identity. This does not denigrate in the least these various expressions of conviction; quite the contrary, each would seem to us salutary and much desired. But apart from certain obvious and depressing instances where reprisal has been visited on ministers who did nothing but affirm that which their congregations opposed, none of these activities appears to involve substantial risk.

When political involvement assumes the form of direct participation, even to the active solicitation of funds, the circumstances have been significantly altered. Political (meaning "party") activity is the first in this series of statements we believe can properly be adjudged "external," and, according to the data, in no denomination could one in five so admit, even when the "activity" in question was left almost totally unspecified. This question of political participation is, for us, an extremely significant one; we would call explicit attention to the quite remarkable consistency of campus clergy responses. Excepting Missouri Synod Lutherans, nearly 50 per cent of them do so participate, a finding that reflects for us as accurate a portrayal of parish-campus differences as any one statement or question examined thus far.

The Emerging Style?

As higher education becomes more cosmopolitan, it withdraws acknowledgment of the campus ministry at the same time it evokes innovative style. To innovative style, however, the denomination responds by reducing its acknowledgment.[12]

Some of the most strategic purposes of both the church and the university cross each other in the campus ministry. . . . The campus ministry does have a significant future . . . as a midwife for a renewed church and a reformulated university.[13]

"When one returns," H. Richard Niebuhr once wrote, "from the hypothetical scheme to the rich complexity of individual events, it is evident at once that no person or group ever conforms completely to a type."[14] Niebuhr's caution is pointedly relevant in this context, where our attempts to categorize and discretely separate remain imperfect and partial. In an often disturbing sense, respondents are captives to the questions and categories imposed by the inquirer, and we are never certain that what we "see" is indeed the more fundamental of numerous possibilities. With Underwood we readily admit that "surveys . . . differentiate only grossly or crudely between individuals within a trend." What is "really out there?" Can we finally speak with any precision about a campus ministry that elicits the wildly differing responses in the statements above? Hammond and Schrading speak a common language; they utilize terms and phrases that are the stuff of this study; but the implications they suggest would seem to vary without hope of synthesis. Wherein is the midwife if the principals do not call?

"Midwife" is potent imagery, but it presupposes an intimacy of relationship and respect that critical inquiry has only rarely discerned,

---

12. Hammond, *op. cit.*, p. 111.
13. Paul Schrading, "A Future for the Campus Ministry?" *Reflection*, Vol. LXVI, No. 2 (January, 1969), p. 8.
14. H. Richard Niebuhr, *Christ and Culture* (New York: Harper, 1951), pp. 43–44.

and we must wonder, as has this entire study, where men do in fact covenant in shared experience and learning. Does the campus ministry really justify Underwood's reasoned and experiential hope that in its many expressions could be seen viable, more richly conceived alternatives to traditional modes, or is it unceremoniously relegated to the fringes of church and university alike, only seeking to rationalize its relative impotence, making theological virtue out of practical necessity?

These are, or ought to be, extremely significant issues for a Protestantism wracked by uncertainty and increasingly bedeviled by that now familiar, if overly simplistic, dichotomy of "challenged" clergy and their "comforted" laity. If we accept one of the basic premises of this study —that the house of intellect is now and shall be vitally central in the shaping of American life and institutions—the church's stake in its ministry to that "house" can hardly be overemphasized. But that is a question with which we began: does the evidence give any support to an "emerging" style that might in actuality be viewed as integral to "the Church's whole ministry to the society," whereby church and campus participate in mutual sharing and enhancement?

We do not really know precisely what it was that Underwood gleaned from the data and would emphasize anew that in no sense do we even attempt to speak in his name. But a number of observations may be appropriate here, if no more than as summary statements permitting us to speculate about and variously interpret the substantial body of quantitative information presented thus far. And if our own opinion and sense of priority are likewise in evidence, we can only trust they are sufficiently informed to warrant their consideration.

No facts initially, if a bit obviously, impose themselves on us quite so forcefully as do the many and substantial areas of disagreement now differentiating parish from the specialized ministries to campuses. Throughout the data these distinctions are ever present, affirming anew what Hammond and Hadden have already demonstrated. No one can possibly speak of parish-campus rapport, about harmony of interest, about shared concerns, without confronting the manifold implications contained therein. Campus pastors *are* more liberal, they *are* relatively more activist and radical, they *are* less committed to given church and institutional forms than are ministers generally.

But that is a generalization, and the data have also demonstrated that "campus ministry" shelters beneath its definitional expansiveness a multiplicity of purpose and structure. We have observed, hence, a sizable number of religious representatives to the university for whom phrases like "crisis of self-definition" and "roles in conflict" have little real meaning. By defining their internal field of action with reference to traditional parish models, they function in sum as priest and pastor, as the church's agent. Demanding little of the university, they imagine little that the university might reasonably expect of them. This view of the minister's charge seems pointedly summarized by the following campus pastor:

> [My task] is to reach into the community, minister to the needs of students where they are in terms they can understand; relate the gospel message in such a way that they can accept it, so it will be meaningful; lead those students to a full conscious commitment to Christ; encourage those students then to let God have full control of their lives and lead them then to commit themselves in a local Baptist Church.[15]

There can be no doubting that the religious center is still a much encountered form and many campus clergy are willing to serve the denominationally few who frequent it. ("The adequacy of my ministry cannot be judged only in terms of numbers.") Return to the parish by such clergy could be explained only as a transition of degree, rather than kind, for he has not, actually, moved outside its defining influence.

Also present have been those for whom adaptation to the mores and value commitments of academic life have been accompanied by overt rejection of orthodox thought and forms, where trenchant dialogue and intense personal encounter have served to emphasize an openness to the university, both in its own right and as a community for Christian concern. John Cantelon gives voice to this commitment.

> The Christian community is coming to a new understanding of itself as the people of God called together in obedience to the gospel within the university. . . . To do this effectively the Christian community must be actively involved in the total life of the university, know where this life is most seriously threatened, and be willing to identify its efforts with concerned secularists in order to preserve the life of the university because God loves it and has purposes for it.[16]

---

15. Quoted in Elden E. Jacobson, *"The Berkeley Crisis: A Case Study of Protestant Campus Ministers"* (Ph.D. dissertation, Yale University, 1966), p. 44.

16. John Cantelon, "Introduction," *A Basis for Study: A Theological Prospectus*

Numerous emphases are apparent in assertions such as this, but the church is not one. No one states the implication of this omission quite so baldly as does Harvey Cox: "What is the role of the church in the University? The 'organizational church' has no role. It should stay out."[17]

Again with reference to the action field, it is the university that principally determines the shape and content of Christian concern. Often innovative and impatient with present patterns, these campus ministers have only the most tangential interest in the parish church, and to the extent that specialized ministries provide opportunity and alternative, that interest seems almost certain to become more minimal still.

Both styles of ministry, then, fall outside the immediate question of comprehensive, collaborative styles: one sees or feels no particular crisis; the other apprehends it so pointedly that tenure in this position is highly uncertain and finally unlikely over time. One *pattern-maintenance*, the other *adaptive*, neither notably successful in resolving the multiple tensions that the entire action field, we would argue, imposes.

But there is yet a third group of campus ministers—that "midwife" again—who understand themselves as relational agents, moving between church and campus, professionals who understand the meaning and substance of both social structures and who provide the bridging link through which one "speaks" to the other. They are, or would hope to be, the church as it ministers to the university; they are, or at least aspire to become, a significant channel through which the church appropriates the knowledge and expertise of the academic world. It is, we would suppose, Underwood's "emerging, mature leadership," ministers who not only recognize but accept the legitimacy of the four historical modes, who recognize that openness to the structures of society does not negate the symbols and ceremony through which faith is proclaimed and the community strengthened. And this style, Underwood believed, is demonstrably present in both the campus *and* the parish.

Let us, then, review briefly the evidence; for all the misgivings we have brought to the endeavor, the data *do* seem to clarify and describe. But not initially. Table after table in these two chapters, we unnecessarily repeat, has dramatized the differences between parish and campus, and among the six denominations; propitious it does not seem to be.

---

for the Campus Ministry (Philadelphia: United Presbyterian Church, USA, 1959), pp. 10–11.

17. Harvey Cox, *The Secular City* (New York: Macmillan, 1965), p. 236.

The areas and intensity of substantive disagreement, however, when the various statements are arranged in somewhat different fashion, become surprisingly specific. In Table 20–10 we have placed, from the many items already offered into evidence in the discussion thus far, those for which campus and parish disagreement, taken collectively, exceed 20 per cent. When considered from this perspective, nearly every state-

TABLE 20–10

(I-7)	A literal interpretation of the Bible
(I-64)	The virgin birth as a biological miracle
(I-15)	Jesus' physical resurrection is an objective historical fact
(I-80)	Adam and Eve are historical persons
(I-111)	Sin is an infraction of God's law
(V-23)	Government is usurping the role of private enterprise
(V-46)	Premarital sexual relations will lead to emotional problems in marriage
(V-49)	College teachers and advisers are too lenient in advising students about premarital sex
(V-54)	It is conceivable that in a given situation, premarital sex might be justified
(V-17)	Obscenity should be banned from the newsstand
(V-20)	Censorship is necessary to protect the public
(III-44)	Campus ministers should win souls for Christ
(III-19)	Campus ministers should protect students from the forces of secularization
(III-38)	Campus ministers have a first responsibility to their own denominational students

ment bespeaks doctrinal disagreement and differing convictions regarding Christian styles of action. These statements reflect, to no one's surprise, the differing thrusts of parish allegiance to pattern maintenance and integration, the campus thrust toward adaptation and distrust of legality. Here are men in the pastorate deeply worried as to the outside parameters of a shifting and ambiguous sexual morality. The debate is almost purely internal as central elements of denominational survival are treated very differently by these respective groups; much of the parish image is simply protective, sustaining the reasonable proposition that parish life must needs depend on retention of its college-bound youth.

These are, without doubt, crucial questions, and we do not wish to mute the problems they present; indeed, we could easily argue that denominational rigidity at precisely these points accounts in significant measure for much of the anguish now expressed by those who avoid the perceived confinement of the parish. But we believe, as did Underwood, that the larger issues lie elsewhere.

In Table 20–11 we have again abstracted from data already in evidence a number of statements with which *at least* two-thirds of *both* campus and parish registered assent.[18]

TABLE 20–11

Agreement

(I-47)	Myth and symbol are important for interpreting biblical literature
(I-16)	Admiration for the honest agnostic
(I-23)	Thinking Christians may have doubt about God's existence
(I-107)	Every area of man's life is corrupted by sin
(I-100)	Ethical decisions, right in one situation, may be wrong in another
(I-5)	The church is true to itself only as it exists for humanity
(I-21)	The church must speak to the great social issues of our day
(I-20)	The church cannot live simply among its own membership
(V-7)	Basic sympathy for the civil rights movement
(V-25)	Medical care for the aged should be provided by the federal government
(V-69)	Public expenditures for welfare should be increased
(III-13)	Universities are major sources of national policy
(III-30)	Universities are neglecting the serious study of moral choices in public policy
(II-19)	There are serious limitations to the scientific method with respect to religious and moral questions
(II-4)	But the scientists' understanding of evolution is an important clue to creation
(III-25)	Major church programs should be shaped by the university's knowledge
(II-13)	Science is essentially a "good thing"
(II-8)	The church must use scientific knowledge if it would express God's love for man
(III-39)	The campus ministry is neither a waste of money nor a frill
(III-40)	The campus minister should help students discover a relevant meaning of God
(III-16)	The campus ministry should increasingly follow functional rather than denominational lines

18. Well, almost two-thirds of both. In several instances, Missouri Synod Lutherans have again been excluded.

To the most casual of readers, it will be evident that the emphases are now elsewhere; doctrinal conflict and the virginity of young people no longer excite and separate. When asked to think about and respond to the larger external environment, several exceedingly central postulates began to emerge.

1. These many statements suggest an epistemological flexibility that acknowledges the multiple sources from which truth derives and express a willingness to utilize the expertise and insights of the academic specialist in discerning the reality of God's ongoing creation. This, we strongly suppose, is in part what Underwood intended when he argued that shifts of ministries "from a stance of proclamation of traditional doctrine to one of inquiry" were demonstrably evident in the data.

2. The church has vital social responsibilities that are not solely expressed through the parish as the one normative form of church life and action.

3. Clergy are becoming increasingly appreciative of situational complexity, and when ideological issues are held in abeyance, specific courses of concrete action do emerge with notable agreement.

4. Clergy express a growing awareness of the university as a social institution of enormous influence for change in the social order; as such, channels of collaboration are vital to the church's own life as it now acknowledges that a religious presence exists in centers of higher education quite as much to educate itself as it does to offer pastoral care for university people.

Lest we be misunderstood, stress must again reside on the aspect of "emergence." All too forcefully do the Enjoyment Scores of several pages back testify to the relatively low esteem in which many of these disparate considerations are held by clergy generally. But for us, the important reality here is that a precondition now seems to exist, a recognition that inquiry is indeed essential to an adequate Christian expression. Relative agreement on the bases of knowledge, the centrality of the university, the church's responsibility in a complicated, technically perplexing society, the emerging complexities of multiple role preferences—these reflect human need and disposition, we would speculate, much more adequately than does stress on theological doctrine or particulars of personal morality. Much too frequently, past debate has been hung on doctrinal purity in argument that moved directly from basic and self-authenticating first principles to evaluation of concrete situations, ignoring and circumventing intermediate levels and criteria of evaluation; in H. D. Aiken's usage, the "levels of discourse" have been ignored.[19] Such situations result in agreement on particular action only after accord has been established regarding the first or ultimate principals involved. Frequently wanting, thus (small wonder), has been the imaginative and useful translation of such "faith statements" into language which makes possible fruitful discussion and understanding with those whose own analyses, ways of thinking, proceed from differing basic presuppositions. Theological description is imagined to be sufficient, and judgment takes place from it.

Yet if we have treated the data at all fairly, the bases for ecumenical conversation and shared concern are much more diverse and immediate than has been commonly supposed; the linear conception of principles that lead into derivative action no longer suffices as a descriptive model. We do not, again, wish to minimize these questions of basic doctrine, but we do suggest that many of the battles need not now be waged on the plains of "my unalterable and courageous principles."

The practical considerations remain staggering. It is one thing to find in the data these "emerging" bases of complementary concern and thought; how they might thus be translated into coherent programs that "move whole institutions and people" is surely something else. If campus ministers really are an integral aspect of the wider church, one might obviously observe that conversation is the critical first requisite. But here the data are most discouraging (Table 20–12).

Two years? We can, certainly, impose any number of extenuating, forgiving circumstances that explain or explain away these extraordinarily limited contacts. But for whatever reason, they remain just that: limited. Campus ministers simply have no sustained commitments or contacts back into the parish.

The problems are in part conceptual. This study, our own individual inquiries, the lives we observe and personally live—each testifies to pervasive longing for "meaning" and symbolic life (the priestly); for genuine forms of community life and participation in the affairs that govern us, for individual integrity of feeling, career, and action (the pastoral); a need for theory and models by which futures are shaped and destinies controlled (governance); a need to relate the heritage we claim as

---

19. See Henry David Aiken's very insightful *Reason and Conduct: New Bearings in Moral Philosophy* (New York: Knopf, 1962), especially pp. 65–84.

TABLE 20-12

"During the past two years have you ever invited a campus minister to describe the intellectual and moral trends in higher education with parents so that they will better understand what is happening to their children?"

	Yes %		Yes %
Episcopal	26	American Baptist	27
Methodist	29	American Lutheran	26
Presbyterian	26	Missouri Synod Lutheran	19

"During the past two years have you ever invited a campus minister to speak with precollege youth about the possibilities of higher education and the criteria for choice of schools?"

	Yes %		Yes %
Episcopal	24	American Baptist	37
Methodist	34	American Lutheran	35
Presbyterian	33	Missouri Synod Lutheran	30

Christians to the modern world as scientifically understood and to see these relations as lived in the lives of these who minister in His name (the prophetic). Yet we seem far from understanding the empirical means by which these four basic needs and modes of ministry might be held in creative tension, how the battles move beyond the specialized rationalities so easily invoked to defend only one, or another.

We seem still to know so precious little about the complexities of governance, of institutional structure and the responsible use of power on sustained bases as the necessary antecedents to effective mission. Again with reference to the data on role preferences, all too few seem willing to undertake the difficult and time-consuming efforts that organization and institutional leadership demand and require.

The church speaks boldly and often about the values by which our lives are ordered, but has said relatively little that makes common cause with the major institutions of the society. We ask the question: with our power to change, have we lost our power to govern? Campus ministers talk of the "healing word to the university," but what has been voiced that informs a morality of knowledge, that speaks with precision and theory to the sources of the sciences and their technological handmaidens? What has the church professed—what can it profess—that informs the processes of discovery and implementation? Wherewith comes the technical competence that will gain for the church a respectable and respectful audience? Again the data are not reassuring.

The problems are in part financial. Campus ministers really are, after all, a privileged lot, only minimally concerned about the financial arrangements that make their continued campus presence possible.[20] How much longer that can remain true seems problematic, given the general retrenching now evident in all main-line Protestant churches. As with most of the church's specialized ministries, an ever more aroused laity is asking "Why?" and "How much?"[21] We might reasonably anticipate that as civil rights and the campus become sources of ever escalating violence, these lay pressures will equally become much more intense. And that may be the most critical consideration of all. As Hadden has pessimistically urged: "It would seem to me that *the only way that clergymen can hope to maintain and further develop their involvement in social issues is to begin to think seriously about a strategy for engaging laity in the struggle.*" (Emphasis in the original.)[22]

As the data convincingly demonstrate, that is not happening, comprehensively and persistently through time. But we have strayed a bit throughout these comments; for to argue that the ministry thinks and dreams too narrowly, that it has confusingly permitted conceptual distinctions of ministerial modes to become dysfunctional realities, is but to argue anew what has already been so convincingly performed throughout this entire study.

We close, then, with three considerations we believe have relevance for further inquiry.

1. We need scarcely reiterate the necessity for more adequate analysis and manipulation of the data that were obtained with this survey instrument. We know of no instance where this amount of ministerial information has been brought together in the confines of a single re-

---

20. In response to the question, "How would you evaluate the problems you encounter in the financial support of your ministry?" The following reported, "A minor problem, taking less than 10 per cent of my time and energy."

Episcopal	77%	American Baptist	69%
Methodist	78%	American Lutheran	95%
Presbyterian	90%	Missouri Synod Lutheran	85%

21. The Presbyterian Lay Committee may simply be the most visible example of this general reaction by laymen.

22. Hadden, *op. cit.*, p. 228.

search endeavor, and we have scarcely begun to exploit its possibilities.

2. We believe, as did Underwood, that an "emerging, mature leadership" was discernible in both the campus and clergy ministries, and a portion of the evidence sustaining this conviction has here been offered. But the analytic subtleties necessary to move beyond easily recognized clergy modal positions, the conservative pastor-preachers and the re-active liberal this-world churchmen, appear now to require the conceptualization of research inquiry rather different than has been utilized thus far. Underwood had himself sought to give additional clarity to this "type" of minister through careful scrutiny of questionnaires from individuals already adjudged, on other and various grounds, to represent balanced appreciation for the four modes in the action field. In our less gifted hands, this procedure has turned to salt; the methodological problems imposed were more than we could resolve in the time available. But the issue remains. How shall we find, and describe, these quantitatively hidden individuals for whom tension and complexity are integral and positive aspects of their ministerial style? Creative re-thinking of present activities, restructuring of seminary emphases and curricula, alternative patterns for parish organization, to suggest but three—these seem desperately dependent on the descriptive precision available. And it is not available now.

3. A third concern flows out of the previous two and harkens to the warning by Hadden above: involvement of laity. As the data show, and as studies of other specialized ministries suggest,[23] laymen, particularly laymen in suburban churches, are not generally understood as integral components in the ministerial images of most ordained clergy who labor outside parish bounds. The literature of recent years abounds in critical assessments of suburban apathy, to which are occasionally offered equally impassioned rejoinders by the wounded. In both instances, however, the depressing impression we bring from them contains precious little of substantive alternative beyond the assertive declaration that men (and ministers) ought somehow to be, or at least do, differently. But men and institutions are more complicated than that; as Underwood has argued,

---

23. Charles A. Ellett, in a recent study of "Urban Mission" in Washington, D.C., reports: "We found that . . . Urban Mission as seen by interviewed leaders, tends to leave out: Baptists, Methodists, suburban clergy, the laity . . . academic centers." *The Field of Urban Mission and Its Leadership* (Washington: Council of Churches of Greater Washington, February, 1969), p. 2.

> One of the conclusions I have reached is that we are in grave need of knowledge, not so much of how we think people in various positions of responsibility ought to act, and what they ought to bring to their actions in the way of religious principles, but of knowledge that tells us the actual basis or grounds of action of men in the major institutions and professions of the society.[24]

This, we need hardly point out, requires careful, patient inquiry into what men really do, into the fears and tenuous hopes by which we all live and work. It does not come through exhortation and demand. Such inquiry is not unknown, of course—much of Underwood's own scholarly activity was given to the critical analysis of the bases of belief and act—but we know few situations where it is now being systematically undertaken for the purposes of creating alternative rationales and instrumentalities. We certainly agree with Hadden: laity ought to be more intimately related to the critical and basic dimensions of church involvement; how, he does not say.

Perhaps we ought to find out, before the circumstances become cataclysmic.

---

24. Kenneth Underwood, "The Campus Ministries and the Ethical Question of the University," paper to Advisory Council on Danforth Programs in Campus Ministries, April, 1965, pp. 13–14.

PART IX

Policy Alternatives in the University and the Church

⤙ 21 ⤚

THE SEMINARY AND PROFESSIONAL EDUCATION

IN THE UNIVERSITY

W<small>E</small> have said that the university is increasingly that place in our society where knowledge is gathered and evaluated, models are formulated, and persons are prepared for making responsible policy decisions for the whole society. The university must thus be seen as a key place where decisions about the mission of the church will be forged in the coming years. What happens to persons in and through the universities shapes what will be happening to persons in church and culture.

Professional Education: Specialized Trap, or the Pay-off for Higher Education?

What, then, does it mean for the ministry that the professional clergy are educated in the university setting? Is the "professional" image, indeed, the concept of the clergy we want? And if we do, in fact, want a professional clergy, what needs to be said about the nature of that profession and its relationships to the whole spectrum and process of professional education in the university?

There are signs that the meaning of "profession" is undergoing a major shift. The clergy are not the only professionals confronted with crises in identification and practice as the society changes around them. Questions are being raised in the universities about the very nature of professional education itself. The professions are highly visible occupations, and professional education uses an overwhelming amount of the space, money, and energy of the American university. It is to be expected, then, that on professional education are focused many of the most stringent criticisms and the most far-reaching dreams of higher education.

Critics of professional education ask first: what does professional education do to the university? Burton Clark sees the "new university" in America becoming a bureaucratized example of the "degree university," characterized by fragmentation and specialization with a loss of "a sense of the social conditions that promote care and affection. One is tempted to say of the gigantic campuses of the near future that there will be no society there." In the "Educational City," the home of specialized labor and segmental involvement, the centrifugal forces of profession and discipline are strong. "The professional school and the department are the basic units for organizing the work, embodying and carrying the diverse expertise of the university. . . . The clusters of experts that we lump together under the heading of faculty take their cues from a very large number of different reference groups—men in their field—and this is the most important of the fragmenting forces in the university."[1] The chief criticisms Clark seems to be making of the professional schools are that they produce a narrowness of vision at the expense of a broader human concern. There is technical expertise unintegrated into an over-all pattern of education for social concern.

The shaping of the student as a professional also draws criticism. Berg proposed that the process of professional socialization leads to an orientation to job technique and loyalty to the organization, with a loss of the sense of vocation that is supposed to characterize the professional. In his doctoral dissertation[2] he demonstrates from a study of the data collected on seminary students[3] that the greater the length of an individual's seminary training, the lower is the incidence of humanitarian-ideational goals and the greater the incidence of bureaucratic goals; the lower is the incidence of charismatic self-conceptions, with a greater emphasis on the mastery of skills in the role of clergyman; and the lower is the degree of "intrinsic religiosity" and the higher the degree of "extrinsic religiosity." The student who may have come to seminary motivated with concern for mankind leaves his training, says Berg, an "organization man" oriented toward success in the opinion of his professional peers and with an increased distance between himself and those whom he will serve.

---

1. Burton Clark, "The New University," *American Behavioral Scientist* (May, 1968).
2. Philip L. Berg, "The Professionalization of Protestant Clergyman," Ph.D. dissertation, University of Nebraska, 1967.
3. Keith R. Bridston and Dwight W. Culver, *The Making of Ministers* (Minneapolis: Augsburg, 1964).

This criticism in a radical form appeared in the "modest proposal" of six Yale Divinity School graduates of 1967 that the seminaries must stop perpetuating a "clergy caste system" which drives a wedge between clergy and laity:

> The church we envision is one in which the priesthood of all believers is taken with utmost seriousness. Such a church is made virtually impossible by the structure of seminary education. Seminaries have endured a lot of criticism in recent years. They are accused of being schizophrenic—of trying to educate scholars as well as professional ministers, and doing a poor job of either or both of these aims. But the issue is not that seminaries should choose to be either a graduate school or a professional school. Rather, seminaries must reject both these roles as they are presently conceived. Instead, they should become centers for the training of all men and women who seek to relate their faith to their future vocation, whatever it might be. The idea that all seminaries should serve to educate professional clergymen is—must be!—a thing of the past.[4]

All these criticisms of professional education seem to be pointing to the separation of the professional from broad human awareness and from those with whom he works. This is a separation produced in the specialized technical training by which he is socialized into the role of a member of a bureaucratic group. The criticisms of seminary education are the more drastic because the clergyman, like perhaps no other professional, is supposed to work in direct identification with a community of people whose common heritage and mission forms the content of his training.

But is the solution this simple—that "human concern" is the opposite of, and the corrective to, technical specialization? To carry the opposition of community and specialization to the extreme of making the tension between them into a dichotomy would be to avoid the issue of professional education by setting the "technician" over against the "friend" and choosing one or the other—neither of which roles is that of the professional.

Another widely expressed view of professional education starts from the assumption that in the kind of society in which we live, decisions are going to have to be made by highly trained people. In the universities, the "pay-off" comes when in professional education the student's exposure to theory is joined with the requirement for disciplined training for specification. Those who take this view of professional education

---

4. George Rupp et al., "A Prescription for Seminaries," *Christianity and Crisis,* Vol. XXVII, No. 10 (1967), pp. 136–139.

speak out of a humanistic concern as genuine as that of those who speak of specialization and community. But their question is this: how can basic *values* and basic *theory* be held together with the requirement for public exercise of *power* in responsible action? Professions are charged with responsibility for major areas of social concern such as health, law, education, or religion; then how can professional education produce persons who understand the broad values and intensive theory of an area of culture and are able to act in social structures along with other responsible leaders? The problem is thus seen as that of placing professional education in the enveloping context of liberal higher education and preparing professionals to take public responsibility for the continuing shaping of the society—not simply as individual practitioners but as members of consciously organized groups who must know how to exercise power informed by their knowledge.

Taking this view, President Kingman Brewster of Yale suggests that specialization is not to be avoided, but placed in a broadened context.

In a society which highly rewards specialized learning, it is increasingly difficult to maintain professional schools which are interested in all aspects of life. Perhaps we need a different sequence of education which aims at the developing of more of a synthesis in the outlook of the student, a synthesis not dominated by any one professional school, department or discipline. . . . We are increasingly aware that exposure of students to different ways of using the mind—which has been commonly called general education—does not mean that the student emerges as a generalist. When the student works on a Ph.D or professional program he is likely to focus on a particular key discipline, and we would not want to disparage this within the life of the university. But we are increasingly aware that the university has to assume responsibility to invent situations where the student, after he has developed his professional competence, is put back into confrontation with problems which involve more than one profession. What we are seeking is not the addition of more professional work in the university, but . . . the encouragement of the student to turn to more problems which involve the synthesis of his knowledge and the relating of the resources and responsibilities of a number of professions. . . . What is needed in the exploration of public problems is an approach which brings people together from different disciplines and professions after they have achieved some rigorous competency and are aware of what their responsibilities and powers may actually be in the areas in which they plan to work and live.[5]

5. From a speech given at Yale Divinity School, New Haven, Connecticut, May 11, 1966.

This kind of synthesis of knowledge from many professions has to go on continually in practice after the completion of basic professional training, says Brewster. He also suggests that a student in his undergraduate education might be exposed to professional education for a year and then come back for a final year of joint reflection with fellow students preparing for different professions.

These two evaluations of professional education—the one condemning professionalism for its technical emphasis at the expense of human concern, the other appreciating the necessity for specialization, but insisting on a broad synthesis of knowledge and a consideration of public responsibility—are not merely opinions raised about two narrow aspects of professionalism. Rather, they must be considered as questions that get at the very heart of what it means to be "professional." They raise and hold before us the dynamic balance of tensions which cannot be reduced if the professions are to function on behalf of society.

These four concerns—concern for persons, trained skills, values and basic theory, and public responsibility—are the central themes of the professional ideology always mentioned in the sociological literature on the professions and in the professions' statements of purpose.[6] Criticisms of professions could easily be interpreted as battles fought by people who consider various ones of these marks of professionalism more important than the others. In concrete practices, however, it is impossible to obtain a general consensus on the meaning of "professionalism" or even an agreement on which occupational groups are professions. What is characteristic of professionals at their best is a quality of *disciplined style*. It is this style or spirit that is the most valuable achievement of professional education and the most difficult thing to program into the process of professional socialization.

What makes a man a professional is the style of action in which he holds all these claims in tension and uses them as resources for service, rather than letting himself be trapped into reducing the tensions by

---

6. The four emphases inside this pattern (specialized training and so on) represent the professions' solutions to the four functional problems of all action systems postulated by Talcott Parsons' general theory of action: that is, integration, pattern maintenance, adaptation, and goal attainment. For a presentation of the professional pattern as a field theory adaptation of Parsons' model, see Hoyt P. Oliver, "Professional Authority and the Professional Ministry: A Study of an Occupational Image," Ph.D. dissertation, Yale University, 1966. This chapter was written in collaboration with Professor Oliver and draws heavily upon his work in this dissertation.

concentrating only on theory, technique, concern, or public leadership. We can also now see from this perspective that the criticisms of professional education to which we have pointed are the kinds of reactions that are to be expected when the professional pattern becomes distorted. These criticisms should actually be seen as demands that professionals be fully professionals, for each criticism is made in the name of a dimension of the professional pattern that is being neglected.

To ask the question of the ministry as a profession in the context of this perspective on the style of professionalism enables us to recognize that the four historic modes of ministry—the pastoral, priestly, prophetic-teaching, and governing modes—correspond to the four dimensions of the professional pattern. Where ministry is present in its fullness, there are the same dynamic and the same spirit that mark professionalism at its best.

The criticisms of professional education for its narrowness, lack of vision, irrelevance to what is going on in the world, and dehumanization of students could, along with the ever increasing concern of seminary students for "worldly presence" and new, nonchurchly forms of mission, be taken as arguments against the continuance of a professional ministry in the church. But we must beware lest such criticisms and new emphases lead to the dissipation of the historic (and professional) dynamic and tension between the demands of the full pattern of ministry. It is also possible, however, to point to these dissatisfactions and at reshaping of professionalism as promising signs of a reawakening of the sense of *vocation* that has ever been the most important mark of the professions. This renewed sense of vocation is appearing here and there all across the spectrum of the major professions, and if ministry is to be renewed, it will be renewed only as a part of the process of renewal of the patterns of professional action wherever trained, responsible people become conscious of their work as mission.

Common Crises in Professional Education: Medical Education as a Case Study—and the Uniqueness of the Ministry

We need now to take a closer look at some of these specific tension points in the professional pattern, the crises that professionals are today facing in common.

Wherever one hears professionals or professional educators raising serious questions about what they are doing, there seem to be present four broad areas of concern: (*a*) the question of the *self-shaping* of the professional person, his taking on a professional identity rather than just being prepared for a role; (*b*) the question of the *view of man* built into professional education—specialized, or comprehensive; (*c*) the question of the *process* of professional education—of what happens when, and who is responsible; and (*d*) the question of the *relationship* of professional education to the university and to the other institutions of society.

Within these four broad areas of concern, each profession faces concrete and confusing alternatives of action. To illustrate, we shall take medical education as a "case study" and then consider the specific ways in which the ministry as a profession is unique, along with the consequences this implies for ministerial education. From these case studies, we can then make some judgment about the meaning of ministerial education carried on in the university setting, as well as the gifts the ministry has to offer to the whole pattern of university professional education.

Medical education is a particularly illuminating illustration of the crises shaking the whole professional structure. This is so not merely because medicine is so very "visible" and in a sense the ideal type profession but also because the changes taking place in medicine are the most rapid and dramatic of all among the human relations professions. This is not to say that the whole body of medical professionals feel themselves shaken by crises; but we need to listen to those who are sensing after the present evidences of contradistinctions that tomorrow will bring conflicts straining the fabric of society.

The problem of shaping the student as an ethical person who knows how to evaluate and to take responsible moral action seems not to be handled very well in the medical schools at present. In half of the medical schools in the United States there is no formal instruction in ethics; and, where ethics is dealt with even perfunctorily, it is most often handled as a matter of *internal* professional ethics: a matter of fees, referrals, conduct, and so on.[7] Even at one medical school where moral and ethical attitudes are explicitly treated as important, "It was found that between freshman and senior year there was really no change in at-

7. Kenneth Underwood, ed., "Trends and Issues in Medical Education," *The Christian Scholar* (Winter, 1967), p. 349.

titudes that have to do with compassion, with understanding the rights of the patients, with accepting responsibility in dealing with patients' problems, or indeed in this matter of respecting the basic human rights of patients."[8] Students tend to identify with the faculty members who teach them basic sciences and clinical techniques, rather than with the practitioners who must make decisions "in the field." And it is not regarded as the faculty members' role to evaluate students as responsible moral actors. George Wolf, in the consultation on medical education sponsored by the Danforth Foundation, suggests that in the future

> it seems to me that the individual faculty member has to take upon himself the responsibility for seeing that the students who graduate from our medical schools are increasingly sensitive to the physician's own responsibilities . . . in ethical matters. We are getting closer to the understanding of many vital processes of the human, but we must not forget our responsibilities for knowledge about those aspects of humanity which are not, at least at the moment, subject to the test tube.[9]

Though medical students, unlike most professional students, are actually involved in offering professional services while they are studying, one of the most pressing criticisms of medical education is that it does not really prepare students for the style of action they will have to adopt in practice. Dr. Paul Sanazaro summarizes the problem in this way:

> As students leave medical school, (*a*) they have a focus that doesn't really orient them to the problems of practice, (*b*) they have not had the opportunity to view medical illness and its consequences in the individual families the way it occurs in practice, and (*c*) the initial stages of becoming a physician in the traditional sense are after a student graduates from medical school.[10]

The students are oriented toward specialization partly because the university teaching hospital connected with the medical school is a key center for research:

> Specialization has gained at the expense of something equally valuable —a sound general view of the patient. The parts have run away with the

---

8. *Ibid.*, p. 354.
9. *Ibid.*, p. 372.
10. *Ibid.*, p. 361.

whole. The medical center has become a specialist's paradise, but not a good place to learn everyday medicine. . . . Concentration on patients' immediate problems, especially the acute and the exotic, has left little time or energy to relate them to the patient's past or future—the dazzling accomplishments of episodic medicine blur the vistas of comprehensive medicine.[11]

Speaking of pediatricians as an example of common experience among doctors, George Harrell remarks, "They are only spending a third of their time with the types of problems that they thought, even as postgraduate students, they would be dealing with."[12] Physicians have not been prepared to deal with families, with nonspecific disturbances, with the social consequences of illness, and with all the other factors of practice which cannot be easily objectified.

Furthermore, the approach of the university medical school tends to lead the student to think that the scientific-technical methodology is a neat system which will also work in practice. It rarely does.

The doctor must take the data he collects on an individual patient from a variety of methods and try to apply them in a variable system. This leads to criteria of action that no one with any conceivable stretch of the imagination could accept as scientific. The application of data to the study of the individual patient is no science and never will be. In the inherent nature of things, medicine is an art.

What is needed in medical education today is an increasing awareness by the student and faculty of the variety of ways of knowing and acting in his own work and life. . . . The faculty needs to study the intellectual process that the student goes through in the community where he practices, and to start him in the most fruitful and adequate intellectual process in the environment under faculty supervision and observation.[13]

Finally, because the student's experience in the applied aspects of medicine has been pushed into the later states of internships and residency training, the "result is that the student, as a student, has only a basic exposure to clinical medicine and it postpones his involvement in the full range of problems inherent in practicing medicine."[14] It also means

---

11. Lester J. Evans, *The Crisis in Medical Education* (Ann Arbor: University of Michigan Press, 1964), pp. 34, 35.

12. Underwood, *op. cit.*, p. 362.

13. *Ibid.*, pp. 358–359.

14. *Ibid.*, p. 351.

that the faculty who teach him the theory of medicine are not the persons who evaluate his actions as a beginning physician. And there is very little feedback built into the process of medical education, where the concrete experiences of students could become a part of the content of that education.

Dr. Sanazaro, in the consultation, describes the tension points in medical education as "factors which either do in fact or potentially influence the medical student in such a way that it is difficult for him to develop a unified view of medicine. By unified view of medicine, I mean not only that he can understand medicine as a profession, but that he comes to develop a clear self-concept of his role and his obligations in medicine."[15] Among these factors influencing medical education, the most impressive change today is the adoption of molecular biology as the central theoretical base for medicine. Basic biologic research, increasingly divorced from research into human problems and from a comprehensive view of illness, is the guiding force in medical education. The changes in new scientific knowledge and new scientific technology are so rapid that one commentator remarks that the doctor of tomorrow will be as different from the one of today as the one of today is different from the one of thirty or forty years ago.[16]

Gains in scientific knowledge cannot be dismissed in favor of a return to the friendly, nonspecialized general practitioner. But the danger inherent in this new scientific base for medical education is that of a reductionism to a specialized view of man, to the detriment of any more comprehensive view. As Sam Banks expresses it:

> On the one hand we have a reductionism, for better or worse, implicit in the movement into an intracellular or subcellular view of man. It doesn't necessarily lead to a philosophical reductionism, but it is certainly a methodological reductionism back into the cell. And it's very easy to jump to a philosophical reductionism in which we say reality occurs only within the cell. On the other hand we have been moving in the direction of seeing reality as occurring in large, global, molar units, such as society. So, I see medicine in a "two-way stretch" which isn't necessarily bad, only fascinating.[17]

---

15. *Ibid.*, p. 349.

16. Evans, *op. cit.*, p. 32.

17. From the full transcript of the Consultation on Trends in Medical Education of Significance to the Campus Ministry, New York, May 7–8, 1965, pp. 42–43.

The recognition of the need for a comprehensive view of man in medical education makes apparent the ways in which the whole medical profession is shaped by the societal definition of illness, by the attitude of society toward the human body in health and disease:

> The values of society permeate medicine—the physician, the medical student. And in fact these may be the most important factors in his making a decision about what questions to ask the patient, about what he should do with a particular patient, or about a choice in life work or specialty, or in personal involvement.[18]

Medical educators are recognizing that the question of what health and disease mean to society, patients, and doctors cannot be answered out of the science of molecular biology. They are asking how to formulate in medical education

> a holistic frame of reference in which the psychological, social and cultural aspects of human behavior are appropriately related to the biological nature of man and the physical environment in which he lives.[19]

The examination of the theory-and-value base of medical education comes to a concrete focus in developing in the individual medical student during the process of his professional socialization a specialized or comprehensive self-image. What has study of the human being really meant to the student by the time he receives his degree? The trend in medical schools has been to attempt to develop in the student a holistic view of medicine by adding courses in psychiatry or the social sciences to the basic biological sciences curriculum. But what happens through this arrangement?

> The student sees from the very beginning two widely divergent trends. He is told that he must be a humanist who looks at the whole patient. Perhaps the behavioral scientist and the psychiatrist introduce him to this concept in the morning. Then in the next period or in the afternoon the student goes into the laboratory where he is told that to be a really good physician he has to be a cool dispassionate objective scientist who evaluates data and makes decisions. Now these emphases are difficult to reconcile in a compatible pattern because the student's emotions are most deeply

---

18. Evan Pattishall, in Underwood, *op. cit.*, p. 386.
19. Straus and Clauson quoted in Evans, *op. cit.*, p. 9.

involved in the one and his mind in the other. But both of these value systems are the facts of medical life.[20]

The departmental autonomy of the basic core courses contributes not only to this division in the medical student's perception but also to a compartmentalization during the clinical years of medical education:

> We've separated each of our clerkships. Students rotate to surgery, internal medicine, psychiatry, pediatrics, etc. We've done this, of course, under the name of education efficiency. But we still have developed almost no relationship among them. [21]

Furthermore, the student's relationship to the practitioner and the patient is often pushed later and later along in his educational program and even then is conditioned by the objective-technical approach:

> The practitioner has less of a role in teaching undergraduate medical education the first four years. The full-time faculty can carry on education in human biology much better than the practitioner. Therefore there is less and less influence of the physician, even the thoughtful physician, who deals with patients, on the thinking of medical students in the early formative years of medicine. . . . The scientific attitude not only permeates the first two years of medical education, but increasingly it is the basic attitude of the so-called clinical years. The emphasis is upon the objective approach, rational analysis of the mechanisms of disease. . . . The progressive divorcement of the undergraduate medical student from the patients, from the discussion of the patient's problems, is also accelerated by the growing number of graduate students in medicine.[22]

All these specific criticisms have tended to consider medical education as an isolated system of theory, students and faculty, and learning process. However, such problems are insoluble apart from viewing medicine as a social phenomenon related complexly to the whole society and specifically to the total process of university education. As Evans remarks, "The professional student may go all the way through his education . . . without ever fully appreciating his role in the ever-expanding and intricate relationships in the scientific and service complex of everyday health and medical activities."[23] The medical school itself is having

20. George Harrell, in Underwood, *op. cit.*, p. 356.
21. Evan Pattishall, *ibid.*, p. 391.
22. Paul Sanazaro, *ibid.*, pp. 351, 352, 353.
23. Evans, *op. cit.*, p. 9.

to expand its role as it is being asked to take public responsibility for models of health care under grants from government-sponsored programs of medical care. This is changing the image of medical education from the former model of preparing individual practitioners to a more complex model where social action is directly programed into the medical school's action.

Thus, in the middle of the process of medical education, there is demanded a continuing evaluation of "medicine" itself as a field:

> Medicine is a social science in itself and therefore incorporates the biologic sciences, the basic behavioral and social sciences, and the applied psychiatric aspects. Everything that occurs in medicine is not just application of technology; it is a social phenomenon. Therefore it should be studied as a social phenomenon, not merely as a surgical technique or an anesthetic technique.[24]

This kind of broad evaluation and intentional study of medicine as a social phenomenon, with explicit consideration of the public effects of medicine, can take place, says Evans, only in the university setting. The university applies knowledge from many disciplines to the study of any phase of man's behavior; it has a responsibility to translate its knowledge into social action through education; and it is unique in that it is obligated to anticipate the future.[25]

In sponsoring the study of health and illness, the university must take a perspective broader than that required merely to teach the skills and techniques of the individual health professions.[26] This perspective, which Evans says might be called "patient-care research," would "foster intensified study of medicine in all dimensions—breadth, depth, and duration. Studies in breadth should include more attention to the patient's environment; those in depth, more consideration of the patient's inner motivations; and those in duration, the relation of the patient's present condition to the past and to the future."[27] One of the fruitful consequences of this approach might be that a new basis could be developed for relationships with the many outside institutions, agencies, and professions with which the university must work to achieve its

---

24. Sanazaro, in the original transcript (mimeographed, May, 1965), p. 42.
25. Evans, op. cit., p. 32.
26. Ibid., pp. 34–35.
27. Ibid.

goals.[28] It would also lead medical educators to the realization that their students could not be educated for this kind of social responsibility in isolation from other professional students faced with their own dimensions of social responsibility. The idea of a professional school with clear, closed boundaries within the university would be exploded.

Education for Professional Ministry: Likenesses and Uniquenesses

Can we identify in education for the ministry crises similar to those in medical education? These same tensions are, indeed, present, shaped in fascinating fashion by the dual relationship of the seminary to the university and the church. First, the conflict in the profession's view of man exemplified by the molecular-molar approaches in medicine appears in the seminary as the problem of *secularization*, the radical redefinition of the church's role that has made belief in a given transcendent revelation no longer to be taken for granted. The clear division between "sacred" and "secular" is no more present; but neither is there present a clear sense of the world as one sacred-secular whole. Ministers and seminarians experience the split between "church" and "world" as an agonizing one. In increasing numbers, they are reacting in two ways: becoming technical experts in the teaching of religion, or choosing "worldly" ministries to inner city and the like over appointments as pastors of local congregations.

The split between *theory and practice* is quite evident in the seminary, with certain faculty members teaching core disciplines and others handling the "practical" courses of field work, Christian education, and so on. Seminary students, like medical students, experience these as two separate kinds of activity. It would be too simple to say that seminary students choose to identify with their professors, rather than with practicing ministers. This happens at schools like Yale, Harvard, or Union Seminary in New York; but in a large number of denominational seminaries, students who may have been preaching in small churches each week end during their training very often fail to develop any identification with the university study of theology and become organization men with little change in self-image. The extremes are the students who come

---

28. *Ibid.*, p. 90.

out of seminary as "idea men" or "career men"—for they have hardly been exposed to ministers in whose work the full range of the historic modes of ministry is present.

While specialization is a growing trend in the seminaries, as it is in other professional schools, the forms of specialization most tempting to the seminary students are outgrowths of the bias of the minister toward being a man who works with *ideas* and *individuals* rather than with the responsible use of power in the structures of society. The "institutional church" appears as a threat to both the student who would rather become a teacher and the student who yearns for the existential closeness of experimental communities. (The campus ministry sometimes, we have noted, combines both of these appeals.)

Seminarians know in a way that perhaps no other professional does that they will function professionally as leaders and members of communities. There are two facts of life about seminary education closely connected with this. The first is the periodic anguish that shakes the seminaries over the "loss of community" between students and between students and faculty. This was voiced at one seminary by a Negro student; and at another, the anguish became a real occasion for self-searching after the death by suicide of a student. The second community anguish comes over the separation of the clergy from the laity. It is an interesting phenomenon in our century that the "theology of the laity" is hailed as the new missional thrust of our times concurrently with the maintenance of the information gap between the laity and ministers to whom the issues raised by Robinson in *Honest to God* were "old stuff," which nevertheless they had not shared with their congregations.

We may mention without elaboration that the seminaries share with other professional schools the tendency to reductionism in epistemology (even to the point of a particular style of theology—neo-orthodoxy—becoming the norm, to say nothing of the practical absence of other basic disciplines of the university from seminary training). They share the tendency to avoid evaluation as a part of the whole process of professional education, though they certainly devote some part of the curriculum to courses in social ethics; and they share the lack of a comprehensive viewpoint of, and evaluation of, the whole field of their practice as a part of their being connected with the university. What President Brewster said about Yale Divinity School is generally true of seminaries over the country: "It has the appearance of great self-containment—it has an Entrance and an Exit, as the signs say."[29]

Seminary education shows some of the same frictions that are present in the other professional schools. But in what ways is the ministry unique among professions?

One of the more obvious differences is that the idea of the ministry as a "profession" is by no means a consensus shared by the churches, many of whom distrust a trained ministry. Even among seminary-educated ministers, the term "professional" is often shunned because of its connotations of "independent expert."

The ministry may also be located along the professional spectrum according to sociological indicators. The minister is among those professionals who work with people, ideas, and symbols; he deals with cultural rather than technical knowledge, and his practice is based on theory held in common by a community. He practices, like the college teacher, in an organization where "clients" are taken in as members; he undergoes isolated socialization, is salaried, appears in the public vision regularly, and performs a group leadership role; and, like no other professional except perhaps the judge, he is expected to exercise moral judgment over others.[30]

Most importantly, the characteristics of the ministry which make that work unique all stem from the fact that the minister works as a member of a community whose life together is constituted by its faith in God. This means that there are differences between the minister's theory, practices, and status and those of other professionals.

The shared "theory" of the Christian community on which the minister's practice is based is *faith-knowledge,* or what Christians have called "revelation"—which H. Richard Niebuhr calls *our* history—history as it is lived and apprehended from within. The rationality of the theory by which the minister practices is more like the rationality of poetry or drama than like that of bridge building or surgery. It is more like a story than a science. Nor is this theory separable into the cognitive realm; it is *self-involving.* This is not to say that faith-knowledge is irrational or that it gives a false interpretation of reality. It is simply to

---

29. Kingman Brewster, from a speech at Yale Divinity School, May 11, 1966.

30. See Oliver, *op. cit.,* Chapter VIII, for an extended discussion of the ministry as a profession.

point to the fact that, however objective the reality the Christian knows, that knowledge is impossible without the involvement of his whole self. This has consequences for the minister's professional preparation. All professional schools teach basic theory, provide practice in skills, and shape the person into his professional identity and role. But in the minister's preparation this self-shaping is the most important factor: the development of a mature selfhood as a "man of faith" whose competence is determined, not solely by what he knows or what he can do, but by who he is. For many, perhaps most, seminary students, their seminary years are a time of real religious identity crisis.

Finally, as the minister's "theory" is the possession not of his profession but of his community, as it is not separable into a cognitive realm, and as it is self-involving, so also it does not specify the particular practice skills which the minister must develop. Ministers study "practical" courses such as homiletics and Christian education, but no claim is made in such courses that the Christian faith demands that just these activities should be done in just such ways. Nor are the "basic content" courses anything more than "language *about*" faith. The actions a minister takes have to be shaped not only by his trained knowledge and skills but also by his personal commitment and by the changing situations he encounters.

Hence the minister does not exercise professional authority as a trained expert called in to furnish technical services based on esoteric theory possessed by his professional group alone. The Protestant minister's authority is assigned to him within a church, not for the sake of the members of that church alone but in order that the whole church may itself minister to others. This suggests that "political images"[31] of the minister as one who must build a constituency, form a consensus, and move people to action need to be joined with the "professional image" of the minister as one specially trained for services to the whole body of the church.

This calling—the enabling of others to be the church as mission—means that the minister's role is that of "man in the middle," the link builder between members, between faith-understandings and persons, between needs and actions. He is not called to perform the whole work

---

31. See James Gustafson, "Political Images of the Ministry," in Volume II.

of ministry himself. But the responsibility is laid on him to make possible the several dimensions of mission as these are carried out by the church community.

The capacity for flexible, moral response in changing situations is developed neither by avoiding the specialized requirements of the four dimensions (pastoral care, priestly and preaching, teaching and inquiry, and governance) of the professional action field nor by choosing one or two demands as more important than the others. The ministry is effective only by holding these demands together in such a way that tension between them becomes an energy resource for action, rather than a source of conflict and frustration.

Education for the Ministry in the University: Demand for Accountability and a Gift to Offer

How is education for the ministry done in relation to education for the other professions in the university setting? The present picture seems to be that, more often than not, there is *no* relationship; the seminaries are perceived by the university community as the most isolated of the professional schools, operating by a different set of standards.

Public criticism comes last to the seminaries. They are not yet, like medical schools, being held accountable for public responsibility through direct involvement in federal funding. The church has not been subject to much external criticism as a public institution. Hence the seminaries tend to pay scant attention to such criticisms as are raised on behalf of the public through the universities.

But we can predict that the time is coming when the university is going to ask: when are the seminaries going to get with the larger educational enterprise? Increasingly, the university has been called into public accountability and made responsible for policy decisions. Its image is no longer that of the isolated community of scholars. In the university, the first place public-policy issues get articulated is in the professional schools; and the universities are going to demand that seminaries become a more integral part of the process of professional education.

This confrontation will be a great occasion for the seminary, for there have been continually raised *from within* in the church's history the same basic concerns of which the university, especially the professional school, is now becoming conscious. The issues of the nature of selfhood, of representational responsibility, of vocation, of the relationship between understanding and action, of value commitment, and of reflection on the ethical dimension of action—all these have been the kinds of hard questions that the church has raised about its own work, and this concern will be the gift the seminaries will bring as they are drawn into the total process of education for decision making in the university. President Brewster held out this hope to the Yale Divinity School community this way:

> Yale Divinity School appears to me potentially to have more and more importance in the forming of the intellectual atmosphere. We are all searching out the roots and structures of faith and purpose in the modern world. It may be that the Divinity School has nothing to say in this search, but this also would be worth finding out. . . . I hope that the Divinity School will be increasingly discovered by the rest of the University. . . . The greater the concern which the University shows for the total man, his whole intellectual powers and for the health of the whole society, the more attentive should be the University to what the Divinity School has to say and vice versa. The church has been through a period of entrancement with sociology and psychology and hopefully now recognizes in the discussions (of professional education) I have been talking about the centrality of theology. Hopefully the church will not try to be an amateur in everything but will develop a professional competence with one discipline, theology, the organizing principle of its thought. There has never been a time for greater and more exciting opportunities to engage in discussion on the kinds of issues I have described.[32]

The discipline of theology about which Brewster speaks here is obviously the activity of *reflection* on the significance of actions in the midst of acting—the discipline of theologizing on the firing line. That very discipline which most easily tempts churchmen to isolate themselves in abstractions can become the seminary's entrance to responsible participation in the total university enterprise on behalf of the world, and it may be demonstrated once more that when one pushes deep enough behind people's worst neuroses, he discovers their greatest gifts.

What will it mean to the seminaries to move into the fast-rushing stream of university education? Surely not simply that they will take more advantage of the "secular" faculty of the university. What the

---

32. Kingman Brewster, from a speech at Yale Divinity School, May 11, 1966.

seminaries, along with the other professional schools, will discover is that the university is a microcosm of the culture, the laboratory in which persons may discover what it means to act flexibly and responsibly in the society. The tensions which shake the world come to a focus in the university; the knowledge which will provide tools for dealing with these conflicts is formulated in the university; the university engages in modeling the future for the society; and in the university are shaped those selves who will be the decision makers. When the seminaries become accountable to the university, and when they take responsibility for what happens there, they will find that they have become accountable to and responsible for the whole world. And this is the object and field of their mission.

The Process of Professional Shaping: Internship and Field Education, or a Comprehensive Model of Learning in Action?

Much that has been written about the reformulation of professional education has been concerned with putting new patches on old garments: tinkering with the contents or the requirements of the curriculum of the schools. Far more important is the consideration of the *process* of professional shaping. Theories and skills will change, but the process of professional education has to be a model for action of the sort that will be continued in practice. A professional school needs to operate out of a model of learning in which the various approaches to knowledge, and the various sections of the student's preparation, are not separated —the humanistic from the scientific, theory from practice, research from application. One way in which the professional schools have tried to accomplish this is through the several forms of "field education": part-time work, internships, residency. How well have these worked to produce competent and sensitive professionals?

The lore and myth surrounding the internship experience of a doctor or minister usually characterize this point in the development and education of a professional or institutional leader as the most crucial and significant one in the whole process of teaching and learning to serve other human beings. This is the time presumably when a young person who has been called to a particular service and educated in its tradition, theory, and skills is placed in his first work situation. He is given the responsibility of meeting genuine needs, and his performance is supervised and evaluated by those considered the most mature and qualified to judge whether a person is ready to do the work of his profession. This certainly has the potential of being the moment of truth both for the new leadership through whom a profession will endure, if at all, and for the older leaders who find in the acceptance or rejection of their advice a clue to whether the coming generation regards what they have learned and done in the past worthy of perpetuation.

Manuals on professional education define internship as a work experience of substantial length, under careful supervision, and through an agency established both to provide a clientele or constituency with the services of a profession and to engage in critical inquiry into the practice of that profession. The internship is that place where the relation between theory and action is explored. It is a period not primarily of observation and reflection, but of an attempt to test the adequacy of one's basic motivation, his theoretical understanding of the service to be rendered to others, the power of habits and affections in crisis and danger, the skills and competencies of professional practice.

But it is precisely because field education and internship have this potentiality for being a moment of truth that they are areas in the life of the university and the co-operating institution of profession characterized by widespread disagreement as to who is responsible for giving shape to the experience and for discovering its consequences to the people involved. Its potentiality for being a moment of truth accounts for the fact that most major reforms in the education and practice of ministers, doctors, lawyers, social workers, and others have taken as their focus the interpretation and conduct of internship and supervised training in the field. Charles Feilding's *Education for Ministry*,[33] for example, reports that there is no agreement in the seminaries on how field work and internships are to be made into educational experiences testing beliefs, theories, and skills valued in the theological schools and no common standards or provisions developed for supervision of such work. Most of the seminaries, he concluded, either apprentice theological students to clergy untrained in supervision and without awareness

---

33. Charles Feilding, "Education for Ministry," *Theological Education*, Vol. III, No. 1 (Autumn, 1966). This study on "Education for the Practice of the Parish Ministry" was conducted by the American Association of Theological Schools and sponsored by the Lilly Endowment, Inc.

of developments in seminary theology and university religious and social studies most influential on student thinking, or assign such supervision to seminary staff in the practical fields who are not able to conduct the research and inquiry necessary to find out what is happening in the situations in which students first try to serve. Feilding concludes:

> It is the negotiation of this (institutional and social) change which calls for the supervision of a special kind of learning. This learning must be securely rooted in theory, that is in clearly perceived views of the nature and purpose of the Christian enterprise, and in accurate knowledge of the various milieus in which that purpose must be realized and of the consequent alternation in church structures that may be necessary. But unless this is accompanied by the courage to act, the ability to assess action, to modify, and to continue it, nothing will be accomplished beyond the frustration in the church. The most desperate cure proposed could easily be worse than the disease, namely to encourage practice without theory, either by reducing academic standards or by deducing the action required from the expressed demands of the surrounding culture—asking the patient instead of the qualified physician to diagnose and prescribe. The answer is to be found not in more, but in better education, in the development of supervision as an educational method new to many areas of church life, though not itself a new method.[34]

These observations are similar to those of scholars studying field education, internships, and residency experience in all the major professions. David F. Cavers, surveying the law schools, concluded that the faculty have "no coherent theory of legal education" and very little knowledge of what the practicing lawyer does with the training he receives and of the styles of thinking and acting that inform the major careers in law, particularly those new areas of public service that break from the forms of law dealing with traditional business and family interests.[35]

Similarly, the Report of the Citizen's Commission on Graduate Medical Education commissioned by the American Medical Association called for the development of a "new body of knowledge in addition to the medical specialities that constitute the bulk" of graduate training.

---

34. Charles R. Feilding, Progress Report to Commerce on Research and Counsel, December 11, 1963 (unpublished).

35. David F. Cavers, "Legal Education in Time of Change," unpublished paper for Conference on Professional Education, Episcopal Theological Seminary, Cambridge, Massachusetts, February, 1967.

This new knowledge was "not yet adequately developed" enough to be defined, but "it would include the medical counterparts of ecology, evaluation, and fundamental theory rather than the specifics of molecular biology, virology, or the physiology of individual organs."[36] The report observed:

> What is needed—and what the medical schools and teaching hospitals must try to develop—is a body of information and general principles concerning man as a whole and man in society that will provide an intellectual framework into which the lessons of practical experience can be fitted. This background will be partly biological, but partly it will be social and humanistic, for it will deal with man as a total, complex, integrated, social being.[37]

The whole thrust of these studies is away from attempts to view specialized services in a profession as a segmented or tandem learning experience and toward placement of training for particular responsibilities and constituencies in the basic processes of teaching and inquiry informing a whole profession. There is a deepened awareness that the epistemologies and learning models which dominate a faculty have profound influence on the practices of the students, often in ways unanticipated by the faculty. The models of knowledge and of learning developed by specialized graduate faculty concerned with a few isolated factors of disease or by poorly informed and uncritical practical, clinical, or diagnostic faculty dominate the educational experience of the professional.

An essential relationship between the theory and doctrine of the university and the practical experience of the actor facing human need is the mark of all great professional practice. When one tries to express in symbols and cognitive form one's deepest convictions and knowledge about human problems and the meeting of them, there is the necessity to act out the meaning in concrete service. And when one is driven to act, the need for the clarification of one's theory or beliefs, the intricacies of human response, the existential limitations, and the personal distortions of reality drive one back to research that isolates and defines factors

---

36. *The Graduate Education of Physicians*, Citizen's Commission on Graduate Medical Education, John S. Miller, Chairman, American Medical Association (Chicago: 1967), p. 51.

37. *Ibid.*, pp. 51–52.

and to reflection that examines presuppositions and relationships between factors.

Most of the seminaries and ministries are just discovering this essential relationship between university and church and what it means not only for a specialized clergy—campus ministries—but for all who claim to be professional leaders in the contemporary world. The whole of seminary education may have to be viewed in the future as a period of theological internship in which the student sees himself in residency in an institution and among laymen he will need to continue to work with all his career. He will see the university as that place providing the major supervision of clinical and intern situations in our society; that is, the place where people become most conscious of, and critical of, the factors (beliefs, theories, data, interests, institutional resources, and skills) that have influenced their past actions and are likely to shape their future conduct.

In this situation, the question becomes important whether ministers are provided in their training with genuine field education in which the responsibility of the school is to explore the relation of belief and theory to modes and forms of actual ministry. Field service may test student commitment or competency, but not be supervised by agents of the school as a test of perspective and learning process formally studied in the curriculum and as part of systematic inquiry.[38] So, too, the question of adequate supervision has come to the fore in the studies of the impact of education on the beliefs, thoughts, and actions of persons in various ministries. Two comments from seminary students working as Danforth Seminary Interns in the campus ministry show the kind of impact an internship can have. One felt that "a lot of the false glamour of the campus ministry has been removed," replaced with "more genuine realism and a truly vibrant vision of the possibilities that exist for the church"; another said, "Being accepted as and treated as an adult and professional has forced me to learn to see my own identity differently."[39]

The Danforth Seminary Interns in the campus ministry felt that one of their recurring problems was that they could not learn to discipline

38. James D. Glass, in Feilding, "Education for Ministry," pp. 227–235, gives a detailed analysis of the distinctions between these three types of field work.

39. The Danforth Seminary Internship report (150 pages, typescript, with tables and graphs) is on file with Danforth Foundation. This study of the Danforth program was done by Kenneth Underwood and Hoyt Oliver in the early stages of the Danforth Study of Campus Ministries.

themselves adequately in their personal study during the intern year. But in two cases, at least, this problem was solved: one in which the intern's supervisor on his campus and his seminary supervisor worked out a study program for him for the intern year and he wrote papers during his work, and another in which a staff member of the Austin Faith and Life Community was assigned to direct the intern in his personal study, which was closely tied in with the work he was doing during the year. Interns began in some cases to realize that they had not left their theology behind as a theory, but had to carry it into their work:

> Theology is more even than a part of general education. As a campus minister, I must also embody "theology" as a way of life, a field of work, a scholarly discipline. It is not enough to have a good general education and a professional training and degree. Even as an "engineer-in-the-field," a "practicing" theologian, I must be a theological scholar.[40]

Another intern speaks out of a sense of what theology feels like in action:

> Rather than convince students that they are in the situation to which I think I know the answer, I have been able to try to see how they view their situation and because I was free from having to fulfill the "student-worker" ideal of the man-of-the-students, I was not even required always to take their problems and their assessment of their situation with as much seriousness as they did. . . . [I have recognized] the importance of a campus minister keeping in touch with the main-stream theologians (if not himself doing creative theological work), not to reduce himself to pursuing and attempting to foster a concern for theological fad literature. Without constant existential groans and screams, without being Christ to every second or third person he meets, part of the campus minister's job is to represent the calm passion, dignity and humor of a great tradition of reflection, a tradition standing in the knowledge of both sin and grace, defeat and victory.[41]

It was our conclusion at the end of our study of the Danforth seminary internship program in campus ministries, however, that the one-man one-supervisor model of internship had run its course, and our vision had to be broadened. Most of the seminary students who were looking for the "exciting," "frontier" ministries and had once looked to the campus as the chief place of action were increasingly turning to the inner

---

40. *Ibid.*
41. *Ibid.*

city or urban church work. As one seminary representative put it, "If someone were to come through here tomorrow offering internships in the inner city, he'd have twenty-five applications before he could get his hat off." This was but one of many indications to us that the intern experience for campus ministers was not able to make significant connections between vast, urgent social problems, university intellectual and research developments, and personal religious beliefs and ministerial competencies.

Some campus ministry interns had valuable learning experiences with their individual supervisors. But we feel that the basic problem is that of providing the beginning minister with this kind of interpersonal communities which sustain him in his search for integrity and wholeness in a career, where fellowship and affection are accompanied by resources for diagnosing the real situation a minister confronts and for evaluating his personal talents and capacities to think about the act in that situation. If the intern has not had the guidance of faculties who are themselves thinking about intellectual developments in the university and are involved in organizing scholars, students, and public leaders to explore basic human problems in the university, no one supervisor can overcome the confusion of the intern. The Danforth intern program went about as far as it could in reorienting students to university and church relations under the present system of theological education. The basic system is due for a radical reshaping so that the student's whole educational experience is one of learning how to use university and church resources in thinking about social action and change.

In the context of supervised internship and field work, the big problem of the seminaries is not, as the Carnegie study concluded, that of "providing a most able core of teaching theologians." Rather, the problem is that of developing educational institutions in which theological activity is carried out as an exploration, as experimentation in modalities of ministry. Thus expression of belief in worship, preaching, and teaching is not to be separated from technical research or operational skills in the development of institutional resources and policy. And a variety of models and settings of learning are to be provided by faculty to students and lay leaders for use in the church. Students preparing for church leadership need to learn particularly from models of interdisciplinary, critical study of the factors influencing past and future actions of Christians in major corporate and professional situations. Such experiences in the relation of theory and practice are less to be viewed as confined to some one year of internship in one form of ministry, but rather woven into a process of education which is a unified whole, planned corporately to give the student an understanding of the varied major types of ministries and resources for enabling the church to fulfill its mission.

The campus ministries have perhaps begun here and there to work out for the churches and the university the kinds of models of learning in action that need to be taken up and built into the whole process of education for ministry in university-connected seminaries. Many of the campus ministers who were thoroughly exposed to the large public universities, particularly to the searching questions of faculties and students as to the facts, theories, and world views on which they based their actions, came to view their ministry as a kind of continuing experience of field education. They found that the university community highly valued awareness of recent scholarly developments not only in theology but in other disciplines. They had to give attention to the kinds of learning experiences not provided in the classroom, such as reflection on social action or university policy issues for which no academic specialty assumed responsibility to study and publicly debate.

Some of the most influential of these campus ministers, such as Robert Bonthius, Parker Rossman, and Al Vastyan have found their careers moving increasingly toward the creation and supervision of centers, institutes, missions, intern programs, whose chief service is a kind of learning that explores the operational-functional relations of word and deed, expression of belief or theory, and instrumental, organizational act. Bonthius, for example, directs an Internship for Clergymen in Urban Mental Health at Case Western Reserve. He takes the clergyman in thirty-two weeks through an educational process which alternates seminars, field experience, independent study and counseling, drawing upon the social sciences and psychology as much as on theology and using community specialists, professional leaders, and public officials as well as faculty and clergy in supervising staff positions. Parker Rossman directs an ecumenical institute for continuing education of ministers, at first associated with Yale Divinity School, but now drawing upon the intellectual resources of many other schools and departments in the university. Al Vastyan is learning from the Hershey Medical School the special co-operation in research and instruction in courses required of doctors participating in the hospital and will expect to develop similar standards for ministers who wish to serve as chaplains associated with the hospital.

The list could include scores of urban training centers, industrial and science missions; preseminary, in-seminary, and postseminary action-study groups; Lutheran, Methodist, and other denominational intern plans. But such careers as those of Bonthius, Rossman, and Vastyan are enough to indicate that a very significant relationship is emerging between campus, urban, and professional ministerial concerns. The proliferation in the past decade of specialties of ministry and of training, and the tightening of funds available for organized religion, are intensifying concern to discover the theoretical and functional connections between these various Christian enterprises.

In short, the calls for a "new knowledge" and "new learning" that are observed in the current self-studies in professional education are actually recognition that faculties in the university will have to assume more responsibility for providing the student with opportunities imaginatively to explore the connections of formal learning and research to his personal and social involvements and that the various church training agencies which have sought to fill educational needs neglected by the universities and seminaries will have to draw much more carefully and comprehensively upon the basic work of major disciplines of the university.

What is at stake is the whole process of seminary education. We could keep on turning out technicians, theoreticians, and organization men—or we could try to set in motion a model of total learning whose most important aim would be to clarify alternatives of action for disciplined professionals. Some of the changes that would have to take place in our present system of seminary education would be drastic. "Field experience" and "internship" no longer would be isolated, segmented actions serving mainly as rites of passage into the ministerial community, but would be integrated with student and faculty study of basic theory, research, and social action; and the data gathered from such experiences on the battle fronts would be fed back into the reflection of the community, so that the models themselves could be modified continually as the consequences of putting them into practice were seen.

The image of the professional as an individual practitioner would be replaced by the image of the professional community taking specific action in its areas of responsibility in close co-operation with other responsible institutional leaders, always aware that specific responsibilities are carried out as a part of the total, complex, human community enterprise. This would mean that supervision of individual students would not be done by individual practitioners, but would follow something of a colloquium process with faculty, church leaders, university staff, and community decision makers all working together with students. Students would find that they could not have "cafeteria-style" education, with separate courses at separate times, but would find themselves involved in theory, action, and ethical reflection all at once. Faculty would not be divided into theorists, researchers, and "practical" teachers. Though there would continue to be special disciplines, every professional school faculty member would be held accountable for evaluation of the process and the results of his work in the actions of students and would share in the evaluation of students as responsible, professional moral actors—as, indeed, the student would be held accountable for evaluating the faculty.

The process of professional shaping would be seen as a lifelong process, not "completed" with the granting of a degree; and the seminaries would be one among a number of centers where continuing professional shaping would be going on. Systems or clusters of seminaries would take responsibility for their regions, with various centers specializing in certain types of work which would be available to all students, faculty, and church and community leaders in the area.

What we are arguing for is a view of learning in action which is not, as field experience or internship has been thought to be, an "embryonic practice" for the professional, but *education at the boundary points* between theory and action, university and church, community and social structure, individual and group, faith and skills. The process of learning in the professional school has to be a model of the style of learning and action that will characterize all of the professional's work. Seminaries can lead the way for the church and the university into the understanding that one neither thinks without acting, nor acts without thinking, nor thinks and learns and *then* acts, but thinks and acts and feels and evaluates together and continually, as one process. This is the criterion by which the church has historically and theologically evaluated its own missional activities: the four primary modes of ministry. Does this education produce the responsible moral actor, whose action grows out of a deep and broad value commitment, whose relationship to those whom he serves is sensitive and accepting, whose vision of the complexities of life is flexible, sharp, and clear, and whose leadership shows an intentionality toward the future and responsible use of power? If it does, the pastor, priest, prophet, and king are merged in the form demanded by our age: the professional.

The Professions, the University, and Social Policy

Thus far, our attention has been focused primarily on the individual professional student and on the separate professional schools. What we have said could have been taken as another set of proposals for the internal reform of the seminary. But now we need to make clear that what we are considering is the impact of the total professional-technical-organizational complex on our whole world. We have finally to say that reform of professional education cannot be accomplished by piecemeal tinkering. Our most fundamental image has to be altered.

What signals are we picking up from our hectic world that confront us with the radical demand for remodeled vision and action? The signals are glaringly evident to all who will see: urbanization, mass society, and global interaction making human relationship a complex, bewildering struggle—and new demands for community being raised from suburbia to Haight-Asbury to Resurrection City; decisions being made by "the experts" or by "the establishment"—and a new resurgence of decisional awareness from the common people across the world; technical know-how making possible abundant resources for people's needs—and the world's population becoming hungrier while nonskilled labor is no longer available in the affluent society; value-absolutes dissolving in church and society alike—and reactions toward normlessness that are retreats into new ideological rigidities; new ecumenical brotherhood among churches—and increasing superficiality of faith-identification; increasingly available higher education—and decreasing consensus on what higher education is about; increasing governmental and organization investment in research—and no process of common evaluation of whether that research should be done.

In short, the battles are being fought in our times over the issues of human relationships in a complex social structure: the issue of decision making and intentional shaping of social action; the issue of value-judgments in the midst of action; the issue of specialization and technical expertise unrelated to comprehensive theory; the issue of governance so that people participate in a continuing education experience. These are precisely the four areas of understanding which are supposed to be the concern of professionals, because they are integrally built into the professional pattern of action by which the professions are supposed to judge their work.

The problem is, however, that at present the professional-technical organization of our society is *part of the social problem*, not part of the answer. We have in effect decided that to be human in our society is to be fitted in at some point in the technical-organizational-professional strata into which our society is divided from top to bottom. And if one is not flowing along with one of these streams, the society does not know what to make of him. William Whyte in *The Organization Man* and Paul Goodman in *Growing Up Absurd* make the point at great length; but we can pick one concrete example to show how the system works. How do we "deal with" the problems of inner-city poverty? We use force to put down rioting, and we set up job-training programs to start the young unemployed on the lower rungs of one or another of the technical ladders—in just the same way as we conduct foreign policy by threat of arms and the offering of technical assistance.

Thus we can see that the problem of departmental and professional school specialization and separation in the universities is not an isolated phenomenon, but the natural, predictable consequence of the designing of higher education by the shape of its social context. The students who come to the universities have been fitted into specialized channels already, and they get in the universities the specialized training to help them perpetuate the segmented society.

Yet professionals know, once they take their work seriously, that they cannot operate *as* dedicated professionals and confine themselves to the offering of narrow technical services. The remaining vision of the professional vocation has at least made them uncomfortable enough to see that what they are doing is not what they ought to be doing, or want to be doing. Then they wonder how they can work with integrity and competence; how can they get hold of the complexity of their situations and make responsible decisions? When a minister tries to work in the inner city, where does he get his insights about social change? How does he relate these insights to his Christian value foundation, and how does he go about focusing his efforts on effective social change? If, like his colleagues in the other professions, he has been educated as an individual practitioner in a professional school isolated from any comprehensive process of education for intentional and corporate social action, he either despairs or works at small problems, chipping around the edges of a social boulder he cannot move.

The professional-technical school complex of the university, because it is that part of the university system where theory, values, and actions are supposed to be joined, is the place where we must start to design a process of education which will enable the university to be the model builder for the society. To say this is to say no one professional school by itself can do the job of educating responsible actors, any more than one individual professional practitioner can by himself provide comprehensive services to persons with all their physical, social, and spiritual needs. We are going to have to start thinking about the design of interprofessional education, where the specialized approaches and resources of the various schools are integrated with a joint program wherein students are made partners in the kinds of societal action they will be performing as colleagues all their lives. (And this has been proposed before; at Yale, for example, a dean of the Law School in the 1930's wanted the new Law School and Divinity School complexes placed on "the hill" in the middle of a slum with the Medical School, but the three schools are now strung out separately along a two-mile line, each isolated.)

This process of model building for the society in the university will take different forms in various universities, as it should. But wherever it goes on, if it remains true to the historic responsibilities of higher education and to the varied and integrated demands of professional practice, it will look like this:

First, there will be an appreciation of a variety of ways of knowing, with specialized faculty sharing their visions and epistemologies and students doing hard work on the synthesis of these approaches. Second, data gathering will be a continuing process, not just as theoretical research but as input from the social events and the consequences of action by professionals in university and out in the field. These data will be part of the content dealt with; there will be no longer a clear separation between theory and practice. Third, the process of evaluation will also be continuous—evaluation not only of the work of students but also of staff; not only of specialized actions but also of the whole broad fields of medicine, religion, law, and so on; not only of practice skills but also of value orientations. Fourth, the forms of community in the professional complex of the university will themselves be models for the kinds of community forms envisioned for the social structure. Fifth, the focus of this education will be on strategic personal and social action, with the university doing the kinds of things that can be tested and evaluated.

This whole process can be looked at scientifically as a cybernetic model, where the basic assumptions are modified by the feedback from action taken on these assumptions. It can also be looked at theologically as a model of what the church is called to be: that sensitive, caring, responsive, missional part of the body of mankind which in response to God's gift of life dares to act on behalf of all men. To this process, the seminary will bring its gift of theologizing, reflecting on the value of action. And it will also bring the gifts of its recognition that no professional, as minister, acts apart from the community of which he is a member and from its vision of the Kingdom, which is finally God's work, for which we work, but then celebrate as it appears in the midst of our struggles unannounced.

⪥ 22 ⪤

THE SEMINARIES AND THE EDUCATIONAL CRISIS

OF THE CHURCH

F ROM the several university centers participating in the Danforth Study of Campus Ministries, we have received news of confusion and uncertainty about how historic modes of ministry can be carried out in a complex and changing social structure. From ministers' responses to the ministry survey, we have seen some radical disjunctures between campus and parish ministers, between ministers of different denominations, and between traditionally and experimentally oriented ministers on matters of beliefs, values, and styles of action, along with signs of significant agreement on shifts in the nature of ministry. From case studies of patterns of ministry in specific situations, we have seen a lack of communication between clergymen and their potential constituents and between clergymen and the persons who are making decisions and exercising leadership in the university. We have observed also that the ministry shares the ambiguity common to all the major professions today, while its quest for integrity is shaped by the unique combination of demands built into the full action field of ministry.

This same confusion is apparent in the efforts of the churches through the seminaries to prepare the ministries of tomorrow. The campus ministry, we have observed, is a rather sensitive indicator of what will be happening in the near future to other forms of ministry. Uncertainty about the campus ministry is common to all the seminaries; we can see it clearly in a case study of what has been one of the seminal programs preparing men for ministry to the university, that of Yale Divinity School.[1]

1. This case study is drawn from a YDS faculty paper, *Religion in Higher Education—Yale Divinity School* (mimeographed, October 10, 1967).

Between 1926 and 1955 there was established in the curriculum of Yale Divinity School a field of religious leadership in higher education available as a distinctive vocational area, alongside training for the parish ministry, foreign missionary service, and religious education in church and schools. Under the primary guidance of Professor Clarence P. Shedd, hundreds of students were trained for specialized ministries as college and university chaplains, YMCA and YWCA secretaries, directors of denominational agencies and foundations, university pastors, teachers of religion, and educational administrators.

Reflecting the changing pattern of American higher education and placing emphasis more on the university context of ministry than on the forms and strategies of specialized ministries, the YDS curriculum during the 1960's changed to include courses in the Cultural History of the University, the Church in the University, the Campus Christian Ministry, Philosophies of Higher Education, and a research seminar on selected topics. Now the program of religion in higher education at Yale is undergoing a still more radical shift. Work at the Ph.D. level in this area has been phased out, and in the Divinity School curriculum students are no longer required to take courses which prepare them for a particular vocation or form of ministry. Responsibility for the preparation of college and university teachers in religious studies has now been moved almost entirely to the Graduate School. Colleges are drawing their chaplains from the ranks of men with Ph.D.'s, and denominations are increasingly requiring pastoral experience and/or graduate degrees for the men they appoint as campus religious workers.

Looking at the field of the campus ministry, the YDS faculty sees an added difficulty in the increasing differentiation between those opting for an "action orientation" and those following other patterns similar to inner-city ministries or more strictly academic models. These trends lead to two differing projections of the future of ministries in higher education. One projection sees the need to raise the perspective of such ministries to the level of institutional interaction, providing "ministries to university structures" with the concern being chiefly with policy issues, including those entailed in university governance, rather than with a pattern of ministry oriented to individuals or groups of persons. The other projection suggests that campus ministries, as we have known them in the past, will be largely extinct in a decade or so. This prophecy is based in part on the difficulty the churches are experiencing in securing funds for this purpose and in part on the need to find new and different ways of relating to the swiftly expanding number of institutions, their changing shape, and their increased size. Whatever position one takes in this debate, say the YDS faculty, it appears certain that the campus ministry will be considerably altered in the near future.

These and other considerations have suggested to the Divinity School faculty that the field of religion in higher education should no longer be regarded primarily as an area of professional training, but as one of the several dimensions of their purview of the relationship of the churches to contemporary culture. But then they ask, what shape should Yale's effort in this area take in the decades ahead? A number of possibilities have been considered: (1) the university at large could be requested to assume responsibility for the specific concerns this area has raised; (2) Yale's efforts could be redefined and merged with those of other schools in the eastern area; (3) other disciplines in the curriculum could include the concerns and needs to which this field has addressed itself; for example, historians could teach the history of the university, and social ethicists could give explicit attention to the policy questions and problems of the "knowledge industry"; (4) the effort of the entire faculty could be enlisted, rather than having one or two experts in the whole vast area of higher education; (5) the Divinity School could specialize in the study of one area of higher education such as seminary education, since foundations and other organizations and agencies are dealing with the field of religion in higher education; or (6) the resources and efforts of YDS could be turned largely to the support of a research institute or center, with the increasing role of higher education in the determination of public policy as the focal point and the effort to meet and serve the needs of seminary students made outside, rather than within, the curriculum.

From this case study we can trace the successive movement of a concept of preparation for ministry in a seminary's program from (i) a specialized effort to meet a perceived need in a new field, to (ii) a consideration of the broader context and issues of the area of society involved, to (iii) a decision point where alternatives of action are open and unresolved. The same story could be told about such fields as pastoral counseling, institutional chaplaincy, and inner-city ministry. What we are realizing, it seems, is that effective ministry can be shaped neither by a specialized preparation for individual roles nor by a study of one specialized context alone; and, increasingly, we are recognizing that preparation for ministry cannot be handled by one specialized institution, the seminary, in isolation from churches, universities, and the other complex social organizations in which ministry must be carried out.

The issues here raised are not merely strategic ones. The perplexity of the church as it shows up in the seminaries is not merely uncertainty over what strategies for ministry are best for our age. The church's whole perception of its relationship to God and to the world is at stake.

We are experiencing in theological education at the most basic level a crisis in contemporary religious commitment and consciousness. This crisis is experienced by clergy and laity as multiform contradictions in the thought and action of the churches consciously trying to live with traditional religious faith in a modern technical society. Much in the present situation is not new to other times of crisis: the anguish of doubt in the midst of faith, the temptation to wholesale anti-institutional attitudes and to moral nihilism. But today these aspects of crisis are expressed in a new setting: a fast-changing, highly specialized, scientifically informed, publicly educated, globally involved society.

Where the church is alive to its mission, all four of the historic modes of ministry—the pastoral, priestly, prophetic, and governing modes—are present and are held together in a dynamic tension that allows each mode its unique expression while it is enacted as an essential part of the full field of ministry. In the seminaries today these modes of ministry are known and recognized as essential; but in the seminaries also there is sincere anguish over the forms these modes of ministry may take and how they may be integrated into the fullness of ministry in response to the actions of God in the reshaping of our world today. Concern in the seminaries about the shaping of ministries is a concrete and specific indication of the wider crisis of religious consciousness we are experiencing in each of the several dimensions of Christian commitment and action: the responsible self, worship, inquiry, and social policy.

In order to act, we must seek clarity and sensitivity of vision. In this chapter of our study, we shall explore our crisis as we perceive it in its several aspects, corresponding to the historic modes of ministry and the dimensions of Christian consciousness as (1) the crisis of integrity and community, (2) the crisis of celebration and conservatism, (3) the crisis of inquiry and understanding, and (4) the crisis of action and governance. It is not our purpose to evaluate the many efforts now being made for the reshaping of education for ministry; we shall present something of what we have learned from our study as evidence of the situation we face and then make a proposal for one specific means of sustaining the continuing process of evaluation and reshaping of the church's learning.

The Crisis of Integrity and Community

The life of the church in mission has at its best manifested a wholeness of style, a pattern of action in which concerned and caring corporate life, worship and celebration of the Christian faith stance, informed and varied ways of knowing the world, and strategic, responsible action for the shaping of the structures of society are all held together in disciplined commitment. The lack of this sense of wholeness in the seminaries and the churches today is the sign of the crisis we are experiencing in the first dimension of Christian commitment—the dimension of responsible selfhood.

The crisis shows up in the powerlessness of the leadership of the churches to integrate religious beliefs, technical theory and data, personal religious experience, and the requirements of social action. Efforts for the renewal of the church in these several directions are not lacking; but the prevailing picture is one of increasing fragmentation and polarization of emphasis. Various groups in the churches claim to have found the one necessary path to renewal in prayer groups or liturgical renewal or revolutionary social action or increased use of social sciences, and much of their time is spent in battles with proponents of other emphases. That sense of the church which would integrate these efforts into one mission is lacking.

This fragmentation is built into the curriculums and the life styles of the seminaries, which share with other professional schools today an isolation from the broader knowledge structures of the universities and from the complex power structures of the society. The historic and the contemporary, the theoretical and the practical, the scientific and the humanistic, all have their advocates—and even their separate courses and departments—in the seminaries as in other professional schools; but hardly to be found is the sense of professional style which encompasses all of these and embodies them in individual and corporate lives. The effects of this disintegrated preparation for ministry can be seen in the conflicts individual clergymen perceive between the several roles they are expected to fulfill: warm and personal pastor, symbolic priestly representative of the faith, informed specialist, and organizational leader moving groups to action.[2]

The data from the Danforth Ministry Survey indicate that ministers' reactions to these contradictions tend toward one of two forms. What is learned in seminary tends either to reinforce traditional, churchly institutionalized forms of ministry or to produce alienation from all institutional structures except for narrow specialization in role and constituency.[3] Clergymen who take the one path concentrate their ministry on the nurturance of church members in the familiar patterns of church structures, as the churches become more and more isolated from the places and the ways in which persons live in the society. The other path, more common to campus ministries, leads to actions shaped by particular situational demands of the moment or by the particular orientations of selected small groups of students or the preferences of individual campus ministers. On the one hand, there appears what has been called "structural fundamentalism," and on the other, ineffectual formlessness; in neither case is the full pattern of ministry present, enabling the corporate and comprehensive mission of the church.

Responsible selfhood for individuals is formed and lived out as they are supported by concerned and sensitive communities. Pastoral care has always been an inseparable, essential part of the life of the Christian church. Yet the crisis in responsible selfhood and pastoral ministry is manifested today in the lack of interpersonal communities which support persons in ministry in their search for integrity and wholeness in a career, where fellowship and affection are accompanied by resources to evaluate personal talents and capacities and integrate individual efforts into the work of ecumenical team ministries. In some cases, seminaries seem to be working with an image of the preparation for ministry as an equipping of individual practitioners, clergymen

2. See Hoyt P. Oliver, "Professional Authority and the Protestant Ministry: A Study of an Occupational Image," Ph.D. dissertation, Yale University, 1966, for an extended analysis of ministers' role conflicts.

3. See Jeffrey K. Hadden, "The House Divided," in Volume II, for some of these data.

whose denominational affiliations, individual knowledge and talents, or specialized roles in institutional settings are what give legitimacy and form to their careers. The concept of the solo practitioner is inappropriate for any modern professional, the clergyman most of all. We have always known from the heritage of the Christian church that the ministry of individual Christians must grow out of—and be held accountable to—the ministry of the corporate body of the church, differing gifts being joined by the same Spirit. Now also we are learning from sensing after the complex variety of our age that there can be no simple, universally applicable model for ministry and that corporate structures of ministry must be imagined to maintain the fullness of mission without losing complexity and individual specialization.

Corporate action is universally agreed upon as a strategic necessity in our world. But Christian ministry is action with an added dimension: it is *caring* corporateness. How this care may be enacted in the structures of a technical, fast-changing, urban society is an agonizing question. The pastoral mode of ministry in our times will be manifested in its historic spirit, but in many new forms and styles through complex, varied structures, institutions, policies, and relationships in the university, community, and society. "Christian fellowship" is for many, perhaps, a watchword expressive of a nostalgic longing for the church of the past or for an ideal; but we have seen the failure of attempts to provide isolated fellowships in the midst of "impersonal structures," and we know that we must find means of evaluating the actual consequences of the patterns of life together that we create in order to help persons take responsibility for these structures of society.[4] For the seminaries, the challenge at hand is that of becoming more open on all sides to church, university, and society and more imaginatively committed to the creation of forms of life together in the seminary community which will serve as models for the varied forms the church will take in its responses to men's needs and the imperatives of the Gospel in a complex world.

The Crisis of Celebration and Conservatism

The church in mission is the signal community, the witness to the world of God's presence, holding up and celebrating in its worship the

---

4. One such attempt at evaluation is made by David Duncombe in "An Experiment in Evaluation of Faith and Life Communities," in Volume II.

newness of life breaking through the barriers men erect to protect themselves in their anxiety. But there is a crisis manifest today in this second dimension of Christian consciousness. The traditional modes of proclaiming the Gospel and celebrating the sacraments (such as evangelism, preaching, and liturgical leadership) have become identified so generally in our society with theological and social conservatism that these are widely rejected not only by the "new breed" of church leadership but by serious, responsible Christians searching for ministries which represent the rich and varied dimensions of contemporary religious and ethical experience and thought they now vaguely perceive.

In the correlations of ministers' responses on the scales of the Danforth Ministry Survey, this identification of traditional religious modes with conservatism shows up strongly. One pattern that emerges from the responses is that of significant positive correlations between biblical fundamentalism, distrust of social sciences, and anticivil rights movement attitude, traditional sex morality, and enjoyment of the roles of evangelist, preacher, priest, traditional pastor, and church administrator. These scales all showed negative correlations with allowance of doubt, salvation in the world rather than in heaven, a welfare responsibility of the government, and enjoyment of the roles of theologian and community leader.

The same linking of theological and social conservatism with traditional ministerial modes is apparent in the comparisons of opinions on the ministry survey received from graduates of various seminaries across the country. To summarize one concrete example from the tables, graduates of one of the more conservative seminaries listed as their most enjoyable roles administering communion and winning a lost soul to Christ, and as their least enjoyable role influencing the policies of major organizations or institutions in the community. They saw the virgin birth and physical resurrection of Jesus as very important beliefs; and they felt that absolute guidance from the past was more reliable than acting in terms of present circumstances, that a faith in God will cure most mental illness, that censorship is often necessary in order to protect the public, that the free enterprise system is the single economic system compatible with the requirements of personal freedom and constitutional government, that most people who live in poverty could do something about their situation if they really wanted to, and that women who engage in premarital sexual intercourse are almost certain to have serious emotional difficulties in marriage.

The tables present the amount of agreement shown in the responses of ministers to a selection of questions from our survey; these are key items which were found to be clues to reactions in whole scales of the questionnaire. Fourteen of the seventy seminaries from which our respondents came have been selected for reporting. These fourteen represent denominational and interdenominational; conservative, liberal, and neo-orthodox-oriented; and weak, middle, and strong academic institutions. The numbers represent the percentage of the sample of ministers graduated from each seminary who answered in the category "definitely agree," that is, responses 5 and 6 on the questionnaire. Though these responses do not tell the whole story, since four numbers in the distribution are missing, yet for purposes of comparison between seminaries they show signicant trends.

The responses to our survey from ministers of widely differing seminary backgrounds show significant polarities of belief about the mission of the church, key theological doctrines, and the roles of ministry. There are evident in the tables the differences of opinion attributable to denominational heritage, regional location, and academic climate of the various seminaries. Yet in the midst of these polarities it is clear that there is also emerging in a great body of the church a consensus of strong saliency on items on which many significant policy actions can be taken. On questions pointing to the reality of human sin and doubt, the relativity of social circumstances, the validity of disciplines other than the theological, and the mission of the church in community polity formation there is strong support among the ministers. The inquiring-teaching roles take precedence over the proclamation by sermon alone, and ministers seem to be aware that along with their priestly and pastoral work they must be willing to exercise and influence institutional power.

It appears in the tables that where seminaries have strong intellectual scholarship balanced with a concern for relevance, they are more sensitive to the epistemological issues of the relations of such disciplines such as the social sciences with theology, and with a recognition of the manifold sources of the knowledge of the will of God. Theologically, many of the seminaries are in a better situation than others in being responsive to the liberal–neo-orthodox dialogue and its changing issues. It is noticeable, however, in the table of ministers' self-perceived theological positions how many seminaries, even such as

TABLE 22–1

Theological and Social Opinions

	Yale	Union	Harvard	Chicago	SMU	Emory	Asbury	General (Episc.)	Seabury Western	North. Bapt.	Luther	Con-cordia	Prince-ton	McCormick
1. The essence of religious truth is more personal than doctrinal.	49	62	60	58	58	53	62	21	24	45	42	18	49	43
4. I accept Jesus' physical resurrection as an objective historical fact in the same sense that Lincoln's physical death was a historical fact.	33	34	32	23	38	57	85	72	82	84	86	93	69	45
5. I would expect a thinking Christian to have doubts about the existence of God.	65	71	72	23	38	57	17	67	58	38	52	43	59	71
7. A vivid or dramatic inner experience of a special call to the ministry should be the controlling factor in deciding whether a man possesses the requisite qualifications for ordination to the ministry.	7	5	5	8	16	30	40	1	2	30	16	4	5	6
8. The discipline and training of the mind is more important than the experience of a dramatic inner call to the ministry.	49	38	38	50	28	16	14	55	42	23	23	45	30	42
12. There is no longer any need for God as a working hypothesis in morals, politics, science, or religion, and in the name of intellectual honesty such working hypotheses should be dropped.	7	11	9	8	4	4	1	46	19	15	28	8	3	2
13. There is no special or divine significance associated with particular institutional forms and structures of the church.	55	56	54	58	51	42	30	12	15	37	48	43	55	49

TABLE 22–1 (Continued)

	Yale	Union	Harvard	Chicago	SMU	Emory	Asbury	General (Episc.)	Seabury Western	North. Bapt.	Luther	Concordia	Princeton	McCormick
18. Whether Jesus was or was not born of a virgin is not very important to my religious beliefs.	86	79	76	96	73	60	16	46	19	15	28	8	53	75
19. Every area of man's life is corrupted by sin.	81	83	82	73	59	55	79	75	77	84	93	95	82	79
21. Our world is changing so fast that a person has to act in terms of circumstances confronting him rather than expecting absolute guidance from the past.	70	76	75	69	64	51	37	58	42	38	45	36	56	64
29. Various disciplines other than theological and biblical studies, such as sociology and psychiatry, may inform the Christian as to the nature of God's action in the world.	89	88	87	89	83	77	65	89	89	60	63	58	82	83
30. Religiously significant knowledge cannot be understood by a social scientist who is not by personal conviction or method a convinced Christian.	24	26	27	23	34	37	49	35	45	45	50	52	35	36
32. Assignments in campus ministries should increasingly follow functional (e.g., assignment to academic disciplines and professional schools) rather than denominational lines, so that ministries are provided to the major structures of the university or college.	67	70	65	73	41	33	21	34	26	43	19	10	53	62
37. Campus ministers would be more effective if they were more concerned with evangelism and winning souls for Christ and less concerned with "making religion relevant to the modern world."	5	3	3	4	7	13	38	10	11	37	28	35	12	5

TABLE 22–1 (*Continued*)

	Yale	Union	Harvard	Chicago	SMU	Emory	Asbury	General (Episc.)	Seabury Western	North. Bapt.	Luther	Con-cordia	Prince-ton	McCormick
38. A faith in God will cure most mental illness if that faith is strong enough.	10	9	9	8	19	27	32	16	18	17	14	18	12	11
40. I am in basic sympathy with northern ministers and students who have gone to the South to work for civil rights.	77	80	79	77	49	25	27	68	52	40	55	38	66	72
41. Censorship is often necessary in order to protect the public.	16	15	17	12	34	47	47	27	29	50	46	48	27	16
42. The free enterprise system is the single economic system compatible with the requirements of personal freedom and constitutional government.	13	14	15	12	43	48	59	28	27	60	44	50	38	19
43. Most people who live in poverty could do something about their situation if they really wanted to.	7	10	11	12	25	29	49	17	23	19	28	30	18	9
45. Women who engage in premarital sexual intercourse are almost certain to have serious emotional difficulties in marriage.	16	16	18	23	32	38	56	16	15	42	32	36	35	22
48. It is conceivable that a particular situation could morally justify extramarital relations.	37	36	35	35	22	16	3	32	13	8	8	6	23	21
49. Christian education needs to bring laymen face to face with urban problems and propose solutions.	83	74	72	77	75	72	66	61	53	55	66	66	69	75

TABLE 22–2
Enjoyment of Roles

	Yale	Union	Harvard	Chicago	SMU	Emory	Asbury	General (Episc.)	Seabury Western	North. Bapt.	Luther	Con-cordia	Prince-ton	McCormick
51. Working with congregational boards and committees.	32	22	22	27	24	29	28	16	19	35	36	28	40	42
52. Playing the conciliator role, seeking to find points of agreement and harmony.	37	41	41	50	30	30	32	36	37	38	33	31	35	40
53. Administering Communion.	68	71	74	73	79	75	80	98	93	75	90	90	85	79
54. Counseling with people about their moral and personal problems.	77	72	73	77	66	70	68	75	77	75	72	69	75	76
55. Winning a lost soul to Christ.	39	46	48	46	74	81	94	67	66	92	86	94	65	52
56. Discussion of contemporary theological issues and viewpoints with educated persons.	81	83	81	85	73	67	57	85	74	75	70	70	79	79
57. Influencing the policies of organizations in my denomination.	42	38	37	38	41	42	30	35	31	43	24	29	39	43
58. Influencing the policies of major organizations or institutions in my community.	52	43	42	42	36	31	26	26	30	27	18	13	37	41

TABLE 22–3
Self-Perceived Theological Positions

F	C	N	L	U	O	F	C	N	L	U	O
Yale						Union					

22. Theological position on entering college.

F	C	N	L	U	O	F	C	N	L	U	O
12	36	5	44	3	0	13	34	5	42	4	3

23. Theological position on entering seminary.

F	C	N	L	U	O	F	C	N	L	U	O
2	12	21	63	1	1	2	14	24	57	3	1

24. Theological position on leaving seminary.

F	C	N	L	U	O	F	C	N	L	U	O
0	5	64	32	0	0	1	6	68	25	0	0

25. Theological position NOW.

F	C	N	L	U	O	F	C	N	L	U	O
0	8	57	31	2	3	1	11	56	30	1	2

Harvard						Chicago U. Div.					

22. Theological position on entering college.

F	C	N	L	U	O	F	C	N	L	U	O
12	29	7	45	4	4	12	50	4	27	0	4

23. Theological position on entering seminary.

F	C	N	L	U	O	F	C	N	L	U	O
0	13	34	49	4	1	15	19	58	4	4	0

24. Theological position on leaving seminary.

F	C	N	L	U	O	F	C	N	L	U	O
0	2	83	15	0	0	8	39	42	4	4	0

25. Theological position NOW.

F	C	N	L	U	O	F	C	N	L	U	O
0	5	65	27	1	2	4	39	50	0	8	0

Perkins						Emory					

22. Theological position on entering college.

F	C	N	L	U	O	F	C	N	L	U	O
36	39	3	20	1	1	32	50	4	13	1	0

23. Theological position on entering seminary.

F	C	N	L	U	O	F	C	N	L	U	O
7	37	12	41	3	0	6	48	13	33	0	0

24. Theological position on leaving seminary.

F	C	N	L	U	O	F	C	N	L	U	O
1	16	46	35	1	2	2	29	37	31	0	0

25. Theological position NOW.

F	C	N	L	U	O	F	C	N	L	U	O
1	20	41	33	0	5	2	34	38	23	0	2

Asbury						General Theological Seminary (Episc.)					

22. Theological position on entering college.

F	C	N	L	U	O	F	C	N	L	U	O
43	54	0	1	0	0	7	48	10	14	1	16

TABLE 22–3 (*Continued*)

F	C	N	L	U	O	F	C	N	L	U	O

23. Theological position on entering seminary.

| 27 | 72 | 0 | 1 | 0 | 0 | 3 | 37 | 17 | 22 | 0 | 21 |

24. Theological position on leaving seminary.

| 19 | 77 | 1 | 4 | 0 | 0 | 0 | 28 | 27 | 22 | 0 | 21 |

25. Theological position NOW.

| 10 | 79 | 4 | 7 | 0 | 0 | 0 | 29 | 17 | 28 | 0 | 26 |

Seabury-Western   Northern Baptist

22. Theological position on entering college.

| 5 | 58 | 5 | 15 | 0 | 21 | 50 | 37 | 2 | 8 | 0 | 2 |

23. Theological position on entering seminary.

| 0 | 53 | 10 | 11 | 2 | 24 | 25 | 75 | 0 | 0 | 0 | 0 |

24. Theological position on leaving seminary.

| 0 | 47 | 21 | 6 | 0 | 26 | 5 | 85 | 7 | 0 | 2 | 2 |

25. Theological position NOW.

| 0 | 45 | 13 | 14 | 0 | 27 | 3 | 77 | 12 | 3 | 0 | 5 |

Lutheran Theol. St. Paul   Concordia Theol. St. Louis

22. Theological position on entering college.

| 36 | 57 | 1 | 4 | 1 | 1 | 26 | 70 | 2 | 1 | 0 | 0 |

23. Theological position on entering seminary.

| 16 | 71 | 10 | 3 | 0 | 1 | 18 | 78 | 2 | 1 | 0 | 0 |

24. Theological position on leaving seminary.

| 7 | 63 | 26 | 4 | 0 | 1 | 10 | 83 | 5 | 1 | 0 | 1 |

25. Theological position NOW.

| 6 | 60 | 29 | 4 | 0 | 1 | 3 | 10 | 87 | 0 | 0 | 0 |

Princeton   McCormick

22. Theological position on entering college.

| 27 | 52 | 5 | 14 | 1 | 2 | 15 | 44 | 10 | 27 | 3 | 2 |

23. Theological position on entering seminary.

| 9 | 57 | 13 | 19 | 0 | 1 | 3 | 40 | 22 | 34 | 1 | 1 |

TABLE 22-3 (*Continued*)

F	C	N	L	U	O	F	C	N	L	U	O

24. Theological position on leaving seminary.

F	C	N	L	U	O	F	C	N	L	U	O
2	42	46	10	0	0	1	17	66	16	0	1

25. Theological position NOW.

F	C	N	L	U	O	F	C	N	L	U	O
1	38	45	15	0	1	0	20	56	22	0	2

Key: The numbers represent percentages in each category. F = Fundamentalist; C = Conservative; N = Neo-Orthodox; L = Liberal; U = Universalist-Unitarian; O = Other.

Yale and Union, have been dominated by a particular theological ethos. The general trend toward neo-orthodoxy from prior positions to the left and right is striking; this may suggest that seminary education presently produces more of a uniformity of orientation among ministers than would perhaps be expected from consideration of the historical and denominational differences between seminaries. Perhaps more difference of opinion, though it lead to conflict, is to be desired.

The agreement of these ministers on directions of mission seems to us more significant than their agreement or disagreement on theological doctrines, for the conviction which this study has supported is that it is finally in the concrete actions of social polity that theological education bears fruit. There is present a keen awareness of the necessity and possibility of action; the task at hand is to build this awareness into shared strategy.

Albert Rasmussen points out in his chapter "Religion and Education in a Secular Society"[5] that a secular trend in culture is describable in two ways. First, religion is increasingly dissociated from aspects of the common life, until it is seen as relevant only to the separated domain of the specifically religious (or spiritual). Second, a secular culture is one in which the value system communicates the belief that religious behavior has no relevance to economic and political action, artistic expression, or other types of activity. We can discern both of these trends in the seminary and the ministry today. On the one hand, there is the conservative reaction which maintains that the established forms of worship and social organization must be preserved as divinely guaranteed absolutes; on the other hand is the reaction toward "worldly"

5. Albert Rasmussen, "Religion and Education in Secular Society," in Volume II.

ministry which at its most extreme seems to lose the dimension of awe and wonder and the ability to celebrate God's presence in the world in the drama of worship.[6]

Worship is the symbolic drama of the Christian community which reminds them of who they are before God, reaffirms the stance to which they have committed themselves, and prepares them for encountering God active in the events and structures of their varying daily activities. Worship is celebration which speaks of what the way of life is really meant to be for men of faith; but today the forms of Christian worship increasingly do not portray what concerns sensitive people, like the students we surveyed at the University of Wisconsin and elsewhere.[7] What we are hearing is not simply demands for internal, direct, and narrow attempts at liturgical renewal in the churches and seminaries (though it is clear that some forms of proclamation such as preaching will not long maintain their centrality in worship). Rather, the church is being called to embody the spirit and style of worship and proclamation—the priestly mode of ministry—which it has received from the Gospel and the Christian heritage in many new forms of celebration in response to the needs of persons and the events of our world, lifting up in the midst of the world the significance of that world as the creation and place of God's action.

The Crisis of Inquiry and Understanding

The third manifestation of the crisis in the church's vision of ministry is that the theological schools have not been able to mobilize adequate resources in the university to inquire into their situation and to understand it. They have been confined in their diagnosis almost entirely to disciplines in the humanities. There is, therefore, under way a shift in the major centers of religious and ethical studies from the seminary to the university. This signifies greater attention to social and behavioral disciplines, to comparative, cross-cultural studies, and to religious phenomena in institutional and professional areas outside the church and clergy.

---

6. Parker Palmer presents these as the "magical" and "secular" world views in "A Typology of World Views," in Volume II.

7. See N. J. Demerath III, and Kenneth Lutterman, "The Student Parishioner: Radical Rhetoric and Traditional Reality," and Julian N. Hartt, "Liturgy and Politics," in Volume II.

Recent developments in the teaching of religion in the universities have made the seminaries aware that the subject matter of their curriculums cannot be taught in isolation from its relationships with the broader context of the many ways of knowing present in the university. Terry H. Foreman points out in an intern-year paper for Union Seminary that the churches gave birth to seminaries in the early part of the nineteenth century as "a new kind of institution, explicitly professional, designed to salvage and safeguard the orthodoxy of the education of the clergy by moving the culmination of that formation within the ecclesiastical preserve."[8] With the onset of new methods of scientific study of religion, new criteria for the construction of curriculums were generated independent of ecclesiastical needs or wants. Now, in the increasing study of religion in the universities, two different paradigms for the organization of curriculums have emerged. The first type organizes its efforts and planning about the basic discipline of *theology*. Found mostly in private colleges and universities, this program offers courses such as would be found in most good seminaries and generally takes into account the confessional allegiances of professors, seeking balance and diversity of beliefs. The other type of curricular paradigm is based on the discipline of the study of *religion*. Departments following this paradigm seem to interpret the study of religion in such a way as to exclude the doing of constructive theology, which is taken to be part of the "practice" of religion, though the historical study of theology is not excluded. When religion is studied according to this model, the principles by which curriculum may be organized are contained in the phenomenon itself: How does the phenomenon of religion divide itself? How does this phenomenon most naturally relate itself to surrounding phenomena?

The coming impact on the seminaries of the study of religion according to this latter model will be upsetting, says Foreman, for in this model, Christian faith-interpretations are examined in the contexts of broad historical religious climates and present interrelated secular disciplines. This approach to the study of religion makes the ecclesiastical parochialisms of seminary education visible; it shows how the study of

8. Terry H. Foreman, "The Study of Religion and Some Imperatives for Theological Education: An Intern Year Project Presented to Dr. Robert W. Lynn, Mr. James W. Berland and the Faculty of Union Theological Seminary," June, 1967.

theology has dominated the seminary curriculum and subjugated all other disciplines to itself, producing questionable methodological orientations among these "ancillary" disciplines. Foreman argues that the seminaries should recognize that the only discipline that is properly the attribute of the church is theology and that the study of theology provides the seminary at present with its unique academic task. Rather than substituting "Church and . . ." courses for exposure to hard-core secular disciplines, the major part of preparation for ministries should be done in the universities, leaving explicitly theological and ecclesiastical training to a context that might be called "Church" rather than university; most seminary faculty would be then appointed to the departments of religious studies of the universities, and the study of theology and practical church training would be done in a following year or in denominational houses close to the university.

Foreman concludes that "the Seminary's value as an institution both to the Church and to society would increase were it to be less an unsatisfactory and perilous hybrid institution than a genuine interface between secular culture and theological reflection, a meeting-place of learning in its most secular purity and the Church at its most faithful." His argument suffers from the assumption of a dichotomy between "church" and "world"; and he is also perhaps too enchanted with the seeming "secular purity" of university learning, for we have received word not only from thoughtful faculty but also from those campus ministers whose work is most sensitive to the issues of university organization and action that the values underlying teaching and research often operate powerfully without being examined in free and critical discussion. But the central point of the argument stands: that ministries cannot be shaped in institutions where theological epistemologies are unrelated to other ways of knowing operating in the university and in the social contexts where ministries must be carried out. Theologizing as a process of critical and committed reflection needs to be related at one pole to the whole spectrum of scholarship and research in the university and at another pole to concrete modes of ministry in the churches' mission in society. *The key task of the seminary is that of developing educational institutions, integral parts of the universities, where the activity of theologizing, of interpretation of the meaning of the faith, explores and experiments with the essential relationship be-*

tween personal calling and community, Christian worship, intellectual inquiry, and social organization.

Most especially, students and faculty in the seminaries need to work with churchmen and public leaders to provide a variety of models of learning for use in the church. Students preparing for leadership in the church need to inculcate into their styles of action that process of many-dimensioned reflection which they will have to foster in the church itself, so that not only the seminary and the university Christian fellowship but also local congregations will be places for continuing inquiry into the implications of Christian faith for concrete corporate action in the shaping of structures of human life.[9]

The Crisis of Action and Governance

H. Richard Niebuhr has given us the image of the church as the "social pioneer": those who represent mankind in responsibility before God, repenting of and repudiating social evil first of all in their own corporate life and then leading the society in responding to the possibilities for new life structures. But the pioneering efforts of the churches in our society seem today not to be very effective. The fourth crisis of the church affecting seminary education is that religious leaders have had great difficulty in making the movement for renewal of the church a model of meaningful governance of major institutions and organizations of the society. The movement for church renewal has taken various forms: ecumenical co-operation, liturgical reshaping, new forms of Christian communities, theology of and for the laity, specialized services, church support of social reform movements, experiments with worldly ministries, and so on. But these efforts seem not to have had the power to move whole congregations, organizations, or cities to action. Even within the churches, differences between the expectations of laymen most active in the church and of ministers seeking radical social change are seldom publicly aired. Significant co-operation between specialized ministries is just beginning (for example, between inner-city ministers engaged in the organization of the poor and sub-

---

9. Two beginning models for such inquiry are Thomas F. Green's "Toward an Action Theory of Learning for the Churches" and David Duncombe's "Toward a Scientific Theory of Experimental Learning for the Churches," in Volume II.

urban ministers exploring with professional and managerial constituencies the religious significance of social protest).

The seminaries are missing an opportunity that is uniquely theirs in the university when they fail to explore the kind of education which links ideas directly to social implementation in organizations, communities, and institutions. The "ivory tower" image is no more true of the university today than is the "cloister" image applicable to the church; but the increasing trend toward seminary students' wanting to remain in the university as teachers of religion can be detrimental if it leads to further communication of ideas without any awareness of the consequences of that communication. The university has a third function besides teaching and research—the function of giving leadership to the community, of expressing a social concern, of shaping the public mind on the issues of the day and the problems of our society.[10] The university by nature is a valuing institution. By definition it cannot be neutral about many of the civilizing values of men. Its very essence demands its acceptance of certain values; and if acceptance, then proclamation and action on their behalf. Even more so is this true for the Church. The truth of the Gospel is enacted truth, not only in individual lives but in the forms of corporate life in the church, and not in the internal life of the church but in the concrete structures of human relationships in society. As a professional school directly related not only to the university but also to the church, the seminary has a mandate to be the explorer, the imaginer, and the builder of models for human life together.

Why have so few of the "experiments" in new forms of ministry succeeded in setting in motion powerful, effective action? It may be that they have not really been undertaken in the style of experiments, after all. That is, there has been built into the design of these ventures no provision for evaluation of the consequences of action, no follow-up on the conditions making for success or failure. Experiments are actions carried out in the framework of energy systems, where a change in one part is initiated with some prediction of consequent changes in the rest of the system. The consequences of changes in the action of the churches are to be sought not alone in internal or religious indicators but in changed patterns of action of individuals and groups in the organizations and institutions of the society. As Robert Lynn observes,

---

10. Merrimon Cuninggim, "The University's Third Function," *Christian Scholar,* Vol. L (Spring, 1967).

we now are operating, especially in the university, as "a ministry on the margin,"[11] which means that we have the gift of the freedom now to be selective, to select that which most needs to be done at this moment. But we have also the obligation to decide how we must act and build into that action the means of learning from our actions.[12]

Our theological understanding of the world today is that it is the place where the Spirit moves, and it is the gift of the Lord to man to shape responsibly. To be obedient to the vocation of being the church today demands that we be strategic and intentional about the concrete embodiments of the Gospel in the shaping of society.

The Shaping of Seminary Education: A Proposal

There are being made, here and there, serious proposals for the reshaping of seminary education to meet the fourfold crisis we have described. Among these is a model for theological curriculum for the 1970's from a task force committee of the American Association of Theological Schools.[13] This proposal envisions theological education as a three-level process: on the first level, that of university undergraduate education, students will gain highly skilled competence in one or more of several broad areas of secular knowledge, with some competence in areas of theological knowledge such as Bible, the history of Christianity, or theological thinking and interpretation. Level II will be specifically education in theological thinking. During this time the student will build on his competence gained in Level I and relate that discipline's conceptions of issues and problems to theology's conceptions and perspectives. It will be an occasion for "practical involvement with the world and problems of contemporary life" with an awareness of relationships between theological conceptions and the historical experience of the community, its present life, and its hopes for and thrusts into the future. The Level II experience would include a "Core" group of ten to twelve students and a faculty member from one of biblical, historical, or theological disciplines meeting several hours each week, and also

---

11. Robert W. Lynn, "A Ministry on the Margin," in Volume II.

12. See David Duncombe, *op. cit.*

13. The Resources Planning Commission, American Association of Theological Schools, "Theological Curriculum for the 1970's," *Theological Education*, Vol. IV, No. 3 (Spring, 1968), pp. 671–705.

traditional course work in knowledge of Bible, church history, history of Christian thought, contemporary Christian thought, contemporary issues confronting Christian faith, and a non-Christian religion. The Core group would deal with specific contemporary problems related to 12 hours of student involvement as volunteers (perhaps part-time remuneration) in community organizations and structures. The sessions would be largely student-directed, with the possibility that other experts might be called in from the university or from public leadership to participate in study and reflection. The Core groups would combine action and reflection and be the site of learning theological thinking, the foundation for various forms of Christian ministry to be chosen in the next level.

Level IIIA, vocational preparation in a variety of professional ministries, would take place in one of three centers related to the "nucleus" of Level II. The emphasis in Level IIIA is on "action informed by theological thought; the student's social identity role; and the relationship of community and world." The three centers suggested for this level are: Family Life Cycle Center, Business and Industrial Community Center, and Theology and the Arts Center. It is proposed that Level IIIA would be eleven months following two years in Level II. Level IIIB is a one-year residency following the doctoral requirements for preparation in teaching and leadership in theological education.

This proposal for the initial preparation of men for ministries has promise, so long as it keeps in balance concern for research and scholarship that has well-developed disciplines that seek to illumine the long-range problems of faith and its corporate forms and are not trivialized by immediate, short-range tactics of church survival. In order to further encourage and support internal reshaping of seminary education, we suggest that there are needed also processes and structures for enabling the continuing evaluation of seminary education as a whole in its relationships to the university, the ministries of the church, and the needs of society. Such evaluative devices are being used in government, in business, and in other fields of professional education and are providing valuable aid from perspectives not readily available to persons whose vision is constricted by the practical exigencies of keeping institutions running.

The Danforth Study of Campus Ministries has used a colloquium approach in several centers of study, where persons concerned with the same issues (but often not in touch with one another) have been drawn together from a variety of involvements in church, seminary, university, and public leadership. This methodology, we feel, could be appropriated as a device for evaluation of seminary education and embodied in institutes for policy research for gathering data, formulating or evaluating and testing models for alternatives of action, and making these models available for responsible decision makers in church, university, and social organizations.

What might such an institute for policy research look like? Drawing upon the whole scope of our findings from the study of campus ministries, we suggest that there are several factors to be taken into consideration in the design of such an institute.

Ministry is the work not of professional individuals alone but of corporate bodies of persons who are intentional about shaping the forms of human life in society in response to their perceptions of the actions of God in the events of the world. The institute would draw together faculty, church leaders, and public decision makers as persons who are engaged in basic research, teaching, and the designing and carrying out of policy. The autonomy of the professional needs to be balanced with his capacity to create communities of specialists, contributing to transformation of religious commitment, knowledge development and transmission, and public participation in the whole culture. One of the tasks of an institute for policy research would be the working out of models for such communities of specialists, trying to find out how they can best be enabled to work together. The provision of funds for task forces of scholars combining evaluative research with advanced learning for those who have to act on the recommendations of the researchers would appear to be a strategic priority.

Forms of ministry change, but the historic modes of ministry must continue and be held together in the full dynamic pattern of ministry. A part of the work of the institute would be the discernment of the variety of ways in which these modes of ministry are being enacted today, and persons exploring new forms of several modes would need to be brought together for the joint enrichment of their visions. The aim of the institute would be, then, to make available to the churches alternative models of learning and acting, reporting on how these models have been used in practice in differing situations. The way the findings of such an institute would be put into practice in the churches and in seminary education would be through encouraging a few institutions to undertake reform action, guided by the continuing research and consultation made available through the institute. Some significant reformulations of ministry are now taking place. The focus of policy research would be on the description and development of such models of ministry and then critical reflection on them so that they could be adapted for wider use.

The process of reflection and evaluation has to proceed at the same time as the process of action. The institute for policy research would function specifically as a continuing evaluative device. Since whole faculties or groups of institutional leaders cannot be expected to take up the process of self-evaluation and accomplish a great deal, the institute could draw together persons from church, seminary, university, and public institutions who can work together from a more comprehensive vision of what the church is about and then carry back into specific institutions suggested models for reform. The institute would seek to find out the effects or consequences of the enactment of such strategic models in the actual work of education and ministry in the seminaries and the churches. It would encourage institutions to undertake the kinds of action that could be tested and evaluated, then recommended to others. The scholars, leaders, and churchmen involved would enter the model-building process at several stages: the gathering of data, the delineating of values underlying alternatives of action, the imagining of strategies, and the reporting back of consequences. Such action would be policy research, not "pure" or abstract research nor the designing of internal policy for one institution alone. Those taking part in such model building would be intentional about looking at the concrete actions of individuals and institutions—and intentional about influencing those actions, knowing that their participation in the examination of processes of action would in itself change both those processes and their own interpretations and recommendations.

The institute for policy research would also seek to serve as a communications bridge between church, university, and seminary. The university is increasingly the place where the shapes of our future society are being worked out. The church needs to test out in the university context the implications and consequences of its faith-understandings, even as it learns from the university about the developments that will affect the forms of church life. The concerns which led to the establishment of professorships in religion and higher education are now seen to be best expressed in the basic scholarship and ways of teaching of the seminary faculty as a whole. The encouragement and enablement of faculty who are willing to assume the task of learning about significant shifts in the relation of the churches to the whole complex system of higher education, especially technical and professional school developments, would be an important function of an institute for policy research.

Strategic action is always specific and concrete, but also always global in import. Institutes for policy research in church, university, and society would need to be regionally grounded, taking on responsibility for policy recommendations for actions of specific groups; but they would report for national use what happens in one region, for they would be acting on behalf of the whole church and society. As an example of how such an institute might be set up, perhaps in the eastern region, one institute, drawing selectively upon faculty from Yale, Harvard, Union Seminary, and other schools, should assume responsibility for advice to other seminary centers in exploring such evaluative policy research, so that some division of intellectual labor on a national level would be possible. Institutes in other regions could specialize in other ways, making use of the advantages of their specific regions, but fitting their efforts into the total picture of evaluation and model building.

There is no question about the fact that the ministry will be radically changed in the coming decades. It is to be hoped that a variety of new models for the preparation of persons for ministry will be worked out, and we suggest that such agencies as institutes for policy research will be needed for encouraging this process of model building. Whatever models emerge will prove their worth by the style in which they hold together in flexible, dynamic patterns of ministry the four historic modes of ministry—pastoral, priestly, prophetic, and governing—generating specific forms of action in response to developing needs of persons in church, university, and society, and finally accountable to the Lord of history to whose actions ours are responses.

CONCLUSION

A Check List of Strategic Decisions for Churches, Universities,

and Foundations in Light of the Whole Study

T HE ministry has been defined in this study as offering ways of action
that promise hope for a better world—hope that is a deliberate, self-
conscious visualization of events that can be made to occur in public
life, which our eyes have not yet fully seen, but which have their attraction because they are a part of what we have already deeply experienced.
Hope in the Christian religious consciousness is not first a fleeting wish.
It is *confidence* felt and thought, added to desire. What can we expect
of the Power that rules the world, and what hope for man's positive response to this Power? We may desire many things in the church or the
university, but dare we try to make them public issues if there is no hope
or expectation that new events can come about?

Lawrence A. Cremin, author of *The Genius of American Education,*
has insisted that education be defined in terms of such hope: "the deliberate, self conscious pursuit of certain intellectual, ethical and esthetic
ideals."[1] To hope is to feel a tension between what is and what ought to
be the glory of a society. The recent theologies of hope have seen the
heart of Christian hope in the Christian's commitment to reform the
power of major institutions in the direction of serving human needs. His
life as a minister, a teacher, a foundation executive is a witness, an
indication of his hope for a more ultimate fulfillment of God's purposes
for the world. What is really good and true will be sustained by the
One who acts in the future, as He has in the past, to correct man's mis-
placed hopes in particular partisan acts. Man's vision is directed to the

---

1. Quoted in Frank G. Jennings[2] guest editorial, "The Education of Educators,"
Saturday Review of Literature, November 19, 1966, p. 79. Lawrence A. Cremin,
The Genius of American Education (New York: Random House, 1966).

larger sweep of historic movement, to the complex configurations of God's work in the world.

Such hopes are the ground of strategic actions. They are to be distinguished from faith and love; yet all have their common origin in God. Paul says, "Love hopes all things." Men are able to help others in politics because they know their neighbors in hope; they know what they are becoming with changes in their work assignments and the resources made available to them. Hope is also, in biblical terms, the first fruit of faith. The hope of the Christian is no longer confined to what the self can do and its programs but rests also in the signs of the appearance of God's Kingdom through policy changes. The Christian makes evident his faith by his participation in the life of the world, with all its brokenness, sorrow, and hatred, because he can also discern and affirm that events are an indication that God is fulfilling His purposes for the world, that passion and feeling for social policies are expressive finally not of varied hopes, but of the *one* true hope in the fidelity of God's concern for the world.

These convictions are being stated in familiar strategic and social terms by the churches. The Board of National Missions of the Presbyterian Church, USA, calls for "policies that affect the entire range of presbytery decision-making, from ministerial relations to development of new congregations."[2] They ask for a "very rapid development of joint structures for ecumenical mission action, that no longer focus on the inner city" but reach for "patterns of interdependence among all churches of a metropolitan area and for mutual involvements of programs of witness and service." These changes are proposed as responses to the "interdependent character of the entire nation" whose problems of housing, transportation, pollution, and so on are dependent for solution on federal programs that activate commerce, banking, communication, universities, and other organizations now linked together in the society. The task of the church is to witness in strategy to the Lordship of Christ over the metropolis through responsible, committed persons whose humane values influence crucial decisions. The churches must develop methods for visualizing the hopeful possibilities in (a) the issues, (b) the structures of power, and (c) the processes of decision of the city.

---

2. "Guidelines for Development of Strategy for Metropolitan Mission," Board of National Missions, United Presbyterian Church, USA, September, 1967. This is one of a series of policy statements on current issues facing the church.

The guidelines support citizens' groups formed by relatively affluent Christians who back with their resources the efforts of poor, racially discriminated people to be self-reliant and productive. Thus the central missions of the church—metropolitan, campus, international—are no longer to be looked upon as separate tasks of the church, but as requiring involvement of all the instruments of the church in carrying out the full witness of God's Kingdom and the achievement of just social policies. These tasks have their own bodies of knowledge and theory, but their object of service is a wider field than acknowledged in the past.

This look at metropolitan mission literature is to remind us again what strategic talk is about. It shows that strategic thinking in campus ministries has its counterparts in other sectors of the church where the revolutionary potential of unsatisfied human rights and unmet obligations is replacing drives toward independence and authoritarianism.

Now let us turn to specific strategic implications of the study.

Policy Research

1. Hopefully the next policy studies of this magnitude will be the consequence of regular, continuing relationships established by religious affairs centers on key campuses for periodic review of church programs and actions. We can hope, too, that they will reflect a new awareness of the methodological choices available to the church and thus draw upon sciences untouched in this study. We can be certain that shortcomings in future studies will, as in this one, necessitate the revision and review that only well-established departments and centers committed to relating thought and action can produce.

Historic Movements

2. The churches are engaged in a massive struggle to turn from denominationalism to ecumenicity, from piecemeal ministry to a restoration of the meaning of its historic modes for contemporary urban society. One guide to the churches' posture in the university is that they, in the spirit of the new University Christian Movement, seek to establish intellectual ecumenes on most major campuses where the diversities of faith are consciously explored in counsel, cult, reflection, and corporate act. The seminaries and colleges should no longer train consecrated function-

aries for denominations, but professionals to serve the ecumenes in all their contemporary complexity.

3. Not all who minister work in churches. The concern of the new centers of policy studies and advanced learning in the church will be with the teaching and training processes which form journalists, television directors, city planners, army generals, textbook publishers, as well as clergy and teachers. Such exploration requires inquiry into the epistemological architecture of education in schools, churches, and everywhere that learning takes place. What disciplines and commitments determine one's knowledge, how he knows it, and what he does with the knowledge? This inquiry includes all the mass media and popular culture, the educational undertakings in government, business, armed forces, law, and other agencies that have emerged with the university as determiners of the quality of knowledge and learning in our society. Today the chief battle is simply that of giving to technical or specialized areas a new consciousness of the human values at stake in their actions. Whether or not this will be the guiding vision of the church in the next two decades is the major strategic decision to be made by the churches. The courts and law schools are to become the subject of controversial attacks and reconciliation by the church leaders, if they administer judicial processes so as to rule out the difficult and important questions of commitment and worth of whole corporate systems and the meaning of collective symbols. So, too, the medical schools and practice are to be taken on when technical reason blinds them to human or social considerations.

4. The campus ministers in the prophetic visions of their founders in the university were to have such a corporate mission and the time and disciplined education to take on such battles. But they never fulfilled this mission, and the society and church suffer the failure. It is not too late—it was never more urgently needed—to have the function performed at every level and mode of ministry: pastoral, priestly, inquiring teacher, and community leader of people.

The stress on the relational aspects of ministry is not intended to denigrate in the least the importance of a corps of professional leaders on each major campus who have a national, disciplined community behind them and a theory of their work and data to support their theory. The churches, seminaries, and universities must provide the conditions which produce such a corps, and the foundations must support only men and women who meet such standards. But they are to keep a fruitful tension between what has to be done in the future and what has been accomplished in the past. There is to be no segregated, elite corps immersed in its own specialty and protection.

Pastoral Care

5. The pastoral role, for all its emphasis in psychological and theological literature in this century, has been mistakenly interpreted and undeveloped in our time. Counseling, group therapy, affections for a supportive small community of persons, must reflect a theology which takes more seriously the self in its social involvements. Hence, foundation support of chaplaincies that encourage faculty or students to do "research" into what happens to religious commitments in the work and life of students is important. A reinterpretation of ego-psychology, counseling, conversion, and personal renewal is going on in the university; the work of scholars such as Erik Erikson and Donald Meyer is of great importance to the churches.

The church in its pastoral emphasis needs to balance the overemphasis in the colleges and universities on the cognitive, adaptive dimensions of higher education. But it must do so in a new way from what we saw in Berkeley. It needs in its counseling to confront the student and professor with the values implicit in professional practices, academic disciplines, ways of learning. It needs to have mastered the relation of pastoral care to other modes of action so it can envision such new relationships in business, law, medicine, and the like. To talk of such balances is the heart of strategic thinking.

Preaching and Worship

6. In this area of policy we are confronted by two extreme strategies: one would make this mode of ministry the chief reliance of the church in its presentation of the Gospel to man, and the other would cease to expect modern man to be convinced by exhortation, ritualistic recall of the past, poetic analogy, or other linguistic associations with the priest and preacher. Neither of these positions is acceptable. The first ignores the repulsion every man experiences when words become cheap substitutes for action or when the deepest events of life are reduced to rote.

The second ignores the pervasive presence of this mode of communication in all areas of our life; it is not an exclusive mode of the church. There are times in every organization when men need to profess their deepest convictions and fears. The mode reflects something universally human.

What is needed in the future, as the Wisconsin-based recommendations sought to convey, is a strategy that makes of priestly functions the expression of new constituencies and new ways of proclaiming the faith without assuming that these people wish to give up exploring the human experiences that produced the rituals and language now part of the Christian community. This is likely to necessitate new organizations, new buildings, new reliance on lay expression of belief and unbelief. These are emerging in the form of centers, institutes, departments, that are more than anything the church has achieved in the past, closely allied with other forces of learning and civic action.

Prophetic Inquiry

7. To talk of such alliances is not to deny the separate and distinctive concerns of churches, universities, and politics in our society. The church should have no place in the university as an institutional agency advertising the superiority of its intellectual and moral attributes. Under study, the vaunted superiority has evaporated, leaving the rancid smell of ecclesiastical imperialism. The university should license or certify *no* denominational church activity in its borders, and it should offer no privately certified surrogate for a church, as though the university were a community with its own *sui generis* religious life. Critical inquiry into the religious life of our society should be explored in free and unpressured settings provided at the initiative and final control of the university, with the actual practice and testing of the consequences of religion to be carried out by the churches.

Extremities of role are evident in the behavior of professional religious leaders who wish to see themselves as faculty more than ministers. They resist, for example, interpretation of the campus ministry in terms which take the integrative, pattern-maintenance, and goal-achievement aspects of the ministry as seriously as prophetic inquiry. These people are going to be increasingly pressured by faculty and administrators to come to terms with the question of whether they are leaders primarily in the church or the university. The prevailing patterns of the future in all colleges and universities will be to separate formally the scholarly study of religion from the ministry and the practice of religion in the church. From the churches the pressures are increasingly for a clarification of the essential functions of campus ministers in the ongoing mission of institutional religion. The churches can encourage these differentiations of functions, so long as they are not expressions of overspecialization and a fear to test thought in action.

8. A continuing analytical task for scholars is that of providing knowledge of whether modes of ministry are being performed competently and of the interconnections of theology, social attitude, and self-perception. The rigor and particularity of these data (two scales in the survey, on Biblical Fundamentalism and Doubt in Midst of Belief, reveal orientations to the world which have significant correlations in about every area of the instrument) may go hard with many who have had a stake in situations where no concrete evaluation of work has been required. In carrying out these recommendations the churches are going to meet considerable resistance, chiefly from the radical left and from very conservative people. For this study does not conceive of the major task of the campus ministry either to radicalize the church or to be a free-floating, vaguely defined professional ministry cut off from the problems of institutional religion and social change.

9. The clergy on campus have considerable stake in the quality and nature of the religious studies which the administration and faculty provide. Great attention should be given by them, therefore, to the funding of *research* into religious phenomena—from both public and private sources. The campus ministries have been myopic here, more concerned often to "teach a little in the college" than to develop criteria of serious study in religion.

The churches and universities need to encourage as a high priority the serious exploration of the ethical and social significance of specific faith traditions in all the structures of higher education, with a special eye to the relations of liberal arts education to technical and professional schools and careers. In our society, we may be reaching the point where the only process by which belief is formed and acted on for most people is that of genuine inquiry in a college or university setting. These inquiries, if they are to gain faculty and student support, need to be placed in a context of comparison with other viable world views and commitments. Too often the pattern-maintenance institutions have tended in the past to identify moral and religious concern with the realities explored only by the classical liberal arts and humanities disciplines, dominating their curriculum in the past century. As a consequence, new, fruitful meanings of faith now being explored by empirical and technical disciplines outside the humanities have been neglected.

Studies such as this one need to be critically assessed as a model for future research enterprises in seminaries, universities, or colleges. For example, consultations with the medical educators have indicated that priority should be given to placement of competent faculty in medical schools capable of bringing disciplined theological and ethical insight to bear in clinical, diagnostic situations. These people are key agents for relating the churches more adequately to the professional world. They probe and form the *technical conscience*, highlighting *relational* problems of self-identity and public policy that cut across disciplines. The universities and colleges are giving increasing attention to this kind of learning and reflection, and some campus ministers are now moving into university-financed work in "discussion" faculties, continuing education centers, clinical faculties, and others.

10. This study has documented the dangers of "tokenism" in the campus ministry; that is, a conception of specialized clergy which does something for the churches in higher education. The greatest failure of campus ministers who are in radical revolt against particular modes of service is their inability to involve the whole church in battles over the quality of higher education, Christian education, foreign missions, and so on. All aspects of the churches have a stake in continuing participation in the life of the university, its policy and evaluative research. The deeper matter is that of involving the laity in such issues of higher education as whether the basic human and public questions of our time are studied and whether students have a chance to explore the alternatives of religious commitment, styles of life, and work.

This study has given some important leads as to how ministers such as Harry Smith, Jack Harrison, and Paul Schrading have taken higher education out of the world of specialized interest, into the world of inner-city and suburban struggles with poverty, into professional sensitivities of lawyers, scientists, and businessmen. Such men need frequent leaves to study, not in anticipation of final degrees, but to permit varied combinations of courses, experiences, and supervision by people who know what is at stake in such education.

If the campus minister is willing to see his task in terms of the kind of provocative, informal, and radical probing that can sometimes go on better outside the classroom than in it, he may be able to make a real contribution to the intellectual development of the student. Too many campus ministries, especially among more conservative groups, wish to plug into the formal credit system of the university. In general, this type of program is a mistake both for the campus minister involved and for the university. But still administrators are sometimes tempted to try this, although they are seldom supported by the faculty, and the campus ministers are strongly tempted to go along. Generally the administrator is interested in destroying the image of the "godless" campus, and the campus minister thinks, mistakenly, that he can be most effective in the classroom because that is where the most important things go on in the university. But the campus minister is as likely to be effective outside as inside the formal classroom or the accredited course.

11. The church is having to move from catechetical images of learning to genuine inquiry which takes on a lot of the aspects of what we identify with scientific and technological disciplines. Students are more interested in the study of religion than they have ever been. This does not mean that they are more religious; but their interest ranges from curiosity to deep probing. Most students are of a "no nonsense" generation; thus catechism and games are out, and the "fundamental" questions are in. Able campus ministers know this and have creatively related themselves to it.

Our survey data also indicate that support for the shift from indoctrination to inquiry is strong among the noncampus clergy. Administrators in denominational centers often talk as if they cannot introduce new programs because there is no great grass-roots support. But in the survey data on clergy, no items are more strongly supported in terms of role than trying to find ways of teaching people to explore the relationship of Christian faith to vocation. Within the campus or parish ministry there is no greater desire than finding some time to get back to the university, to do some fresh additional work. It is true one can talk about these as popular reflections of education as a social mobility factor and other forces in the culture. But a lot of people recognize a shift in the concept of learning and epistemology, and the shift is seen as what God wills.

Urban trends indicate that more and more college youth and academic staff are going to be served religiously by regular parishes which specialize somewhat in strong programs of religious education. Specialization in meeting the specific needs of a locality is now well advanced in urban ministries, and it is increasingly difficult to duplicate the full institutional apparatus of the strong parish churches inside the university or any other institution. The ministries on campus must, therefore, be highly involved in developments of parish churches and in providing services to them.

Most metropolitan students, faculty, and administrators are now full-time commuters. Ministry to this group is increasingly being based in the local churches, and the meaningful participation of these people in local parishes—acquainting them with theological, ethical, and social developments in education—should be encouraged by campus ministries. The abilities of the ordinary parish to respond to interests of large potential campus clientele are usually slight, and many frustrated campus ministers would do well to seek flexible and resourceful positions in a combination of parish churches or a large parish church bringing the university and churches into greater interaction. Such work could be abetted by the establishment of one or two metropolitan university religious centers to program for the city as a whole, engage in periodic re-evaluations of work being done, co-ordinate resources, and bring about enduring relations between selected parishes and university groups.

12. A crisis in theological education is manifested in varied ways. The leadership of the churches lacks the power to integrate religious beliefs, technical theory and data, and the varied modes of ministry. What is learned in seminary tends either to reinforce traditional ministries or produce alienation from all institutional structures except for narrow specialization in role and constituency. The church response needed in the situation is leadership perceiving God at work redeeming all modes of ministry in the church and all structures of human existence. Such a field encompasses the major dimensions of Christian commitment and action: the responsible self, worship, inquiry, and social policy. The crisis of religious commitment is manifested further in the lack of interpersonal communities which sustain ministries in their search for

integrity and wholeness in a career, where fellowship and affection are accompanied by resources to evaluate personal talents and capacities in ecumenical team ministries.

We predict there will be few seminaries of importance in the next two decades which will not consider transforming their academic programs into residential internships for ministry to the university as its most manageable access to the society as a whole. This will come about as attempts are made to use limited resources of leadership effectively in an increasingly complex and sophisticated society. Yet, more and more the seminaries will send people out into university structures in a systematic way so that important aspects of society will not be ignored. Teachers will confer with students as to what they are learning, and this knowledge can be widely shared and acted on in policy terms. Such internships in the university are the most manageable entry into the world for the churches to develop for their leaders. The Jesuits might well consider making their whole order a campus ministry in this sense, focusing on education of the educators, and Protestant denominations could well consider the same priorities in use of their most intelligent and balanced leadership.

If Christians will come to know what the university is about, they may be able to say something in the modern world. Proliferation of ill-defined activities in inner-city work and dabbling with suburban institutes for businessmen without strong ties to the university must be regarded as playing around with issues and problems. In short, we do not see how the church, with its limited resources, can enter into the major institutions of the society in any effective way unless it moves out through the structures of the university which have been set up to reflect on just those major institutions.

The university departments, in turn, need this intern or residency development. To give one example of what has happened to the disciplines in the seminaries specially charged with responsibility to cross the boundaries of departments, we can note the state of social ethics. The work of Daniel Patrick Moynihan, a social scientist, and Ralph Nader, a lawyer, alone have acocunted for more public attention to crucial social issues of irresponsible corporate behavior than the Association of Professors of Christian Social Ethics over the past decade. Most writing of these faculty is like the fancy footwork of a fighter who never gets into the ring. They never get beyond the methodological problems to clarification of human choices in the major technical and professional schools that surround them.

13. Foundation funding in the seminaries needs primarily to establish conditions for continuing research and consultation to encourage reform action by a few institutions. Some significant reformulations of ministry are now taking place. The focus would be on the description and development of models of such ministry and then critical reflection on them. The research and consultation being developed by professional schools such as the American Medical Colleges may provide some standards. Professional schools such as medicine and law are increasingly aware that the realities they profess to serve (such as life and health, just public law) are undergoing radical reformulation and that the intellectual disciplines dominating the curriculums are not responsive to the changing needs of society, particularly in the reorganization of modes of service and provision for continuing education.

In many ways the ministry's distinctive historical concern that clergy and laity share in the discernment of God's action in the world has taken on great contemporary relevance. All professionals are involved more and more in explaining their ways of thinking and acting to clients and to sources of public and financial support for the functions performed. The autonomy of the professional needs to be balanced with his capacity to create communities of specialists, contributing to transformation of religious commitment, health, and public engagement in the whole culture. The provision of funds for "task forces" of scholars combining evaluative research with advanced learning for those who have to act on the recommendations of the research would appear to be a strategic priority in foundation grants.

Furthermore, the placement of this action in the context of awareness of similar problems and developments in other professional schools is important. This approach reduces defensiveness and supplies knowledge of human needs to be met by common endeavors of major specializations in our society. The ministry, which rightly fears narrow technical training and seeks reformation of the self for free and responsible action in the world, can gain most in insight and compassion from a multiple-professional approach to the clergy.

The concerns which led to the establishment of professorships in religion and higher education are now best expressed in the basic scholarship and ways of teaching of the seminary faculty as a whole.

There can be performed an enabling function by faculty with responsibilities in such an area, providing opportunities for learning about significant shifts in the relation of the churches to the whole complex system of higher education, with perhaps particular attention to the technical and professional school developments. Special funds are needed to aid (a) in arranging for consultation and reflection with persons having insight crucial to future scholarship and teaching and outside one's routine contacts and (b) in assuring greater flexibility and co-operative work on intellectual problems and developments more sustained than ordinary leave time and teaching arrangements permit.

The primary focus of those involved in the use of such funds and enabling personnel would be on understanding and evaluating the influence of seminary education on all kinds of church and university leadership.

The seminaries would gain greatly if one institute—drawing, for instance, selectively upon Yale, Harvard, Union faculty—were to assume responsibility for advising other seminary centers given help by the Danforth Foundation in exploring evaluative policy research, so that some division of intellectual labor on a national level might result. Such institutes would not administer extensive "adult" or continuing education programs, but would relate the thought and research of the seminary and university to church policy and ministerial action. Perhaps, in time, funds would come from a variety of sources—university, church, foundations, and others. Such institutes should be kept small administratively and in program; they are not a substitute for the ongoing, basic work of the faculty of a seminary and university. When they ceased to serve to inform that work, their activities should be curtailed or ended.

One or two seminaries or graduate departments of religious studies ought to assume responsibility for providing special instruction in developments in the campus ministry. They would act as clearing centers for information on career posibilities, academic leave programs, research in process on new developments in education, and so forth. Most of this information should be communicated in special, intensive study programs of continuing education, thus alowing ample time for the student to experience technical school work, departments of higher education and urban studies, extension education, and the like. These are the places where he will develop disciplined knowledge of the university and of his special work. No seminary should undertake this task with only its own faculty. The "briefing" responsibility should be assumed only in seminaries intimately associated with university work in an intern-residency program. As the Very Rev. H. C. Williams has noted:

> The problems of the modern world cannot be solved by good intentions or pious principles alone. An awesome body of technical, statistical, historical, psychological, aesthetic and political knowledge is necessary, in addition to a theological grasp of goals and ethics, for any constructive intervention in the major processes of today's society. Yet, too few clergymen have enough training and experience in these areas of knowledge. Without such knowledge, the church's mission remains an ineffective or even an impeding influence in the world's revolution.[3]

14. The seminaries, churches, and foundations, in recruiting new ministerial leadership, need to play down the concept of a single, lifetime, one-job church occupation and to concentrate on the innovative and historically rich quality of theological training as a preparation for intelligent decision making in all fields and professions. Many students should be encouraged to think of theological education as a background for professional choices other than the clergy. The recruitment of future qualified students will be dependent chiefly on the transformation of the educational quality of church-sponsored learning; this explains our concentration in strategy on the inquiring mode of ministry. The best people to be sent into new mission fields are articulate, enthusiastic, and disciplined students; hence our emphasis on the phenomenology of student religious commitment. The faculty are the best source of information on this. So larger allocations of church funds for specific policy studies and continuing education work by faculty should appear in future national, regional, and metropolitan budgets. A variety of paths through religious studies and seminaries should be encouraged, since personal maturity, vocational assurance, and religious commitments vary greatly among students. Yet, for almost all of them today and in the foreseeable future, the quality of ministry will be judged by a person's ability to participate responsibly in shaping the society of his time and in serving the needs of his neighbor.

---

3. H. C. N. Williams, "Some Starting Points for Christian Renewal," *Church in Metropolis* (Fall, 1966), p. 35.

Governance and Power

15. The learning situations which the church should seek to provide need to assume that our society has great difficulty in placing account-ability for concrete actions that affect the lives of others. A church that still sees the reality of sin in the world will explore the self-deceptions and cultural illusions by which people hide from what they do to others in their indifference and their "business as usual" practices. In our society the church tends to organize discussions on the "ultimate issues" of death and eternal life, sin and the tolerance of pain and hardship, civil order and obedience. The professional-technical schools tend to study the specialized, manageable issues of an academic discipline. And no one assumes responsibility to clarify the "middle range" issues, the "nitty-gritty" problems where religious faith, technical fact, skill, and moral concern must come together. These questions have to do with the financ-ing, locating, organizing of professional practice, for example. These are precisely the kinds of issues the church must now prepare itself to take up; and the institutes of Christian Faith and Higher Education (Harrison), the programs of religion and society (Shriver), the civic centers of public affairs (Halvorsen), point the way. The strategic re-sponsibility of the corporate church is to prepare and support high-level general practitioners, overseers of ministries, who can harness the re-sources of the church to face accountability in these terms. The hardest task of the minister is to sense the conflicts of role in our society and thus to pierce the polytheistic and henotheistic structures of faith with the Gospel of Jesus Christ as Lord.

16. The problem of Protestantism in its ministry of governance is one of inability to relate highly moral goals to the means available in the institutional church for achieving these objectives. In recent years elaborate theologies have been developed to exempt religious leaders from responsibility for goal achievement. They do not want to be prag-matic, compromise their ideals, or mix religion and politics, power and conviction. But to be is to have power to achieve goals. The old doctrines of providence and redemption in Calvinism and Liberal Protestantism saw men building the city of man with confidence that thus God acted in history. But in recent years the theologies of alienation and personal angst have turned attention from what makes for effective organization in the achievement of high purpose.

There is today no morale in men and women who think they serve in marginal roles isolated from the forces that are changing people in the world. Either ministerial roles will be found that influence people in a way which can be objectively verified, or the people who wish to do something significant with their lives will evade church careers. If the church can only fulfill the negative role of trying to keep the church from impeding the work of the university, why give one's life to work in the ranks of campus ministry?

A reallocation and retraining of people in the ministry is necessary in the next few years. This can be done with one eye on institutional policy and the other eye on personal needs. Sizable numbers of "sick" and disoriented men are located in both parish and campus ministries— men who on the pattern-maintenance–priestly side have hidden from the world in certain doctrinal formulations, and on the governance side have lost any theological grounds for action, and are highly moralistic and manipulative of people for private career ambitions. They are incapable of being "team men"; yet the various types of actions we see as essential to the whole mission of the church cannot be performed by one man, but only by selected groups of professional ministries leading and activating the whole lay resources of the church. Foundations, churches, and universities should not encourage ministries of "private enterprise," but the enhancement of communities. They should assume responsibility to distinguish and discourage incompetent people who are not capable of, or interested in, doing tasks for communities which serve whole metropolitan areas and whole structures of education.

Some pastors should go into teaching and other fields on other incomes than that of the church, but remain, hopefully, in "ecumenical" orders of the church as laymen. (Arthur Brandenburg's "ecumenical community" is now this kind of mix of clergy and laity in New Haven, Connecticut.) The church, with its emerging theology of mission and its financial limitations, cannot support professional clergy who do not have competencies and functions that develop the capacities of the laity to do the work formally considered to be "the pastor's concern," such as inquiring into the religious-moral dimensions of technical areas of the university and of the society. Some of the ministers who are most pretentious in their ideology of service to the university and are the most persistent memorandum writers about radical change turn out, as we have seen in our clergy survey, to be suspicious—even hateful—of persons and as of now not capable of working in a community ministry. Such men often have little to give but the capacity to be "around where the action is," to bring people together and "trust in the dialogue," to parrot to the church a mishmash of jargons from the technical areas in which they were last "present."

The problem of leadership is not lack of people who claim to be servants of others or wish to improve the quality of higher education. The problem is the small number of those with competence to serve. The most able leaders in the church need more financial support, public recognition, and serious study than in the past. They are embarrassed and frustrated by the people in the ministry who need to be subjects of affection and care, who cannot be expected to tolerate ambiguity of faith or change of role and, hence, should not be charged with church leadership. There is a hard task of describing, so others can identify them, the people who perform no respected, needed function in the eyes of conscientious lay faculty administrators who know what viable programs, responsible counseling, and rigorous thinking look like. The provision in foundations or church for a little money for a great number of mediocre churchmen must be weighed against careful support of the very best professional leaders, in hopes of changing the public image of the church and the processes by which mediocre and mentally handicapped leadership is attracted to the clergy.

Denominational leaders should be encouraged in critical reappraisal of the use of their funds and selection of personnel so that they can serve in the long-range work of the United Ministries in Higher Education. In time, it seems likely, such an organization can provide experts for very private consultations, using the data now available on personality and role. Remember Dentler's report on metropolitan New York in Chapter 17: eighteen people trying to minister to a fifth of the student body of this country, half-time "Y" secretary the only professional Protestant leader for a third of the engineering students in this country. Such is the fate of men without policy leadership. What happens to men in situations like these? They play games, or they go to pieces. Why do dedicated, educated people not catch on that they have been had, that they do not work in strategic situations? What is there in the seminary education that will produce the kind of man who will work in such situations for years without effective protest to the people who put him there and administer without really knowing what they want done?

The churches now face in the younger generations membership

with considerably more knowledge of career alternatives, of the nature of policy, and of the disciplines that inform professional leadership. The administrator's most devastating action could be indifference to clergy who know they do not have adequate criteria for their own career evaluation and want effective aid in changing the clergy's working situation. The initiative for such reform must still come from the clergy itself who recognize that they, too, live in bureaucracies that have lost direction and are surviving on the strength of past decades.

Foundation Influence

17. Policy leads can be provided by carefully planned consultations and by conferences carried out by foundation staffs. Clusters of faculty, ministers, and public leaders must be found who see their own deepest concerns expressed through use of funds supervised by a foundation. Through convening of consultations and providing a "setting of persuasion," these people can get the implications of their work acted on by university, church, and other institutional leadership. Model programs and activities can be developed in a few key centers of higher education and national life. They will need to be chosen so that these components are present: strong seminaries and universities, strong ministries on campus and in the city, evidencing the power to co-operate functionally and to agree on some manageable priorities of social policy concern. The leadership of two or three men whom a foundation trusts and who wish to implement the Danforth Study is needed in these areas. The centers evaluate, report, and provide the fresh, continuing educational materials and leadership needed to train others.

A priority project for funding and administrative support by the Danforth Foundation, to be more concrete, might be the establishment of four or five metropolitan-wide organizations that provide the arrangements for leaders in the universities, churches, and public life to engage in evaluation of *past* church actions and to make imaginative judgments as to future corporate action. These would be for the church what RAND-type organizations are for business. They would not administer programs, but would bring together in ecumenical co-operation, the best leadership in the campus ministries, inner city and other clergy for the purpose of relating university thought and research to institutional policy and action. They would use faculty and students in speculative, exploratory, interdisciplinary ways that formal, traditional university organizations do not permit. Faculty would be involved not simply as specialists but as participants in provocative, probing, free-wheeling inquiry sufficiently different from the university, and expressive enough of church concerns in learning, to be challenging. The funds would come from a variety of sources, including universities, churches, and foundations. In some cases these would be outgrowths or elaborations of going operations; others would be newly fashioned.

18. The Protestant and Roman Catholic leaderships need to heighten their understanding of their stuations by more comparative studies and more sharing of literature on re-evaluation procedures being undertaken in each communion. An inquiry by Catholic educators in Boston revealed their overdependence on formal religious knowledge and instruction. They found that Protestant campus ministers were relying much more on the transmission of religious tradition by extracurricular activities and achieving less alienation of laymen from the clergy. The simplicism and overrationalism of manual- or catechetical-oriented teaching in Catholicism and Protestant fundamentalism was brought into sharp relief by our studies. Some Protestant existentialists and romantics also found the extreme revolt of many Catholic radicals against the institutional church and its structures of authority a sobering study of the consequences of their own position. The outcome of strategic reviews in Catholic schools has resulted in the disciplines of phiolosophy, theology, and ethics being taught less in the mode of apologetics and more in terms of inviting an inquiry by the lay student and faculty into the nature of the Christian ethos in the modern world. Also, less attention is being given to the immediately pragmatic career and vocational concerns of students and more attention to the implication of religious education for the whole style of personal and social life.

In comparing Catholic and Protestant practice in higher education, strategies colloquia came to support the development of high-quality theological and moral inquiry in centers near the best graduate study programs of public universities as a substitute for poor-quality church-sponsored graduate institutions in highly technical and expensive areas of education. Areas of church life never previously studied by Catholic faculty and clergy, such as policies for "senior citizens'" homes, raised new questions as to what the good life is like at various stages of one's life development and what encouragement the churches gave to the participation of older people in higher education. Elderly students are often worried about different issues than the undergraduate students;

they have questions unanswered as to the meaning of pain, as to what creative, enduring, healing forces their lives are linked to. These questions pervade and go beyond issues of community organization and violent protest to more ultimate questions which have always been central to the Scriptures.

19. The churches need considerable flexibility in their programs for higher education, while following broad strategic guidelines. The state colleges, for example, that have burgeoned in the past two decades are different in their grasp of religious policy alternatives from the more established public universities. The administrators are often timid, uneasy men when they approach church-state issues. They still think the courts and law experts in the area forbid teaching about religion, when in fact they encourage it. They know little about theological and pedagogical trends such as we have described. For such leaders, a concerted review of our findings will need to be undertaken by campus ministers.

20. The surveys of the clergy indicate widespread and growing polarization on many traditional theological and social issues among conservatives and liberals in the church. But there is also abundant evidence that on the new frontiers of religious thought and ministerial action, a solid basis of ecumenical belief is emerging for strategies such as we are recommending. No denominational executive can any longer claim that he opposes radical increases in funds for research, continuing education, or reorientation of discussions toward technical and professional issues freighted with public controversy, because clerical and lay support is present.

21. If the church is to be a significant part of university life, it will need to reconstitute the four fundamental historic modes as its witness, knowing that they have as much relevance to the life of education as they do to the church. (For example, we cannot understand the Berkeley rebellion except as an effort to restate pastoral care in education.) A theology of ministry which pulls together all the classic dimensions of pastoral care, priestliness, prophetic inquiry, and governance into a viable and workable organization is essential to the ministry today.

A Theology of Hope

Some final words can be said about the shape of that theology. It will have at the center of the meaning of each mode of ministry a message of Christian hope. Christian hope is the fulfillment of time at the end of time, some theologians tell us. Christian hope is in the action of God in each present moment of time, others tell us. Or Christian hope is in the acts of Christ in the past—now finished. The point that brings these emphases together is that God holds all time in His hands; hope in Him is not confined to one particular time. Yet there is a point of emphasis we would make. The temporal descriptions of Christian hope vary, but a direction of the movement remains; namely, the *towardness* of the hope. Christian hope, where it permeates a society, gives it an impetus toward the future and a confidence in it. After the Resurrection experience, for example, the morale of the early Christian community was that of an awakened people. Every historical event in a sense became eschatological and prophetic for them, opening the way for other events to come after, which would be unlike the great events of the past and yet a fulfillment of them.

The Christian ethos is determined as much by the compelling power of things to come as it is by memory of events of the past. For the God who has acted in fulfillment of His promises in the past acts now and in the future. Thus the Christian, if he enjoys the gift of hope, has the assistance, the patience, the readiness to leave the past for an unknown future, to surrender visible securities for the sake of "things not seen." For hope in the consummation of God's work in the world, toward a perfect Kingdom of God, is the object of the Christian's courage.

There is nothing quiescent in this style of life. Maximum boldness is called for in all public acts. The Christian has been informed of the whole purpose of God from "the foundation of the world" and to the "end of time." He should have the confidence and assurance to seek a pattern to events and to impart a sense of direction to his colleagues. If he is a policy maker, he is not simply to concede to the various appeals of groups around him, but to express his own view of national purpose with all the clarity at his command. The object of hope is salvation, and salvation is nothing less than full and unceasing participation in the destiny of God's people. A mark of this participation is not the fragmenting of life into a whole series of repetitive and separate decisions, but the relating of one's acts to some significant purpose and direction.

The man who looks upon the world as a scene of hope knows that the events of the future will not be simply what he wants. They will judge him and promise even more judgment to come. The civil war in

Vietnam, the rise of black and student power—these are events of the past few years which few Americans could have predicted. They are painful events for us to face, for they represented in part the failure of American social policies and in part the unfolding of forces beyond our control or knowledge. But insofar as we see them hopefully as meaningful judgments upon us, they became the occasion for our reconsideration of our public acts.

Once historical events became the source of judgment, and their uniqueness an occasion for review of assumptions which do not quite fit reality, time loses its monotony, its quality of uniform succession. History takes on excitement and hope; and events, mystery and depth. This is the context of a creative society. Men no longer just endure time; they have problems to solve, issues to win, causes to espouse.

The Christian deals not primarily with the many successive and competing hopes of public affairs, but with a single hope: the whole being and work of God as disclosed in Jesus Christ and made accessible to man in the Holy Spirit. This one hope encompasses the destiny of all men of whatever race or age, whether or not they are ignorant of this unique hope. He who is the ground of hope deals with the beginning and end of life and beyond. No hope that is contingent on specific political or social fortunes can claim this comprehensiveness or singularity. The Christian hope consequently stands in opposition to all politics which claim that man's hope is contingent on the victory of a particular party, people, or sequence of social change. It rejects all human claims to provide for the absolute, final, complete future of mankind.

It is thus apparent that the relation between the Christian's hope and his social acts will always be indirect. Christian hope can give no precise answers to any of the problems of social policy, but Christian hope does provide direction, understanding, and commitment in which concrete relationships are worked out.

The Christian does not have the resources within his faith alone to construct a view of social change, but he is able to press for a realism that embraces the fact of estrangement and exploitation in the world as well as the possibilities for the mitagation of social conflict through the just acts of men. Further, the Christian is able to cast doubt on the notion that Americans can ever meet their obligations in the world simply by reacting to Communist hopes. The Christian can urge the American people to re-examine the grounds of their own hopes for the world and to discover in an ultimate hope in God the certainty to act, to maneuver, to adapt to new situations, to run risks of their own.

Christian hope prospers in the midst of adversities and affliction; other hopes grow strong only in proportion to human resources and historical opportunities. How can we explain this fact? It can be explained only by the character of Christian hope as a gift of grace. God is not so niggardly as to give hope only to those who are winning wars; He does not dole it out according to men's merit or power. The gift of hope is available to those who will become His people.

APPENDIX

Iₙ the appendix of this volume are the three questionnaires prepared
for surveys of students and clergy. The first, devised by Parker Palmer
and his associates in the San Francisco Bay Area Colloquium, gives
much wider range and depth to the personal and group dimensions of
student life and to the questions of how students come to know what
they know than does the other student questionnaire. It has its own
unique and irreplaceable qualities about it and deserves, as do the
other instruments of study, use in its own right. We have not reproduced the whole questionnaire used in California, but only those
parts which are significantly different from the Wisconsin instrument
and not incorporated in it.

The second questionnaire on student perspectives was chiefly developed by Professors N. J. Demerath III and Kenneth Lutterman, of the
University of Wisconsin department of sociology, but it represents a
composite, complex instrument which grew up during debates over the
content of the Bay instrument and of the clergy survey questionnaire.

This third instrument was chiefly the product of Jeffrey Hadden and
the director of the study for use with clergy. It can be seen, then, that
these instruments all have an intellectual connection with one another,
but also reflect particular concerns of the scholars involved.

Each survey bore introductory statements explaining the sponsorship of the study, its scientific objectives, and the fact that all responses
would be anonymous. The point was made in each statement that the
instrument sought to place religious and ethical convictions within a

wider context of social, political, and educational issues, that it was intended to provide an opportunity for different positions on such issues to be given expression, and that it was not being prepared or interpreted under the auspices of a particular religious body, but by a group of scholars from a number of disciplines. The covering letters, since they carried those same themes, are not reproduced in the Appendix.

DANFORTH BAY AREA QUESTIONNAIRE
FOR STUDENTS

Almost all the questions can be answered by drawing a circle around one or more numbers in the left-hand margin of the questionnaire. Thus:

I am now: (circle one)

1. . . A student in high school
2. . . A student in college
3. . . A student in graduate or professional school

Please note that after each question there are instructions in parentheses. Sometimes you will be asked to circle only one response, sometimes "as many as apply"; and occasionally you will be asked to rank two or three items in a given order. Please follow these instructions closely, as they are very important for data processing.

A. 1. Which of the following best describes your current relations with your parental family? (circle one)

1. . . My family and I are very close.
2. . . My family and I are cordial.
3. . . My family and I continue to be in touch but there are no close ties.
4. . . My relations with my family are somewhat cool.
5. . . My family and I do not get along.
6. . . My family and I are hostile.
7. . . Does not apply—both parents dead.

2. While you were growing up, what was your and your parents' religious affiliation? (circle one in each column)

	Mother	Father	Self
Baptist	1	1	1
Congregational	2	2	2

Episcopal	3	3	3
Jewish	4	4	4
Lutheran	5	5	5
Methodist	6	6	6
Presbyterian	7	7	7
Roman Catholic	8	8	8
None	9	9	9
Other	0	0	0

If "Other," please specify:

Father _____

Mother _____

Self _____

3. How frequently did you and your parents attend church or synagogue while you were growing up? (circle one in each column)

	Mother	Father	Self
Frequently	1	1	1
Occasionally	2	2	2
Seldom	3	3	3
Never	4	4	4

4. While you were growing up, did your parents insist that you attend religious instruction (e.g., Sunday School)? (circle one)

1. . . Yes

2. . . No

5. Which of the following best characterizes your parents' attitude toward *your* religious beliefs as a child? (circle one)

1. . . My parents insisted that I believe as they did.

2. . . My parents insisted that I expose myself to religious beliefs but never attempted to dictate what I should believe.

3. . . My parents were indifferent to what I believed.

4. . . My parents wanted to discourage me from holding religious beliefs.

5. . . Other (Please specify: _____).

6. Which of the following best characterizes the nature of your parents' religious beliefs during your childhood? (circle one)

    1. .. My parents held certain religious beliefs which they were convinced were the only true ones.

    2. .. My parents held religious beliefs which they were convinced were true but felt that there might be other true beliefs as well.

    3. .. My parents held religious beliefs not because they were so convinced of their truth but because to do so was the accepted thing.

    4. .. My parents had nothing I could call "religious beliefs."

7. At present I would say that I: (circle one)

    1. .. Wholly reject the religious tradition in which I was reared.

    2. .. Partially agree with it but have important reservations.

    3. .. Am in substantial agreement with that position.

    4. .. Was not reared in a "religious tradition."

8. When you were living at home, what was the *most frequent* topic of conversation at mealtime? (circle one)

    1. .. The events of that day in the family's life.

    2. .. Current affairs (e.g., the newspaper stories that day).

    3. .. The occupation of the head of the household.

    4. .. The children's schoolwork.

    5. .. Intellectual topics.

    6. .. Religion.

    7. .. We had very little conversation.

    8. .. Other (Please specify: _____).

9. When you, as a child, would ask your parents questions which were important to you, how did they generally handle them? (circle one)

    1. .. They "brushed me off."

    2. .. They would talk to me but they did not take the questions very seriously.

    3. .. They would talk to me and they took the questions very seriously.

    4. .. I don't recall.

10. Do you feel that your parents understand and appreciate your current academic and vocational interests? (circle one)

    1. .. Definitely yes.

    2. .. Probably yes.

    3. .. Probably not.

    4. .. Definitely not.

11. How well acquainted are (were) you with your grandparents; i.e., how well do you feel you know (knew) them as people? (circle one)

    1. .. Very well.

    2. .. Fairly well.

    3. .. Not too well.

    4. .. Not well at all.

12. Do you feel that you have a strong sense of "family heritage"? (circle one)

    1. .. Definitely so.

    2. .. Somewhat so.

    3. .. Definitely not.

13. What are the current political affiliations of your parents and yourself? (circle one in each column)

	Mother	Father	Self
Republican	1	1	1
Democrat	2	2	2
Independent	3	3	3
Other	4	4	4

If "Other," please specify:

Father _____

Mother _____

Self _____

14. How do your opinions on issues of racial relations compare with your parents' opinions? My parents' opinions are: (circle one)

    1. .. More liberal than mine.

    2. .. About the same as mine.

    3. .. More conservative than mine.

    4. .. One parent more liberal; the other more conservative.

B. 1. Have you taken courses at college which you felt were especially influential in your life? If so, please indicate the names of these courses and the departments in which they were offered in the spaces provided below. If there is no such course in your experience, please check here. _____

1st most influential _____

2nd most influential _____

3rd most influential _____

2. What were the *two* most important ways these courses influenced you? (circle two)

   1. . . By opening up new vocational opportunities.
   2. . . By giving me new knowledge.
   3. . . By teaching me to think and use my mind.
   4. . . By bringing me into contact with an important professor.
   5. . . By challenging my basic values.
   6. . . By offering me new values.
   7. . . By bringing me into contact with interesting students.
   8. . . By tapping some hidden abilities of mine.
   9. . . Other (Please specify: _____).

3. There seem to be some professors whose lives and personalities become totally identified with their subject matter. Do you know a professor like this at your college of whom it might be said, "He embodies his field"? (circle one)

   1. . . Yes, I know several.
   2. . . Yes, I know one.
   3. . . No, I don't know any.

4. If you answered "Yes" to the question above, please indicate the field(s) in which this man (these men) teaches. _____

   _____

5. If there have been professors who have been particularly influential in your life, what would you say were their *two* most important characteristics? (Please give a "1" to the most important and a "2" to the second most important.)

   _____1. . . Mastery of their subject matter.
   _____2. . . Warm, personal approach to students.
   _____3. . . Academic eminence in their fields.
   _____4. . . Excellence in lecturing.
   _____5. . . Sensitivity to human values.

_____6. . . . Good sense of humor.

_____7. . . . Ability to make ideas come alive.

_____8. . . . Profound religious or philosophical convictions.

_____9. . . . Personal enthusiasm about their subject matter.

_____0. . . . Other (Please specify: _____).

6. Whether or not you know a professor at your college who possesses them, what do you think are the two most important qualities of a good professor?

1st most important _____

2nd most important _____

7. Is there any particular person on the faculty of your college whom you think of as a model to emulate in your career? (circle one)

1. . . Yes, a particular younger faculty member.

2. . . Yes, a particular senior faculty member.

3. . . No particular person but a composite of two or more.

4. . . No.

8. About what proportion of the faculty members in (1) the college as a whole and (2) your major department would you say are really interested in students and their problems? (circle one in each column)

	College as a Whole	Your Major Dept.
Almost all	1	1
Over half	2	2
About half	3	3
Less than half	4	4
Very few	5	5
None	6	6

9. When you had a particularly troublesome problem, which of the following people would you generally approach first? (circle one)

1. . . A student friend at my college.

2. . . A student friend at another college.

3. . . A faculty member.

4. ... Dean of Students (Dean of Men, Dean of Women).
5. ... One or both parents.
6. ... Counselor (Counseling Center).
7. ... A minister, priest, or rabbi.
8. ... A psychiatrist.
9. ... No one.
0. ... Other (Please specify: _____).

10. Is there any faculty member at your college to whom you have felt particularly responsible and who you believe feels particularly responsible to you? (circle one)

1. ... Yes, there is one.
2. ... Yes, there are several.
3. ... No, there isn't any.

11. Has any professor in your college experience ever singled you out for special academic work or asked you to help him on something in his academic line? (circle one)

1. ... Yes, this has happened several times.
2. ... Yes, this has happened once.
3. ... No, this has never happened.

12. How do you feel about your intellectual capacity and potential in comparison with that of your professors? (circle one)

1. ... I am inferior to most of my professors in this respect.
2. ... I am about on a level with most of my professors in this respect.
3. ... I am superior to most of my professors in this respect.

13. How do most of your professors regard you in terms of intellectual capacity and potential? (circle one)

1. ... They regard me as an intellectual equal.
2. ... They regard me as intellectually inferior to them.
3. ... I don't know.

14. How do you feel about your intellectual capacity and potential in comparison with that of your fellow students? (circle one)

1. ... I am inferior to most of my fellow students in this respect.
2. ... I am about on a level with most of my fellow students in this respect.
3. ... I am superior to most of my fellow students in this respect.

C. 1. Aside from the formal groups above is there an informal group of friends at your college with whom you spend a fair amount of time? (circle one)

1. .. Yes, there is one such group.
2. .. Yes, there are several such groups.
3. .. No.

If Yes, which *three* of the following are the most important characteristics of that group? (circle three)

1. .. We are all in the same major field.
2. .. We have common vocational interests.
3. .. We participate in social life together.
4. .. We share similar intellectual concerns.
5. .. We share similar religious commitments.
6. .. We trust each other.
7. .. We have diverse points of view and enjoy arguing them.
8. .. We share similar extracurricular interests.
9. .. We are all from the same area of the country.
0. .. We are all the same year in school.
X... We have a deep interest in each other's lives.
Y... Other (Please specify: —————————————).

2. Of all the groups you are involved in, formal and informal, which *one* would you call "most important" to you?

Name and/or description of group: —————————

———————————————————————

———————————————————————

3. Thinking again of that group which you would call "most important" to you—why does it occupy that status in your life? Please rank the three most important reasons in the list below, giving a "1" to the most important reason, a "2" to the second most important, and a "3" to the third most important.

_____1. .. Because it gives me an opportunity to be with interesting people.
_____2. .. Because it enables me to get training in certain important skills.
_____3. .. Because it gives me support in facing problems.
_____4. .. Because it furthers my education.

_____5. . . . Because in it I can be myself.

_____6. . . . Because it gives me an opportunity to meet important people.

_____7. . . . Because it is a group with great prestige.

_____8. . . . Because it is one of the few places I've found to make friends.

_____9. . . . Because it gives me a feeling of belonging.

_____0. . . . Because it gives me an opportunity to do the kind of thing I hope to do in my vocation.

_____X. . . Because it gives me an opportunity to express my basic concerns in life.

_____Y. . . Other reasons (Please specify: _____).

4. "This group has its own personality, something over and above the individual members of it." Does this statement express the way you feel about any of the following groups? (circle as many as apply)

1. . . Your college or university.

2. . . Your immediate family.

3. . . Your church or religion.

4. . . Your nationality.

5. . . A group of friends you go around with.

6. . . Your fraternity or sorority.

7. . . Your team(s).

8. . . Your club(s).

9. . . Your anticipated profession.

0. . . Other (Please specify: _____).

X. . . None.

5. Are there groups of students on campus who seem very interested in movements in modern art, literature, etc.? (circle one)

1. . . Yes.

2. . . No.

IF YES: How do you feel about the students in these groups? (circle one)

3. . . I am one of them.

4. . . I am sympathetic toward them.

5. . . I am indifferent toward them.

6. . . I feel negatively toward them.

7. . . I don't know anything about them.

6. Are there groups of students on campus who seem very interested in movement for political or social change? (circle one)

   1. . . Yes.

   2. . . No.

IF YES: How do you feel about the students in these groups? (circle one)

   3. . . I am one of them.

   4. . . I am sympathetic toward them.

   5. . . I am indifferent toward them.

   6. . . I feel negatively toward them.

   7. . . I don't know anything about them.

7. Are there groups of students on campus who seem very interested in religion? (circle one)

   1. . . Yes.

   2. . . No.

IF YES: How do you feel about the students in these groups? (circle one)

   3. . . I am one of them.

   4. . . I am sympathetic toward them.

   5. . . I am indifferent toward them.

   6. . . I feel negatively toward them.

   7. . . I don't know anything about them.

8. Which of the following best characterizes you in relation to the rest of the student body at your college? (circle one)

   1. . . I share most of the characteristics of the typical student there.

   2. . . I am not typical of students there.

9. What is your present feeling about your college or university? (circle one)

   1. . . I have a very strong attachment to it.

   2. . . I like it, but my feelings are not strong.

   3. . . I don't feel much about it one way or another.

   4. . . I don't like it, but my feelings are not strong.

   5. . . I thoroughly dislike it.

10. College students have different ideas about the main purposes of a college education. Some of these ideas are listed below. As

you read this list, please rank the two goals most important to you by writing a "1" next to the most important and a "2" next to the second most important.

_____1. . . Provide vocational training; develop skills and techniques directly applicable to your career.

_____2. . . Develop your ability to get along with different kinds of people.

_____3. . . Provide a basic general education and appreciation of ideas.

_____4. . . Develop your knowledge of and interest in community and world problems.

_____5. . . Prepare you to serve your immediate community.

_____6. . . Prepare you to serve mankind.

_____7. . . Help develop your moral capacities, ethical standards and values.

_____8. . . Prepare you for a happy marriage and family life.

_____9. . . Advance learning and stimulate the production of new knowledge.

_____0. . . Other (Please specify: _____).

11. Which of the goals of college education in the list above would you say is most important to the faculty and administration at your college? Enter the number of that goal (numbered above) in the following space: _____

D. 1. Listed below are a number of areas for which college might prepare a person. For each area please indicate how well you feel your college has prepared you. (circle one in each row)

	Very Well	Fairly Well	Not Too Well	Not Well
Family life	1	1	1	1
Use of leisure time	2	2	2	2
Personal relations	3	3	3	3
Use of your mind	4	4	4	4
Vocational aims	5	5	5	5
Moral issues	6	6	6	6
Civic affairs	7	7	7	7
Earning a living	8	8	8	8

2. Which would you say is more important to you: ideas or people?
   1. ... Ideas are much more important to me than people.
   2. ... Ideas are somewhat more important to me than people.
   3. ... Ideas and people are equally important to me.
   4. ... People are somewhat more important to me than ideas.
   5. ... People are much more important to me than ideas.

3. Which of these statements comes closer to your own view?
   (circle one)
   1. ... Students should be given very great freedom in choosing their subjects of study and in choosing their own areas of interest within those subjects.
   2. ... There is a body of knowledge to be learned, and the faculty is more competent than the student to direct the student's course of study, through required courses, prerequisites, and the like.

4. Which of these statements comes closer to your own views?
   (circle one)
   1. ... A college education should be aimed at transmitting the knowledge which men have developed over the years.
   2. ... A college education should be aimed at preparing students to become producers of new knowledge.

5. Suppose you were studying for a very important exam to be given the next day, and a friend came into your room with an urgent personal problem. If it looked as though you would have to spend the rest of your waking hours until the exam helping your friend, what would you *prefer* to do and what would you be *most likely* to do? (circle one in each column)

	Prefer to do	Likely to do
a. Would definitely continue studying and be unable to help the friend	1	1
b. Would probably continue studying and be unable to help the friend	2	2
c. Would probably stop studying and help the friend	3	3
d. Would definitely stop studying and help the friend	4	4

6. How difficult would this decision be for you? (circle one)

1. ... Very difficult.
2. ... Somewhat difficult.
3. ... Not too difficult.
4. ... Not difficult at all.

E. 1. Listed below are three occupations and a number of characteristics which might apply to any occupation. For each occupation, circle whatever characteristics you think apply to it. (circle as many as apply in each column)

	Business-man	Pro-fessor	Clergy-man
Intense competition	1	1	1
Plenty of leisure time	2	2	2
Complete freedom of expression	3	3	3
High social status	4	4	4
Great creative opportunities	5	5	5
Social usefulness	6	6	6
Good relations with co-workers	7	7	7
Freedom from supervision	8	8	8
A secure future	9	9	9
Lack of high-pressure work	0	0	0

2. Which three of the following characteristics would be most important to you in picking a job or career? Place a "1" in front of the most important, a "2" in front of the second most important, and a "3" in front of the third most important.

_____1. ... Making an above-average living.

_____2. ... Opportunities to be original and creative.

_____3. ... Opportunities to be helpful to others or useful to society.

_____4. ... Avoiding a high-pressure job which takes too much out of you.

_____5. ... Living and working in the world of ideas.

_____6. . . Freedom from supervision in my work.

_____7. . . Opportunities for moderate but steady progress rather than the chance of extreme success or failure.

_____8. . . A chance to exercise leadership.

_____9. . . Opportunity to work with people rather than things.

_____0. . . Opportunities to advance an ideal or cause.

_____X. . . Other (Please specify: _____).

3. Which three things or activities do you expect to give you the most satisfaction in your life? Please mark your 1st, 2nd, and 3rd choices as in the question above.

_____1. . . Career or occupation.

_____2. . . Family relationships.

_____3. . . Leisure-time recreational activities.

_____4. . . Religious beliefs or activities.

_____5. . . Participation as a citizen in the affairs of your community.

_____6. . . Participation in activities directed toward national or international betterment.

_____7. . . Literature, art, or music.

_____8. . . Meaningful friendships.

_____9. . . Other (Please specify: _____).

F. 1. Listed below are a number of statements dealing with personal beliefs, attitudes, and experiences. In the space to the left of each statement, we would like you to indicate whether you *agree, disagree,* or are *uncertain* about the statement AND whether you find the content or subject of the statement *very important* or *not too important* to you. We ask you to use these unusual response categories because we believe that a person may agree with two statements but find the content of one much more important than the content of the other. Thus, you may agree that "the moon is not made of blue cheese" and that "murder is not good for mankind." But you will probably find the content of the former statement much less important than the content of the latter. Therefore, we are asking you to mark each of the following statements with the appropriate number from the following list of response categories:

1. I *agree* with this, and it is *very important* to me.
2. I *agree* with this but it is *not very important* to me.
3. I am *uncertain* about this, but it is *very important* to me.
4. I am *uncertain* about this, but it is *not very important* to me.
5. I *disagree* with this, and it is *very important* to me.
6. I *disagree* with this, but it is *not very important* to me.

The following statement, for which the response categories above are to be used, begins with number "7" for tabulation purposes only.

7____There are many important things which will probably never be understood by the human mind.

8____If a man is to accomplish his mission in life, it is sometimes necessary to risk everything.

9____It is often necessary to pursue your own goals even if someone else gets hurt.

10____If you really take the trouble to be scientific, it is not so difficult to make perfectly rational decisions about your future.

11____No difficulty will hold us back if we have enough will power.

12____Personal survival is generally less important than the survival of the group.

13____Although a college degree is required to *get* a good job today, the education behind the degree is not usually necessary to *do* the work involved.

14____I never accept anything which my mind cannot understand.

15____Life becomes most meaningful only when a person is grasped by an ideal or a cause.

16____I have certain aspirations which I regard as so important that I would not give them up for anything.

17____I see life as a series of problems for which there are rational solutions.

18____The businessman and the manufacturer are more important to society than the artist.

19____There are certain groups in my life without which I could not get along.

20____Attending classes is often a waste of time.

21____While children may have a "sense of mystery" about life, this is totally inappropriate for an adult.

22____I am unwilling to be "swept off my feet" by anything, because that kind of experience is generally so irrational.

23____Everything people do is rooted basically in self-interest.

24____The universe is essentially impersonal.

25____While the use of force is wrong, by and large, it is sometimes the only possible way to advance an ideal, and we should accept it as such.

26____Anything we do for a cause which will benefit others is justified.

27____The person who lacks a college education is not adequately prepared for living a broad, well-rounded life.

28____Men are involved with powers greater than themselves.

29____A work of art should have a definite message.

30____It's only natural that a person should take advantage of every opportunity to promote his own welfare.

31____There is but one sure road to truth—the road of patient, co-operative inquiry, operating by means of observation, experiment, and controlled reflection.

32____You can't blame people for taking all they can get.

33____As a rule, the interests of the group should take precedence over the interests of the individual.

34____The requirements in most college courses do not really contribute to the intellectual development of the student.

35____With his proven ability to control the forces of nature, man is potentially the greatest power in the universe.

36____I enjoy just contemplating questions which have no answer.

37____The main thing in life is to do something important on your own.

38____There is no power in the universe which man theoretically cannot someday control.

39____There are truths which no one but a poet can express adequately.

40___Important as social groups are, they are really valuable only if they serve some higher purpose.

41___In my college, cheating is the only way the average student can be sure of success.

42___There is nothing in the world beyond the natural order.

43___I am deeply moved by great music.

44___If I had to choose between friendly relations with other people and personal greatness, I'd choose greatness.

45___The world is our "oyster" if only we will develop the skill to open it.

46___It's who you know rather than what you know that's important in getting ahead.

47___I am involved in at least one group for which I would give up a great deal.

48___In college, the person who follows the rules is run over by those who don't.

49___There is something about life to which man can respond only with awe and wonder.

50___Sometimes we should do things even though they have no pay-off for us.

51___A person should be prepared to give up his personal goals for the sake of an ideal.

52___There is nothing which science cannot eventually comprehend.

53___The true joy in life is being used for a purpose recognized by yourself as a mighty one.

54___A group which tolerates too much difference of opinion between its members cannot last for long.

55___The kind of knowledge acquired in most college classes is of doubtful value outside the college doors.

56___I am often struck by my own powerlessness in the face of life.

57___Faith is a poor substitute for assurance and knowledge.

58___Anyone can succeed by his own hard work.

59___Science is capable of disproving religion, even though people may go on believing in it.

60____The thought of being at the mercy of forces beyond
my control is intolerable to me.

61____I would never be able to give myself completely to any
social group.

62____Making good grades is useless if one does not also learn
to win friends and influence people.

The University of Wisconsin Survey Instrument on

UNIVERSITY & SOCIETY: STUDENT PERSPECTIVES

I. Of course, one of our major interests is to get your reaction to college itself. This section contains several questions on the subject. But first, since we are asking students in several different schools to help us, what college or university are you currently enrolled in?

1. _____
   (write in name of college or university)

2. Now, if you were perfectly free to choose (i.e. if there were no financial considerations and no family pressures) which one of the following would you most prefer to do? (Circle one)

   1. Stay at my present school and follow my present plan of studies
   2. Stay at my present school but change my plan of studies
   3. Transfer to another school
   4. Drop out of school temporarily
   5. Drop out of school permanently
   6. Other (Please specify) _____

2a. If you would like to transfer to another school, which of the following would you be primarily looking for in the new school? (Use a "1" for the most important consideration and a "2" for the second.)

   ____1. A larger school than my present one
   ____2. A smaller school than my present one
   ____3. A school in an urban setting
   ____4. A school in a rural or small town setting
   ____5. A church-related school
   ____6. A private school without religious ties

_____7. A public university

_____8. A school that is stronger academically

_____9. Other (Please specify) _____

3. College life obviously has a number of different aspects. Some of these are listed below. For each of them, please indicate (1) how important an aspect it is to you, and (2) how happy you are with this particular aspect at your college or university. (Circle)

	Very Impor- tant	Fairly Impor- tant	Not Too Impor- tant
Extracurricular Activities	1	2	3
Social Life	1	2	3
Campus Cultural Oppor- tunities	1	2	3
Political Debate & Activity on Social Issues	1	2	3
Vocational Training	1	2	3
Contact with Faculty	1	2	3
Religious Vitality	1	2	3
Classroom Vitality	1	2	3

	Very Happy	Fairly Happy	Not Too Happy
Extracurricular Activities	1	2	3
Social Life	1	2	3
Campus Cultural Oppor- tunities	1	2	3
Political Debate & Activity on Social Issues	1	2	3
Vocational Training	1	2	3
Contact with Faculty	1	2	3
Religious Vitality	1	2	3
Classroom Vitality	1	2	3

4. What is your major field of study (or anticipated major)? (Circle one)

11. English

12. Language Area (e.g. French, Russian, Chinese)

13. Philosophy and Ethics	35. Mathematics
14. History	41. Engineering
15. Classics	42. Commerce or Business
21. Sociology	43. Education
22. Psychology	44. Journalism
23. Geography	45. Nursing
24. Political Science	46. Social Work
25. Economics	51. Agriculture Economics
26. Religion, Theology	52. Rural Sociology
31. Biology, Zoology	53. Home Economics
32. Geology	54. Agriculture
33. Chemistry	60. Other (Please specify)
34. Physics	_____

5. College students have different ideas about the main purpose of a college education. As you read the list below, rank the two goals most important to you by putting a "1" next to the most important and a "2" next to the second most important.

_____ 1. Develop skills and techniques which are directly applicable to my intended career

_____ 2. Advance learning and stimulate the discovery of new knowledge through research

_____ 3. Develop my ability to get along with different kinds of people

_____ 4. Obtain a degree so that I may qualify for the kinds of jobs I am considering

_____ 5. Provide a basic general education and appreciation of ideas

_____ 6. Help develop the meanings and values for my life

_____ 7. Prepare myself to serve others and remedy major social problems

_____ 8. Prepare me to act responsibly in family, business and political relations

_____ 9. Other (Please specify) _____

5a. List the number of the goal above which you think is most important: to the faculty? _____ (Number)

5b. To the administration? _____ (Number)

6. Which of the following characteristics do you feel are most

important in distinguishing a good professor from one that is mediocre or poor? (Place a "1" by the most important; a "2" by the second most important)

_____1. Extensive research experience and competence in the subject

_____2. A greater interest in raising questions than in providing answers

_____3. Deep sensitivity to human needs and values

_____4. Willingness to give special help to individual students

_____5. Good sense of humor in his teaching

_____6. Ability to relate theory to action

_____7. Willingness to admit his own lack of knowledge and errors

6a. Which one of the above do you feel to be the *least* important?

_____

7. Have you ever had a professor who made a particularly strong impression upon you and who earned your respect? (Circle one)

   1. Yes, several
   2. Yes, one
   3. No, none in particular
   4. No, I don't really respect any of my professors

8. About what proportion of the professors from whom you have taken courses are really interested in students and their problems?

   1. All
   2. A very high proportion
   3. More than half
   4. About half
   5. Less than half
   6. Very few
   7. None

9. Increasing numbers of students are being taught by graduate students serving as quiz instructors. Which of the following has been your experience here:

   1. I have had no experience with quiz instructors and cannot evaluate them first-hand.

2. I have had many quiz instructors and found them generally good as teachers.

3. I have had a few quiz instructors and found them generally good as teachers.

4. I have had many quiz instructors and found them generally poor as teachers.

5. I have had a few quiz instructors and found them generally poor as teachers.

10. What is your current college living arrangement? (Circle one)
   1. College dormitory
   2. Private residence hall
   3. Fraternity or sorority
   4. Cooperative rooming house
   5. Single apartment
   6. Apartment with roommates
   7. Apartment or house with spouse
   8. At home with parents
   9. Other (Please specify) _____

11. What was your approximate over-all grade average during your last complete semester? (Circle one)
   1. A
   2. A—
   3. B+
   4. B
   5. B—
   6. C+
   7. C
   8. C—
   9. D+ or below

12. Now we are interested in your participation in campus activities, if any. For each of the activities below, circle the appropriate column to the right.

	Not Involved	A Partici-pant	Highly Involved
1. Music or dramatic group ..1		2	3
2. Fraternity or sorority 1		2	3
3. Civil rights action group 1		2	3

4. Partisan political group	1	2	3
5. Student government	1	2	3
6. Religious group	1	2	3
7. Club connected with an academic subject	1	2	3
8. Hobby club	1	2	3
9. Athletic organization	1	2	3
0. Other (Please specify)	_____		

12a. Which one of the above is it most important for you to participate in? _____ (Number)

12b. Which one of these groups do you feel most at home in? _____ (Number)

Following is a series of brief statements about higher education. For each statement, please indicate your opinion by circling the appropriate number, ranging from 1 (strongly agree) to 6 (strongly disagree) with 3 indicating tentative agreement and 4 indicating tentative disagreement.

	Strongly Agree					Strongly Disagree
13. The person who lacks a college education is not adequately prepared for living a full, well-rounded life 1		2	3	4	5	6
14. I am often reluctant to speak out in class for fear of appearing foolish 1		2	3	4	5	6
15. The intellectual issues of the university have little bearing on matters of religious faith 1		2	3	4	5	6
16. Research competence is more important to good teaching than a personal interest in students 1		2	3	4	5	6
17. Given the pressures of college life today, I can understand and condone some kinds of cheating 1		2	3	4	5	6

18. I prefer to keep my distance
from professors 1 2 3 4 5 6

19. The kind of knowledge
acquired in most college
classes is of doubtful value
outside the college doors 1 2 3 4 5 6

20. Significant learning may take
place even if the professor
does not know or relate to the
student as an individual 1 2 3 4 5 6

21. I think of myself as an
"intellectual" 1 2 3 4 5 6

22. Courses and research in
theology and religion should
be available in public colleges
and universities 1 2 3 4 5 6

23. It is proper to seek knowledge
for knowledge's sake and not
merely for the improvement
of human and public affairs 1 2 3 4 5 6

24. College professors are usually
hostile to religious faith 1 2 3 4 5 6

25. Many scientific disciplines are
gaining exactitude at the
expense of what is relevant
and human 1 2 3 4 5 6

26. College education does more
to break down values than to
build up ideals 1 2 3 4 5 6

27. If I felt strongly about a
cause, I would be willing to
participate in a public
demonstration 1 2 3 4 5 6

28. Research is just as important
as teaching in the life of the
university 1 2 3 4 5 6

29. Theology should be taught as
a formal discipline within
the university 1 2 3 4 5 6

30. I have found my study in scientific disciplines to be as personal and creative as study in humanities and the arts 1 2 3 4 5 6

31. My college courses provide almost no discussion or controversy over basic values or commitments in life 1 2 3 4 5 6

32. There exist plenty of channels of communication between the students and the administration, if only people would use them 1 2 3 4 5 6

33. My professors seem very concerned about political issues and social problems 1 2 3 4 5 6

34. Students sometimes state that education at their schools has become "depersonalized." How depersonalized would you say education at your school is? (Circle one)
    1. Very
    2. Fairly
    3. Not too
    4. Not at all

34a. If you believe education at your school has undergone some degree of depersonalization, which two of the following are most characteristic of that fact? Put a "1" by the most important and a "2" by the next most important.

_____1. Faculty have little time for students

_____2. Professors don't put themselves into their teaching

_____3. Academic work seems to have little to do with real life

_____4. There is too much competition between students

_____5. The pressures of college life leave too little time for personal life

_____6. The school is run like a machine

_____7. Other (Please specify) _____

II. Now we would like to learn something about your background, your future plans and your views on other kinds of issues.

35. First, what is your sex? (Circle)
    1. Male
    2. Female

36. How old are you? _____

37. What year are you in school? (Circle)
    1. Freshman
    2. Sophomore
    3. Junior
    4. Senior
    5. First-year graduate student
    6. Second-year graduate student
    7. Third-year graduate student or beyond

38. What is your race? (Circle)
    1. Negro
    2. White
    3. Oriental
    4. Other (Please specify) _____

39. Are you a citizen of:
    1. U.S.
    2. Other (Please specify) _____

40. What is your current marital status? (Circle one)
    1. Single
    2. Single but going steady
    3. Engaged
    4. Married without children
    5. Married with children
    6. Divorced or separated
    7. Widowed

41. In what kind of community did you live for the longest time while growing up? (Circle one)
    1. Rural farm, village
    2. Small town (under 10,000)
    3. Medium-sized town (10,000 to 50,000)

4. Small city (50,000 to 100,000)
5. Medium-sized city (100,000 to 500,000)
6. Large city (over 500,000)
7. Suburb of a large city

42. What is your anticipated occupation? (Please give what you expect to be your long-run career. If you are a woman, indicate "housewife" only if you do not expect to work full-time until you have children). Please specify as closely as possible in the spaces allotted. _____

_____

_____

_____

43. Which of the following statements best characterizes your choice of occupation? (Circle one)
   1. This occupation is my first choice and there are no others that I would really consider.
   2. While this would not be my first choice, my real preference requires a kind of talent and capacity that I don't really have.
   3. While this would not be my first choice, my real preference requires more money for training than is available to me.
   4. While this would not be my first choice, my real preference would require too much work and time away from my family; it would not be worth it to me.
   5. I really don't have any clear preferences and my current plans are quite tentative and subject to change.

44. Which of the following do you expect will provide you with the greatest satisfaction in life? Pick two, placing a "1" next to the most satisfying and a "2" by the next most satisfying.
   _____1. Artistic and intellectual activities
   _____2. Sports and hobbies
   _____3. Family relationships
   _____4. Occupational career
   _____5. Political activities
   _____6. Relation to God or ultimate reality
   _____7. Civic activities and community associations
   _____8. Friends

_____9. Worship and church involvement

_____0. Other (Please specify) _____

44a. Of all the ones above, which do you expect to provide you the least satisfaction? _____ (Number)

45. What is (or was) your father's principal occupation? (Circle one)

1. Manager, official or proprietor of large business
2. Professional
3. Manager, official or proprietor of small business
4. Government civil service employee
5. Farm owner or farm manager
6. Craftsman, technical worker or foreman
7. Sales worker
8. Clerical worker
9. Unskilled laborer

46. Does your mother have a job or career (even part-time) outside the home?

1. Yes
2. No
3. Did, now retired or deceased

47. Indicate the highest educational attainment of both your father and your mother. (Circle one)

	Mother	Father
1. Grade school	_____1.	_____1.
2. Some high school	_____2.	_____2.
3. High school graduate	_____3.	_____3.
4. Some college	_____4.	_____4.
5. College graduate	_____5.	_____5.
6. Graduate or professional education ..	_____6.	_____6.

48. Which of the following best represents the total yearly income of your parents? (Circle one)

1. Less than $4,000
2. 4,000 to 5,999
3. 6,000 to 7,999
4. 8,000 to 9,999
5. 10,000 to 14,999

6. 15,000 to 25,000
7. Over 25,000

49. Are both your parents currently living and together? (Circle one)

   1. Yes, both living and together
   2. No, parents separated or divorced
   3. Mother dead
   4. Father dead
   5. Both parents dead
   6. Other (Specify) _____

50. Which of the following best describes your current relations with your parents? (Circle one)

   1. Does not apply—both parents dead
   2. My parents and I are very close to each other
   3. My parents and I are cordial
   4. My parents and I continue to be in touch but there are no close ties
   5. My parents and I do not get along
   6. My parents and I are hostile

51. Which of the following political positions best describes yourself and your parents? (Circle one for each person)

	Self	Mother	Father
1. Socialist 1		1	1
2. Liberal Democrat 2		2	2
3. Conservative Democrat 3		3	3
4. Independent—leaning toward Democrat 4		4	4
5. Independent—leaning toward Republican 5		5	5
6. Liberal Republican 6		6	6
7. Conservative Republican 7		7	7
8. John Birch Society supporter ... 8		8	8
9. Other (Please specify) _____ 9		9	9

52. How much have your earlier political beliefs changed since you entered college or in the last few years? (Circle one)

1. My views have changed a great deal in a more liberal direction
2. My views have changed somewhat in a more liberal direction
3. My views have remained about the same
4. My views have changed somewhat in a more conservative direction
5. My views have changed a great deal in a more conservative direction

Now we would like your reaction to a number of political, social and philosophical issues. As before, please place yourself on the scale from 1 (strongly agree) to 6 (strongly disagree).

	Strongly Agree					Strongly Disagree
53. People should do what is morally right regardless of the consequences	1	2	3	4	5	6
54. I believe there is at least a 50-50 chance of a nuclear war in the next ten years	1	2	3	4	5	6
55. In all human relations, men are involved in the control and manipulation of others, no matter how permissive they claim to be	1	2	3	4	5	6
56. I believe that a larger proportion of the Federal Government's budget should be allocated to poverty, medical care, education, etc.	1	2	3	4	5	6
57. I personally feel a need to believe in some sort of religious faith or philosophy	1	2	3	4	5	6
58. The businessman and the manufacturer are more important to society than the artist and the scholar	1	2	3	4	5	6

59. The United States should try
to initiate negotiations in an
area like Vietnam and should
avoid further military partici-
pation 1 2 3 4 5 6

60. The thought of being at the
mercy of uncontrollable forces
is intolerable to me 1 2 3 4 5 6

61. Negroes would be better off
if they would take advantage
of the opportunities that have
been made available rather
than spending so much time
protesting 1 2 3 4 5 6

62. Although never a totally satisfactory answer to family problems, divorce is sometimes the
best solution 1 2 3 4 5 6

63. Federal funds should be provided to parochial schools on
the same basis as to public
schools 1 2 3 4 5 6

64. In view of past discrimination,
Negroes should now be given
jobs ahead of Whites 1 2 3 4 5 6

65. You can't blame people for
taking all they can get 1 2 3 4 5 6

66. Science and technology have
enriched rather than debased
human life 1 2 3 4 5 6

67. Our major institutions are too
rigidly bureaucratic and depersonalized to be significantly
changed by actions from
within them 1 2 3 4 5 6

68. I favor having our government
continue to give economic aid to
other countries such as India ...1 2 3 4 5 6

69. My interest in religion has increased since I have been in college or in the last few years . . 1 2 3 4 5 6

70. I am in basic sympathy with northern students who have gone to the South to work for civil rights 1 2 3 4 5 6

71. The most rewarding thing a woman can do is be a totally dedicated mother and wife 1 2 3 4 5 6

72. Science is capable of disproving religion even though many people may go on believing in it 1 2 3 4 5 6

73. American culture is sick and moving along the road to destruction 1 2 3 4 5 6

74. There is one group in my life whose survival is more important than my survival as an individual 1 2 3 4 5 6

75. There is no power in the universe which man, theoretically, cannot some day control 1 2 3 4 5 6

76. Bible reading and prayer for all students do not belong in public schools 1 2 3 4 5 6

77. There are situations which morally justify one's having sexual relations with someone other than one's own wife or husband 1 2 3 4 5 6

78. Faith is a poor substitute for assurance and knowledge 1 2 3 4 5 6

79. There is one group in my life without which I could not get along 1 2 3 4 5 6

80. Our society should be more understanding and less punitive in dealing with homosexual activity 1 2 3 4 5 6

81. It's who you know rather than what you know that's important in getting ahead 1 2 3 4 5 6

82. It is wrong for two people who are in love and totally committed to each other to have sexual relations without marriage 1 2 3 4 5 6

83. With his proven ability to control the forces of nature, man is potentially the greatest power in the universe 1 2 3 4 5 6

84. A person's ethical concern and activity are the crucial measures of his religiousness and therefore even a strict atheist may be more religious than a devout church goer 1 2 3 4 5 6

85. The racial crisis in the U.S. should be resolved on a local level without the intervention of the Federal government 1 2 3 4 5 6

86. There is nothing which science cannot eventually comprehend ..1 2 3 4 5 6

87. A married couple who feel they have as many children as they want are not doing anything wrong when they use birth control techniques such as the pill, the diaphragm, etc. 1 2 3 4 5 6

88. I believe there is a definite plan or purpose which is working out in the world 1 2 3 4 5 6

89. An ethical or moral decision
    which may be right in one situ-
    ation may be wrong in another
    situation 1   2   3   4   5   6

90. To what degree do you feel religious faith has been an influ-
    ence in your life, in the lives of your mother and your father?
    (Circle one for each)

	Self	Mother	Father
1. No influence	1	1	1
2. Slight influence	2	2	2
3. Some influence	3	3	3
4. Quite influential	4	4	4
5. Great influence	5	5	5

91. How has the influence of religious faith in your life changed
    since you entered college or in the last few years? (Circle
    one)

    1. Increased greatly
    2. Increased some
    3. No change
    4. Decreased some
    5. Decreased greatly

92. What about your church or synagogue attendance? How often
    did you attend services while growing up and how often do
    you attend now? (Circle one for each)

	While Growing Up	Now
1. Once a week or more	1	1
2. Two or three times a month	2	2
3. About once a month	3	3
4. Several times a year	4	4
5. Hardly ever	5	5
6. Never	6	6

93. Were you confirmed or did you celebrate Bar Mitzva (or
    equivalent)?

    1. Confirmed
    2. Bar Mitzva
    3. Neither

94. What, if any, is your religious affiliation and that of your parents? (Circle one)

	Self	Mother	Father
01. No affiliation 01		01	01
11. Roman Catholic 11		11	11
21. Reform Judaism 21		21	21
22. Conservative Judaism ...22		22	22
23. Orthodox Judaism 23		23	23
31. Baptist-Northern (American Baptist Convention) 31		31	31
32. Baptist-Southern Baptist .32		32	32
33. Disciples of Christ 33		33	33
34. Methodist 34		34	34
35. Evangelical and Reformed 35		35	35
36. Lutheran-Missouri, Wisconsin Synod 36		36	36
37. Lutheran-United, American 37		37	37
41. Episcopalian 41		41	41
42. Presbyterian 42		42	42
43. United Church of Christ 43		43	43
44. Congregational 44		44	44
51. Unitarian-Universalist ...51		51	51
52. Ethical Culture Movement 52		52	52
60. Other (Please specify) ..60		60	60

94a. IF PROTESTANT DENOMINATION, would you regard yourself as a: (Circle one)

1. Fundamentalist
2. Conservative
3. Neo-orthodox
4. Liberal
5. These categories are not clear to me.

95. Which one of the following statements comes closest to expressing what you now believe about God or ultimate reality? Which would have come closest when you were about 13 years old? (Circle one in each of the two age columns)

	Now	Age 13
1. I have faith in God as a person who is concerned about me and all mankind and to whom I am accountable	1	1
2. I don't believe in God as a person, but I do believe in a higher power or being of some kind	2	2
3. Ultimate reality for me is love for other human beings but I do not believe in God or a higher power or being	3	3
4. Ultimate reality is represented for me in the natural and physical laws which man is able to discover	4	4
5. I have many values and trust many beings, but no one is superior to or pervades all others	5	5
6. I don't know whether there is a God or ultimate reality, and I don't believe there is any way to find out	6	6
7. I don't believe there is a God or any ultimate reality	7	7
8. Other (Please specify) _____	8	8

96. How certain are you about the belief or views which you indicated in the previous question about God or ultimate reality? (Circle one)

1. I have no doubts about this faith or belief
2. I sometimes have doubts
3. I often have doubts
4. I find that I believe this some of the time but not at other times

97. People have had various views of the essential or basic nature

of man. Do you think that man is essentially or basically: (Circle one)

1. Good
2. Evil
3. Neither essentially good nor evil, but depends on social factors

98. Sin is an old concept in the Judeo-Christian tradition, but we would like to know how the concept is understood today. Which one of the following statements *comes closest* to *your* understanding of what sin is? (Circle one)

1. Not obeying the 10 Commandments
2. Violation of the social norms or mores
3. The wrong or misuse of good things and relationships
4. The absence of justice and concern for others in human relationships
5. Inability to recognize the wrong I have done others, to seek restitution and ask forgiveness
6. Alienation or separation from God
7. None of these

99. How important is the idea or reality of sin in your life?

1. The idea of sin means very little to me
2. I accept the idea of sin, but do not really think about it very much
3. The idea of sin is rather important to me
4. The concept of sin is central to my own self-understanding

III. Listed below are a number of varied experiences which some peo-have reported having. Please indicate whether you have ever had these experiences since becoming an adult, and how sure you are that you have had them. (Circle the appropriate number for each item)

	Yes, I'm sure I have	Yes, I think I have	No
1. A sense of sharing in a great purpose or historic destiny	1	2	3
2. A sense of joy and exhilaration over human life	1	2	3

3. A feeling that you were some-
how in the presence of God ...   1   2   3
4. A feeling of deep identification
with the suffering of others   1   2   3
5. A basic reorientation of your life   1   2   3
6. A feeling of being afraid of God   1   2   3
7. A sense of being saved in Christ   1   2   3

8. Which of the following comes closest to your view of what the church should devote its greatest attention? (Circle one)

1. Witness for God and save souls
2. Deal with problems such as unwed mothers, juvenile delinquency and crime
3. Provide religious education and a place of worship and fellowship for its members
4. Help people to act more responsibly with such problems as civil rights, nuclear war, poverty
5. Reconciling people to one another and estabishing the conditions for new life in this world

9. Which of the following would best characterize your views of the relation between Christianity and our society? (Circle one)

1. The two are so bound up together that we really have a Christian society
2. We don't really have a Christian society, but we should work to achieve one
3. We don't really have a Christian society but this is not an important consideration
4. We have a society which people refer to as Christian but they should not do so
5. Christianity is counter to our society and should be opposed in its efforts to gain influence

10. Please list the names of the four New Testament Gospels:

1. _____   3. _____
2. _____   4. _____

IV. Now we would like your reaction to a number of specific statements about religion, religious doctrine and religious institutions.

Here as before we have provided a six-point scale ranging from strongly agree to strongly disagree. If a statement is obscure to you, try to answer it as best you can. If there is no way to express your view exactly, remember that even an approximation is important to us since we are studying students generally and not one or two single individuals.

	Strongly Agree				Strongly Disagree
11. Organized religion is irrelevant today when it tries to deal with political and economic problems in religious terms 1	2	3	4	5	6
12. I believe in a divine judgment after death where some shall be rewarded and others punished 1	2	3	4	5	6
13. I believe in the demonic or evil as a personal power in the world 1	2	3	4	5	6
14. Religion provides important criteria for helping us decide how we should act 1	2	3	4	5	6
15. A person cannot be a Christian and believe in the evolution of mankind 1	2	3	4	5	6
16. Ambiguity and uncertainty as to what one is to believe and do are signs of faithlessness to God 1	2	3	4	5	6
17. The church is holy and not to be equated with other human institutions 1	2	3	4	5	6
18. For me salvation refers more to the possibility of living a fully human life, rather than to a life after death 1	2	3	4	5	6
19. Regardless of one's own beliefs, he should expose his children to Christian doctrine ..1	2	3	4	5	6

20. The separation of life and
things into the sacred and
the secular is a false dichotomy . . 1   2   3   4   5   6

21. I often find myself in agreement with religious doctrine
but opposed to the policies
of churches and ministers 1   2   3   4   5   6

22. Jesus was God's only Son, sent
into the world by God to
redeem me and all mankind . . . 1   2   3   4   5   6

23. Religion hampers man's
development by making him
dependent on a higher power . . 1   2   3   4   5   6

24. Atheists should not try to
convince others of their
beliefs or to seek changes
in society which reflect
their interests 1   2   3   4   5   6

25. I expect to live after death 1   2   3   4   5   6

26. I think that all who live a
good moral life are Christians . . 1   2   3   4   5   6

27. I would expect a thinking religious person to have doubts
about the existence of God 1   2   3   4   5   6

28. I think of religion primarily
as a set of beliefs or
doctrines which one
either accepts or rejects 1   2   3   4   5   6

29. The discipline and training
of the mind is more important
for becoming a minister than
the experience of a definite
inner call 1   2   3   4   5   6

30. The way to be justified
before God is to try
sincerely to live a good life 1   2   3   4   5   6

31. We will see and recognize our
families some time after death . . 1   2   3   4   5   6

32. Only in Christianity is the
one true God revealed
and confessed 1   2   3   4   5   6
33. Adam and Eve were two
historical persons 1   2   3   4   5   6
34. The only way I can think of
Hell is the experience of self-
estrangement, guilt and
meaningless in this life 1   2   3   4   5   6
35. Private prayer or meditation
is an important activity
in my daily life 1   2   3   4   5   6
36. Reading the Bible is an
important and frequent
activity for me 1   2   3   4   5   6
37. Men cannot fulfill them-
selves in the world without
believing in God 1   2   3   4   5   6
38. Christian theology has overemphasized the evil of man and
has neglected the goodness of
the world—including man 1   2   3   4   5   6
39. It is impossible for a person
to be genuinely religious and
rich in material possessions 1   2   3   4   5   6
40. The extension of human
powers to know and control
natural and social forces in
the world are expressive of
God's purpose in history 1   2   3   4   5   6
41. Christ vicariously atoned
for our sins by his death
and resurrection 1   2   3   4   5   6
42. I often feel guilty for things
I do or fail to do 1   2   3   4   5   6

Now that you have gone through the items, we would like you to
think of them in another way. In any list this size, some of your
positions (whether in agreement or disagreement with a state-

ment) will seem more important to your own beliefs than others. For example, you may strongly agree with an item on intellectual grounds and yet this position may not be the one that you feel often or that informs your everyday activity. Hence:

43. WHICH OF THE FOLLOWING BEST REPRESENTS YOUR REACTION TO THE BELIEFS YOU HAVE INDI-CATED? (Questions 11–42)

   1. I feel that all of the positions I took are central and urgent in my life.
   2. I feel that some of the positions I took are central and urgent in my life but not others.
   3. I feel that none of the positions I took are really central or urgent to my life, though my religious beliefs are ade-quately represented there.
   4. I feel that the list of items completely bypassed my beliefs.

(IF YOUR ANSWER TO THE ABOVE WAS #2, THEN PLEASE GO BACK AND CIRCLE THE NUMBERS TO THE LEFT OF THE ITEMS THAT ARE PARTICULARLY URGENT TO YOU.)

44. Now that we have dwelt upon your specific beliefs, we would like to get your feeling about values in general. Which of the following statements best expresses your view? (Circle one)

   1. There are fundamental value principles in human life which are not man-made and which exist whether man ac-knowledges them or not.
   2. Values are totally man-made; they have no objective existence of their own.
   3. I am uncertain about the objective status of values.

V. Now we would like to get your judgments concerning religion on your campus. Campus religion—the lack of it, the revival of it—has been much debated. Again, we need information to substitute for speculation. Remember that this is all anonymous. Take heart since the end of the questionnaire is fast approaching.

45. First, regardless of whether you think that campus religious faith has increased or decreased, we would like your impres-sion of a number of factors that have been related to it. For

each factor, indicate whether you think it has influenced students strongly toward religious faith, moderately toward, has no effect, moderately away from religious faith, or strongly away from. (Circle one for each letter)

		Strongly Toward Religious Faith		No Effect		Strongly Away From Religious Faith
A.	Exposure to science and scientific method	1	2	3	4	5
B.	Student relation to parents and home community	1	2	3	4	5
C.	Campus clergymen	1	2	3	4	5
D.	Knowledge of other religions and other cultures	1	2	3	4	5
E.	Faculty's general orientation toward religion	1	2	3	4	5
F.	Demands of course work and other career decisions	1	2	3	4	5
G.	Attempts by secular scholars and writers to interpret the world	1	2	3	4	5
H.	Theological debate, its vitality and relevance or lack of them	1	2	3	4	5
I.	Religious views of students in general and the student "culture"	1	2	3	4	5
J.	Religious symbols and worship services available	1	2	3	4	5

46. Again regardless of whether you think religious faith has increased or decreased, which one of the following best represents your view concerning the consequences of a loss of faith? (Circle one)

1. It is desirable for a student to lose his religious faith permanently since it is an obstacle to intellectual maturity.
2. It is not terribly important one way or the other since religious faith is not a crucial factor in life.
3. It is desirable for a student to lose his faith so that he may develop a more mature faith for adulthood.
4. Loss of faith is entailed in religious life—the "death of gods" leads to more adequate religious views.
5. Loss of faith is serious since the student is losing the prime way of coping with life in meaningful terms.
6. It is crucial if a student loses his faith since he is jeopardizing his own salvation.

47. Conformity on this campus is more likely to involve: (Circle one)

1. Declaring oneself religious
2. Declaring oneself unconcerned about religion
3. Declaring oneself irreligious

48. Below are several groups of student attributes. From each group, circle the one which you think most likely to characterize the students who participate in religious activities. (Circle one from each set)

A. 1. Good student
   2. Poor student
   3. No difference
B. 1. Parents of high social status
   2. Parents of low social status
   3. No difference
C. 1. Interested in sports
   2. Not interested in sports
   3. No difference
D. 1. Fraternity or sorority member
   2. Not a member of fraternity or sorority
   3. No difference

E. 1. Politically active on national issues
   2. Politically inactive
   3. No difference
F. 1. Concerned with music, the arts, and theatre
   2. Not concerned
   3. No difference
G. 1. Active in campus affairs and other organizations
   2. Inactive in campus affairs and other organizations
   3. No difference
H. 1. Has a lot of friends on campus
   2. Has few friends on campus
   3. No difference
I. 1. Is an "intellectual"
   2. Is not an "intellectual"
   3. No difference

49. How much knowledge would you say you have about campus religious groups, their programs or activities? (Circle one)
    1. A great deal of knowledge about several groups
    2. A great deal of knowledge about one group in particular
    3. Some knowledge of several groups
    4. Some knowledge of one group in particular
    5. No real knowledge about any group's program

50. Think now of your five closest friends on this campus. How many are active in a campus religious activity? (Circle one)
    1. Five   4. Two
    2. Four   5. One
    3. Three   6. None

51. Would you have any qualms about marrying a person who considered himself (herself) to be an atheist? (Circle one)
    1. Yes   2. No

52. Would you have any qualms about marrying a person who was devoutly religious and clamed that his (her) relation to God was the most crucial aspect of life? (Circle one)
    1. Yes   2. No

53. Which one of the following best describes you own contact with campus religious groups or campus clergymen? (Circle one)

1. I have had no contact at all with any religious group while on campus.
2. I have received notification of meetings and activities but have never attended.
3. I have not participated in any campus activity, but I do participate in a non-campus community church.
4. I have not participated in any campus activity, but I have had personal contact with a campus clergyman.
5. I have attended one or more meetings or activities but have never actually joined a campus religious group.
6. I am a member of a group but not really involved in it.
7. I am a member of a group and am moderately involved in it.
8. I am a member of a group and am highly involved in it.
9. I was a member of a group at one time, but I no longer participate.

THE NEXT (AND LAST) SECTION IS ONLY FOR THOSE WHO HAVE ANSWERED THE ABOVE QUESTION WITH RESPONSES 4, 5, 6, 7, 8, OR 9. ALL OTHERS SKIP TO THE LAST PAGE FOR MAILING INSTRUCTIONS.

54. First, which religious group and/or campus clergymen have you had the most contact with?

|—————————————————

What is the denominational affiliation of the group and clergyman you have had the most contact with? (Circle one)

01. No formal affiliation
11. Roman Catholic
21. Reform Judaism
22. Conservative Judaism
23. Orthodox Judaism
31. Baptist—Northern, American Baptist Convention
32. Southern Baptist
33. Disciples of Christ
34. Methodist
35. Evangelical and Reformed
36. Lutheran—Missouri, Wisconsin Synod
37. Lutheran—United, American
41. Episcopalian

42. Presbyterian
43. United Church of Christ
44. Congregational
51. Unitarian-Universalist
52. Ethical Culture
61. Inter-Varsity Christian Fellowship
71. YMCA-YWCA
90. Other (Please specify) ──────────────

55. Does the campus group or religious center that you have had the most contact with have:

A. An elected group of local student officers? (Circle one)
   1. Yes, but I have not been one.
   2. Yes, and I have been one.
   3. No.

B. A formal schedule of worship services? (Circle one)
   1. Yes, and I participate rather regularly.
   2. Yes, but I do not participate regularly.
   3. No.

C. Seminars or courses led by a campus religious leader? (Circle one)
   1. Yes, and I have been a member of one or more.
   2. Yes, but I have not been a member of any.
   3. No.

D. Informal student discussion groups which meet regularly? (Circle one)
   1. Yes, and I have participated in one or more.
   2. Yes, but I have not participated.
   3. No.

E. Social hours, teas, parties, etc.? (Circle one)
   1. Yes, and I have attended rather frequently.
   2. Yes, but I have not attended often.
   3. No.

F. Groups that work with the mentally ill or mentally retarded, or the aged? (Circle one)
   1. Yes, and I have participated in one or more.

    2. Yes, but I have not participated.

    3. No.

G. Ecumenical meetings, courses or retreats? (Circle one)

    1. Yes, I have participated in one or more.

    2. Yes, but I have not participated.

    3. No.

H. Social action programs, i.e. civil rights, poverty, foreign policy? (Circle one)

    1. Yes, I have participated in one or more.

    2. Yes, but I have not participated.

    3. No.

56. About how many hours per week do you spend with this group or at its meeting places? (Circle one)

1. Reside there	6. Five to ten hours
2. Thirty hours or more	7. Two to five hours
3. Twenty to thirty hours	8. Less than two hours,
4. Fifteen to twenty hours	worship services only
5. Ten to fifteen hours	9. No time recently

57. How close do you feel to the religious leader of your group? If there are several, pick the one you know best. (Circle one)

    1. I feel very close to the campus clergyman

    2. I feel somewhat close

    3. I really don't know him well

    4. I tend to avoid him

    5. I actually feel hostile towards him

58. Have you ever had a personal conference with a campus clergyman about matters of religious faith generally or about religious faith and course work? (Circle one)

1. Yes, many times	3. Yes, once
2. Yes, several times	4. No

59. Have you ever had a personal conference about a personal or moral problem (e.g. sex, cheating, vocational choice, your relation to your parents, etc.) (Circle one)

1. Yes, many times	3. Yes, once
2. Yes, several times	4. No

59a. If you have had any sort of personal conferences with a campus clergyman, how helpful do you think these conferences have been? (Circle one)
1. Very helpful
2. Somewhat helpful
3. Only slightly helpful
4. Not helpful at all
5. Actually made matters worse

Now we would like you to respond to a number of statements about religious activities or campus ministers and students. Again, indicate your views on the six-point scale ranging from 1 (strongly agree) to 6 (strongly disagree).

	Strongly Agree					Strongly Disagree
60. One activity I would like to see emphasized is religiously sponsored "coffee houses" where students of all views can have informal bull sessions	1	2	3	4	5	6
61. My campus religious group is very receptive to change and experimentation	1	2	3	4	5	6
62. Many of the students in my group are active for primarily social reasons	1	2	3	4	5	6
63. My campus clergyman encourages students to use their intellectual training to criticize and reform the church	1	2	3	4	5	6
64. The campus minister should seek to bring his students a program as nearly as possible like that of the students' home church	1	2	3	4	5	6
65. There are strong inhibitions in my group about expressing religious doubt	1	2	3	4	5	6

66. Faculty members need a better understanding of theology and this should be one of the principal concerns of campus ministers 1   2   3   4   5   6

67. It is important for the minister and students in a campus religious group to reach close agreement on religious issues ..1   2   3   4   5   6

68. I would like to be able to participate in a campus religious community in which students live and eat in order to promote more intensive discussion 1   2   3   4   5   6

69. The students in my group have many different religious beliefs 1   2   3   4   5   6

70. My campus minister enourages our participation in civil rights activities and/or political movements 1   2   3   4   5   6

71. A major purpose of campus religious groups ought to be to keep students from being swept off their feet by forces of secularization in the university 1   2   3   4   5   6

72. Campus ministers spend too much time keeping student religious organizations going on a state and national level ...1   2   3   4   5   6

73. Campus religious groups would be better if they included more of the political activists among students (e.g. civil rights workers) 1   2   3   4   5   6

74. Campus ministers are usually the most outstanding men in the clergy 1   2   3   4   5   6

75. My campus minister is very
    strict in his interpretation of
    theology and religious doctrine . . 1   2   3   4   5   6
76. Many campus ministers are
    too radical in their political
    and social views 1   2   3   4   5   6
77. The students in my campus
    religious group have very little
    interest in theological issues . . .1   2   3   4   5   6

78. Now how important are the following factors to your involvement in religious activities on campus. Pick the two most important reasons, putting a "1" by the first most important and a "2" by the next most important.

     _____ 1. Parental pressure

     _____ 2. The personal magnetism of campus clergyman

     _____ 3. A particular program sponsored by the group

     _____ 4. Chance to relate classroom ideas to personal and social issues

     _____ 5. Close ties with other student members

     _____ 6. The intellectual challenge of the new theology

     _____ 7. Need for counsel in a period of religious doubt and confusion

     _____ 8. Desire to continue my religious contacts with my denomination

     _____ 9. My need for some meaningful group involvement in a large university

     _____ 0. Other (Please specify) _____

79. Finally, consider the following in terms of a) the degree to which they are the official or *expressed* goals of your campus religious group; b) the degree to which they seem to be the *actual goals* even though they may be unexpressed; and c) the degree to which you *personally prefer them as goals*. In column a) below, indicate the goal *that is most expressed* with a "1," and the goal that is next most expressed with a "2." In column b), indicate the goal *that is actually most prevalent* with a "1" and the goal that is second-most prevalent with a "2." In column c) indicate the goal *that you personally would most prefer* with a "1" and your second choice with a "2".

	a) Group's Expressed Goals	b) Group's Actual Goals	c) My Preferred Goals
1. Giving the student a home away from home ..	___	___	___
2. Helping the student to attain salvation in God ..	___	___	___
3. Furthering ecumenical contact between different religious groups	___	___	___
4. Encouraging the student to bring his academic specialty to bear upon the church and his religious activity	___	___	___
5. Providing individual counseling for the student's personal problems, religious and non-religious	___	___	___
6. Maintaining and enriching the student's ties to his particular denomination	___	___	___
7. Exploring and ameliorating major social problems (e.g. poverty, civil rights, foreign policy issues)	___	___	___
8. Furthering contact between students, faculty, administrators, public leaders, and professionals for more responsible action in all areas	___	___	___

9. Aiding the student in his education, even at

the expense of religious
orthodoxy . . . . ____   ____   ____

0. Trying to bring religion
to the non-religious and
combat the pervasive
secularism of the college
campus . . . . ____   ____   ____

Today's date is ————————————————, 196__.

This completes the questionnaire. You may feel the winner (or the loser) in an endurance contest. But we are grateful to you for staying with it and answering all the questions.

Note that a stamped addressed envelope accompanies the questionnaire. Simply insert the questionnaire in the envelope and mail it as soon as possible, or follow the directions given you for returning it.

Thank you again for your cooperation. If you have any over-all comments, either attach them here or take a while and send them at your leisure. BUT PLEASE RETURN THE QUESTIONNAIRE ITSELF IMMEDIATELY.

SURVEY OF PROTESTANT CLERGY: RELIGIOUS BELIEFS, VALUES, AND SOCIAL ATTITUDES

Sponsored by the Danforth Study of Campus Ministries

INSTRUCTIONS

1. Most of the items in this questionnaire are attitude, belief, or evaluative statements to which you are asked to agree or disagree. For each item we ask you to indicate the position on a six-point scale that most nearly represents your own view by circling the appropriate number. If you *strongly* disagree or agree with a statement, you should respond by circling 1 or 6 respectively. Rankings of 2 and 5 mean that you disagree or agree with the statement, but you do not feel as strongly about these statements as those you circled 1 and 6. Rankings of 3 and 4 are almost neutral, but 3 means you *probably* do not agree with the statement and 4 means you *probably* do agree with the statement.
2. We emphasize that these middle positions are almost neutral. They should be used for those statements which you do not think are very relevant or important for you, and for those statements on which you are not sure how you stand. In the latter case, we ask you not to ponder over the statement, but to give your immediate reaction. There are likely to be several such items, and if you stop to ponder each, the time it will take to complete the questionnaire is likely to become excessive. This, in turn, decreases the chances that we will get a completed questionnaire from you.
3. *Please answer all questions.* If you wish to modify or explain an answer, make a note to that effect in the margin next to the ques-

tion, but still mark the answer that comes closest to being your answer.

4. We invite your comments on the questionnaire in general or to specific questions. Individual reaction to the questionnaire constitutes an important aspect of our analysis, we ask that you complete the questionnaire and return it at your earliest convenience. In order to proceed with our analysis on schedule, we need your completed questionnaire now. We can make use of your comments even if they are not received for several months.

5. The small numbers in the margins and next to the answer categories have been placed there to increase the efficiency and reliability of electronic data processing. Just disregard them in answering questions.

6. While the length of this questionnaire is admittedly long, answering the questions actually goes very quickly. In our pretests of this instrument, some ministers were able to complete it in an hour. The average time, however, was about an hour and a half.

7. When you have completed the questionnaire, place it in the return envelope that has been provided. No postage is necessary. If you would like a copy of the questionnaire for your files, we will be pleased to send you one upon request.

PART 1. Religious Beliefs

The statements in this first section describe various views toward the nature of God, the way the Diety is known, and the relationship between faith and the contemporary world. For each statement please indicate the position which most nearly represents your own view by circling the appropriate number following the instructions on the inside cover.

	Definitely Disagree					Definitely Agree	01
1. What a man believes about God doesn't matter a great deal as long as he leads a life of concern for others.	1	2	3	4	5	6	1
2. The essence of religious truth is more personal than doctrinal.	1	2	3	4	5	6	2
3. Only in Christianity is the one true God revealed and confessed.	1	2	3	4	5	6	3
4. The Christian style of life is one of contentment with one's wordly possessions, forbearance toward others, and certainty of eternal life.	1	2	3	4	5	6	4
5. The Christian church can only be its true self as it exists for humanity.	1	2	3	4	5	6	5
6. Intercessory prayer has no efficacy, except for some possible influence on the petitioner himself.	1	2	3	4	5	6	6
7. I believe in a literal or nearly literal interpretation of the Bible.	1	2	3	4	5	6	7
8. I don't feel Jesus to be the Son of God any more than all men are children of God.	1	2	3	4	5	6	8
9. The most reliable way to judge whether a certain action is good or bad is to consider the consequences.	1	2	3	4	5	6	9
10. Nothing of real value can be accomplished without suffering.	1	2	3	4	5	6	10
11. Man by himself is incapable of anything but sin.	1	2	3	4	5	6	11
12. Ambiguity and uncertainty as to what one is to believe and do are signs of faithlessness and indifference to God.	1	2	3	4	5	6	12

	Definitely Disagree					Definitely Agree	
13. The church should be a place of refuge and of quiet reflection away from the world.	1	2	3	4	5	6	13
14. Hell does not refer to a special location after death, but to the experience of self-estrangement, guilt, and meaninglessness in this life.	1	2	3	4	5	6	14
15. I accept Jesus' *physical* resurrection as an objective historical fact in the same sense that Lincoln's physical death was a historical fact.	1	2	3	4	5	6	15
16. I have greater admiration for an honest agnostic seeking truth than a man who is certain that he has the complete truth.	1	2	3	4	5	6	16
17. My understanding of the central doctrines of the Christian faith has changed considerably during my ministry.	1	2	3	4	5	6	17
18. The primary mission of the church is to save sinners.	1	2	3	4	5	6	18
19. The mission of the church is to bring new awareness of the possibilities of life and to prepare people to serve the world.	1	2	3	4	5	6	19
20. The primary task of the church is to live the Christian life among its own membership and activities rather than to try and reform the world.	1	2	3	4	5	6	20
21. The church must speak to the great social issues of our day, or else its very existence is threatened.	1	2	3	4	5	6	21
22. My relationship to God is immediate and direct, having little to do with my feeling of identity with the church.	1	2	3	4	5	6	22
23. I would expect a thinking Christian to have doubts about the existence of God.	1	2	3	4	5	6	23
24. Following completely rigid moral rules may cause more harm than good.	1	2	3	4	5	6	24
25. There can be no love of God apart from compassion for one's fellow man.	1	2	3	4	5	6	25

26.	Christ's coming into the world represents for me a radical break from what men knew about God before his coming.	1	2	3	4	5	6
27.	There was a distinct occasion or period in my life when I made a definite decision to become vitally committed to God.	1	2	3	4	5	6
28.	Belief in God eases the pain of decision-making.	1	2	3	4	5	6
29.	God can only be talked about by analogy or in various pictures or imagery.	1	2	3	4	5	6
30.	For Christ to be really present in the sacraments, the Christian must believe that he is present.	1	2	3	4	5	6
31.	As one whose life is dedicated to serving the Lord and trained to do so, I often feel that my work is frustrated by too many overseers.	1	2	3	4	5	6
32.	For the Christian, the Bible has a primacy over all other sources of knowledge of God.	1	2	3	4	5	6
33.	Jesus was more concerned with others than with the truth of a belief.	1	2	3	4	5	6
34.	The Vatican Council appears to make possible a more ecumenical witness to the Gospel.	1	2	3	4	5	6
35.	I believe in a divine judgment after death where some shall be rewarded and others punished.	1	2	3	4	5	6
36.	The corporate body of the church, not the individual, should be charged with the responsibility to discern the nature of the call and the ordaining of a minister.	1	2	3	4	5	6
37.	A vivid or dramatic inner experience of a special call to the ministry should be the controlling factor in deciding whether a man possesses the requisite qualifications for ordination to the ministry.	1	2	3	4	5	6
38.	The discipline and training of the mind is more important than the experience of a dramatic inner call to the ministry.	1	2	3	4	5	6

	Definitely Disagree					Definitely Agree	
39. Private prayer is one of the most important and satisfying activities in my daily life.	1	2	3	4	5	6	39
40. We need greater emphasis on the joy and delight which comes from living in this world rather than on joy to be found after death.	1	2	3	4	5	6	40
41. Miracles happen more often than most people realize.	1	2	3	4	5	6	41
42. The church should be taking a much more active role in the struggle for world peace.	1	2	3	4	5	6	42
43. Norman Vincent Peale's positive thinking is the kind of religion quite often present in my own sermons.	1	2	3	4	5	6	43
44. Men can live creative lives in the world without believing in Jesus Christ and without despair or guilt over rejection of such belief.	1	2	3	4	5	6	44
45. I find it often very difficult to discern God's will and presence.	1	2	3	4	5	6	45
46. Scriptures are the inspired and inerrant Word of God not only in matters of faith but also in historical, geographical, and other secular matters.	1	2	3	4	5	6	46
47. An understanding of the language of myth and symbol are as important for interpreting biblical literature as history and archaeology.	1	2	3	4	5	6	47
48. The Old Testament is not really an essential part of the Christian Bible. ..	1	2	3	4	5	6	48
49. As described in Revelation, Christ and his saints will historically rule the earth during the millennium.	1	2	3	4	5	6	49
50. There should be a stricter observance of the Sabbath, the religious day of rest.	1	2	3	4	5	6	50
51. For the Christian, God is both revealed and hidden in the words and acts of Jesus.	1	2	3	4	5	6	51
52. I do not find the concept of the Trinity to be very meaningful.	1	2	3	4	5	6	52

53.	There is no longer any need for God as a working hypothesis in morals, politics, science, or religion, and in the name of intellectual honesty such working hypotheses should be dropped.	1	2	3	4	5	6	53
54.	I think of God more as a merciful helper and friend rather than as the powerful majestic King.	1	2	3	4	5	6	54
55.	Churches are often built for the glorification of the men who build them.	1	2	3	4	5	6	55
56.	Young people abandon religion because Christians fail to provide clear-cut positive answers to their doubts and moral confusions.	1	2	3	4	5	6	56
57.	The church is holy, and not to be equated with other human institutions. ..	1	2	3	4	5	6	57
58.	A noninstitutional Christianity is impossible.	1	2	3	4	5	6	58
59.	There is no special or divine significance associated with particular institutional forms and structures of the church.	1	2	3	4	5	6	59
60.	Everyone who is baptized is a member of the church, and no one else is. ..	1	2	3	4	5	6	60
61.	Religious institutions often show indifference to human suffering.	1	2	3	4	5	6	61
62.	Being a part of the community of forgiven sinners is as important a dimension of the Christian life as the assurance of my personal forgiveness.	1	2	3	4	5	6	62
63.	Organized religion is the one sure infallible foundation of life.	1	2	3	4	5	6	63
64.	I believe that the virgin birth of Jesus was a biological miracle.	1	2	3	4	5	6	64
65.	God always answers our prayers, although the answers may not always be those we desire.	1	2	3	4	5	6	65
66.	The central theological issue today is justification through grace by faith alone.	1	2	3	4	5	6	66
67.	The cross of Jesus Christ is the central act of God in history, for in that event Jesus vicariously atoned for man's sin.	1	2	3	4	5	6	67

		Definitely Disagree					Definitely Agree	
68.	I feel that Jesus was a great man and very holy, but I don't feel him to be the Son of God any more than all men are the children of God.	1	2	3	4	5	6	68
69.	The spiritual healing of Oral Roberts is a modern example of the supernatural presence of God in this world.	1	2	3	4	5	6	69
70.	I find it difficult to accept the doctrine of the *physical* resurrection of Christ.	1	2	3	4	5	6	70
								02
71.	People outside the church often respond more quickly to needs of people in the world than do church members.	1	2	3	4	5	6	1
72.	I am no longer certain of many of the doctrines I once thought were central to the Christian faith.	1	2	3	4	5	6	2
73.	Everyone should believe in and practice some religion.	1	2	3	4	5	6	3
74.	Christian theology has overemphasized the evil of man and has neglected the goodness of the created world—including man.	1	2	3	4	5	6	4
75.	Heaven and hell are not geographical places, but concern relationships with God both here and hereafter.	1	2	3	4	5	6	5
76.	There is no moral rule which can be applied in every situation.	1	2	3	4	5	6	6
77.	The church is often the place where many of us make our last-ditch stand against God.	1	2	3	4	5	6	7
78.	Billy Graham is one of the best interpreters and spokesmen for the Christian faith.	1	2	3	4	5	6	8
79.	I understand the Resurrection of Jesus as a symbol of God's sovereignty over both death and life.	1	2	3	4	5	6	9
80.	Adam and Eve were individual historical persons.	1	2	3	4	5	6	10

81. We must try to translate the language of biblical faith into meaningful contemporary symbols because biblical faith is not rigid doctrine.	1	2	3	4	5	6	11
82. I do not like to put intercessory petitions or prayers for the sick in my worship services.	1	2	3	4	5	6	12
83. Local ministers would be more effective if they had less supervision by regional and national denominational officials.	1	2	3	4	5	6	13
84. The meaning of the Incarnation is that God can be known in the relationships between men.	1	2	3	4	5	6	14
85. Christ is really present in the Eucharist of Holy Communion of the church.	1	2	3	4	5	6	15
86. Theology is the proper task not of individuals, but of the whole corporate body of the church—laity as well as clergy.	1	2	3	4	5	6	16
87. There is probably as much blasphemy in the pulpit on Sunday mornings as in taverns on Saturday nights.	1	2	3	4	5	6	17
88. Many loyal churchgoers are using religion as an escape from their responsibilities in the world.	1	2	3	4	5	6	18
89. I expect to live after death.	1	2	3	4	5	6	19
90. I believe in the demonic as a personal power in the world.	1	2	3	4	5	6	20
91. No Christian should claim that his official responsibilities, for example as a businessman nor politician, justify actions which he would not take as an individual.	1	2	3	4	5	6	21
92. People should do what is morally right without giving thought to the consequences.	1	2	3	4	5	6	22
93. Christianity helps people by reconciling them to death and suffering.	1	2	3	4	5	6	23
94. I find it increasingly difficult to believe in God.	1	2	3	4	5	6	24
95. The pastor has a special authority to transmit blessings and to forgive sins.	1	2	3	4	5	6	25

	Definitely Disagree				Definitely Agree		
96. Salvation in the Christian sense refers to the possibility of living a fully human life, rather than to a life after death.	1	2	3	4	5	6	26
97. Mystery is a quality I experience in the common things of life as much as the uncommon.	1	2	3	4	5	6	27
98. The faith of the Christian protects him from suffering, doubt, or fear that he might have to endure if he was not a Christian.	1	2	3	4	5	6	28
99. Whether Jesus was or was not born of a virgin is not very important to my religious beliefs.	1	2	3	4	5	6	29
100. An ethical decision which may be right in one situation may be wrong in another situation.	1	2	3	4	5	6	30
101. The Vatican Council represents the discovery—although somewhat late—of what Protestants have been saying all along.	1	2	3	4	5	6	31
102. Creeds and practices of churches are likely to be marks of irreligion as well as religion.	1	2	3	4	5	6	32
103. I don't think it is as important to worry about life after death as about what one can do in this life.	1	2	3	4	5	6	33
104. There is no Christian support for novelists and dramatists who see the world as absurd, idiotic, and sick.	1	2	3	4	5	6	34
105. Much of the traditional religious language (such as "Heavenly Father" or "Salvation") is not very meaningful to me.	1	2	3	4	5	6	35
106. I believe that the principal value of prayer is that it provides a psychological outlet for pent-up emotions.	1	2	3	4	5	6	36
107. Every area of man's life is corrupted by sin.	1	2	3	4	5	6	37
108. God's creation is continuous, and the world is still in the making.	1	2	3	4	5	6	38

109. I believe Christ was identified and recognized by his disciples after his death, but this does not necessitate a corporal appearance. 1 2 3 4 5 6   39

110. Christian ethics involves a faith in redemptive love in race and international relations, and is not to be equated with the proximate justice achieved through the compromising of vested interests. 1 2 3 4 5 6   40

111. Sin is primarily the infraction of God's law. 1 2 3 4 5 6   41

112. Our world is changing so fast that a person has to act in terms of circumstances confronting him rather than expecting absolute guidance from the past. 1 2 3 4 5 6   42

113. I consider legal restriction on business activity on the Sabbath to be desirable. 1 2 3 4 5 6   43

114. In worship I prefer to lead Christians in celebrating God's creation rather than in petition for forgiveness of their sins in a fallen world. 1 2 3 4 5 6   44

115. The amount of success or effectiveness a clergyman has in his church is generally proportionate to the amount of effort he expends. 1 2 3 4 5 6   45

Admittedly, there are difficulties associated with describing oneself in terms of broad theological positions. However, within the following categories, which of the following best describes your own theological positions at each point in your career?

	On Entering College	On Entering Seminary	On Leaving Seminary	Now
Fundamentalist	1	1	1	1
Conservative	2	2	2	2
Neo-orthodox	3	3	3	3
Liberal	4	4	4	4
Universalist-Unitarian	5	5	5	5
Other (Circle and Specify) ————	6	6	6	6

Following is a list of theologians. For each name please indicate (1) whether you have read one or more books by the person by placing a check mark in the box beside the name, and (2) the extent to which your own theological position agrees or disagrees with each person.

Have Read		Definitely Disagree			Not Familiar With			Definitely Agree	
☐	1. Karl Barth	1	2	3	4	5	6	7	50
☐	2. Louis Berkof	1	2	3	4	5	6	7	51
☐	3. Dietrich Bonhoeffer	1	2	3	4	5	6	7	52
☐	4. Edgar S. Brightman	1	2	3	4	5	6	7	53
☐	5. Emil Brunner	1	2	3	4	5	6	7	54
☐	6. Martin Buber	1	2	3	4	5	6	7	55
☐	7. Rudolf Bultmann	1	2	3	4	5	6	7	56
☐	8. Gerhard Ebeling	1	2	3	4	5	6	7	57
☐	9. Harry Emerson Fosdick	1	2	3	4	5	6	7	58
☐	10. Billy Graham	1	2	3	4	5	6	7	59
☐	11. Carl McIntire	1	2	3	4	5	6	7	60
☐	12. H. Richard Niebuhr	1	2	3	4	5	6	7	61
☐	13. Reinhold Niebuhr	1	2	3	4	5	6	7	62
☐	14. Warren H. Orcutt	1	2	3	4	5	6	7	63
☐	15. Norman Vincent Peale	1	2	3	4	5	6	7	64
☐	16. Francis Pieper	1	2	3	4	5	6	7	65
☐	17. John A. T. Robinson	1	2	3	4	5	6	7	66
☐	18. Joseph Sittler	1	2	3	4	5	6	7	67
☐	19. Paul Tillich	1	2	3	4	5	6	7	68
☐	20. Henry N. Wieman	1	2	3	4	5	6	7	69

PART II. Religion and Science

There is much concern today about the relation between science and religion. Below are a number of statements that reflect different orientations toward this problem. For each statement please circle the position that most nearly reflects your own view.

	Definitely Disagree					Definitely Agree	O3
1. Man's knowledge of God comes wholly and exclusively from God in special revelation.	1	2	3	4	5	6	1
2. Christianity and science are completely compatible if properly understood. ..	1	2	3	4	5	6	2
3. The Christian is confined to no single method of gaining knowledge, but can make use of a plurality of methods revelant to the judgment to be made or the question under study.	1	2	3	4	5	6	3
4. The scientist's understanding of evolution is an important clue to the way God creates in the world.	1	2	3	4	5	6	4
5. Science is the most positive expression of Christianity that the world has seen.	1	2	3	4	5	6	5
6. Christian theology ought to demand clarification of its premises and as rigorous a scrutiny of its methods as science.	1	2	3	4	5	6	6
7. I heartily approve of efforts of science to create life.	1	2	3	4	5	6	7
8. If the church is going to express God's love for man in the modern world, it will need to make use of specialized knowledge developed by scientists. ..	1	2	3	4	5	6	8
9. The impact of science demands that we carefully and critically re-examine every aspect of the Christian faith.	1	2	3	4	5	6	9
10. The supernatural power of God in the world is shown in those events for which there is no scientific explanation.	1	2	3	4	5	6	10

	Definitely Disagree				Definitely Agree		
11. Many of the doctrines of the church have little revelance to the modern world.	1	2	3	4	5	6	11
12. Theology alone can provide an adequate basis for moral judgment.	1	2	3	4	5	6	12
13. Science has made it possible for people to turn away from preoccupation with mere survival toward issues of intellectual attainment, friendship, and participation in civic life.	1	2	3	4	5	6	13
14. Various disciplines other than theological and biblical studies, such as sociology and psychology, may inform the Christian as to the nature of God's action in the world.	1	2	3	4	5	6	14
15. Science is a faith feeding false hopes to men.	1	2	3	4	5	6	15
16. Religiously significant knowledge cannot be understood by a social scientist who is not by personal conviction or method a convinced Christian.	1	2	3	4	5	6	16
17. Many scientific disciplines of the university are gaining exactitude at the expense of what is relevant and human.	1	2	3	4	5	6	17
18. The views of psychology and sociology that hold that men are not responsible for their behavior are fundamentally at odds with the Christian view of guilt and personal accountability.	1	2	3	4	5	6	18
19. There are serious limitations to the scientific method, particularly in respect to moral and religious questions.	1	2	3	4	5	6	19
20. Most students have been sold on the position that science has the answers to all human problems.	1	2	3	4	5	6	20
21. It is impossible for the sociologist to fully comprehend the meaning and significance of religion unless he is himself a member of the faith.	1	2	3	4	5	6	21
22. In the last analysis, human behavior is very unpredictable.	1	2	3	4	5	6	22

23. Most scientists pay lip service to the ideal of being value free in their work, but in reality are not really value free. 1 2 3 4 5 6 23

24. No matter what the possibilities for advancement of scientific knowledge are, human beings should never be experimented upon without their consent. ... 1 2 3 4 5 6 24

25. The biblical account of creation provides us with the clearest evidence that Darwin's theory of evolution is wrong. 1 2 3 4 5 6 25

PART III. Religion and Higher Education

Another important contemporary problem is the relationship of religion to higher education. The following set of questions deal with the place of religion in higher education, the role of the campus minister, and the strategy of religious institutions toward higher education. For each item indicate the response that most nearly represents your own view by circling the appropriate number.

	Definitely Disagree				Definitely Agree		

1. Higher education in our society is the central place where Christians are engaged in study of and learning the human needs and developments in all other institutions. 1 2 3 4 5 6 26

2. University professors are usually hostile to the Christian faith. 1 2 3 4 5 6 27

3. The presuppositions, values, and faith of faculty members influence their teaching, as much as similar factors influence the preaching and teaching of ministers. 1 2 3 4 5 6 28

4. The ideal of scientific objectivity or detachment falsifies the inevitably personal nature of all inquiry. 1 2 3 4 5 6 29

5. The pluralism of disciplines and religions in the university helps the student to see the limits of each. 1 2 3 4 5 6 30

	Definitely Disagree					Definitely Agree	
6. The chief responsibility of college faculty should be to develop new knowledge in their own disciplines.	1	2	3	4	5	6	31
7. Knowledge should be sought in the university not simply for the sake of knowledge but for the improvement of human and public affairs.	1	2	3	4	5	6	32
8. Higher education in the United States has abdicated its responsibility of dealing with vital moral issues in its teaching and research.	1	2	3	4	5	6	33
9. Scientific knowledge is both subjective and objective; that is, it is gained by a responsible act of selecting tools and ordering data to establish contact with universal reality outside the self.	1	2	3	4	5	6	34
10. Campus ministers should have a Th.D. and be as well trained in theology as professors in colleges and universities are in their own disciplines.	1	2	3	4	5	6	35
11. Campus ministers should give more attention to educating faculty in theology than to teaching and working with students.	1	2	3	4	5	6	36
12. Theology is a rational intellectual discipline and should be taught in the university as any other discipline.	1	2	3	4	5	6	37
13. The universities have become major sources of national policy for the major institutions in our society.	1	2	3	4	5	6	38
14. The campus ministries should be launching pads for wide-ranging experimental educational programs.	1	2	3	4	5	6	39
15. The campus minister should seek to bring his students a program as nearly as possible like that of the student's home church.	1	2	3	4	5	6	40
16. Assignments in campus ministries should increasingly follow functional (e.g., assignment to academic disciplines and professional schools) rather than denominational lines, so that ministries are provided to the major structures of the university or college.	1	2	3	4	5	6	41

No.	Statement	1	2	3	4	5	6	
17.	Campus ministers should give their chief attention to freshmen and other new students who are away from home and church ties for the first time. ...	1	2	3	4	5	6	42
18.	Significant learning takes place only if the student knows that the teacher fully accepts and is seriously interested in him as a person.	1	2	3	4	5	6	43
19.	A major purpose of campus ministries ought to be to keep students from being swept off their feet by the forces of secularization in the university. ..	1	2	3	4	5	6	44
20.	One needs more formal educational preparation to be a competent campus minister than to serve a resident parish or congregation.	1	2	3	4	5	6	45
21.	Campus ministers have less clarity as to their mission and more tensions than ministers in regular parish situations.	1	2	3	4	5	6	46
22.	Small church-related colleges provide more opportunity for interpersonal relations between students and faculty than large public universities.	1	2	3	4	5	6	47
23.	The campus minister should be primarily a professor of theology engaged in teaching and research.	1	2	3	4	5	6	48
24.	For the most part, the campus ministry is a waste of time and denominational money.	1	2	3	4	5	6	49
25.	Major programs and policies of the church in foreign missions, inner-city work, and adult education should now be significantly shaped by knowledge and research from the colleges and universities.	1	2	3	4	5	6	50
26.	The intellectual disciplines of the university have little or no bearing upon matters of faith.	1	2	3	4	5	6	51
27.	The churches, in their approach to higher education, should concentrate their funds and professional personnel in the small, liberal arts, church-related colleges.	1	2	3	4	5	6	52
28.	Learning to get along with people should be the chief object of higher education.	1	2	3	4	5	6	53

	Definitely Disagree				Agree Definitely		
29. The next break-through in adult Christians education will come with campus ministers bringing faculty, students, and lay adults together to study what can be done to meet serious public problems.	1	2	3	4	5	6	54
30. The universities are neglecting serious study of the moral choices which confront men in areas where we face major public problems.	1	2	3	4	5	6	55
31. A teacher can know nothing and care nothing about the personal background of a student outside of his interest in the teacher's own field of knowledge, and still teach the student well.	1	2	3	4	5	6	56
32. The humanities are producing disproportionate numbers of dilettantes and vague generalists in comparison with the sciences.	1	2	3	4	5	6	57
33. A person who does not believe in God should not be allowed to teach in a denominational college or university.	1	2	3	4	5	6	58
34. The best place for ministers who feel themselves prepared and interested in teaching the Word of God would be the college or seminary and not the local church.	1	2	3	4	5	6	59
35. It is more important for the churches to support systematic research into religion and its significance for contemporary problems than to build more student centers.	1	2	3	4	5	6	60
36. The campus minister should be free from denominational restraints in developing his program.	1	2	3	4	5	6	61
37. Teaching is one of the most important activities of my ministry.	1	2	3	4	5	6	62
38. The first responsibility of a campus minister is that of keeping in touch with the spiritual needs of students of his own denomination.	1	2	3	4	5	6	63
39. The campus ministry is in general a "frill" in the church, a program designed for college students who are perhaps already the most pampered group in America.	1	2	3	4	5	6	64

40. A principal task of the campus minister should be to help students discover a new meaning of God that is relevant for the modern world. 1 2 3 4 5 6 65

41. Religion can be taught and studied with objectivity and fairness comparable to that of other disciplines. 1 2 3 4 5 6 66

42. Liberals, who significantly distort the meaning of the Christian faith, have captured a very large percentage of the campus ministry positions of my denomination. 1 2 3 4 5 6 67

43. Theology is primarily a discipline of the church and proceeds by confession and witness to personal belief. 1 2 3 4 5 6 68

44. Campus ministers would be more effective if they were more concerned with evangelism and winning souls for Christ and less concerned with "making religion relevant to the modern world." 1 2 3 4 5 6 69

45. The campus minister's teaching is different from the university professor's in that the minister makes clear that he is committed to one faith rather than another, and that he hopes to persuade others of the truth of his faith. 1 2 3 4 5 6 70

PART IV. *Counseling*

Many ministers are involved in one form of counseling or another. In this section we would like to know something about your own attitudes toward and experience with counseling. The first set of items are to be answered in the same manner as the items in the first three parts. These are followed by a few questions that, for the most part, can be answered by making a check in the appropriate box.

	Definitely Disagree				*Definitely Agree*		

1. As a counselor, a minister should be nonjudgmental, reflecting what the layman says so that he the better sees himself. 1 2 3 4 5 6 04 1

2. Ministers would probably do a better job counseling if they put away their psychology books and turned to God for His guidance. 1 2 3 4 5 6 2

	Definitely Disagree					Definitely Agree	
3. My training as a counselor is often woefully inadequate for many of the types of problems I am called upon to help with.	1	2	3	4	5	6	3
4. As much as possible, I try to refer emotionally disturbed cases to someone who is better qualified than I to deal with the problem.	1	2	3	4	5	6	4
5. I would welcome the opportunity to learn more about psychology and counseling.	1	2	3	4	5	6	5
6. Most people with problems need a deeper and better faith rather than a psychiatrist.	1	2	3	4	5	6	6
7. One important contribution the church can make to society is to provide laymen with opportunities for discussions where they can "blow off steam," confess their failures to one another.	1	2	3	4	5	6	7
8. A faith in God will cure most mental illness if that faith is strong enough.	1	2	3	4	5	6	8
9. If a minister cannot solve his own mental problems, he cannot help others solve theirs.	1	2	3	4	5	6	9
10. Worry about career and social status problems causes most of the mental breakdowns that do occur.	1	2	3	4	5	6	10
11. I sometimes feel that I should seek the help of a psychiatrist or psychologist.	1	2	3	4	5	6	11
12. Anguish and loneliness may be characteristic of responsible moral action, not mental illness.	1	2	3	4	5	6	12
13. When personal guilt is the crucial problem, the practice of penance and confession may be more helpful than professional psychiatric aid.	1	2	3	4	5	6	13
14. The problem of guilt and sin is central in most mental illness.	1	2	3	4	5	6	14
15. A man can be devoutly religious and still become mentally ill.	1	2	3	4	5	6	15

16

1. Approximately what percent of your working time do you spend in some form of counseling?

0☐ None, or almost none
1☐ Less than 5%
2☐ 5%–10%
3☐ 10%–20%
4☐ 20%–35%
5☐ 35%–50%
6☐ More than 50%

17

2. Over the past five years, have the demands on your time for counseling:

0☐ Increased
1☐ Remained about the same
2☐ Decreased

18-20

3. During an average month, how many people would you estimate that you counsel with? _____

21

4. The time you devote to counseling may not necessarily reflect the importance you attribute to this activity. Check the category below that best describes your own feeling regarding counseling.

0☐ Little or no importance to my ministry.
1☐ Some importance, but minor relative to other responsibilties.
2☐ Rather important, but there are several more important aspects to my ministry.
3☐ Ranks with several other activities as one of my more important responsibilities.
4☐ One of my most important responsibilities.
5☐ Definitely the most important aspect of my ministry.

22

5. Have you received any formal training in guidance and counseling?

0☐ Yes
1☐ No

5a. If yes, was this (check as many as apply):

☐ as an undergraduate   23

☐ in seminary   24

☐ in graduate training   25

☐ other (specify) _____   26

Indicate courses, majors, degrees, or nature of training in counseling. (*Be as specific as possible.*)   27-36

6. Assume someone came to you who in your judgment had very serious emotional or psychic disturbances. Please rank-order your preference for handling this person. Let "1" stand for your most preferred way, "2" for your next choice, and "3" for your third choice.

_____ Refer to a Christian psychiatrist or psychologist of my own denomination   37

_____ Refer to a Christian psychiatrist or psychologist of another denomination   38

_____ Refer to a non-Christian psychiatrist or psychologist   39

_____ Refer to a psychiatrist or psychologist of outstanding capability; even though he might not be a Christian   40

_____ Handle the case myself   41

_____ Other (specify) _____   42

PART V. *Social Issues*

Much has been written by individual ministers about the vital social issues of our day. However, as a group, little is known about ministers' attitudes toward these vital issues. This section deals with a broad range of questions revolving around politics, economics, family life, civil rights, and church and state. For each statement, indicate the position that most nearly represents your own view by circling the appropriate number.

	Definitely Disagree					Definitely Agree	
1. Bible reading and prayer for all students do not belong in public schools.	1	2	3	4	5	6	1
2. Use of governmental funds to provide transportation for denominational schools should be permitted as long as all religions are treated alike.	1	2	3	4	5	6	2
3. The use of government money to support religious organizations should be strictly forbidden.	1	2	3	4	5	6	3
4. I have some sympathy with the position that the tax exemption for churches should be eliminated.	1	2	3	4	5	6	4
5. Federal funds should be provided to denominational colleges and universities on the same basis as they are provided to public universities, since both are involved in the important task of educating American youth.	1	2	3	4	5	6	5
6. Negroes would be better off if they would take advantage of the opportunities that have been made available rather than spending so much time protesting.	1	2	3	4	5	6	6
7. I basically disapprove of the Negro civil rights movement in America.	1	2	3	4	5	6	7
8. The racial crisis in the U.S. would probably be much less serious if the federal government had not intervened.	1	2	3	4	5	6	8
9. For the most part, the churches have been woefully inadequate in facing up to the civil rights issues.	1	2	3	4	5	6	9

	Definitely Disagree					Definitely Agree	
10. I am in basic sympathy with northern ministers and students who have gone to the South to work for civil rights.	1	2	3	4	5	6	10
11. There is little hope of changing the segregationist feelings of whites in this country during the next generation.	1	2	3	4	5	6	11
12. The real obstacle to integration in this country is political leadership and not the people themselves.	1	2	3	4	5	6	12
13. Many whites pretend to be very Christian while in reality their racial attitudes demonstrate their lack of or misunderstanding of Christianity.	1	2	3	4	5	6	13
14. Negroes could solve many of their own problems if they would not be so irresponsible and carefree about life.	1	2	3	4	5	6	14
15. The economic and psychological disabilities of the masses of Negroes become greater almost daily in the United States.	1	2	3	4	5	6	15
16. Freedom of speech should include the right for someone to make speeches against religion.	1	2	3	4	5	6	16
17. Publications that dwell on sex and use obscene language should be banned from the newsstand.	1	2	3	4	5	6	17
18. Congressional investigations into un-American activities are essential to our nation's security.	1	2	3	4	5	6	18
19. Students receiving any financial aid from the government should be required to swear that they are not members of the Communist party.	1	2	3	4	5	6	19
20. Censorship is often necessary in order to protect the public.	1	2	3	4	5	6	20
21. The free enterprise system is the single economic system compatible with the requirements of personal freedom and constitutional government.	1	2	3	4	5	6	21
22. The war against poverty can best be fought by the federal government's leaving private enterprise alone so that they can create more jobs.	1	2	3	4	5	6	22

23. The government is providing too many services that should be left to private enterprise. 1 2 3 4 5 6

24. I am not nearly so concerned with the amount of power of the federal government as I am with the irresponsibility of many government officials. 1 2 3 4 5 6

25. Adequate medical care for the aged through some kind of governmental program is badly needed. 1 2 3 4 5 6

26. Most people who live in poverty could do something about their situation if they really wanted to. 1 2 3 4 5 6

27. I would tend to distrust the political judgments of a person who did not believe in Jesus Christ 1 2 3 4 5 6

28. Ministers should not publicly indicate their views on political issues. 1 2 3 4 5 6

29. Any means must, if necessary, be used to preserve America from the menace of atheistic Communism. 1 2 3 4 5 6

30. There can never be a complete reduction in nuclear arms so long as there are Communist nations in the world. 1 2 3 4 5 6

31. If the Republicans had nominated a moderate or "main-stream" candidate for President I would have voted for the Republican candidate in the recent election. 1 2 3 4 5 6

32. The John Birch Society and other extremist groups constitute a grave threat to our society. 1 2 3 4 5 6

33. Red China should be admitted to the United Nations. 1 2 3 4 5 6

34. I believe that I am politically and economically more liberal than the majority of the members of my congregation. 1 2 3 4 5 6

35. I believe that there is at least a 50-50 chance of a nuclear war breaking out in the next ten years. 1 2 3 4 5 6

	Definitely Disagree				Definitely Agree		
36. The identification of Goldwater with extremist groups during the recent election was nothing more than a great political smear by his opposition. . .	1	2	3	4	5	6	36
37. The philosophy of modern liberalism is leading to an alteration of family, morals, law, and order.	1	2	3	4	5	6	37
38. A person who does not believe in God should not be permitted to hold public office.	1	2	3	4	5	6	38
39. The only real victory over Communism is total victory.	1	2	3	4	5	6	39
40. During the recent campaign I endorsed one of the Presidential candidates from the pulpit or at some other religious gathering.	1	2	3	4	5	6	40
41. Most people will give you a hard time if you give them a chance.	1	2	3	4	5	6	41
42. In all human relations, men are involved in the control and manipulation of others, no matter how permissive they claim to be.	1	2	3	4	5	6	42
43. It is often who you know rather than what you know that is important in getting ahead.	1	2	3	4	5	6	43
44. Most people you meet want to get something out of you.	1	2	3	4	5	6	44
45. Although never a totally satisfactory answer to family problems, divorce is sometimes the best solution.	1	2	3	4	5	6	45
46. Women who engage in premarital sexual intercourse are almost certain to have serious emotional difficulties in marriage.	1	2	3	4	5	6	46
47. The most rewarding thing a woman can do is to be a totally dedicated mother and wife.	1	2	3	4	5	6	47
48. Parents are too easy on their children these days.	1	2	3	4	5	6	48
49. College teachers and counselors are too lenient in advising students about premarital sex.	1	2	3	4	5	6	49

#	Statement	1	2	3	4	5	6	
50.	Parents should give their children more direction than they do.	1	2	3	4	5	6	50
51.	Although popular views on sex have changed in the past quarter of a century, procreation is still the major purpose and intercourse between marital partners should be carried out with moderation.	1	2	3	4	5	6	51
52.	Women who really desire full-time careers should not marry because the roles of wife-mother and career woman are basically incompatible.	1	2	3	4	5	6	52
53.	The churches should initiate inquiries into the implications of Christian convictions for the relations of the sexes, not assuming that there is any actual consensus in the churches on sexual morality.	1	2	3	4	5	6	53
54.	It is conceivable that a particular situation could morally justify extramarital relations.	1	2	3	4	5	6	54
55.	The primary meaning of sexual intercourse is that two individuals have made a total commitment to each other.	1	2	3	4	5	6	55
56.	For two people in our society to be totally committed to each other, they must acknowledge this with a marriage ceremony, rather than simply relying on a private commitment of love.	1	2	3	4	5	6	56
57.	Until the children are grown, a woman's place is in the home.	1	2	3	4	5	6	57
58.	The use of birth control should be governed only by the needs of the persons involved.	1	2	3	4	5	6	58
59.	I do not believe in spanking children. Rewarding proper behavior and setting a good example are always more effective.	1	2	3	4	5	6	59
60.	Birth control information should be available to all persons.	1	2	3	4	5	6	60
61.	It is always better to explain to a child why his behavior is wrong rather than to punish him.	1	2	3	4	5	6	61
62.	The changes in our society affecting sexual relations are so profound that old patterns of morality are not adequate for the future.	1	2	3	4	5	6	62

	Definitely Disagree					Definitely Agree	
63. The suburban churches have become a force for retreat from urban responsibilities and realities.	1	2	3	4	5	6	63
64. Suburban people have enough community problems to meet without accepting any more economic and political burdens of the central city.	1	2	3	4	5	6	64
65. The modern saints of the ministry are those who are staying in the central city.	1	2	3	4	5	6	65
66. Christian education needs to bring laymen face to face with urban problems and propose solutions.	1	2	3	4	5	6	66
67. I enjoy a ministry that is situated in the midst of a city where all types of activities go on in close proximity.	1	2	3	4	5	6	67
68. The reason the Jews are having so much trouble is because God is punishing them for rejecting Jesus.	1	2	3	4	5	6	68
69. I believe that a larger proportion of the federal government's budget should be allocated for public welfare expenditures such as schools, hospitals, parks, etc.	1		3	4	5	6	69
70. Couples have a moral obligation to limit their family size to the number of children they can afford to care for.	1	2	3	4	5	6	70

PART VI. *Professional Activities and Missions*

The items in this section describe many of the activities that ministers frequently do. We would like for you to respond to each statement in terms of the enjoyment or personal satisfaction you gain from the activity, independent of the time you may devote to it. The same principle of response is followed here as in earlier sections, except you are responding in terms of liking or disliking an activity. Try to keep in mind that you are implicitly rating an activity against all other activities. Therefore, you should reserve the category 6 for those activities you *most* enjoy.

	Definitely Do Not Enjoy				*Definitely Enjoy*		
1. Teaching children.	1	2	3	4	5	6	1
2. Leading public worship.	1	2	3	4	5	6	2
3. Ministering to the sick, dying, and bereaved.	1	2	3	4	5	6	3
4. Counseling with people facing the major decisions of life, e.g., marriage, vocation.	1	2	3	4	5	6	4
5. Fostering fellowship at church gatherings.	1	2	3	4	5	6	5
6. Teaching young people (i.e., junior high and high school).	1	2	3	4	5	6	6
7. Talking with individuals about their spiritual development.	1	2	3	4	5	6	7
8. Visiting new residents and recruiting new members.	1	2	3	4	5	6	8
9. Supplying ideas for new activities and projects	1	2	3	4	5	6	9
10. Working with congregational boards and committees.	1	2	3	4	5	6	10
11. Recruiting, training, and assisting lay leaders and teachers.	1	2	3	4	5	6	11
12. Managing the church office—records, correspondence, information center, etc.	1	2	3	4	5	6	12

	Definitely Disagree				Definitely Agree		
13. Preaching sermons.	1	2	3	4	5	6	13
14. Following a definite schedule of reading and study.	1	2	3	4	5	6	14
15. Developing more effective adult teaching and study programs.	1	2	3	4	5	6	15
16. Teaching undergraduates and graduate students.	1	2	3	4	5	6	16
17. Playing the conciliator role, seeking to find points of harmony and agreement.	1	2	3	4	5	6	17
18. Promoting and creating enthusiasm for church activities.	1	2	3	4	5	6	18
19. Maintaining a disciplined life of prayer and personal devotion.	1	2	3	4	5	6	19
20. Helping manage church finances.	1	2	3	4	5	6	20
21. Administering Communion.	1	2	3	4	5	6	21
22. Teaching and working directly with adults.	1	2	3	4	5	6	22
23. Counseling with people about their moral and personal problems.	1	2	3	4	5	6	23
24. Participating in community projects and organizations.	1	2	3	4	5	6	24
25. Maintaining harmony, handling troublemakers, averting or resolving problems.	1	2	3	4	5	6	25
26. Organizing and helping groups who are victims of social neglect or injustice.	1	2	3	4	5	6	26
27. Speaking to community and civic groups.	1	2	3	4	5	6	27
28. Visiting regularly in the homes of the congregation.	1	2	3	4	5	6	28
29. Raising money for special church projects.	1	2	3	4	5	6	29
30. Winning a lost soul to Christ.	1	2	3	4	5	6	30
31. Participating in evangelistic meetings.	1	2	3	4	5	6	31
32. Ministering to the aged.	1	2	3	4	5	6	32

		1	2	3	4	5	6	
33.	Helping people come to grips with the problems involved in the relationship between the Christian heritage and the modern scientific world.	1	2	3	4	5	6	33
34.	Preparing sermons.	1	2	3	4	5	6	34
35.	Organizing or administering local community projects.	1	2	3	4	5	6	35
36.	Helping a young person make a decision to enter the ministry.	1	2	3	4	5	6	36
37.	Privately encountering God through prayer.	1	2	3	4	5	6	37
38.	Seeing a major building project to completion.	1	2	3	4	5	6	38
39.	Giving theological interpretations of *avant-garde* movies and other art forms.	1	2	3	4	5	6	39
40.	Participating in state, regional, and national denominational activities.	1	2	3	4	5	6	40
41.	Helping a person or family resolve a serious problem, whether it be spiritual, social, psychological, or economic.	1	2	3	4	5	6	41
42.	Taking a firm stand on some issue confronting the life of the church.	1	2	3	4	5	6	42
43.	Reading the Holy Bible.	1	2	3	4	5	6	43
44.	Discussing contemporary theological issues and viewpoints with educated persons.	1	2	3	4	5	6	44
45.	Conducting a baptismal service.	1	2	3	4	5	6	45
46.	Participating in a local ecumenical ministerial association.	1	2	3	4	5	6	46
47.	Influencing the policies of organizations in my denomination.	1	2	3	4	5	6	47
48.	Influencing the policies of major organizations or institutions in my community.	1	2	3	4	5	6	48
49.	Teaching people to use their Bibles in personal meditations.	1	2	3	4	5	6	49
50.	Spotting the key places in the community where decisions influencing our common life are being made and informing church members of this.	1	2	3	4	5	6	50

	Definitely Disagree					Definitely Agree	
51. Creating an agenda for my supervisory or advisory boards which open up new ideas and programs for the church.	1	2	3	4	5	6	51
52. Participating in creating plans for improvement of city life.	1	2	3	4	5	6	52

How desirous are you of doing the following:

	Definitely Do Not Desire					Definitely Desirous	
1. Specialize in one particular aspect or role of the ministry, such as preacher, counselor, evangelist, etc.	1	2	3	4	5	6	53
2. Learn to balance and co-ordinate better the various roles of the minister (such as preacher, administrator, counselor), so as to become a sort of pastor director.	1	2	3	4	5	6	54
3. Be a theologian of the congregation, helping laymen to think theologically.	1	2	3	4	5	6	55
4. Obtain a teaching position in a college or seminary.	1	2	3	4	5	6	56
5. Be more concerned with the qualities of human experience commonly called secular than with manifestations of religion in creeds and church institutional structures.	1	2	3	4	5	6	57
6. Provide in the church greater opportunity for adult study and reflections. ..	1	2	3	4	5	6	58
7. Obtain a pastorate with a more liberal and progressive congregation.	1	2	3	4	5	6	59
8. Obtain more information as to what developments are taking place in education of significance to my congregation.	1	2	3	4	5	6	60
9. Find a ministry in which my role and functions are more clearly defined or established.	1	2	3	4	5	6	61
10. Engage the adults of my congregation in a search for the concrete meaning of their Christian commitment for responsibilities in various aspects of their work and leisure.	1	2	3	4	5	6	62

11. Obtain a position that would provide more time for personal study.	1	2	3	4	5	6	63
12. Relocate in another parish.	1	2	3	4	5	6	64
13. Take advantage of opportunities to advance my own career.	1	2	3	4	5	6	65
14. Obtain more formal education or a sabbatical for personal study.	1	2	3	4	5	6	66
15. Receive a higher salary.	1	2	3	4	5	6	67
16. Be appointed as pastor to a large and prestigeful church.	1	2	3	4	5	6	68
17. Experiment with new worship forms, such as drama, jazz music, etc.	1	2	3	4	5	6	69

PART VII. *How You See Yourself*

In order to have a complete picture of Protestant ministers, it is important to know something about how they see themselves. It should be emphasized that we are interested in how *you* see *yourself*, not how you feel others may see you. Please respond to each item in terms of the same principle used above.

	Definitely Disagree					*Definitely Agree*	07	
1. I make friends easily.	1	2	3	4	5	6	07	1
2. I usually act on the spur of the moment.	1	2	3	4	5	6		2
3. My moods seem to go up and down.	1	2	3	4	5	6		3
4. I take the lead in a group when it is necessary to get something done.	1	2	3	4	5	6		4
5. I often think of myself as a failure.	1	2	3	4	5	6		5
6. I enjoy intellectual pursuits.	1	2	3	4	5	6		6
7. I often feel that I have more problems than other people.	1	2	3	4	5	6		7
8. I am not nice to people I don't like.	1	2	3	4	5	6		8
9. I don't get upset easily.	1	2	3	4	5	6		9

	Definitely Disagree				Definitely Agree		
10. I enjoy reading books.	1	2	3	4	5	6	10
11. Sometimes I feel I am just no good.	1	2	3	4	5	6	11
12. When I am in a group that is discussing a problem, I do not do much of the talking.	1	2	3	4	5	6	12
13. I am often tense, even when there is no reason to be.	1	2	3	4	5	6	13
14. My interest shifts quickly from one thing to another.	1	2	3	4	5	6	14
15. People must often get the feeling that I am not well adjusted.	1	2	3	4	5	6	15
16. Most people bore me.	1	2	3	4	5	6	16
17. I often feel blue or sad.	1	2	3	4	5	6	17
18. I find it difficult to concentrate on reading anything longer than a newspaper article.	1	2	3	4	5	6	18
19. I rarely get nervous.	1	2	3	4	5	6	19
20. I rarely think things out in detail before I act.	1	2	3	4	5	6	20
21. I am easy-going, even under pressure.	1	2	3	4	5	6	21
22. I don't like discussions about serious problems or world affairs.	1	2	3	4	5	6	22
23. People think I am unpredictable in my moods.	1	2	3	4	5	6	23
24. I do not find it easy to speak publicly.	1	2	3	4	5	6	24
25. I am impulsive about most things.	1	2	3	4	5	6	25
26. I get discouraged easily.	1	2	3	4	5	6	26
27. I am not good-natured when someone is giving me a hard time.	1	2	3	4	5	6	27
28. When I am by myself, I often get depressed.	1	2	3	4	5	6	28

	Does Not Describe Me				Describes Me Well		
29. I enjoy planning work carefully before carrying it out.	1	2	3	4	5	6	29
30. I seem to withdraw in many situations when I should really be speaking up.	1	2	3	4	5	6	30
31. I have a great deal of self-control.	1	2	3	4	5	6	31
32. Sometimes the deep personal guilt I feel is almost more than I can bear.	1	2	3	4	5	6	32
33. I frequently feel the anxiety of being alone and helpless in this world.	1	2	3	4	5	6	33
34. My hardest battles are with myself.	1	2	3	4	5	6	34
35. I hardly ever reveal my innermost feelings to others.	1	2	3	4	5	6	35
36. If something important needs to be done, I don't mind breaking a few rules or raising a few eyebrows to do it.	1	2	3	4	5	6	36
37. I seem quite incapable of having good friends without getting emotionally involved in their troubles.	1	2	3	4	5	6	37
38. I like to have a definite course of action in my ministry rather than be vacillating among several possibilities.	1	2	3	4	5	6	38
39. It is better to keep on with the present methods of doing things than to take a way that might lead to chaos.	1	2	3	4	5	6	39
40. I experience moments of great exultation and great despair in my ministry.	1	2	3	4	5	6	40

Generally, I . . .

	Does Not Describe Me				Describes Me Well		
1. am very active.	1	2	3	4	5	6	41
2. am friendly.	1	2	3	4	5	6	42
3. am intelligent.	1	2	3	4	5	6	43
4. am very tense.	1	2	3	4	5	6	44

	Does Not Describe Me				Describes Me Well		
5. am interested in getting things done.	1	2	3	4	5	6	45
6. am authoritarian.	1	2	3	4	5	6	46
7. am pleasant.	1	2	3	4	5	6	47
8. am rational and logical.	1	2	3	4	5	6	48
9. get upset easily.	1	2	3	4	5	6	49
10. pay attention to the task.	1	2	3	4	5	6	50
11. do most of the talking.	1	2	3	4	5	6	51
12. am likable.	1	2	3	4	5	6	52
13. am clear-minded.	1	2	3	4	5	6	53
14. am nervous.	1	2	3	4	5	6	54
15. accept responsibilities.	1	2	3	4	5	6	55
16. am assertive.	1	2	3	4	5	6	56
17. support others.	1	2	3	4	5	6	57
18. am mature.	1	2	3	4	5	6	58
19. am emotional.	1	2	3	4	5	6	59
20. am conscientious.	1	2	3	4	5	6	60

PART VIII. *Personal Background Information*

Finally, we would like to have just a few items of background information about yourself, your family, your job, etc. Please be as accurate as possible and please do not leave any questions blank.

08

1. Your age: _____ 1-2

2. Your sex: 3

0☐ Male
1☐ Female

3. Your race: 4

0☐ White
1☐ Negro
3☐ Other (specify) _____

4. Your marital status: 5

0☐ Married
1☐ Single
2☐ Widowed
3☐ Separated
4☐ Divorced

IF MARRIED:
4a. When did you marry? _____ month _____ year

4b. Is this your only marriage?

0☐ Yes
1☐ No

4c. How many children do you have? _____
4d. What are their birth dates?

	MONTH	YEAR
1.	_____	_____
2.	_____	_____
3.	_____	_____
4.	_____	_____
5.	_____	_____
6.	_____	_____
7.	_____	_____

5. What is (was) your father's occupation? (Be as specific as possible.)

_____

6. Which of the following general categories best describes your father's occupation?

0☐ Manager, Official, or Proprietor of Large Business
1☐ Professional (nonminister)
2☐ Minister
3☐ Manager, Official, or Proprietor of Small Business
4☐ Government Civil Service Employee
5☐ Farm Owner, or Farm Manager
6☐ Craftsman, Technical Worker, or Foreman
7☐ Sales Worker
8☐ Clerical Worker
9☐ Unskilled Laborer

7. How do you think the general social standing of your father's occupation compares with the social standing of your own occupation?

0☐ Father's occupation was much lower socially
1☐ Father's occupation was somewhat lower socially

8-9

10-11

12-14

2☐   Father's occupation about the same socially

3☐   Father's occupation was somewhat higher socially

4☐   Father's occupation was much higher socially

8. How many children did your parents have, counting yourself? _____

9. What was your birth order? (i.e., were you the first child, second child, etc.) _____

10. What was the highest educational attainment for the following:

	Father	Mother	Spouse
8th grade or less	0☐	0☐	0☐
Some high school	1☐	1☐	1☐
High school graduate	2☐	2☐	2☐
Some college	3☐	3☐	3☐
Bachelor's degree	4☐	4☐	4☐
Master's degree	5☐	5☐	5☐
Doctor's degree	6☐	6☐	6☐
Not Married			7☐

15

11. What was the approximate size of the community you lived in during most of your childhood?

0☐   Farm or rural community less than 2,500

1☐   2,500– 10,000

2☐   10,000– 25,000

3☐   25,000– 50,000

4☐   50,000–250,000

5☐   250,000–500,000

6☐   500,000 or more

16

12. What is the highest educational level you attained?

0☐   High school graduation or less

1☐   Some college or post-high school training

2☐ Bible school training
3☐ College graduation
4☐ Some college plus full three-year seminary
5☐ College graduation plus some seminary
6☐ College graduation plus graduation from three-year seminary
7☐ College and seminary graduation, plus additional graduate work

13. Degrees held, including undergraduate:

College, University, Seminary	Degree	Date Awarded	Field in which Degree granted

14. What was the total cash salary you received last year, and in addition, any "anniversary" or "appreciation" gifts? (If you serve more than one parish, include total income, but *do not* include allowances such as gas mileage.)

$ _____ Cash salary, last year 17-19
$ _____ "Anniversary" or "appreciation" gifts 20-22
$ _____ Total cash income last year 23-25

15. Do you have other sources of income such as your wife's employment, inheritance, endowment, investments, etc.? 26

0☐ Yes
1☐ No

15a. If yes, what is the approximate *annual* amount of these other sources: $ _____ 27-29

16. Are you presently provided with a parsonage or housing allowance? `30`

    0☐ Yes
    1☐ No

16a. If yes, what is the approximate rental value of the parsonage *per year* (includes utilities if paid by the church), or what is the amount of the housing allowance? $ _____ `31-33`

17. During the past year, how many of the following activities did you participate in? (Check as many as apply.) `34-36`

    ☐ I discussed political issues with friends `37`
    ☐ I attended or listened to speeches and discussion programs dealing with national and international problems at least once a month. `38`
    ☐ I followed national and international events in the newspapers daily and the magazines weekly. `39`
    ☐ I read one or more books about politics. `40`
    ☐ I signed a petition for or against some legislation. `41`
    ☐ I wrote a letter or sent a telegram to a public official. `42`
    ☐ I contributed money to some political cause or group. `43`
    ☐ I collected money for some political cause or group. `44`
    ☐ I voted in the last national election. `45`
    ☐ I participated in the activities of a political group. `46`
    ☐ I ran for or held an elective office during the past five years. `47`

18. Do you usually consider yourself as: `48-49`

    0☐ Republican `50`
    1☐ Independent
    2☐ Democrat

19. In the recent election did you favor:

    0☐ Goldwater `51`
    1☐ Johnson

20. Approximately how large is the community in which you currently reside? `52`

Farm or rural community less than 2,500

- 0☐
- 1☐ 2,500– 5,000
- 2☐ 5,000– 10,000
- 3☐ 10,000– 25,000
- 4☐ 25,000– 50,000
- 5☐ 50,000– 250,000
- 6☐ 250,000– 500,000
- 7☐ 500,000–1,000,000
- 8☐ 1,000,000 or more

20a. Is this community a suburb of a larger metropolitan center? `53`

- 0☐ Yes
- 1☐ No

21. What region of the country do you currently reside in? `54`

- 0☐ East-Northeast
- 1☐ Midwest
- 2☐ South
- 3☐ West

22. Are you ordained? `55`

- 0☐ Yes
- 1☐ No

22a. If yes, in what year were you ordained? _____ `56-57`

23. In total, how many years have you been in the ministry? _____ `58-59`

24. How long have you served in your current position? _____ `60-61`

25. What is the total number of ministerial positions you held prior to the present one? _____ `62-63`

26. Have you ever considered leaving the ministry for some other vocation? | 64

  0☐ Yes, very seriously
  1☐ Yes, but not seriously
  2☐ The thought has occurred to me, but I can't say I've *really* considered leaving the ministry.
  3☐ No, definitely not

PARISH MINISTERS (If you have no duties as a parish minister, please skip to question No. 36.) | 09

27. What is the average attendance at Sunday morning worship in your church? _____ | 1-4

28. How many persons do you have on your active church rolls? _____ | 5-8

29. What is your annual church budget? $ _____ | 9-12

30. How much does your church give annually to support home and foreign missions? $ _____ | 13-15

31. How much does your church give annually to support campus ministries? $ _____ | 16-18

32. Is your parish located near a college or university? | 19

  0☐ Yes
  1☐ No

32a. *If yes*, what is the average number of students in attendance on an average Sunday morning in which the college or university is in session? _____ | 20-22

33. During the past two years have you ever invited campus ministers to describe the intellectual and moral trends in higher education with parents so that they will better understand what is happening to their children? | 23

  0☐ Yes
  1☐ No

34. During the past two years have you ever invited a campus minister to speak with precollege youth about the possibilities of higher education and the criteria for choice of schools? | 24

  0☐ Yes
  1☐ No

35. Which of the following categories *best* describes the occupational background of the members of the church you currently serve?

- 0☐ The majority are professional and managerial.
- 1☐ The majority are salaried white-collar workers, but there are also a considerable number of professional and managerial people.
- 2☐ The majority are salaried white-collar workers, but there are also a considerable number of blue-collar workers.
- 3☐ The majority are blue-collar workers, but there are some white-collar, professional, and managerial people.
- 4☐ The membership is predominantly blue-collar.
- 5☐ None of the above. My church draws membership about equally from all occupational groups.

CAMPUS MINISTERS (If *any* aspect of your normal ministerial duties involves working with students in higher education, please complete this section.)

36. What is the nature of your current employment?

- 0☐ Full-time campus minister serving one campus.
- 1☐ Full-time campus minister serving two or more campuses.
- 2☐ Ecclesiastically appointed chaplain to college or university.
- 3☐ University- or college-appointed chaplain.
- 4☐ Local pastor with at least ¾ time devoted to campus ministry.
- 5☐ Local pastor with ¼ to ¾ time devoted to campus ministry.
- 6☐ Local pastor with ¼ time or less devoted to campus ministry.
- 7☐ Other (specify) _____

37. Number of full-time students in the college or university you serve. If you serve more than one campus, please report for the campus on which you serve most time):

- 0☐ Less than 500
- 1☐ 500– 1,000
- 2☐ 1,000– 1,500

3☐ 1,500– 4,000
4☐ 4,000– 7,500
5☐ 7,500–10,000
6☐ 10,000–15,000
7☐ 15,000 and over

38. What is the highest academic degree offered by the college or university you serve?   28

0☐ Diploma (Jr. College)
1☐ Professional or Trade
2☐ Bachelor's
3☐ Master's
4☐ Doctor's

39. What is the type of school you serve?   29

0☐ Private with significant denominational tie
1☐ Private with nominal denominational tie
2☐ Private nondenominational
3☐ State teachers college
4☐ Municipal college or university
5☐ State college or university
6☐ Other (specify)

40. Sex of the undergraduate student body: 30

0☐ Coed
1☐ Male
2☐ Female

41. Approximately how many students are there on the campus(es) where you work who are members of the   31-33
denomination(s) which support your work? (If no data, please estimate.) ——————

42. Approximately how many students participate in some way in the ministry in which you are engaged? ——————   34-36

43. How many students are *regularly* and *actively* involved in some facet of your campus ministry? _____   37-39

44. How many times during the past three months have you seen members of the faculty or administration of the school(s) you serve in relation to issues such as student problems, health services, speaker advice, etc?   40

- 0 ☐ None
- 1 ☐ One
- 2 ☐ Two
- 3 ☐ Three
- 4 ☐ Four
- 5 ☐ Five
- 6 ☐ Six to Nine
- 7 ☐ Ten to Twenty
- 8 ☐ Twenty or More

45. How many times in the past three months have you engaged in intellectually oriented discussions with members of the faculty of the school(s) you serve about the relation of the Christian faith to the academic enterprise?   41

- 0 ☐ None
- 1 ☐ One
- 2 ☐ Two
- 3 ☐ Three
- 4 ☐ Four
- 5 ☐ Five
- 6 ☐ Six to Nine
- 7 ☐ Ten to Twenty
- 8 ☐ Twenty or More

46. How many members of the faculty of the school(s) you serve have seen in in a counseling situation in relation to their personal or intellectual problems in the past three months?   42

- 0 ☐ None
- 1 ☐ One
- 2 ☐ Two
- 3 ☐ Three
- 4 ☐ Four
- 5 ☐ Five
- 6 ☐ Six to Nine
- 7 ☐ Ten to Twenty
- 8 ☐ Twenty or More

47. How would you evaluate the problems you encounter in the financial support of your ministry?   43

- 0 ☐ A most serious problem, taking 50% or more of my time and energy.
- 1 ☐ A major problem, taking 25–49% of my time and energy.
- 2 ☐ A considerable problem, taking 10–24% of my time and energy.

3☐ A minor problem, taking less than 10% of my time and energy.
4☐ No problem, as others bear this responsibility.
5☐ Other (specify) _____

44-45

48. How many years have you been in the campus ministry? _____

46-47

49. How many campus ministry positions have you held? _____

48

50. Do you intend to remain in the campus ministry?

0☐ Yes, indefinitely.
1☐ Yes, for a while at least
2☐ Uncertain
3☐ No, want to do something else eventually
4☐ No, want to get out in near future

You have now completed the questionnaire. Before placing the questionnaire in the return envelope, would you please go back over the questions to see that they are all answered and in accord with their directions? *We sincerely appreciate your attention and cooperation.*

If you have any comments you would like to make about the questionnaire, please use this space.

BIBLIOGRAPHY

PUBLISHED WORKS

Aiken, Michael; Demerath, N. J. III; and Marwell, Gerald. *Conscience and Confrontation*. East Lansing: Christian Faith and Higher Education Institute, 1965.

American Academy of Arts and Sciences. "The Contemporary University." *Daedalus*, 94 (Fall, 1964).

American Academy of Arts and Sciences. "The Professions." *Daedalus*, 92 (Fall, 1963).

*Apter, David E. *Politics of Modernization*. Chicago: University of Chicago Press, 1965.

Arendt, Hannah. *The Human Condition*. Chicago: University of Chicago Press, 1958.

Ashbrook, James B. "Ministerial Leadership in Church Organization." *Ministry Studies*, 1 (May, 1967).

Austin, Grey. *A Century of Religion at the University of Michigan*. Ann Arbor: University of Michigan Press, 1957.

Averell, Lloyd J. "Christian Values in the Student Personnel Program." *Liberal Education*, 49 (March, 1963).

Bailyn, Bernard. *Education in the Forming of American Society*. New York: Vintage Books, 1960.

Baker, James C. *The First Wesley Foundation*. Nashville: Methodist Publishing House, 1960.

Baker, Ray Palmer. *After One Hundred Years*. Troy, N.Y.: Rensselaer Polytechnic and Engineering Series, no. 29, 1930.

Belgum, David. *Guilt: Where Pyschology and Religion Meet*. Englewood Cliffs, N.J.: Prentice-Hall, 1963.

*Bell, Daniel. *The Reforming of General Education*. New York: Columbia University Press, 1966.

Bellah, Robert N., ed. *Religion and Progress in Modern Asia*. New York: The Free Press, 1965.

Bennett, John C. *Christian Ethics and Social Policy*. New York: Charles Scribner's Sons, 1946.

Berg, Philip L. "The Professionalization of Protestant Clergymen." Ph.D. dissertation, University of Nebraska, 1967.

Bloy, Myron. *The Crisis of Cultural Change: A Christian Viewpoint.* New York: Seabury Press, 1965.

Board of National Missions, United Presbyterian Church, USA. *Guidelines for Development of Strategy for Metropolitan Mission.* New York: United Presbyterian Church, 1967.

Bochenski, Joseph M. *The Logic of Religion.* New York: New York University Press, 1965.

Bosc, Jean. *The Kingly Office of the Lord Jesus Christ.* London: Oliver and Boyd, 1959.

Boyd, Malcolm. *Are You Running With Me, Jesus?* New York: Holt, Rinehart and Winston, 1965.

Brameld, Theodore. *Education for the Emerging Age.* New York: Harper & Row, 1950.

Bronfenbrenner, Urie. "The Split-Level American Family." *Saturday Review,* 7 October 1967.

Bridston, Keith R., and Culver, Dwight W. *Pre-Seminary Education.* Minneapolis: Augsburg Publishing House, 1965.

Bridston, Keith R., and Culver, Dwight W. *The Making of Ministers.* Minneapolis: Augsburg Publishing House, 1964.

Buerk, John A. *Personnel Services and the Campus Ministry.* Buffalo: Department of Campus Ministries, Buffalo Council of Churches, 1968.

Bultmann, Rudolph. *Jesus and the Word.* New York: Charles Scribner's Sons, 1934.

Calvin, John. *The Institutes of the Christian Religion.* Translated by John Allen. 2 vols. Philadelphia: Presbyterian Board of Christian Education, 1936.

Cantelon, John. "Introduction." *A Basis for Study: A Theological Prospectus for the Campus Ministry.* Philadelphia: Board of Education, United Presbyterian Church, USA, 1969.

―――. *A Protestant Approach to the Campus Ministry.* Philadelphia: Westminster Press, 1964.

Campbell, Alexander. *The Millenial Harbinger.* Series 3, vol. 7 (1850); Series 4, vol. 5 (1855); Series 5, vol. 3 (1860).

Carmichael, Oliver C. *Graduate Education.* New York: Harper & Row, 1961.

Chamberlain, J. Gordon. *Churches and Campus.* Philadelphia: Westminster Press, 1963.

Citizen's Commission of Graduate Medical Education. *The Graduate Education of Physicians.* Chicago: American Medical Association, 1967.

Clark, Burton R. *Educating the Expert Society.* San Francisco: Chandler Publishing Co., 1962.

Clark, Burton R. "The New University." *American Behavioral Scientist* (May, 1968).

Clark, Henry, ed. *Manpower for Mission.* New York: Council Press, 1968.

Cox, Harvey. *The Secular City.* New York: The Macmillan Company, 1965.

Cremin, Lawrence A. *The Genius of American Education.* New York: Vintage Books, 1966.

Cuber, John F., and Harroff, Peggy B. *Sex and the Significant Americans: A Study of Sexual Behavior Among the Affluent.* Baltimore: Penguin Books, 1967.

Cuninggim, Merrimon. "The University's Third Function." *The Christian Scholar,* 50 (Spring, 1967).

De Vane, William C. *Higher Education in Twentieth Century America.* Cambridge; Harvard University Press, 1965.

Dondeyne, Albert. *Faith and the World.* Pittsburgh: Duquesne University Press, 1963.

Doxiadis, Constantine A. "Anthropocosmos: The World of Man." Paper read at Aspen Institute, Aspen, Colorado, summer, 1966.

Earnshaw, George L. *The Campus Ministry.* Valley Forge: The Judson Press, 1964.

Eddy, Edward D., Jr. *The College Influence on Student Character.* Washington: American Council on Education, 1959.

Eddy, John Paul. "Public School Directors of Religious Affairs." Ph.D. dissertation, Southern Illinois University, 1968.

Edwards, Richard Henry. *Cooperative Religion at Cornell University.* Ithaca: Cornell Cooperative Society, 1939.

Ellett, Charles A. *The Field of Urban Mission and its Leadership.* Washington: Council of Churches of Greater Washington, February, 1969.

Emmett, Dorothy. *Rules, Roles and Relations.* New York: St. Martin's Press, 1966.

Erikson, Erik H. *Identity and the Life Cycle.* Psychological Issues, monograph no. 1. New York: International Universities Press, 1959.

Evans, Lester J. *The Crisis in Medical Education.* Ann Arbor: University of Michigan Press, 1964.

Feilding, Charles R. "Education for Ministry." *Theological Education* 3 (Autumn, 1966).

Fichter, J. H. "Integrative Functions of Metropolitan Religion." *Harvard Divinity Bulletin* (April, 1964).

Fleming, Don. "The University Parish Pastor." Th.D. dissertation, Pacific School of Religion, 1961.

Forell, George W. *The Protestant Faith.* Englewood Cliffs, N.J.: Prentice-Hall, 1960.

Fowler, Newton B., Jr., ed. *Consultation on the Church's Ministry in Higher Education.* Mimeographed. East Lansing: Kellogg Center for Continuing Education, Michigan State University, 1964.

Freeman, Roger A. *Crisis in College Finance.* Washington: Institute for Social Science Research, 1965.

Fridrichsen, Anton, ed. *The Root of the Vine: Essays in Biblical Theology*. London: Dacre Press, Black, Ltd., 1953.

Gabor, Dennis. "An Ethical Quotient." *Technology and Human Values*. Santa Barbara: Center for the Study of Democratic Institutions, 1966.

Gauss, Christian, ed. *The Teaching of Religion in American Higher Education*. New York: Ronald Press, 1951.

Geier, Woodrow A. *The Campus Ministry of the Methodist Church*. Nashville: The Board of Education, The Methodist Church, 1967.

Gibson, Samuel N. *A Study of the Wesley Foundations and the Campus Ministry of the Methodist Church*. Nashville: The Board of Education, The Methodist Church, 1967.

Gilkey, Langdon. *How the Church Can Minister to the World Without Losing Itself*. New York: Harper & Row, 1964.

Gilliam, Harold. "The Fallacy of Single-Purpose Planning." *Daedalus*, 106 (Fall, 1967).

Glock, Charles Y., and Stark, Rodney. *Christian Beliefs and Anti-Semitism*. New York: Harper & Row, 1966.

Goode, William J. "The Protection of the Inept." *American Sociological Review* (Feb., 1967).

Goodman, Paul. "Student Chaplains." *The New Republic*. 7 January 1967.

Green, Thomas F. "A Typology of the Teaching Concept." *Studies in Philosophy and Education*, 3 (Winter, 1964).

Greer, Scott. *The Emerging City*. New York: The Free Press, 1962.

Gross, Neal; Mason, Ward S; and McEachern, Alexander. *Explorations in Role Analysis*. New York: John Wiley and Sons, 1958.

Gustafson, James M., and Laney, James T., eds. *On Being Responsible*. New York: Harper & Row, 1968.

Hadden, Jeffrey K. "A Study of the Protestant Ministry of America." *Journal for the Scientific Study of Religion*, 5, no. 1 (1955).

————. *The Gathering Storm in the Churches*. Garden City. Doubleday & Company, 1969.

————, and Rymph, Raymond C. "Social Structure and Civil Rights Involvement: A Case Study of Protestant Ministers." *Social Forces*, 45:1 (September, 1966).

Halleck, Seymour. "The Source of Student Alienation." *New York Times*, 12 May 1967.

Hallett, Stanley. "Working Papers in Church Planning, Columbia, Maryland." New York: National Council of Churches, 1964.

Hammond, Phillip E. *The Campus Clergyman*. New York: Basic Books, 1966.

Hampshire, Stuart. *Thought and Action*. New York: Viking Press, 1960.

Hartt, Julian N. *A Christian Critique of American Culture*. New York: Harper & Row, 1967.

Harvey, Van A. *The Historian and the Believer: The Morality of Historical*

Knowledge and Christian Belief. New York: The Macmillan Company, 1966.

Hechinger, Fred M. "A Call for the 'Urban Grant' College." *New York Times,* 22 October 1967.

Hofstadter, Richard. *Academic Freedom in the Age of the College.* New York: Columbia University Press, 1955.

Holbrook, Clyde. *Religion as a Humanistic Discipline.* Englewood Cliffs, N.J.: Prentice-Hall, 1963.

Holloman, J. Herbert. "Literate Engineering." *Saturday Review,* 1 July 1967.

Hopkins, C. H. *History of the YMCA in North America.* New York: Association Press, 1951.

Houtart, François. *The Challenge to Change.* New York: Sheed and Ward, 1964.

————. *The Church Confronts the Future.* New York: Sheed and Ward, 1964.

Hutchison, Russell. "A Study of Needs in Christian Adults." *Religious Education,* 60 (September-October, 1965).

Jacob, Philip. *Changing Values in College.* New York: Harper & Row, 1957.

Jacobson, Elden E. "The Berkeley Crisis: A Case Study of Protestant Campus Ministers." Ph.D. dissertation, Yale University, 1967.

Jacobson, Robert L. "The Role of Higher Education in Solving the Urban Crisis." Paper at Morgan State College Conference on Higher Education and the Challenge of the Urban Crisis, 1967.

Jenkins, Daniel. *Beyond Religion: The Truth and Error in Religionless Christianity.* Philadelphia: Westminster Press, 1962.

Jennings, Frank G. "The Education of Educators." *Saturday Review,* 19 November 1966.

Johnstone, John W., and Ribers, Ramon. *Volunteers for Learning: A Study of Educational Pursuits of American Adults,* National Opinion Research Center Monographs in Social Research, no. 4. Chicago: Aldine Publishing Co., 1965.

Kadushin, Charles. "Power, Influence and Social Circles: A New Methodology for Studying Opinion Makers." *American Sociological Review,* xxxiii-5 (October, 1968).

Katz, Joseph; Koln, Harold A.; and Levin, Max M. *Growth and Constraint in the College Years.* Institute for Study of Human Problems, Stanford University. New York: Oxford University Press, 1967.

Kean, Richard. "The University in a Cybernated Era." *motive* (March-April, 1967).

Kelsey, David H. *The Fabric of Paul Tillich's Theology.* New Haven: Yale University Press, 1967.

Kennan, George. "Rebels Without a Program." *New York Times Magazine,* 21 January 1968.

Kerr, Clark. *The Uses of the University.* Cambridge: Harvard University Press, 1963.

Kimball, Solon T., and McClellan, James E., Jr. *Education and the New America*. New York: Random House, 1962.

Kinnane, Mary. "The Chaplain: Perceptions of His Role; A Comparison by College Staff Members and Undergraduates." *Humanity* (Spring, 1966).

Klotche, J. Martin. *The Urban University*. New York: Harper & Row, 1966.

Kneller, George F. *Existentialism and Education*. New York: John Wiley & Sons, 1958.

Kubler, George. *The Shape of Time*. New Haven: Yale University Press, 1962.

Lampe, M. Willard. *The Story of an Idea: History of the School of Religion at the State University of Iowa*. Bulletin no. 704. Iowa City: State University of Iowa, March, 1955.

Lane, Robert E. *The Liberties of Wit, Humanism, Criticism and the Civic Mind*. New Haven: Yale University Press, 1961.

Laney, James T. "A Critique of the Ethics of the Radical Contextualists." Ph. D. dissertation, Yale University, 1966.

Lenski, Gerhard. *The Religious Factor*. Garden City: Doubleday & Company, 1961.

Lerner, Daniel, and Lasswell, Harold D. (eds.). *The Policy Sciences: Reports on Developments in Scope and Method in the Behavioral and Social Sciences*. Stanford: Stanford University Press, 1951.

Leypoldt, Martha. "An Analysis of Seminary Courses in Christian Adult Education." *Religious Education*, 60 (September-October, 1965).

Lipset, Seymour Martin, and Wolin, Sheldon S. (eds.). *The Berkeley Student Revolt*. Garden City: Doubleday & Company, 1965.

Llewellyn, Karl N. *The Bramble Bush*. New York: Oceana Publications, 1951.

Long, Edward L., Jr. *A Survey of Christian Ethics*. New York: Oxford University Press, 1967.

Luecke, Richard. *New Meanings for New Beings*. Philadelphia: Fortress Press, 1964.

Lynch, William F., S. J. *Images of Hope: Imagination as a Healer of the Hopeless*. Baltimore-Dublin: Helicon Press, 1965.

Lynn, Robert W. *Education in the New America*. New York: Department of Higher Education, National Council of Churches, 1966.

McCoy, Charles S., and Kolb, William L. "The Campus Ministries in the Context of Higher Education." Mimeographed. St. Louis: The Danforth Foundation, 1964.

McGhee, Larry T. "Higher Education and Human Depravity on the Antebellum Frontier." Ph.D. dissertation, Yale University, 1967.

———. (ed.) "The Work of the University in the United States." Mimeographed. East Lansing: Christian Faith and Higher Education Institute, 1964.

McLean, Milton D., and Kimler, Harry H. *The Teaching of Religion in State Universities*. Ann Arbor: University of Michigan Press, 1960.

McLean, Stuart D. "The Campus Ministry." Mimeographed. New York: United Church of Christ, 1962.

McLuhan, Marshall, *Understanding Media*. New York: McGraw-Hill Book Company, 1964.

McNeill, Robert. *God Wills Us Free: The Ordeal of a Southern Minister*. New York: Hill and Wang, 1965.

Marty, Martin. *Varieties of Unbelief*. New York: Holt, Rinehart, and Winston, 1964.

Meeks, Wayne A. *Jesus as Prophet in the Fourth Gospel*. Leiden: Brill, 1967.

Meland, B. E. *Higher Education and the Human Spirit*. Chicago: University of Chicago Press, 1958.

Merleau-Ponty, M. *Phenomenology of Perception*. Translated by Colin Smith. London: Routledge and Kegan Paul, 1962.

Michaelsen, Robert. *The Study of Religion in American Universities: Ten Case Studies with Special Reference to State Universities*. New Haven: The Society for Religion and Higher Education, 1965.

Miller, Michael V., and Gilmore, Susan. *Revolution at Berkeley*. New York: Dell Publishing Company, 1965.

Miller, Perry. *The New England Mind: The Seventeenth Century*. Cambridge: Harvard University Press, 1954.

Miller, William R. *The New Christianity*. New York: Delacorte Press, 1967.

Molnar, Thomas. *The Future of Education*. New York: Grosset and Dunlap, 1961.

Monane, Joseph. *Sociology of Human Systems*. New York: Appleton-Century-Crofts, 1967.

Moore, Allen. "The Role of Religious Education in Theological Education." *Religious Education*, 60 (Sept-Oct, 1965).

Morison, Elting E. *Men, Machines and Modern Times*. Cambridge: M. I. T. Press, 1966.

Morison, Samuel Eliot. *Three Centuries of Harvard*. Cambridge: Harvard University Press, 1937.

Morton, A. Q., and McLeman, James. *Christianity in the Computer Age*. New York: Harper & Row, 1964.

Mowrer, O. Hobart. *The Uses of Psychiatry and Religion*. Princeton: D. Van Nostrand Co., 1961.

Moynihan, Daniel P. "The Professionalization of Reform." *The Public Interest* (Fall, 1965).

Muirhead, Jan A. *Education in the New Testament*. New York: Association Press, 1965.

Natanson, Maurice. *Philosophy in the Social Sciences*. New York: Random House, 1963.

Niebuhr, H. Richard. *Christ and Culture*. New York: Harper & Row, 1951.

――――. *The Purpose of the Church and its Ministry*. New York: Harper & Row, 1956.

————. *Radical Monotheism and Western Culture.* New York: Harper & Row, 1960.

————.*The Responsible Self.* New York: Harper & Row, 1963.

————, and Williams, D. D. (eds.). *The Ministry in Historical Perspectives.* New York: Harper & Row, 1956.

————; Williams, D. D.; and Gustafson, James G. *The Advancement of Theological Education.* New York: Harper & Row, 1957.

Niebuhr, Richard R. "A Power and a Goodness. How I am Making up My Mind." *The Christian Century* (1 December 1965).

————. *Schleiermacher on Christ and Religion: A New Introduction.* New York: Charles Scribner's Sons, 1964.

O'Dea, Thomas F. *American Catholic Dilemma: An Inquiry into the Intellectual Life.* New York: Sheed and Ward, 1958.

Oliver, Hoyt P. "Professional Authority and the Professional Ministry: A Study of an Occupational Image." Ph. D. dissertation, Yale University, 1966.

Paige, John W. "Commuting to New York Colleges." *University of the State of New York Bulletin* (1 July 1946).

Parsons, Talcott, "Pattern Variables Revisited: A Response to Robert Dubin." *American Sociological Review* (August, 1960).

Patillo, Manning M., Jr., and MacKenzie, Donald M. *Church Sponsored Higher Education in the United States.* Washington, D.C.: American Council on Education, 1966.

Pearl, Arthur, and Riessman, Frank. *New Careers for the Poor.* New York: The Free Press of Glencoe, 1965.

Peerman, Dean (ed.). *Frontline Theology.* Richmond: John Knox Press, 1967.

Perkins, James A. *The University in Transition.* Princeton: Princeton University Press, 1966.

Perry, John. *The Coffee House Ministries.* Richmond: John Knox Press, 1966.

Phenix, Phil. *Education and the Common Good.* New York: Harper & Row, 1961.

Polanyi, Michael. *Personal Knowledge.* Chicago: University of Chicago Press, 1958.

————. *Science, Faith and Society.* Chicago: University of Chicago Press, 1964.

Pope, Liston. *Millhands and Preachers.* New Haven; Yale University Press, 1942.

Ramsey, Paul (ed.) *Faith and Ethics: The Theology of H. Richard Niebuhr.* New York: Peter Smith, 1959.

———— (ed.) *Religion.* Englewood Cliffs, N.J.: Prentice-Hall, 1965.

Raushenbush, Esther. *The Student and His Studies.* Middletown, Conn.: Wesleyan University Press, 1964.

Resources Planning Commission, American Association of Theological Schools, "Theological Curriculum for the 1970's". *Theological Education,* 4:3 (Spring, 1968).

Richardson, Herbert W. *Toward an American Theology.* New York: Harper & Row, 1967.

Ripley, S. Dillon, and Buechner, Helmut K. "Ecosystem Science as a Point of Synthesis." *Daedalus* 106 (Fall, 1967).

Rossi, Peter. "Researchers, Scholars, and Policy Makers." *Daedalus,* 94 (Fall, 1964).

Rossman, Parker. "The Denominational Chaplain in the State University." *Religious Education,* 55 (1960).

Rudolph, Frederick. *The American College and University.* New York: Vintage Books, 1965.

Rupp, George, et al. "A Prescription for Seminaries." *Christianity and Crisis,* 27:10 (1967).

Sanford, Nevitt (ed.). *The American College.* New York: John Wiley & Sons, 1962.

Savio, Mario. "An End to History." *Humanity* (December, 1964).

Schmidt, George P. *Old Time College President.* New York: AMS Press, 1930.

Schrading, Paul. "A Future for the Campus Ministry?" *Reflection,* LXVI–2 (January, 1969).

Seeley, John R.; Sim, R. Alexander; and Loosley, Elizabeth W. *Crestwood Heights: A Study of the Culture of Suburban Life.* New York: Basic Books, 1956.

Shedd, Clarence P. *Two Centuries of Student Christian Movements: Their Origin and Intellectual Life.* New York: Association Press, 1934.

Silberman, Charles. *Crisis in Black and White.* New York: Random House, 1964.

Smith, Harry. "The Secular Theologians and Higher Education in the United States." Ph. D. dissertation, Drew University, 1967.

Smith, Seymour. *The American College Chaplaincy.* New York: Association Press, 1954.

———. *Religious Cooperation in the State Universities.* Ann Arbor: University of Michigan Press, 1957.

Smith, Wilson. *Professors and Public Ethics: Studies of Northern Moral Philosophers Before the Civil War.* Ithaca: Cornell University Press, 1956.

Spilhaus, Athelstan. "The Experimental City." *Daedalus, 106* (Fall, 1967).

Stroup, Herbert. *Bureaucracy in Higher Education.* New York: The Free Press, 1966.

Szasz, Thomas S. *The Myth of Mental Illness.* New York: Harper & Row, 1961.

Tarcher, Martin. *Leadership and the Power of Ideas.* New York: Harper & Row, 1966.

Teller, Azrield. "Air-Pollution Abatement." *Daedalus, 106* (Fall, 1967).

TeSelle, Sallie MacFague. *Literature and the Christian Life.* New Haven: Yale University Press, 1967.

Tewksbury, Donald G. *The Founding of American Colleges and Universities Before the Civil War.* New York: Columbia University Press, 1932.

Theobald, Robert. *An Alternative Future for America: Essays and Speeches.* Edited by Kendall College. Chicago: Swallow Press, 1968.

Thomas, M. M. (ed.). *The Idea of a Responsible University in Asia Today.* Geneva: World Student Christian Federation.

Tillich, Paul. *The Protestant Era.* Chicago: University of Chicago Press, 1948.

Tinder, Glenn. *The Crisis of Political Imagination.* New York: Charles Scribner's Sons, 1964.

Underwood, Kenneth W. *Protestant and Catholic.* Boston: Beacon Press, 1957.

————. "Protestant Political Thought." *International Encyclopedia of the Social Sciences.* New York: The Macmillan Company and Free Press, 1968.

————. (ed.). "Trends and Issues in Medical Education." *Christian Scholar* (Winter, 1967).

Vernon, Raymond, and Hoover, Edgar Malone. *Anatomy of a Metropolis.* Cambridge: Harvard University Press, 1959.

Walter, Erich A. *Religion and the State University.* Ann Arbor: University of Michigan Press, 1964.

Welch, Claude, and Dillenberger, John. *Protestant Christianity.* New York: Charles Scribner's Sons, 1954.

Whitley, Oliver Read. *Religious Behavior: Where Sociology and Religion Meet.* Englewood Cliffs, N.J.: Prentice-Hall, 1965.

Wiebe, G. D. "Some Implications of Separating Opinions from Attitudes." *Public Opinion Quarterly* (Fall, 1963).

Wilkinson, John. "Futuribles: Innovation vs. Stability." *Center Diary* (Santa Barbara: Center for the Study of Democratic Institutions), March-April, 1967.

Williams, Colin W. *What in the World.* New York: Council Press, 1964.

Williamson, René de Visme. *Independence and Involvement: A Christian Reorientation in Political Science.* Baton Rouge: Louisiana State University Press, 1964.

Willie, Charles V. "Evaluation Resources and Their Use." *Information Service* (12 February 1966).

Windsor, James C. "The American Higher Education Chaplaincy." *College and Chapel* (Spring, 1963).

Wollman, Nathaniel. "The New Economics of Resources." *Daedalus, 106* (Fall, 1967).

World Council of Churches. *Church as Mission.* Geneva: World Council of Churches, 1967.

World Student Christian Federation. "The Christian Community in the Academic World." Geneva: World Student Christian Federation, 1964.

Wren-Lewis, John, et al. *Faith, Fact and Fantasy.* Brooklyn: Fontana Books, 1964.

Zahn, Gordon. *In Solitary Witness.* New York: Holt, Rinehart, and Winston, 1964.

Zeigler, Jerome M. "Continuing Education in the University." *Daedalus,* 94 (Fall, 1964).

PAPERS PRESENTED IN THE VARIOUS CENTERS OF STUDY

Boston Colloquium: Changing Expectation of the Campus Minister in the Urban Setting of Higher Education, December 1963–March 1965.

Horn, Henry. "Paper on Institutionalism."

Overholt, William. "What Is the Campus Ministry/Minister?"

Stotts, Herbert. "Assumptions on Anti-Institutionalism."

Boston College Colloquium: The Catholic University as an Arena for Exploring the Relation Between Catholic Theology and Concrete Moral Action. February-June 1964.

Devine, J. Frank, S. J. "Contemporary Christian Commitment: Some Reflections."

Molloy, Francis P., S. J. "Relation of Catholic Faith and Morality to Scientific Epistemologies."

Sheehan, Robert Louis. "A Proposal for Extending Participation of the Lay Faculty in the Religious Life of the Boston College Campus."

Von Hildebrand, Dietrich. "The Conception of a Catholic University."

Walsh, John. "Report of Study of Beliefs and Values of Boston College Students from the Survey Data."

Champaign-Urbana Colloquium: The Relation of Campus Ministries at the University of Illinois to Student Morality, October 1963–January 1965.

Durham-Chapel Hill Colloquium: The Campus Ministry in a Secular University. January-June 1964.

Beach, Waldo. "Theological Views of Secularization."

Dixon, John W. Jr. "Notes on the Problems of the University."

Schnorrenberg, John M. "The Significance and Knowledge of the Bible in the Secular University."

Smith, Harry. "Concepts of Secularization and Implications for Campus Ministry."

———. "Secularization and the American University."

White, W. D. "The Study of Religion and the Liberal Arts."

——— "Preaching the Word in the Liberal University Which Has Lost its Biblical Understanding."

M. I. T. Colloquium: Religion and Community Cooperation in Planning, Housing, and Architecture, July 26–30, 1967.

Abrams, Charles. "The Churches' Opportunity under Federal Housing Programs."

Adams, Frederick J. "Scope and Objectives of Comprehensive Planning."

Appleyard, Donald S. "Urban Design in the Future City."

Beshers, James M. "The Role of Church in Defining Urban Social Problems."

Colcord, Frank C., Jr. "The Politics of Urban Change."

Cox, Harvey. "The Crisis in the Secular City."

Frieden, Bernard J. "Emerging Public Policies that Affect Urban Areas."

Hallett, Stanley J. "Ethical Issues in Urban Planning and Development."

Millon, Henry A. "The Role of Architecture in the Planning of Future Urban Centers."

Oppermann, Paul. "Metropolitan Communities as Appropriate Units of Comprehensive Urban Region Plans."

Revelle, Roger. "Three Main Population Problems in the U.S."

Medical Consultation: Trends and Issues in Medical Education of Significance to the Campus Ministry, May 7–8, 1965.

Banks, Samuel, and Pattishall, Evan. "Effect upon Physicians of Current Ethical Questions in Medicine."

Sanazaro, Paul. "Major Issues in Medical Education."

Stumpf, Samuel. "Moral Dimensions in Medicine."

Underwood, Kenneth. "Significance of This Consultation for Churches and Ministries."

Wolf, George. "Ethical Guidelines for Use of Human Beings in Experimentation and Teaching."

Barth, Phebe, and Underwood, Kenneth. "Transcript of the Consultation Discussions."

Michigan Colloquium: Response of Protestant Churches to Changes in Michigan Higher Education, January 1964–February 1965.

Baker, William. "Decision Making and Action in Protestant Churches."

Bloy, Myron T. "Christianity and Technology."

Dobyns, Lester L. "A Review of Campus Ministries in Michigan."

Green, Thomas. "The Relation of Faith to the Educational Process."

Hannahs, Eugene. "Experimental Ministry in Business and Engineering Education."

Hazard, John. "Ethical-Theological Inquiry in Business Education."

Soleau, John. "The Relation of Ethical Disciplines to the Total Curriculum for Training for Industrial Leadership."

New Haven Colloquium: The University as the Arena for Christian Ministry; The Response of Yale Divinity School to Changes in Higher Education. 1964–1967.

Johnson, Robert C. "Religion in Higher Education: Yale Divinity School."

New York Study: The Contribution of the Protestant Campus Ministry to Social Action in the Great Metropolis, 1963–1966.

McFarlane, Alan R., and Dentler, Robert A. "The Protestant Campus Ministry in a Northern Metropolitan Area."

Pittsburgh Colloquium: Can Roman Catholic and Protestant Leadership Provide a Constructive Critique of the Role of Higher Education in the Renewal of Urban Pittsburgh?, April-November 1964.

Berkowitz, Morris, and Walsh, James Leo. "Convergences in Religious Attitudes: Protestant, Catholic and Jew."

Bodine, John. "Liberal Education for Urban Responsibility."

Bowen, Charles. "Community."

Cramer, John E. "The Faculty Study."

Egan, Edmund J. "Ethics and the Campus Ministry."

Ham, Clifford. "The Campus Ministry and the Urban Renaissance."

———. "The Neighborhood Church in Urban Extension."

Hill, Warren. "A Long Look at the New Look in Sex."

Pittman, J. Ronald. "The University's Responsibility and Role in Minority Group Relocation."

Schrading, Paul E. The Protestant Campus Ministry in Pittsburgh."

———. "Summary and Personal Reflections."

Stoutamyer, Joyce. "Community and Campus Ministry."

Walsh, Philip. "The Oratory."

San Francisco Bay Area Colloquium: The Nature of the Religious Commitment in the Churches and Universities of the San Francisco Bay Area, December 1963–June 1965.

Gaff, Jerry C. "The Danforth Study of Campus Ministries: A Report to the University of the Pacific Community."

McCoy, Charles S. "Religious Commitment and Realms of Actuality."

Palmer, Parker J. "A Typology of World Views: Some Concepts for the Sociology of Religion."

———, "Studying Commitments on Campus."

———, "Report of the First Meeting of the Bay Area Research Colloquium of the Danforth Study of Campus Ministries."

Danforth Bay Area Questionnaire for Students.

University of Wisconsin Colloquium: Study of the Religious Institutional Involvements and Beliefs of the Students at University of Wisconsin, 1964–1967.

Aiken, Michael; Demerath, N. J. III; and Marwell, Gerald. "Conscience and Confrontation."

Demerath, N. J. III, and Levinson, Richard M. "Baiting the Dissident Hook: Some Effects of Bias in Measuring Religious Beliefs."

———, and Lutterman, Kenneth. "The Student Parishioner: Radical Rhetoric and Traditional Reality."

———, Lutterman, Kenneth; and Lyons, Judith. " 'So What' and 'That Too': Twin Problems in the Measurement of Religious Beliefs."

Moore, Daniel E. "The Campus Clergyman and His Student Parishioner: A Comparison."

University of Wisconsin Student Survey: *University and Society: Student Perspectives*. Madison, 1965.

UNPUBLISHED PAPERS WRITTEN AND COLLECTED FOR THE STUDY STAFF

Adams, James Luther. "The Social Import of the Professions." Paper to 21st Meeting of American Association of Theological Schools, Boston School of Theology, June 1958.

Campus Ministry Committee. "Report of the Committee to Study the Campus Ministry." Annual Conference, Methodist Church of California, February 1967.

Cavers, David F. "Legal Education in Time of Change." Paper to Conference on Professional Education, Episcopal Theological Seminary. Cambridge, Mass., February 1967.

Daly, John W. "Results of Survey to Determine Characteristics of Existing University Related Research and Industrial Park Programs." Albuquerque Industrial Development Service, 1966.

Dobyns, Lester. "A Report to the Churches from the Association for Ecumenical Ministries." A report given in Ann Arbor, spring, 1967.

Feilding, Charles R. "Progress Report to Commission on Research and Counsel." Report to American Association of Theological Schools. 11 December, 1963.

Foreman, Terry H. "The Study of Religion and Some Imperatives for Theological Education." Union Theological Seminary, June 1967.

Gelwick, Richard L. "A Paradigm of Freedom." Sermon. Danforth Associates Conference, Ojai, Calif., March 1966.

Green, Thomas. "Work, Leisure and Structure of Hope." Syracuse, New York: Syracuse University, 1965.

Hadden, Jeffrey K. "The Crisis in Professional Identity: The Clergy as a Clue to its Nature." Case Western Reserve University, 1967.

———. "Structural Restraints on Ministers in Civil Rights." Case Western Reserve University, 1966.

Harrison, Jack. "Dwelling with Man." Christian Faith and Higher Education Institute, East Lansing, Mich. 4 March 1967.

Harrison, Paul M. "Scholarship in the Public Domain and Some Implications for Church and Seminary." Consultation on Study of Religion in College and University. Department of Higher Education, National Council of Churches, January, 1967.

Hartt, Julian N. "The University: The Dilemmas of Academic Life in American Culture and Politics." Paper to Institute of Ethics and Politics, Wesleyan University, Middletown, Conn.

Katz, Joseph. "The Role of the Student Dean in Educational Innovation." Paper at Annual Conference, College Student Personnel Institute, Claremont, Calif., 2 November 1965.

Kolb, William. "American Higher Education Today." Report of the First Phase of the Danforth Study of Campus Ministries. St. Louis, 1963.

Lehman, Edward C., Jr. "Religion and the North Carolina State University Faculty." Science and Theology Discussion Group, North Carolina State University, 1966.

Lowell, Earl, and Monick, Eugene. "Beginning Statements on Theology, Philosophy, Strategy, Structure and Budget Relative to the Proposed Ecumenical Foundation for Higher Education." Working paper for United Ministries in Higher Education, New York, 1964.

Michaelsen, Robert. "Present Scope and Development of the University Study of Religion." Consultation on Study of Religion in College and University. Department of Higher Education, National Council of Churches. January, 1967.

Ransome, Eugene Arthur. "A Study of the Role of the Campus Ministries in a Selected Sample of Colleges and Universities." Ph. D. dissertation, University of Michigan, 1964.

Ramshaw, Warren. "Study of Religion of Students at Monteith College (Wayne State) and University of Illinois." Wayne State University, 1964.

Rossman, Parker. "Campus Ministry Study Programs." Paper written for the initial stages of the study. New Haven, fall, 1964.

————, and Baker, William. "The Worldly Ministry" New Haven, book manuscript in process.

Shriver, Don. "Reports of Programs." Experimental Study of Religion and Society, North Carolina State University, February 1964–1967.

————. "What Is Ethics?" Research Group in Ethics and Decision Making. North Carolina State University, April, 1965.

Scott, Anne Frior. "Sex and Society." Durham, Duke University, 1965.

Underwood, Kenneth. "The Campus Minister and Ethical Problems of the University." New Haven, Danforth Study of Campus Ministries, 1965.

————. "The New Ethics of Personal and Corporate Responsibility." Third Centennial Symposium on the Responsible Individual, University of Denver, April 1964.

————. "Occasions for Decision-Making in Campus Ministries." New Haven: Danforth Study of Campus Ministries, 1966.

————. "Social Change and American Protestantism." New Haven, Danforth Study of Campus Ministries, 1965.

————. "Statement for Exploratory Committee of Danforth Foundation on Theological Education." New Haven, Danforth Study of Campus Ministries, March 1967.

————. "The University as Moral Critic of American Business." 1963 Meeting of Association of College and University Chaplains, spring 1963.

————. "Value Contexts for Decision Making." Paper for fourth Quadrennial

Convocation, Council of Protestant Colleges and Universities, Richmond, Ind., June 1966.

————, and Oliver, Hoyt. "The Danforth Seminary Internship Report." Report to the Danforth Foundation, St. Louis, December 1964–February 1965.

United Campus Christian Fellowship. "A Statement of Policy and Strategy." St. Louis, United Campus Christian Fellowship, 1964.

University of Wisconsin Extension. "Education for Continuing Change." Madison, Wisconsin: University of Wisconsin Extension, 1962.

Wheaton, William L. C. "The Role of the University in Urban Affairs." Paper delivered at Arlington State College, October 1966.

Williams, Daniel Day. "Metaphysics of Love." Union Theological Seminary, April 1967.